Autodesk Inventor for Designers
Release 5

Sham Tickoo

Professor
Department of Mechanical Engineering Technology
Purdue University Calumet
Hammond, Indiana
U.S.A.

CADCIM Technologies

(www.cadcim.com)
U.S.A.

CADCIM Technologies

Autodesk Inventor for Designers: Release 5
Sham Tickoo

ISBN 0-9663537-1-4

Cover designer: *CADCIM Technologies*
Copy editor: *Vivek Kumar*
Cover illustration: *Created by Deepak Maini and Puja Bahl Manchanda using Inventor and MAX software*
Technical editors: *Deepak Maini, Abhinav Rai, Gurpreet Singh*
Typeface: *10/12 New Baskerville Bt*

www.cadcim.com

Teaching Aids for Faculty

The following teaching aids are available to faculty:

1. All Part files (.ipt), Assembly files (.iam), Presentation files (.ipn), and Drawing files (.idw) used for tutorials and exercises in this book.

2. PowerPoint presentations for every chapter of the book.

3. Instructor's Guide with answers to review questions and solution to exercises.

4. Course outlines

5. Students projects

6. Free online technical support by contacting cadsoft@vsnl.com

To access the web site that contains these teaching aids, please contact the author, Prof. Sham Tickoo, at the following address:

> **stickoo@calumet.purdue.edu**
> or
> **tickoo@cadcim.com**

Engineering Services Offered by CADCIM Technologies

The following are the services offered by CADCIM Technologies:

Solid Modeling, MAX/VIZ

CADCIM Technologies specializes and undertakes the following solid modeling related projects:
- Conversion of 2D drawings to 3D solid/surface models using Mechanical desktop (MDT), Autodesk Inventor, Pro/ENGINEER, I-DEAS, CATIA, SolidWorks, and AutoCAD.
- Conversion of 3D models to 2D drawings.
- Generation of assembly models.
- Animation and rendering using 3D Studio VIZ/MAX.
- Animation of assemblies using Inventor and SolidWorks.

Training and Technical Documentation

CADCIM Technologies offer training on the following software packages:
- AutoCAD, • Mechanical Desktop (MDT), • Autodesk Inventor, • Pro/ENGINEER, and • SolidWorks

CADCIM Technologies also offers services in developing technical documents, study/training materials, and brochures.

For more information, please visit www.cadcim.com

Table of Contents

Chapter 3: Editing, Extruding, and Revolving the Sketches

Chapter 4: Other Sketching and Modeling Options

Chapter 5: Advanced Modeling Tools-I

Chapter 6: Editing Features and Adding Automatic Dimensions to the Sketch

Chapter 11: Drawing Mode-II

Chapter 12: Presentation Mode

Appendices

Index

Author's Web Sites

For Faculty: Please contact the author at **stickoo@calumet.purdue.edu** or **tickoo@cadcim.com** to access the web site that contain the PowerPoint presentations, solid models used in the text book, Instructor's Guide, and other related material.

For Students: You can download solid modeling exercises, tutorials, and special topics by accessing the author's web site at **www.cadcim.com**.

Preface

AUTODESK INVENTOR 5

Autodesk Inventor, developed by Autodesk Inc., is one of the world's fastest growing solid modeling softwares. It is a parametric feature-based solid modeling tool and it not only unites the 3D parametric features with 2D tools but also addresses every design-through-manufacturing process. The adaptive technology of this solid modeling tool allows you to handle an extremely large assembly with tremendous ease. Based mainly on the solid modeling users' feedback, this solid modeling tool is remarkably user-friendly and it allows you to be productive from day one.

This solid modeling tool allows you to easily import the AutoCAD, the AutoCAD Mechanical, and the Mechanical Desktop files with an amazing compatibility. The parametric features and assembly parameters are retained when you import the Mechanical Desktop files in Autodesk Inventor.

The 2D drawing views of the components are automatically generated in the layouts. The drawing views that can be generated include detailed, orthographic, isometric, auxiliary, section, and so on. You can use any predefined drawing standard files for generating the drawing views. You can display the model dimensions in the drawing views or add reference dimensions whenever you want. The bidirectional associative nature of this software ensures that any modification made in the model is automatically reflected in the drawing views and any modification made in the dimensions in drawing views automatically updates the model.

Autodesk Inventor for Designers is a book that is written with an intent of helping the people who are into 3D design. This book is written with the tutorial point of view with learn-by-doing as the theme. The mechanical engineering industry examples and tutorials are used in this book to ensure that the user can relate his knowledge of this book with the actual mechanical industry designs. The main features of the book are as follows:

- **Sheet Metal Mode.**

  This is one of the very few books that includes the complete coverage of the Sheet Metal mode of Autodesk Inventor. Fifty-six pages of heavily illustrated text on Sheet Metal mode has each and every tool of this mode discussed in detail.

- **Tutorial approach.**

  The author has adopted the tutorial point-of-view with learn-by-doing as the theme throughout the book. This approach will guide the users through the process of creating the model in the tutorial.

- **Real-World Projects as Tutorials.**

     The author has used the real-world mechanical engineering projects as tutorials in this book so that the reader can correlate the tutorials in this book with the real-time models in the mechanical engineering industry.

- **Coverage of all Autodesk Inventor modules.**

     All the modules of Autodesk Inventor are covered in this book including the **Presentation** module for animating the assemblies and the **Sheet Metal** module for creating the sheet metal components.

- **Tips and Notes.**

     The additional information related to the topics is provided to the users in the form of tips and notes.

- **Learning Objectives.**

     The first page of every chapter provides in brief the topics that will be covered in that chapter. This will help the users to easily refer to a topic.

- **Tools section.**

     Every chapter begins with the tools section that provides the detailed explanation of the Autodesk Inventor tools.

- **Self-Evaluation Test, Review Questions, and Exercises.**

     Every chapter ends with a Self-Evaluation Test so that the users can assess their knowledge of the chapter. The author has given the answers of the Self-Evaluation Tests so that the users can compare their answers with the correct answers. The Review Questions and Exercises are also given at the end of each chapter and can be used by the Instructors as test questions and exercises in the classroom.

- **Heavily illustrated text.**

     The text in this book is heavily illustrated with the help of around 700 line diagrams and 500 photos that support the tools sections and tutorials.

Introduction

AUTODESK INVENTOR R5

Welcome to the world of Autodesk Inventor. If you are new to the world of 3D design then you have joined hands with thousands of people worldwide who are already into 3D designing. If you are already using some of the other solid modeling tools then you will find this solid modeling tool more adaptive to your use. You will find tremendous improvement in the duration of completing the design using this solid modeling tool.

Autodesk Inventor is a parametric and feature-based solid modeling tool. It allows you to convert the basic 2D sketch into a solid model using a very simple but highly effective modeling commands. This solid modeling tool do not restricts its capabilities to the 3D solid output, but also extends them to the bidirectional associative drafting. This means that all you have to do is to create the solid model. The documentation of the solid model in the form of the drawing views is easily done by this software package itself. You just have to specify the type of view you require. This solid modeling tool can be specially used at the places where the concept of **"collaborative engineering"** is brought into use. Collaborative engineering is a concept that allows more than one user to work on the same design at the same time. This solid modeling tool allows more than one user to simultaneously work on the same design.

As a product of Autodesk, this software package allows you to directly open the drawings of the other Autodesk softwares like AutoCAD, Mechanical Desktop, AutoCAD LT, and so on. This interface is not only restricted to the Autodesk softwares. You can very easily import and export the drawings from this software package to any other software package and vice versa.

To reduce the complicacies of the design, this software package has provided you with different design environments. This helps you to capture the design intent easily by individually incorporating the intelligence of each of the design environment into the design. The different design environments that are available in this solid modeling tool are as follows:

Part Mode

This is a parametric and feature-based solid modeling environment. This environment allows you to create solid models. The sketches for the models can be drawn fairly easily. All the applicable constraints will be applied to the sketch automatically and will be displayed on the sketch. You do not have to invoke an extra command to apply the constraints. Once the basic sketches are drawn, you can convert them into solid models using simple but highly effective modeling commands. One of the major advantages of using Autodesk Inventor is the availability of the Design Doctor. The Design Doctor is used to calculate and describe the errors, if any, in the sketch. You will also be provided with the remedy for removing the errors from the sketch so that they can be converted into features. The complicated features can be captured in this mode and can be later used in other parts. This appreciably reduces the time taken to create the designer model. In the same mode you can also create the sheet metal components. These components can be created using the same principles as that of creating the solid models.

Assembly Mode

This mode helps you to create the assemblies by assembling the components of the assemblies. This mode supports both the Bottom-up approach as well as the Top-down approach of creating the assemblies. This means that you can either copy the external components into the assembly mode or create the components in the assembly mode itself. You are allowed to assemble the components using the smart assembly constraints. All the assembly constraints can be added using just a single dialog box. You can even preview the components before they are actually assembled. This solid modeling tool supports the concept of making a part or a feature in the part adaptive. An adaptive feature or a part is the one that can change its actual dimensions based upon the need of the environment.

Presentation Mode

One of the major limitations of most of the solid modeling tools is their limitation to display the working of an assembly. The most important question asked by the customers in today's world is how to show the working of any assembly. Most of the solid modeling tools do not have an answer to this question. The reason for this is that they do not have proper tools to display any assembly in motion. Therefore, in return, the designers cannot show the working of the assemblies to their clients. In cases where it is necessary to show the animation, they have to take the help of some other software packages like the 3D Studio MAX or 3D Studio VIZ. However, keeping this problem of the users in mind, this software package has provided you with a mode called the **Presentation** mode. In this mode you can animate the assemblies created in the **Assembly** mode and view their working. You can also view if there is any interference during the operation of the assembly. The assemblies can be animated using the unbelievably easy steps.

Drawing Mode

This mode is used for the documentation of the parts or the assemblies in the form of the drawing views. You can also create the drawing views of the presentation created in the **Presentation** mode. All the parametric dimensions added to the components in the **Part** mode during the creation of the parts can be displayed on their drawing views in this mode.

Sheet Metal Mode

This mode is used for the creating the sheet metal component. When you invoke a sheet metal file, the sketching environment is activated by default. You can draw the sketch of the base sheet in this mode and then proceed to the sheet metal mode to covert the sketch into the sheet metal component.

SYSTEM REQUIREMENTS

The system requirements to ensure smooth running of Autodesk Inventor on your system are:

- Windows NT 4.0, Windows 98.
- Pentium 200MHz Processor, with 96MB RAM (Minimum).
- Pentium II, Pentium III 333MHz Processor, with 128MB RAM (Recommended).
- Pentium II, Pentium III 450MHz Processor, with 512MB RAM (Preferred).

GETTING STARTED WITH AUTODESK INVENTOR

Install Autodesk Inventor on your system and then start it by double-clicking on the Autodesk Inventor shortcut icon on the desktop of your computer. This icon will be automatically created when you install the software on to your system. You can also start Autodesk Inventor by using the taskbar shortcuts. Choose the **Start** button available on the lower left corner of the screen. Choose **Programs** to display the **Program** menu. In the **Program** menu, choose **Inventor 5** to display the cascading menu. In this cascading menu, choose **Autodesk Inventor 5** as shown in Figure I-1.

Figure I-1 Starting Autodesk Inventor using the taskbar shortcuts

The system will now prepare to start Autodesk Inventor by loading all the required files. After the completion of the loading of the required files, the **Open** dialog box will be displayed. Choose **New** from the **What To Do** area to display the **Default**, **English**, and **Metric** tabs for selecting a new file. Choose the **Metric** tab and then double-click on the **Standard (mm).ipt** template to open a default metric template, see Figure I-2.

A new part file with the default name of **Part1.ipt** will be opened and now you can start working in this file. The initial screen appearance of Autodesk Inventor is shown in Figure I-3. This figure also displays various components of this screen.

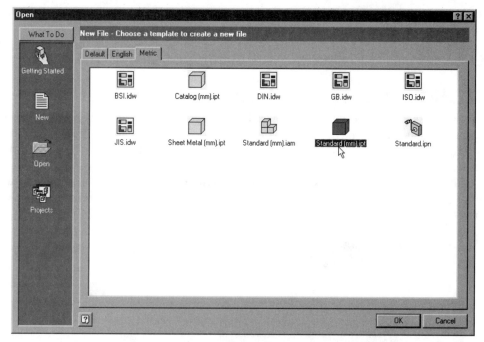

Figure I-2 *Selecting* ***Standard (mm).ipt*** *template from* ***Metric*** *tab*

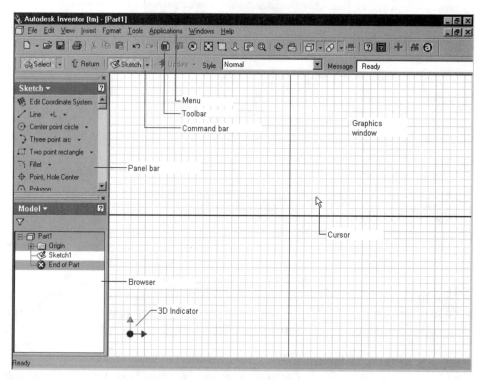

Figure I-3 *Initial screen appearance of Autodesk Inventor along with the components*

It is evident from Figure I-3 that the screen of Autodesk Inventor is quite user friendly. Apart from the components shown in Figure I-3, you are also provided with different shortcut menus. The shortcut menus are displayed upon right-clicking the mouse. The type of the shortcut menu and its options will depend upon where or when you are trying to access this menu. For example, when you are inside any command, the options displayed in the shortcut menu will be different from the options that will be displayed when you are not inside any command. These shortcut menus will be discussed when they are used in the book.

TOOLBARS

You might have noticed that there is no command prompt in Autodesk Inventor. The complete designing process is carried out by invoking the commands from the toolbars. Therefore, Autodesk Inventor provides you with different types of toolbars while working with different design environments. This means that the toolbars that will be available while working with the **Part**, **Assembly**, **Drawing**, **Sheet Metal**, and **Presentation** mode will be different.

Part Mode Toolbars

There are a number of toolbars that can be invoked in the **Part** mode. The toolbars that will be extensively used during the designing process in this environment are described below:

Standard Toolbar

This toolbar is common in all the design environments of Autodesk Inventor. However, some of these options will not be available in all the environments. The **Standard** toolbar with the various buttons that are available in it is shown in Figure I-4.

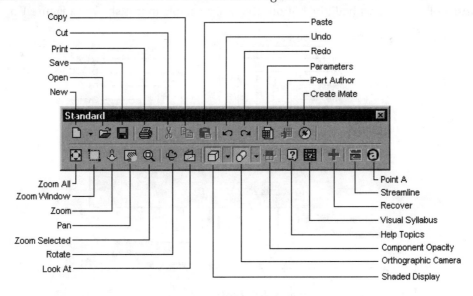

Figure I-4 Standard toolbar

Sketch Toolbar

This is one of the most important toolbar in the **Part** mode. You will choose all commands for creating the sketches of the parts from this toolbar. The **Sketch** toolbar along with all the buttons that are available in it is shown in Figure I-5.

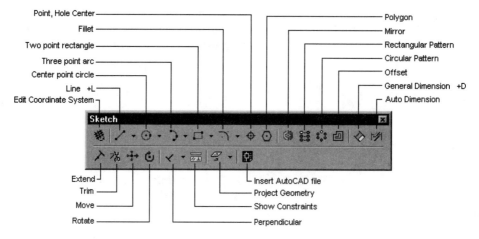

Figure I-5 Sketch toolbar

Features Toolbar

This is the second most important toolbar provided in the **Part** mode. Once the sketch is completed, you need to convert it into a feature using the modeling commands. This toolbar provides all the modeling commands that can be used to convert the sketch into a feature. The **Feature** toolbar along with all the buttons that are available in it is shown in Figure I-6.

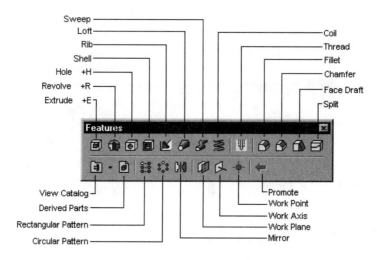

Figure I-6 Features toolbar

Precise Input Toolbar

You are now aware of the fact that Autodesk Inventor does not provide you with any command prompt. Because of this you will be restricted from entering the precise values of the sketcher entities. But this problem was foreseen and has been taken care of in Autodesk Inventor by providing you with a very important toolbar called the **Precise Input** toolbar. This toolbar is used to enter the precise values for the coordinates of the sketcher entities. This toolbar is also available in the **Drawing** and the **Assembly** mode for providing the precise values. The **Precise Input** toolbar is shown in Figure I-7.

Figure I-7 Precise Input toolbar

Sheet Metal Toolbar

This toolbar provide the commands that are used in creating the sheet metal parts. This toolbar will be available only when you are in the sheet metal environment. You can proceed to the sheet metal environment by choosing **Sheet Metal** from the **Application** menu. The **Sheet Metal** toolbar is shown in Figure I-8.

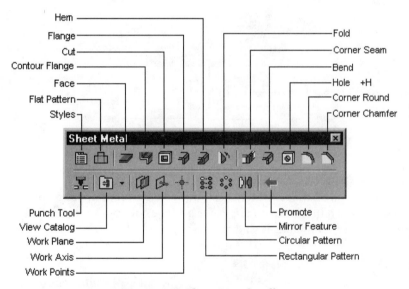

Figure I-8 Sheet Metal toolbar

Assembly Mode Toolbars

All the above-mentioned toolbars are also available in this environment. In addition to these toolbars, this environment also provides the **Assembly** toolbar, see Figure I-9.

Drawing Mode Toolbars

The **Standard**, **Sketch**, and **Precise Input** toolbars are also available in this environment. In addition to these toolbars the **Drawing Mode** also provides you with the following two toolbars:

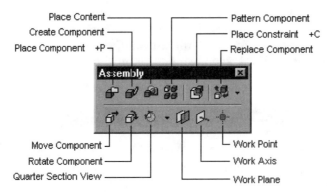

Figure I-9 Assembly toolbar

Drawing Management Toolbar

This toolbar is extensively used in the **Drawing** environment for generating the drawing views. All the tools required to generate the drawing views are available in this toolbar. The **Drawing Management** toolbar is shown in Figure I-10.

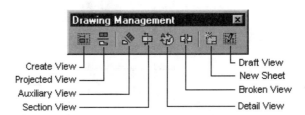

Figure I-10 Drawing Management toolbar

Drawing Annotation Toolbar

This is the second toolbar that is widely used in this environment. This tollbar provide you with the tools that are required to create different types of annotation in the drawing views. The **Drawing Annotation** toolbar is shown in Figure I-11.

Presentation Mode Toolbar

The **Standard** toolbar is also available in this environment. In addition to this toolbar, the **Presentation** mode also provides you with the **Presentation View Management** toolbar as shown in Figure I-12.

Command Bar

In addition to these toolbars, Autodesk Inventor also displays the **Command Bar**, see Figure I-13.

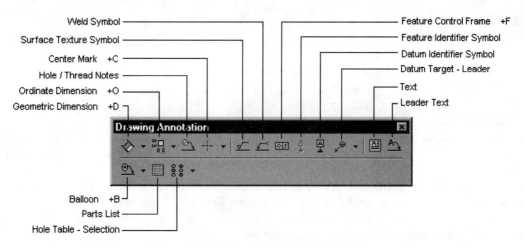

Figure I-11 Drawing Annotation toolbar

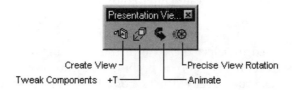

Figure I-12 Presentation View Management toolbar

The **Command Bar** is also a toolbar and is referred to a lot during the designing process using Autodesk Inventor.

The **Command Bar** is displayed in all the environments of Autodesk Inventor, with some modifications. The options in this toolbar are discussed next.

Figure I-13 Command Bar

Select

This tool is used to set the selection priority. When you choose the down arrow on the right of this button, three more buttons will be displayed. These buttons are **Feature Priority**, **Face Priority**, and **Sketch Priority**. The **Feature Priority** button is chosen to set the selection priority to features. If this button is chosen, you can select any feature in the model. The **Face Priority** button is chosen to set the priority to faces. If this button is chosen, you can select the faces of the features. The **Sketch Priority** button is chosen to set the priority to sketches. If this button is chosen, you can select the entities of the sketches in the sketcher environment.

Return

This button is chosen to exit the sketching environment. Once you have finished the sketch, choose this button to proceed to the **Part** mode where you can convert the sketch into a feature using the required tools. When you choose this button, the **Sketch** panel bar is replaced by the **Features** panel bar.

Sketch

This button is chosen when you want to draw a sketch. This button is chosen by default when you start a new file in the **Part** mode. This enables you to draw the sketches as in most of the designs, the first feature is a sketched feature. Once you have completed a sketch, you can either choose the **Return** button or choose this button again to exit the sketching environment. Whenever you need to draw the sketch for another feature, choose this button. You will be prompted to select the plane for sketching the feature. Once you define the new sketching plane, the sketching environment will be activated.

Update

This button is chosen to update the design after editing.

Style

This drop-down list is used to select the style of the sketching entities. In the sketching environment you can select either the normal or the construction option from this drop-down list. In the **Drawing** mode, you can select the line or edge styles from this drop-down list. In the **Part** or the **Assembly** mode, this drop-down list is replaced by the **Color** drop-down list. You can select the color for the selected models using this drop-down list.

Message

The **Message** box is used to display the messages and prompts. If you move the cursor on any tool or button, this box displays the function of that tool. If you choose a tool or a button, all the prompt sequences related to it will be displayed in this box. For example, if you choose the **Line** tool in the sketching environment, all the prompts related to drawing the lines will be displayed in this box. Similarly, in the **Part** mode, all the prompts related to the creation of the selected feature will be displayed in this box.

Tip. *All the messages and prompts displayed in the **Message** box are also displayed on the lower left corner of the Autodesk Inventor window.*

In almost all the toolbars you will notice that there are some buttons that have an arrow on the right. These arrows are called the down arrows. When you choose these arrows, some more related buttons will be displayed, see Figure I-14.

ADDITIONAL DESIGN TOOLS

Autodesk Inventor has gone a step ahead from the other solid modeling tools in making the design intent easier. This is done by introducing the **Panel Bar** and the **Browser** to invoke the commands or to perform an operation. Both of these additional tools make the design intent a lot more easier and also appreciably reduces the time consumed in completing the design.

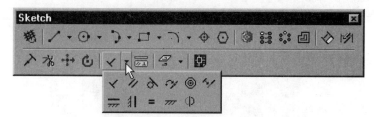

Figure I-14 *More buttons displayed upon choosing the down arrow on the right of the **Perpendicular** button*

Panel Bars

The panel bars are generally provided on the left of the drawing window. The panel bar provides only those tools that will be required to complete the design at that step. For example, when you are in the sketching mode, at that time only the tools that are required for sketching will be available in the panel bar. Similarly, when you want to convert the sketch into a feature, at that time only the solid modeling tools will be available. This implies that the tools available in the panel bar will be different for each of the designing environment of Autodesk Inventor. Figure I-15 to Figure I-20 shows the panel bars in the different designing environments.

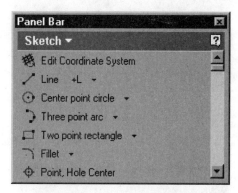

Figure I-15 *Sketch* *panel bar*

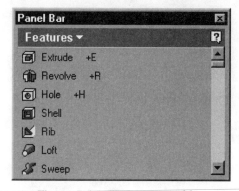

Figure I-16 *Features* *panel bar*

Figure I-17 Sheet Metal panel bar

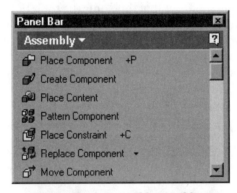

Figure I-18 Assembly panel bar

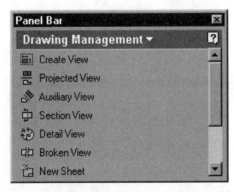

Figure I-19 Drawing Management panel bar

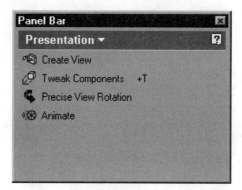

Figure I-20 Presentation panel bar

Browser

This is the second additional tool that is provided to make the designing process easier. The browser is also available on the left side of the drawing window and below the panel bar. It displays all the operations that were performed during the designing process in the order in which they were performed. All these operations are displayed in the form of a tree view. The contents of the browser are different for different environments of Autodesk Inventor. For example, in the **Part** mode, it displays various operations that were used in creating the part. Similarly, in the **Assembly** mode, it displays all the components along with the constraints that were applied on them in order to assemble them.

UNITS FOR DIMENSIONS

While installing Autodesk Inventor on your system, you can specify the units that will be used for dimensioning the models in inches or in millimeters. If you select inches as the units, the English standard will be followed in Autodesk Inventor and if you select millimeter as the units, Metric standard will be followed. This book follows the units in millimeter. Therefore, it is recommended that you install Autodesk Inventor for Metric standards by selecting the units in millimeter.

IMPORTANT TERMS AND THEIR DEFINITIONS

Before you proceed further in Autodesk Inventor, it is very important for you to understand the following terms. These terms will be widely used in this book.

Featured-based Modeling

Feature is defined as the smallest building block that can be modified individually. In Autodesk Inventor, the solid models will be created by integrating a number of these building blocks. Therefore, you can say that the model in Autodesk Inventor is a combination of a number of individual features. These features understand their fit and function properly, and therefore, can be modified any time during the designing process. Generally, these features automatically adjust their values if there is any change in their surrounding. This provides greater flexibility to the design. For example, a feature created by cutting right through the base feature will automatically adjust its depth if you increase the depth of the base feature.

Parametric Modeling

The parametric nature of a software package is defined as its ability to use the standard properties or parameters in defining the shape and size of a geometry. The main function of this property is to derive the selected geometry to the new size or shape without considering its original size or shape. For example, you can derive a line of say 20 mm that was initially drawn at an angle of 45° to a line of 50 mm and change its orientation to 90°. This property make the designing process very easy. This is because now you do not have to draw the sketch to the actual dimensions that are required. All you have to do is to draw the sketch to some relative dimensions and then this solid modeling tool will derive it to the actual values you require.

Bidirectional Associativity

As mentioned earlier, this solid modeling tool does not restrict its capabilities to the 3D solid output. It is also capable of highly effective assembly modeling, drafting, and presentations. There exists a bidirectional associativity between all these environments of Autodesk Inventor. This means that at every point of time there exists a link between all the environments of Autodesk Inventor. This link ensures that if any modification is made in the model in any one of the environment, it is automatically reflected in the other environments immediately.

Adaptive

This is a new but highly effective property that is included in the designing process of this solid modeling tool. You are aware of the fact that there are a number of components that can be used at various places in the design with a small change in their shape and size. This property makes the part or the feature adapt to its environment. This property also ensures that the adaptive part changes its shape and size as soon as it is constrained to other parts. This considerably reduces the time and effort required in creating similar parts in the design.

Design Doctor

The design doctor is one of the most important part of the designing process using this solid modeling tool. It is a highly effective tool provided to you to ensure that the entire design process is error free. The main purpose of the design doctor is to make you aware if there exists a problem in the design. The design doctor works in the following three steps:

Selecting the Model and Errors in the Model

In this step the design doctor selects the sketch, part, assembly, and so on and finds out all the errors in it.

Examining the Errors

In this step it examines all the errors in the selected design. Each of the error is individually examined so that it can come up with a solution for each of the error.

Providing the Solutions for the Errors

This is the last step of the working of the design doctor. Once it has individually examined each of the errors, it comes up with solutions for them. It provides you with a list of methods that can be utilized in order to remove the errors from the design.

Constraints

These are the logical operations that are performed on the selected design to make it more accurate or define its position with respect to the other design. There are two types of constraints that are available in Autodesk Inventor. Both of these types are explained below:

Geometry Constraints

These logical operations are performed on the basic sketching entities to relate them to the standard properties like collinearity, concentricity, perpendicularity, and so on. Autodesk Inventor automatically applies these geometric constraints to the sketcher entities at the time of their creation. You do not have to use an extra command to apply these constraints on to the sketcher entities. However, you can also manually apply these geometry constraints on to the sketcher entities. There are eleven types of the geometric constraints. They are

Perpendicular

This constraint is used to make the selected line segment perpendicular to another line segment.

Parallel

This constraint is used to make the selected line segments parallel.

Tangent

This constraint is used to make the selected line segment or curve tangent to another curve.

Coincident

This constraint is used to make two points or a point and a curve coincident.

Concentric

Applying this constraint forces two selected curves to share the same center point. The curves that can be made concentric are arcs, circles, or ellipses.

Colinear

Applying this constraint forces two selected line segments or ellipse axes to be placed in the same line.

Horizontal

This constraint forces the selected line segment to become a horizontal line.

Vertical

This constraint forces the selected line segment to become a vertical line.

Equal

This constraint forces the selected line segments to become of equal length. This constraint can also be used to force two curves to become of equal radius.

Fix

This constraint is used to fix the selected point or curve to a particular location with respect to the coordinate system of the current sketch.

Symmetric

This constraint is used to force the selected sketched entities to become symmetrical about a sketched line segment. The line segment may or may not be a center line.

Assembly Constraints

The assembly constraints are the logical operations performed on the components in order to bind them together to create an assembly. These constraints are applied to reduce the degrees of freedom of the components. There are four types of assembly constraints. They are

Mate

The **Mate** constraint is used to make the selected faces of different components coplanar. The model can be placed facing in same direction or facing in opposite direction. You can also specify some offset distance between the selected faces.

Angle

The **Angle** constraint is used to place the selected faces of different components at some angle with respect to each other.

Tangent

The **Tangent** constraint is used to make the selected face of a component tangent to the cylindrical, circular, or conical faces of the other component.

Insert

The **Insert** constraint is used to force two different circular components to share same orientation of the central axis. It also makes the selected faces of the circular components coplanar.

Motion Constraints

The motion constraints are the logical operations performed on the components that are assembled using the assembly constraints. There are two types of motion constraints. They are discussed next.

Rotation

The **Rotation** constraint is used to rotate one component of the assembly in relation with the other component. Both the components rotate about the specified central axis.

Rotation-Translation Constraint

The **Rotation-Translation** constraint is used to rotate the first component in relation with the translation of the second component.

Transitional Constraints

The transitional constraints are also applied on the assembled components and used to ensure that the selected face of the cylindrical component maintains the contact with the selected faces of the other component when you slide the cylindrical component.

Note

The motion and the transitional constraints are applied on the components that are already assembled using the assembly constraints. Therefore, these constraints work along the degrees of freedom of the components that are not restricted.

Consumed Sketch

A consumed sketch is a sketch that has been converted into a feature using the tools like **Extrude**, **Revolve**, **Sweep**, **Loft**, and so on.

CYCLING THROUGH THE ENTITIES

While working with the complicated models, you have to sometimes select the entities that are not visible in the current view or are hidden behind other entities. To select these type of entities, Autodesk Inventor allows you to cycle through the entities using a cycling tool. This tool is displayed automatically when you hold the cursor at a point where more than one entity are available. You can also display the cycling tool by pressing the SPACEBAR on the keyboard.

This cycling tool consists of two arrows at each end and a rectangle in between. The left arrow is used to cycle through the previous entities, the right arrow is used to cycle through the next entities, and the rectangle is used to select the highlighted entity. The current entity will be highlighted and displayed in red color. Once the entity that you want to select is highlighted, move the cursor over the rectangle in the cycling tool and select it using the left mouse button. The highlighted entity will be selected and will be displayed in blue color. Figure I-21 shows the cycling tool displayed in the sketching environment to cycle through the sketched entities. You can use this tool in all the modes and environments of Autodesk Inventor.

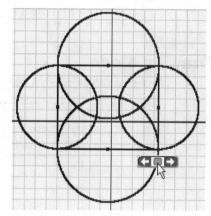

Figure I-21 *Cycling through the entities*

HOT KEYS

As mentioned earlier, there is no command prompt in Autodesk Inventor. However, you can still use the keys on the keyboard to invoke some tools. The keys that can be used to invoke the tools are called the hot keys. Remember that the working of the hot keys will be different in the different environments. All the hot keys that can be used in different environments are discussed below:

Part Mode

The hot keys that can be used in the **Part** mode are

D	Dimensioning The Sketched Entities
E	Extruding The Sketch
H	Placing The Hole
L	Invoking The Line Command
R	Revolving The Sketch

Assembly Mode

The hot keys that can be used in the **Assembly** mode are

| C | Placing The Constraints |
| P | Placing The Components |

Drawing Mode

The hot keys that can be used in the **Drawing** mode are

B	Adding The Balloons
C	Placing Center Marks
D	General Dimensions
O	Ordinate Dimensions
F	Feature Control Frame

Presentation Mode

The hot keys that can be used in the **Presentation** mode are

| T | Tweaking The Component |

In addition to these keys, you can also use some other keys for the ease of designing. Note that you will have to hold some of these keys down and use them in a combination of the pointing device in order to use them. These hot keys are

F1	Help
F2	Pan Realtime
F3	Zoom Realtime
F4	Rotate
F5	Previous View
SHIFT+F5	Next View
CTRL	Command Modifier
SHIFT	Command Modifiers
ESC	Abort The Command

COLOR SCHEME

Autodesk Inventor allows you to use different color schemes as the background color of the screen and for displaying the entities on the screen. However, this book uses the **Presentation** color scheme and the **Background Gradient** check box is cleared. To change the color scheme, choose **Tools > Application Options** from the menu bar. The **Options** dialog box will be displayed. In this dialog box choose the **Colors** tab to display different predefined colors. Select the required color scheme from the **Color Scheme** list box.

Chapter 1

Drawing Sketches for the Solid Models

Learning Objectives

After completing this chapter you will be able to:
- *Open a new template file for drawing the sketches.*
- *Set up the sketching environment.*
- *Know about various drawing display options.*
- *Know about the sketcher environment in the Part mode.*
- *Get acquainted with the sketcher entities.*
- *Draw the sketches using the different sketcher entities.*
- *Delete the sketched entities.*

THE SKETCHING ENVIRONMENT

Most of the designs you create are a combination of sketched, placed, and work features. The placed and the work features can be created directly without creating sketches, but the sketched features require sketches. Generally, in most of the designs the first or the base feature has to be a sketched feature. Therefore, in any design the first and the foremost point of concern is to draw the basic sketch of the base feature. Later you can add more features to the base feature to complete the design. In the sketching environment you will learn to draw the sketches for the base features. The same concept can also be used later to add more sketched features to the base feature for completing the design. A sketch is nothing but the basic contour for the solid model. For example, consider the model shown in Figure 1-1.

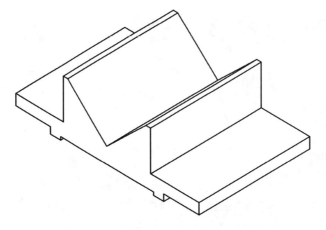

Figure 1-1 *A solid model*

This model is created using a sketched feature. The basic sketch for the sketched feature is shown in Figure 1-2. Once you have drawn the basic sketch, you just have to convert it into a solid model using simple but highly effective solid modeling tools.

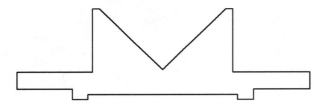

Figure 1-2 *The basic sketch for the solid model*

The sketching environment of Autodesk Inventor can be invoked at any time in the **Part** mode or in the **Assembly** mode. Unlike the other solid modeling tools, here you just have to specify that you want to create a sketch, and the sketcher mode will be activated. Also when you start a new file in the **Part** mode, first the sketching environment will be active. You can draw the sketch in this environment and then proceed to the part modeling environment for converting the sketch into a solid model. The different options in the sketching environment will be discussed later in this chapter.

OPENING A NEW FILE

The first step after you start any solid modeling tool is to open a new file. As mentioned in Introduction, when you start Autodesk Inventor, the **Open** dialog box will be displayed. The different options of this dialog box are discussed next.

Getting Started

The options that are displayed when you choose **Getting Started** from the **What To Do** area are used to select different types of help topics for working in Autodesk Inventor, see Figure 1-3. You can find out the latest enhancements in this release, open a tutorial mode that will guide you through different steps of creating solid models, browse the help topics of Autodesk Inventor, or directly start using Autodesk Inventor. All this can be done using the links provided on the right side of the dialog box. You can also proceed to the **Autodesk Point A** or the **Autodesk Streamline** web sites using the option provided in the lower portion of this dialog box.

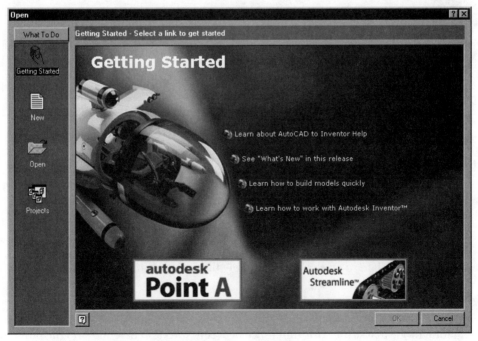

Figure 1-3 Getting Started options of the Open dialog box

New

The options that are provided when you choose **New** will be extensively used during the designing process using Autodesk Inventor. These options are used to select a template file for starting the design. You can select a template in the **Default** standard, the **English** standard, or the **Metric** standard. If you have installed Autodesk Inventor by selecting millimeter as the unit for measurement, the standards under the **Default** tab are used for the designing purpose. However, if you have installed Autodesk Inventor by selecting inch as the unit for measurement, you will select templates from the **Metric** tab, see Figure 1-4. The different types of templates that are available when you choose the **Metric** tab are discussed next.

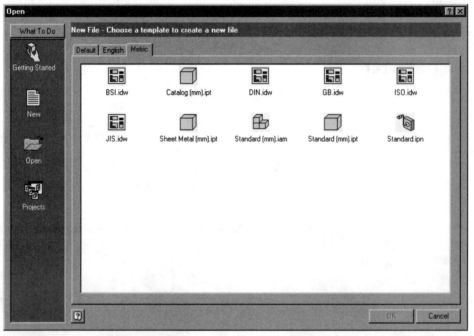

*Figure 1-4 Default templates displayed under the **Metric** tab of the **Open** dialog box*

.ipt Template

Select the .ipt template to open a new part file for creating a solid model or a sheet metal component. When you open this file, the sketching environment will be automatically active and you can directly start drawing the sketches.

.iam Template

Select the .iam template to open a new assembly file for assembling different part files.

.ipn Template

Select the .ipn template to open a new presentation file for animating the assemblies. The **Presentation** mode marks the basic difference between Autodesk Inventor and the other design tools. This mode allows you to animate the assemblies created in the **Assembly** mode. For example, you can create a presentation that shows a Drill Press Vice assembly in motion. The presentations are created using simple but highly effective tools provided in the **Presentation** mode.

.idw Template

Select the .idw template to open a new drawing file for generating the drawing views. You can use the drawing templates of different standards that are provided in this tab such as ISO, DIN, GB, JIS, and BSI.

Open

The options that are provided when you choose this option are used to open the existing files, see Figure 1-5. You can select the file to open from the list that is available in the upper part of the dialog box. The preview of the selected file will be displayed in the preview window provided in the lower left portion of this dialog box. By default, you can open any file created using Autodesk Inventor. The reason for this is that by default, the **Files of type** drop-down list displays the **Inventor Files (*.iam;*.idw;*.ipt;*.ipn;*.ide)** option. However, you can also open the files created in other solid modeling tools such as AutoCAD or Pro/ENGINEER by selecting their respective options from the **Files of type** drop-down list.

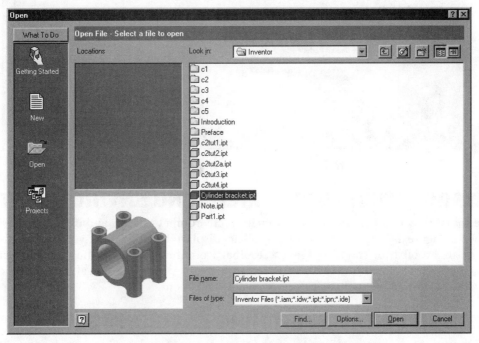

Figure 1-5 **Open File** *options of the* **Open** *dialog box*

Projects

This option is chosen to change the current project directory and the project files. All the available project directories will be displayed in the upper half of the dialog box and the options of the project folder will be displayed in the lower half of the folder. If the desired project folder is not displayed in the list, choose the **Browse** button to display the

Choose project file dialog box and then select the project folder using this dialog box. Once you have selected the project folder, it will be added in the upper part of the **Open** dialog box. Its path will also be displayed in the upper part of the dialog box. When you select a project, the options related to it are shown in the lower part of the dialog box. You can add various search paths for this project using the button provided on the right of the lower part. The **Open** dialog box with the various **Projects** options is shown in Figure 1-6.

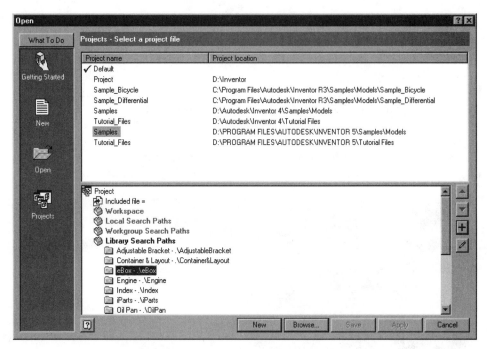

Figure 1-6 *Projects* options of the *Open* dialog box

INTRODUCTION TO THE SKETCHING ENVIRONMENT

The initial screen appearance in the sketching environment of a **Standard (mm).ipt** file is shown in Figure 1-7. In addition to the toolbars displayed in the figure, you can also invoke the desired toolbar by choosing **View > Toolbar** from the menu bar. These toolbars can be placed at any location by dragging them to the desired location. You can also double-click on the blue portion of the toolbars to automatically dock them.

SETTING UP THE SKETCHING ENVIRONMENT

It is very important for you to first set up the sketcher environment. This has to be done before you start drawing the sketches. Setting up the sketcher environment includes increasing the limits of the drawing. It is not always possible that the designs you want to create consist of small limits. You will come across a number of designs that have large dimension values. Therefore, before starting the drawing you need to set the limits of the sketching environment. These limits will depend upon the dimensions of the design. The process of increasing the limits of the drawing is discussed next.

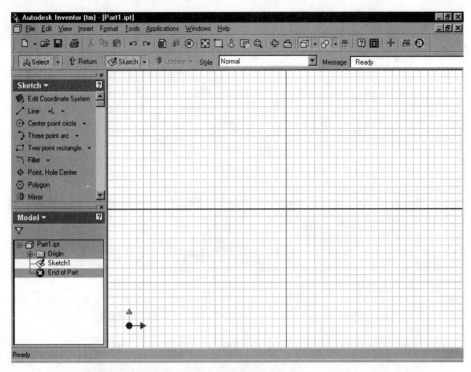

Figure 1-7 Initial screen appearance in the sketch mode

Modifying the Limits of the Drawing

You might have noticed that the drawing window in the sketch mode consists of a number of light and dark lines that are drawn normal to each other. These normal lines are called grid lines. The grids are used as reference for drawing the sketches and to modify the limits of the drawing. To modify the limits, choose **Document Settings** in the **Tools** menu. When you choose this option, the **Document Settings** dialog box will be displayed. In this dialog box choose the **Sketch** tab to display the options related to the sketching environment, see Figure 1-8. The options provided under this tab are discussed next.

Snap Spacing Area

The options under this area are used to specify the snap and grid spacing.

X

This edit box is used to specify the grid spacing in the X direction. More the spacing, bigger will be the limits of the drawing along the X axis direction.

Y

This edit box is used to specify the grid spacing in the Y direction. More the spacing, bigger will be the limits of the drawing along the Y axis direction.

Grid Display Area

The options under this area are used to control the number of major and minor lines. The

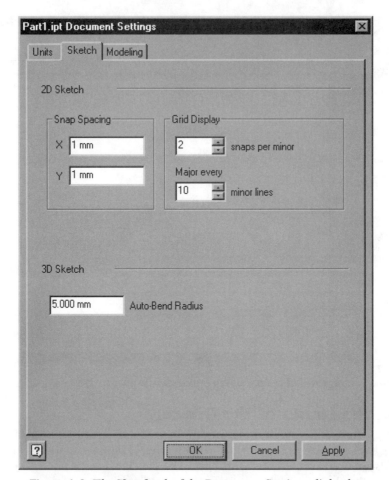

*Figure 1-8 The **Sketch** tab of the **Document Settings** dialog box*

minor lines are the light lines that are displayed inside the dark gray lines. The dark gray lines are called the major lines.

snaps per minor Lines
This spinner is used to specify the number of snap points between each minor line.

Major every minor lines
This spinner is used to specify the number of minor lines between the major lines.

Note
You will have to increase the drawing display area after increasing the grid spacing. The options that will be used to increase the drawing display area are discussed next.

Tip. *You can also turn off the display of the major and minor grid lines and the axes. To turn off the display, choose **Application Options** from the **Tools** menu. The **Options** dialog box will be displayed. Choose the **Sketch** tab and clear the **Grid Lines**, **Minor Grid Lines**, and the **Axes** check boxes in the **Display** area.*

LEARNING ABOUT DIFFERENT DRAWING DISPLAY TOOLS

The various drawing display tools are an integral part of any design software. These options are extensively used during the designing process. The various drawing display tools that are available in Autodesk Inventor are discussed next.

Zoom All

Menu:	View > Zoom All
Toolbar:	Standard > Zoom All

The **Zoom All** tool is used to increase the drawing display area so that all the sketched entities are included in the current display. Note that if a drawing consists of dimensions that are beyond the current display, invoking this tool does not necessarily include them in the current display.

Zoom Window

Menu:	View > Zoom Window
Toolbar:	Standard > Zoom Window

The **Zoom Window** tool is used to define an area to be magnified and viewed in the current drawing. The area is defined using two diagonal points of a box (called window) in the drawing area. The area that is inscribed inside the window will be magnified and displayed.

Tip. *The size of the dimension text always remains constant even if you magnify the area that include some dimensions.*

*To switch to the previous view, right-click in the drawing area and then choose **Previous View** from the shortcut menu, or press the F5 key.*

Zoom

Menu:	View > Zoom
Toolbar:	Standard > Zoom

The **Zoom** tool is used to interactively zoom in and out of the drawing. When you choose this button, the cursor is converted into an arrow. You can zoom into the drawing by pressing the left mouse button and dragging it down. Similarly, you can zoom out of the drawing by pressing the left mouse button and then dragging it up. You can exit this tool by choosing the button for the new tool or by pressing ESC. You can also choose **Done** from the shortcut menu that is displayed upon right-clicking in this drawing display option.

Tip. *You will have to increase the drawing display area by zooming out from the drawing using the **Zoom** tool after increasing the limits of the drawing with the help of the **Grid** button.*

Pan

Menu:	View > Pan
Toolbar:	Standard > Pan

 The **Pan** tool is used to drag the current view in the drawing area. This option is generally used to display the contents of the drawing that are outside the drawing without actually changing the magnification of the current drawing. It is just like holding a portion of the drawing and dragging it across the drawing window.

Zoom Selected

Menu:	View > Zoom Selected
Toolbar:	Standard > Zoom Selected

 When you choose the **Zoom Selected** button, you will be prompted to select the entity to zoom. The entity then selected will be magnified to the maximum extent and placed at the center of the drawing window.

 Note

The other drawing display tools will be discussed in later chapters.

GETTING ACQUAINTED WITH THE VARIOUS SKETCHING TOOLS

Getting acquainted with the different sketcher entities is a very important part of learning process using this book. A major part of the design will be created using the sketcher entities. Therefore, this section can be considered as one of the most important sections of the book. In Autodesk Inventor, any sketched entity can be of two types: **Normal** and **Construction**. The type of entity you want to draw can be selected from the **Style** drop-down list in the **Command Bar**. The normal entities can be converted into a feature but the construction entities are drawn just for reference purpose and cannot be converted into a feature. The various sketcher entities that can be drawn in Autodesk Inventor are discussed next.

Drawing Lines

Toolbar:	Sketch > Line
Panel Bar:	Sketch > Line

Lines are the basic and one of the most important entities in the sketching environment. As mentioned earlier, you can draw either normal lines or construction lines. A line is defined as the shortest distance between two points. The two points are the start point and the endpoint of the line. Therefore, the main point of concern in drawing a line is defining these two points. As you are aware of the fact that Autodesk Inventor is parametric in nature, therefore, you can draw an initial line of any length or at any angle by just picking the points on the screen and then driving it to a new value using the respective tool. However, you can also directly create the line of the actual length and angle using the **Precise Input** toolbar. Both these methods of drawing the lines are discussed next.

Drawing Lines by Picking the Points on the Screen

This method is a very convenient method of drawing lines and is extensively used in drawing the sketches of the models. When you invoke the **Line** tool from the **Sketch** toolbar or panel bar, the cursor (that was initially an arrow) is replaced by a crosshair with a yellow circle at the intersection of crosshair and you will be prompted to select the start point of the line. The point of intersection of the X and Y axes (drawn with dark black color) is the origin point. If you move the cursor close to the origin point, it snaps to the origin point automatically. The coordinates of the points where the cursor moves are displayed on the lower right corner of the Autodesk Inventor screen. To start the line, pick a point anywhere in the drawing window. As soon as you pick the start point of the line, a rubber-band line will start from that point. One end of this rubber-band line will be fixed at the point you picked on the screen and the second end will be fixed with the yellow circle in the crosshair.

Now, the lower left corner of the Autodesk Inventor screen will display three columns. The first column will display the coordinates of the current location of the cursor, the second column will display the current length of the line, and the third column will display the current angle of the line. Taking the reference from these columns you can now move the cursor to a new location to define the endpoint of the line.

The line drawing does not end after you have specified the endpoint of the line. When you pick the endpoint of the last line, it will be drawn and a new rubber-band line will be started. The start point of the new rubber-band line will be the endpoint of the last line and you will be prompted to specify the endpoint of the line. As mentioned earlier, when you draw the entities, the valid constraints will be automatically applied to the entities. Therefore, when you create the continuous lines, the perpendicular and the parallel constraints will be automatically applied to the lines. The symbol of the constraint that is applied will be displayed on the lines. Similarly, you can create as many lines a you want by specifying continuous endpoints. At any time you can exit the line drawing by pressing the ESC key or by choosing any other button. Figure 1-9 and Figure 1-10 display the perpendicular and parallel constraints that are applied to the lines when they are drawn.

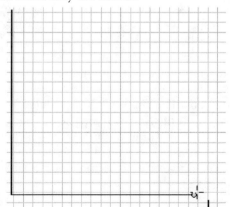

Figure 1-9 *Applying the perpendicular constraint*   **Figure 1-10** *Applying the parallel constraint*

Note
*The various prompt sequences are displayed in the **Message** box of the **Command Bar**.*

Tip. *You can turn off the automatic applications of the constraints on to the lines by holding down the CTRL key while drawing the lines.*

Drawing Lines by Specifying the Exact Values

This is the second method of drawing lines in Autodesk Inventor. This method uses the **Precise Input** toolbar to define the coordinates of the start point and the endpoint of the lines. As mentioned earlier, the origin of the drawing lies at the intersection of the X and Y axes. The X and Y coordinate of this point is 0,0. Taking the reference of this point you can draw the lines. There are two methods of defining the coordinates using this toolbar. Both of these methods are discussed next.

Specifying the Coordinates with Respect to the Origin. This system of defining the coordinates is also termed as the **absolute coordinate system**. In this system the coordinates of the point are defined with respect to the origin of the drawing. By default, the origin lies at the intersection of the X and Y axes. All the points in this system are defined with respect to this origin. To define the points you can use the following four methods:

Defining the Absolute X and Y Coordinates. In this method you will define the X and Y coordinates of the new point with respect to the origin. To invoke this method, choose the **Indicate a point location by typing the X and Y values** button in the **Precise Input** toolbar. The exact X and Y coordinates of the point can be entered in the X and Y edit boxes provided in this toolbar.

Defining the Absolute X Coordinate and the Angle from the X Axis. In this method you will define the absolute X coordinate of the new point with respect to the origin and the angle that will be made by the line with the X axis. The angle will be calculated in the counterclockwise direction from the positive side of the X axis. To invoke this method, choose the down arrow besides the **XY** button in the **Precise Input** toolbar and then choose the **Specify a point using X coordinate and angle from X-axis** button. The X coordinate of the new point and the angle can be defined in the respective edit boxes that are available in the **Precise Input** toolbar.

Defining the Absolute Y Coordinate and the Angle from the X Axis. In this method you will define the absolute Y coordinate of the new point with respect to the origin and the angle that will be made by the line with the X axis. The angle will be calculated in the counterclockwise direction from the positive side of the X axis. To invoke this method, choose the down arrow besides the **XY** button in the **Precise Input** toolbar and then choose the **Specify a point using Y coordinate and angle from X-axis** button. The Y coordinate of the new point and the angle can be defined in the respective edit boxes that are available in the **Precise Input** toolbar.

Specifying the Length of the Line and the Angle from the X Axis. In this method you will define the length of the line and the angle that will be made by the line with the X axis. To invoke this method, choose the down arrow besides the XY button in the **Precise Input** toolbar and then choose the **Specify a point using distance from the**

origin and angle from X-axis button. The length of the line and the angle can be defined in the respective edit boxes.

Specifying the Coordinates with Respect to the Last Point. This system of specifying the coordinates is also termed as the **relative coordinate system**. In this type of system the coordinate of the next point is specified with respect to the last specified point. Note that this system of defining the points cannot be used for specifying the first point (the start point of the line). All the above-mentioned absolute coordinate methods for specifying the point can also be used with respect to the last specified point by choosing the **Delta Y Delta X** button along with the button of the respective method. This button is provided on the left of the **XY** button in the **Precise Input** toolbar. This button will be available only after you have specified the start point of the first line.

Note

*The **Precise Input** toolbar can also be used to draw other sketcher entities. The use of options available under this toolbar for drawing other sketcher entities will be discussed along with the respective tools.*

Drawing Circles

In Autodesk Inventor you can draw circles using two methods. You can either draw a circle by defining the center and the radius of the circle or draw a circle that is tangent to three specified lines. Both these methods of drawing the circle are discussed next.

Drawing a Circle by Specifying the Center Point and the Radius of the Circle

Toolbar:	Sketch > Center point circle
Panel Bar:	Sketch > Center point circle

This is the default option of drawing circles. In this method you have to define the center point and the radius of the circle. When you choose the **Center point circle** button, you will be prompted to locate the center of the circle. As soon as you specify the center point of the circle, you will be prompted to specify a point on the circle. The point on the circle will define the radius of the circle. You can also specify the center and the radius of the circle using the **Precise Input** toolbar. Figure 1-11 shows a circle drawn by specifying the center and the radius of the circle.

Drawing Circles Using Three Tangent Lines

Toolbar:	Sketch > Center point circle > Tangent circle
Panel Bar:	Sketch > Center point circle > Tangent circle

This is the second method of drawing circles. In this method you will draw a circle that is tangent to three selected lines. To invoke this option, choose the down arrow besides the **Center point circle** in the **Sketch** toolbar and then choose the **Tangent circle** button. When you invoke this option, you will be prompted to select the tangent lines one by one. As soon as you specify the three lines, a circle will be drawn that is tangent to all the three specified lines. Figure 1-12 shows a circle drawn using this method.

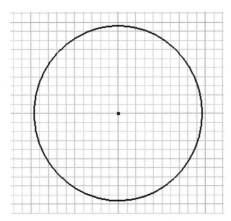 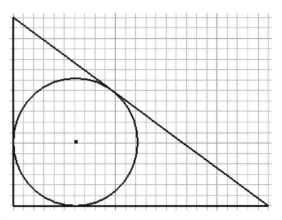

Figure 1-11   *Circle drawn using the center point and the radius of the circle*

Figure 1-12   *Circle drawn using three lines*

Drawing Ellipses

Toolbar:	Sketch > Center point circle > Ellipse
Panel Bar:	Sketch > Center point circle > Ellipse

To draw an ellipse, choose the down arrow besides the **Center point circle** in the **Sketch** toolbar and then choose the **Ellipse** button. When you choose this button, you will be prompted to specify the center of the ellipse, a point on the first axis of the ellipse, and a point on the ellipse. You can also specify all these points using the **Precise Input** toolbar. However, keep in mind that you cannot use the relative options for defining the points of the ellipse. Therefore, if you use the **Precise Input** toolbar for drawing the ellipse, all the values will be specified from the origin, see Figure 1-13.

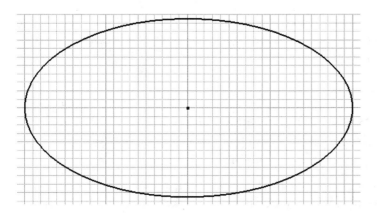

Figure 1-13   *Drawing the ellipse*

Drawing Arcs

Autodesk Inventor provides you with three methods for drawing arcs. All these three methods are discussed next.

Drawing an Arc Using Three Points

Toolbar:	Sketch > Three point arc
Panel Bar:	Sketch > Three point arc

This is the default method of drawing arcs. In this method you will draw an arc by specifying three points. The first point is the start point of the arc, the second point is the endpoint of the arc, and the third point is a point on the arc. You can also specify all these points using the **Precise Input** toolbar. Figure 1-14 shows an arc drawn using the three points method.

Drawing an Arc Tangent to an Existing Entity

Toolbar:	Sketch > Three point arc > Tangent arc
Panel Bar:	Sketch > Three point arc > Tangent arc

Using this method you can draw an arc that is tangent to an existing open entity. The open entity can be an arc or a line. To invoke this method, choose the down arrow besides the **Three point arc** button and then choose the **Tangent arc** button. When you choose this button you will be prompted to select the start point of the arc. The start point of the arc has to be the start point or the endpoint of an existing open entity. Once you specify the start point, a rubber-band arc will start from that point and tangent to the selected entity. You will then be prompted to specify the endpoint of the arc. It is very important to mention here that you cannot use the **Precise Input** toolbar to select the start point of this arc. However, you can use this toolbar to specify the endpoint of this arc. Figure 1-15 shows an arc drawn tangent to the line.

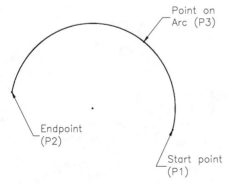

Figure 1-14 Drawing the three point arc

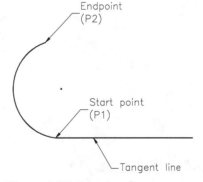

Figure 1-15 Drawing the tangent arc

Drawing an Arc Using the Center, Start and Endpoint of the Arc

Toolbar:	Sketch > Three point arc > Center point arc
Panel Bar:	Sketch > Three point arc > Center point arc

To invoke this method, choose the down arrow besides the **Three point arc** button in the **Sketch** toolbar and then choose the **Center point arc** button. This method allows you to draw an arc by specifying the center point of the arc, the start point of the arc, and the endpoint of the arc. When you choose this button, you will be prompted to specify the center point of the arc. Once you specify the center of the arc, you will be prompted to specify the start point of the arc and then the endpoint of the arc, see Figure 1-16. You can also use the **Precise Input** toolbar to specify these three points of the arc. As you define the center point of the arc and the start point of the arc in this method, the radius of the arc is automatically calculated. Therefore, the third point is just used to define the arc length. If the endpoint of the arc is more than the radius of the circle, then an imaginary line is drawn from that point to the center of the arc. The point at which the arc cuts the imaginary line will then be taken as the endpoint of the arc, see Figure 1-17.

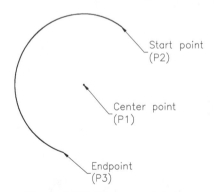

Figure 1-16 The center point arc

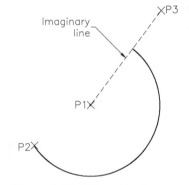

Figure 1-17 The center point arc

Drawing Rectangles

In Autodesk Inventor, rectangles can be drawn using the following two methods.

Drawing Rectangles Using the Two Opposite Corners

Toolbar:	Sketch > Two point rectangle
Panel Bar:	Sketch > Two point rectangle

This is the default method of drawing rectangles. In this method a rectangle is drawn by specifying the two opposite corners of the rectangle. When you choose the **Two point rectangle** button, you will be prompted to specify the first corner of the rectangle. Once you specify the first corner, you will be prompted to specify the opposite corner of the rectangle. Figure 1-18 shows a rectangle drawn using the **Two point rectangle** method.

Drawing Rectangles Using Three Points on a Rectangle

Toolbar:	Sketch > Two point rectangle > Three point rectangle
Panel Bar:	Sketch > Two point rectangle > Three point rectangle

You can invoke this method by choosing the down arrow besides the **Two point rectangle** button in the **Sketch** toolbar and then choosing the **Three point rectangle** button. This method allows you to draw a rectangle using three points. The first two points are used to define the size of one of the sides of the rectangle and the third point is used to define the size of the other side of the rectangle. When you invoke this method, you will be prompted to specify the first corner of the rectangle. Once you specify the first corner, you will be prompted to specify the second corner of the rectangle. Both of these corners are along the same direction and, therefore, are used to calculate the size of one of the sides of the rectangle. Upon specifying the second corner, you will be prompted to specify the third corner. This third corner will be used to calculate the size of the other side of the rectangle. Note that if you specify the second corner at a certain angle then the resultant rectangle will also be inclined. You can also specify all these three points for drawing the rectangle using the **Precise Input** toolbar. Figure 1-19 shows an inclined rectangle drawn using the **Three point rectangle** method.

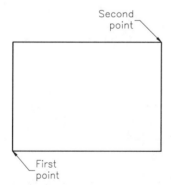
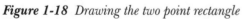

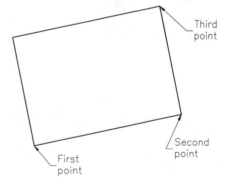

Figure 1-18 *Drawing the two point rectangle*

Figure 1-19 *Drawing the three point rectangle at an angle*

Tip. *You can move the sketched entities by just selecting them using a window or a crossing and then dragging them to a new location. You can move the lines by picking them and dragging. However, when you pick the arcs or circles and drag them then instead of moving from their original location they will just change their radius. But when you pick them and select their center point, they will move.*

You will learn about selecting objects using window and crossing later in this chapter.

Drawing Polygons

Toolbar:	Sketch > Polygon
Panel Bar:	Sketch > Polygon

 The polygons drawn in Autodesk Inventor are regular polygons. A regular polygon is a multisided geometric figure in which the length of all sides and the angle between all sides are same. In Autodesk Inventor, you can create a polygon with the number of sides ranging from 3 to 120. You cannot create a polygon with the number of sides less than 3 or more than 120. When you invoke the **Polygon** tool, the **Polygon** dialog box will be displayed as shown in Figure 1-20 and you will be prompted to select the center of the polygon. The options in this dialog box are discussed next.

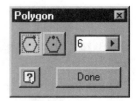

Figure 1-20 Polygon dialog box

Inscribed

This is the first button in the **Polygon** dialog box and is chosen by default. This option is used to draw an inscribed polygon. An inscribed polygon is a polygon that is drawn inside an imaginary circle such that the vertices of the polygon touch the circle. Once you have specified the center of the polygon, you will be prompted to specify a point on the polygon. In case of an inscribed polygon, the point on the polygon will define one of the vertices of the polygon, see Figure 1-21.

Circumscribed

This is the second button in the **Polygon** dialog box and is used to draw a circumscribed polygon. A circumscribed polygon is a polygon that is drawn outside an imaginary circle such that the edges of the polygon are tangent to the imaginary circle. In case of a circumscribed polygon, the point on the polygon will be the midpoint of one of the edges of the polygon, see Figure 1-22.

Number of Sides

This edit box is used to specify the number of sides of the polygon. The default value in this edit box is 6. You can enter any value ranging from 3 to 120 in this edit box.

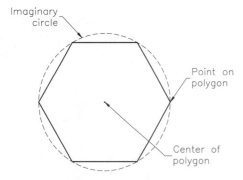

Figure 1-21 Drawing a six sided inscribed polygon

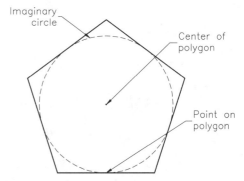

Figure 1-22 Drawing a five sided circumscribed polygon

Note
The rectangles and polygons drawn in Autodesk Inventor are a combination of individual lines. All the lines can be separately selected or deleted. However, when you select one of the lines and drag, the entire rectangle or polygon will be considered as a single entity. Therefore, instead of only one line moving, the entire object will be moved or stretched.

Placing the Points/Hole Centers

Toolbar:	Sketch > Point, Hole Center
Panel Bar:	Sketch > Point, Hole Center

In Autodesk Inventor, holes will be created using only a sketched point or a hole center. These sketched points or the hole centers can be placed using the **Point, Hole Center** button in the **Sketch** toolbar. When you choose this button, you will be prompted to specify the center point of the hole. You can specify the location of the point or the hole center by picking a point using the left mouse button. You can also specify the exact location using the **Precise Input** toolbar.

Tip. *You can redefine the origin of the current drawing by placing a point at the desired origin and then relocating the origin. To relocate the origin, choose the coordinate system button available at the extreme left of the **Precise Input** toolbar and then place the coordinate system icon at the desired point. You can relocate the origin to the actual origin by again choosing the coordinate system button.*

Creating Fillets

Toolbar:	Sketch > Fillet
Panel Bar:	Sketch > Fillet

Filleting is defined as the process of rounding the sharp corners and sharp edges of models. This is basically done to reduce the area of stress concentration in the model. This tool in the sketch mode is used to round the corners of the sketch by creating an arc tangent to both the selected curves. The portions of the selected curves that comprise the sharp corners are trimmed when the fillet is created. When you choose this button, the **2D Fillet** toolbar will be displayed with the current fillet radius (see Figure 1-23) and you will be prompted to select the lines or the arcs to fillet. You can change the value of the fillet radius by selecting the preset values from the list that is displayed by choosing the arrow provided on the right side of the edit box. You can also directly enter the desired value in the edit box. As many fillets of similar or different radius can be created in a single attempt using the **Fillet** button. You can fillet parallel or perpendicular lines (Figure 1-24 and Figure 1-25), intersecting lines or arcs,

Figure 1-23 2D Fillet toolbar

noninteresecting lines or arcs, and between a line and an arcs.

Drawing Splines

Toolbar:	Line > Spline
Panel Bar:	Line > Spline

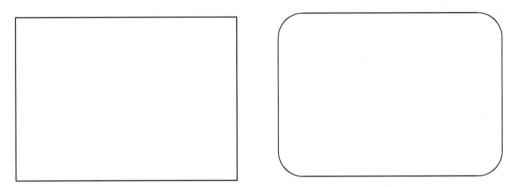

Figure 1-24 *Rectangle before filleting*   *Figure 1-25* *Same rectangle after filleting*

To draw a spline, choose the down arrow besides the **Line** button in the **Sketch** toolbar and choose the **Spline** button. When you choose this button, you will be prompted to specify the start point of the spline. After specifying the start point, you will be prompted to specify the next point of the spline. This procedure will continue until you terminate spline creation. To end the spline at the current point, right-click to display the shortcut menu and choose **Create**. Note that if you choose **Done** from the shortcut menu, the spline will not be drawn. You can also end spline creation by pressing the ENTER key. You can undo the last drawn spline segment when you are still inside the spline drawing options. This can be done by choosing **Backup** from the shortcut menu displayed upon right-clicking.

You can also draw a spline tangent to an existing entity. To draw the tangent spline, select the point where the spline should be tangent and then drag it. A construction line will be drawn that displays the possible tangent directions for the spline. Drag the mouse in the required direction to draw the tangent spline. Figure 1-26 shows a spline drawn by specifying different points and Figure 1-27 shows a spline drawn tangent to an existing line.

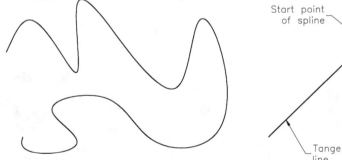

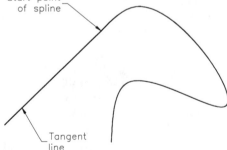

Figure 1-26 *Drawing a spline*   *Figure 1-27* *Drawing a tangent spline*

DELETING THE SKETCHED ENTITIES

To delete the sketched entity, first ensure that no drawing tool is active. If there is a drawing tool active, press the ESC key. Now, pick the entity you want to delete using the left mouse button and then right-click to display the shortcut menu. In this menu choose **Delete**. If you want to delete more than one entity, you can use a window or a crossing.

Deleting the Entities Using a Window

A window is defined as the box created by pressing the left mouse button and dragging it from left to right in the drawing window. A window has a property that all the entities that lie completely inside the window will be selected. All the selected entities will be displayed in light gray color. After selecting the entities, right-click and choose **Delete** from the shortcut menu to delete all the selected entities.

Deleting the Entities Using a Crossing

A crossing is defined as the box created by pressing the left mouse button and dragging it from right to left in the drawing window. A crossing has a property that all the entities that lie completely or partially inside the crossing, or the entities that touch the crossing will be selected. Once the entities are selected, right-click and choose **Delete** from the shortcut menu.

Tip. *You can add or remove an entity from the selection set by pressing the SHIFT key and then selecting the entity using the left mouse button. If the entity is already in the current selection set, it will be removed from it. If it is not in the current selection set, it will be added to it.*

You can also delete the entities by using the DELETE key on the keyboard. Select the entities that you want to delete and then press the DELETE key.

TUTORIALS

Although Autodesk Inventor is parametric in nature, in this chapter you will use the **Precise Input** toolbar to draw objects. This is to make you comfortable with the various drawing options in Autodesk Inventor. From next chapter onwards, you will use the parametric nature of Autodesk Inventor for dragging the entities to the desired dimension values.

Tutorial 1

In this tutorial you will draw the sketch for the model shown in Figure 1-28. The sketch is shown in Figure 1-29. Do not dimension the sketch as the dimensions are just for reference.

(Expected time: 30 min)

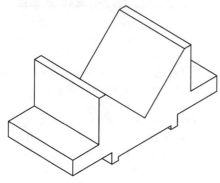

Figure 1-28 Model for Tutorial 1

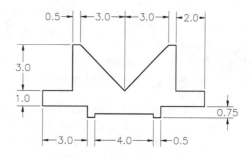

Figure 1-29 Sketch of the model

The steps that will be followed for completing the tutorial are listed below.

a. Open a new standard metric template file and then invoke the **Precise Input** toolbar
b. Invoke the **Line** tool and specify the coordinates of points in the **Precise Input** toolbar.
c. Save the sketch with the name **Tutorial1.ipt**.

Starting Autodesk Inventor

1. Start Autodesk Inventor either by double-clicking on its shortcut icon on the desktop of your computer or by using the **Start** menu.

2. The **Open** dialog box will be displayed. Choose **New** to display the **Default, English**, and **Metric** tabs. Choose the **Metric** tab to display metric templates, see Figure 1-30.

3. Double-click on the **Standard (mm).ipt** icon to open a standard metric template.

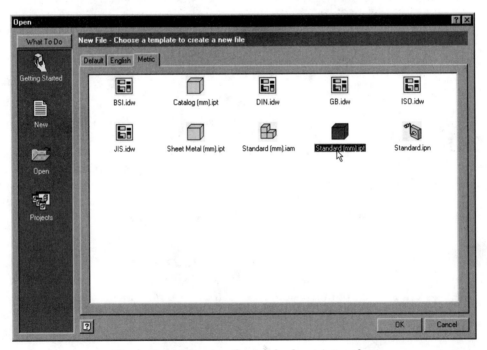

Figure 1-30 Opening the standard metric template

 Note
*If you have installed Autodesk Inventor by selecting millimeter as the measurement unit, you can also open a standard metric template by selecting **Standard.ipt** from the **Default** tab.*

The **Part** mode of the Autodesk Inventor with the sketching environment will be opened with various sketching tools, see Figure 1-31. On the left of the screen is the **Sketch** panel bar and the browser and on the right side is the drawing window. You will also see the major and minor grid lines in the drawing window and the X and Y axes.

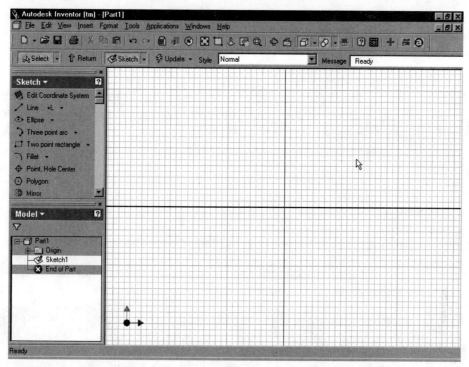

Figure 1-31 *Initial screen appearance in the **Part** mode with the sketching environment*

Drawing the Sketch

1. As mentioned earlier, Autodesk Inventor is parametric in nature, therefore, you can start drawing the sketch from any point in the drawing window. However, it is recommended that you should initially use the **Precise Input** toolbar for specifying the points. Once you are conversant with this design tool, you can specify the points directly in the drawing window. To display the **Precise Input** toolbar, choose **View > Toolbar > Precise Input** from the menu bar. Double-click on the blue portion of this toolbar to dock it. If you want, you can also leave this toolbar floating on the screen.

   Initially, no option of the **Precise Input** toolbar will be available. The options in this toolbar will be available only when you choose any drawing tool. Now, as all the initial settings are adjusted, you can start drawing the sketch.

2. Choose **Line** from the **Sketch** panel bar to start drawing the lines. You will notice that the various options in the **Precise Input** toolbar are now available.

   When you choose **Line** from the **Sketch** panel bar, the cursor that was initially an arrow will be replaced by a drawing cursor and a yellow circle will be attached at the intersection of the crosshair. This yellow circle is used to snap on to the various points.

3. Specify the start point of the sketch as **0** and **0** in the **X** and **Y** edit box of the **Precise Input** toolbar and then press ENTER. You will be prompted to specify the endpoint of the line.

4. Enter **-3** in the **X** edit box and **3** in the **Y** edit box of the **Precise Input** toolbar to define the endpoint of the line. This will draw the first line of the sketch. You will now be prompted to select the endpoint of the next line.

    You will notice that the line is very small. The reason for this is that the dimensions of the sketch are very small and the drawing display area is large. Therefore, you will have to decrease the drawing display area using the drawing display options. To decrease the drawing display area, use the **Zoom** drawing display option.

5. Choose the **Zoom** button from the **Standard** toolbar. The drawing cursor will be converted into an arrow. Move the cursor to the top of the drawing window. Now, press the left mouse button and drag the cursor towards the lower portion of the drawing window. Stop dragging once you feel the display is adjusted to your desire.

6. Right-click to display the shortcut menu and then choose **Done** to exit the **Zoom** tool.

    You will notice that line creation will resume and you will be prompted to specify the endpoint of the next line.

 Tip. *You can use the TAB key on the keyboard to move from the X edit box to the Y edit box and vice versa in the* **Precise Input** *toolbar.*

7. The coordinates of the remaining points in the sketch are as follows:

Point	Coordinates (X,Y)
3	-3.5,3
4	-3.5,0
5	-5.5,0
6	-5.5,-1
7	-2.5,-1
8	-2.5,-1.75
9	-2,-1.75
10	-2,-1.5
11	2,-1.5
12	2,-1.75
13	2.5,-1.75
14	2.5,-1
15	5.5,-1
16	5.5,0
17	3.5,0
18	3.5,3
19	3,3
20	0,0

8. Once you have specified all these points, right-click to display the shortcut menu. In this menu choose **Done** to exit the **Line** tool.

While specifying various points you will notice that some of the constraints are automatically applied to the lines as you sketch them. These constraints help you in reducing the number of dimensions that are required to complete the sketch.

Note
You can also force some more constraints such as equal length, collinear, parallel, and so on. The method of applying additional constraints will be discussed in Chapter 2.

9. The final sketch after drawing should look similar to the one shown in Figure 1-32.

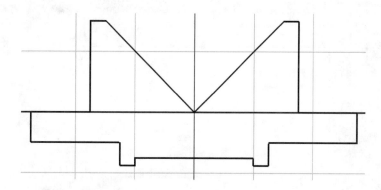

Figure 1-32 Complete sketch for Tutorial 1

Remember that you cannot save a sketch in the sketching environment because in Autodesk Inventor, the sketching environment is just a part of the **Part** mode. This environment is used only for drawing the sketches of the features. Therefore, you will have to exit the sketching environment to save the sketch for further use. The sketches in the **Part** mode are saved in the **.ipt** format.

10. You can exit the sketching environment by choosing the **Return** button from the **Command Bar** toolbar.

When you choose the **Return** button in the **Command Bar**, you will notice that in place of the **Sketch** panel bar, the **Features** panel bar is displayed. This panel bar provides the options for creating features. The options under this panel bar will be discussed in later chapters.

11. Now, to save the sketch, choose the **Save** button from the **Standard** toolbar. The **Save As** dialog box will be displayed.

By default, whenever you invoke the **Save As** dialog box for the first time, the current directory that is opened for saving the sketch is **My Documents** directory. Create a new directory with the name **PersonalProject** in this directory using the **Create New Folder** button in the **Save As** dialog box. You can either save the sketch in this directory or create another subdirectory in this directory. It is recommended that you create separate subdirectories for all the chapters in this book. The reason for this is that if you create separate subdirectories for all the chapters, you can save all the tutorials of various chapters in their respective subdirectories. This way it will be easier for you to refer to the sketches or models at later stages.

12. Create a directory with the name c01 inside the **PersonalProject** directory as shown in Figure 1-33 and save the sketch with the name **Tutorial1.ipt**. The path for restoring this sketch at a later stage is \PersonalProject\c01**Tutorial1.ipt**.

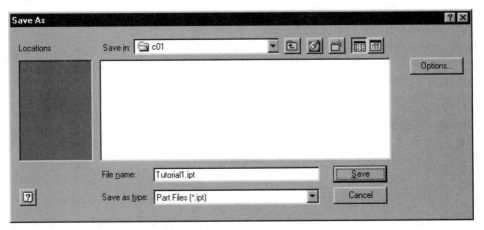

Figure 1-33 Save As dialog box

Tutorial 2

In this tutorial you will draw the sketch for the model shown in Figure 1-34. The sketch is shown in Figure 1-35. Do not dimension the sketch. The solid model and dimensions are for reference only.   **(Expected time: 45 min)**

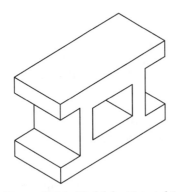

Figure 1-34 Model for Tutorial 2

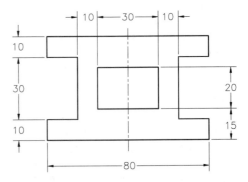

Figure 1-35 Dimensioned sketch for Tutorial 2

The steps that will be followed to complete this tutorial are listed below:

a.   Open a new standard metric template file and invoke the **Precise Input** toolbar.
b.   Specify the coordinates of points of both the loops in the **Precise Input** toolbar.
c.   Save the sketch with the name **Tutorial2.ipt**.

Starting a New File

1.   Choose the **New** button from the **Standard** toolbar to display the **Open** dialog box. Choose **New** to display the **Default**, **English**, and **Metric** tabs.

If you are starting a new session of Autodesk Inventor, you do not have to choose the **New** button. This is because the **Open** dialog box will be automatically displayed when you start a new session of Autodesk Inventor.

2.   Choose the **Metric** tab to display metric templates. Double-click on **Standard (mm).ipt** to open a new metric part file.

Drawing the Sketch

As shown in Figure 1-35, this sketch consists of two closed loops, one inside the other. When you draw two closed loops, one inside the other, and extrude, the inner closed loop can be subtracted from the outer closed loop. Thus, the cavity in the model will be created automatically as you extrude the sketch. This will reduce the time and effort required in creating the inner cavity as another feature. Therefore, for this tutorial you can draw both the closed loops shown in Figure 1-35 together.

1.   Choose **Line** from the **Sketch** panel bar. You will be prompted to specify the start point of line. The points and their coordinates that you have to enter in the **Precise Input** toolbar are given below.

Points	Coordinates (X,Y)
1	-40,-25
2	40,-25
3	40,-15
4	25,-15
5	25,15
6	40,15
7	40,25
8	-40,25
9	-40,15
10	-25,15
11	-25,-15
12	-40,-15
13	-40,-25

2.   After you have specified all these points, right-click to display the shortcut menu. Choose **Done** to exit line creation. You can also press the ESC key to exit the **Line** tool.

3. Choose **Two point rectangle** from the **Sketch** panel bar. You will be prompted to specify the first corner of the rectangle. Enter the start point of the rectangle as **-15,-10** in the **Precise Input** toolbar.

4. You will be prompted to specify the opposite corner of the rectangle. The opposite corner can be defined relative to the first corner of the rectangle. Choose the **Delta Y Delta X** button available on the left of the **X** edit box in the **Precise Input** toolbar to use the relative coordinates option.

    When you choose the **Delta X Delta Y** button, you will notice that a small coordinate system icon is attached to the start point of the rectangle (at point **-15,-10** in this case). This means that the next point will be defined taking the last point as the origin point.

5. Enter the coordinates of the other corner of the rectangle as **30,20**. After drawing all the lines and the rectangle the sketch should look similar to the one shown in Figure 1-36.

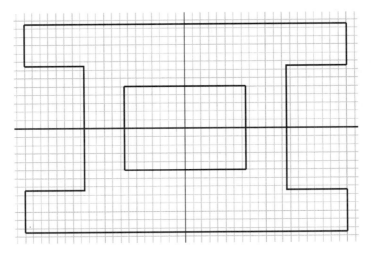

Figure 1-36 Complete sketch for Tutorial 2

6. Choose the **Return** button from the **Command Bar** toolbar to exit the sketching environment.

7. Save this sketch with the name given below:

    \PersonalProject\c01**Tutorial2.ipt**

Tutorial 3

In this tutorial you will draw the sketch for the model shown in Figure 1-37. The sketch for the model is shown in Figure 1-38. Do not dimension the sketch as these dimensions are just for reference.   **(Expected time: 30 min)**

The steps that will be followed to complete this tutorial are listed next.

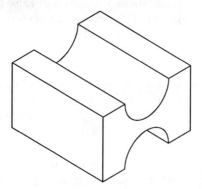

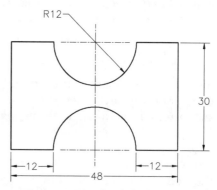

Figure 1-37 Model for Tutorial 3   *Figure 1-38* Sketch for Tutorial 3

a.   Open a new standard metric template and invoke the **Precise Input** toolbar.
b.   Draw the sketch using the **Arc** and the **Line** tool.
c.   Save the sketch with the name **Tutorial3.ipt**.

Starting a New File

1.   Open a new standard metric template by double-clicking on the **Standard (mm).ipt** in the **Metric** tab of the **Open** dialog box. The **Metric** tab is displayed when you choose **New** in the **Open** dialog box.

Drawing the Sketch

1.   The upper arc in the sketch can be easily drawn by specifying the center point, start point, and the endpoint. Therefore, choose the down arrow on the right of the **Three point arc** in the **Sketch** panel bar and choose **Center point arc**.

2.   You will be prompted to specify the center of the arc. Enter the coordinates of the center of the arc as **0,15** in the **Precise Input** toolbar.

3.   Once you enter the coordinates of the center of the arc, you will be prompted to specify the start point of the arc. Specify the start point as **-12,15** in the **Precise Input** toolbar.

4.   Now, enter the coordinates of the endpoint of the arc as **12,15** in the **Precise Input** toolbar. The upper arc will be drawn.

5.   Choose **Line** from the **Sketch** panel bar. You will be prompted to specify the start point of the line.

It is evident in Figure 1-37 that the line should start from the endpoint of the arc. Therefore, you can either specify the coordinates of the start point of the arc in the **Precise Input** toolbar or select the start point of the line in the drawing window. **Here, it is recommended that you should select the start point of the line in the drawing window.** This is because when you choose any sketching tool from the **Sketch** panel bar, a yellow circle appears on the cursor. Now, when you move the cursor close to any endpoint, the yellow circle at the end of the cursor automatically snaps to the endpoint and turns green. You will also notice that the symbol of the coincident constraint is displayed. This symbol suggests that the coincident constraint will be automatically applied to the endpoint of the arc and the start point of the line.

6. Move the cursor close to the left endpoint of the arc until the yellow circle snaps to the endpoint of the arc. When the yellow circle turn green, it indicates that the cursor has snapped to the endpoint of the arc. Press the left mouse button to select this point as the start point of the line.

7. Since it is easier to define the points by using the relative coordinates, therefore, choose the **Delta Y Delta X** button in the **Precise Input** toolbar to use the relative coordinates. Enter the coordinates of the endpoint of the line as **-12,0** in the **Precise Input** toolbar.

8. Enter the second point as **0,-30** and the third point as **12,0** in the **Precise Input** toolbar.

    Even while drawing lines, Autodesk Inventor provides you with the option of drawing an arc tangent or normal to the line. This is done by dragging the cursor from the point where you want to draw the arc. At this point you have to draw an arc that is normal to the last drawn line. To draw this arc, you do not have to exit the **Line** tool and invoke the options for drawing the arcs. You can directly draw the arc using the options for drawing the lines.

9. Move the cursor close to the right endpoint of the latest line until the yellow circle snaps to that point. As soon as the yellow circle snaps to the endpoint of the line, it will turn gray. Now, press and hold the left mouse button down and drag the mouse upwards.

    You will notice that four imaginary lines are displayed, showing the four directions in which you can draw the arc.

10. Since you have to draw the arc normal to the line, therefore, move the cursor in the direction of the vertical imaginary line in the upward direction to a small distance and then drag the cursor towards right.

    You will notice that an arc normal to the last line is being created as you move the cursor. Remember that you have to drag the mouse upwards only to a small distance and then drag the mouse towards right, without releasing the left button of the mouse. **Note that the point at which you release the left mouse button will be taken as the endpoint of the arc**. Therefore, you will have to be very careful in specifying the endpoint of the arc.

    While drawing the arc by dragging the cursor, you cannot use the **Precise Input** toolbar. This us because as soon as you release the left mouse button, that point will be taken as the endpoint of the arc. Therefore, it is very difficult to define the endpoint of the arc precisely. This problem can be solved by using the **temporary tracking** option. The temporary tracking option allows you to select a point by using two different points. For example, in this case, the right endpoint of the lower arc has to be vertically in the same line as that of the right endpoint of the upper arc and horizontally in the same line as that of the start point of the lower arc. Now, imagine a vertical imaginary line drawn from the right endpoint of the upper arc and a horizontal imaginary line drawn from the start point of the lower arc. Both these imaginary lines intersect at a point that is essentially the endpoint of the lower arc. **The temporary tracking option draws these imaginary lines for you and removes the imaginary lines after you have selected the point**.

11. To use the temporary tracking option, drag the mouse close to the right endpoint of the upper arc. The cursor snaps to the endpoint of the arc and turns green. Now, move the cursor downwards.

    You will notice that a vertical imaginary line is being drawn from the right endpoint of the arc. You do not have to snap to the horizontal point since this point was automatically selected when you started drawing the arc. As you move downwards, you will notice a point where both the vertical and horizontal imaginary lines intersect, see Figure 1-39. This point is the endpoint of the lower arc. The cursor will automatically snap to the point where both the imaginary lines intersect. Do not release the left mouse button until this entire process is completed.

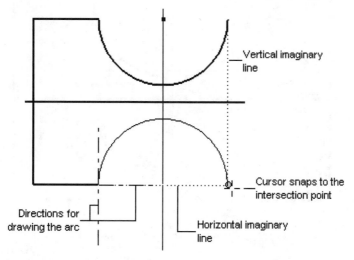

Figure 1-39 Figure showing the use of the temporary tracking option

Note
In Figure 1-39, the major and minor grid lines are not displayed for better display of the sketch and the imaginary lines.

12. When the cursor snaps to the intersection point of the imaginary lines, release the cursor to draw the lower arc.

13. Enter the coordinates of the next point as **12,0** in the **Precise Input** toolbar.

14. For the next point you can either enter the coordinates in the **Precise Input** toolbar or use the temporary tracking option. To use this option, move the cursor close to the right

endpoint of the upper arc. Once the cursor snaps to this point and turns green, move it in the horizontal direction. You will notice a horizontal imaginary line being drawn. Using the left mouse button, select the point where both the vertical and horizontal imaginary lines meet. This point will be the endpoint of the right vertical line.

Note
While using the temporary tracking option in drawing lines, you do not have to press the left mouse button and drag it. You have to press the left mouse button only once to select the endpoint of the line after you get the intersection point of the imaginary lines.

15. Complete the sketch by snapping to the right endpoint of the upper arc as the endpoint of the next line. Right-click to display the shortcut menu and choose **Done** to exit the **Line** tool.

16. The final sketch should look similar to the one shown in Figure 1-40.

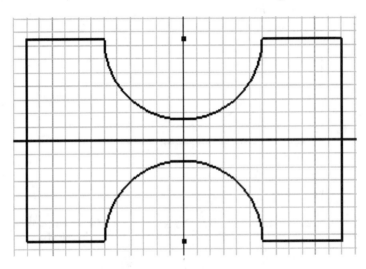

Figure 1-40 *Final sketch for Tutorial 3*

17. Choose the **Return** button in the **Command Bar** toolbar to exit the sketching environment. Save the sketch with the name given below:

\PersonalProject\c01**Tutorial3.ipt**

Tutorial 4

In this tutorial you will draw the basic contour of the revolved solid model shown in Figure 1-41. The contour that you have to draw for creating this revolved solid is shown in Figure 1-42. Do not dimension the sketch as these dimensions are for reference only. **(Expected time: 45 min)**

The steps that will be followed to complete the tutorial are listed next.

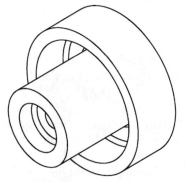

Figure 1-41 *Revolved model for Tutorial 4*   **Figure 1-42** *Sketch for the revolved model*

a. Open a new metric template file.
b. Invoke the **Line** tool and specify the coordinates of points in the **Precise Input** toolbar.
c. Save the sketch with the name **Tutorial4.ipt**.

Starting a New File

1. Choose the **New** button from the **Standard** toolbar to display the **Open** dialog box. Choose the **Metric** tab to display the standard metric templates. Double-click on **Standard (mm).ipt** to open a new metric part file.

Drawing the Sketch

1. Choose **Line** from the **Sketch** panel bar. You will be prompted to specify the start point of the line. Enter the coordinates of the start point in the **Precise Input** toolbar as **22,0**.

2. You will be prompted to specify the endpoint of this line. In this sketch you can specify the coordinates of the next point relative to the previous point as this makes it easier to define the points. Choose the **Delta X Delta Y** button on the left of the **X** edit box in the **Precise Input** toolbar. The coordinates of the remaining points in the sketch are as follows:

Point	Coordinates (X,Y)
2	0,30
3	-20,0
4	0,-5
5	16,0
6	0,-9
7	-40,0
8	0,-6
9	8,0
10	0,-6
11	14,0
12	0,-4
13	22,0

3. Right-click to display the shortcut menu and choose **Done** to complete the sketch. The sketch should look similar to the one shown in Figure 1-43. For reference, the lines in the sketch are numbered.

    The arcs at the end of lines 4 and 5, 5 and 6, and 8 and 9 will be created using the **Fillet** tool. This tool will draw the arcs at the point of intersection of the lines and remove the sharp corners.

4. Choose **Fillet** from the **Sketch** panel bar. The **2D Fillet** toolbar will be displayed with some default fillet radius. Enter the value of the fillet radius in this toolbar as **1.5**.

5. Select line 4 and then line 5. The fillet will be created between these lines and the fillet radius will be displayed in the sketch, see Figure 1-44.

6. Similarly, select lines 5 and 6, and then lines 8 and 9 to create the fillet between these lines.

    Since all the lines were filleted with same radius value, therefore other fillets will not display the fillet radius. This completes the sketch. The final sketch for Tutorial 4 after filleting should look similar to the one shown in Figure 1-44.

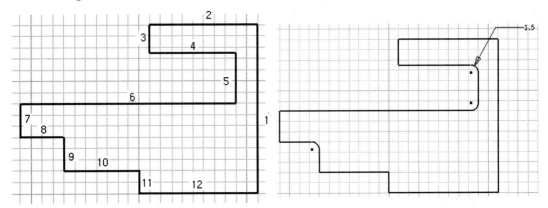

Figure 1-43 Sketch after drawing the lines   *Figure 1-44 Sketch after filleting*

Note
In Figure 1-43 and Figure 1-44, the display of axes is turned off for clarity in displaying the lines of the sketch.

7. Choose the **Return** button from the **Command Bar** to exit the sketching environment.

8. Save this sketch with the name given below:

    \PersonalProject\c01**Tutorial4.ipt**

Self-Evaluation Test

Answer the following questions and then compare your answers with the answers given at the end of the chapter.

1. Most of the designs are a combination of sketched, placed, and work features. (T/F)

2. When you start a new file in the **Part** mode, first the sketching environment will be active. (T/F)

3. You cannot turn off the display of the grid lines. (T/F)

4. You cannot draw an arc from within the line drawing options. (T/F)

5. The two type of sketching entities that can be drawn in Autodesk Inventor are _____ and _____.

6. In Autodesk Inventor, the holes can be created using only _____.

7. Filleting is defined as the process of _____ the sharp corners and sharp edges of models.

8. You can also delete the sketched entities by pressing the _____ key on the keyboard.

9. The rectangles in Autodesk Inventor are drawn as a combination of _____ entities.

10. You can undo the last drawn spline segment when you are still inside the spline drawing option by choosing _____ from the shortcut menu displayed upon right-clicking.

Review Questions

Answer the following questions.

1. Generally, in most of the designs the first or the base feature has to be the placed feature. (T/F)

2. You can also invoke the options related to the sheet metal parts from the **.ipt** file. (T/F)

3. You can change the current project directory and the project files by choosing **Projects** in the **Open** dialog box. (T/F)

4. You cannot control the display of grid lines. (T/F)

5. In Autodesk Inventor you can save a file in the sketching environment. (T/F)

6. Using which option in the **View** menu can you invoke additional toolbars?

    (a) **Isometric**   (b) **Tools**
    (c) **Toolbars**   (d) **You cannot invoke additional toolbars**

7. Which one of these tabs is not available when you choose **New** in the **Open** dialog box?

    (a) **Default**   (b) **Projects**
    (c) **Metric**   (d) **English**

8. Using which of the following drawing display options can you interactively zoom in and out of the drawing?

    (a) **Zoom All**   (b) **Pan**
    (c) **Zoom**   (d) **Zoom Window**

9. Using which key on the keyboard can you restore the previous view?

    (a) **F5**   (b) **F6**
    (c) **F7**   (d) **F4**

10. Which of the following drawing display options prompts you to select an entity whose magnification will be increased?

    (a) **Zoom**   (b) **Pan**
    (c) **Zoom Selected**   (d) **None**

Exercises

Exercise 1

Draw the basic sketch for the model shown in Figure 1-45. The sketch that you have to draw is shown in Figure 1-46. Do not dimension the sketch as these dimensions are just for reference.

(Expected time: 30 min)

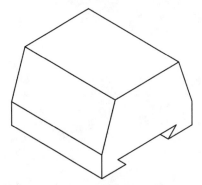

Figure 1-45 *Model for Exercise 1*

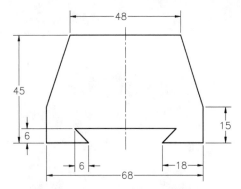

Figure 1-46 *Sketch for Exercise 1*

Exercise 2

Draw the basic sketch for the model shown in Figure 1-47. The sketch that you have to draw is shown in Figure 1-48. Do not dimension the sketch as these dimensions are just for reference.

(Expected time: 45 min)

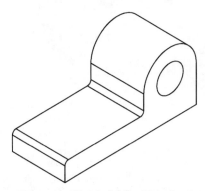

Figure 1-47 *Model for Exercise 2*

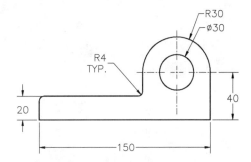

Figure 1-48 *Sketch for Exercise 2*

Note

The solid model and the dimensions in Exercise 1 and Exercise 2 are given for reference only. You do not have to dimension the sketches.

Answers to Self-Evaluation Test

1. T, **2**. T, **3**. F, **4**. F, **5**. normal, construction, **6**. hole center or sketch point, **7**. rounding, **8**. Delete, **9**. individual, **10**. **Backup**

Chapter 2

Adding Constraints and Dimensions to the Sketches

Learning Objectives

After completing this chapter you will be able to:
- *Add different geometric constraints to the sketch.*
- *View and delete the constraints from the sketch.*
- *Dimension the sketches.*
- *Modify the dimensions of the sketches.*
- *Measure distances and angles in the sketch.*

ADDING THE GEOMETRY CONSTRAINTS TO THE SKETCH

As mentioned in Introduction, there are eleven types of geometric constraints that can be applied to the sketched entities. Most of these constraints are automatically applied to the entities at the time of their creation. However, sometimes you may have to apply some additional constraints. All these constraints are discussed next.

Perpendicular

Toolbar:	Sketch > Perpendicular
Panel Bar:	Sketch > Perpendicular

The **Perpendicular** constraint forces the selected entity to become perpendicular to the specified entity. To use this constraint choose the **Perpendicular** button from the **Sketch** toolbar or choose **Perpendicular** from the **Sketch** panel bar. When you invoke this constraint, you will be prompted to select the first line or ellipse axis. Once you select an entity, you will be prompted to select the second line or ellipse axis. Figure 2-1 shows two lines before and after adding this constraint.

Parallel

Toolbar:	Sketch > Perpendicular > Parallel
Panel Bar:	Sketch > Perpendicular > Parallel

The **Parallel** constraint forces the selected entity to become parallel to the specified entity. The entities to which this constraint can be applied are lines and ellipse axes. You can apply this constraint by choosing the down arrow provided on the right of the **Perpendicular** button in the **Sketch** toolbar and choosing the **Parallel** button. Similarly, choose the down arrow on the right of **Perpendicular** in the **Sketch** panel bar and choose **Parallel** to invoke this constraint. When you invoke this constraint, you will be prompted to select the first line or ellipse axis. Once you select an entity, you will be prompted to select the second line or ellipse axis. Figure 2-2 shows two lines before and after adding this constraint.

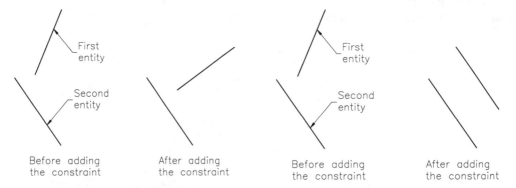

Figure 2-1 *Applying the* ***Perpendicular*** *constraint*   *Figure 2-2* *Applying the* ***Parallel*** *constraint*

Tangent

Toolbar:	Sketch > Perpendicular > Tangent
Panel Bar:	Sketch > Perpendicular > Tangent

The **Tangent** constraint forces the selected line segment or curve to become tangent to another curve. Choose the down arrow on the right of the **Perpendicular** button in the **Sketch** toolbar or the **Sketch** panel bar to apply this constraint. When you invoke this constraint, you will be prompted to select the first curve. Once you select the first curve, you will be prompted to select the second curve. The curves can include lines, circles, ellipses, or arcs. Figure 2-3 and Figure 2-4 show the use of tangent constraint.

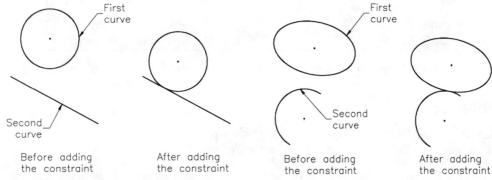

First curve		First curve	
Second curve		Second curve	
Before adding the constraint	After adding the constraint	Before adding the constraint	After adding the constraint

*Figure 2-3 Applying the **Tangent** constraint*   *Figure 2-4 Applying the **Tangent** constraint*

Coincident

Toolbar:	Sketch > Perpendicular > Coincident
Panel Bar:	Sketch > Perpendicular > Coincident

The **Coincident** constraint is used to force two points or a point and a curve to become coincident. Choose the down arrow on the right of the **Perpendicular** button in the **Sketch** toolbar or the **Sketch** panel bar to apply this constraint. When you invoke this constraint, you will be prompted to select the first curve or point. Once you specify the first constraint or point, you will be prompted to specify the second constraint or point. Note that either the first or the second entity selected should be a point. The points include the endpoints of a line or an arc, or the center points of circles or arcs.

Concentric

Toolbar:	Sketch > Perpendicular > Concentric
Panel Bar:	Sketch > Perpendicular > Concentric

The **Concentric** constraint is used to force two curves to share the same center points. The curves that can be made concentric include arcs, circles, and ellipses. When you invoke this constraint, you will be prompted to select the first arc, circle, or ellipse. After making the first selection you will be prompted to select the second arc, circle, or ellipse.

Note

If you apply a constraint that is not required in the sketch, Autodesk Inventor will display a message box informing you that adding this constraint will over-constrain the sketch, see Figure 2-5. Over-constrained is a situation where the number of dimensions or constraints have exceeded the number that are required in the sketch.

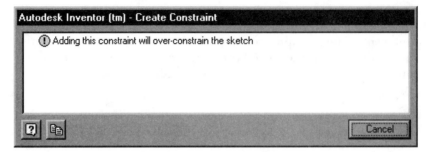

Figure 2-5 *The message box informing that the sketch is over-constrained*

Collinear

Toolbar:	Sketch > Perpendicular > Collinear
Panel Bar:	Sketch > Perpendicular > Collinear

The **Collinear** constraint forces the selected line segments or ellipse axes to be placed in the same line. When you invoke this constraint, you will be prompted to select the first line or ellipse axis. After making the first selection you will be prompted to select the second line or ellipse axis.

Tip. *To select an ellipse axis, move the cursor close to the ellipse. Depending upon whether the cursor is close to the major axis or the minor axis, it will be highlighted. When the required axis is highlighted, select it using the left mouse button.*

Horizontal

Toolbar:	Sketch > Perpendicular > Horizontal
Panel Bar:	Sketch > Perpendicular > Horizontal

The **Horizontal** constraint forces the selected line segment, ellipse axis, or two points to become horizontal irrespective of their original orientation. When you invoke this constraint, you will be prompted to select a line, an ellipse axis, or the first point. If you select a line or an ellipse axis, it will become horizontal. If you select a point, you will then be prompted to select a second point. The points in this case can also include the center points of arcs, circles, or ellipses.

Vertical

Toolbar:	Sketch > Perpendicular > Vertical
Panel Bar:	Sketch > Perpendicular > Vertical

The **Vertical** constraint is similar to the **Horizontal** constraint with the only difference being that this constraint will force the selected entities to become vertical.

 Tip. *You can use the **Horizontal** or the **Vertical** constraint to line up arcs, circles, or ellipses in the same horizontal or vertical direction. This can be done by choosing the center points of the arcs, circles, or ellipses.*

Equal

Toolbar:	Sketch > Perpendicular > Equal
Panel Bar:	Sketch > Perpendicular > Equal

The **Equal** constraint can be used either for line segments or for curves. If you select two line segments, this constraint will force the length of one of the selected line segment to become equal to the length of the other selected line segment. In case of curves, this constraint will force the radius of one of the selected curves to become equal to the radius of the other selected curve. Note that the size of the entity drawn last will be changed when you apply this constraint. Also, if the first selection includes a line, the second selection also has to be a line. Similarly, if the first selection includes a curve, the second selection also has to be a curve.

Fix

Toolbar:	Sketch > Perpendicular > Fix
Panel Bar:	Sketch > Perpendicular > Fix

This constraint is used to fix the orientation or location of the selected curve or point with respect to the coordinate system of the current drawing. If you apply this constraint to a line or an arc, you cannot move them from their current location. However, you can change their length by selecting one of their endpoints and then dragging it. If you apply this constraint to a circle or an ellipse, you cannot edit them by dragging. Once you apply this constraint to an entity, its color changes from blue to black.

Symmetric

Toolbar:	Sketch > Perpendicular > Symmetric
Panel Bar:	Sketch > Perpendicular > Symmetric

This constraint is used to force the selected sketched entities to become symmetrical about a selected sketched line segment. This constraint is used in the sketches of the models that are symmetrical about a line. When you invoke this constraint, you will be prompted to select the first sketched entity. Note that you can select only one entity at a time to apply this constraint. Once you have selected the first sketched entity, you will be prompted to select the second sketched entity. Then you will be prompted to select the symmetry line. As soon as you select the line of symmetry, the second selected entity will be modified such that its distance from the line of symmetry becomes exactly equal to that of the first entity. After you have applied this constraint to one set of entities, you will again be prompted to select the first and second sketched entities. However, this time you will not be prompted to select the line of symmetry. The last line of symmetry will be automatically selected to add this constraint. Similarly, you can continue to select the set of entities to apply the symmetric constraint until this constraint is applied to all the entities in the sketch.

Note

*If the line of symmetry is different for applying the symmetric constraint to different entities in the sketch, you will have to restart the process of applying this constraint by choosing the **Symmetric** button. This is because the first symmetry line is used to apply this constraint to all the sets of entities you select. However, if you restart applying this constraint, you will be prompted to select the line of symmetry again.*

VIEWING THE CONSTRAINTS APPLIED TO THE SKETCH

Toolbar:	Sketch > Show Constraints
Panel Bar:	Sketch > Show Constraints

You can view all constraints that are applied to the entities of the sketch. This can be done by choosing the **Show Constraints** button in the **Sketch** toolbar or by choosing **Show Constraints** from the **Sketch** panel bar. When you invoke this tool and take the cursor close to any sketched entity, it will be highlighted and a box will be displayed showing the symbols of all the constraints that are applied to that entity. The number of constraints that are applied to the highlighted entity will also be displayed in the **Message** box of the **Command Bar**. If you want that the box displaying the symbol of constraints should remain on the screen, select the entity using the left mouse button. Figure 2-6 shows the box displaying all the constraints applied to the line. You can move this box by selecting it at its left end and dragging. To close this box, choose the cross (X) on the extreme right of this box.

As you move the cursor close to any of the constraint in the box, a square will appear around the constraint and the position and reference of that constraint will be highlighted. For example, if you take the cursor close to the perpendicular constraint, the vertical line will also be highlighted along with the horizontal line suggesting that the horizontal line is perpendicular to the vertical line. Similarly, if

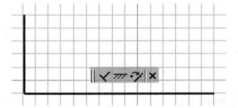

Figure 2-6 The box showing the constraints

you take the cursor close to the coincident constraint, the point at which this line is coincident with the vertical line will be highlighted.

Tip. *You can also display the constraints applied to all the entities in the drawing. To display all the constraints, first make sure no tool is selected. Then, right-click to display the shortcut menu and choose **Show All Constraints**. Separate boxes for all the entities will be displayed showing the constraints on all the entities. Similarly, to hide all the constraints, right-click and choose **Hide All Constraints** from the shortcut menu.*

DELETING THE CONSTRAINTS

You can also delete one or all constraints applied to the selected entities. To delete the constraints you have to first invoke the constraint box using the **Show Constraints** button. Once the box is displayed, move the cursor close to the constraint in the box that you want to delete. A square will appear around the constraint. At this moment, right-click to display the shortcut menu. In this shortcut menu, choose the **Delete** option, see Figure 2-7. The selected constraint will be deleted and will also be removed from the constraint box that is displayed on the screen. Similarly, you can delete all the unwanted constraints in the sketch.

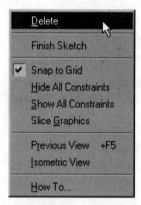

Figure 2-7 Deleting the constraints using the shortcut menu

Tip. *When you move the cursor close to the constraint in the constraint box, its reference will be highlighted in the sketch. For example, if you move the cursor close to the coincident constraint, the points on which this constraint is applied will be highlighted. This allows you to confirm that the constraint selected is correct.*

DIMENSIONING THE SKETCHES

Toolbar:	Sketch > General Dimension
Panel Bar:	Sketch > General Dimension

After drawing the sketches, dimensioning is the second most important step in creating a design. As mentioned earlier, Autodesk Inventor is parametric in nature. The parametric nature of this software package ensures that irrespective of the original size, the selected entity is driven by the dimension value you specify. Therefore, whenever you dimension an entity, it is forced to change its size in accordance with the specified dimension value. The type of dimension that will be applied varies depending upon the type of entity selected. For example, if you select a line segment, linear dimensions will be applied and if you select a circle, diameter dimensions will be applied. Note that all these types of dimensions can be applied using the same dimensioning tool. While dimensioning, you can set the priority for editing the dimension value as soon as you place it. To set this priority, choose the **General Dimension** button from the **Sketch** toolbar or choose **General Dimension** from the **Sketch** panel bar and then right-click to display the shortcut menu. In this menu, choose **Edit**

Dimension such that when you right-click again, this option is checked, see Figure 2-8. Now, as soon as you place the dimension, the **Edit Dimension** toolbar will be displayed as shown in Figure 2-9. The selected entity will be driven to the size defined in this toolbar.

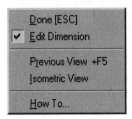

Figure 2-8 *Setting the priority for editing the dimensions as they are placed*

Figure 2-9 *The **Edit Dimension** toolbar*

You can enter a new value for the dimension or choose the button on the right of this toolbar to accept the default value. If you do not want to edit the dimension after you place them, invoke the **General Dimension** option and then right-click to display the shortcut menu. Clear the check mark on the left of **Edit Dimension** option by choosing it again. When you place a dimension now, the **Edit Dimension** toolbar will not be displayed. However, if you want to edit the dimension value, double-click on it. The **Edit Dimension** toolbar will be displayed so that you can edit the dimension value. The various dimensioning types are discussed next.

Linear Dimensioning

Linear dimensions are defined as the dimensions that define the shortest distance between two points. You can apply linear dimensions directly to a line. You can also apply this dimension to two points or two objects. The points can be the endpoints of lines or arcs, or the center points of circles, arcs, or ellipses. You can dimension a vertical or a horizontal line by directly selecting them. As soon as you select them, the dimension will be created and will be attached to the cursor. You can place the dimension to any desired location. If the priority for editing the dimensions is set, the **Edit Dimension** toolbar will be displayed as soon as you place the dimension. To place the dimension between two points, select the points one by one. After selecting the second point, right click to display the shortcut menu, see Figure 2-10. In this menu choose the type of dimension you want to display. If you choose **Horizontal**, the horizontal dimension between the two selected points will be created. If you choose **Vertical**, the vertical dimension between two points will be placed. If you choose **Inclined**, the inclined dimension between the two points will be placed. Figure 2-11 shows linear dimensioning of lines and Figure 2-12 shows linear dimensioning of two points.

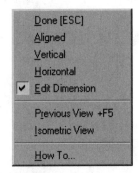

Figure 2-10 *Shortcut menu with the options to dimension two points*

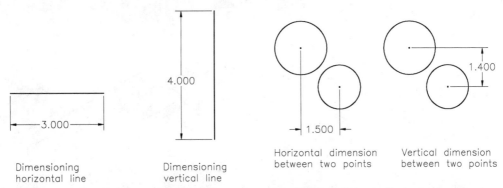

Dimensioning horizontal line	Dimensioning vertical line

Figure 2-11 *Linear dimensioning of lines*

Horizontal dimension between two points   Vertical dimension between two points

Figure 2-12 *Linear dimensioning of points*

You can also apply horizontal or vertical dimension to an aligned line, see Figure 2-13. To apply these dimensions, select the inclined line and then right-click. A shortcut menu similar to the one shown in Figure 2-10 will be displayed. In this menu choose **Horizontal** to place horizontal dimension and choose **Vertical** to place the vertical dimension.

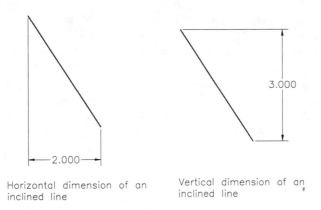

Horizontal dimension of an inclined line   Vertical dimension of an inclined line

Figure 2-13 *Linear dimensioning of an inclined line*

Aligned Dimensioning

Aligned dimensions are used to dimension lines that are neither parallel to the X axis nor to the Y axis. This type of dimensioning measures the actual distance of the inclined lines or the lines that are drawn at a certain angle. You can directly select the inclined line to apply this dimension or select two points. The points that can be used to apply aligned dimension include the endpoints of lines or arcs and the center points of arcs, circles, or ellipses. If you select two points to apply the aligned dimensions, right-click to display the shortcut menu. In this menu choose **Aligned** to apply the aligned dimension. Figure 2-14 and Figure 2-15 show the aligned dimensions applied to various objects.

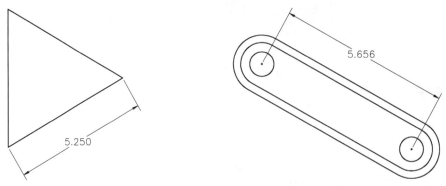

Figure 2-14 *Aligned dimensions of a line*   **Figure 2-15** *Aligned dimensions using two points*

Angular Dimensioning

Angular dimensions are used to dimension angles. You can directly select two line segments to apply this dimension or use three points to apply the angular dimensions. You can also use the angular dimensioning to dimension an arc. All these options of angular dimensioning are discussed next.

Angular Dimensioning using Two Line Segments

You can directly select two line segments to apply angular dimensions between them. Invoke the **General Dimension** tool and then select a line segment using the left mouse button. Now, instead of placing the dimension, select the second line segment. Now, place the dimension to measure the angle between the two lines. While placing the dimension you will have to be very careful. This is because depending upon the location of the dimension placement, the interior or the exterior angle will be displayed. Figure 2-16 shows the interior angular dimension between two lines and Figure 2-17 shows the exterior angular dimension between two lines.

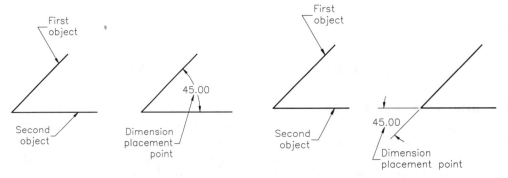

Figure 2-16 *Interior angular dimensioning*   **Figure 2-17** *Exterior angular dimensioning*

Also, depending upon the location of the dimension the major or the minor angle value will be displayed. Figure 2-18 shows the major angle dimension between two lines and Figure 2-19 shows the minor angle dimension between the same set of lines.

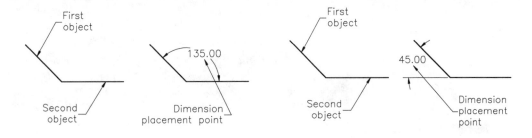

Figure 2-18 *Major angle dimension*   **Figure 2-19** *Minor angle dimension*

Angular Dimensioning using Three Points

You can also apply angular dimensions using three points. You have to remember that the three points should be selected in either the clockwise sequence or the counterclockwise sequence. The points that can be used to apply the angular dimensions include the endpoints of lines or arcs or the center points of arcs, circles, and ellipses. Figure 2-20 shows the angular dimensioning using three points.

Angular Dimensioning of an Arc

You can use angular dimensions to dimension an arc. In case of arcs, the three points that should be used are the endpoints of the arc and the center point of the arc. Note that the points should be selected in either the clockwise sequence or the counterclockwise sequence. Figure 2-21 shows the angular dimensioning of an arc.

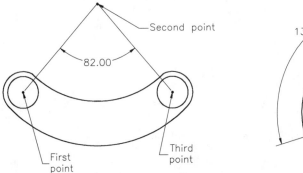

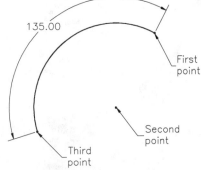

Figure 2-20 *Angular dimensioning using three points*   **Figure 2-21** *Angular dimensioning of an arc*

Tip. *In Autodesk Inventor, the ellipses are dimensioned in terms of half of the major and minor axes distances. To dimension an ellipse, invoke the **General Dimension** tool and then select the ellipse. Now, if you move the cursor along the X axis, the axis of the ellipse along the X axis will be dimensioned in terms of its half length. Similarly, if you move the cursor along the Y axis, the axis of the ellipse along the Y axis will be dimensioned it terms of its half length.*

Tip. *After invoking the **General Dimension** tool as you take the cursor close to the sketched entities, a small symbol will be displayed close to the cursor. This symbol displays the type of dimension that will be applied. For example, if you select a line, the linear dimensioning or aligned dimensioning symbol will be displayed. If you move the cursor close to another line after selecting one, the symbol of angular dimensioning will be displayed. These symbols help you in judging the type of dimensions that will be applied.*

Diameter Dimensioning

Diameter dimensions are applied to dimension a circle or an arc in terms of its diameter. In Autodesk Inventor, by default, when you select a circle to dimension, the diameter dimension is applied to it. However, when you select an arc, the radius dimension is applied to it. You can also apply diameter dimensions to an arc. To apply diameter dimensions to an arc, invoke the **General Dimension** tool and then select the arc. Now, right-click to display the shortcut menu, see Figure 2-22. Choose **Diameter** from this menu to apply the diameter dimension to an arc. Figure 2-23 shows a circle and an arc with diameter dimensions.

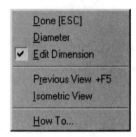

Figure 2-22 Shortcut menu for applying diameter dimensions to an arc

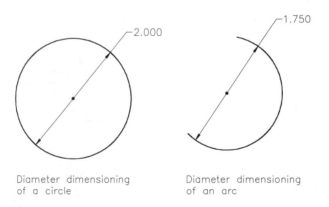

Figure 2-23 Diameter dimensioning of a circle and an arc

Radius Dimensioning

Radius dimensions are applied to dimension an arc or a circle in terms of its radius. As mentioned above, by default, the circles will be assigned diameter dimensions and the arcs will be assigned radius dimensions. However, you can also apply radius dimensions to a circle. To apply radius dimension to a circle, invoke the **General Dimension** tool and then select the circle. Now, right-click to display the shortcut menu, as shown in Figure 2-24. Choose **Radius**

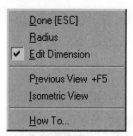

Figure 2-24 *Shortcut menu for applying radius dimensions to a circle*

from this menu to apply radius dimension to a circle. Figure 2-25 shows an arc and a circle with radius dimensions.

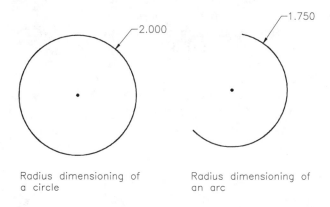

Radius dimensioning of a circle

Radius dimensioning of an arc

Figure 2-25 *Radius dimensioning of a circle and an arc*

 Tip. *To distinguish whether the dimension applied to an arc or a circle is radius or diameter, try to locate the number of arrowheads in the dimension. If there are two arrowheads in the dimension and the dimension is placed inside the circle or arc, it is a diameter dimension. The radius dimension has one arrowhead and is placed outside the circle or the arc.*

Linear Diameter Dimensioning

Linear diameter dimensioning is used to dimension revolved components. The sketch for a revolved component is drawn using simple sketcher entities. For example, if you draw a rectangle and revolve, it will result in a cylinder. Now, if you dimension the rectangle using the linear dimensions, the same dimensions will be displayed when you generate the drawing views of the cylinder. Also, the same dimensions will be used while manufacturing the component. But these linear dimensions will result in a confusing situation in manufacturing. This is because while manufacturing a revolved component, the dimensions have to be in terms of the diameter of the revolved component. The linear dimensions will not be acceptable during the manufacturing of a revolved component. To overcome this confusing situation, the sketch for the revolved features are dimensioned using the linear diameter dimensions. These dimensions display the distance between two selected line segments in terms of diameter, that is, double the original length. For example, if the original dimension between two entities is 10 mm, the linear dimension will display it as 20 mm. This is because when you revolve a rectangle with 10 mm width, the diameter of the resultant cylinder will be 20 mm. To apply linear diameter dimensions, invoke the **General Dimension** tool. You will be prompted to select the first geometry to dimension. Select the first line.

After you have selected the first line, you will be prompted to select the second geometry to dimension. Select the second line with reference to which you want to apply the linear diameter dimensions. Now, right-click to display the shortcut menu. In this shortcut menu, choose **Linear Diameter**, see Figure 2-26. You will see that the distance between the two lines is now displayed in terms of double the distance. Also, the dimension value is preceded by the Ø symbol, suggesting the linear diameter dimension. In this type of dimension Autodesk Inventor makes an assumption. It assumes that the line selected first will act as the axis of revolution for the sketch and the line selected

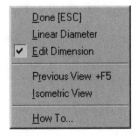

Figure 2-26 Choosing the option for applying linear diameter dimension

last will result in the outer surface of the revolved feature. This means that the line selected last will be the one that will be dimensioned. Figure 2-27 and Figure 2-28 show the use of linear diameter dimensioning.

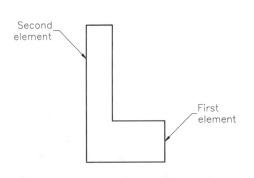

Figure 2-27 Selecting the elements for linear diameter dimensions

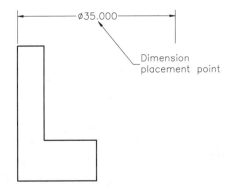

Figure 2-28 The linear diameter dimension

MEASURING DISTANCES

Menu Bar:	Tools > Measure Distance
Shortcut Menu:	Measure Distance

Autodesk Inventor allows you to measure the length of a line segment, radius of an arc, diameter of a circle, minimum distance between two entities, or the coordinates of a point. All this can be done using the **Measure Distance** tool. When you invoke this tool, the **Measure Distance** toolbar will be displayed and you will be prompted to select the first entity. The **Measure Distance** toolbar will be modified depending upon the type of entities selected to measure. The methods of measuring the distances between different entities are discussed next.

Measuring the Length of a Line Segment

When you invoke the **Measure Distance** tool, the **Measure Distance** toolbar will be displayed and you will be prompted to select the first entity. If you select a line segment at this point, the **Measure Distance** toolbar will be changed to the **Length** toolbar and the length of the selected line segment will be displayed in this toolbar, see Figure 2-29.

*Figure 2-29 The **Length** toolbar displaying the length of the line*

 Tip. *To restart the measuring of distances, choose the arrow on the right of the **Measure Distance** toolbar to display the shortcut menu. Choose **Reset** in this menu to restart the process. You will be prompted to select the first element.*

Measuring the Distance Between Two Line Segments

To measure the distance between two line segments, invoke the **Measure Distance** tool and then select the first line segment. The **Measure Distance** toolbar will be changed to the **Length** toolbar and you will be prompted to select the second entity. Select the second line. The **Length** toolbar will be changed to the **Minimum Distance** toolbar. This toolbar will display the minimum distance between the two lines and also the length of the second line, see Figure 2-30.

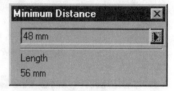

*Figure 2-30 The **Minimum Distance** toolbar displaying the distance between the lines*

Finding the Coordinates of a Point

To find out the coordinates of a point with respect to the current coordinate system, invoke the **Measure Distance** tool. You will be prompted to select the first element. Select the point whose coordinates you want to know. The points that can be selected include the endpoints of lines, arcs, or splines, or the center point of arcs, circles, or ellipses. When you select the point, the **Measure Distance** toolbar is changed to the **Position** toolbar and the X, Y, and Z coordinates of the current position of the selected point with respect to the current coordinate system will be displayed, see Figure 2-31.

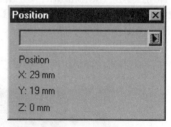

*Figure 2-31 The **Position** toolbar displaying the coordinates of a point*

Measuring the Distance Between Two Points

During the designing process there might arise a situation where you have to calculate the distance between two points. This can be done using the **Measure Distance** tool. Invoke this tool and then select the first point. The **Measure Distance** toolbar will change to the **Position** toolbar and you will be prompted to select the second element. Select the second point. The **Position** toolbar will be changed to the **Minimum Distance** toolbar. This toolbar will display the distance between the two points. This toolbar will also display the coordinates of the second point. You will also notice the **Delta X**, **Delta Y**, and **Delta Z** values in this toolbar, see Figure 2-32. These values are the distances between the two selected points along the X, Y, and Z axes.

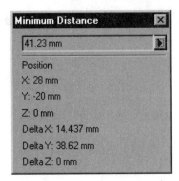

*Figure 2-32   Toolbar displaying the minimum distance
between two points, coordinates of the second points and
the delta X, Y, and Z distances between the two points*

Tip. *You would have noticed that the Z coordinates or the Z distances are zero at all
the places. This is because by default, when you start a new drawing, the sketches
are drawn in the XY plane. You can also draw the sketches on the other planes. You
will learn more about these sketching planes in later chapters.*

Calculating the Radius of an Arc or the Diameter of a Circle

You can also calculate the radius of an arc or the diameter of a circle using the **Measure
Distance** tool. When you invoke this tool, the **Measure Distance** toolbar will be displayed and
you will be prompted to select the first element. If you select an arc, this toolbar is changed to
the **Radius** toolbar and will display the radius of the arc, see Figure 2-33. If you select a circle,
this toolbar is changed to the **Diameter** toolbar and will display the diameter of the circle, see
Figure 2-34. Note that when you select an arc or a circle, you are not prompted to select the
second element. This is because when you select an arc or a circle, you cannot calculate any
value other than their radius or diameter.

*Figure 2-33 The **Radius** toolbar
displaying the radius of an arc*

*Figure 2-34 The **Diameter** toolbar
displaying the diameter of a circle*

Tip. *You can make sure that no sketching tool is selected by looking at the **Select**
button in the **Command Bar**. If the **Select** button in the **Command Bar** is chosen,
this means that no sketching tool is selected. If this button is not chosen, this means
that some sketching tool is active. Right-click and choose **Done** to close the sketching
tool that is active. You will notice that the **Select** button is chosen automatically
when you exit the sketching tool.*

MEASURING ANGLES

Menu Bar:	Tools > Measure Angle
Shortcut Menu:	Measure Angle

To measure an angle, choose **Measure Angle** from the **Tools** menu. The **Measure Angle** toolbar will be displayed. Using this tool you can measure the angle between two line segments or between three points. Both these methods for measuring the angles are discussed next.

Measuring the Angle Between Two lines

To measure the angle between two lines, invoke the **Measure Angle** tool. The **Measure Angle** toolbar is displayed and you will be prompted to select the first element. Select the first line. You will be prompted to select the second element. Select the second line. The **Measure Angle** toolbar will be changed to the **Angle** toolbar and the angle between the selected line segments will be displayed, see Figure 2-35.

Figure 2-35 The Angle toolbar displaying the angle between two lines

Measuring Angles using Three Points

You can also measure the angle using three points. Note that the points must be selected in either the clockwise sequence or the counterclockwise sequence. When you invoke this tool, you will be prompted to select the first element. If you select a point in this case, you will be prompted to select the next point. After you select the second point, you will again be prompted to select the next point. Select the third point. Once you have selected three points, Autodesk Inventor draws imaginary lines between the first and second point and between the second and third point. Now, the angle between these two imaginary lines will be calculated (Figure 2-36 and Figure 2-37) and displayed in the **Angle** toolbar.

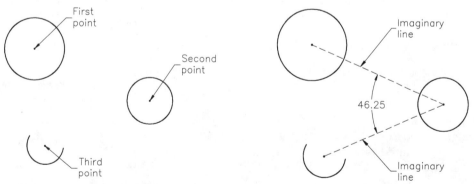

Figure 2-36 Selecting three points   *Figure 2-37 Angle between the imaginary lines*

Tip. *Autodesk Inventor allows you to switch from the distance measuring tool to the angle measuring tool, and vice versa. This is done using the shortcut menu displayed upon choosing the arrow on the right of the toolbar of any of these tools. If you choose the arrow in the **Measure Distance** toolbar, the shortcut menu will display the option of measuring angle. If you choose the arrow in the **Measure Angle** toolbar, the option to measure distance will be displayed in the shortcut menu.*

TUTORIALS

This chapter onwards, you will use the parametric nature of Autodesk Inventor in drawing the sketches and creating the features. The following tutorials will explain the method of drawing the sketches to some arbitrary dimensions and then driving them to the dimension values required in the model

Tutorial 1

In this tutorial you will draw the sketch shown in Figure 2-38. This sketch is the same as that drawn for Tutorial 2 of Chapter 1. However, you will not use the **Precise Input** toolbar while drawing the sketch now. After drawing the sketch, add the required constraints and then dimension the sketch. Save the sketch with the name given below:

\PersonalProject\c02**Tutorial1.ipt**   **(Expected time: 30 min)**

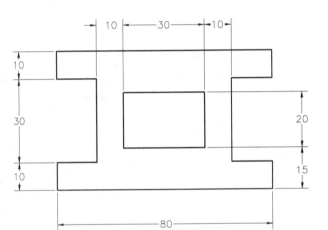

Figure 2-38 *Dimensioned sketch for Tutorial 1*

Before you start drawing the sketch, it is recommended that you outline the steps that will be followed to complete the tutorials. The steps that will be followed are listed below.

a.   Open a new metric template part file.
b.   Draw the rough sketch using the **Line** and the **Two point rectangle** tool.
c.   Add the required constraints and dimensions to complete the sketch.
d.   Save the sketch with the name **Tutorial1.ipt**.

Starting Autodesk Inventor

1.   Start Autodesk Inventor by double-clicking on its shortcut icon on the desktop of your computer or by using the **Start** menu.

2.   Choose **New** in the **Open** dialog box to display various tabs. Choose the **Metric** tab to display the metric templates. Double-click on the **Standard (mm).ipt** in the **Metric** tab to open the standard metric part file. By default, the sketching environment will be active.

Drawing the Sketch

1. Using the **Line** tool and the **Two point rectangle** tool draw the required sketch similar to the one shown in Figure 2-38. You do not need to draw the sketch to the exact length and can use the temporary tracking option for drawing the sketch. For your reference, all lines in the sketch have been assigned a number, see Figure 2-39. In this sketch, the X and Y axes are not displayed.

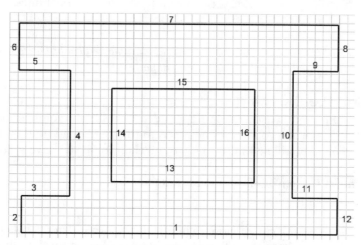

Figure 2-39 *Sketch after drawing*

Adding Constraints to the Sketch

It is evident in Figure 2-39 that some of the lines have to be of the same length. For example, lines 1 and 7, lines 2 and 6, lines 8 and 12, and so on have to be of the same length. Now, one option is that you assign dimensions to all these lines. But this will increase the number of dimensions in the sketch. The other option is that you apply constraints that will force the lines to maintain equal length.

In this case you can apply the **Equal** constraint to all the lines that should have the same length. The **Equal** constraint will relate the length of one of the lines with respect to the other line. Now, if you dimension any one of the related lines, all other lines that are related to it are forced to acquire the same dimension value. The **Equal** constraint is applied in pairs.

1. Choose the down arrow on the right of the **Perpendicular** button in the **Sketch** toolbar to display the other constraints. Choose **Equal** to invoke this constraint. You can also invoke this constraint by choosing **Perpendicular > Equal** from the **Sketch** panel bar.

When you invoke this constraint, you will be prompted to select the first line, circle, or arc.

 Note
*By default, the **Perpendicular** constraint will be displayed in the **Sketch** panel bar or toolbar. However, when you select any other constraint by choosing the down arrow on the right of this constraint, it will become active and will be displayed in the **Sketch** panel bar or toolbar.*

2. Select line 2. The color of this line will be changed to blue. You will be prompted to select the second line, circle, or arc. Select line 6. The **Equal** constraint will be applied to lines 2 and 6. You will again be prompted to select the first line, circle, or arc. Select line 6 as the first line and then select line 8 as the second line.

3. Similarly, select lines 8 and 12, 1 and 7, 3 and 5, 5 and 9, 9 and 11, and then lines 10 and 4. This will apply the **Equal** constraint to all these pairs of lines.

Note

While drawing the sketch if any line was not applied the vertical or horizontal constraint, you can apply it manually using the respective buttons.

Dimensioning the Sketch

Once all the required constraints are applied to the sketch, you can dimension it. As mentioned earlier, when you add dimensions to the sketch and modify the value of the dimension, the entity will be forced to the dimension value you have specified.

1. Choose **General Dimension** from the **Sketch** panel bar. You will be prompted to select the geometry to dimension. Select line 1.

As soon as you move the cursor close to line 1, it will turn red and a small symbol will be displayed suggesting that linear dimension will be applied to this line. It is important to modify the value of the dimensions after it is placed so that the geometries are driven to the values that you require. Therefore, after selecting line 1, right-click to display the shortcut menu. In this menu choose **Edit Dimension**. If it is already selected, press the ESC once. This will make sure that the **Edit Dimension** toolbar is displayed when you place the dimension. This toolbar allows you to modify the dimension value.

2. Place the dimension below line 1. When you place the dimension, the **Edit Dimension** toolbar will be displayed. Enter **80** as the length of line 1 in this toolbar and then choose the check mark button on the right of this toolbar.

You will notice that the length of the line is modified to 80 units. Also, notice that the length of line 7 is modified because of the **Equal** constraint (refer to Figure 2-41).

3. Since you are still in the **General Dimension** tool, you will again be prompted to select the geometry to dimension. Select line 2 and place the dimension on left of this line. The **Edit Dimension** toolbar will be displayed. Change the length of this line in this toolbar to **10**.

You will notice that the length of lines 6, 8, and 10 will also be forced to change to **10** units. This is because of the **Equal** constraint applied to all these lines.

4. Select line 4 and place the dimension on the left of this line. Modify the dimension value to **30** in the **Edit Dimension** toolbar. Notice that the length of line 10 is also modified.

5. Select line 16 and place the dimension outside the sketch on the right side. Modify the dimension value in the **Edit Dimension** toolbar to **20**.

6. Select line 15 and place the dimension outside the sketch on the top. Modify the dimension value to **30** in the **Edit Dimension** toolbar.

7. Now, to dimension the distance between lines 4 and 14, select them one by one. Place the dimension outside the sketch on the top and then change the dimension value to **10** in the **Edit Dimension** toolbar.

8. Similarly, select lines 16 and 10 and place the dimension outside the sketch on the top to dimension the distance between these two lines. Change the dimension value to **10** in the **Edit Dimension** toolbar. You will notice that the length of lines 5, 9, 3, and 11 are automatically adjusted due to the **Equal** constraint.

9. To locate the inner rectangle vertically from the outer loop, select lines 1 and 13 and then place the dimension on the right of the sketch. Modify the dimension value in the **Edit Dimension** toolbar to **15**.

With this you have applied all the required constraints and dimensions to the sketch. Now, this sketch is ready to be converted into a feature. If you try to add more constraints or dimensions to this sketch, Autodesk Inventor will display an error message dialog box with the message that adding this dimension or constraint will over-constrain the sketch, see Figure 2-40. If you still want this dimension to be displayed, choose the **Accept** button in this message box. The dimension will be added as a **driven dimension**. A driven dimension is placed inside parentheses and is not used during the manufacturing process. These dimensions are used only for reference. Note that you cannot edit the value of a driven dimension.

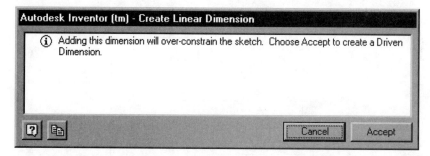

Figure 2-40 *Autodesk Inventor message box*

10. The final sketch for Tutorial 1 after applying all the dimensions and constraints should look similar to the one shown in Figure 2-41.

11. Choose the **Return** button in the **Command Bar** to exit the sketching environment. You can also right-click in the drawing window and choose **Finish Sketch** from the shortcut menu to exit the sketching environment. Choose the **Save** button from the **Standard** toolbar and save this sketch with the name given below:

\PersonalProject\c02**Tutorial1.ipt**.

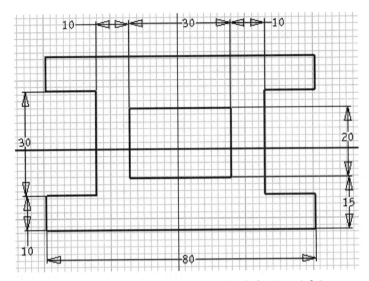

Figure 2-41 *Final dimensioned sketch for Tutorial 1*

Tutorial 2

In this tutorial you will draw the sketch shown in Figure 2-42. This sketch is the same as the one you had drawn for Tutorial 4 of Chapter 1. While drawing this sketch now, you will not use the **Precise Input** toolbar. After drawing the sketch, you will apply the required constraints and dimensions to this sketch.   **(Expected time: 30 min)**

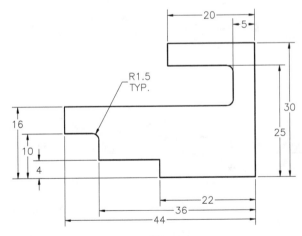

Figure 2-42 *Sketch for Tutorial 2*

The steps that will be followed to complete the tutorial are listed below.

a.   Open a new metric template file and draw the rough sketch using the **Line** tool.
b.   Add linear diameter dimensions to the sketch by using the **General Dimension** tool.
c.   Add the fillets and then save the sketch with the name **Tutorial2.ipt**.

Starting a New File

1. Choose the **New** button in the **Standard** toolbar and open a new metric part file using the **Metric** tab of the **Open** dialog box.

Drawing the Sketch

1. Draw the sketch shown in Figure 2-43 using the **Line** tool. You can use the object snap option to join the last line with the first line. For reference, the lines in the sketch are numbered.

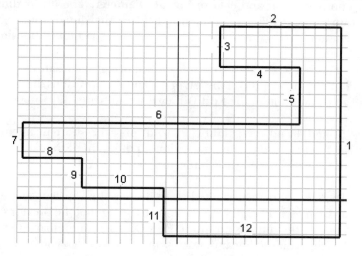

Figure 2-43 *Numbering the lines in the sketch*

Dimensioning the Sketch

The dimensions shown in Figure 2-42 are linear dimensions. But since the sketch is for a revolved feature, you will add linear diameter dimensions to the sketch. It is recommended to first apply all the dimensions to the sketch and then add the fillets. This is because the sketch generally changes its size after dimensioning. Before proceeding with adding the dimensions to a revolved section, it is important for you to find out which line segment will act as the revolution axis for revolving the sketch. If you refer to Figure 1-38 and Figure 1-39 in Chapter 1, you will notice that for this model, line 12 will act as the axis for revolving the sketch. Therefore, while applying linear diameter dimensions, line 12 should be selected first.

1. Choose **General Dimension** from the **Sketch** panel bar. Right-click to display the shortcut menu and choose **Edit Dimension** if it is not already chosen. If it is already chosen, press the ESC key once to exit the shortcut menu. You will be prompted to select the geometry to dimension. Select line 12. You will again be prompted to select the geometry to dimension. Select line 10 and then right-click to display the shortcut menu. In this menu choose **Linear Diameter**. You will notice that the dimension is displayed as the double of the actual length. Place the dimension on the left of the sketch. When you place the dimension, the dimension value will be preceded by the Ø symbol, suggesting that it is linear a diameter dimension.

2. The **Edit Dimension** toolbar will be displayed as soon as you place the dimension.

Figure 2-42 shows this value as 4. But since the linear diameter dimensions are placed as the double of the original length, therefore, enter **8** in the **Edit Dimension** toolbar. The vertical distance between lines 12 and 10 will be automatically adjusted to match the value entered.

3. Since you are inside the **General Dimension** tool, you will again be prompted to select the first geometry to dimension. Select line 12 and then select line 8. Now, right-click to display the shortcut menu and choose **Linear Diameter**. The linear dimension will be converted into a linear diameter dimension. Place the dimension on the left of the previous dimension. Modify the value of the dimension in the **Edit Dimension** toolbar to **20**.

4. Select lines 12 and 6. Right-click to display the shortcut menu and then choose **Linear Diameter**. Place the dimension on the left of the and then previous dimension and change the value of the dimension in the **Edit Dimension** toolbar to **32**.

5. Select lines 12 and 4 and then right-click to display the shortcut menu. In this menu choose **Linear Diameter**. Place the dimension on the right of the sketch and change the value of the dimension in the **Edit Dimension** toolbar to **50**.

6. Select lines 12 and 2 and then right-click to display the shortcut menu. In this menu choose **Linear Diameter**. Place the dimension on the right of the previous dimension and change the value of the dimension in the **Edit Dimension** toolbar to **60**. With this you have applied all the required linear diameter dimensions. Now, you have to add the linear dimensions.

Tip. *Autodesk Inventor allows you to invoke the drawing display options even when any of the sketching environment tool is active. This is done using a combination of the hot keys and the left mouse button. For example, if the **General Dimension** tool is active, you can use the **Pan** option by holding the F2 key down and then pressing the left mouse button and dragging. Similarly, you can dynamically zoom in and out of the sketch by holding the F3 key down and then pressing the left mouse button and dragging.*

7. Select line 1 and line 5 and then place the dimension above the sketch. Modify the dimension value in the **Edit Dimension** toolbar to **5**.

8. Select line 2 and then place the dimension above the previous dimension. Modify the value of the dimension in the **Edit Dimension** toolbar to **20**.

9. Select line 12 and then place the dimension below the sketch. Modify the value of the dimension in the **Edit Dimension** toolbar to **22**.

10. Select lines 1 and 9 and place the dimension below the previous dimension. Modify the value of the dimension in the **Edit Dimension** toolbar to **36**.

11. Select lines 1 and 7 and place the dimension below the previous dimension. Modify the value of the dimension in the **Edit Dimension** toolbar to **44**.

12. The sketch after adding all the dimensions should look similar to the one shown in Figure 2-44.

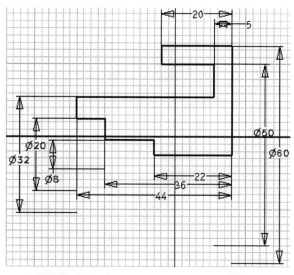

Figure 2-44 *The sketch after dimensioning*

Adding Fillets to the Sketch

Once all dimensions are applied, you can fillet the sketch.

1. Choose **Fillet** from the **Sketch** panel bar. The **2D Fillet** toolbar will be displayed. Set the value of fillet in this toolbar to **1.5**. Now, select lines 8 and 9. The fillet will be automatically applied between these two lines and the fillet dimension will be displayed.

2. Similarly, select lines 5 and 6, and lines 4 and 5 to apply fillet between these lines. The final sketch after applying all fillets should look similar to the one shown in Figure 2-45. In this figure, the X and Y axes are not displayed for clarity.

   Notice that the radius of fillet is displayed only on the fillet that was created first. This is because all fillets have the same radius. If you modify this fillet radius, all other fillets will change automatically.

Saving the Sketch

1. Choose **Return** from the **Command Bar** to exit the sketching environment.

2. Save this sketch with the name given below:

   \PersonalProject\c02**Tutorial2.ipt**.

 Tip. *When you are applying linear diameter dimensions, the line selected first will be considered as the center line and the dimension will be applied to the line selected second. Therefore, while applying linear diameter dimensions, the first line should be the one around which the sketch will be revolved.*

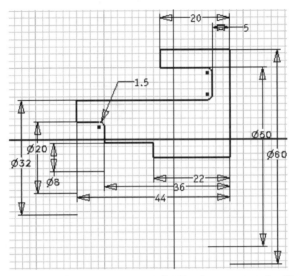

***Figure 2-45** Final dimensioned sketch after creating the fillets*

Tutorial 3

In this tutorial draw the sketch for the model shown in Figure 2-46. After drawing the sketch, add the constraints and then dimension it. The basic dimensioned sketch that is required for the model is shown in Figure 2-47. Figure 2-46 shows the solid model created after extruding the sketch. The solid model is shown for reference only. **(Expected time: 30 min)**

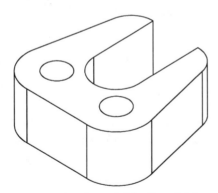

***Figure 2-46** Model for Tutorial 3*

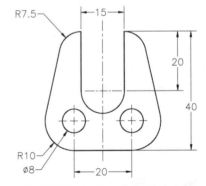

***Figure 2-47** Dimensioned sketch for the model*

The sketch shown in Figure 2-46 is a combination of multiple closed loops; the outer closed loop and the inner circles. As the number of closed loops increases, the complexity of the sketch also increases. This is because the number of constraints and dimensions in the sketch increases in case of multiple closed loops. Now, if you are not using the **Precise Input** toolbar for drawing the sketches, it is recommended that you first draw the outer closed loop and add constraints and dimensions to it. This is because once the outer closed loop is constrained and dimensioned, the inner closed loops can be easily constrained and dimensioned with reference to the outer loop.

The steps that will be followed to complete this tutorial are listed below.

a.   Open a new metric template and create the outer loop of the sketch.
b.   Add the required dimensions and constraints to the outer loop.
c.   Create the inner circles and add constraints and dimensions to them.
d.   Finally, save the sketch with the name **Tutorial3.ipt**.

Starting a New File

1.   Choose the **New** button in the **Standard** toolbar to invoke the **Open** dialog box. Choose the **Metric** tab and open a standard metric part file.

Drawing the Outer Loop

1.   Using the **Line** tool, draw the rough sketch for the model as shown in Figure 2-48.

You can use the option of drawing the tangent arcs using the **Line** tool for drawing this sketch. This can be done by pressing the left mouse button and then dragging in the required direction. (Refer to Tutorial 3 of Chapter 1 to learn more about drawing this type of arc.) For reference, all the geometries in the sketch are numbered. The inner holes in the sketch will be drawn after dimensioning the sketch.

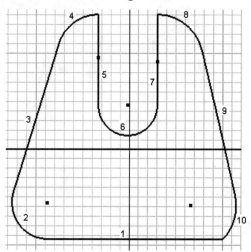

Figure 2-48 *Initial sketch with numbered geometries*

Adding Constraints to the Sketched Entities

As evident in Figure 2-48, some of the constraints like tangent and equal are missing in the sketch. You will have to manually add these constraints to the sketch. You can view the constraints applied on the various geometries using the **Show Constraint** tool.

1.   It is evident in Figure 2-48 that the tangent constraint is missing between line 1 and arc 10. To add this constraint, choose the down arrow on the right of the **Perpendicular** button in the **Sketch** panel bar and choose **Tangent**. You will be prompted to select the first curve. Select arc 10 and then select line 1 as the second curve. Similarly, add this constraint at all the places where it is missing in the sketch.

The geometries 5 and 7, and 3 and 9 are lines and must be of equal length. Also, geometries 2 and 10, and 4 and 8 are arcs that must be of equal radius. Therefore, you will have to add the **Equal** constraint to all these geometries.

2. Choose the down arrow on the right of **Tangent** in the **Sketch** panel bar and choose **Equal**.

3. Select line 5 as the first line and then select line 7 as the second line. This will apply the **Equal** constraint to these lines. Autodesk Inventor will again prompt you to select the first entity. Select line 3 and then select line 9 to apply the **Equal** constraint to these lines.

4. You will be prompted to select the first entity again. Select arc 2 and then arc 10 to apply this constraint to these arcs.

   Applying the **Equal** constraint to the arcs or circles forces their radius or diameter to be equal.

5. Similarly, apply this constraint on arcs 4 and 8. The sketch after applying all the constraints should look similar to the one shown in Figure 2-49.

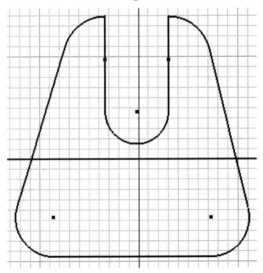

Figure 2-49 *Sketch after applying all the constraints*

Note
The shape of the sketch that you have may be a little different at this stage. This is because of the difference in specifying the points while drawing the sketch. However, once all the dimensions are applied, the shape of the sketch will become similar.

Dimensioning the Sketch

1. After adding all the constraints, you have to dimension the sketch. Choose **General Dimension** in the **Sketch** panel bar. Right-click to display the shortcut menu. In this menu choose **Edit Dimension** if it is not already selected. If it shows the check mark, press

the ESC key once to exit the shortcut menu. You will be prompted to select the geometry to dimension. Select line 1 and place the dimension below the sketch. Modify the value of this dimension in the **Edit Dimension** toolbar to **20**.

As mentioned earlier, you can use a combination of hot keys and mouse button to modify the drawing display. At this stage hold the F3 key down to invoke the **Zoom** tool. Press the left mouse button and drag it upwards to reduce the size of display. After getting the desired size, hold the F2 key down to invoke the **Pan** tool. Press the left mouse button and drag it to pan the display to the desired point.

2. As soon as you release the F2 key, the dimensioning process will resume and you will be prompted to select the geometry to dimension. Select arc 4 and place the dimension on the left of the sketch. This will place the radius dimension for the sketch. Modify the dimension value in the **Edit Dimension** toolbar to **7.5**. You will notice that the size of arc 8 will also be changed due to the **Equal** constraint.

3. Select arc 2 and place the dimension on the left of the sketch. Modify the dimension value in the **Edit Dimension** toolbar to **10**. You will notice that the size of arc 10 will also be changed due to the **Equal** constraint.

4. Select line 5 and then line 7 and place the dimension above the sketch. Modify the value of this dimension in the **Edit Dimension** toolbar to **15**.

5. Select line 7 and place the dimension on the right of the sketch. Modify the value of this dimension in the **Edit Dimension** toolbar to **20**.

6. Select the upper endpoint of line 7 and then select line 1 and place the dimension on the right of the previous dimension. Modify the value of this dimension in the **Edit Dimension** toolbar to **40**.

    With this, all the dimensions are applied, except the horizontal dimension between center points of arcs 4 and 6.

7. Since you are already inside the **General Dimension** tool, you will be prompted to select the geometry to dimension. Select the center point of arc 4 and then the center point of arc 6.

    As you have selected two points that are not horizontally or vertically aligned, you can apply horizontal, vertical, or aligned dimensions to these points. However, in this sketch you require only the horizontal dimension. Therefore, you will use the shortcut menu.

8. Right-click and choose **Horizontal** from the shortcut menu. Place the dimension above the sketch and modify the dimension value to 7.5.

    You will notice that all the other arcs are also aligned automatically. This is due to other constraints and dimensions that are already applied to the sketch. The dimensioned sketch should look similar to the one shown in Figure 2-50.

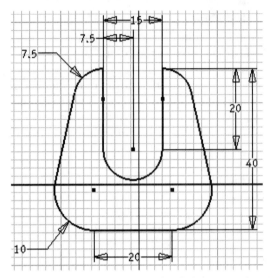

Figure 2-50 *Dimensioned sketch for Tutorial 3*

Drawing the Circles

Once all the required dimensions and constraints are applied, you will have to draw the circles. Figure 2-47 suggests that the circles are concentric with arcs 2 and 10.

1. To draw the concentric circles, choose **Center point circle** from the **Sketch** panel bar. You will be prompted to select the center of the circle. Take the cursor close to the center of arc 2. The cursor will snap to the center point of arc 2 and will turn green. Once the cursor turns green, press the left mouse button to select it as the center of the circle. Now, move the cursor away from the center to size the circle. Again press the left mouse button to give an approximate size to the circle.

2. Similarly, taking the reference of the center of arc 10, draw another circle.

Adding Constraints to the Circles

Since both the circles have the same diameter, you can apply the **Equal** constraint to them. This way you have to apply dimension to just one of them. The other circle will be automatically forced to the specified diameter value because of the **Equal** constraint.

1. Choose **Equal** from the **Sketch** panel bar. This button replaces the **Vertical** button in the **Sketch** panel bar as it was the last constraint that was used. Select the first circle and then select the second circle to apply this constraint.

Dimensioning the Circle

1. Choose **General Dimension** from the **Sketch** panel bar and select the left circle. Place the dimension on the left of the sketch. Change the value of the diameter of the circle in the **Edit Dimension** toolbar to **8**.

You will notice that the dimension of the other circle is automatically modified to match the dimension of the first circle. This is because of the **Equal** constraint. This completes the dimensioning of the sketch. The final sketch for Tutorial 3 after drawing and dimensioning the circles should look similar to the one shown in Figure 2-51.

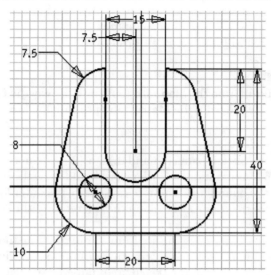

Figure 2-51 *The final dimensioned sketch for Tutorial 3*

Saving the Sketch

1. Choose the **Return** button in the **Command Bar** to exit the sketching environment. Save this sketch with the name given below:

    \PersonalProject\c02**Tutorial3.ipt**.

Tutorial 4

In this tutorial you will draw the sketch for the model shown in Figure 2-52. The dimensioned sketch of the model is shown in Figure 2-53. After drawing the sketch, add constraints and then dimension it. The solid model is given for reference only.   **(Expected time: 30 min)**

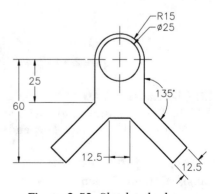

Figure 2-52 *Model for the sketch of Tutorial 4*   **Figure 2-53** *Sketch to be drawn*

The steps that will be followed to complete this tutorial are listed below.

a. Open a new metric template and create the outer loop of the sketch.
b. Add the required dimensions and constraints to the sketch.
c. Add the inner circle and add the dimension to it.
d. Finally, save the sketch with the name **Tutorial4.ipt**.

Starting a New File
1. Choose the **New** button from the **Standard** toolbar to display the **Open** dialog box. Open a new metric template file from the **Metric** tab of this dialog box.

Drawing the Outer Loop
1. Choose **Line** from the **Sketch** panel bar and draw an approximate sketch for the model as shown in Figure 2-54. As mentioned earlier, you should draw the inner loop after drawing and dimensioning the outer loop. This is because once the outer loop is fully constrained, you can directly draw the inner loop taking the reference of the outer loop.

   You can use the option of drawing the arc from within the **Line** tool to draw the arc in the sketch. You can also use the temporary tracking option for drawing this sketch. For your reference, various geometries in the sketch are numbered, see Figure 2-54.

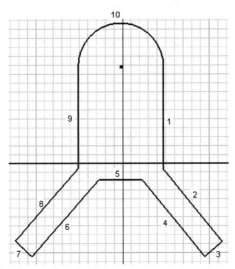

Figure 2-54 Initial sketch with the geometries numbered

Adding Constraint to the Sketch
1. Add the **Equal** constraint to lines 1 and 9, lines 2 and 8, lines 3 and 5, lines 5 and 7, and lines 4 and 6. Also, add the **Perpendicular** constraint to lines 2 and 3 and lines 7 and 8.

Dimensioning the Sketch
1. Choose **General Dimension** from the **Sketch** panel bar. You will be prompted to select the geometry to dimension. Select line 9 and place the dimension on the left of the sketch.

Modify the dimension value in the **Edit Dimension** toolbar to **25**.

2. Select the center of the arc and then select the lower endpoint of line 6. Place the dimension on the left of the previous dimension. Modify the dimension value in the **Edit Dimension** toolbar to **60** .

3. Select line 3 and then right-click to display the shortcut menu. Choose **Aligned** from this shortcut menu and then place the dimension below the sketch. Modify the dimension value in the **Edit Dimension** toolbar to 12.5.

   You will notice that the length of lines 5 and 7 is also modified due to the **Equal** constraint.

4. Select lines 1 and 2 and then place the angular dimension on the right of the sketch. Modify the value of the angular dimension in the **Edit Dimension** toolbar to **135**.

5. Select arc 10 and then place the radius dimension above the sketch. Modify the value of the radius of the arc in the **Edit Dimension** toolbar to **15**.

   With this you have added all the required dimensions to the sketch. You can now draw the inner circle taking the center of the arc as the center of the circle.

Drawing the Inner Circle

1. Choose **Center point circle** from the **Sketch** panel bar. You will be prompted to select the center of the circle. Take the cursor close to the center of the arc. The cursor will snap on to that point and will turn green. Select this point as the center of the circle and then move the cursor away from the center to size the circle. Specify a point to give an approximate size to the circle.

Dimensioning the Circle

1. Choose **General Dimension** from the **Sketch** panel bar and select the circle. Place the diameter dimension below the arc dimension. Enter the diameter of the circle as **25** in the **Edit Dimension** toolbar.

   This completes the sketch for Tutorial 4. The final dimensioned sketch should look similar to the one shown in Figure 2-55.

Saving the Sketch

1. Choose the **Return** button in the **Command Bar** to exit the sketching environment and then save this sketch with the name given below:

   \PersonalProject\c02**Tutorial4.ipt**.

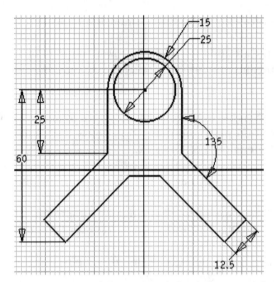

Figure 2-55 *Final dimensioned sketch for Tutorial 4*

Self-Evaluation Test

Answer the following questions and then compare your answers with the answers given at the end of the chapter.

1. The **Perpendicular** constraint forces the selected entity to become normal to another specified entity. (T/F)

2. The **Coincident** constraint can be applied to two line segments. (T/F)

3. The **Collinear** constraint can be applied only to line segments. (T/F)

4. If you apply a constraint that is not required in the sketch, Autodesk Inventor will display a message box informing you that adding this constraint will over-constrain the sketch. (T/F)

5. The _____ nature of Autodesk Inventor ensures that irrespective of the original size, the selected entity is driven to the dimension value you specify.

6. When you select a circle to dimension, by default, the _____ dimension is applied to it.

7. The _____ dimension has one arrowhead and is placed outside the circle or the arc.

8. The _____ dimensions display the distance between two selected line segments in the terms of diameter, that is double the original length.

9. Using the _____ tool you can measure the radius of an arc.

10. To measure the angle between three points, the points must be selected either in the _____ sequence or in the _____ sequence.

Review Questions

Answer the following questions.

1. You cannot apply **Concentric** constraint between a point and a circle. (T/F)

2. You can use the **Horizontal** or the **Vertical** constraint to line up arcs, circles, or ellipses in the same horizontal or vertical direction. (T/F)

3. You can view all or some of the constraints applied to the sketch. (T/F)

4. There are twelve types of geometric constraints that can be applied additionally to the sketched entities. (T/F)

5. The linear dimensions are defined as the dimensions that define the shortest distance between two points. (T/F)

6. The situation where the number of dimensions or constraints have exceeded the number that are required in the sketch is called

    (a) Constraint   (b) Under-constrained
    (c) Over-constrained   (d) None

7. When you invoke the **Measure Distance** tool and select two lines, the **Measure Distance** toolbar changes into which of the following toolbar?

    (a) **Length**   (b) **Distance**
    (c) **Minimum Distance**   (d) Remains the same

8. Whenever you select an arc to dimension, by default, which of the following types of dimension is applied to it?

    (a) **Radius**   (b) **Diameter**
    (c) **Linear**   (d) **Linear Diameter**

9. In addition to the lines, which of the following entity can be selected to apply the collinear constraint?

    (a) Arc   (b) Circle
    (c) Ellipse   (d) Ellipse axis

10. Which of the following combination of entities cannot be used to apply the tangent constraint?

    (a) Line, Line   (b) Line, Arc
    (c) Circle, Circle   (d) Arc, Circle

Exercises

Exercise 1

Draw the basic sketch for the model shown in Figure 2-56. The sketch to be drawn is shown in Figure 2-57. After drawing the sketch, add the required constraints and then dimension it.

(Expected time: 30 min)

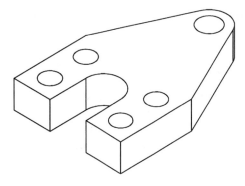

Figure 2-56 Model for Exercise 1

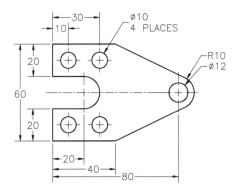

Figure 2-57 Sketch for Exercise 1

Exercise 2

Draw the basic sketch for the model shown in Figure 2-58. The sketch is shown in Figure 2-59. After drawing the sketch, add the required constraints and then dimension it.

(Expected time: 30 min)

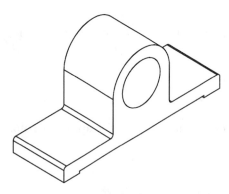

Figure 2-58 Model for Exercise 2

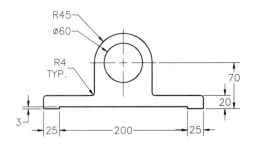

Figure 2-59 Sketch for Exercise 2

Exercise 3

Draw the basic sketch for the model shown in Figure 2-60. The sketch is shown in Figure 2-61. After drawing the sketch, add the required constraints and then dimension it.

(Expected time: 30 min)

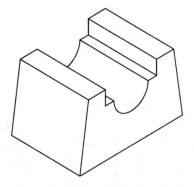

Figure 2-60 Model for Exercise 3

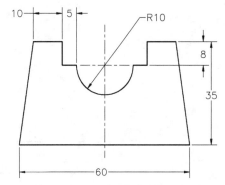

Figure 2-61 Sketch for Exercise 3

Exercise 4

Redraw the sketch for Exercise 1 of Chapter 1 without using the **Precise Input** toolbar. After drawing the sketch, add the required constraints to it and then dimension it. The dimensioned sketch is shown in Figure 2-62.

(Expected time: 30 min)

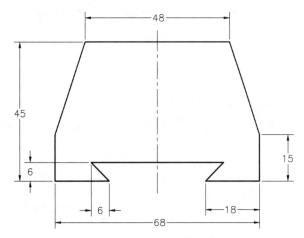

Figure 2-62 Dimensioned sketch for Exercise 4

Exercise 5

Redraw the sketch for Exercise 2 of Chapter 1 without using the **Precise Input** toolbar. After drawing the sketch, add the required constraint to it and then dimension it. The dimensioned sketch is shown in Figure 2-63.   **(Expected time: 30 min)**

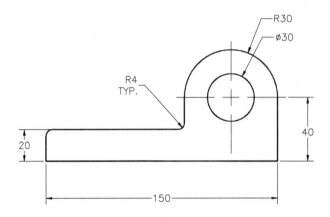

Figure 2-63 *Dimensioned sketch for Exercise 5*

 Note
The solid models in Exercises 1, 2, and 3 are given for reference only.

Answers to Self-Evaluation Test
1. T, **2.** F, **3.** F, **4.** T, **5.** parametric, **6.** diameter, **7.** radius, **8.** linear diameter, **9. Measure Distance**, **10.** clockwise, counterclockwise.

Chapter 3

Editing, Extruding, and Revolving the Sketches

Learning Objectives

After completing this chapter you will be able to:

- *Edit the sketches using various editing tools.*
- *Create rectangular and circular patterns.*
- *Convert the sketches into base features using the Extrude tool.*
- *Convert the sketches into base features using the Revolve tool.*
- *Dynamically rotate a model in 3D space and use the existing common views to view the model from various directions.*

EDITING THE SKETCHED ENTITIES

Autodesk Inventor provides you with a number of tools that can be used to edit the sketched entities. All these options are discussed next.

Extending the Sketched Entities

Toolbar: Sketch > Extend
Panel Bar: Sketch > Extend

This tool is used to extend or lengthen the selected sketched entity. The selected entity will be extended up to a specified boundary. Therefore, to use this tool, you should have at least two entities such that when extended, these entities meet at a point. Taking the reference of one of the entities the other will be extended. The entities that can be extended are lines and arcs. When you choose this button, you will be prompted to select the curve to be extended. When you take the cursor close to the curve to be extended, the original curve will be displayed in red color and the portion that will be extended will be displayed in black color. To exit this command, select another button, press ESC, or right-click to display the shortcut menu and then choose **Exit**. While extending the arcs, the point from where you select the arc will define the side of the arc that will be extended. Figure 3-1 and Figure 3-2 show the curves before and after extending.

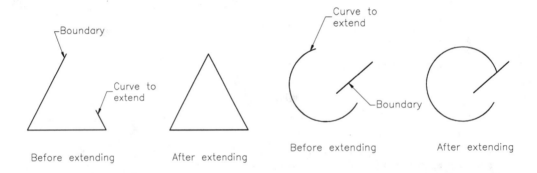

Figure 3-1 Line before and after extending   *Figure 3-2 Arc before and after extending*

Trimming the Sketched Entities

Toolbar: Sketch > Trim
Panel Bar: Sketch > Trim

This tool can be considered as the opposite of the extend tool. This tool is used to chop the selected sketched entity by using an edge (also called the knife edge). The knife edge may or may not actually touch the entity to be trimmed. However, when extended the knife edge must intersect the entity to be trimmed. When you choose **Trim** from the **Sketch** panel bar, you will be prompted to select the portion of the curve to be trimmed. As you take the cursor close to the curve, the portion to be trimmed will be displayed in dashed lines of red color and the remaining curve will be displayed in a continuous line of red color.

You can select the side of the curve to be trimmed by selecting that side of the curve. Figure 3-3 shows the curves to be selected for trimming and Figure 3-4 shows the sketch after trimming the edges.

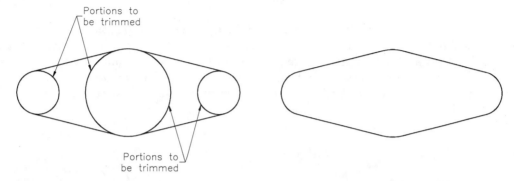

Portions to
be trimmed

Portions to
be trimmed

Figure 3-3 Selecting the edges for trimming   *Figure 3-4* Sketch after trimming the edges

Tip. *If you are inside any one of the* **Trim** *or the* **Extend** *editing operation, you can switch to the other by using the shortcut menu that is displayed upon right-clicking. The active operation will have a check mark in front of it. You can choose the other operation to shift to that command.*

If you are inside the **Extend** *or the* **Trim** *editing operation, you can also momentarily switch to the other one by just pressing the SHIFT key. For example, if the active editing operation is* **Trim** *and you press and hold the SHIFT key down, it will act as the* **Extend** *operation. When you release the SHIFT key, the original operation will resume its function of trimming. Similarly, vice versa.*

Offsetting the Sketched Entities

Toolbar:	Sketch > Offset
Panel Bar:	Sketch > Offset

Offsetting is one of the easiest methods of drawing parallel lines or concentric arcs and circles. You can select the entire loop as a single entity to offset or select the individual entities to offset. When you choose **Offset** from the **Sketch** panel bar, you will be prompted to select the curve to be offset. At this point if you right-click, a shortcut menu will be displayed as shown in Figure 3-5.

The **Loop Select** option is chosen as shown in Figure 3-5. This option allows you to select the entire loop as a single entity. However, if this option is cleared then the entire loop will be considered as a combination of individual segments and you will be allowed to select individual entities. The **Constraint Offset** option applies the constraints automatically when the loop or the individual entity is offset.

Figure 3-5 Offset Shortcut menu

If you select the **Loop Select** option, then once you have selected the loop, you will be prompted to specify the offset position for the new loop. If you specify the location to be inside the original loop, then the new loop will be smaller than the original loop. If you specify the location to be outside the original loop, then the new loop will be bigger than the original loop.

In case of individual entities, once you have selected the entity to be offset, right-click to display the shortcut menu and choose **Continue**, or press the ENTER key to continue. You will be prompted to specify the location for the new entity. If the selected entity is a line segment then its length will remain the same and if it is an arc or a circle then the size of the new entity will depend upon the location of the new point. Figure 3-6 shows offsetting of a loop and Figure 3-7 shows offsetting of an individual entity.

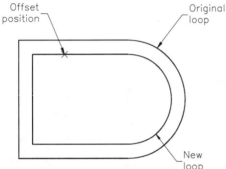

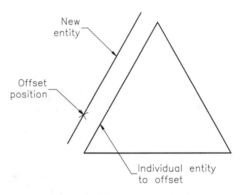

Figure 3-6 *Creating a new loop by offsetting the original loop*

Figure 3-7 *Offsetting an individual line segment to a new location*

Mirroring the Sketched Entities

Toolbar:	Sketch > Mirror
Panel Bar:	Sketch > Mirror

 The **Mirror** tool can be used to create a mirror image of the selected entities. The entities are mirrored about a straight line segment. This tool is used to draw sketches that are symmetrical about a line or sketches that have some portion symmetrical about a line. When you invoke this tool, the **Mirror** dialog box will be displayed, see Figure 3-8. The **Select** button will be chosen in this dialog box and you will be prompted to select the entities to be mirrored. You can select as many entities as you want to mirror. Once you have selected all the entities to be mirrored, choose the **Mirror line** button. You will be prompted to select the line about which the entities should be mirrored. After selecting the mirror line, choose the **Apply** button. The selected entities will be mirrored about the mirror line. If the

Figure 3-8 *Mirror dialog box*

mirror line is at an angle, the resultant entities that will be created upon mirroring will also be at an angle. Choose the **Done** button to exit this dialog box.

Figure 3-9 shows different sketched entities selected for mirroring and the mirror line that will be used to mirror the entities and Figure 3-10 shows the entities created after mirroring. Figure 3-11 shows the entities selected to mirror about an inclined mirror line and Figure 3-12 shows the entities created after mirroring.

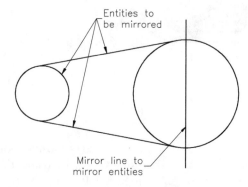

Figure 3-9 *Selecting the geometries to be mirrored about the mirror line*

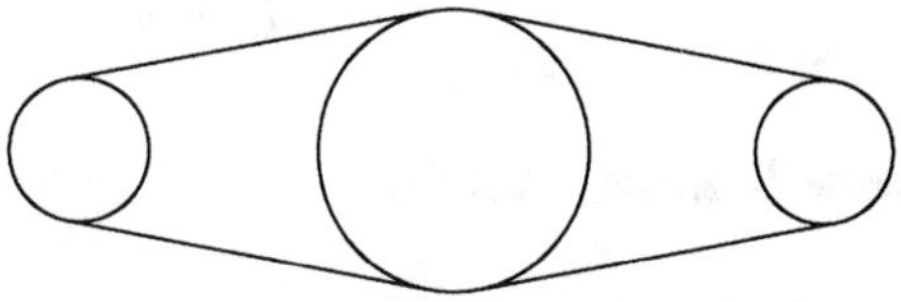

Figure 3-10 *Sketch after mirroring the geometries and deleting the mirror line*

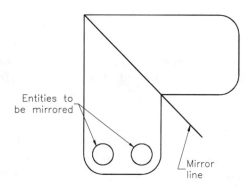

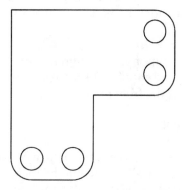

Figure 3-11 *Selecting the geometries to be mirrored about the mirror line*

Figure 3-12 *Sketch after mirroring the geometries and deleting the mirror line*

Moving the Sketched Entities

Toolbar:	Sketch > Move
Panel Bar:	Sketch > Move

The **Move** tool is used to move one or more selected sketched entities from one specified point to the other. The points that can be used to move the entities include the sketched points/hole centers, endpoints of lines, arcs, and splines, and the center points of arcs, circles, and ellipses. When you invoke this command, the **Move** dialog box will be displayed as shown in Figure 3-13. You can even use this dialog box to create copies of the selected entities. The various options provided under the **Move** dialog box are discussed next.

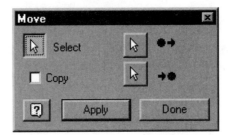

Figure 3-13 Move dialog box

Move Dialog Box Options

Select
This button is chosen to select the entities to be moved. When you invoke the **Move** tool, this button is automatically chosen. You can select more than one object by using the Window or Crossing options or by selecting them one by one using the left mouse button.

Copy
This check box is chosen to create a copy of the selected entities as they are moved. If this check box is selected, a copy of the selected entities will be created and placed at the destination point, keeping the original entities intact at their original location.

From Point
This button is chosen to specify the point that will act as the base point for moving the selected entities. Once you have selected all the entities to be moved, choose this button to select the from point.

To Point
This button is chosen to specify the destination point to which the selected entities will be moved. As soon as you specify the from point for moving the entities, this button is automatically chosen in the dialog box and you will be prompted to specify the point to which the selected entities will move.

Apply
This button is chosen to apply the move operation to the selected entities such that they are moved from the specified from point to the specified to point. Until this button is chosen, the objects will not be moved from their original location. After you have applied the move operation by choosing this button, the **Select** button is again chosen so that you can select another set of entities for moving.

Done
This button is chosen to exit the **Move** dialog box, thus exiting the **Move** tool.

Figure 3-14 through Figure 3-17 show moving and copying of various sketched entities from one specified point to the other specified point.

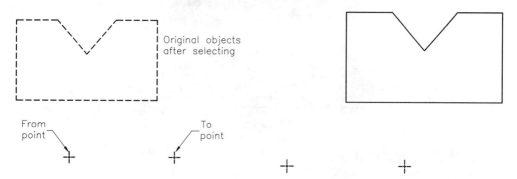

Figure 3-14 *Moving the entities using the sketch points*

Figure 3-15 *Objects after moving*

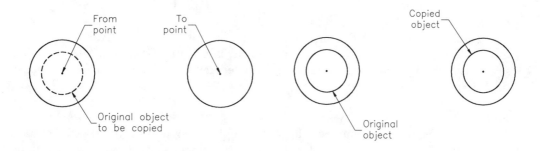

Figure 3-16 *Moving and copying the entities using the center points of circles*

Figure 3-17 *Objects after moving and copying*

 Note
Remember that the behavior of the selected entities is also governed by the constraints that are applied to them. If the selected entities have some constraints applied to them, those constraints will also move along with the entities even if they are not selected. For example, consider a case where a circle is drawn at the endpoint of one of the lines of a rectangle, with the coincident constraint applied to the endpoint of line and the center of circle. Now, the circle will also move if you move the line of the rectangle on which the coincident constraint is applied.

Rotating the Sketched Entities

Toolbar:	Sketch > Rotate
Panel Bar:	Sketch > Rotate

The **Rotate** tool is used to rotate the selected sketched entities about a specified center point. You can also use this tool to create a copy of the selected entities by rotating them, keeping the original entities intact at their original location. When you invoke this tool, the **Rotate** dialog box will be displayed as shown in Figure 3-18. The options provided under the **Rotate** dialog box are discussed next.

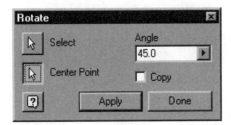

Figure 3-18 Rotate dialog box

Rotate Dialog Box Options

Select

This button is chosen to select the entities to be rotated. When you invoke this tool, the **Rotate** dialog box will be displayed with the **Select** button automatically chosen. You can use any object selection technique to select one or more objects.

Center Point

This button is chosen to define the base point around which the selected entities will be rotated. This point can also be referred to as the base point of rotation. After you have selected all the entities to be rotated using the **Select** button, choose this button to specify the base point of rotation.

Angle

This edit box is used to define the value of the angle through which the selected entities will be rotated. You can enter the value directly in this edit box or choose the arrow on the right of this edit box to specify the predefined angle values. Remember that a positive angle value will rotate the selected entities in the counterclockwise direction and a negative angle value will rotate the selected entities in the clockwise direction.

Copy

This check box is chosen to create a copy of the selected entities as they are rotated. If this check box is selected, a copy of the selected entities will be created and will be placed at the angle value you have defined in the **Angle** edit box. The original entities will be intact at their original location.

Apply

This button is chosen to apply the rotate operation to the selected entities such that they are rotated through the specified angle. Until this button is chosen, the selected entities will not be rotated. After you apply the rotate operation by choosing this button, the **Select** button is again chosen so that you can select a new set of entities for rotating.

Done

This button is chosen to exit the **Rotate** dialog box, thus exiting the **Rotate** tool.

Figure 3-19 shows the rotation of the selected entities at different angles.

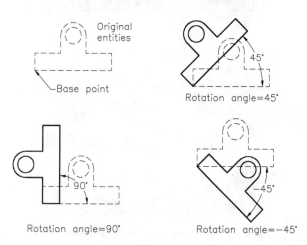

Figure 3-19 *Rotating the entities at different angles*

Tip. *You can also create a copy of the sketched entities using the shortcut menu. Select the sketched entities and right-click to display the shortcut menu. In this menu choose* **Copy**. *Again, right-click to display the shortcut menu and choose* **Paste** *to paste the selected entities, thus creating a copy of the selected entities.*

CREATING PATTERNS

Generally, in the mechanical industry, you come across various designs that consist of multiple copies of a sketched feature arranged in a particular fashion. For example, it can be multiple noncircular sketched grooves around an imaginary circle. It can also be along the edges of an imaginary rectangle, such as the grooves in the Pedestal Bearing. Drawing all the sketches again and again is a very tedious and time-consuming process. To avoid this lengthy process, Autodesk Inventor provides you with an option of creating patterns of the sketched entities during the sketching stage itself. The patterns are defined as the sequential arrangement of the copies of selected entities. You can create the patterns in a rectangular fashion or a circular fashion. Both these types of patterns are discussed next.

Creating Rectangular Patterns

Toolbar:	Sketch > Rectangular Pattern
Panel Bar:	Sketch > Rectangular Pattern

Rectangular patterns are the patterns that arrange the copies of the selected entities along the edges of an imaginary rectangle. When you invoke this tool, the **Rectangular Pattern** dialog box will be displayed as shown in Figure 3-20. The options provided under this dialog box are discussed next.

Geometry

This button is chosen to select the entities to be patterned. When you invoke this tool, the **Geometry** button is automatically chosen. After you have selected all the entities to be patterned, choose this button again to proceed with pattern creation.

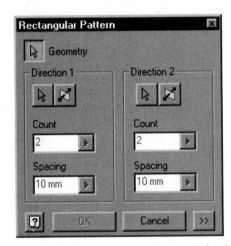

Figure 3-20 Rectangular Pattern dialog box

Direction 1 Area

This area provides the option of defining the first direction of pattern creation, the number of copies to be created in this direction, and the spacing between the entities. All these options are discussed next.

Direction

This is the button with an arrow. This button is chosen to select the first direction for arranging the items in a rectangular pattern. The other options in **Direction 1** area will be available only when you define the first direction of pattern creation. The direction can be defined by a line segment. The line segment can be at any angle. The resultant pattern will also be created at an angle if the line selected to specify the direction is at an angle. As you define the first direction, you can preview the pattern on the graphics screen as it will be created using the current values. Pattern creation will be dynamically modified as you change the values in this dialog box.

Flip Direction

This is the button on the right of the **Direction** button. This button is chosen to reverse the direction of pattern creation. When you define the first direction of pattern creation using the **Direction** button, an arrow appears on the sketch that displays the direction in which the items of the pattern will be arranged. If you choose this button, the direction will be reversed and the arrow will point in the opposite direction.

Count

This edit box is used to specify the number of items in the pattern along the first direction. Remember that this value includes the original selected entities also. As you increase the value in this edit box, you can dynamically preview the increased items in the pattern on the graphics screen. You can also select a predefined number of items by choosing the arrow on the right of this edit box. However, if you are using this tool for the first time in the current session of Autodesk Inventor, this arrow will not provide any value.

Spacing

This edit box is used to define the distance between the individual items of the pattern in the first direction. You can directly enter a value in this edit box or use the **Measure** or the **Show Dimension** options to define this value. The **Measure** option allows you to select a line segment, the length of which will define the distance between the individual items. The **Show Dimension** option allows you to use an existing dimension to define the distance between the individual items of the pattern. The selected dimension will be entered in the edit box in terms of parameter. You will have to delete the existing value in this edit box to use the dimension value.

Note

You will learn more about parameters in later chapters.

Direction 2 Area

This area provides the option of defining the second direction of pattern creation, the number of copies to be created in this direction, and the spacing between the entities. All these options are discussed next.

Direction

This button is chosen to select the second direction for arranging the items of rectangular pattern. The direction can be defined by a line segment. Similar to the first direction, the line segment can be at any angle. It is not necessary that the first direction and the second direction for arranging the items of the pattern should be normal to each other. These directions can be at any angle to each other. If the lines selected to define the directions are at some angle, the resultant pattern will also be created at an angle. As you define the second direction, you can preview the pattern on the graphics screen as it will be created using the current values. Pattern creation will be dynamically modified as you change the values in this dialog box.

Flip Direction

This is the button on the right of the **Direction** button. This button is chosen to reverse the second direction of pattern creation. When you define the second direction of pattern creation using the **Direction** button, another arrow appears on the sketch that displays the second direction in which the items of the pattern will be arranged. If you choose this button, the direction will be reversed and the arrow will point in the opposite direction.

Count

This edit box is used to specify the number of items in the pattern along the second direction. Remember that this value also includes the original entities. As you increase the value in this edit box, you can dynamically preview the increased items in the pattern on the graphics screen. Similar to the **Count** edit box in the **Direction 1** area, here also you can also select a predefined number of items by choosing the arrow on the right of this edit box. However, if you are using this tool for the first time in the current session of Autodesk Inventor, this arrow will not provide any value.

Spacing

This edit box is used to define the distance between the individual items of the pattern in the second direction. Similar to the **Spacing** edit box in the **Direction 1** area, you can directly enter a value in this edit box or use the **Measure** or the **Show Dimension** options to define this value.

Figure 3-21 shows various parameters involved in creating a rectangular pattern having three items along direction 1 and four items along direction 2.

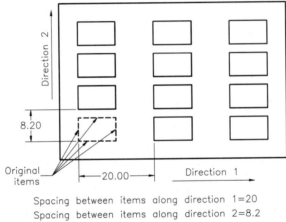

Spacing between items along direction 1=20
Spacing between items along direction 2=8.2

Figure 3-21 Creating a rectangular pattern

More

This is the button provided on the lower right corner of the **Rectangular Pattern** dialog box. When you choose this button, this dialog box expands, providing you with more options for creating the pattern, see Figure 3-22. These options are discussed next.

*Figure 3-22 The **More** options of the **Rectangular Pattern** dialog box*

Suppress

This button is chosen to suppress the selected item from the pattern. When you select any item of the pattern by using this button, it will change into dashed lines. Although the items suppressed using this button will be displayed in the pattern, these items will not participate in feature creation when you finish the sketch. However, you can unsuppress these items later if you need them.

Note
Editing the sketches of features will be discussed in later chapters.

Associative

This check box is selected so that all the items of the pattern are associated with each other. All the items of the associative pattern are automatically updated if any one of the entity is modified. For example, if you modify the dimension of any of the item of the pattern, the dimensions of all the other items are also modified. However, if you clear this check box before creating the pattern, all the items will be individual entities and can be modified individually.

Fitted

This option works in combination with the **Spacing** option in the **Direction 1** and the **Direction 2** areas. If you select this option, a specified number of items will be created such that the distances specified in the **Spacing** edit boxes in both **Direction 1** and **Direction 2** areas define the included distance between all the items instead of the incremental distance between each item. Figure 3-22 shows the pattern created by clearing this check box (spacing is incremental) and Figure 3-23 shows the pattern created by selecting this check box (included spacing between all the items).

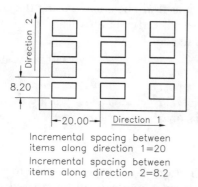

Incremental spacing between items along direction 1=20
Incremental spacing between items along direction 2=8.2

Figure 3-22 *Pattern created with* **Fitted** *check box cleared*

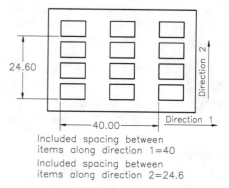

Included spacing between items along direction 1=40
Included spacing between items along direction 2=24.6

Figure 3-23 *Pattern created with* **Fitted** *check box selected*

Creating Circular Patterns

Toolbar:	Sketch > Circular Pattern
Panel Bar:	Sketch > Circular Pattern

Circular patterns are the patterns created around the circumference of an imaginary circle. To create the circular pattern, you will have to define the center of that imaginary circle. When you invoke this tool, the **Circular Pattern** dialog box will be displayed, see Figure 3-24. The options provided under this dialog box are discussed next.

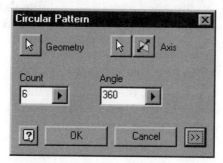

Figure 3-24 **Circular Pattern** *dialog box*

Geometry

This button is chosen to select the entities to be patterned. Most of the other options in this dialog box will be available only after you have selected the entities to be patterned. As you select the individual entities, they turn blue in color, indicating that they are selected. After you have selected all the entities to be patterned, choose this button again to proceed with pattern creation.

Axis

This is the button with an arrow and is provided on the right of the **Geometry** button. This button is chosen to select the center of the imaginary circle around which the circular pattern will be created. The points that can be used to define the center of pattern creation are the endpoints of lines, splines, and arcs, center points of arcs, circles, and ellipses, and the points/ hole centers. You can dynamically preview the pattern as it will be created using the current values. If you modify the other values in this dialog box, pattern creation will also be modified, and it can be dynamically previewed on the graphics screen.

 Tip. *If you select an arc or a circle to define the axis of circular pattern, its center will be automatically selected as the center of the circular pattern. However, this is not possible in the case of an ellipse. You cannot select an ellipse to define the center of the circular pattern. You will have to directly select the center of ellipse.*

Flip Axis

This is the button provided on the right of the **Axis** button. This button is chosen to reverse the direction of pattern creation. By default, the circular pattern will be created in the counterclockwise direction. If you choose this button, the circular pattern will be created in the clockwise direction.

 Tip. *If the circular pattern is created through the complete 360°, you cannot find a difference in changing the direction of pattern creation from counterclockwise to clockwise. However, if the pattern is created through an angle less than 360°, you can find out the difference of changing the direction of pattern creation.*

Count

This edit box is used to specify the number of items in the circular pattern. You can directly enter a value in this edit box or choose the arrow provided on the right of this dialog box for using the predefined values, or for using the **Measure** or the **Show Dimension** options. These options are the same as those discussed in the rectangular pattern.

Angle

This edit box is used to define the angle for creating the circular pattern. You can directly enter an angle value in this edit box or use the predefined values by choosing the arrow on the right of this edit box. You can also use the **Measure** or the **Show Dimension** option to define the angle value. Figure 3-25 and Figure 3-26 show the circular patterns created using different angle values.

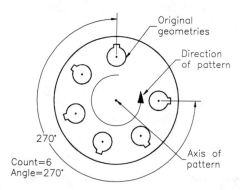

Figure 3-25 *Circular pattern with 6 items and 270° angle*

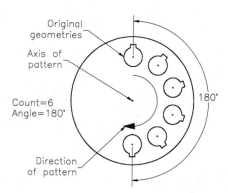

Figure 3-26 *Circular pattern with 6 items and 180° angle*

More

This is the button with two arrows and is provided on the lower right corner of the **Circular Pattern** dialog box. When you choose this button, the **Circular Pattern** dialog box expands, providing more options, see Figure 3-27. These options are discussed next.

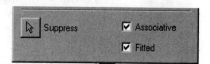

Figure 3-27 *More options of the Circular Pattern dialog box*

Suppress

This button is chosen to suppress the selected item from the pattern. Similar to the rectangular pattern, when you select any item of the circular pattern using this button, it will change into dashed lines. Although the items suppressed using this button will be displayed on the graphics screen, these items will not participate in feature creation when you finish the sketch. However, you can unsuppress these items later if you need them.

Associative

This check box is selected so that all the items of the pattern are associated with each other. All the items of the associative pattern are automatically updated if any one of the entity is modified. If you clear this check box before creating the pattern, all the items will be individual entities and can be modified individually.

Fitted

This option works in combination with the **Angle** edit box. If you select this option, a specified number of items will be created such that the angle specified in the **Angle** edit box defines the included angle between all the items. This check box is selected by default in the **Circular Pattern** dialog box. If you clear this check box, the angle that you specify in the **Angle** edit box will be considered as the incremental angle between each item. Figure 3-28 shows the pattern created by selecting this check box (included angle between all the items) and Figure 3-29 shows the pattern created by clearing this check box (angle is incremental).

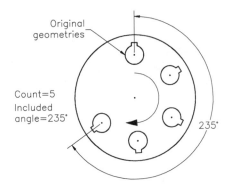

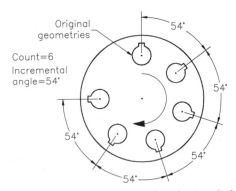

Figure 3-28 *Pattern created with* **Fitted** *check box selected*

Figure 3-29 *Pattern created with* **Fitted** *check box cleared*

Tip. *If you are creating a circular pattern through an angle of 360° and clear the* **Fitted** *check box, you will see only one item on the graphics screen. The reason is that since the incremental angle between the individual items is 360°, all the items will be arranged one over the other, displaying only one copy.*

EDITING THE SKETCHED ENTITIES BY DRAGGING

You can also edit the sketched entities by dragging them. Depending upon the type of entity selected, and the point of selection, the object will be moved or stretched. For example, if you select a circle at its center and drag, it will be moved. However, if you select the same at a point on its circumference, it will be stretched to a new size. Similarly, if you select a line at its endpoints, it will be stretched and if you select a line at a point other than its endpoints, it will be moved. Therefore, editing the sketched entities by dragging is entirely based on selection points. The following table gives you the details of the operation that will be performed when you drag various objects.

Object	Selection point	Operation
Circle	On circumference	Stretch
	Center point	Move
Arc	On circumference	Stretch
	Center point	Move
Single line or multiple lines selected together	Anywhere other than any endpoint	Move
	Endpoint	Stretch
Single line	Any point other than the endpoints	Move
	Endpoints	Stretch
Rectangle	All lines selected together	Move
	Any one line or any endpoint	Stretch

CONVERTING THE BASE SKETCH INTO A BASE FEATURE

As mentioned earlier, any design is a combination of various sketched, placed, and work features. The first feature, generally, is a sketched feature. In the previous chapters you have learned to draw the sketches for these base features and dimension them. After you have finished drawing and dimensioning the sketch, choose the **Return** button on the **Command Bar**. When you choose this button, you will exit the sketching environment and will enter the **Part** mode. You will also notice that the **Sketch** panel bar is replaced by the **Features** panel bar. Autodesk Inventor provides you with a number of tools such as **Extrude**, **Revolve**, **Loft**, **Sweep**, and so on to convert these base sketches into base features. However, in this chapter you will learn the use of only the **Extrude** and the **Revolve** tools for converting the base sketch into a base feature. The remaining tools will be discussed in later chapters.

Tip. *You can also proceed to the **Part** mode from the sketching environment by using the shortcut menu. Right-click in the graphics window and choose **Finish Sketch**. The sketching environment will be automatically exited and you will enter the **Part** mode.*

Note

*It is advised that as soon as you enter the **Part** mode, you should change the current view to the Isometric view. This is because you can dynamically preview the result of the **Extrude** or the **Revolve** tools while you are defining the values in their respective dialog boxes. If the view is not set to the Isometric view, you cannot preview the result of these tools. To change the current view to the Isometric view, right-click in the graphics window and choose **Isometric View**.*

Extruding the Base Sketch

Toolbar:	Features > Extrude
Panel Bar:	Features > Extrude

The **Extrude** tool is the most extensively used tool for creating a design. Extrusion is defined as a process of adding or removing material, defined by the sketch, along the Z axis of the current coordinate system. Since you are creating the first feature, you will be given the option of just adding the material and not removing it. This is because there is no existing feature from which you can remove the material. When you invoke this tool, the **Extrude** dialog box will be displayed, see Figure 3-30. The options provided under the **Extrude** dialog box are discussed next.

Shape Area

The options provided under this area are used to select the sketch to be extruded and to define the taper angle.

Profile

This button is chosen to select the sketch to be extruded. If the drawing consists of a single closed loop, it will be automatically selected when you invoke this tool. Since the sketch is already selected, this button will not be chosen. However, if the drawing consists of more than one closed loop, this button will be chosen and you will be prompted to select the profile you want to extrude. As you move the cursor close to any of the closed loop, it will

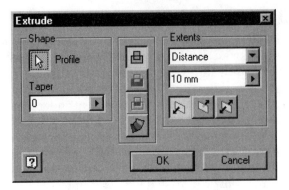

Figure 3-30 Extrude dialog box

be highlighted. After you have selected the sketch to be extruded, choose this button again. The preview of the resultant solid can be displayed on the graphics screen. Note that if you select any of the inner closed loops, only that single loop will be extruded. Also, after the extrusion of one of the inner closed loops, the remaining loops will no more be displayed on the screen. However, if you select the profile by specifying a point inside the outer closed loop but outside the inner closed loops, the sketch will be extruded such that the resultant solid will have all the inner closed loops subtracted from the outer closed loop, see Figure 3-31 and Figure 3-32.

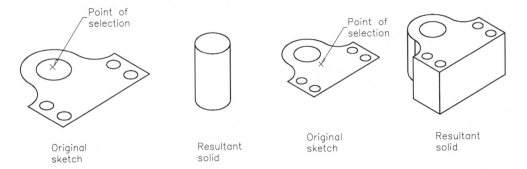

Figure 3-31 Specifying the selection point in the sketch and the resultant solid

Figure 3-32 Specifying the selection point in the sketch and the resultant solid

Taper

This edit box is used to define the taper angle for the resultant solid model. Taper angles are generally provided to solid models for their easy withdrawal from the castings. A negative taper angle will force the resultant solid to taper inwards, thus creating a negative taper. A positive taper angle will force the resultant solid to taper outwards, thus creating a positive taper. When you define a taper angle, an arrow is displayed in the preview of the solid model on the graphics screen. Depending upon the positive or negative value of the taper angle, this arrow will point inwards or outwards from the sketch. Figure 3-33 and Figure 3-34 show the model created using the negative and positive taper angles.

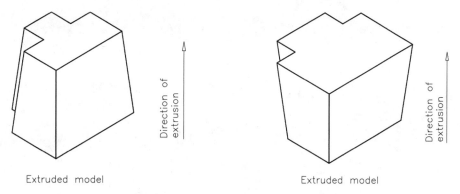

Extruded model   Extruded model

Figure 3-33 *Extruding the model with negative taper angle*

Figure 3-34 *Extruding the model with positive taper angle*

Join

This is the first button provided in the area between the **Shape** and the **Extents** area. This button is chosen to create a feature by adding the material defined by the sketch. Since this is the first feature, there will only be two buttons available in this area.

Surface

The **Surface** button is the last button provided below the **Join** button and is chosen to create surface models. If this button is chosen, the resultant feature will be a surface and not a solid. Remember that the sketches for surface models should not necessarily be closed loops.

Note
The other buttons in this area will not be available.

Extents Area

The options under this area are used to specify the termination of the extruded feature.

Distance

This drop-down list is used to select the method of specifying extrusion termination. By default, the **Distance** option is selected in this drop-down list. This option is used to define the extrusion depth by specifying its value. The value of extrusion can be specified in the **Depth** edit box available below this drop-down list. You can select a predefined distance value by choosing the arrow on the right of the **Depth** edit box or use the **Measure** or the **Show Dimension** options to specify the depth of extrusion. When you select the **Distance** option, there will be three buttons provided below the **Depth** edit box. These buttons are used to specify the direction of extrusion. The current direction will be displayed by the first button. You can reverse the direction of feature creation by choosing the second button. The third button that is available extrudes the feature equally in both directions from the current sketch plane. This button is also called the **Mid-plane** button. For example, if the extrusion depth you have specified is 20 mm, the resultant feature will be created such that it is extruded 10 mm above the current sketch plane and 10 mm below the current sketch plane. Figure 3-35 shows a feature created by extruding the sketch using the **Mid-plane** button and with a positive taper angle.

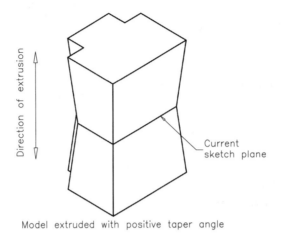

Direction of extrusion

Current
sketch plane

Model extruded with positive taper angle

Figure 3-35 *Model extruded with a positive taper angle and using*
*the **Mid-plane** button*

To

This is the second option in the **Distance** drop-down list. This option is used to define
the termination of the extruded feature by using a work plane, planar face, or extended
face. When you select this option, all the other options in the **Extents** area are removed
and only the **Select surface to end the feature creation** button is displayed. As soon as
you select the plane or the face to terminate extrusion, the **Check to terminate feature on
the extended face** check box is displayed. This check box is selected to terminate the
feature on the plane that will be created when you extend the plane or planar face that was
selected to terminate the feature.

From To

This is the third option in the **Distance** drop-down list. This option uses two planes to
define feature. The first plane defines the plane from which the feature will start. The
second plane defines the plane for terminating the feature. When you select this option,
all the remaining options in the **Extents** area are replaced by two buttons. The upper
button is the **Select surface to start the feature creation** button and is used to define the
plane where the feature starts. The lower button is the **Select the surface to end the
feature creation** button and is used to define the plane where the feature terminates.

Note
*The methods of creating work planes will be discussed in later chapters. The **Distance** drop-down
list will display more options once you have created the base feature. These options will be
discussed in later chapters.*

Tip. *You will notice that as soon as the sketch is converted into a feature, its color is
changed and it is assigned a material. By default, it is assigned the **By Material**
color. However, you can also change the color of the feature. To change the color,
choose the **Select** button from the **Command Bar** that enables you to select the
object. Now, select the model. The face from which the model is selected will be
highlighted. Choose the color from the **Color** drop-down list in the **Command Bar**.*

Revolving the Base Sketch

Toolbar: Features > Revolve
Panel Bar: Features > Revolve

The **Revolve** tool is the second most extensively used method of creating features. This tool is generally used to create circular features like shafts, couplings, pulleys, and so on. You can also use this tool for creating the cut features that are circular in shape. A revolved feature is created by revolving the sketch about an axis. You can use the straight edges of the sketch as the axis for revolving the sketch. When you invoke this tool, the **Revolve** dialog box will be displayed as shown in Figure 3-36. The options provided under this dialog box are discussed next.

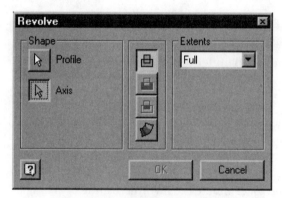

Figure 3-36 Revolve dialog box

Shape Area

The buttons available in this area are used to select the sketch to be revolved and the axis for revolving the sketch.

Profile

This button is chosen to select the sketch to be revolved. If there is only one closed loop on the graphics screen, it will be automatically selected when you invoke this tool and this button will not be chosen. However, if there are more than one closed loops, this button will be chosen and you will be prompted to select the profile to be revolved.

Tip. *To remove the closed loop that has been selected using the **Profile** button, hold down the SHIFT key and then select the closed loop to be removed. You will notice that the selected closed loop is no more highlighted, suggesting that it has been removed from the selection set.*

Axis

This button is chosen to select the axis for revolving the sketch. As mentioned earlier, you can select a straight line segment in the sketch as the axis for creating the revolved feature. When you select the axis, the preview of the feature that will be created using the current values will be displayed on the graphics screen.

Join

This is the button provided on top of the area between the **Shape** area and the **Extents** area. This button is chosen to create the revolved feature by adding the material defined by the sketch. This is the option you will be using for creating the base feature.

Surface

This button is chosen to create a surface by revolving the sketch about the defined axis. If you choose this button, the resultant model will be a surface model and not a solid model.

 Note
Since the feature you are creating is the base feature, no other button in this area will be available. Once you have created the base feature, the remaining buttons in this area will also be available for use.

Extents Area

The drop-down list provided under this area is used to specify the methods of termination of a revolved feature. These options are discussed next.

Full

This option is chosen to create a feature by revolving the sketch through a complete 360°. This is the default option.

Angle

This option is used to terminate the revolved feature at an angle less than 360°. The angle of revolution can be defined in the edit box displayed below this drop-down list when you select this option. You can use a predefined value by choosing the arrow provided on the right side of this edit box. You can also use the **Measure** and the **Show Dimensions** options to define the angle of revolution.

Also, when you select this option, three buttons will be displayed in this area. These buttons are used to define the direction of rotation. You can also revolve the sketch equally in both the directions by choosing the **Mid-plane** button. Figure 3-37 and Figure 3-38 show the features created by revolving the sketches through different angles.

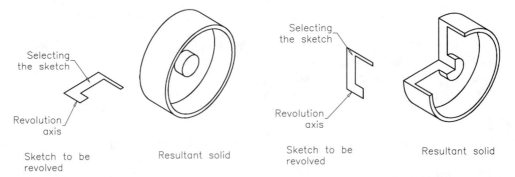

Figure 3-37 Revolving the sketch through 360°   *Figure 3-38 Revolving the sketch through 270°*

ROTATING A MODEL IN 3D SPACE

Autodesk Inventor provides you with an option of rotating a solid model freely in 3D space. This makes it possible for you to visually maneuver around the solid model and view it from any direction and angle. To invoke this option, choose the **Rotate** button from the **Standard** toolbar. When you choose the **Rotate** button, a circle is displayed with small lines at all four quadrant points and a cross at the center of the circle. The circle is called the **rim**, the small lines at four quadrants are called **handles**, and the cross at the center is called the **center point**. Also, when you invoke this tool, the cursor is changed. The new shape of this cursor depends upon its current position. For example, if the cursor is inside the rim, it shows two elliptical arrows, suggesting that the model can be freely rotated in any direction. If you move the cursor close to the horizontal handles, the cursor is changed to a horizontal elliptical arrow. The various methods using which you can rotate a model are discussed next.

Rotating a Model Freely in 3D Space

To freely rotate a model, move the cursor inside the rim. The cursor will be replaced by two elliptical arrows. Now, select a point inside the rim and then drag it anywhere on the graphics screen. The model will dynamically rotate as you drag the cursor around the graphics screen.

Rotating a Model Around the Horizontal Axis

To rotate a model around the horizontal axis, move the cursor close to one of the horizontal handles. The cursor will be replaced by a horizontal elliptical arrow. Now, select a point and drag the cursor to rotate the model along the horizontal axis.

Rotating a Model Around the Vertical Axis

To rotate a model around the vertical axis, move the cursor close to one of the vertical handles. The cursor will be replaced by a vertical elliptical arrow. Now, select a point and drag the cursor to rotate the model along the vertical axis.

Rotating a Model Around the Center Point

To rotate a model around the center point of the view, which is also normal to the view, move the cursor close to the rim. As soon as you move the cursor close to the rim, the cursor will be replaced by a circular arrow. Now, select a point and drag the cursor. The model will be rotated around the center point.

Figure 3-39 shows the model being rotated freely in 3D space.

To exit this tool, right-click to display the shortcut menu. In this menu choose **Done** and this tool will be exited. This shortcut menu also displays some more options. These options are discussed next.

Common View (SPACE)

If you choose this option, a cube is displayed at the center of the graphics screen. All the eight vertices and the six faces of this cube have green arrows. You can choose any of these arrows

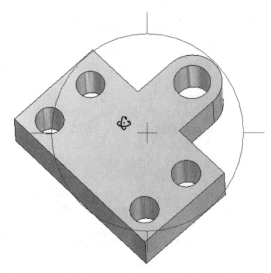

Figure 3-39 *Rotating the model freely in 3D space*

and the model will be displayed from that direction. Figure 3-40 shows the common views that can be used to reorient the model. Once you exit this tool in the **Common View** mode, the next time when you invoke this tool, the **Common View** option will be invoked and not the **Free Rotation** mode. The **Free Rotation (SPACE)** option replaces the **Common View (SPACE)** option in the shortcut menu when you choose this option. If you choose the **Free Rotation (SPACE)** option, you will again switch to the **3D Rotate** mode.

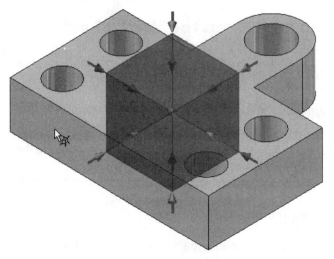

Figure 3-40 *Reorienting the model using the common views*

Redefine Isometric

This option is used in combination with the **Common View** option. Modify the viewing direction by using the **Common View** option and then choose this option from the shortcut menu. The current view will be displayed whenever you invoke the Isometric view.

Previous View

When you choose this option, the previous view displaying the orientation of the model will be displayed again. The **Next View** option is added to the shortcut menu when you choose this option. The **Next View** option is used to activate the view that was current before you chose the **Previous View** option. You can also invoke the previous view by pressing the F5 key and the next view by holding down the SHIFT key and then pressing the F5 key.

Isometric View

This option is chosen to reorient the model such that it is displayed in the Isometric view.

Note

*The **Pan** and the **Zoom** options are the same as those discussed in Chapter 1, Drawing Sketches for the Solid Models.*

Tip. *Autodesk Inventor provides you with an option to change the display type of the model. The default display type is shaded. This means that the model will be assigned a material and will behave as a solid model with an opaque material assigned to it. However, you can also change this display type. To change the display type, choose the arrow on the right of the **Shaded Display** button in the **Standard** toolbar. The **Shaded Display** flyout will be displayed with two more options. The other two options that are available are **Hidden Edge Display** and the **Wireframe Display**. The **Hidden Edge Display** displays the model with a material applied to it and also the hidden edges in light color. The **Wireframe Display** displays the model in a wireframe mode and you can see through the model.*

*You can also change the camera type from the default orthographic to the perspective camera. This is done by choosing the arrow on the right of the **Orthographic Camera** button in the **Standard** toolbar. The flyout will be displayed with a second option of **Perspective Camera**. Choose this button to display the model through a perspective camera.*

TUTORIALS

Tutorial 1

In this tutorial you will open the sketch drawn in Tutorial 1 of Chapter 2. You will then convert this sketch into a solid model by extruding it to a distance of 10 mm. After creating the solid model, you will change the color of the model to **Metal-Steel (Polished)** and rotate it in 3D space using the **3D Rotate** option.   **(Expected time: 30 min)**

Before you start creating the model, it is recommended that you outline the steps that will be required to complete the tutorial. The steps that will be used to complete this tutorial are listed below.

a. Save the sketch from the c02 directory to the c03 directory with another name.
b. Open the sketch and extrude it to a distance of 10 mm using the **Extrude** tool.
c. Change the color of the model by using the **Color** drop-down list in the **Command Bar**.
d. Rotate the model in 3D space using the **Rotate** tool.

Opening the Sketch Drawn in Chapter 2

1. Start Autodesk Inventor by double-clicking on its shortcut icon on the desktop of your computer or by using the **Start** menu.

2. The **Open** dialog box will be displayed. Choose **Open** to display the **Open File - Select a file to open** options.

3. Open the directory **\PersonalProject\c02** and then open the file **Tutorial1.ipt**.

   When you open an existing part drawing, you are by default in the **Part** mode, even if the drawing is just a sketch. Also, the sketch will be displayed in the Isometric view, see Figure 3-41.

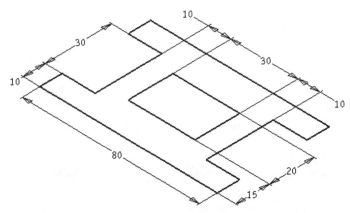

Figure 3-41 *The sketch displayed in Isometric view when opened*

Saving the Sketch with Another Name

After opening the sketch, you will have to first save it with another name so that the original sketch drawn in Chapter 2 is not modified. Remember that in Autodesk Inventor, when you save the file with another name, a new file is created and saved but the original file is still open. You will have to carefully close the original file and then open the new file using the **Open** dialog box.

1. Choose **Save Copy As** from the **File** menu. The **Save Copy As** dialog box is displayed.

2. Select the directory **\PersonalProject\c03** from the **Save in** drop-down list.

Tip. *If you have not created the c03 directory, you can create it using the* ***Save Copy As*** *dialog box also. Select the PersonalProject directory from the* ***Save in*** *drop-down list. It will now be displayed in the* ***Save in*** *drop-down list. Choose the* ***Create New Folder*** *button and specify c03 as the name of the directory.*

3. Save the sketch with the name **Tutorial1.ipt**.

4. Now, choose **Close** from the **File** menu to close this file. You will be prompted to specify whether or not you want to save the changes in this file. Choose **No**.

5. Choose the **Open** button from the **Standard** toolbar to display the **Open** dialog box. Open the file **\PersonalProject\c03\Tutorial1.ipt**.

Extruding the Sketch

As mentioned earlier, when you open an existing part file, you are by default in the **Part** mode and the sketch is displayed in the Isometric view. Sometimes, the dimensions of the sketch are not fully displayed in the current view. You can use the **Zoom** tool to increase the drawing display area so that all the dimensions are displayed in the current view. Now, since you are in the **Part** mode, all the tools of this mode are available in the **Features** panel bar. You do not have to activate the **Features** panel bar.

1. Choose the **Extrude** button from the **Features** toolbar to invoke the **Extrude** dialog box or choose **Extrude** from the **Features** panel bar.

   Since the sketch consists of two closed loops, the sketch will not be automatically selected. The **Profile** button in the **Shape** area will be chosen and you will be prompted to select the profile to be extruded.

2. Select the sketch by defining a point outside the inner closed loop but inside the outer closed loop. The sketch will be highlighted as shown in Figure 3-42.

   As shown in Figure 3-42, the inner closed loop is not selected. This suggests that the selected sketch when extruded will have a cavity in the center. This cavity is defined by the inner closed loop.

3. Choose the **Profile** button again to proceed with the extrusion process. The preview of the model, as it will be created using the current distance value, is displayed on the screen.

4. Enter **20** in the **Depth** edit box available below the **Distance** drop-down list.

   You will notice that the depth of the model in the preview will be increased since the original depth was 10 mm.

5. Choose the **OK** button to create the model and exit the **Extrude** tool. The extruded model is shown in Figure 3-43.

Changing the Color of the Model

When the model is created, it is applied a default color **As Material**. However, as mentioned earlier, you can change this material and use one of the colors or materials that are provided in Autodesk Inventor.

1. Select the model by specifying a point on any one of the faces of the model.

   As you specify a point on any face of the model, it is highlighted and turned blue in color.

2. Select **Metal-Steel (Polished)** from the **Color** drop-down list in the **Command Bar**. The color of the model will change to the new selected color.

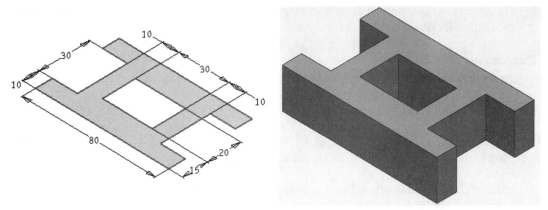

Figure 3-42 *Selecting the sketch to be extruded*   **Figure 3-43** *The extruded model*

Rotating the Model in 3D Space

1. Choose the **Rotate** button from the **Standard** toolbar. The rim with four handles will be displayed.

2. Move the cursor inside the rim and then drag it to rotate the model freely in 3D space, see Figure 3-44.

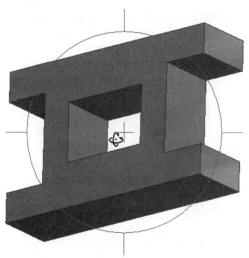

Figure 3-44 *Rotating the model freely in 3D space*

3. Now, move the cursor outside the rim and drag it to rotate the model. Notice the difference between rotating the model by dragging inside the rim and dragging outside the rim. Right-click to display the shortcut menu and choose **Done** to exit this tool.

Saving the Model

1. Choose the **Save** button in the **Standard** toolbar to save the model. Now, choose **Close** from the **File** menu to close this file.

Tutorial 2

In this tutorial you will open the sketch drawn in Tutorial 2 of Chapter 2 and then convert it into a fully revolved model. After creating the revolved model, change the camera type to perspective and then view the model.   **(Expected time: 30 min)**

The steps that will be followed to complete the tutorial are listed below.

a. Open the sketch from the c02 directory and save it in the c03 directory.
b. Revolve the sketch through an angle of 360° by using the **Revolve** tool.
c. Change the camera type from the **Standard** toolbar and view the model.

Opening the Sketch Drawn in Chapter 2

1. Choose the **Open** button in the **Standard** toolbar to display the **Open** dialog box. Using this dialog box, open the file **\PersonalProject\c02\Tutorial2.ipt**. The sketch will be displayed in the **Part** mode in the Isometric view.

Saving the Sketch with Another Name

1. Choose **Save Copy As** from the **File** menu. The **Save Copy As** dialog box is displayed.

2. Select the directory **\PersonalProject\c03** from the **Save in** drop-down list. Save the sketch with the name **Tutorial2.ipt**.

    Since the current file is the original Chapter 2 file, you will have to close it and open the Chapter 3 file.

3. Choose **Close** from the **File** menu to close this file. Now, choose the **Open** button to display the **Open** dialog box and open the file **\PersonalProject\c03\Tutorial2.ipt**.

    The dimensions of the sketch might not be displayed completely inside the current display. Increase the drawing display area using the **Zoom** and **Pan** tools to fit the dimensions in the current view, see Figure 3-45.

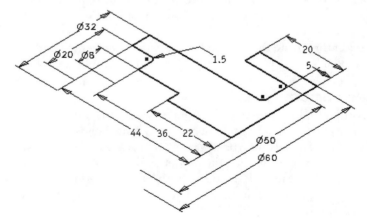

Figure 3-45 Sketch displayed in the Isometric view

Revolving the Model

As mentioned earlier, to revolve a model you need an axis of revolution. This axis can be a sketched line segment. In this case, the revolution axis will be the line that measures 22 mm and the sketch will be revolved about this line.

1. Choose the **Revolve** button from the **Features** toolbar to display the **Revolve** dialog box.

   Since the sketch has just one closed loop, it will be automatically selected and highlighted. Also, the **Profile** button in the **Shape** area will not be chosen. Instead, the **Axis** button will be chosen.

2. Select the bottom horizontal line that measures 22 mm as the axis of revolution.

   When you move the cursor close to this line, it will be highlighted and will turn red in color. As soon as you select this line, the preview of the model that will be created using the current values will be displayed on the graphics screen.

3. Accept the default values and choose the **OK** button to complete the process of creating the revolved model.

Changing the View of the Model

The current view in which the model is displayed does not show the model properly. Therefore, you will have to change the view of the model.

1. Choose the **Rotate** button from the **Standard** toolbar. But you will not be rotating the model by using this tool. You will use the shortcut menu to use the common views for displaying the model.

2. Right-click to display the shortcut menu. Choose **Common View (SPACE)** from this shortcut menu to display a cube with arrows in different directions.

3. Select the arrow on the upper left vertex on the left face of the cube, see Figure 3-45. When you move the cursor close to this arrow, it turns red in color.

4. When you select this arrow, the revolved model will be reoriented and you will get a better view of the model, see Figure 3-46. Right-click and choose **Done** to exit this tool.

Changing the Camera Type

By default, orthographic camera type is used to display the model. In this type of viewing, the parallel lines in the model do not meet at any point. This is the reason it is also termed as parallel viewing. The second type of camera that is available for displaying the model is perspective. In this type of viewing, the model on the graphics screen is displayed exactly as it would be displayed in real 3D space. In this type of viewing, the lines in the model, when extended, meet at three points. Therefore, this type of viewing is also called three-point perspective.

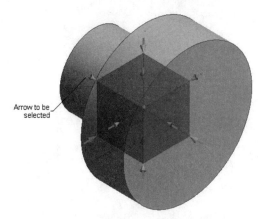

Figure 3-45 *Selecting the arrow*

Figure 3-46 *Viewing the model from a new direction*

1. Choose the down arrow on the right of the **Orthographic Camera** button in the **Standard** toolbar. From this flyout, choose the **Perspective Camera** button. The model will now be displayed using the perspective camera, see Figure 3-47.

Figure 3-47 *Viewing the model using the perspective camera*

Saving the Model

1. Choose the **Save** button in the **Standard** toolbar to save the model.

2. Now, choose **Close** from the **File** menu to close this file.

Tutorial 3

In this tutorial you will create the model shown in Figure 3-48. The dimensions for the model are given in Figure 3-49. The extrusion height for the model is 10 mm.

(Expected time: 45 min)

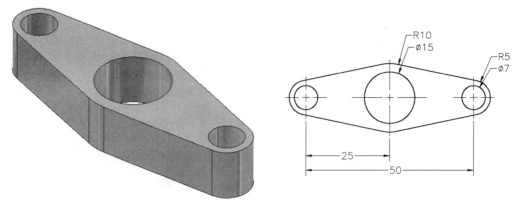

Figure 3-48 *Model for Tutorial 3*   **Figure 3-49** *Dimensions for the model*

The steps that will be followed to complete this tutorial are listed below.

a.   Open a new metric part file. Draw the sketch of the outer loop and add the constraints.
b.   Draw the inner circles and add the required constraints. Dimensions the complete sketch.
c.   Extrude the sketch to a distance of 10 mm by using the **Extrude** tool.

Opening a New Part File

If you have installed Autodesk Inventor with millimeter as unit of measurement, you can directly open a new metric part file, thus avoiding the use of **Open** dialog box for opening a new part file. This is done using the down arrow available on right of the **New** button in the **Standard** toolbar. Note that this method is not applicable for opening a metric template if you have not installed Autodesk Inventor with millimeter as unit for measurement.

1.   Choose the down arrow on the right of the **New** button in the **Standard** toolbar. A flyout will be opened displaying the buttons for part, assembly, drawing and presentation files.

2.   Choose the **Part** option to open a new metric part file. If Autodesk Inventor was not installed with millimeter as measurement unit, you will have to use the **Metric** tab of **Open** dialog box for opening a new metric part file.

Drawing the Sketch of the Model

As shown in Figure 3-49, the sketch is a combination of four closed loops. First you will draw the outer closed loop. This outer loop will be drawn by drawing three circles, two at the ends and one at the center. Then you will draw tangent lines that will join the left circle with the middle circle and the middle circle with the right circle. After this you will trim the unwanted portions of the circles.

1.   Draw the sketch that is a combination of three circles and tangent lines. Add the **Tangent** constraint to the lines wherever it is missing. Also, add the **Equal** constraint to all the four lines and to the circles on the left and right. The sketch after drawing and adding all the constraints should look similar to the one shown in Figure 3-50.

Now, you will have to remove the unwanted portions of the circles by using the **Trim** tool.

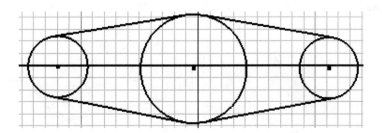

Figure 3-50 *Sketch after adding all constraints*

2. Choose the **Trim** button from the **Sketch** toolbar. You can also invoke this tool by choosing **Trim** from the **Sketch** panel bar. When you invoke this tool, you will be prompted to select the portion of the curves to be trimmed.

3. Move the cursor close to the right half of the circle on the left of the sketch.

    As you move the cursor close to the circle, the circle will turn red in color and the right portion of the circle will be changed into dotted lines. This suggests that if you select the circle at this point, the portion displayed as dotted lines will be trimmed. In this case the left tangent lines will be taken as the cutting edges.

4. Specify a point on the right half of the circle that is on the left of the sketch. The portion on the right of this circle will be trimmed. Similarly, select other points as shown in Figure 3-50 to trim the circles.

5. Now, taking the center of the previously drawn circles, draw the remaining circles. Add the **Equal** constraint to the smaller circles. The sketch after drawing the circles and applying the **Equal** constraint should look similar to the one shown in Figure 3-52.

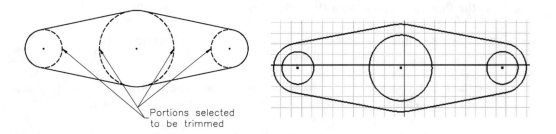

Figure 3-51 *Selecting the portions to be trimmed*   **Figure 3-52** *Sketch after trimming the circles and drawing the remaining circles*

Dimensioning the Sketch

1. Add the required dimensions to the sketch. The sketch after adding all the dimensions should look similar to the one shown in Figure 3-53.

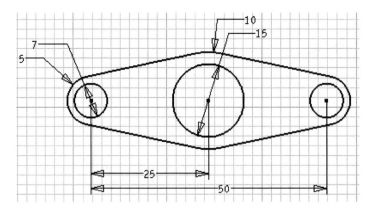

Figure 3-53 Sketch after applying the dimensions

Extruding the Sketch

The sketch drawn consists of four closed loops: the outer closed loop and the three circles. When you extrude this sketch, the three circles will be automatically subtracted from the outer closed loop, resulting in the required figure. However, this is possible only if you specify the point for selecting the closed loop inside the outer closed loop but outside all the inner closed loops.

1. Choose **Return** on the **Command Bar** to exit the sketching environment.

   As mentioned earlier, before proceeding with converting the sketch into a model, it is better to change the view to the Isometric view. This is because you can preview the depth of the model only if you are viewing the model from the Isometric view.

2. Right-click in the graphics window to display the shortcut menu. Choose **Isometric View** from the shortcut menu to view the model from the Isometric view.

3. Choose the **Extrude** button from the **Features** toolbar or choose **Extrude** from the **Features** panel bar to invoke the **Extrude** dialog box, see Figure 3-54.

   Since the sketch consists of more than one closed loop, the **Profile** button in the **Shape** area will be selected and you will be prompted to select the profile to be extruded.

4. Select the profile to be extruded by specifying the selection point anywhere inside the outer closed loop but outside all the three circles.

   The selected profile will be highlighted and shaded. You will notice that the area inside all

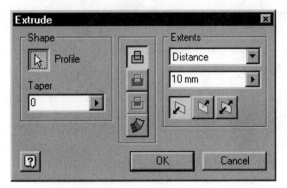

Figure 3-54 *Extrude dialog box*

the three circles is not shaded. This suggests that the area inside these circles will not be extruded. This is also one of the methods to cross check whether the sketch selected is the one you want to extrude or not.

5. Choose the **Profile** button again to proceed with the process of extruding the model.

    The preview of the model that will be created using default extrusion depth is displayed on the graphics screen.

6. Accept the default values that will extrude the model through a depth of **10 mm**. The final model should look similar to the one shown in Figure 3-55.

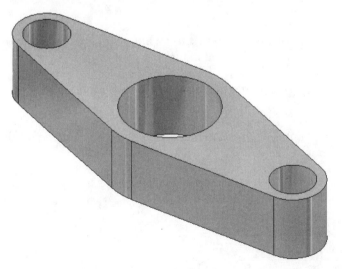

Figure 3-55 *Final model for Tutorial 3*

Saving the Model

1. Choose the **Save** button in the **Standard** toolbar and save the model with the name:

    \PersonalProject\c03**Tutorial3.ipt**

Self-Evaluation Test

Answer the following questions and then compare your answers with the answers given at the end of this chapter.

1. The line once drawn in Autodesk Inventor cannot be reduced in length. You will have to delete the line and then redraw a line of smaller length. (T/F)

2. The copies of the sketched entities can be arranged along the length and width of an imaginary rectangle using the **Circular Pattern** tool. (T/F)

3. When you select the profile by using a point that is inside the outer closed loop but outside the inner closed loops, the resultant solid will have the inner closed loops subtracted from the outer closed loop. (T/F)

4. To mirror the sketched entities, you necessarily require a mirror line. (T/F)

5. The _____ option should be cleared from the shortcut menu to select only one entity to offset from a closed loop.

6. To create a copy of an existing sketched entity by rotating it, select the _____ check box in the **Rotate** dialog box.

7. Autodesk Inventor allows you to create two types of patterns. They are _____ patterns and _____ patterns.

8. The _____ option allows you to select a line segment, the length of which will define the distance between the individual items.

9. The _____ angles are generally provided to solid models for their easy withdrawal from the castings.

10. If the _____ button in the **Extrude** dialog box is chosen, the resultant feature will be a surface and not a solid.

Review Questions

Answer the following questions.

1. You can invoke the **Trim** tool from within the **Extend** tool by pressing the SHIFT key. (T/F)

2. Offsetting is one of the easiest methods of drawing parallel lines or concentric arcs and circles. (T/F)

3. If you select a circle from a point on its circumference and drag, it will be moved from its location. (T/F)

4. Selecting a line at its endpoint and dragging will stretch it. (T/F)

5. The preview of a model as it will be created after extruding or revolving is available on the graphics screen even before you exit the **Extrude** or the **Revolve** dialog box. (T/F)

6. Which one of the following tools can be used to reposition the sketched entity from one place to the other using two points?

   (a) **Move**   (b) **Rotate**
   (c) **Mirror**   (d) **Extend**

7. Which one of the following tools can be used to arrange multiple copies of the sketched entities around an imaginary circle?

   (a) **Move**   (b) **Rotate**
   (c) **Rectangular Pattern**   (d) **Circular Pattern**

8. Which of the following options allow you to use an existing dimension to define the distance between the individual items of a pattern.

   (a) **Dimension**   (b) **Show Dimensions**
   (c) **Measure**   (d) **None**

9. Which one of the following check boxes is selected to ensure that all the items in the pattern are automatically updated if any one of the entity is modified.

   (a) **Associative**   (b) **Fitted**
   (c) **Suppress**   (d) **None**

10. Which one of the following options is added to the shortcut menu after you choose the **Previous View** option from it?

   (a) **Isometric View**   (b) **Common View**
   (c) **Pan**   (d) **Next View**

Exercises

Exercise 1

In this exercise you will extrude the sketch drawn in Exercise 1 of Chapter 2, see Figure 3-56. The extrusion depth for the model is 15 mm.   **(Expected time: 30 min)**

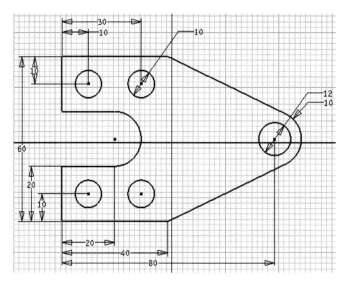

Figure 3-56 *Sketch of Exercise 1*

Exercise 2

In this exercise you will extrude the sketch drawn in Exercise 2 of Chapter 2, see Figure 3-57. The extrusion depth for the model is 80 mm.   **(Expected time: 30 min)**

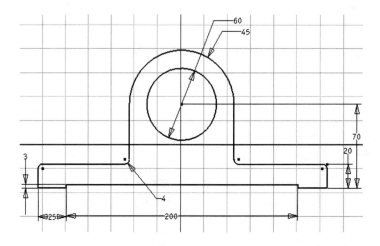

Figure 3-57 *Sketch of Exercise 2*

Exercise 3

In this exercise you will extrude the sketch drawn in Exercise 3 of Chapter 2, see Figure 3-58. The extrusion depth for the model is 40 mm. **(Expected time: 30 min)**

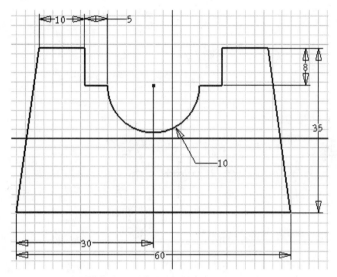

Figure 3-58 *Sketch of Exercise 3*

Exercise 4

In this exercise you will extrude the sketch drawn in Exercise 4 of Chapter 2, see Figure 3-59. The extrusion depth for the model is 35 mm. **(Expected time: 30 min)**

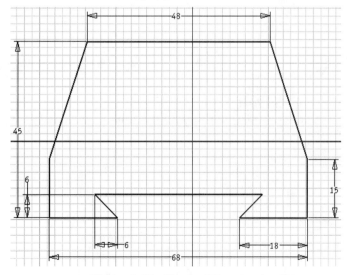

Figure 3-59 *Sketch of Exercise 4*

Exercise 5

In this exercise you will extrude the sketch drawn in Exercise 5 of Chapter 2, see Figure 3-60.
The extrusion depth for the model is 65 mm.   **(Expected time: 30 min)**

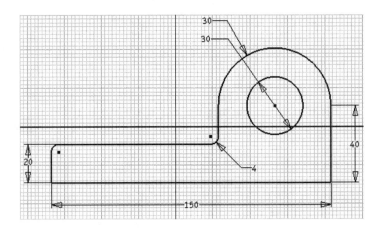

Figure 3-60 *Sketch of Exercise 5*

Note

*When you extrude the sketches of Exercises 2, 3, 4, and 5 and change the view to Isometric view,
the model will not be displayed as in the figures of exercises in Chapter 2. The reason is that these
sketches are created on the default XY plane, which is a horizontal plane. You will learn to draw
sketches on other planes in the next chapter.*

Answers to Self-Evaluation Test

1. F, **2.** F, **3.** T, **4.** T, **5. Loop Select, 6. Copy, 7.** Rectangular, Circular, **8. Measure, 9.** taper,
10. Surface

Chapter 4

Other Sketching and Modeling Options

Learning Objectives

After completing this chapter you will be able to:

- *Create features on planes other than the default XY plane.*
- *Create work features such as work planes, work axes, and work points.*
- *Use other extrusion and revolution options for creating models.*

WHY DO YOU NEED OTHER SKETCHING PLANES?

All the mechanical designs consist of a number of sketched, work, and placed features integrated together. The base feature is the first feature in a model. After creating the base feature, you have to add more features to it. By default, when you open a new file, the features are created on the XY plane. However, most of the times, the additional features are not created on the default plane on which the base feature is created, for example, the model shown in Figure 4-1.

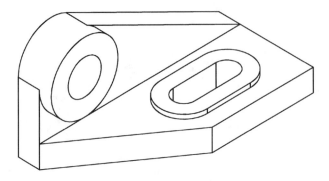

Figure 4-1 Model created by combining various features

The base feature for this model is shown in Figure 4-2. The sketch for the base feature is drawn on the XY plane. After creating the base feature you will have to create three join features, one cut feature, and a hole feature, see Figure 4-3. Now, the cut feature and all the join features are sketched features and require sketching planes where you can draw their sketches.

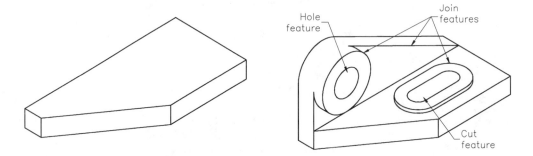

Figure 4-2 Base feature for the model   *Figure 4-3 Model after adding other features*

As visible in Figure 4-3, all these features are not created on the same plane as that of the sketch for the base feature. Therefore, to draw the sketches of all the sketched features, you will have to define new sketching planes that are different from the default XY plane. The method of specifying a new sketching plane is discussed next.

Defining a New Sketch Plane

In Autodesk Inventor, defining a new sketch plane is a very easy process. All you need to do is to specify the plane that you want to select for drawing the sketch. The selected plane will be automatically made the current sketching plane. Once you have finished creating the base feature, choose **Sketch** from the **Command Bar**. You will be prompted to select the plane on which you want to draw the new sketch. Specify a point on the plane you want to select as the new sketching plane. When you take the cursor close to the plane, it will be highlighted. As soon as you select the new sketching plane, the sketching environment will be activated and the grid lines will be displayed on that plane. Also, the **Features** panel bar will be replaced by the **Sketch** panel bar.

Note

Generally, before creating a feature, the view is changed to the Isometric view. Now, when you define a new sketch plane to draw the sketch for the next feature, the sketching environment is activated. However, Isometric view is still the current view. Before proceeding with drawing the sketch, you will have to change the current view such that you are viewing the new sketch plane

*from the top. You can change the Isometric view to the plan view by choosing the **Look At** button from the **Standard** toolbar. This tool is used to reorient the view using an existing plane or sketched entity. When you invoke this tool, you will be prompted to select the entity to look at. The current view will be automatically changed to the plan view of the selected plane or entity.*

WORK FEATURES

Work features are parametric features that are associated with a model. Autodesk Inventor has provided three work features to assist you in the process of creating a design. The three work features that are available in Autodesk Inventor are

*   **Work Planes**
*   **Work Axes**
*   **Work Points**

The methods of creating these work features are discussed next.

Creating Work Planes

Toolbar:	Features > Work Plane
Panel Bar:	Features > Work Plane

Work planes are similar to sketch planes and are used to draw sketches for sketched features or used to create placed features like holes. The reason you need work planes is that the sketch planes have a lot of limitations. For example, it is not possible to define a sketch plane that is at some offset distance from the existing plane. Also, it is not possible to define a sketch plane that is tangent to a cylindrical feature. But in all such situations it is possible to define a work plane. In Autodesk Inventor, there are twelve possible combinations of creating the work planes. The eleven possible combinations are discussed next and the remaining combination will be discussed in later chapters.

Note

The new sketch planes that you will define will not be visible on the screen or in the browser. However, the new work plane will be displayed on the screen as a shaded plane and will also be displayed in the browser. You can turn off the display of these work planes also. Turning off the display of work planes will be discussed later in this chapter.

Creating a Work Plane using Two Edges

This option is used to create a work plane that passes through two selected edges. Both the edges may or may not lie in the same plane. If the two edges do not lie in the same plane, the resultant work plane will be inclined, see Figure 4-4 and Figure 4-5.

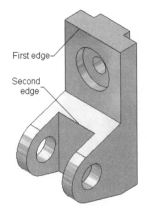

Figure 4-4 Selecting the edges to define the work plane

Figure 4-5 Resultant work plane

 Tip. *You can also select two axes instead of two edges to define the work plane in the above-mentioned situation.*

Creating a Work Plane using Three Vertices

This option allows you to create a work plane using three vertices. The three vertices that are required can be the vertices of the model or the point/hole centers. When you move the cursor close to the vertex, a yellow circle with a cross is placed on it, suggesting that the vertex has been selected. Figure 4-6 shows three points selected to create the work plane and Figure 4-7 shows the resultant work plane.

Creating a Work Plane Parallel to a Plane/Planar Face and Passing through an Edge/Axis

This option allows you to create a work plane that is parallel to an existing plane or planar face and is passing through the selected edge or axis. The planar face can be an existing work plane or the planar face of an existing feature. Remember that to use this option you will have to first select the plane or planar face to which the resultant plane should be parallel and then

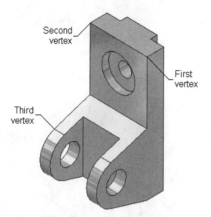

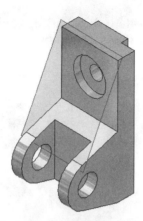

Figure 4-6 *Selecting the vertices to define the work plane*

Figure 4-7 *Resultant work plane*

select the edge through which the new work plane should pass. Figure 4-8 shows a planar face and an edge selected for creating the work plane and Figure 4-9 shows the resultant work plane.

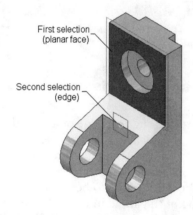

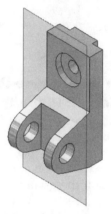

Figure 4-8 *Selecting a planar face and an edge to define the work plane*

Figure 4-9 *Resultant work plane*

Creating a Work Plane Normal to a Plane/Planar Face and Passing through an Edge/Axis

Using this option you can create a work plane that is normal to an existing plane or planar face and is passing through the selected edge or axis. The planar face can be an existing work plane or the planar face of an existing feature. Remember that to use this option you will have to first select the edge through which the work plane will pass and then select the plane or planar face to which the new work plane will be normal. After you select the plane or planar face, the **Angle** toolbar will be displayed. The default value of the angle in this toolbar will be **90**. This value will create a work plane that is at an angle of 90° to the selected plane or planar face. Figure 4-10 shows an edge and a planar face selected for creating the work plane and Figure 4-11 shows the resultant work plane.

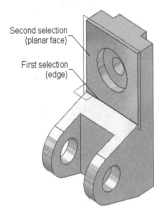

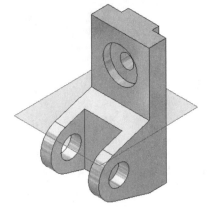

Figure 4-10 *Selecting an edge and a planar face to define the work plane*

Figure 4-11 *Resultant work plane*

Tip. *You can also use the above-mentioned method to create a work plane parallel to the selected planar face and passing through the selected edge. This is done by setting the value in the **Angle** toolbar to **0**.*

Creating a Work Plane Passing through an Edge/Axis and at an Angle to the Selected Plane/Planar Face

This option allows you to create a work plane that passes through an edge or axis and is at an angle to an existing plane or planar face. This option is similar to the previous option, with the only difference being that in the **Angle** toolbar, you will set the angle through which the new work plane will be rotated. You can preview the work plane that will be created using the current values on the graphics screen. If you want the work plane to be rotated through a specified angle in the opposite direction, set the value of the angle in negative. Figure 4-12 shows an edge and a planar face selected to create the work plane and Figure 4-13 shows a work plane created at an angle to -30° to the selected planar face by setting the value in the **Angle** toolbar to **-30**.

Creating a Work Plane Passing through a Point and Parallel to the Selected Plane/Planar Face

This option allows you to create a work plane that passes through a specified point and is parallel to the selected plane or planar face. To define this plane you can select the point and the plane or planar face in any sequence. You can either select the point first and then the plane or planar face to which the new work plane will be parallel, or select the plane or planar face first and then the point through which the work plane will pass. Figure 4-14 shows a point and a planar face selected to define the work plane and Figure 4-15 shows the resultant work plane.

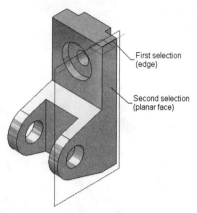

Figure 4-12 *Selecting an edge and a planar face to define the work plane*

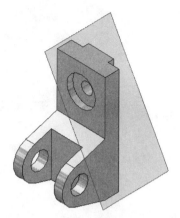

Figure 4-13 *Resultant work plane*

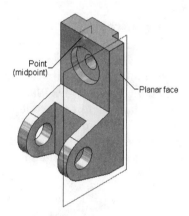

Figure 4-14 *Selecting a point and a planar face to define the work plane*

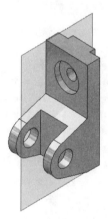

Figure 4-15 *Resultant work plane*

Creating a Work Plane Tangent to a Circular Feature and Parallel to a Plane/Planar Face

This option allows you to create a work plane that is tangent to the selected circular feature and is parallel to the selected plane or planar face. Figure 4-16 shows the circular feature to which the new work plane will be tangent and the planar face to which the resultant work plane will be parallel. Figure 4-17 shows the resultant work plane.

Tip. *To create a work plane tangent to a cylinder, select the cylindrical face and then select the XY, YZ, or XZ plane to which the resultant work plane should be parallel. To select any of the XY, YZ, or XZ planes, click on the + sign on the left of* **Origin** *in the browser. The three default planes along with the three axes will be displayed. You can now select the required plane from the browser.*

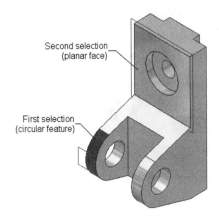

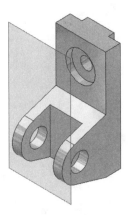

Figure 4-16 *Selecting a circular feature and a planar face to define the work plane*

Figure 4-17 *Resultant work plane*

Creating a Work Plane Tangent to a Sketched Circle

This option is used to create a work plane that is tangent to a sketched circle. Remember that you cannot create the work plane directly. You also need to draw a centerline from the center of the circle to the point at which the work plane should be tangent. After drawing the circle and the centerline, exit the sketching environment and then invoke the **Work Plane** tool. You will be prompted to select the geometry to create the work plane. Select the centerline and then select the intersection point of the centerline and the circle. The work plane will be created tangent to the circle and will pass through the intersection point of the centerline and circle. Also, the new work plane will be normal to the centerline, see Figure 4-18 and Figure 4-19.

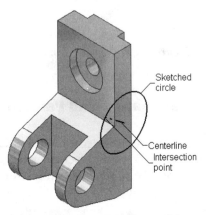

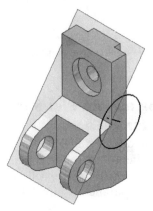

Figure 4-18 *Selecting centerline and intersection point to define the work plane*

Figure 4-19 *Resultant work plane*

Creating a Work Plane Tangent to a Circular Face and Passing through the Selected Edge/Axis

This option allows you to create a work plane that is tangent to the selected circular face and passes through the selected edge. Figure 4-20 shows the circular face and the edge selected to create the work plane and Figure 4-21 shows the resultant work plane.

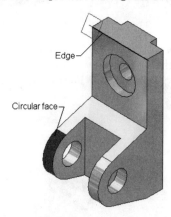
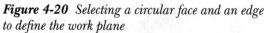

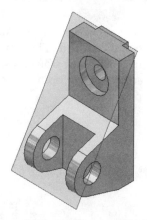

Figure 4-20 *Selecting a circular face and an edge to define the work plane*

Figure 4-21 *Resultant work plane*

Creating a Work Plane Parallel to a Plane/Planar face and at an Offset

This option is used to create a work plane that is parallel to an existing plane or planar face and at some offset from the selected plane or planar face. To create this work plane, select the plane or planar face and then drag it. As soon as you start dragging, the **Offset** toolbar will be displayed. The current offset value will be displayed in this toolbar. This value will change dynamically as you drag the plane further. You can also enter the offset value directly in this toolbar. If you enter a negative value in this toolbar, the work plane will be offset in the opposite direction. Figure 4-22 shows the plane selected to define the new work plane and Figure 4-23 shows the new work plane created at an offset of 30 mm.

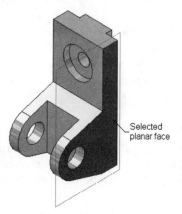

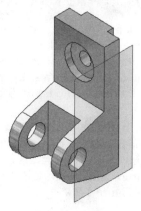

Figure 4-22 *Selecting a planar face to define the offset work plane*

Figure 4-23 *Resultant work plane*

Creating a Work Plane Normal to an Edge/Axis and Passing through a Point

This option allows you to create a work plane that is normal to the selected edge and passes through a specified point. The point can be any vertex in the model, a sketched point/hole center, or the work point. You can select the point and the edge in any sequence. Figure 4-24 shows the edge and the point selected to create the work plane and Figure 4-25 shows the resultant work plane.

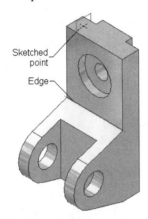

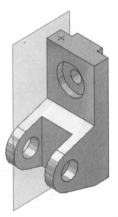

Figure 4-24 *Selecting an edge and a point to define the work plane*

Figure 4-25 *Resultant work plane*

Creating Work Axes

Toolbar:	Features > Work Axis
Panel Bar:	Features > Work Axis

Work axes are parametric lines passing through a model or a feature. A work axis is used to create work planes, work points, and circular patterns. The work axis will be displayed in the model as well as in the browser and is automatically modified when you edit the circular features. In Autodesk Inventor you can create a work axis using four methods. All these methods are discussed next.

Creating a Work Axis on a Circular Feature

This method allows you to create a work axis passing through the center of a circular feature. When you invoke the **Work Axis** tool, you will be prompted to select the geometry. Select the circular feature and the work axis will be created passing through the center of the circular feature, see Figure 4-26.

Creating a Work Axis Normal to a Plane/Planar Face and Passing through a Point

This method allows you to create a work axis normal to a plane or planar face and passing through a specified point. After invoking this tool, select the plane to which the axis will be normal and then select the point through which the axis will pass, see Figure 4-27.

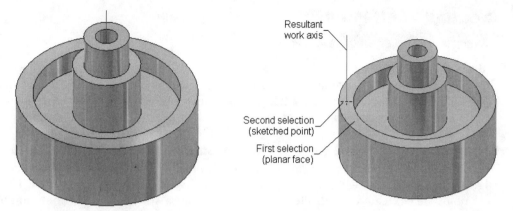

Figure 4-26 *Work axis passing through the center of a circular feature*

Figure 4-27 *Creating work axis using a planar face and a sketched point*

Creating a Work Axis Passing through the Intersection of Two Planes/ Planar Faces

This option is used to create a work axis that passes through the intersection of two planes or planar faces. If you select two planar faces that do not intersect in the model, but when extended will intersect, the resultant axis will pass through the extended intersection, see Figure 4-28.

Creating a Work Axis Passing through Two Points

This option is used to create a work axis that passes through two specified points. The points that can be used are the vertices of a model, midpoints of the edges of the model, sketched points/hole centers, or work points. Figure 4-29 shows a work axis created using the midpoints of two edges of a model.

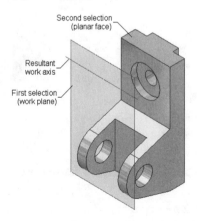

Figure 4-28 *Work axis passing through the intersection of two planes*

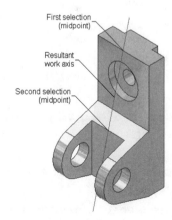

Figure 4-29 *Creating a work axis using the midpoints of two edges*

Creating Work Points

Toolbar:	Features > Work Point
Panel Bar:	Features > Work Point

 Work points are parametric points that can be created on an existing model and are used as an aid in creating work planes, work axes, or other features. In Autodesk Inventor, you can create a work point using the following four methods.

Creating a Work Point on a Vertex or on the Midpoint of an Edge

This option is used to create a work point on any vertex of a model or on the midpoints of the edges of the model. Invoke this tool and then select any of the vertices of the model. The new work point will be created on the selected vertex. To create a work point at the midpoint of the selected edge, move the cursor close to the midpoint of the edge. The midpoint will be highlighted. You can also use the SPACEBAR to cycle through various entities and select the midpoint as and when it is displayed. Figure 4-30 shows work points created at the vertices of a model and at the midpoints of the edges of the model.

Creating a Work Point at the Intersection of Two Edges/Axes

This option is used to create a work point at the intersection or extended intersection of two edges or axes. The edge selected for creating the work point should not necessarily be a linear edge, see Figure 4-31.

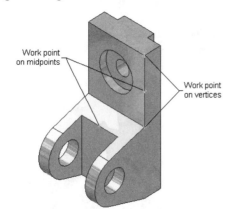

Figure 4-30 *Work points on the vertices and midpoints of edges*

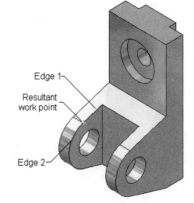

Figure 4-31 *Work point at the intersection of two edges*

Creating a Work Point at the Intersection of a Plane/Planar Face and an Edge/Axis

Using this option you can create a work point at the intersection of a plane or planar face and an edge or axis, see Figure 4-32.

Creating a Work Point at the Intersection of Three Planes/Planar Faces

Using this option you can create a work point at the intersection of three planes or planar faces, see Figure 4-33.

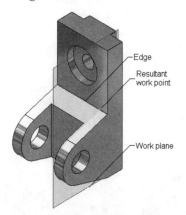

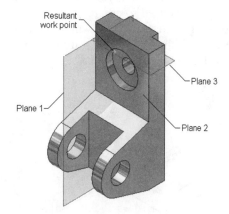

Figure 4-32 *Work point at the intersection of an edge and a work plane*

Figure 4-33 *Work point at the intersection of three planes*

Tip. *All the work features can also be created **in-line**. The in-line features are the features that are created while you are inside the process of creating some other feature. For example, during the process of creating a work axis, if you right-click, a shortcut menu will be displayed. This shortcut menu will provide the options of creating a work plane and a work point. The work plane and the work point created using this shortcut menu will be in-line work features. Note that all the in-line features are dependent on the original features inside which they were created.*

OTHER EXTRUSION OPTIONS

As mentioned in the previous chapter, some of the options of the **Extrude** dialog box will not be available until you have created the base feature. Once the base feature is created, all the remaining options in this dialog box will be available, see Figure 4-34. These options are discussed next.

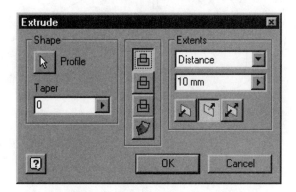

Figure 4-34 Extrude *dialog box*

Cut

This is the second button in the area between the **Shape** and the **Extents** area. This button will be available only when you are creating another feature after creating the base feature. The **Cut** option is used to create an extruded feature by removing the material from an existing feature. The material that will be removed will be defined by the sketch you have drawn. Figure 4-35 shows a join feature created using a sketch and Figure 4-36 shows a cut feature created using the same sketch.

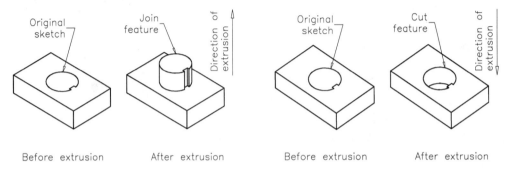

Figure 4-35 Extruding the sketch using the **Join** option

Figure 4-36 Extruding the sketch using the **Cut** option

Intersect

This button is available below the **Cut** button. This button is chosen to create an extruded feature by retaining the material common to the existing feature and the sketch, see Figure 4-37.

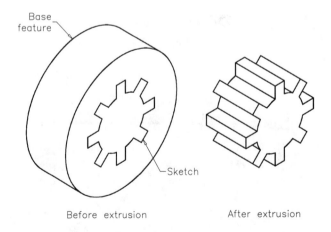

Figure 4-37 Extruding the sketch using the **Intersect** option

Extents Area

Once you have created the base feature, two more options will be available in the **Distance** drop-down list in this area. These options are discussed next.

To Next

This option is used to terminate the extruded feature to the first plane or planar face it comes across in the specified direction. When you select this option, two buttons will be displayed in this area. These buttons are used to define the direction of extrusion.

Note

*When you select the **To Next** option, the **Mid-plane** button will not be provided along with the two direction buttons. This is because you cannot select planes or planar faces in both the directions of the current sketch plane in a single attempt. You will have to define the direction of extrusion in either direction of the current sketch plane using the two buttons that will be available when you select this option.*

All

This option is combined with the **Cut** or the **Intersect** operations. The **All** option is used to create a feature by cutting right through all the features that it will come across on its way to the last face of the model. The material that will be removed is defined by the sketch. You can cut the material in either direction of the current sketch plane using the direction buttons that will be available in the **Extents** area when you invoke this option. You can also remove the material in both the directions of the current sketch plane by choosing the **Mid-plane** button.

OTHER REVOLUTION OPTIONS

Once you have created the base feature, the **Cut** and the **Intersect** buttons will also be available in the **Revolve** dialog box, see Figure 4-38. The function of both these buttons is discussed next.

Figure 4-38 Revolve dialog box

Cut

This is the second button in the area between the **Shape** and the **Extents** area. This button will be available only when you are creating another feature after creating the base feature. The **Cut** option is used to create a revolved feature by removing material from an existing feature.

The material that will be removed will be defined by the sketch you have drawn and the axis of revolution.

Intersect

This button is available below the **Cut** button. The **Intersect** option is used to create a revolved feature by retaining the material common to the existing feature and the sketch.

Note
*The remaining options of the **Extrude** and the **Revolve** dialog box were discussed in Chapter 3, Editing, Extruding, and Revolving the Sketches.*

THE CONCEPT OF SKETCH SHARING

Generally, while creating a design, you will come across a lot of situations where you have to use a consumed sketch for creating another feature in the same plane and along the same direction of extrusion. As mentioned in the Introduction, a consumed sketch is a sketch that has already been converted into a feature. For example, consider a case where you have to create a join feature by extruding the sketch to different distance values in both the directions about the current sketch plane.

Now, in most of the other solid modeling tools, if you have to use the consumed sketch, you will have to copy it to the new location. After placing the sketch, you will have to add the dimensions to locate it on its exact location. However, in Autodesk Inventor, you can directly use the same sketch by sharing it. This concept of using the consumed sketch again is termed as sharing the sketches. This concept has drawn a very distinctive line between Autodesk Inventor and the other solid modeling tools as it reduces the designing time appreciably.

Sharing the Sketches

As mentioned in Introduction, all the operations that were used to create a model are displayed in form of a tree view in the browser. All these operations will be arranged in the sequence in which they were performed on the model. Also, once the sketch is converted into a feature, the sketch will be hidden and the feature will be displayed in the browser. For example, when you create the sketch for the base feature, the browser will display **Sketch1** below **Origin**. When this sketch is extruded and is converted into the base feature, the browser will display **Extrusion1** below **Origin**. **Extrusion1** will have a plus sign (+) located on the left. If you click on this plus sign, it will expand and will also display **Sketch1** now. Similarly, if you click on the plus sign of any sketched feature, it will expand and display the sketch.

To share the sketch, right-click on the sketch you want to share to display the shortcut menu, see Figure 4-39. In this shortcut menu choose **Share Sketch**. Another sketch with the same name will be displayed in the browser. Also, the shared sketch will be displayed in the graphics window. You can now convert this sketch into a feature.

Figure 4-39 Sharing the sketch using the shortcut menu

Note

By default the visibility of the shared sketch is set to on. This means that after the shared sketch is converted into a feature, the sketch will also be displayed along with the new feature. You will have to manually turn off the visibility of this sketch. This is done by using the shortcut menu displayed upon right-clicking on the sketch. In this shortcut menu, the **Visibility** *option will have a check mark in front of it. Choose this option again to turn off the visibility. You will notice that the sketch is no more visible on the screen. Similarly, right-click on any of the work feature and turn off their visibility using the* **Visibility** *option in the shortcut menu.*

TUTORIALS

Tutorial 1

In this tutorial you will create the model of the Standard Bracket shown in Figure 4-40a. The dimensions of model are shown in Figure 4-40b, Figure 4-40c, and Figure 4-40d. After creating the model, change its color to Metal-AL-6061 (Polished) and save it with the following name:

\PersonalProject\c04**Tutorial1.ipt**   (**Expected Time: 30 min**)

It is clear in the model that it is a combination of various extruded features. Also, all the features are sketched features. All these sketched features will be created on different sketch planes. The first feature will be created on the default XY plane. The remaining features will be added to the base feature. Whenever you start creating a model, you will have to first determine the number of features in the model and then the sequence in which they will be created. The model for this tutorial comprises of three features, including the base feature. The following is the list of features that need to be created for the given model.

a. Create the base feature with two holes on the XY plane.
b. Define a new sketch plane on the back face of the base feature and add the join feature with a hole on the back face of the base feature.
c. Define a new sketch plane on the front face of the model and create the rectangular join feature on the front face.

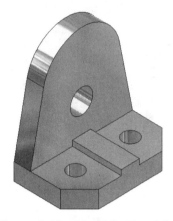

Figure 4-40a *Model for Tutorial 1*

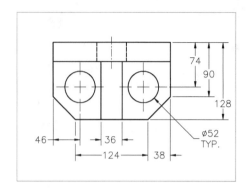

Figure 4-40b *Top view of the model*

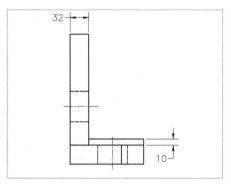

Figure 4-40c *Left side view of the model*

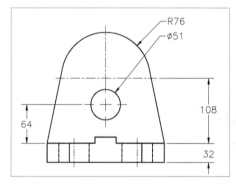

Figure 4-40d *Front view of the model*

Creating and Dimensioning the Sketch for the Base Feature

1. Start Autodesk Inventor and then open a new metric part file using the **Open** dialog box.

    As mentioned earlier, whenever you open a new metric file, by default, you start sketching in the XY plane. In this tutorial, the base feature will be created on the XY plane. Therefore, you can directly start drawing the sketch when you open the new file.

2. Draw the sketch for the model using various sketching tools.

3. Add the required constraints and dimensions to the sketch as shown in Figure 4-41.

4. Choose the **Return** button in the **Command Bar** to exit the sketching environment.

Extruding the Base Sketch

Change the current view to the Isometric view by using the shortcut menu displayed upon right-clicking in the drawing area.

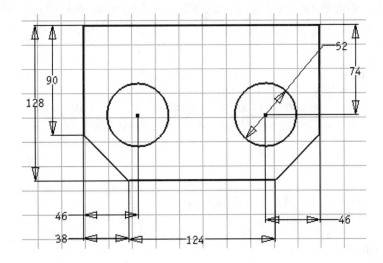

Figure 4-41 *Sketch for the base feature*

1. Using the **Extrude** tool, extrude the sketch to a distance of 32 mm.

    Since the sketch has multiple closed loops, you will have to specify the sketch to be extruded in the **Extrude** dialog box. Select the sketch by specifying a point outside the circles but inside the outer closed loop.

2. Using the **Color** drop-down list in the **Command Bar**, change the color of the model to Metal-AL-6061 (Polished). Change the current view to Isometric view. The model after changing the color and view is shown in Figure 4-42.

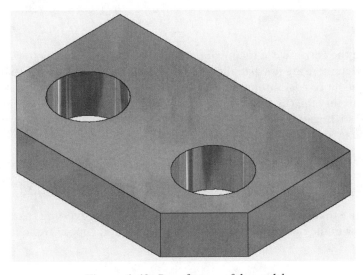

Figure 4-42 *Base feature of the model*

Creating the Feature on the Back Face of the Model

To create the feature on the back face of the model, you will have to first define the sketch plane on the back face of the model.

1. Using the **Rotate** tool, rotate the model such that the back face of the model is visible.

2. Choose the **Sketch** button from the **Command Bar**. You will be prompted to select the plane on which the sketch will be created.

3. Select the back face of the model.

   As soon as you select the back face, the sketching environment will be activated and the grid lines will be displayed in the drawing area. Now, since the current view was invoked using the **Rotate** tool, it will not be a proper view for creating the sketch. The reason for this is that the **Rotate** tool is used to arbitrarily rotate the model and the rotation is not to any exact value.

4. Choose the **Rotate** button and then right-click to display the shortcut menu. In this menu choose **Common View**.

   A cube will be displayed with arrows on all the vertices and faces.

5. Select the arrow that points in the middle of the face of the cube that is parallel to the back face of the model.

   The model will be reoriented such that the back face will be parallel to the screen. Also, the cube will now be displayed as a rectangle. Now, sometimes, when the model is reoriented, the X axis of the model (displayed in red) becomes vertical. You can again reorient the model such that the X axis become horizontal using the cube that is still displayed on the screen.

   If you move the cursor close to any of the edges of the cube, that is now a rectangle, you will notice that there are not actually four edges, but eight. This means that each edge is a combination of two edges, separated by an arrow. All these eight edges are used to rotate the model around the current view direction. The current view direction is normal to the screen, and so the model will be rotated about an axis normal to the screen. The direction in which the model will be rotated is displayed by a small arrow that appears on the cursor when you move it close to any of the eight edges.

6. Choose the lower right vertical edge of the rectangle to reorient the model.

   You will notice that the red arrow has become horizontal, suggesting that the X axis of the model is now in the horizontal direction. Right-click and choose **Done** to exit the **Rotate** tool.

Whenever you define a sketch plane to create a sketch on a planar face, you will notice that a sketch comprising of some sketcher entities is automatically drawn. This sketch will define the contour of the sketching plane. For example, in this case the sketch will be a rectangle defining the back face of the model. The entities that are used to create this sketch are called reference geometries. These entities can also participate in feature creation but cannot be dimensioned. You can use this entire sketch or a part of this sketch and create the remaining part yourself. The part that you do not need can be selected and deleted. However, if you do not delete these entities, they will become a part of the sketch.

7. Delete both the vertical edges of the contour and the lower horizontal edge and then create the remaining portion of the sketch.

8. Add the required constraints and then dimension the sketch. The sketch after dimensioning should look similar to the one shown in Figure 4-43.

9. Choose the **Return** button from the **Command Bar** and exit the sketching environment.

Extruding the Sketch

1. Change the current view to Isometric view and then extrude the sketch using the **Extrude** tool to a distance of 32 mm. The model after creating the feature on the back face should look similar to the one shown in Figure 4-44.

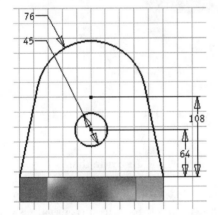
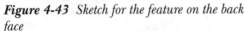

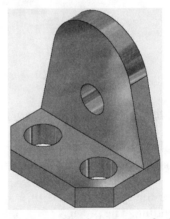

Figure 4-43 *Sketch for the feature on the back face*

Figure 4-44 *Model after creating the feature*

Creating the Feature on the Front Face of the Model

1. Choose the **Sketch** button from the **Command Bar**. You will be prompted to select the plane on which the sketch will be created. Select the front face of the model.

   The sketching environment will be activated and a rectangle defining the contour of the front face will be created. Delete this rectangle.

2. Choose the **Look At** button and then select the front face of the model. Choose the **Zoom All** button to increase the drawing display area.

The model will be reoriented such that the front face is parallel to the screen and the X axis of the model is in the horizontal direction.

3. Draw the rectangle and then add the **Collinear** constraint between the lower edge of the rectangle and the upper edge of the front face of the model.

4. Add the required dimensions to the model. The model after adding the dimensions should look similar to the one shown in Figure 4-45.

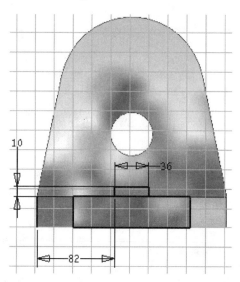

Figure 4-45 Dimensioned sketch for the feature on the front face

5. Exit the sketching environment and then change the current view to Isometric view.

Extruding the Sketch

1. Choose **Extrude** from the **Features** panel bar to invoke the **Extrude** dialog box.

    Since the sketch consists of a single closed loop, it will be automatically selected for extruding. The preview of the feature as it will be created using the current values will be displayed on the graphics screen.

2. Select **To** from the **Distance** drop-down list in the **Extents** area.

    The **Select surface to end the feature creation** button will be displayed below the drop-down list. This button will be chosen automatically.

3. Select the front face of the feature created on the back face of the base feature as the face to terminate the current feature.

    The selected face will be highlighted and will turn blue in color. Also, the **Check to terminate feature on the extended face** check box will be displayed. Since the current feature will terminate on the selected face, you do not have to select this check box.

4. Choose the **OK** button. The final model for Tutorial 1 should look similar to the one shown in Figure 4-46.

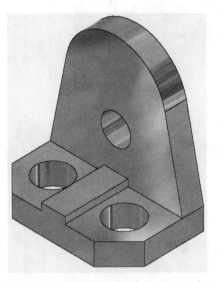

Figure 4-46 Final model for Tutorial 1

Saving the Model

1. Save the model with the name given below:

\PersonalProject\c04**Tutorial1.ipt**

Note
*The holes shown in the model for Tutorial 1 can also be drawn directly using the **Hole** tool. The use of this tool will be discussed in later chapters.*

Tutorial 2

In this tutorial you will create the model shown in Figure 4-47a. The dimensions of the model are shown in Figure 4-47b, Figure 4-47c, and Figure 4-47d. After creating the model, save it with the name given below:

\PersonalProject\c04**Tutorial2.ipt**   **(Expected time: 30 min)**

Before creating the model, it is important to determine the number of features in the model. The model for this tutorial is a combination of a base feature and four cut features. The list of features that need to be created for the model is given next.

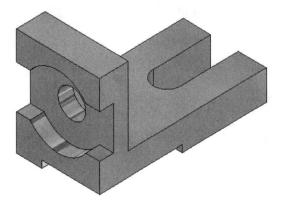

Figure 4-47a *Model for Tutorial 2*

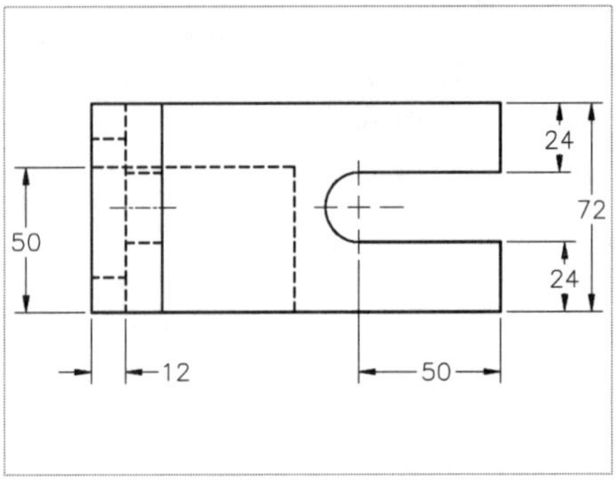

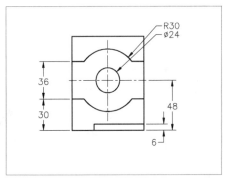

Figure 4-47c *Left side view of the model*

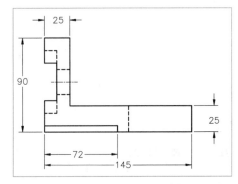

Figure 4-47b *Top view of the model*

Figure 4-47d *Front view of the model*

a. Create the base feature on YZ plane by defining a new sketch plane on this plane.
b. Define a new sketch plane on the front face of the model and create the cut feature.
c. Create the next cut feature by defining a new sketch plane on the back face of the model.
d. Define a new sketch plane on the new face that is exposed by creating the last cut feature and create the circular cut feature.

Changing the Sketch Plane

The base feature for this model is a L-shaped feature. The L-shaped base feature cannot be created on the XY plane. This feature will be created on the YZ plane. Therefore, you will have to change the sketching plane before creating the base sketch.

1. Open a new metric part file. Choose the **Return** button from the **Command Bar** to exit the current sketching environment.

This is needed because you do not want to draw the sketch in the current sketching plane, that is, the XY plane. It has to be drawn on the YZ plane.

2. Change the view to the Isometric view and then click on the plus sign (+) located on the left of the **Origin** directory in the browser.

   This directory will expand and will display the YZ, XZ, and XY planes and the X, Y, and Z axes. The center point will also be displayed.

3. Choose the **Sketch** button from the **Command Bar**. You will be prompted to select the plane to create the sketch. Select the YZ plane from the browser.

   The sketching environment will be activated and all the tools for creating a sketch will be displayed. However, the Isometric view will still be the current view. You will have to change the current view such that the sketching plane becomes parallel to the screen.

4. Choose the **Look At** button from the **Command Bar**. You will be prompted to select the entity to look at. Select YZ plane from the browser.

   The YZ plane will become parallel to the screen and you can draw the sketch on this plane.

Creating and Dimensioning the Sketch for the Base Feature

1. Create the L-shaped sketch for the base feature. Add the required constraints.

2. Add the dimensions to the sketch. The sketch after adding the dimensions should look similar to the one shown in Figure 4-48.

3. Choose the **Return** button from the **Command Bar** to exit the sketching environment. Change the current view to Isometric view.

Extruding the Sketch

1. Choose **Extrude** from the **Features** panel bar to invoke the **Extrude** dialog box. Extrude the sketch to a distance of 72 mm. Use the **Mid-plane** button to extrude the sketch. Choose the **Zoom All** button. The base feature is shown in Figure 4-49.

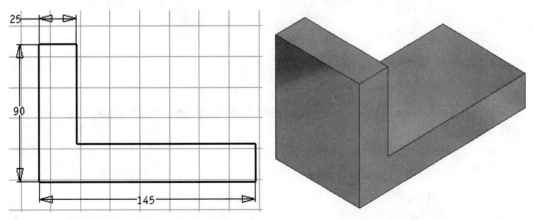

Figure 4-48 Sketch for the base feature   *Figure 4-49* Base feature

Creating the Cut Feature on the Front Face

The next feature that is to be created is a rectangular cut feature on the front face of the base feature. But before creating the feature, you will have to define the sketch plane on the front face.

1. Choose the **Sketch** button from the **Command Bar**. You will be prompted to select the sketching plane. Select the front face of the model. The sketching environment will be activated.

2. Using the **Look At** tool and **Common View** option, reorient the model. Delete the reference geometries created when you defined the sketch plane.

3. Create the sketch for the model and then add the required constraints and dimensions to it. The dimensioned sketch is shown in Figure 4-50.

4. Choose the **Return** button from the **Command Bar** and then change the current view to Isometric view.

Extruding the Sketch

1. Extrude the sketch using the **Cut** operation to a distance of 50 mm. The model after creating the cut feature is shown in Figure 4-51.

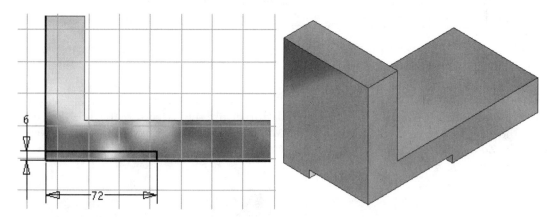

Figure 4-50 Sketch for the cut feature   *Figure 4-51* Model after creating the cut feature

Creating and Dimensioning the Sketch for the Cut Feature on the Left Face

The next feature is the cut feature that has to be created on the left face of the model. Before creating the sketch, you will have to define the sketch plane on the left face.

1. Choose the **Sketch** button from the **Command Bar**. You will be prompted to select the plane for creating the sketch. Select the left face of the model. The sketching environment will be activated.

2. Choose the **Look At** button from the **Standard** toolbar and select the left face of the model. The model will be reoriented such that the left face becomes parallel to the screen.

3. Delete the reference geometries and then create the sketch for the cut feature. Add the required constraints and then dimension the sketch as shown in Figure 4-52.

4. Exit the sketching environment and then change the current view to Isometric view.

Extruding the Sketch

1. Extrude the sketch using the **Cut** operation to a distance of 12 mm. The model after creating this cut feature is shown in Figure 4-53.

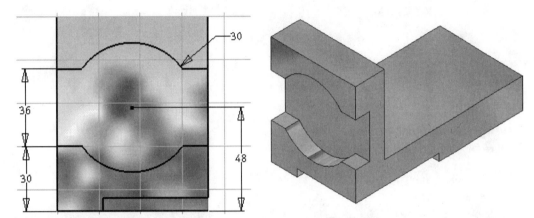

Figure 4-52 Sketch for the cut feature   *Figure 4-53 Model after creating the cut feature*

Creating the hole

1. Define a new sketch plane on the face that is exposed after creating the last cut feature.

2. Create the circle and then add dimensions to it. Extrude it using the **Cut** operation. Select the **All** option from the **Distance** drop-down list in the **Extents** area.

Creating the Last Cut Feature

1. Define a sketch plane on the lower horizontal face of the base feature and then reorient the model using the combination of the **Look At** tool and the **Common View** options.

2. Delete the reference geometries and then create the sketch for the cut feature. Add the required constraints and dimensions to the sketch.

3. Extrude the sketch using the **Cut** operation. Use the **All** option from the **Distance** drop-down list in the **Extents** area. The final model for Tutorial 2 is shown in Figure 4-54.

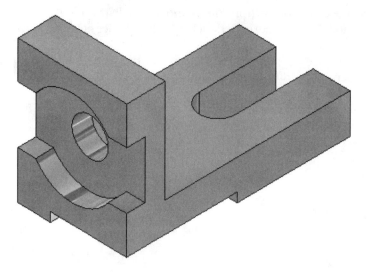

Figure 4-54 *Solid model for Tutorial 2*

Saving the Model

1. Save the sketch with the name given below:

\PersonalProject\c04**Tutorial2.ipt**.

Tip. *You can also apply the* **Collinear** *constraint between a sketched line and a linear edge of the model. However, when you apply this constraint between one of the sketched lines and an edge, another line will be created defining the linear edge selected to apply the* **Collinear** *constraint. It is recommended that you do not delete this line, because if you delete this line, the* **Collinear** *constraint will also be deleted along with the line.*

Tutorial 3

In this tutorial you will create the model shown in Figure 4-55a. The dimensions for the model are shown in Figure 4-55b, Figure 4-55c, and Figure 4-55d. Change the material of the model to Metal-AL-6061 (Polished). After creating the model, change the camera type to perspective. Save the model with the name given below:

> \PersonalProject\c04**Tutorial3.ipt**   **(Expected time: 35 min)**

The model for this tutorial is a combination of three join features, including the base feature and six cut features (holes). The list of features that need to be created for the model is given next.

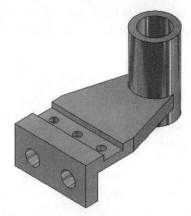

Figure 4-55a *Model for Tutorial 3*

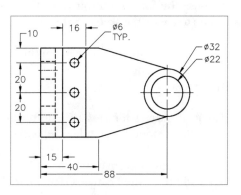

Figure 4-55b *Top view of the model*

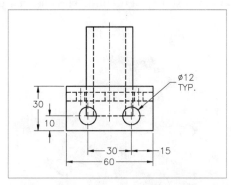

Figure 4-55c *Left side view of the model*

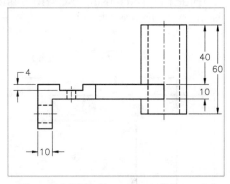

Figure 4-55d *Front view of the model*

a.   Create the base feature on YZ plane.
b.   Create the next join feature on the top face of the base feature.
c.   Create a work plane at an offset of 10 mm from the bottom face of the second join feature. Define a new sketch plane on this work plane and create the cylindrical join feature.
d.   Create a hole in the cylindrical feature by defining a new sketch plane on the top face of the cylindrical feature.
e.   Create two holes by defining a sketch plane on the left face of the model.
f.   Define a new sketch plane on the top face of the groove on the top face of the model and create three holes on it.

Creating the Base Feature

1.   Open a new metric part file and choose the **Return** button to exit the sketching environment.

2.   Change the current view to Isometric view and then click on the plus sign (+) located on left of the **Origin** directory in the browser. The default planes, axes, and the center point will be displayed.

3. Choose the **Sketch** button from the **Command Bar**. You will be prompted to select the plane to create the sketch. Select the YZ plane. The sketcher environment will be activated.

4. Choose the **Look At** button from the **Standard** toolbar and then select the YZ plane from the browser. The current view will be reoriented such that the YZ plane is now parallel to the screen.

5. Create the sketch for the base feature and then add the required constraints and dimensions. The dimensioned sketch for the base feature is shown in Figure 4-56.

6. Exit the sketching environment and then change the current view to Isometric view. Choose **Extrude** from the **Features** panel bar. The **Extrude** dialog box will be displayed.

   Since the sketch has a single closed loop, it will be automatically selected.

7. Extrude the sketch using the **Mid-plane** option to a distance of 60 mm. The base feature is shown in Figure 4-57.

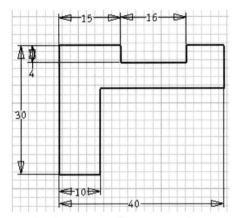 

Figure 4-56   *Sketch for the base feature*   *Figure 4-57*   *Base feature*

Creating the Next Join Feature on the Top Face

1. Choose the **Sketch** button from the **Command Bar** and select the top face of the base feature as the new sketching plane.

2. Reorient the model using the **Look At** tool and the **Common View** options. Create the sketch for the next feature and add the required constraints and dimensions as shown in Figure 4-58.

3. Exit the sketching environment and then extrude the sketch to a distance of 10 mm. Change the current view to Isometric view, see Figure 4-59.

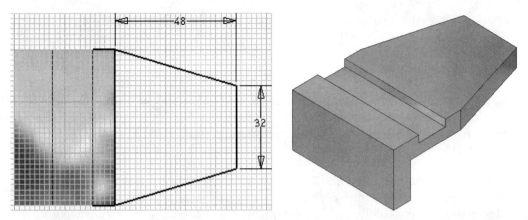

Figure 4-58 *Sketch for the next feature*   *Figure 4-59* *Model after creating next feature*

Creating the Cylindrical Feature

As shown in Figure 4-55d, the cylindrical feature starts at a distance of 10 mm below the bottom face of the feature you just created. Since it is not possible to define a sketch plane at an offset, therefore, you will have to define a work plane and use it to create the sketch. As mentioned earlier, the work plane can be defined at an offset from the selected planar face. In this model, the planar face will be the bottom face of the second feature. But first you will have to change the orientation of the model such that the bottom face of the second feature is visible.

1. Reorient the model using the **Rotate** tool such that the bottom face of the second feature is visible.

2. Choose **Work Plane** from the **Features** panel bar. Select the bottom face of the second feature and then drag it downwards.

    As soon as you start dragging the mouse, the **Offset** toolbar will be displayed. Release the left mouse button when the **Offset** toolbar is displayed.

3. Enter **10** as the offset distance in the **Offset** dialog box and press ENTER. A work plane will be created at an offset of 10 mm from the bottom face of the base feature.

4. Choose the **Sketch** button from the **Command Bar** and select the new work plane as the plane for sketching the new feature. Reorient the model using the **Look At** tool and the **Common View** options. Using the **Zoom All** tool, increase the drawing display area.

5. Draw a circle and then add the required constraints and dimensions to it, see Figure 4-60.

6. Exit the sketching environment and then change the current view to Isometric view.

7. Extrude the sketch to a distance to 60 mm. Increase the drawing display area.

After extruding the sketch you will notice that the work plane is still visible on the screen. Now, since there is no use of this work plane, it should not be displayed on the screen. Therefore you will have to turn off the display of this work plane. This is done using the browser.

8. Right-click on **Work Plane1** in the browser to display the shortcut menu.

    In the shortcut menu, there will be a check mark in front of the **Visibility** option. This suggests that the work plane is visible on the screen.

9. Choose the **Visibility** option in the shortcut menu. The check mark will be cleared and the work plane will not be displayed on the screen any more. Figure 4-61 shows the model after turning off the visibility of the work plane and changing the view to Isometric view.

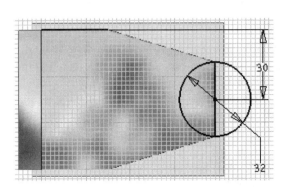

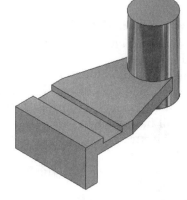

Figure 4-60 *Sketch for the cylindrical feature*   *Figure 4-61* *Model after creating the cylindrical feature*

Creating the Remaining Cut Features

1. Create the remaining cut features by creating their respective sketches on the sketching planes. The final model after creating all the cut features is shown in Figure 4-62.

Saving the Model

1. Save the model with the name given below:

    \PersonalProject\c04**Tutorial3.ipt**

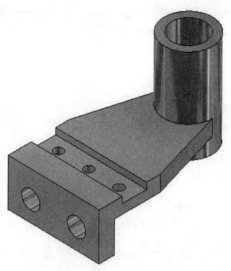

Figure 4-62 *Final model for Tutorial 3*

Self-Evaluation Test

Answer the following questions and then compare your answers with the answers given at the end of this chapter.

1. In a design, all the features are created on the XY plane. (T/F)

2. As soon as you select a sketching plane, the sketching environment is activated. (T/F)

3. You cannot define a sketch plane on the circular face of a cylindrical feature. (T/F)

4. The visibility of the shared sketches is turned off by default. (T/F)

5. The work axes are the _____ lines passing through the model or the feature.

6. The _____ tool and the _____ options are used to reorient the model such that the selected plane becomes parallel to the screen.

7. While defining a work plane, when you select a planar face or plane and start dragging it, the _____ toolbar is displayed.

8. The features that are created while you are inside the process of creating some other feature are called _____ features.

9. When you select the **To Next** option in the **Extrude** dialog box, the _____ button will not be provided along with the two direction buttons.

10. The _____ planes are not visible on the screen, whereas the _____ planes are visible on the screen as well as in the browser.

Review Questions

Answer the following questions.

1. Whenever you open a new file, by default you start drawing in the XY plane. (T/F)

2. You can create a work plane tangent to a cylinder by selecting the cylindrical face and then the XY, YZ, or XZ plane to which the resultant work plane should be parallel. (T/F)

3. You can create a work axis on a cylindrical feature by directly selecting it. (T/F)

4. The **All** option in the **Distance** drop-down list of the **Extents** area in the **Extrude** dialog box cannot be combined with the **Join** operation. (T/F)

5. A consumed sketch can be used again for creating another feature. (T/F)

6. Which of the following features is not a work feature?

    (a) Work Line   (b) Work Axis
    (c) Work Plane   (d) Work Point

7. How many planes are displayed when you click on the plus sign on the left of the **Origin** directory in the browser?

    (a) 2   (b) 3
    (c) 4   (d) 1

8. Which one of the following options of the shortcut menu is used to turn off the display of the work features?

    (a) **Display**   (b) **Show**
    (c) **Visible**   (d) **Visibility**

9. Which of the following operations is used to create a feature by retaining the material common to the existing feature and the sketch?

    (a) **Cut**   (b) **Join**
    (c) **Intersect**   (d) None

10. In Autodesk Inventor, you can create a work axis using how many methods?

    (a) Four   (b) Five

    (c) Six   (d) Three

Exercises

Exercise 1

Create the model shown in Figure 4-63b. The dimensions for the model are given in 4-63a, Figure 4-63c, and Figure 4-63d. Save the model with the name given below:

\PersonalProject\c04**Exercise1.ipt**   **(Expected time: 45 min)**

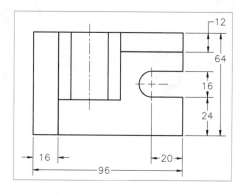

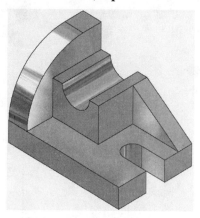

Figure 4-63a *Top view of the model*   **Figure 4-63b** *Model for Exercise 1*

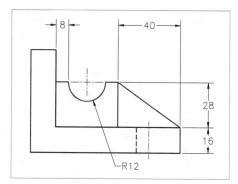

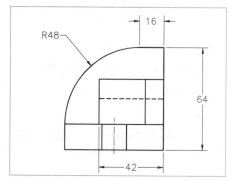

Figure 4-63c *Front view of the model*   **Figure 4-63d** *Right side view of the model*

Exercise 2

Create the model shown in Figure 4-64. The dimensions for the model are given in 4-65a and Figure 4-65b. Save the model with the name given below:

\PersonalProject\c04**Exercise2.ipt**   **(Expected time: 30 min)**

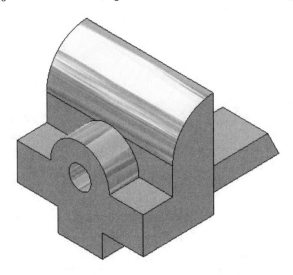

Figure 4-64 Solid model for Exercise 2

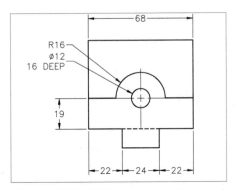

Figure 4-65a Left side view of the model

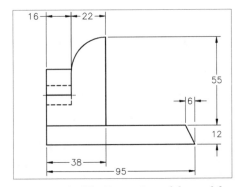

Figure 4-65b Front view of the model

Answers to Self-Evaluation Test
1. F, **2.** T, **3.** T, **4.** F, **5.** parametric, **6. Look At, Common View**, **7. Offset**, **8.** in-line, **9. Mid-plane**, **10.** sketch, work

Chapter 5

Advanced Modeling Tools-I

Learning Objectives

After completing this chapter you will be able to:

- *Use the Hole tool for creating different types of holes.*
- *Fillet the edges of a model.*
- *Chamfer the edges of a model.*
- *Mirror the features.*
- *Create rectangular patterns of the features.*
- *Create circular patterns of the features.*
- *Create rib features.*

ADVANCED MODELING TOOLS

Autodesk Inventor has provided a number of advanced modeling tools to assist you in creating a design. These advanced modeling tools appreciably reduce the time taken in creating the features in the models, thus reducing the designing time. For example, if you have to create a hole in a cylindrical feature, one option is that when you are sketching the cylindrical feature, you sketch the hole at the same time. But if you have to edit the dimensions of the hole, you will have to edit the complete sketch. Also, if the hole is drawn along with the sketch of the cylindrical feature, it will be extruded to the same distance. However, if you want the hole to terminate before the end of the cylindrical feature, you will have to draw another sketch. But if you use the **Hole** tool, you can directly create different types of holes and control their depth along with the other parameters.

The various advanced modeling tools that are available in Autodesk Inventor are

1. **Hole**
2. **Fillet**
3. **Chamfer**
4. **Mirror**
5. **Rectangular Pattern**
6. **Circular Pattern**
7. **Rib**
8. **Sweep**
9. **Loft**
10. **Coil**
11. **Thread**
12. **Shell**
13. **Face Draft**
14. **Split**

In this chapter, the first seven advanced modeling tools will be discussed. The remaining tools will be discussed in later chapters.

Note

All the features created using the advanced modeling tools are parametric in nature and can be modified at any time.

Creating Holes

Toolbar:	Features > Hole
Panel Bar:	Features > Hole

 Holes are the circular cut features that are created on an existing feature. Holes are generally provided for the purpose of assembling the model. In an assembly, another component like the bolt or the shaft is inserted into the hole. In Autodesk Inventor you can create holes only on the points/hole centers, endpoints of lines and arcs, or at the center of arcs, circles, or ellipses. This means that before creating a hole you will have to either place a point at which the hole will be created or create a sketched entity like arc, circle, ellipse, line, and so on. When you invoke this tool, the **Holes** dialog box will be displayed, see Figure 5-1. The options provided under this dialog box are discussed next.

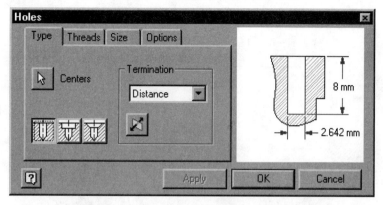

Figure 5-1 *Type tab of the* *Holes* *dialog box*

Type Tab

The options under this tab are used to specify the type of holes and the type of termination of the hole. The options under this tab are discussed next.

Centers

The **Centers** button is chosen to specify the center of the hole. If a model has one or more than one hole centers, they will be automatically selected as centers for the holes. You can preview the hole as it will be created using the current values. However, if there are one or more sketched lines, arcs, or circles, and their center points or endpoints have to be used to define the centers of holes, you will have to select them manually using this button.

 Tip. *To remove any of the hole centers from being selected for creating the holes, press the SHIFT key and then select them once again. You will notice that the preview of hole creation is not displayed. This suggests that the hole center is removed from the selection set and no hole will be created on it.*

Drilled

This is the first button below the **Centers** button. This button is chosen by default and is used to created a drilled hole. A drilled hole is a hole that has a uniform diameter throughout the length of the hole. The diameter of the hole and the depth of the hole has to be specified in the preview window on the right of this dialog box. Figure 5-2 shows the section view of a drilled hole.

Counterbore

This is the button next to the **Drilled** button. This button is chosen to create a counterbore hole. A counterbore hole is a stepped hole and has two diameters, a bigger diameter and a smaller diameter. The bigger diameter is called the counter diameter and the smaller diameter is called the drill diameter. In this type of hole, you will also have to specify two depths. The first depth is the counter depth. The counter depth is the depth up to which the bigger diameter will be defined. The second depth is the depth of the hole, including the counter depth. All these values are defined in the preview window on the right of the **Holes** dialog box. Figure 5-3 shows the section view of a counterbore hole.

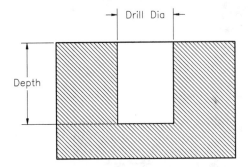

Figure 5-2 Drilled hole

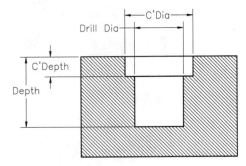

Figure 5-3 Counterbore hole

Countersink

This button is provided on the right of the **Counterbore** button and is used to create a countersink hole. A countersink hole also has two diameters but the transition between the bigger diameter and the smaller diameter is in the form of a tapered cone. In this type of hole, you will have to define the counter diameter, the drill diameter, the depth of the hole, and the countersink angle. All the values except that for the countersink angle are defined in the preview window. The countersink angle value is defined in the **Options** tab of the **Holes** dialog box. Figure 5-4 shows the sectioned view of a countersink hole.

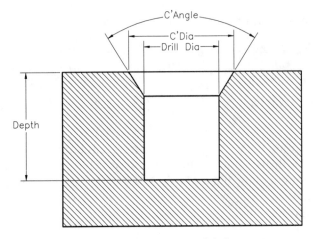

Figure 5-4 Countersink hole

Termination Area

The drop-down list provided under this area is used to define the termination of the holes.

Distance. The **Distance** option is used to create a hole by defining the depth of the hole in the form of a numeric value. The depth of the hole is defined in the preview window. You can reverse the direction of the hole by choosing the **Flip** button below this drop-down list.

Through All. The **Through All** option is used to create a hole that is cut through all the features. When you select this option, the option to define the depth of the hole is no more displayed in the preview window. The direction of the hole can be reversed using the **Flip** button.

To. The **To** option is used to terminate the hole feature at a specified plane, planar face, or an extended face. When you select this option, the **Flip** button is replaced by the **Select surface to end the feature creation** button. Using this button you can select the face to terminate the hole feature.

Threads Tab

The options under the **Threads** tab are used to specify the parameters for creating threaded holes, see Figure 5-5. These options are discussed next.

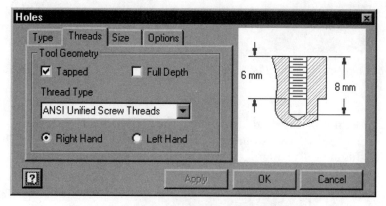

Figure 5-5 Threads tab of the Holes dialog box

Tapped

The **Tapped** check box is selected to create threaded holes. The options under the **Threads** tab will be available only if this check box is selected.

Full Depth

If the **Full Depth** check box is selected, the threads will run through the length of the hole. If this check box is not selected, you will have to specify the depth to which the threads will be created in the hole. This length is defined in the preview window on the right side of the **Holes** dialog box.

Thread Type

The **Thread Type** drop-down list is used to select the type of threads. The types that are available are **ANSI Unified Screw Threads** and the **ANSI Metric M Profile**.

Right Hand
The **Right Hand** radio button is used to create right handed threads. A right handed thread enters a nut when you turn it in the clockwise direction.

Left Hand
The **Left Hand** radio button is used to create left handed threads. A left handed thread enters a nut when you turn it in the counterclockwise direction.

Figure 5-6 shows a hole without threads and Figure 5-7 shows a hole with threads.

Figure 5-6 Counterbore hole without threads   *Figure 5-7 Counterbore hole with threads*

Size Tab
The options under this tab are used to define the size of the threads, see Figure 5-8. Depending upon the type of thread selected from the **Thread Type** drop-down list in the **Threads** tab, the options under this tab will change.

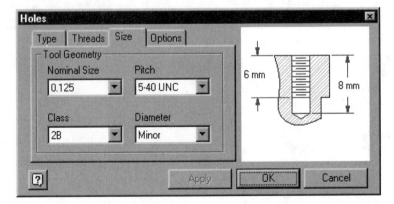

*Figure 5-8 **Size** tab of the **Holes** dialog box*

Nominal Size
This drop-down list is used to select the nominal size of the threads. The pitch and the class value will be different for different nominal sizes.

Pitch
This drop-down list is used to select the pitch value for the threads. The pitch is defined as the distance between a specified point on the thread and its corresponding point on the next or the previous thread when calculated parallel to the central axis of the hole.

Class
The **Class** drop-down list is used to select the class of the threads. Alphabet A suggests that the threads are external and alphabet B suggests that the threads are internal. Also, higher the numeric value in this drop-down list, more accurate is the fitting.

Diameter
The **Diameter** drop-down list is used to specify whether the diameter defined for creating the threads is the major, minor, pitch, or drill diameter of the original hole. You can select the required option from this drop-down list.

Options Tab
Most of the options under the **Options** tab (Figure 5-9) will be available only if the **Through All** option from the **Termination** area in the **Type** tab is not selected.

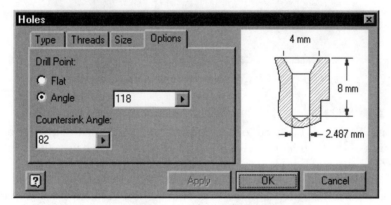

Figure 5-9 Options tab of the Holes dialog box

Drill Point: Flat
If this radio button is chosen, the end of the hole will be a flat plane.

Drill Point: Angle
If this radio button is chosen, the end of the hole will be tapered and will converge to a point. The angle of the taper can be defined in the edit box provided on the right of this radio button. The default value in this edit box is 118.

Countersink Angle
This edit box is used to define the countersink angle for a countersink hole. The default value in this edit box is 82.

Creating Fillets

Toolbar:	Features > Fillet
Panel Bar:	Features > Fillet

In Autodesk Inventor, you can add fillets or rounds using the **Fillet** tool. Fillets are generally used to apply curves on the interior edges of a model and rounds are generally used to apply curves on the exterior edges. When you invoke this tool, the **Fillet** dialog box will be displayed as shown in Figure 5-10. The options under the various tabs of this dialog box are discussed next.

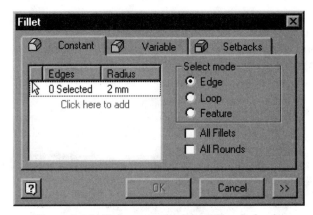

*Figure 5-10 **Constant** tab of the **Fillet** dialog box*

Constant Tab

The options under this tab are used to fillet the selected edges such that they have a constant fillet radius throughout their length. However, different edges can have a different fillet radius.

Edges

When you invoke the **Fillet** tool, the **Fillet** dialog box will be displayed and you will be prompted to select the edges to be blended. The number of edges you select to apply the fillet will be displayed under this column. However, note that all the edges selected will have the same fillet radius. If you want to specify different fillet radii, click on the text **Click here to add**. Another row will be added. Now, if you select an edge, it will be displayed in the second row. The second row can be assigned a different fillet radius.

Radius

You can specify the fillet radius for the selected edges in this column. Different rows can have different radii.

Select Mode

The options under this area are used to set the priorities of selection for filleting.

Edge. If the **Edge** radio button is selected, you can select the individual edges of a model for filleting. As you move the cursor close to any of the edges of the model, the edge will be highlighted.

Loop. If the **Loop** radio button is selected, all the edges in the selected face will be automatically selected for filleting. Remember that all the edges selected using this option will have the same fillet radius.

Feature. If this option is selected, all the edges in the selected feature will be selected for filleting. However, all the selected edges will be applied the same fillet radius.

All Fillets
The **All Fillets** check box is selected to apply the fillet to all the interior edges of a model. Note that the fillet radius will be the same at all the places. Figure 5-11 shows a model with fillets.

All Rounds
The **All Rounds** check box is selected to apply the rounds to all the exterior edges of a model. All the exterior corners will also be curved if you select this check box. The radius for all the rounds will be the same. Figure 5-12 shows a model with rounds.

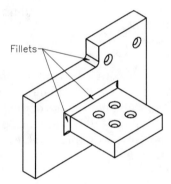

Figure 5-11 Creating fillets

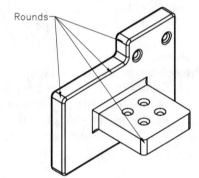

Figure 5-12 Creating rounds

Variable Tab
The options under the **Variable** tab (Figure 5-13) are used to fillet the selected edges such that they can be applied different radius values along the length. By default, there will be two points on the selected edge. You can add more points by specifying their desired location on the edge.

Edges
This column displays the number of edges selected to fillet. You can select more edges by clicking on **Click to add**.

Point
This column displays the points selected on the edge. By default, there will be only two points, **Start** and **End** at the start point of the edge and at the endpoint of the edge, respectively. However, as soon as you add a point by specifying its location on the edge, it will be added in this column.

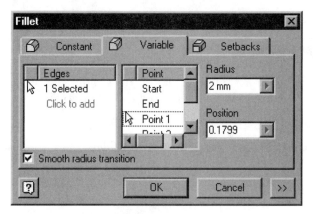

*Figure 5-13 **Variable** tab of the **Fillet** dialog box*

Radius

The **Radius** edit box displays the radius of the selected point. This edit box will not be available until you select a point in the **Point** column. To define variable radius, select a point and then enter the value of fillet radius in this edit box.

Position

This edit box is used to define the position of the point selected in the **Point** column. This edit box will not be available until you select a point other than the default points in the **Point** column. This edit box defines the point in terms of the percentage of the length of the selected edge. The length of the selected edge is taken as 1 (100%) and the position of the new point will be defined anywhere between 0 and 1. For example, a value of 0.5 will suggest that the point is placed at the midpoint of the edge.

Figure 5-14 and Figure 5-15 show the variable filleting of the edges of a model.

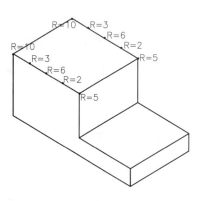

Figure 5-14 Defining the fillet radius

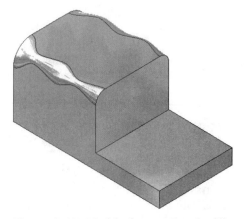

Figure 5-15 Model after creating the fillet

Smooth radius transition

This check box is selected to allow smooth transition between all the points you have defined in the edge. If this check box is selected, there will be a smooth blending between all the points. If this check box is cleared, the blending between all the points will be linear, see Figure 5-16 and Figure 5-17.

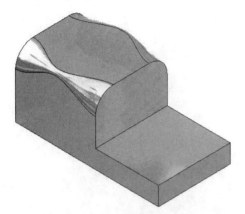

Figure 5-16 *Smooth transition*

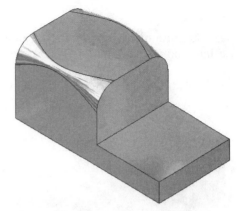

Figure 5-17 *Linear transition*

Setbacks Tab

The options under the **Setbacks** tab (Figure 5-18) are used to specify the setbacks of the transition between the three edges that comprise the vertex. You will have to first select the three edges using the **Constant** tab and then invoke the **Setbacks** tab. The options under this tab are discussed next.

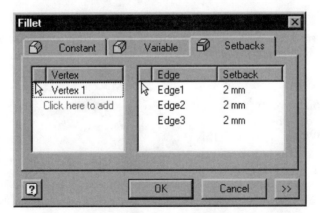

Figure 5-18 *Setbacks* tab of the *Fillet* dialog box

Vertex

After you have selected the three edges using the **Constant** tab, invoke this tab. You will be prompted to select the common vertex to add the setback. Select the vertex common to the three selected edges. The selected vertex will be displayed in this column. You can also add more vertices by clicking on **click here to add**.

Edge

This column displays the edges common to the vertex selected in the **Vertex** column. The edge that will have the arrow in front will be highlighted in the drawing window.

Setback

This column displays the setback value for the transition along the edge selected in the **Edge** column. You can modify this value by clicking on it.

Figure 5-19 and Figure 5-20 show the fillet created using different setback values.

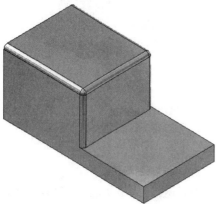
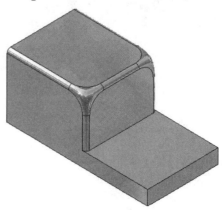

Figure 5-19 *Fillet with setback =2*   *Figure 5-20* *Fillet with setback =10*

Note
*Using the **Setbacks** tab you cannot set the radius of the fillet. The radius of the fillet will be set in the **Constant** tab where you have selected the edges.*

More

This is the button with two arrows provided on the lower right corner of the **Fillet** dialog box. When you choose this button, the **Fillet** dialog box expands providing you with more options, see Figure 5-21. All these options are discussed next.

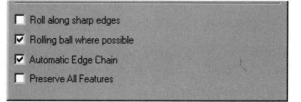

*Figure 5-21 **More** options of **Fillet** dialog box*

Roll along sharp edges

This check box is selected to modify the radius of the fillet in order to retain the shape and the sharpness of the edges of adjacent faces. If this check box is cleared, the adjacent faces will extend in case the fillet radius is more than what can be adjusted in the current face. Figure 5-22 shows the fillet created with the **Roll along sharp edges** check box cleared and Figure 5-23 shows the fillet created with this check box selected.

Rolling ball where possible

This check box is selected to create a rolling ball fillet wherever it is possible. If this check

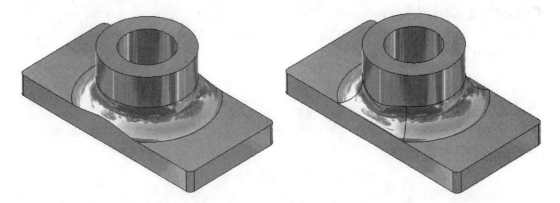

Figure 5-22 Adjacent face extended   *Figure 5-23 Fillet radius adjusted to retain the sharpness of the edge*

box is cleared, the transition at the sharp corners will be continuously tangent. Figure 5-24 shows the rolling ball fillet created by selecting this check box and Figure 5-25 shows the tangent fillet created by clearing this check box.

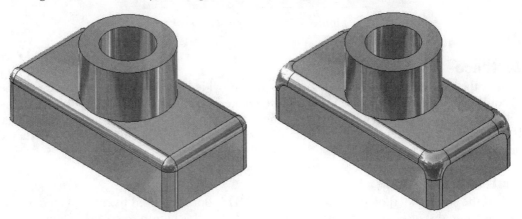

Figure 5-24 Rolling ball fillet   *Figure 5-25 Tangent fillet*

Automatic Edge Chain
If this check box is selected, all the tangent edges will also be selected when you select an edge to fillet.

Preserve All Features
This check box is selected to calculate the intersection of all the features that intersect with the fillet. If this check box is cleared, the intersection of only the edges that are a part of the fillet will be calculated.

Creating Chamfers

Toolbar:	Features > Chamfer
Panel Bar:	Features > Chamfer

Chamfering is defined as the process of bevelling the sharp edges of a model in order to reduce the area of stress concentration. In Autodesk Inventor, the chamfers are created using the **Chamfer** tool. When you invoke this tool, the **Chamfer** dialog box will be displayed, see Figure 5-26, and you will be prompted to select the edges to be chamfered. The options under this dialog box are discussed next.

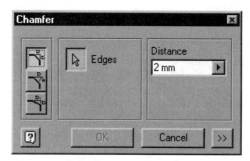

Figure 5-26 Chamfer dialog box

Distance

This is the first button in the dialog box and is provided on the upper left corner of the **Chamfer** dialog box. This button is chosen to create a chamfer such that the distance of the selected edge is equal from both the faces. The chamfer thus created will be at 45° angle. Since both the distance values are same, therefore, there will be only one edit box in the **Distance** area. You can specify the chamfer distance in this edit box.

Distance and Angle

This is the second method of creating chamfers. This option is used to create a chamfer by defining one distance and one angle. When you choose this button to create a chamfer, you will be prompted to select the face to be chamfered. This is the face from which the angle will be calculated. After selecting the face, you will be prompted to select the edge to be chamfered. The distance and the angle value can be specified in their respective edit boxes. These edit boxes will be displayed in the **Distance** area when you choose this button.

Two Distances

This button is chosen to create a chamfer using two different distances. The distances can be specified in the **Distance1** and **Distance2** edit boxes that are displayed in the **Distance** area when you choose this button. The face along which the distance 1 value will be calculated will be highlighted. You can select the other face by choosing the **Flip** button. This button is available below the **Edge** button.

Figure 5-27 shows the model before chamfering and Figure 5-28 shows the model after chamfering.

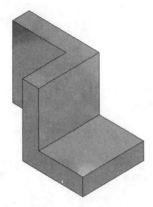

Figure 5-27 *Model before chamfering*

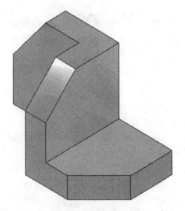

Figure 5-28 *Model after chamfering*

More

This is the button with two arrows and is provided
on the lower right corner of the dialog box. When
you choose this button, the **Chamfer** dialog box
will expand, displaying more options, see
Figure 5-29. These options are discussed next.

Figure 5-29 *The **More** options of **Chamfer**
dialog box*

Edge Chain Area

The buttons in this area are used to set the priorities for selecting the edges to be chamfered.
If you select the first button, all the edges that are tangent to the selected edge will also be
selected for chamfering. If you choose the second button, the tangent edges will be ignored.

Setback Area

The buttons in this area are used to specify whether or not the setback will be applied to
the model. If you choose the first button, the setback will be applied and the vertex will be
flattened. However, if you choose the second button, the setback will not be applied and
the vertex will be pointed. Figure 5-30 shows the chamfer created with setback and
Figure 5-31 shows the chamfer without setback.

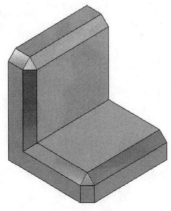

Figure 5-30 *Chamfer with setback*

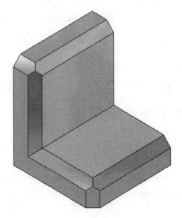

Figure 5-31 *Chamfer without setback*

Mirroring the Features

Toolbar: Features > Mirror Feature
Panel Bar: Features > Mirror Feature

 This tool is used to create a mirror image of the selected features using a mirror plane. The plane that can be used to mirror the features can be a planar face, or a work plane. An exact replica of the selected entities will be created at a distance from the mirror plane. This distance will be equal to the distance between the original selected entities and the mirror plane. When you invoke this tool, the **Mirror Pattern** dialog box will be displayed (Figure 5-32) and you will be prompted to select the feature to be patterned. The options in the **Mirror Pattern** dialog box will be discussed next.

Figure 5-32 Mirror Pattern dialog box

Features

The **Features** button is chosen to select the features to be mirrored. When you invoke this tool, this button is chosen automatically.

Mirror Plane

The **Mirror Plane** button is chosen to select the plane about which the selected features will be mirrored. After you have selected all the features to be mirrored, choose this button. You will be prompted to select the plane about which the features will be mirrored. The preview of the mirrored feature will be displayed on the graphics screen as soon as you specify the mirror plane.

More

This is the button with two arrows and is provided in the lower right corner of the **Mirror Pattern** dialog box. If you choose this button, the **Mirror Pattern** dialog box expands, providing you with more options, see Figure 5-33. These options are discussed next.

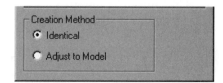

Figure 5-33 The More options

Identical

This radio button is chosen if you want the mirrored feature to be exactly similar to the original feature, even if they intersect other features.

Adjust to Model

This radio button is chosen if the mirror feature terminates at a planar face of the model. In this case, the mirror feature will be modified such that it adjusts in the model.

Figure 5-34 shows the features being selected for mirroring and Figure 5-35 shows the model created by mirroring the features.

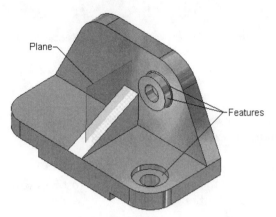

Figure 5-34 *Selecting features to be mirrored and the mirror plane*

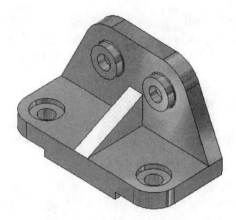

Figure 5-35 *Model after mirroring the features and hiding the work plane*

Creating Rectangular Patterns

Toolbar:	Features > Rectangular Pattern
Panel Bar:	Features > Rectangular Pattern

In the **Part** mode, you can use the **Rectangular Pattern** tool for arranging the selected features along the edges of an imaginary rectangle, thus creating a rectangular pattern. When you invoke this tool, the **Rectangular Pattern** dialog box will be displayed, see Figure 5-36.

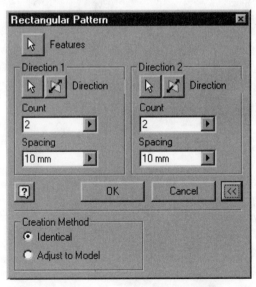

Figure 5-36 *Rectangular Pattern dialog box*

Since most of the options in this dialog box are exactly similar to those discussed in the **Rectangular Pattern** dialog box in the sketching environment, they will not be discussed here.

Features

This button is chosen to select the features to be patterned. When you invoke the **Rectangular Pattern** tool, the **Rectangular Pattern** dialog box will be displayed and this button will be chosen automatically. You will be prompted to select the features to be patterned.

Creation Method

This area will be displayed when you choose the button with two arrows provided in the lower right corner of this dialog box. The options under this area are discussed next.

Identical

The **Identical** radio button is chosen if you want the patterned features to be exactly similar to the original feature, even if they intersect other features.

Adjust to Model

The **Adjust to Model** radio button is chosen if any of the patterned feature terminates at a planar face of the model. In this case, the patterned features will be modified such that they adjust in the model.

Figure 5-37 shows the hole selected for creating a rectangular pattern and Figure 5-38 shows the model after creating a rectangular pattern.

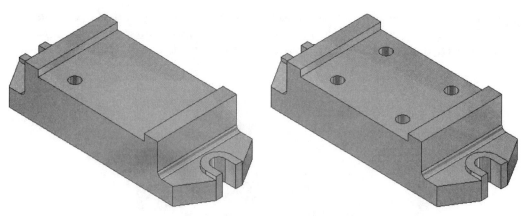

Figure 5-37   *Model before creating the pattern*   *Figure 5-38*   *Model after creating the pattern*

Note
*The remaining options in the **Rectangular Pattern** dialog box are similar to those discussed under the **Rectangular Pattern** dialog box in Chapter 3.*

Creating Circular Patterns

Toolbar:	Features > Circular Pattern
Panel Bar:	Features > Circular Pattern

 In the Part mode, you can use the **Circular Pattern** tool for arranging the selected features around the circumference of an imaginary circle, thus creating a circular pattern. When you invoke this tool, the **Circular Pattern** dialog box will be displayed, see Figure 5-39. The options in this dialog box are discussed next.

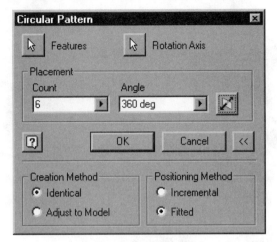

Figure 5-39 Circular Pattern dialog box

Features

This button is chosen to select the features to be patterned. This button is chosen by default when you invoke this dialog box.

Rotation Axis

The **Rotation Axis** button is chosen to select the axis about which the features will be arranged. The entities that can be selected as rotation axis include a work axis or a linear edge of any face of the model. You can also select a cylindrical feature, the central axis of which will be selected as the axis of rotation.

Creation Method Area

The options under this area will be displayed when you choose the button with two arrows provided in the lower right corner of this dialog box. These options are discussed next.

Identical

This radio button is chosen if you want the patterned features to be exactly similar to the original feature, even if they intersect other features.

Adjust to Model

This radio button is chosen if any of the patterned feature terminates at a planar face of the model. In this case, the patterned features will be modified such that they adjust in the model.

Figure 5-40 shows a model before creating a circular pattern and Figure 5-41 shows the model after creating a circular pattern. In this case the cylindrical feature is selected for defining the axis of rotation. By selecting the cylindrical feature, you will select its central axis as the axis of rotation.

Figure 5-40 *Model before creating the pattern*   **Figure 5-41** *Model after creating the pattern*

Note
*The remaining options in the **Circular Pattern** dialog box are similar to those discussed under the **Circular Pattern** dialog box in Chapter 3.*

Creating Rib Features

Toolbar:	Features > Rib
Panel Bar:	Features > Rib

Ribs are defined as thin wall-like structures used to bind the joints together so that they do not fail under an increased load. In Autodesk Inventor, ribs are created using an open profile, see Figure 5-42 and Figure 5-43.

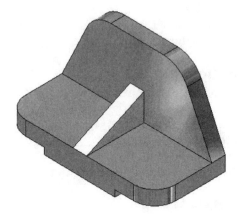

Figure 5-42 *Sketch for the rib feature*   **Figure 5-43** *The rib feature*

Remember that before invoking the **Rib** tool, you must have an unconsumed sketch. When you invoke the **Rib** tool, the **Rib** dialog box will be displayed, see Figure 5-44. Using this dialog box you can create a rib or a web. A web is similar to a rib, with the only difference being that the web is an open feature. Web features are created by adding material to a specified distance. The options under this dialog box are discussed next.

Figure 5-44 Rib dialog box

Shape Area

The options under this area are used to select the profile of the rib or the web feature and the direction of feature creation. These options are discussed next.

Profile

The **Profile** button is chosen to select the sketch of the rib or the web feature. If there is a single unconsumed sketch, it will be automatically selected when you invoke this tool.

Direction

The **Direction** button is chosen to define the direction in which the rib or the web feature will be created. The feature can be created in a direction normal to the selected sketch or parallel to it. If you take the cursor close to the selected sketch, the directions will be displayed using green arrows. A dynamic preview of the resultant feature could also be seen along with the direction.

Thickness Area

The options under this area are used to define the thickness of the rib or the web feature. The thickness is specified in the **Thickness** edit box. This area also has three buttons. These buttons are used to define the direction in which the thickness will be applied. You can apply the thickness on either side of the sketch or equally in both the directions.

Extents Area

The buttons in this area are used to specify whether the feature will be extended to the next face or to a specified distance. The two buttons that are provided in this area are discussed next.

To Next

If this button is chosen, the rib or the web feature will be created such that it merges with the next face, see Figure 5-45.

Finite

The **Finite** button is chosen to create the rib or the web feature to a specified distance, see Figure 5-46. The distance is specified in the edit box that will be displayed in this area when you choose this button. The direction is controlled using the **Direction** button in the **Shape** area.

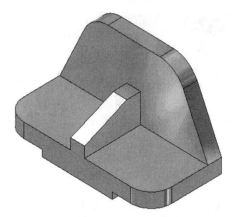 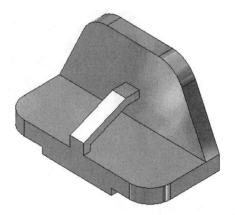

Figure 5-45 *Rib created by extending the sketch to the next face*

Figure 5-46 *Rib created by extending the sketch to a specified distance*

Extend Profile

This check box will be displayed below the **Shape** area. This check box will be displayed when you select the direction of applying the thickness parallel to the sketch or choose the **Finite** button from the **Extents** area. If this check box is selected, the sketch will be extended such that it intersects with the face.

TUTORIALS

Tutorial 1

In this tutorial you will create a model of Fixture Base shown in Figure 5-47a. The dimensions for the model are given in Figure 5-47b, Figure 5-47c, and Figure 5-47d. After creating the model, save it with the name given below:

\PersonalProject\c05**Tutorial1.ipt**   (**Expected time: 45 min**)

Before you start creating the model, it is recommended that you outline the procedure for creating the model. The steps that will be followed to complete this tutorial are listed below.

a. Open a new part file and exit the sketching environment. Create a sketch for the base feature on the XZ plane and extrude it to a distance of 102 mm.
b. Define a new sketch plane on the back face of the base feature and create the join feature on the back face of the base feature.
c. Create the two cylindrical features with a hole on the front face of the second feature.
d. Create the fillet on the base feature.
e. Define a new sketch plane on the top face of the base feature and taking the center points of fillets on the top face, create two counterbore holes using the **Hole** tool.
f. Finally draw an open sketch and convert it into a rib using the **Rib** tool to complete the model.

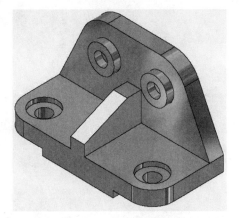

Figure 5-47a Model for Tutorial 1

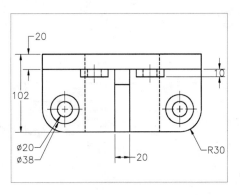

Figure 5-47b Top view of the model

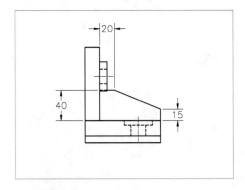

Figure 5-47c Left view of the model

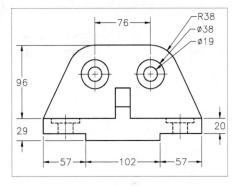

Figure 5-47d Front view of the model

Creating the Base Feature

Since the base feature will be created on the XZ plane, you will have to exit the sketching environment without drawing anything. Then define a new sketch plane on the XZ plane for drawing the sketch. The reason for this is that if you directly start drawing the sketch in the new file, it will be created on the XY plane and not on the plane you actually want to draw on.

1. Open a new metric template and draw the sketch for the base feature on the XZ plane. Add the required constraints and dimensions to it. The sketch after adding the constraints and dimensions is shown in Figure 5-48.

2. Exit the sketching environment. Extrude the sketch to a distance of 102 mm using the **Extrude** tool to create the base feature. The base feature is shown in Figure 5-49.

Creating a Join Feature on the Back Face of the Base Feature

1. Define a new sketch plane on the back face of the base feature. Draw the sketch for the join feature and then add the required constraints and dimensions. The sketch after adding

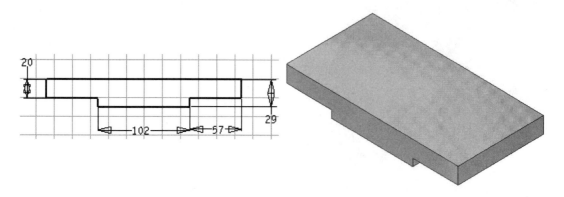

Figure 5-48 *Sketch for the base feature*   **Figure 5-49** *Base feature*

the constraints and dimensions is shown in Figure 5-50.

2.   Exit the sketching environment and then extrude the sketch to a distance of 20 mm. The
model after creating the join feature is shown in Figure 5-51.

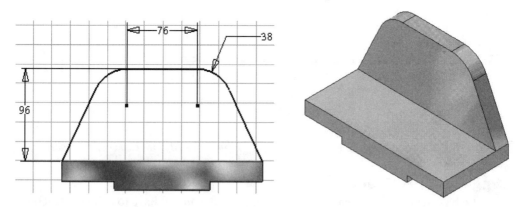

Figure 5-50 *Sketch for the join feature*   **Figure 5-51** *Model after creating the join feature*

Creating the Cylindrical Features on the Front Face of the New Feature

To create the cylindrical features, you can draw the sketch for both the features at the same
time. Each sketch will consist of two circles. The reason for this is that both the cylindrical
features are to be extruded to the same distance.

1.   Draw the sketch for both the cylindrical features. Extrude the sketches to a distance of
10 mm.

While selecting the sketches for extruding, make sure that you select a point outside the
inner circles but inside the outer circles so that when you extrude them, the inner circles
are subtracted from the outer circles, thus creating the holes. The model after creating the
cylindrical features is shown in Figure 5-52.

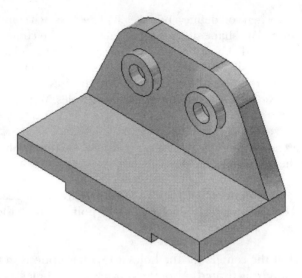

Figure 5-52 Model after creating the cylindrical features

Creating Fillets

The vertical edges of the front face of the base features have to be filleted so that you can use the center point of fillets to define the counterbore holes.

1. Choose **Fillet** from the **Features** panel bar. The **Fillet** dialog box will be displayed.

2. The **Constant** tab will be active and you will be prompted to select the edges to blend. Select both the vertical edges on the front face of the base feature.

    As soon as you select the edges, the **Edges** column will display 2 edges. The preview of the fillet will be displayed on the model using the default radius value, that is 2 mm.

3. Click on the default radius in the **Radius** column to edit the radius value. Change this value to 30 mm.

    You will notice that the fillet in the preview of the model has also increased.

4. Choose the **OK** button to exit the **Fillet** dialog box. The fillets will be created.

Creating Counterbore Holes

As mentioned earlier, holes in Autodesk Inventor are created on points. The points that can be used to create holes include the endpoints of lines, arcs, or splines, center points of arcs or circles, or sketched points/hole centers. To draw any of these points, you will have to define a sketch plane on the face where the holes have to created.

1. Choose the **Sketch** button from the **Command Bar** and define a sketch plane on the top face of the base feature.

As mentioned earlier, when you define a new sketch plane, a sketch comprising the reference entities will be drawn. The shape of this sketch will define the contour of the face where the sketch plane is defined. Therefore, when you define a sketch plane on the top face of the base feature, a sketch will be drawn. This sketch comprises of two horizontal lines, two vertical lines, and two arcs. Also, the center points of the arcs will be drawn. These center points of the arcs can be used for creating counterbore holes. You will not have to draw the hole centers.

2. Delete all the reference entities except the arcs because you need only the center points of arcs for creating the holes.

3. Exit the sketching environment and then choose **Hole** from the **Features** panel bar to invoke the **Holes** dialog box. Select the center points of both the arcs as the centers of the holes.

    As soon as you select the centers for the holes, the other options in the **Type** tab of the **Holes** dialog box will be activated. Also, the preview of the holes as they will be created using the current value will be displayed on the model.

4. Choose the **Counterbore** button. Note that the preview of hole on the graphics screen will still show the drilled hole. The reason is that the preview will always display drilled hole even if you choose the **Counterbore** or the **Countersink** button.

5. Select **Through All** from the drop-down list in the **Termination** area.

6. Modify the value of counter diameter in the preview window to 38 mm. Similarly, modify the value of bore diameter to 20 mm and counter depth to 6 mm.

7. Choose the **OK** button to exit the **Holes** dialog box. The model after creating the holes is shown in Figure 5-53.

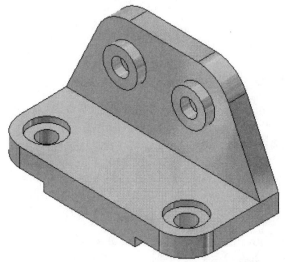

Figure 5-53 Model after creating the fillets and the holes

> **Tip**. *Even if you select the option to create a counterbore or a countersink hole, the preview on the model will display the drilled hole. But that is just for the display and when you exit the **Holes** dialog box, the resultant hole will be the one you had actually selected from the **Types** tab.*

Creating the Rib Feature

The rib feature is created in the middle of the model. Therefore, you will have to define an offset work plane in the middle of the model on which the rib feature will be created.

1. Create a work plane at an offset from the right face of the base feature. The offset distance should be -108 mm. The negative value will ensure that the work plane is created inside the model. Choose this work plane as the sketching plane.

> **Tip**. *If the sketch plane is defined inside the model, the sketched entities are hidden by the faces of the model that are between the user and the sketch. Therefore, it is sometimes hard to dimension such sketches. To avoid this confusing situation, Autodesk Inventor provides you with an option of temporarily slicing the portion of the model that is in between the user and the sketch. The model will be restored as soon as you exit the sketching environment. To slice the model, right-click in the graphics window and choose the **Slice Graphics** option from the shortcut menu.*

2. In the sketching environment, right-click to display the shortcut menu. Choose **Slice Graphics** option. The portion of the model that lies between the sketch plane and the user will be temporarily sliced.

3. Draw the open sketch for the rib feature and then add the required constraints and dimensions to it. The sketch after adding dimensions and constraint is shown in Figure 5-54.

    When you apply the **Coincident** constraint between the lines in the sketch and the edges of the model, the lines defining the edges will be drawn. Make sure these lines are not selected when you are selecting the sketch for the base feature.

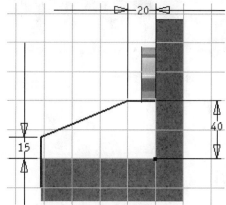

Figure 5-54 Sketch for the rib feature

4. Exit the sketching environment and choose **Rib** from the **Features** panel bar to display the **Rib** dialog box. You will be prompted to select the sketch for the rib feature. Select the open profile.

5. Set the value in the edit box in the **Thickness** area to 20 mm. Choose **OK** to exit the **Rib** dialog box. The final model after creating all the features is shown in Figure 5-55.

6. Save the model with the name \PersonalProject\c05**Tutorial1.ipt**.

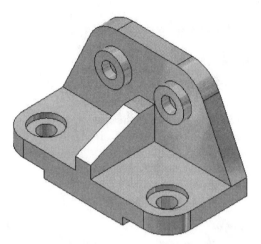

Figure 5-55 *Final model for Tutorial 1*

Tutorial 2

In this tutorial you will create a model of Pivot Base shown in Figure 5-56a. The dimensions for the model are given in Figure 5-56b, Figure 5-56c, and Figure 5-56d.   **(Expected time: 45 min)**

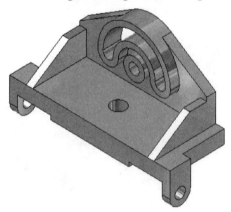

Figure 5-56a *Model for Tutorial 2*

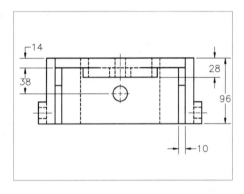

Figure 5-56b *Top view of the model*

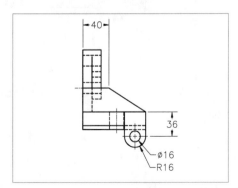

Figure 5-56c *Left view of the model*

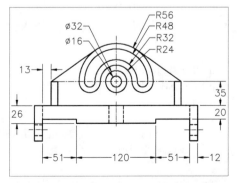

Figure 5-56d *Front view of the model*

The model for this tutorial is a combination of a number of join and cut features. Also, the model has a rib feature and two holes. As shown in Figure 5-56a, there are two instances of the rib feature and the feature on the right face of the model. However, you will create both these features and then mirror them on the other side using a work plane that will be defined in the middle of the model.

Creating the Base Feature

1. Open a new metric part file and then change the sketching plane to the XZ plane.

2. Draw the sketch for the base feature on the XZ plane. Extrude the sketch to a distance of 96 mm. The base feature of the model is shown in Figure 5-57.

Creating a Join Feature on the Back Face of the Base Feature

1. Specify a new sketch plane on the back face of the base feature.

2. Draw the sketch for the next feature on the back face and then extrude it to a distance of 14 mm, see Figure 5-58.

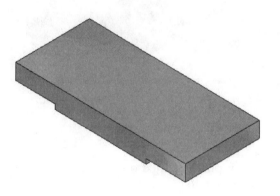
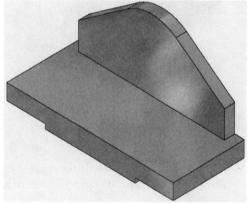

Figure 5-57 Base feature   *Figure 5-58 Model after creating the join feature*

Creating the Next Join Features

1. Define a new sketch plane on the front face of the last feature.

2. Draw the sketches for both the join features. Extrude both the sketches to a distance of 14 mm. The model after creating the join features is shown in Figure 5-59.

Creating the Cut Features

Now, you need to create cut features that will remove the material from the circular feature and the semicircular feature last created. You can draw the sketch of both the cut features at the same time and extrude them using the **Cut** operation. Since both the sketches are to be extruded through the model, you can select both of them together while selecting the sketch for creating the cut feature. However, since both the sketches were selected together while creating the cut feature, they will be displayed as a single feature in the browser.

1. Define a new sketch plane on the front face of the semicircular feature. Draw the sketch for the cut feature and the circle for the hole.

   When you define the sketch plane on the semicircular feature, a sketch defining the semicircular feature will be drawn. Offset this sketch inside and then delete. Since you have used a reference entity to draw the inner sketch, you will have to specify just one dimension value, that is the radius of any of the arcs.

2. Extrude the sketch and the circle using the **Cut** operation through the model to create the cut features, see Figure 5-60.

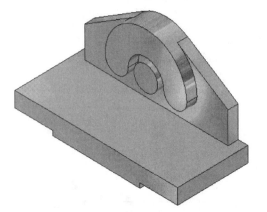 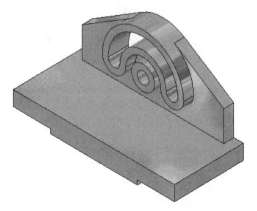

Figure 5-59 *Join feature on the front face of the second feature*   *Figure 5-60* *After creating the Cut features*

Creating the Rib Feature

The sketch for the rib will be created on a sketch plane defined on the left face of the second feature. The sketch will be extruded toward left to create the feature.

1. Define a new sketch plane on the right face of the second feature and draw the sketch of the rib feature. Add the required dimensions and constraints to the sketch.

2. Exit the sketching environment and choose **Rib** from the **Features** panel bar. The **Rib** dialog box will be displayed and you will be prompted to select the sketch for the rib feature.

3. Select the open sketch and all other options in this dialog box will be made available. Enter 10 mm in the edit box available in the **Thickness** area.

4. Choose the second button in the **Thickness** area to extrude the feature toward the left side. Choose the **Direction** button from the **Shape** area to define the direction of the rib feature. Move the cursor close to the open sketch and select it when the green arrow is pointing downwards. This will ensure that the rib feature is created properly.

   The preview of the rib feature will be displayed showing the sketch extruded toward the left side of the sketch.

5. Choose **OK** to exit the **Rib** dialog box. The rib feature will be created.

Creating the Join Feature on the Right Face of the Base Feature

1. Define a new sketch plane on the right face of the base feature.

2. Draw the sketch for the next feature. Draw a circle inside the sketch so that when extruded, the hole is automatically created. Add the required constraints and dimensions to it.

3. Extrude the sketch to create the feature. Make sure that you select the sketch using a point inside the outer closed loop but outside the circle. The model after creating the feature is shown in Figure 5-61.

Mirroring the Features

The second set of rib and join features will be created by mirroring them on the other side. These features will be mirrored using a work plane that is defined in the middle of the model. Therefore, you will have to first create an offset work plane in the middle of the model.

1. Create an offset work plane inside the model using the right face of the base feature. The offset distance is -111 mm.

2. Choose **Mirror Feature** from the **Features** panel bar to display the **Mirror Pattern** dialog box. You will be prompted to select the features to be patterned. Select the rib feature and the feature created on the right face of the base feature.

3. Choose the **Mirror Plane** button and select the offset work plane as the mirror plane. The preview of the mirrored features will be displayed on the model. Choose **OK** to exit this dialog box. Right-click on the work plane in the browser to display the shortcut menu. Choose the **Visibility** option to make the work plane invisible. The model after mirroring the features is shown in Figure 5-62.

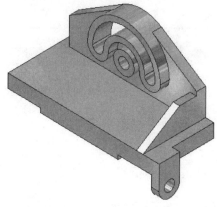

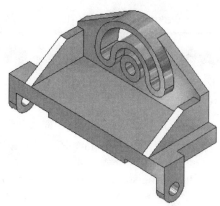

Figure 5-61 *Model after creating rib and join features*

Figure 5-62 *Model after mirroring the features*

Creating a Hole on the Top Face of the Base Feature

1. Define a new sketch plane on the top face of the base feature. Draw a hole center and then add the required dimensions to it.

2. Exit the sketching environment and then choose **Hole** from the **Features** panel bar to invoke the **Holes** dialog box.

3. The hole center will be automatically selected for creating the hole. Select **Through All** from the drop-down list in the **Termination** area.

4. Set the value of the diameter of the hole in the preview window to 22 mm. The diameter of the hole in the preview will also increase automatically.

5. Choose the **OK** button. The final model for Tutorial 2 is shown in Figure 5-63.

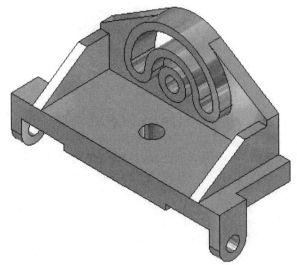

Figure 5-63 Final model for Tutorial 2

6. Now, save the model with the name \PersonalProject\c05**Tutorial2.ipt**.

Tutorial 3

In this tutorial you will create the model shown in Figure 5-64a. The dimensions for the model are given in Figure 5-64b and Figure 5-64c. After creating the model save it with the name given below:

\PersonalProject\c05**Tutorial3.ipt**   **(Expected time: 30 min)**

The following steps outline the procedure for creating the model.

a. Create the sketch for the base feature on the YZ plane and extrude it midplane.
b. Create the second feature on the YZ plane and extrude it midplane.

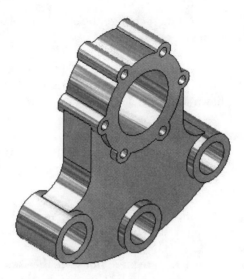

Figure 5-64a *Model for Tutorial 3*

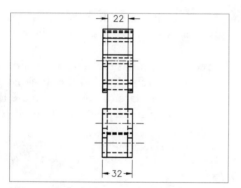

Figure 5-64b *Left side view of the model*

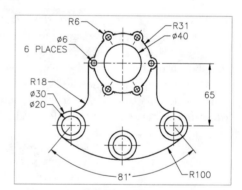

Figure 5-64c *Front view of the model*

c.   Create one of the holes on the front face of the second feature and then create a circular pattern of this hole.
d.   Create the cylindrical join feature and then create a hole in it.
e.   Create the circular pattern of the last join feature and the hole.

To draw this model you will use the **Copy** option of the **Rotate** tool in the sketching environment and the **Circular Pattern** tool in the **Part** mode. The base feature of this model will be created on the YZ plane. Also, all features in this model will be extruded using the **Mid-plane** option. This is because all features are extended equally from the front face and the back face of the base feature.

Creating the Base Feature

The base feature for this model will be created on the YZ plane. Therefore, you will have to exit the sketching environment of the new file and then define a new sketch plane on the YZ plane.

1.   Open a new metric part file and then change the sketching plane to the YZ plane. Draw the sketch for the base feature.

2.   Add the required constraints and dimensions to it. Exit the sketching environment and then extrude the sketch to a distance of 22 mm using the **Mid-plane** option. The base feature of the model is shown in Figure 5-65.

Creating the Next Join Feature

Since the last feature was created on the YZ plane and was extruded using the **Mid-plane** option, you can create the other features also in the same plane and extrude using the **Mid-plane** option.

1.   Choose the **Sketch** button from the **Command Bar**. You will be prompted to select the plane or planar face to create the sketch on. Select the YZ plane from the browser.

The sketching environment will be activated. But since the sketch will be drawn inside the model, it will be hidden by the faces that lie between the sketch and the user. Therefore, you will have to slice the model.

2.   Right-click in the graphics window to display the shortcut menu. In this menu choose **Slice Graphics**. Draw the sketch for the next feature that consists of six semicircular curves.

You can draw the central circle and then add the required dimensions and constraints to it. After adding the dimensions, draw one of the smaller circle and add the dimensions and constraints to it. Then using the **Copy** option of the **Rotate** dialog box, create the other five instances of the smaller circle. Finally, trim the unwanted portions of the sketch.

 Tip. *If you create a circular pattern of any entity, you cannot trim its instances. This is because Autodesk Inventor does not allow you to trim an entity that has been created using the **Circular Pattern** tool.*

3.   Exit the sketching environment and then extrude the sketch using the **Mid-plane** option to a distance of 32 mm. The model after creating the next feature is shown in Figure 5-66.

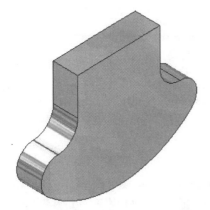

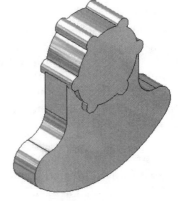

Figure 5-65 *Base feature of the model*   ***Figure 5-66*** *Model after creating the next feature*

Creating the Hole Pattern

The new feature that you have created consists of six holes created through the feature. Instead of creating all the holes, you can create one of the holes and then create a circular pattern of the holes. However, to create the pattern, you will have to create at least one hole by defining the sketch plane on the front face of the new feature.

1. Define a new sketch plane on the front face of the new feature.

    The reference entities will be created. You can use the center points of any of the reference arcs for creating the holes.

2. Exit the sketching environment and then choose **Hole** from the **Features** panel bar. The **Holes** dialog box will be displayed.

3. Select the center point of any one of the smaller arcs as the center of the hole. Select **Through All** from the drop-down list in the **Termination** area.

4. Modify the value of the diameter of the hole in the preview window to 6 mm. Choose **OK** to exit the dialog box and create the hole. The model after creating the hole is shown in Figure 5-67.

5. Choose **Circular Pattern** from the **Features** panel bar to display the **Circular Pattern** dialog box.

6. You will be prompted to select the feature to pattern. Select the hole. Choose the **Rotation Axis** button and select the outer circular edge of the second join feature.

    As soon as you select the circular edge to specify the rotation axis, an axis will be displayed passing through its center and the preview of the pattern as it will be created will be displayed on the model. A copy of the hole will be displayed on each of the semicircular features.

7. Accept the default values and choose **OK** to exit this dialog box and create the hole pattern. The model after creating the hole pattern is shown in Figure 5-68.

Creating the Next Join Feature

The next join feature will also be created on the YZ plane and will be extruded using the **Mid-plane** option.

1. Define a new sketch plane on the YZ plane and then slice the graphics. Draw the circle as the sketch for the cylindrical join feature. Add the required constraints and dimensions to the sketch.

2. Exit the sketching environment and then extrude the circle using the **Mid-plane** option to a distance of 32 mm.

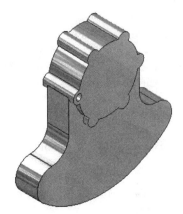

Figure 5-67 *Model after creating the hole*

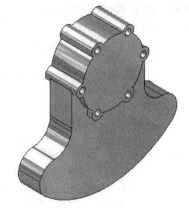

Figure 5-68 *Model after creating the hole pattern*

Creating the Hole in the Join Feature

1. Define a new sketch plane on the front face of the new join feature.

    A reference circle will be drawn. You can use the center of this circle as the center point for the hole.

2. Exit the sketching environment and then choose **Hole** from the **Features** panel bar. The **Holes** dialog box will be displayed.

3. Select the center of the circle as the hole center. Select **Through All** from the drop-down list in the **Termination** area.

4. Modify the value of the diameter of the hole in the preview window to 20 mm. Choose **OK** to exit the dialog box and create the hole. The model after creating the hole on the join feature is shown in Figure 5-69.

Creating Circular Pattern

1. Choose **Circular Pattern** from the **Features** panel bar. The **Circular Pattern** dialog box will be displayed and you will be prompted to select the feature to pattern.

2. Select the join feature and the hole to pattern. Both the features will be displayed with a blue outline.

3. Choose the **Rotation Axis** button and select the lower curved edge of the base feature to define the axis of rotation for the pattern.

    The preview of the pattern with six items arranged through an angle of 360° will be displayed on the model. But since this is not the pattern you need, you will have to modify the other values.

4. Enter 3 in the **Count** edit box and 81 in the **Angle** edit box under the **Placement** area.

5. Accept the other default values and choose **OK** to create the circular pattern. The model after creating the pattern is shown in Figure 5-70.

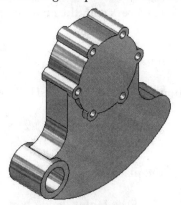

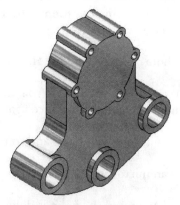

Figure 5-69 *Model after creating the hole on the join feature*

Figure 5-70 *Model after creating the circular pattern of the join feature and the hole*

Creating the Hole

1. Define a new sketch plane on the front face of the second feature. The reference sketch will be drawn.

2. Exit the sketching environment and choose **Hole** from the **Features** panel bar. The **Holes** dialog box will be displayed. Select the point at the center of the bigger circular feature.

3. Select **Through All** from the drop-down list in the **Termination** area. Modify the value of the diameter of the hole in the preview window to 40 mm.

4. Choose **OK**. The final model for Tutorial 3 is shown in Figure 5-71. Save the model with the name \PersonalProject\c05**Tutorial3.ipt**.

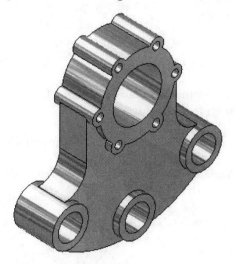

Figure 5-71 *Final model for Tutorial 3*

Self-Evaluation Test

Answer the following questions and then compare your answers with the answers given at the end of this chapter.

1. The hole created using the **Hole** tool is parametric in nature. (T/F)

2. You can remove any entity from the current selection set by pressing the SHIFT key and then selecting the entity once again. (T/F)

3. You can create both fillets and rounds using the same **Fillet** dialog box. (T/F)

4. You can mirror the features using the work plane or the planar face. (T/F)

5. The diameter of the holes is defined in the _____ of the **Holes** dialog box.

6. _____ is defined as the process of bevelling the sharp edges of the model in order to reduce the area of stress concentration.

7. The rib feature is created using an _____ sketch.

8. The _____ radio button is chosen in the **Mirror Pattern** dialog box to create a mirrored feature exactly similar to the original feature, even if they intersect other features.

9. _____ are defined as the thin wall-like structures used to bind the joints together so that they do not fail under an increased load.

10. A _____ hole is a stepped hole and has two diameters, a bigger and a smaller.

Review Questions

Answer the following questions.

1. In Autodesk Inventor, you can create holes only on the points/hole centers. (T/F)

2. In the Part mode, you can use the **Circular Pattern** tool for arranging the selected features around the circumference of an imaginary circle. (T/F)

3. The chamfer created using the **Distance** button will be at a 45° angle. (T/F)

4. The options under the **Variable** tab are used to fillet the selected edges by applying different radius values along the length of the edge. (T/F)

5. The options under the **Threads** tab of the **Holes** dialog box are used to define the size of the threads. (T/F)

6. Which of the following is not a type of hole?

(a) Counterbore   (b) Countersink
(c) Countercut   (d) Drilled

7. Which one of the following tabs provides with an option of creating a flat base hole?

     (a) **Type**   (b) **Options**
     (c) **Size**   (d) **Thread**

8. How many edges are used to define the setback for a vertex?

     (a) 2   (b) 3
     (c) 1   (d) 4

9. Which check box is displayed in the **Rib** dialog box when you select the direction of applying thickness parallel to the sketch or choose the **Finite** button from the **Extents** area?

     (a) **Extend Profile**   (b) **Clear Profile**
     (c) **Trim Profile**   (d) **None**

10. How many type of methods are provided for creating a chamfer?

     (a) 2   (b) 3
     (c) 1   (d) 4

Exercises

Exercise 1

Create the model shown in Figure 5-72. The dimensions for the model are given in Figure 5-72b and Figure 5-72c. Save this model with the name \PersonalProject\c05**Exercise1.ipt**.

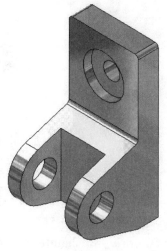

Figure 5-72a *Model for Exercise 1*

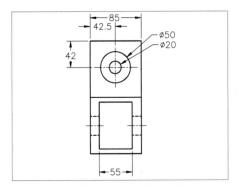

Figure 5-72b *Left side view of the model*

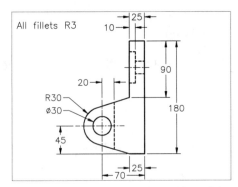

Figure 5-72c *Front view of the model*

Exercise 2

Create the model shown in Figure 5-73a. The dimensions for model are given in Figure 5-73b, Figure 5-73c, and Figure 5-73d. Save it with the name \PersonalProject\c05**Exercise2.ipt**.

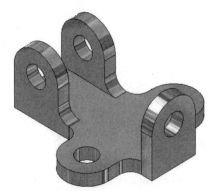

Figure 5-73a *Model for Exercise 2*

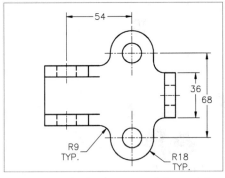

Figure 5-73b *Top view of the model*

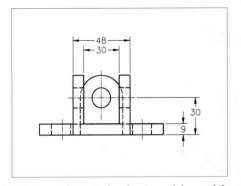

Figure 5-73c *Left side view of the model*

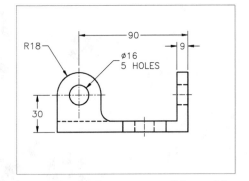

Figure 5-73d *Front view of the model*

Answers to Self-Evaluation Test
1. T, **2.** T, **3.** T, **4.** T, **5.** preview window, **6.** Chamfering, **7.** open, **8. Identical**, **9.** Ribs, **10.** counterbore

Chapter 6

Editing Features and Adding Automatic Dimensions to the Sketch

Learning Objectives

After completing this chapter you will be able to:

- *Edit the features in a model.*
- *Update the model after editing.*
- *Edit the sketches of the sketched features.*
- *Suppress the features.*
- *Unsuppress the Features.*
- *Delete the Features.*
- *Copy the Features.*
- *Add automatic dimensions to the sketches.*

EDITING THE FEATURES IN A MODEL

Editing is one of the most important part of designing. Most of the designs require editing, either during creation or after creation. As mentioned earlier, Autodesk Inventor is a feature-based solid modeling tool. This means that the model created in Autodesk Inventor is a combination of various features integrated together. All these features are individual components and can be edited separately. This property gives this solid modeling software a cutting edge over the other non-feature-based solid modeling tools. For example, Figure 6-1 shows a cylindrical part with six countersink holes created at some pitch circle diameter (PCD).

Now, in case you have to edit the features such that the number of holes is increased to eight and the countersink holes are changed into counterbore holes, all you need to do is to use two editing operations. The first editing operation will open the **Holes** dialog box where you can modify the countersink holes to counterbore holes. You can specify the various parameters for the counterbore hole in this dialog box. When you exit this dialog box, all the six countersink holes will be modified into counterbore holes. The second editing operation will open the **Circular Pattern** dialog box. In this dialog box you can change the number of instances to eight, see Figure 6-2.

Figure 6-1 *Part with six countersink holes*   *Figure 6-2* *Modified part with counterbore holes*

Similarly, you can also edit work features or the sketches of the sketched features. The features created using the work features will be modified automatically when you edit the work features. For example, if you have created a feature on a work plane that is at an offset of 100 mm, the feature will be automatically repositioned if you change the offset value of the work plane. In Autodesk Inventor, all the editing operations are performed using the browser.

Performing the Editing Operations

As mentioned earlier, all the editing operations will be performed using the browser. To edit a feature, select it in the browser. The selected feature will be highlighted in the model. Right- click on the selected feature in the browser or in the model to display the shortcut menu. In this shortcut menu, choose **Edit Feature**, see Figure 6-3. Depending upon the feature selected for editing, the corresponding dialog box will be displayed. For example, if you right-click on an extruded feature, the **Extrude** dialog box will be displayed. The dialog box will also have the

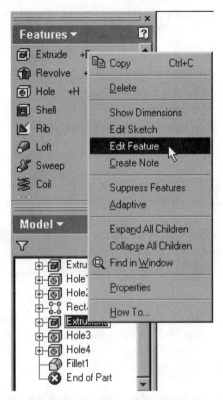

Figure 6-3 *Editing a feature using the browser*

sequence number of the feature. This means that if you right-click on the fifth extruded feature in a model to display the shortcut menu and choose **Edit Feature**, the **Extrude : Extrusion5** dialog box will be displayed, see Figure 6-4.

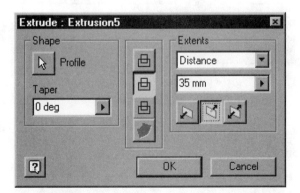

Figure 6-4 Extrude : Extrusion5 *dialog box for editing an extruded feature*

You can perform the required editing operation using this dialog box. Some of the editing operations that can be performed using this dialog box include changing the sketch to be extruded, modifying the taper angle, changing the type of operation, and so on. Similarly, if you right-click on a hole feature and then choose **Edit Feature** from the shortcut menu, the **Holes** dialog box will be displayed, see Figure 6-5.

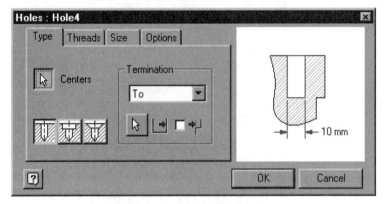

Figure 6-5 Holes : Hole4 dialog box

You can also edit a hole feature by right-clicking on it in the browser and then choosing **Show Dimensions**. All the dimensions related to the hole will be displayed on the model. Double-click on the diameter dimension and the **Hole Dimensions** dialog box will be displayed. The options in this dialog box will be available depending upon whether the hole is drilled, countersink, or counterbore. Figure 6-6 shows the **Hole Dimensions** dialog box for a counterbore hole.

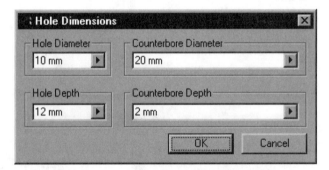

Figure 6-6 Hole Dimensions dialog box

Tip. *You can also display the dimensions of a feature on the model by double-clicking on it in the browser.*

*When you choose the option of displaying the dimensions of the feature for editing, the dimensions will be retained on the screen even after the editing operation is over. To clear these dimensions from the screen, either choose **Update** from the **Command Bar** or select another feature from the browser.*

Updating the Features

If you edit a feature using the browser, you do not have to update the feature to view the effect of the editing operation. This is because as soon as you exit the editing operation, the feature will be automatically updated. However, if you modify the feature using the dimensions, you will have to update the feature manually. Until the feature is updated after editing, it will not display the modified values. The features can be modified by choosing the **Update** button in the **Command Bar**. This button will be activated when you modify the dimensions of any of the feature.

Editing the Sketches of the Features

Autodesk Inventor also provides you with the flexibility of editing the sketches of the sketched feature. You can add additional entities to the sketch or remove some of the entities from the sketch. Once you have made the necessary changes, you just have to update the sketched feature using the **Update** button in the **Command Bar**. However, you have to make sure that the sketch after editing remains a closed loop. In case the sketch is not a closed loop, the **Autodesk Inventor - Update Part Document** dialog box will be displayed. This dialog box will give an error message that the loop could not be repaired after editing.

To edit the sketch of a sketched feature, right-click on it in the browser to display the shortcut menu. In this shortcut menu choose **Edit Sketch**, see Figure 6-7. When you choose the **Edit Sketch** option from the shortcut menu, the sketching environment will be activated. The **Features** panel bar will be replaced by the **Sketch** panel bar and all the sketching environment tools will be activated. Once you have made the necessary changes, choose the **Update** button from the **Command Bar**.

Figure 6-7 *Editing a sketch using the browser*

SUPPRESSING THE FEATURES

Sometimes, there may be a situation where you want that some of the features should not show up in the drawing views of the model or in the printout of the model. In any of the non-feature-based solid modeling tool, you will have to either delete the feature or create the feature after taking the printout. However, in Autodesk Inventor, you can simply suppress that feature. Once the feature is suppressed, it will neither be displayed in the drawing views nor in the printout of the model. You can anytime resume the feature by unsuppressing it. As soon as you unsuppress the feature, it will be displayed in the drawing views. To suppress a feature, right-click on it in the browser and then choose **Suppress Features** from the shortcut menu, see Figure 6-8.

Figure 6-8 *Suppressing a feature using the browser*

Note
If the feature that you select to suppress has some dependent features, they will also be suppressed. All the features that are suppressed will be displayed in light grey color in the browser. Also, all the suppressed features will have a line that will strike through the name of the feature in the browser.

UNSUPPRESSING THE FEATURES

The suppressed features can be resumed using the browser. Right-click on the suppressed feature in the browser to display the shortcut menu. In this shortcut menu, choose **Unsuppress Features**, see Figure 6-9. The selected feature will be displayed in the model again.

Tip. *If you have generated the drawing views of the current model, as soon as you suppress any feature in the model, it will not be displayed in the drawing views. Similarly, as soon as you unsuppress the feature, it will be displayed in the views.*

Figure 6-9 *Unsuppressing a feature using the browser*

DELETING THE FEATURES

The unwanted feature can be deleted from the model using the browser. Right-click on the feature to be deleted in the browser to display the shortcut menu. In this menu, choose the **Delete** option. When you choose this option, the **Delete Features** dialog box will be displayed as shown in Figure 6-10.

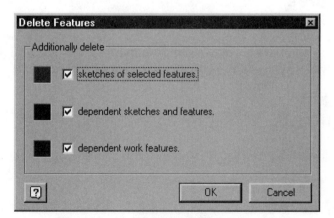

Figure 6-10 *Delete Features dialog box*

This dialog box will prompt you to specify whether or not you want to delete the dependent features and sketches. The options that you can select for deleting include the sketch of the feature, the dependent sketches and features, and the dependent work features.

COPYING THE FEATURES

Autodesk Inventor allows you to copy a feature from the current file to any file or to some other place in the same file. However, the method of copying a feature in Autodesk Inventor is different from that in other solid modeling tools. To copy a feature, right-click on it in the browser and choose **Copy** from the shortcut menu. If you want to paste the feature in another file, open it. Right-click in the graphics window to display the shortcut menu and then choose **Paste** from it. The **Paste Features** dialog box will be displayed as shown in Figure 6-11 and the dynamic preview of the feature will be displayed on the screen.

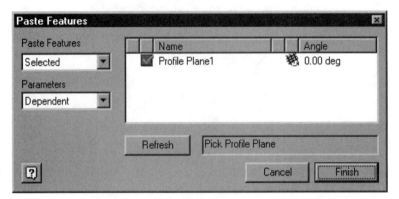

Figure 6-11 Paste Features dialog box

By default, the feature will be attached to any planar face in the model. However, you can attach the feature to the desired face using the options in the **Paste Features** dialog box. The options under this dialog box are discussed next.

Paste Features

This drop-down list is used to select the option for pasting the features. By default, only the selected feature will be pasted and the features that are dependent on the selected features will not be pasted. The reason for this is that by default, the **Selected** option in this drop-down list is selected. However, if you want to paste all the dependent features also, select **Dependent** from this drop-down list.

Parameters

This drop-down list is used to select whether the parameters of the feature should be independent or dependent. You can select the required option from this drop-down list.

Name

This column displays the plane on which the feature will be pasted. When you invoke this dialog box, by default the feature will be temporarily pasted on any plane. As you move the mouse on any plane, the feature will be temporarily pasted on that plane. You can view all this in the dynamic preview of the feature on the model. Once you select the plane on which the feature should be pasted using the left mouse button, dynamic preview will fix to that plane. Until you select the plane to paste the feature, an icon will be displayed on the left of the profile plane in this column. This icon will display an arrow on the face of a box. This suggests that you have not selected the plane for placing the feature. When you select the plane, this icon is replaced by a box that has a check mark, suggesting that the plane for placing the feature has been selected. In case you want to change the plane for the feature placement, click on the **Profile Plane** in this column.

Angle

This column is used to rotate the pasted feature through an angle. You can specify the angle in this column. The preview of the feature will be dynamically rotated through the specified angle.

Refresh

The **Refresh** button will be available only after you have selected the plane for pasting the feature. This button is chosen to refresh the feature such that it adjusts to the selected plane. For example, if a feature has a dependent feature that is cut using the **All** option, the preview of the model will display the cut feature extending beyond the plane on which the feature is pasted, see Figure 6-12. However, when you choose the **Refresh** button, the cut feature will be adjusted such that it is not extended beyond the selected plane, see Figure 6-13.

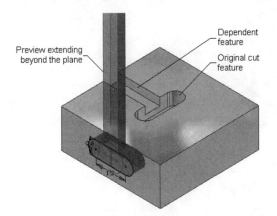
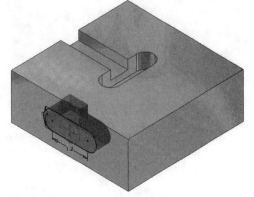

Figure 6-12 *Preview of the dependent cut feature extending beyond the selected plane*

Figure 6-13 *Preview of the dependent cut feature adjusted to fit the plane*

Finish

The **Finish** button is used to paste the feature on the selected face. The paste operation will be completed only after you choose this button. Figure 6-14 shows a model before copying the feature and Figure 6-15 shows the model after copying the original cut feature and the dependent cut feature on two different planes.

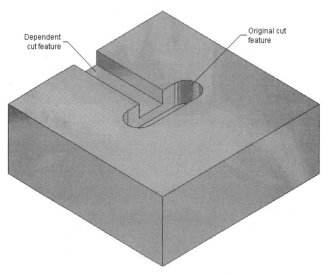

Figure 6-14 *Model with original cut feature and dependent cut feature*

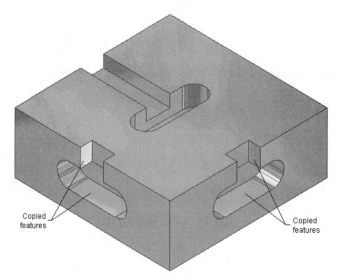

Figure 6-15 *Cut features copied on two different faces of the model*

ADDING AUTOMATIC DIMENSIONS TO THE SKETCH

Toolbar:	Sketch > Auto Dimension
Panel bar:	Sketch > Auto Dimension

The auto dimensions are the dimensions that are added automatically to the sketch by Autodesk Inventor. Note that the you cannot apply all the dimensions required in the sketch using only the automatic dimensions. These dimensions are used in association with the general dimensions to fully constrain the sketch. In Autodesk Inventor, the automatic dimensions are added using the **Auto Dimension** tool. When you invoke this tool, the **Auto Dimension** dialog box will be displayed as shown in Figure 6-16. The options under this dialog box are discussed next.

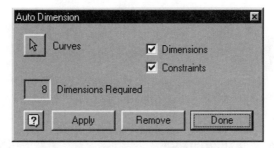

Figure 6-16 Auto Dimension dialog box

Curves

The **Curves** button is chosen to select the sketch for applying the automatic dimensions. Choose this button and then select the sketch from the graphics screen. The selected sketch will be highlighted and turned blue in color. After selecting the sketch, choose the **Apply** button to apply the automatic dimensions to the sketch.

Dimensions Required

The **Dimensions Required** box will display the number of dimensions that are required in the sketch. You cannot modify the value in this box. When you select the sketch and apply the automatic dimensions using the **Apply** button, the number of dimensions that are still required in the sketch will be displayed in this box.

Dimensions

The **Dimensions** check box is selected to apply the automatic dimensions to the sketch. If this check box is cleared, the dimensions will not be applied to the sketch.

Constraints

The **Constraint** check box is selected to also apply the constraints to the sketch while applying the automatic dimensions. If this check box is cleared, the constraints will not be applied to the sketch.

Apply

The **Apply** button is chosen to apply the automatic dimensions to the selected sketch. Select the sketch from the graphics screen using the **Curves** button and then choose this button to add the dimensions. Note that until this button is chosen, the automatic dimensions will not be applied to the sketch.

Remove

The **Remove** button is chosen to remove the automatic dimensions from the sketch.

Done

The **Done** button is chosen to exit the **Auto Dimension** dialog box.

TUTORIALS

Tutorial 1

In this tutorial you will create a model of the Gear-shifter link shown in Figure 6-17a. The dimensions of the model are shown in Figure 6-17b, Figure 6-17c, and Figure 6-17d. After creating the model, save it with the name given below:

\PersonalProject\c06**Tutorial1.ipt**   **(Expected time: 45 min)**

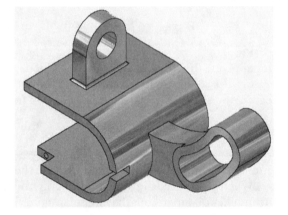

Figure 6-17a Model for Tutorial 1

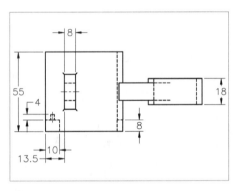

Figure 6-17b Top view of the model

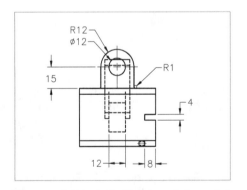

Figure 6-17c Left side view of the model

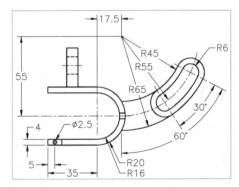

Figure 6-17d Front view of the model

Before you start creating the model, it is recommended that you outline the procedure for creating the model. The steps that will be followed to complete this tutorial are listed below.

a. Create the base feature that is a reverse C-like feature on the XZ plane and extrude this feature using the **Mid-plane** option.

b. Define a new sketch plane for the curved feature on the XZ plane and add the curved features on the circular face of the base feature.

c. Again define a new sketch plane on the XZ plane and create the sketch for the third feature. Extrude this feature also using the **Mid-plane** option.

d. Define a new sketch plane on the front face of the third feature and draw the sketch for the cut feature. Extrude this sketch using the **Cut** operation.

e. Suppress all features except the base feature and then define a work plane at an offset of 17.5 mm from the left face of the base feature. Draw the sketch for the feature on the top face of the base feature and extrude it using the **Mid-plane** option.

f. Suppress the last feature and create the slots and hole on the front face of the base feature.

g. Finally Unsuppress all features to complete the model.

Creating the Base Feature

1. Open a new part file and then create the sketch for the base feature on the XZ plane.

2. Exit the sketching environment and then extrude the sketch using the **Mid-plane** option to a distance of 55 mm. The base feature of the model is shown in Figure 6-18.

Figure 6-18 Base feature of the model

Creating the Curved Features

Since the base feature was created on the XZ plane and was extruded using the **Mid-plane** option, you can create the sketch for the curved features also on the same plane and then extrude it to the required distance using the **Mid-plane** option.

1. Select the same XZ plane as the plane for creating the sketch for the curved feature. Draw the sketch for the feature and then add the required constraints and dimensions to it. The sketch for the curved feature after applying all the dimensions and constraints is shown in Figure 6-19.

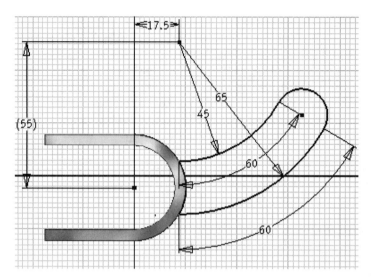

Figure 6-19 Sketch for the curved feature

2. Exit the sketching environment and then extrude it using the **Join** operation to a distance of 12 mm. Use the **Mid-plane** option for creating the feature. The join feature in Isometric view is shown in Figure 6-20.

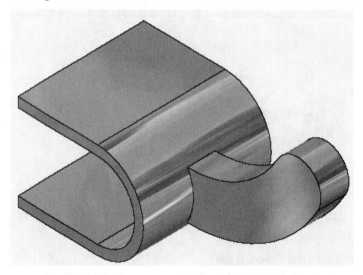

Figure 6-20 Feature created after extruding the sketch

3. Using the same sketching plane, create the sketch for the other join feature as shown in Figure 6-21. You can draw the sketch and then apply the concentric and equal constraints to the sketch and the existing feature.

4. Exit the sketching environment and then extrude it using the **Join** operation and **Mid-plane** option to a distance of 18 mm, see Figure 6-22.

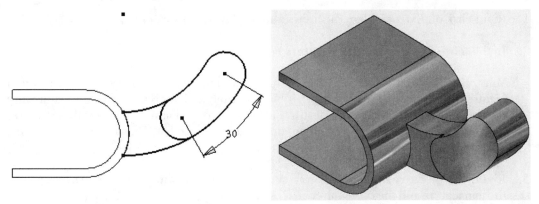

Figure 6-21 *Sketch for the next join feature in wireframe display*

Figure 6-22 *Model after creating the second join feature*

5. Specify a new sketch plane on the front face of the new join feature and then draw the sketch for the cut feature.

    The reference geometries that are created when you define the sketch plane can be offset and then dimensioned for creating the sketch of the cut feature.

6. Extrude the sketch using the **Cut** operation and **All** option to create the cut feature.

7. The model after creating the cut feature is shown in Figure 6-23.

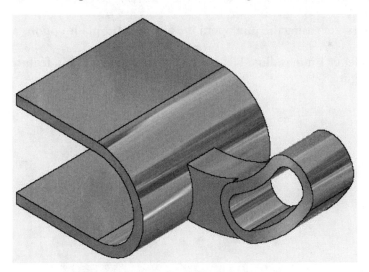

Figure 6-23 *Model after creating the cut feature*

Suppressing the Feature

As mentioned earlier, in a complicated model, it is better to suppress the features that are not required in creating the other features. Once all the features are created, you can unsuppress the suppressed features. In Autodesk Inventor, the features are suppressed using the browser.

1. Right-click on **Extrusion2** in the browser to display the shortcut menu.

2. In the shortcut menu, choose **Suppress Features**.

   You will notice that the second join feature is no more visible. However, the third join feature and the cut feature will still be visible on the model. This is because these features are not dependent on the second join feature. Therefore, you will have to suppress these features also. Since the cut feature is dependent upon the third join feature, when you suppress it, the cut feature will be suppressed automatically.

3. Right-click on **Extrusion3** in the browser and then choose **Suppress Features** to suppress the join feature and the cut feature.

   The only feature that will be visible now will be the base feature of the model.

Creating the next Join Feature

The next join feature will be created on an offset work plane. This work plane will be offset from the left face of the base feature to a distance of -17.5 mm. The negative value will make sure that the work plane is offset inside the model.

1. Define a new work plane at an offset of -17.5 mm from the left face of the base feature. Create the sketch for the join feature.

   Create the circle inside the sketch so that the hole is also created at the same time.

2. Extrude the sketch using the **Join** operation and the **Mid-plane** option.

3. Create a fillet of 1 mm radius. The model after creating the join feature and the fillet is shown in Figure 6-24.

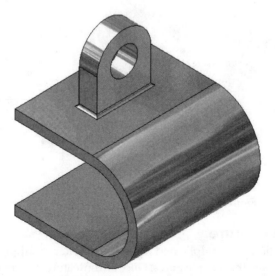

Figure 6-24 Model after creating the next join and fillet feature

Suppressing the Last Join Feature

1. Right-click on **Extrusion5** in the browser to display the shortcut menu. Choose **Suppress Features** from this menu.

   The fillet feature will also be suppressed because the fillet feature is dependent on the join feature. The only feature that will be visible will be the base feature.

Creating the Slots and the Hole

Next, the slots will be created on the front face of the base feature. Since both the slots will be cut to the same distance, you can draw the sketch for both the slots together and then extrude them using the **Cut** operation.

1. Define a new sketch plane on the front face of the base feature.

2. Draw the sketch for both the cut features and then extrude them using the **Cut** operation to a distance of 8 mm.

3. Define a new sketch plane on the back face of the slot on the left side. Place the hole center and then draw a drilled hole of 2.5 mm diameter. The depth of the hole is 4 mm. The model after creating the slots and hole is shown in Figure 6-25.

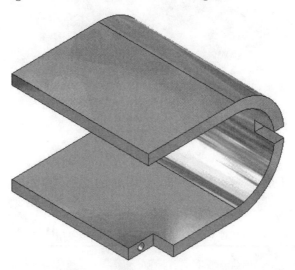

Figure 6-25 *Model after creating the cut and hole feature*

Note

*The viewing direction of Figure 6-25 is changed using the **Common Views** options.*

Unsuppressing the Features

Once all the features of the model are created, you can unsuppress the suppressed features and save the model. As mentioned earlier, the features are unsuppressed by using the browser. All the features that are suppressed will be displayed in light gray color and will have a line that strikes through their names in the browser.

1. Right-click on the **Extrusion2** in the browser and choose **Unsuppress Features** from the shortcut menu.

2. The **Autodesk Inventor - Unsuppress Feature** dialog box will be displayed.

    This dialog box will inform you that some errors occurred while unsuppressing the features. It will also display the sketches and features that could not be unsuppressed.

3. Choose **Accept** in this dialog box. The second join feature and the fillet will be unsuppressed.

4. Similarly, unsuppress the remaining suppressed features. Choose **Accept** in the **Autodesk Inventor - Unsuppress Feature** dialog box whenever it is displayed.

5. The final solid model of the Gear-shifter link is shown in Figure 6-26.

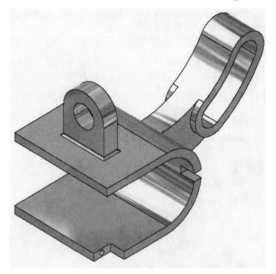

Figure 6-26 *Final solid model of the Gear-shifter link*

Saving the Model

1. Save the model with the name \PersonalProject\c06**Tutorial1.ipt**.

Tutorial 2

In this tutorial you will create the model shown in Figure 6-27a. The dimensions for the model are shown in Figure 6-27b, Figure 6-27c, and Figure 6-27d. After creating the model, save it with the name given below:

> \PersonalProject\c06**Tutorial2.ipt**   **(Expected time: 45 min)**

Before you start creating the model, it is recommended that you outline the procedure for creating the model. The steps that will be followed to complete this tutorial are listed below.

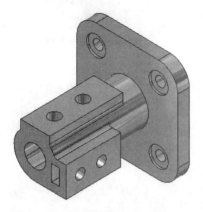

Figure 6-27a *Model for Tutorial 2*

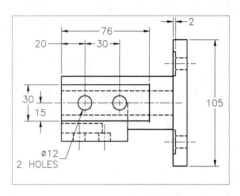

Figure 6-27b *Top view of the model*

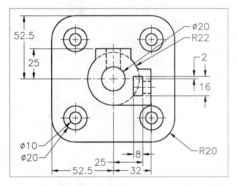

Figure 6-27c *Left side view of the model*

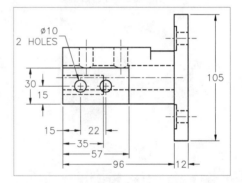

Figure 6-27d *Front view of the model*

a.   Create the sketch for the base feature on the XZ plane. The sketch consists of a square with fillet on all the four corners.

b.   On the front face of the base feature, create the counterbore holes by using the center points of fillets as center of holes.

c.   Suppress the holes and create the cylindrical join feature on the front face of the base feature.

d.   Add two rectangular join features to the cylindrical feature and create the rectangular cut feature on one of the rectangular join feature.

e.   Finally create all drilled holes by defining the sketch plane on the required planes. Once all the features are created, unsuppress the holes on the base feature.

Creating the Base Feature

1.   Open a new part file and then draw the sketch for the base feature on the XZ plane.

   The sketch for the base feature will be a square of side 105 mm and with all the four corners filleted with radius 20 mm.

2.   Exit the sketching environment and extrude the sketch to a distance of 12 mm. The base feature of the model is shown in Figure 6-28.

Creating the Holes

The base feature has four counterbore holes. When you define a new sketch plane on the front face of the model, a sketch will be created using the reference geometries. The sketch will also include four arcs defining the fillet at the four corners. You can use the center points of these arcs for creating the counterbore holes. You can also create one of the holes and then create a rectangular pattern for creating the remaining three holes.

1. Define a new sketch plane on the front face of the base feature and then use the center points of the reference arcs for creating the counterbore holes. The model after creating the counterbore holes is shown in Figure 6-29.

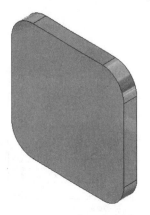   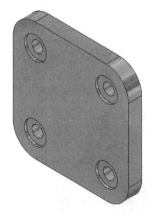

Figure 6-28 Base feature of the model   *Figure 6-29 Model after creating counterbore holes*

Suppressing the Holes

The browser will display only one hole operation with the name **Hole1** and not four. This is because all the holes were created in a single attempt, and therefore, all the holes are a part of one hole operation. For this reason, all the four holes will be suppressed using **Hole1** option in the browser.

1. Right-click on **Hole1** in the browser to display the shortcut menu. In the shortcut menu, choose **Suppress Features**.

You will notice that all the four holes are no more visible on the model. The only feature that is visible is the base feature.

Creating the Cylindrical and Rectangular Join Features

1. Define a new sketch plane on the front face of the base feature and then draw a circle that will define the sketch for the cylindrical feature.

2. Extrude the circle to a distance of 96 mm.

3. Define a new sketch plane on the front face of the cylindrical feature and then create one of the rectangular join features. Similarly, define a new sketch plane again on the same plane and then create the other rectangular join feature. The model after creating both the join

features is shown in Figure 6-30.

Creating the Cut Feature and Holes

1. Define a new sketch plane on the front face of the cylindrical feature and then create the rectangular cut feature.

2. One by one define new sketch planes on both the rectangular join features and create the holes. The model after creating the holes and the cut feature is shown in Figure 6-31.

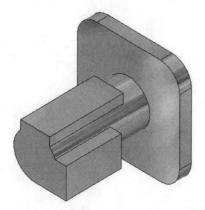 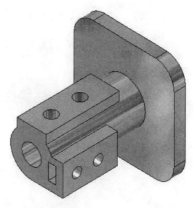

Figure 6-30 Model after creating join features   *Figure 6-31* After creating the cut feature and holes

Unsuppressing the Counterbore Holes

1. Right-click on **Hole1** in the browser and choose **Unsuppress Features** from the shortcut menu. The final model for Tutorial 2 is shown in Figure 6-32.

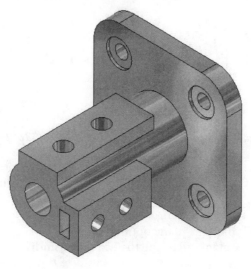

Figure 6-32 Final model for Tutorial 2

2. Save the model with the name \PersonalProject\c06**Tutorial2.ipt**.

Tutorial 3

In this tutorial you will create the model of the Body of Butterfly Valve assembly shown in Figure 6-33a. The dimensions of the model are shown in Figure 6-33b, Figure 6-33c, and Figure 6-33d. After creating the model, save it with the name \PersonalProject\c06**Tutorial3.ipt**. After creating the model, you will modify the 175 mm dimension of curved feature on the top face of the model to 200 mm. The dimensions of the remaining five instances should also change automatically. **(Expected time: 45 min)**

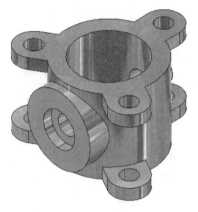

Figure 6-33a Model for Tutorial 3

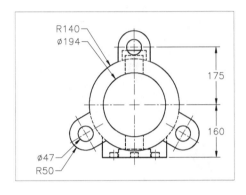

Figure 6-33b Top view of the model

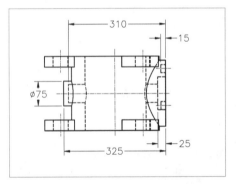

Figure 6-33c Left side view of the model

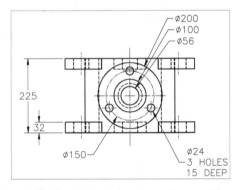

Figure 6-33d Front view of the model

Before you start creating the model, it is recommended that you outline the procedure for creating the model. The steps that will be followed to complete this tutorial are listed below.

a. Create the sketch for the base feature on the XY plane. The sketch consists of two circles and will be extruded using the **Mid-plane** option.
b. Define new offset work planes to create the two join cylindrical features on the cylindrical face of the base feature.
c. Add the counterbore hole and three smaller holes on the front face of the second feature.
d. Suppress the second and third features and then create the curved sketch feature with a hole on the top face of the model.

e. Pattern the last feature using the **Circular Pattern** tool. Finally, you will mirror all the three instances of the circular pattern on the bottom face of the model.

f. After creating the feature you will edit them as mentioned in the tutorial.

Creating the Base Feature

1. Open a new part file and then create the base feature on the XY plane. Take the origin as the center of the two circles in the sketch of the base feature.

> **Tip**. *While creating the sketch for the base feature, it is recommended that you select the origin as the center of both the circles. The origin is the point at which the X and Y axes meet in the drawing window. The reason for this is that the origin is not only the point at which the X and Y axes meet in the sketching environment, but also the point at which all the three planes meet in the **Part** mode. Now, if this point is selected as the center of the base feature, you can use the default XZ plane to create the offset planes. If this point is not selected as the center of the base feature, you will have to first create a work plane tangent to the cylindrical face of the base feature. After creating a tangent work plane, you will have to use it to define the offset work plane.*

2. Extrude the sketch to a distance of 225 mm using the **Mid-plane** option.

The reason of extruding the sketch using the **Mid-plane** option is that you can use the XY plane as the plane for mirroring the features on the top face of the model to the bottom face of the model. If the base feature is not extruded using the **Mid-plane** option, you will have to create a new work plane for mirroring the features. The base feature of the model is shown in Figure 6-34.

Figure 6-34 Base feature of the model

Creating the Join Features on the Cylindrical Faces of the Base Feature

Since the base feature was created taking the origin as the center of the circles, you can use the XZ plane to create the offset work plane.

1. Create a new work plane at an offset of -160 mm from the XZ plane.

    The negative value will ensure that the work plane is created toward the front side of the base feature and not toward the back side.

2. Define a new sketch plane on **Work Plane1** and draw the sketch of the next feature. Use the origin of new sketch plane for drawing circle. Extrude it using the **To Next** extents option.

3. Similarly, define a new work plane at an offset of 325 mm from **Work Plane1**. Define a new sketch plane on **Work Plane2** and create the second join feature. The model after creating the two join features is shown in Figure 6-35.

Creating the Counterbore Hole and Drilled Holes on the Front Face of the Second Feature

1. Define a new sketch plane on the front face of the second feature. Use the center of the reference circle to create the counterbore hole.

2. Similarly, create one of the three smaller holes on the front face of the second feature.

3. Create a circular pattern containing three instances of the holes. The model after creating the counterbore hole and the three smaller drilled holes is shown in Figure 6-36.

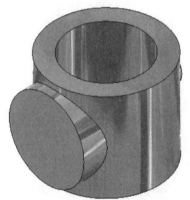 

Figure 6-35 *Model after creating the join features*   *Figure 6-36* *Model after creating the holes*

Suppressing the Features

Since the features other than the base feature are not required in creating the remaining features in the model, you can suppress them. This will reduce the complicacy of the model and it will be easier for you to create the remaining features.

1. Right-click on **Extrusion2** in the browser and choose **Suppress Features**.

    You will notice that the counterbore hole and the three drilled holes are also suppressed. This is because these holes are dependent on the second join feature as they are created on it.

2. Similarly, right-click on **Extrusion3** in the browser and choose **Suppress Features**.

Creating the Join Feature on the Top Face of the Model

1. Define a new sketch plane on the top face of the model and draw the sketch of the join feature. Include the circle in the sketch so that the hole is created automatically.

2. Extrude the sketch to a distance of 32 mm. The model after creating the join feature on the top face of the model is shown in Figure 6-37.

Creating the Circular Pattern of the Feature

1. Create circular pattern of the feature on the top face of the model. The circular pattern should have three instances as shown in Figure 6-38.

Figure 6-37 *Join feature on the top face*   *Figure 6-38* *After creating the circular pattern*

Mirroring the Features on the Bottom Face of the Model

Since the base feature was extruded using the **Mid-plane** option, you can use the XY plane for mirroring the feature on the bottom face of the model. This is because the base feature is extruded equally in both the directions of the XY plane.

1. Invoke the **Mirror Feature** tool and then select the join feature on the top face of the model and the circular pattern as the features to be mirrored.

2. Select the XY plane as the mirror plane and then mirror the features and choose **OK**.

Tip. *You can specify the features to be mirrored by selecting them on the graphics screen or in the browser.*

Unsuppressing the Features

1. Right-click on **Extrusion2** in the browser and choose **Unsuppress Features**. The second feature as well as the holes will be unsuppressed.

2. Right-click on **Extrusion3** and then choose **Unsuppress Features** from the shortcut menu to unsuppress the third feature also. The model after creating all the features is shown in Figure 6-39.

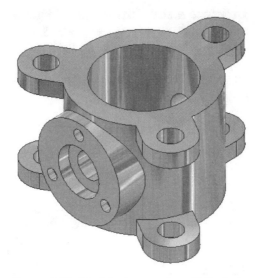

Figure 6-39 *Model after creating all the features*

Modifying the Dimensions of the Feature on the Top Face of the Model

Out of the three instances of the join feature on the top face of the model and three instances on the bottom face, only one was actually sketched. Rest all were either created using the **Circular Pattern** tool or the **Mirror Feature** tool. Therefore, if you modify the original feature, rest of the features will be automatically modified.

1. Right-click on **Extrusion4** in the browser to display the shortcut menu. In this menu, choose **Show Dimensions**, see Figure 6-40.

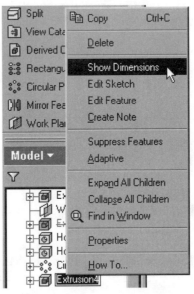

Figure 6-40 *Editing the feature using the browser*

The basic sketch of the feature will be displayed on the feature along with the dimensions. You can double-click on any dimension to display the **Edit Dimension** toolbar. This toolbar can be used to edit the selected dimension value.

2.   Double-click on the 175 mm dimension to display the **Edit Dimension** toolbar.

3.   In this toolbar, enter the dimension value as 200 mm. Press the ENTER key.

You will notice that the temporary sketch of the feature that is displayed on the screen is modified due to the change in the dimension value. However, the features are not modified. This is because the features will be modified only when you choose the **Update** button from the **Command Bar**.

4.   Choose the **Update** button from the **Command Bar**. All six instances of the feature will be automatically modified. The final model for Tutorial 3 is shown in Figure 6-41.

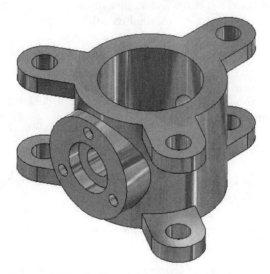

Figure 6-41 Final model after editing the features

Note
While drawing the sketch for the feature that you edited in the last step, if you do not apply the coincident constraint between the lower endpoint of lines of sketch and the outer circle of the base feature, the feature will be separated from the base feature when you edit it. You can also apply the concentric constraint between the arc of the sketch and the outer circle of the base feature to avoid separation.

5.   Save the model with the name given below:

\PersonalProject\c06**Tutorial3.ipt**

Self-Evaluation Test

Answer the following questions and then compare your answers with the answers provided at the end of this chapter.

1. Most of the designs require editing, either during creation or after creation. (T/F)

2. In Autodesk Inventor, all the editing operations are performed using the toolbars. (T/F)

3. You can also edit a hole feature by right-clicking on it in the browser and then choosing **Show Dimensions**. (T/F)

4. You can also display the dimensions of a feature on the model by double-clicking on it in the browser. (T/F)

5. If you right-click on the third extruded feature in a model and choose **Edit Feature** from the shortcut menu, the _____ dialog box will be displayed.

6. The features edited using the dimensions can be updated by choosing the _____ button from the _____.

7. The features in the model can be suppressed by right-clicking on them and choosing _____ from the shortcut menu.

8. The _____ dialog box is used to paste the copied features in a new file.

9. The _____ button in the **Paste Features** dialog box is chosen to adjust the preview of the pasted feature on the selected plane.

10. If the feature that you select to suppress has some dependent features, they will also be _____.

Review Questions

Answer the following questions.

1. Autodesk Inventor allows you to copy the features from one file to the other. (T/F)

2. Autodesk Inventor allows you to edit the sketches of the sketch features. (T/F)

3. When you choose the option of displaying the dimensions of the feature for editing, the dimensions will be retained on the screen even after the editing operation is over. (T/F)

4. The feature to be copied can be rotated at any angle. (T/F)

5. After editing the sketch of the feature, you have to make sure the sketch is still a closed loop. (T/F)

6. The dependent features will also be suppressed along with the parent feature. (T/F)

7. You can specify whether or not you want to delete the dependent sketches and features. (T/F)

8. In the **Paste Features** dialog box, you can specify whether you want to paste only the selected feature or the dependent features also. (T/F)

9. All the suppressed features are displayed in light gray color in the browser. (T/F)

10. If you edit a feature using the browser, you do not need to update it to view the effect of the editing operation. (T/F)

Exercises

Exercise 1

Create the model of Slide Bracket shown in Figure 6-42a. The dimensions of the model are shown in Figure 6-42b, Figure 6-42c, and Figure 6-42d. After creating the model, save it with the name given below:

\PersonalProject\c06**Exercise1.ipt**   (**Expected time: 45 min**)

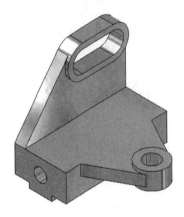

Figure 6-42a *Model for Exercise 1*

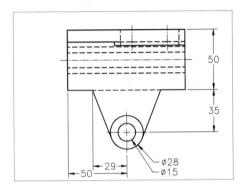

Figure 6-42b *Top view of the model*

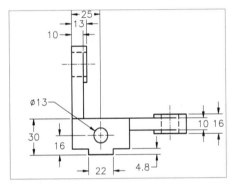

Figure 6-42c *Left side view of the model*

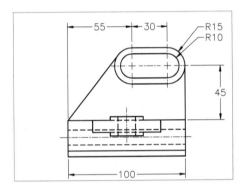

Figure 6-42d *Front view of the model*

Exercise 2

Create the model shown in Figure 6-43a. The dimensions of the model are shown in Figure 6-43b, Figure 6-43c, and Figure 6-43d. After creating the model, save it with the name given below:

\PersonalProject\c06**Exercise2.ipt**   **(Expected time: 45 min)**

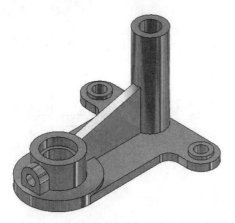

Figure 6-43a *Model for Exercise 2*

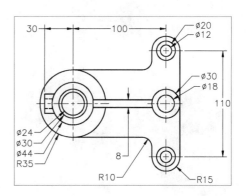

Figure 6-43b *Top view of the model*

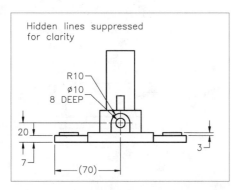

Figure 6-43c *Left side view of the model*

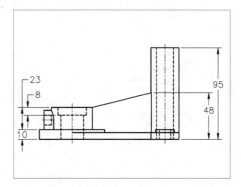

Figure 6-43d *Front view of the model*

Exercise 3

Create the model shown in Figure 6-44a. The dimensions of the model are shown in Figure 6-44b, Figure 6-44c, and Figure 6-44d. After creating the model, save it with the name given below:

\PersonalProject\c06**Exercise3.ipt**   **(Expected time: 45 min)**

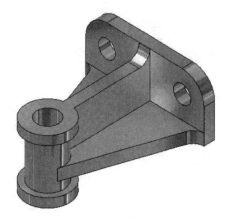

Figure 6-44a *Model for Exercise 3*

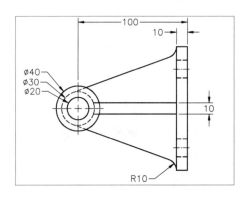

Figure 6-44b *Top view of the model*

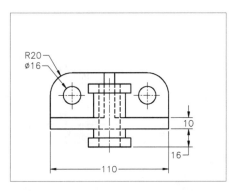

Figure 6-44c *Left side view of the model*

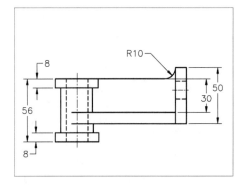

Figure 6-44d *Front view of the model*

Exercise 4

Create the model shown in Figure 6-45a. The dimensions of the model are shown in Figure 6-45b, Figure 6-45c, and Figure 6-45d. After creating the model, save it with the name given below:

\PersonalProject\c06**Exercise4.ipt**   **(Expected time: 45 min)**

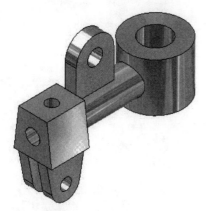

Figure 6-45a *Model for Exercise 4*

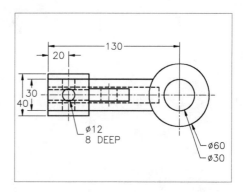

Figure 6-45b *Top view of the model*

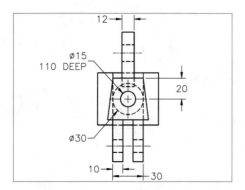

Figure 6-45c *Left side view of the model*

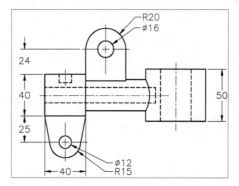

Figure 6-45d *Front view of the model*

Answers to Self-Evaluation Test
1. T, **2.** F, **3.** T, **4.** T, **5. Extrude: Extrusion3**, **6. Update, Command Bar**, **7. Suppress Features**, **8. Paste Features**, **9. Refresh**, **10.** suppressed

Chapter 7

Advanced Modeling Tools-II

Learning Objectives

After completing this chapter you will be able to:

- *Sweep the sketches and create sweep features.*
- *Create lofted features.*
- *Create coils.*
- *Create internal or external threads.*
- *Create shell features.*
- *Apply drafts on the faces of a model.*
- *Split the faces of a model or the complete model.*

ADVANCED MODELING TOOLS

The first seven advanced modeling tools were discussed in Chapter 5, Advanced Modeling Tools-I. In this chapter you will learn about the remaining advanced modeling tools.

Creating Sweep Features

Toolbar:	Features > Sweep
Panel bar:	Features > Sweep

The next advanced modeling tool is the **Sweep** tool. This tool is used to create sweep features. A sweep feature is created when a closed sketch is extruded along an open or a closed path. Therefore, to create the sweep feature, you need two unconsumed sketches: a closed sketch (also called profile) and a path. Remember that in Autodesk Inventor, the sweep feature will be created only if the profile and the path intersect at a point. If the profile do not intersect with the path, the sweep feature will not be created. The path for the sweep feature is created using the usual method of creating the sketches. It can be a combination of the sketcher entities like lines, arcs, circles, splines, and ellipses.

As mentioned earlier, the profile and the path should intersect. Therefore, after you have finished drawing the path, create a work plane using the start point of the path and then create the profile on that work plane. To create a work plane using the path, exit the sketching environment. Choose **Work Plane** from the **Features** panel bar. Now, select the start point of the path and then select a line segment to which the resultant work plane will be normal. However, if the path does not have a straight line segment, from the browser select a plane to which the resultant work plane will be parallel. Figure 7-1 shows a profile and a 2D path and Figure 7-2 shows the resultant sweep feature.

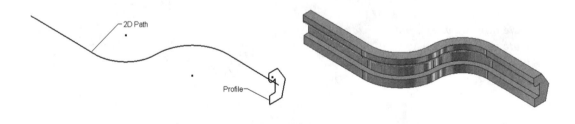

Figure 7-1 Path and profile for sweep   *Figure 7-2 Resultant sweep feature*

To create the sweep feature, choose **Sweep** from the **Features** panel bar. The **Sweep** dialog box will be displayed as shown in Figure 7-3. The options under this dialog box are discussed next.

Shape Area

The options under this area are used to select the profile and the path of the sweep feature.

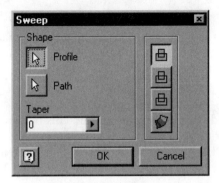

Figure 7-3 **Sweep** *dialog box*

You can also specify taper angle for the sweep feature using the options in this area. The options under this area are discussed next.

Profile

The **Profile** button is chosen to select the profile for the sweep feature. Remember that the profile has to be a closed loop for creating the solid sweep feature. When you invoke the **Sweep** dialog box, the **Profile** button will be selected by default and you will be prompted to select the profile for the sweep feature.

Path

The **Path** button is chosen to select the path for the sweep feature.

Taper

The **Taper** edit box is used to define the taper angle for the sweep feature. A positive taper angle will taper the sweep feature outwards and a negative taper angle will taper the sweep feature inwards. Figure 7-4 shows a sweep feature with a positive taper angle and Figure 7-5 shows the sweep feature with a negative taper angle.

Figure 7-4 *Sweep feature created with a positive taper angle*

Figure 7-5 *Sweep feature created with a negative taper angle*

Join

The **Join** button is the first button provided under the area that is on the right side of the **Shape** area. This button is chosen to create a sweep feature by adding material to the model. Figure 7-6 shows the sweep feature created using the **Join** operation.

Cut

The **Cut** button is provided below the **Join** button. This button is chosen to create a sweep feature by removing material from the model. If the sweep feature is the first feature, this button will not be available. Figure 7-7 shows the sweep feature created using the **Cut** operation.

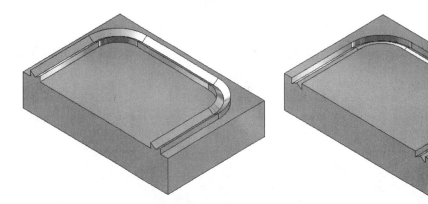

Figure 7-6 *Sweep feature created using the* ***Join*** *operation*   *Figure 7-7* *Sweep feature created using the* ***Cut*** *operation*

Intersect

The **Intersect** button is provided below the **Cut** button and is used only when you have an existing feature. This means that this button will not be available if the sweep feature is the first feature in the model. This operation is used to create a sweep feature such that the material common to the profile and the existing feature is retained. The remaining material is removed from the model.

Surface

The **Surface** button is provided below the **Intersect** button and if chosen, the resultant sweep will be a surface model. The profile for the sweep surface can be an open entity.

Creating Lofted Features

Toolbar:	Features > Loft
Panel bar:	Features > Loft

 Lofted features are the features that are created by blending more than one dissimilar geometries together. These dissimilar geometries may or may not be parallel to each other. The sketches for the solid loft features should be closed profiles. However, if you are creating a surface model, the sketches can be open profiles. Figure 7-8 shows three dissimilar sketches before lofting and Figure 7-9 shows the resultant lofted feature.

Figure 7-8 *Three dissimilar sketches before blending*

Figure 7-9 *Feature created after blending the sketches*

In Autodesk Inventor, lofted features are created using the **Loft** tool. When you invoke this tool, the **Loft** dialog box is displayed as shown in Figure 7-10. The options under this dialog box are discussed next.

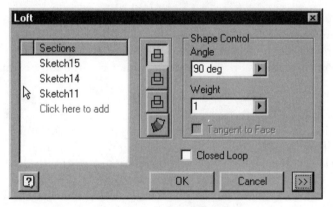

Figure 7-10 *Loft dialog box*

Sections Area

When you invoke the **Loft** dialog box, you will be prompted to select the sketches for creating the loft feature. The **Sections** area displays all the sketches that you have selected for creating the loft feature. When you select the sketches, an arrow is displayed on the graphics screen. This arrow displays the path for the loft feature. For example, if you select Sketch15, Sketch14, and Sketch11 in the same sequence, there will be two arrows. The first arrow will point from Sketch15 to Sketch14 and the second arrow will point from Sketch14 to Sketch11. This suggests that the resultant loft feature is a blending between Sketch15 - Sketch14 and Sketch14 - Sketch11.

Tip. *You can also modify the sequence in which the sketches are selected using the **Sections** area. To modify the sequence, select the sketch and drag it above or below the other sketch. The arrow direction will also change automatically in the preview of the model.*

Join

The **Join** button is the first button in the area provided on the right of the **Sections** area. This button is chosen to create a loft feature by adding material to the model.

Cut

The **Cut** button is provided below the **Join** button. This button is chosen to create a loft feature by removing material common to the loft and the model. This button will not be available if the loft feature is the first feature.

Intersect

The **Intersect** button is provided below the **Cut** button and is chosen to create a loft feature by retaining the material common to the loft and the model. The remaining material will be removed from the model. This button will also not be available if the loft feature is the first feature.

Surface

The **Surface** button is provided below the **Intersect** button and is chosen to create a lofted surface. The sketches for creating lofted surfaces can be open profiles.

Shape Control Area

The options in the **Shape Control** area are used to control the shape of the lofted feature. You can control the angle, weight, and tangency of the lofted feature using the options provided under this area. All the options for controlling the shape of the lofted feature are discussed next.

Angle

The **Angle** edit box will be available only when the value in the **Weight** edit box is more than zero (default value). This edit box is used to define the angle at the start and end section of the loft. Remember that you cannot define an angle for the intermediate sketches. To specify the value of the angle at the start section, select the first sketch from the **Sections** area and then set the value in this edit box. Similarly, to specify the value of the angle at the end section, select the last sketch from the **Sections** area and then set the value in this edit box. Figure 7-11 shows different angle values at the start and end sections of the loft.

> **Tip**. *An angle value greater than 90° will create an obtuse section in the loft feature. Similarly, an angle value less than 90° will create an acute section in the loft feature.*

Weight

The **Weight** edit box is used to specify the distance to which the resultant feature will maintain the angle value at the start or the end sections. Greater the value of weight, more will be the distance to which the angle value will be maintained. Similar to the angle values, this value can also be defined only for the first and the last sketch. You cannot define this value for the intermediate sketches. To define the weight value, select the first or the last sketch from the **Sections** area and then define the value in this edit box. Figure 7-11 shows different weight values at the start and end sections of the loft.

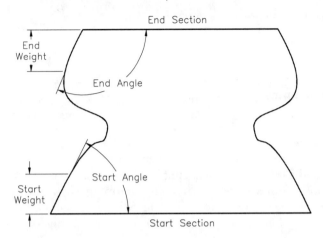

Figure 7-11 *Parameters associated with loft feature*

Tangent to Face
The **Tangent to Face** check box will be available only if the sketch for the start or the end section is created on the planar face of an existing feature. If this check box is selected, the resultant loft feature will be tangent to the adjacent faces of the planar face on which the sketch was drawn. Remember that you cannot define the angle for the section if the **Tangent to Face** check box is selected. This means that the **Angle** edit box will not be available if this check box is selected.

Closed Loop
The **Closed Loop** check box is selected to close the loft feature by joining the end section with the start section. Figure 7-12 shows a loft feature created with this check box cleared and Figure 7-13 shows a loft feature created with this check box selected.

Figure 7-12 *Open-ended loft feature*

Figure 7-13 *Closed-ended loft feature*

More

The **More** button is the button with two arrows and is provided on the lower right corner of the **Loft** dialog box. When you choose this button, the **Loft** dialog box expands displaying the **Point Mapping** area, see Figure 7-14.

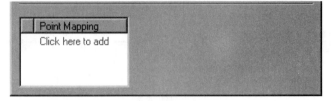

*Figure 7-14 **Point Mapping** area displayed upon choosing the **More** button*

Point Mapping Area

The **Point Mapping** area is used to select the points on the sketches that will be used to map the shape of the loft feature. Mapping in a lofted feature is generally done to reduce the twist in the loft feature. To select a point for mapping, click on **Click here to add**. You will be prompted to select a point for mapping. Select one point each on all the sketches. The loft feature will follow the path created by the mapping points, see Figure 7-15 through Figure 7-18.

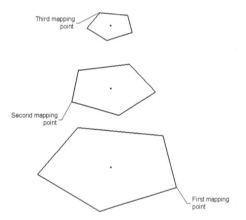

Figure 7-15 Defining the mapping points

Figure 7-16 Resultant loft feature

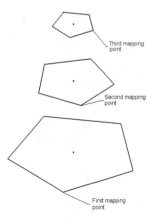

Figure 7-17 Defining the mapping points

Figure 7-18 Resultant loft feature

Creating Coil Features

Toolbar:	Features > Coil
Panel bar:	Features > Coil

 A coil feature is created by sweeping a profile about a helical path. Examples of the coil feature are springs, filaments of light bulbs, and so on. A spring created using the coil feature is shown in Figure 7-19.

Figure 7-19 Spring created using the coil feature

The coil features are created with the help of the **Coil** dialog box, see Figure 7-20. This dialog box is displayed by using the **Coil** tool. To create a coil feature in Autodesk Inventor, you need just the profile. Depending upon the parameters defined in the **Coil** dialog box, an imaginary helical path will be created and the profile will be swept about that path. Therefore, to create a coil feature you need only one unconsumed sketch. This sketch will define the profile of the coil section. The options under the **Coil** dialog box are discussed next.

Coil Shape Tab

The options under this tab are used to select the profile of the coil feature and the axis about which the imaginary helical path will be created. You can also specify whether the coil will be created in clockwise direction or counterclockwise direction using the options in this tab. All the options under this tab are discussed next.

Shape Area

The options under this area are used to select the profile and the axis of the coil.

Profile. The **Profile** button is chosen to select the profile of the coil. If the drawing consists of a single unconsumed sketch, it will be automatically selected as the profile of the coil feature.

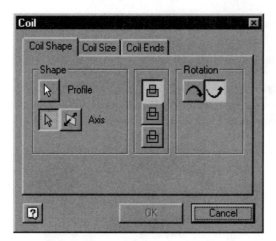

Figure 7-20 Coil Shape tab of the Coil dialog box

Axis. The **Axis** button is chosen to select the axis for creating the coil feature. When you select the axis, an imaginary helical path will be created around the selected axis. The preview of the path will be displayed in the graphics window. The entities that can be selected as the axis for creating the coil feature are work axes, linear edges of a model, line segments, and so on. You can reverse the direction of the path by choosing the **Flip** button provided on the right of the **Axis** button.

Join

The **Join** button is the first button in the area between the **Shape** area and the **Rotation** area. This operation is used to create a coil feature by adding material to the model, see Figure 7-21.

Cut

The **Cut** button is provided below the **Join** button. This operation is used to create a coil feature by removing material from the model, see Figure 7-22.

Figure 7-21 Coil feature created on a cylinder using the Join operation

Figure 7-22 Coil feature created on a cylinder using the Cut operation

Note

*The **Cut** operation of the **Coil** tool can be used for creating internal or external threads in the model. However, Autodesk Inventor provides the **Thread** tool for directly creating the threads. The use of this tool will be discussed later in this chapter.*

Intersect

The **Intersect** button is provided below the **Cut** button. This operation is used to create a coil feature by retaining material common to the model and the coil. The remaining material will be removed.

Note

*The area with the **Join**, **Cut**, and the **Intersect** button will not be available if the coil is the first feature.*

Coil Size Tab

The options under this tab are used to define the type of method and the other parameters that will be used for creating the coil, see Figure 7-23.

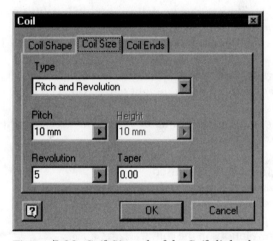

Figure 7-23 Coil Size tab of the Coil dialog box

Type

The **Type** drop-down list is used to select the method for creating the coil feature. The various types of methods that are available in this drop-down list for creating the coil are discussed next.

> **Pitch and Revolution**. The **Pitch and Revolution** method is used to create the coil by defining the pitch and the number of revolutions in the coil. The pitch value can be defined in the **Pitch** edit box and the number of revolutions can be defined in the **Revolution** edit box. Both these edit boxes will be available when you select the **Pitch and Revolution** option from the **Type** drop-down list. You can also define a taper angle for the coil feature in the **Taper** edit box. A positive taper angle will taper the coil out and a negative taper angle will taper the coil in. Figure 7-24 shows a coil created with a positive taper and Figure 7-25 shows a coil created with a negative taper.

Figure 7-24 *Coil feature created with a positive taper angle*

Figure 7-25 *Coil feature created with a negative taper angle*

Revolution and Height. The **Revolution and Height** method is used to create the coil by defining the number of revolutions in the coil and the total height of the coil. The number of revolutions can be defined in the **Revolution** edit box and the height of the coil can be defined in the **Height** edit box. Both these edit boxes will be available when you select the **Revolution and Height** option from the **Type** drop-down list.

Pitch and Height. The **Pitch and Height** method is used to create the coil by defining the pitch of the coil and the total height of the coil. The value of pitch can be defined in the **Pitch** edit box and the height of the coil can be defined in the **Height** edit box. Both these edit boxes will be available when you select the **Pitch and Height** option from the **Type** drop-down list.

Spiral. The **Spiral** method is used to create a spiral coil in a single plane. The spiral coil can be created using only the pitch of the coil and the number of revolutions in the coil. Since the spiral coil is created in a single plane, the **Height** edit box will not be available when you use this method. Also, you cannot define the taper angle for a spiral coil and so the **Taper** edit box also will not be available. Figure 7-26 shows a spiral coil.

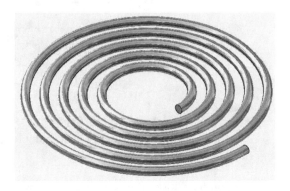

Figure 7-26 *Spiral coil*

Coil Ends Tab

The options under this tab are used to specify the type of ends of the imaginary helical path that will be used to create the coil, see Figure 7-27. These options are discussed next.

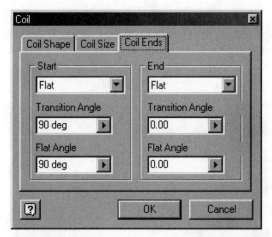

*Figure 7-27 **Coil Ends** tab of the **Coil** dialog box*

Start Area

The options under the **Start** area are used to specify the end type at the start section of the imaginary helical path. The type of start section can be selected from the drop-down list in this area. These options are discussed next.

> **Natural**. The **Natural** option is the default option that is selected in this drop-down list. If this option is selected, no other option in this area is available.

> **Flat**. If the **Flat** option is selected, you can specify a different start section of the helical path. The other options in this area will be available only if this option is selected.

> **Transition Angle**. The **Transition Angle** edit box is used to specify the angle of transition of the coil at the start section of the coil. This option works in association with the number of revolutions in the coil and is generally used in coils with less than one revolution. The value of the transition angle can vary from 0° to 360°.

> **Flat Angle**. The **Flat Angle** edit box is used to specify the angle through which the coil will extend beyond the transition at the start section of the coil. The value of the transition angle can vary from 0° to 360°.

End Area

The options under the **End** area are similar to those discussed under the **Start** area. The only difference being that these options are used to specify the end type at the end section of the imaginary helical path.

Creating Threads

Toolbar:	Features > Threads
Panel bar:	Features > Threads

Autodesk Inventor allows you to directly create internal or external threading in a model. Internal threads are the threads that are created on the inner surface of a feature. For example, the threads created on the hole inside a cylinder are called internal threads, see Figure 7-28. External threads are the threads that are created on the outer surface of a feature or a model. For example, the threads created on a bolt, see Figure 7-29.

Figure 7-28 *Internal threads in a cylinder*   **Figure 7-29** *External threads on a bolt*

You can create the threads using the **Thread** tool. When you invoke this tool, the **Thread Feature** dialog box is displayed. The various options provided under different tabs of the **Thread Feature** dialog box are discussed next.

Location Tab

The options under the **Location** tab are used to define the location, length, and offset of the threads, see Figure 7-30. These options are discussed next.

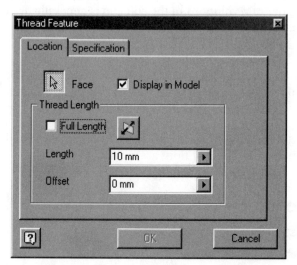

Figure 7-30 **Location** *tab of the* **Thread Feature** *dialog box*

Face

The **Face** button is chosen to select the face on which the threads will be created. When you invoke this dialog box, this button will be automatically chosen and you will be prompted to select the face on which the threads will be created.

Display in Model

The **Display in Model** check box is selected to display the threads in the model. If this check box is cleared, the threads will be created but will not be displayed in the model. The threads will be displayed only in the browser.

Thread Length Area

The options under the **Thread Length** area are used to specify the length of the threads. These options are discussed next.

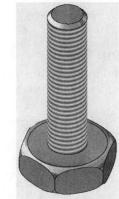

Full Length. The **Full Length** check box is selected to create the threads through the length of the selected face. By default, this check box is selected and therefore, no other option in the **Thread Length** area will be available. Figure 7-31 shows a bolt with the threads created through the length of the bolt. If you clear this check box, the remaining options in this area will be activated.

Flip. The **Flip** button is chosen to reverse the direction of thread creation.

Figure 7-31 Full length threads on a bolt

Length. The **Length** edit box is used to define the length to which the threads will be created on the selected face.

Offset. The **Offset** edit box is used to define the distance by which the threads should be offset from the starting edge of the face selected for creating the threads. By default, the value of the offset distance is zero. If you define any offset value, the start point of the threads will move away from the start of the face selected for threading. Figure 7-32 shows the threads created at an offset distance of 0 mm and Figure 7-33 shows the threads created at an offset distance of 20 mm.

Note

*You cannot define a negative value for the length of the threads or the offset of the threads. If you want to create the threads in the opposite direction, choose the **Flip** button. The direction of creating the threads will reverse automatically.*

Figure 7-32 *Threads at on offset of 0 mm*   *Figure 7-33* *Threads at on offset of 20 mm*

Specification Tab

The options under this tab are used to define the type of threads that will be created and the other parameters related with the type of threads, see Figure 7-34.

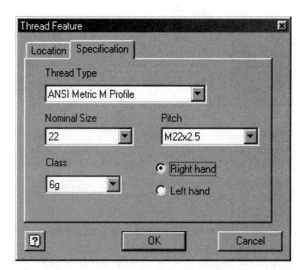

Figure 7-34 Specification tab of the Thread Feature dialog box

Thread Type

The **Thread Type** drop-down list is used to select the predefined thread types. There are some predefined thread types that are saved in a spreadsheet. This spreadsheet is stored in the directory \Autodesk\Inventor\Design Data. You can also add customized thread types in this spreadsheet and use them in the model.

Nominal Size

The **Nominal Size** drop-down list is used to select the nominal diameter of the threads. Depending upon the type of thread selected from the **Thread Type** drop-down list, the values in this drop-down list will change. You can select the required value of the diameter of the threads from this drop-down list.

Pitch
The **Pitch** drop-down list is used to select the pitch of threads. The pitch value will depend upon the type of threads and the nominal diameter of the threads.

Class
The **Class** drop-down list is used to select the predefined class of threads. The class of the threads will depend upon the face on which the threads will be created.

Note
*For some of the thread types, the **Pitch** and the **Class** drop-down lists will not be available.*

Creating Shell Features

Toolbar:	Features > Shell
Panel bar:	Features > Shell

Shelling is defined as the process of scooping out material from a model and making it hollow from inside. The resultant model will be just a structure of walls with cavity inside. You can also remove some of the faces of the model or apply different wall thicknesses to different faces of the model. Figure 7-35 shows a model with shelling and with the front face removed.

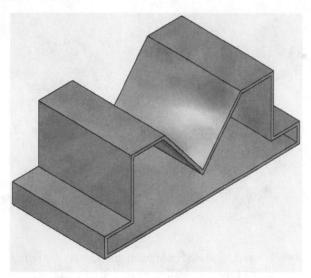

Figure 7-35 Model after creating the shell feature

In Autodesk Inventor, the shell feature is created using the **Shell** tool. When you invoke this tool, the **Shell** dialog box is displayed, see Figure 7-36. The options under this dialog box are discussed next.

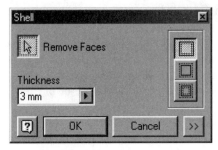

*Figure 7-36 **Shell** dialog box*

Remove Faces

The **Remove Faces** button is used to select the faces of the model that you want to remove. When you invoke this dialog box, this button will be chosen by default and you will be prompted to select the faces to be removed from the model. The selected faces will be displayed in blue color. Figure 7-37 shows the face selected to be removed and Figure 7-38 shows the resultant hollow model.

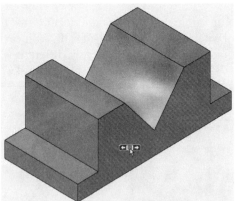
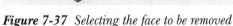

Figure 7-37 Selecting the face to be removed

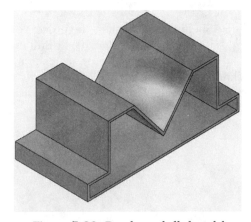

Figure 7-38 Resultant shelled model

Tip. *If by mistake you have selected a wrong face to remove, you can remove it from the selection set. This is done by pressing the SHIFT key and selecting the face again. The face will be removed from the current selection set.*

Thickness

The **Thickness** edit box is used to specify the wall thickness of the resultant hollow model. The resultant shell feature will have the wall thickness that you specify in this edit box.

Inside

The **Inside** button is the first button in the area provided on the right of the **Shell** dialog box. This button is chosen to define the wall thickness inside the model with respect to the outer faces of the model. In this case, the outer faces of the model will be considered as the outer walls of the resultant shell feature.

Outside

The **Outside** button is provided below the **Inside** button. This button is chosen to define the wall thickness outside the model with respect to the outer faces of the model. In this case, the outer faces of the model will be considered as the inner walls of the resultant shell feature.

Both

The **Both** button is provided below the **Outside** button and is chosen to calculate the wall thickness equally in both the directions of the outer faces of the model.

More

The **More** button is the button with two arrows and is provided on the lower right corner of the **Shell** dialog box. When you choose this button, the **Shell** dialog box will expand and display the **Unique face thickness** area, see Figure 7-39. Using the options in this area you can select the faces and apply different wall thicknesses to them. To select the faces, click on **Click here to add**. You will be prompted to select the surfaces to apply different wall thicknesses. The thicknesses of these

Figure 7-39 More options

selected surfaces can be defined in the **Thickness** column of the **Unique face thickness** area. Figure 7-40 shows a model with different wall thicknesses applied to different faces.

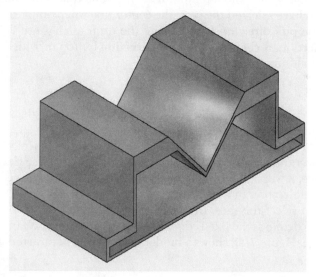

Figure 7-40 Shell feature with different wall thicknesses

Applying Face Draft

Toolbar:	Features > Face Draft
Panel bar:	Features > Face Draft

Face draft is a process of tapering the outer faces of a model for its easy removal from casting during manufacturing. In Autodesk Inventor, face draft can be applied with the help of the **Face Draft** tool. When you invoke this tool, the **Face Draft** dialog box will be displayed, see Figure 7-41. The options under this dialog box are discussed next.

*Figure 7-41 **Face Draft** dialog box*

Pull Direction

The **Pull Direction** is the direction defined by a plane that will be used to apply the face draft. The draft angle for the selected faces will be calculated using the plane selected to define the pull direction. When you invoke the **Face Draft** dialog box, this button will be automatically chosen and you will be prompted to select the pull direction. If you move the cursor close to any face, it will be highlighted and a temporary center line that is normal to the face will be displayed. Once you have selected the face, the center line will be replaced by an arrow. This arrow will define the pull direction for applying the draft angles, see Figure 7-42. You can reverse the pull direction by choosing the **Flip Direction** button provided on the right of the **Pull Direction** button.

Faces

The **Faces** button is chosen to select the faces on which the draft angle will be applied. If the selected face has some tangent faces, they will also be selected for applying the face draft. After you have selected the pull direction, this button will be automatically chosen and you will be prompted to select the faces and the fixed edges to apply the face draft. If you move the cursor close to a face, it will be highlighted and an arrow will be displayed on that face. This arrow will define the direction in which the draft angle will be applied. Depending upon the point that is used to select the face, the nearest edge parallel to the pull direction will be selected. This edge is define as the fixed edge. The direction of the draft angle will be calculated using this fixed edge. Figure 7-42 shows a model with various parameters associated with the face draft.

Draft Angle

The **Draft Angle** edit box is used to specify a draft angle for the selected faces. Remember that the value of the draft angle should be more than 0° but less than 90°.

Note
*The face draft feature will be displayed as **TaperEdge** in the browser.*

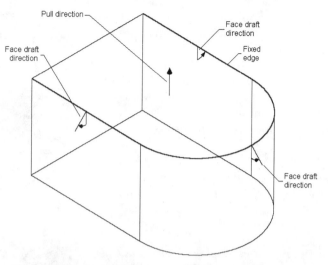

Figure 7-42 Various parameters associated with face draft

Figure 7-43 shows a model after applying the face draft using the tangent edge of the top face as the fixed edge and with pull direction upwards. Figure 7-44 shows a model after applying the face draft using the same fixed edge but after reversing the pull direction using the **Flip Direction** button. In both these figures the value of the draft angle is 8°.

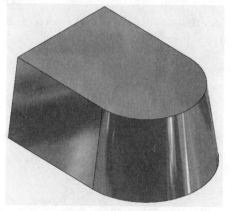

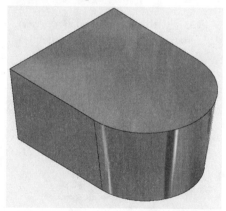

Figure 7-43 Face draft with pull direction upwards   *Figure 7-44 Pull direction downwards*

Creating Split Features

Toolbar:	Features > Split
Panel bar:	Features > Split

 In Autodesk Inventor, the **Split** tool can be used for splitting the entire part or for splitting the faces of the part. The two uses of the **Split** tool are discussed next.

Splitting the Faces

The **Split** tool allows you to split all or selected faces of a model. Generally, the faces of the model are split in order to apply different draft angles to both the sides of the model. When you invoke the **Split** tool, the **Split** dialog box will be displayed. By default, the **Split Face** button will be chosen from the **Method** area, see Figure 7-45. This button is chosen to split the faces of the model. Since the **Split Face** button is chosen in the **Split** dialog box, the options for splitting the faces will be available in this dialog box. These options are discussed next.

Figure 7-45 Face Split options in the Split dialog box

Split Tool

The **Split Tool** button is chosen to select the tool that will be used to split the faces of the model. The tools that can be used to split the faces are the sketched lines, planar faces, or work planes.

Tip. *If you want to use a sketched line to split the faces of the model, make sure the sketched line intersects the faces to be split in its current form or when it is projected normal to the plane on which it is sketched.*

Faces Area

The options under this area are used to select all the faces of the model for splitting or specify the faces for splitting. These options are discussed next.

All. If the **All** button is chosen, all the faces that the splitting tool intersects in its current form or when projected will be selected for splitting.

Select. The **Select** button is chosen to select the faces for splitting. The faces can be selected by choosing the **Faces to Split** button provided in the **Faces** area. When you choose the **Faces to Split** button, you will be prompted to select the faces that will be split. Only the faces that you select will be split and the remaining faces will remain unchanged even if they intersect the split tool. Figure 7-46 shows the sketched lines that will be used for splitting the model and Figure 7-47 shows the split faces.

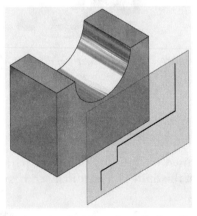

Figure 7-46 Sketched lines for splitting the faces of the model

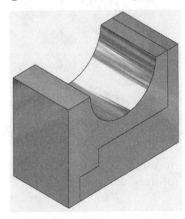

Figure 7-47 Model after splitting the faces and making the work plane invisible

Splitting the Model

The same **Split** tool can also be used to split the model. This is done by choosing the **Split Part** button from the **Method** area of the **Split** dialog box. When you choose this button, the options related to splitting the part will be displayed, see Figure 7-48. These options are discussed next.

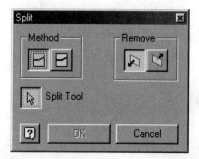

*Figure 7-48 **Part Split** options in the **Split** dialog box*

Split Tool

The **Split Tool** button is chosen to select the tool for splitting the model. Similar to splitting the faces, here also you can use either the sketched lines, planar faces, or work planes for splitting the model.

Remove Area

The buttons provided in this area are used to select the portion of the model to be removed after splitting. When you select the splitting tool, an arrow will appear on the model. This arrow will point toward the portion of the model that will be removed after splitting. If you want to remove the other portion, choose the other button in the **Remove** area.

Figure 7-49 shows the model before splitting and the work plane that will be used to split the model. Figure 7-50 shows the model after splitting and making the work plane invisible.

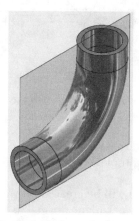

Figure 7-49 Model before splitting and the work plane for splitting the model

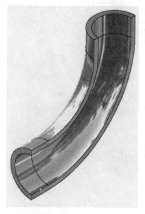

Figure 7-50 Model after splitting and making the work plane invisible

TUTORIAL

Tutorial 1

In this tutorial you will create the model shown in Figure 7-51a. The dimensions for the model are given in Figure 7-51b, Figure 7-51c, and Figure 7-51d. After creating the model, save it with the name given below:

\PersonalProject\c07**Tutorial1.ipt**   (**Expected time: 45min**)

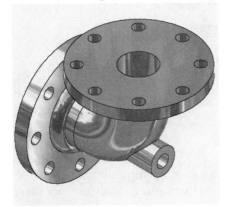

Figure 7-51a Model for Tutorial 1

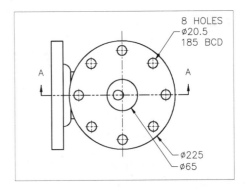

Figure 7-51b Top view of the model with hidden lines suppressed for clarity

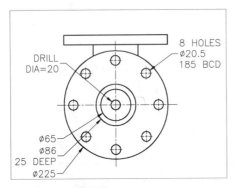

Figure 7-51c Left side view of the model with hidden lines suppressed for clarity

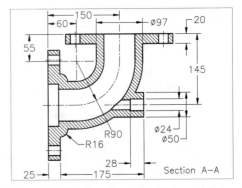

Figure 7-51d Sectioned front view of the model

Before you start creating the model, it is recommended that you outline the procedure for creating the model. The steps that will be followed to complete this model are listed below.

a. The base feature for the model is a sweep feature and will be created on the XZ plane. Create the path of the sweep feature and then define a work plane normal to the path and positioned at the start point of the path. Create the profile of the sweep feature on this work plane. Use the **Sweep** tool to create the sweep feature.

b. Create the inner cavity using the **Shell** tool.
c. Add the remaining join features on both ends of the sweep feature.
d. Create the hole patterns on both ends.
e. Define a work plane at an offset of 200 mm from the front face of the circular feature on the left face of the model. Create the join feature and counterbore hole on this plane.

Creating the Path for the Sweep Feature

As mentioned earlier, the base feature of the model is a sweep feature. To create the sweep feature, you will first create the path of the sweep feature. This path will be created on the XZ plane. The path for the sweep feature is a combination of two lines and an arc.

1. Open a new standard template and then create the path for the sweep feature on the XZ plane. Add the required dimensions. Exit the sketching environment and change the view to Isometric view. The path of the sweep feature is shown in Figure 7-52.

Creating a Work Plane Normal to the Start Section of the Path

After creating the path you will have to create a work plane normal to the start section of the path and positioned at the start point of the path. This work plane will be used to draw the profile for the sweep feature. The start section of the path can be either the line of 19 mm length or the line of 35 mm length. In this tutorial the line with 19 mm length is considered as the start section of the path.

1. Choose **Work Plane** from the **Features** panel bar. You will be prompted to define a work plane by highlighting and selecting the geometry.

2. Select the line of 19 mm length. You will again be prompted to define a work plane by highlighting and selecting the geometry. Select the start point of this line.

As you move the cursor close to the start point of the line, you will notice that the preview of the work plane is displayed at the start point of the path. As soon as you select the start point of the line, a work plane will be created that is normal to the line and is positioned at the start point of the line. The work plane at the start point of the path is shown in Figure 7-53.

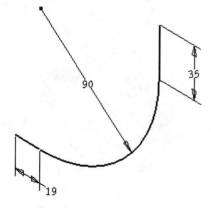

Figure 7-52 Path for the sweep feature

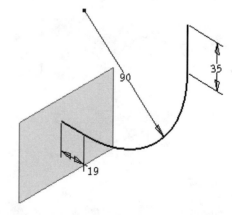

Figure 7-53 Work plane normal to the path

Creating the Profile for the Sweep Feature

The profile for the sweep feature will be created on the new work plane. Therefore, you will have to define a sketch plane on the new work plane.

1. Choose the **Sketch** button from the **Panel Bar** and then select the new work plane as the plane for sketching.

   As soon as you select the new work plane as the plane for sketching, the sketching environment will be activated. You will notice that the origin of the sketching environment coincides with the start point of the start section of the path. This will help you in positioning the profile of the sweep feature.

2. Create the sketch for the profile of the sweep feature. This profile will be a circle. Take the origin of the sketching environment as the center of the circle. Exit the sketching environment and change the view to Isometric view. The profile of the sweep feature is shown in Figure 7-54. In this figure, the work plane is made invisible.

 Tip. *You can avoid the shell feature by creating two circles as the profile for the sweep feature. When you sweep both the circles, the inner circle will be subtracted from the outer one. This way the inner cavity will be created automatically. However, in this tutorial, the **Shell** tool will be used to create the inner cavity.*

Sweeping the Profile

1. Choose the **Sweep** button from the **Features** panel bar to display the **Sweep** dialog box.

   Since the sweep is the first feature and there are only two unconsumed sketches, the profile will be automatically selected and highlighted. The path will also be selected automatically and displayed in blue color.

2. Choose **OK** in the **Sweep** dialog box. The sweep feature after changing the viewing direction is shown in Figure 7-55.

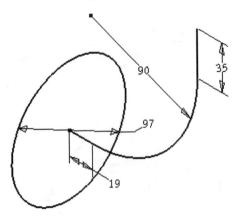

Figure 7-54 Profile for the sweep feature

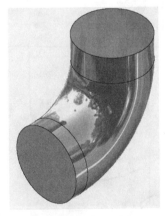

Figure 7-55 Sweep feature

Creating the Shell Feature

The shell feature will scoop out material from the sweep feature and will leave behind some wall thickness. However, you will have to remove the front face and the top face of the sweep feature in order to view the cavity inside.

1. Choose the **Shell** button from the **Features** toolbar to display the **Shell** dialog box. You will be prompted to select the surfaces to be removed.

2. Select the front and the top face of the sweep feature. Both the selected faces will be highlighted and displayed in blue color.

   The diameter of the inner cavity is 65 mm and the diameter of the sweep feature is 97 mm. Therefore, the resultant wall thickness is 32 mm. Since this value is in terms of diameter, the radius value will be 16 mm. Therefore, the resultant wall thickness is 16 mm.

3. Enter 16 mm in the **Thickness** edit box and choose the **OK** button. The model after creating the shell feature is shown in Figure 7-56.

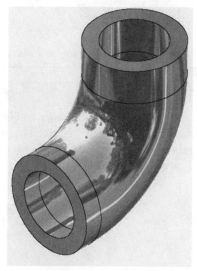

Figure 7-56 Base feature after creating the shell feature

Creating the Remaining Features

1. Create the remaining features by defining new sketch planes at the required faces. To create the join feature with fillet on the left face of the base feature, draw a circle of 129 mm diameter and extrude it to a distance of 16 mm. Then create the fillet of 16 mm on the outer edge of this feature.

   The join feature at the cylindrical tangent edge can be created by defining an offset work plane. The smaller holes can be copied from one of the cylindrical feature to the other using the **Paste Features** dialog box. The final model for Tutorial 1 is shown in Figure 7-57.

2.   Save the model with the name given below:

\PersonalProject\c07**Tutorial1.ipt**

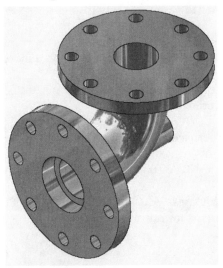

Figure 7-57 Final model for Tutorial 1

Tutorial 2

In this tutorial you will create a model of the joint shown in Figure 7-58a. The dimensions for the model are shown in Figure 7-58b and Figure 7-58c. The threads to be created are **ANSI Metric M Profile** with nominal size of 14 and pitch value of 14x2. The class of the threads is 6g. Make sure that the threads are right handed.   **(Expected time: 30 min)**

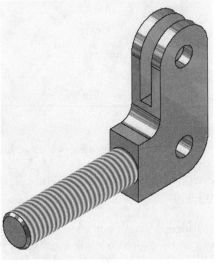

Figure 7-58a Solid model of the joint

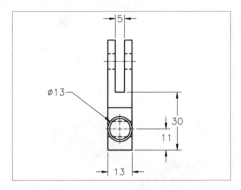

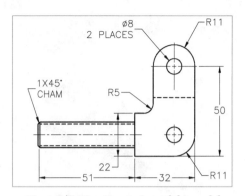

Figure 7-58b Left side view of the model

Figure 7-58c Front view of the model

As mentioned earlier, you should first outline the procedure for creating the model. The steps that will be followed to complete the model are listed below:

a. Create the base feature of the model on the YZ plane.
b. Define a new sketch plane on the right face of the base feature and create the cut feature.
c. Create the cylindrical join feature on the left face and then create the chamfer feature.
d. Finally, using the **Thread** tool, create the threads on the cylindrical join feature.

Create the Base Feature

1. Create the base feature of the model on the YZ plane as shown in Figure 7-59.

Creating the Cut Feature in the Base Feature

1. Create the cut feature by defining a sketch plane on the right face of the base feature as shown in Figure 7-60.

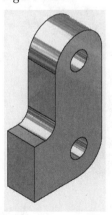

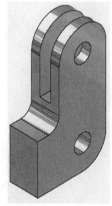

Figure 7-59 Base feature for the model

Figure 7-60 Model after creating the cut feature

Creating the Join Feature and the Chamfer Feature

1. Create the cylindrical join feature as shown in Figure 7-61.

2. Create the chamfer feature at the end face of the cylindrical feature, see Figure 7-62.

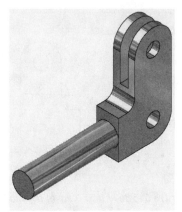
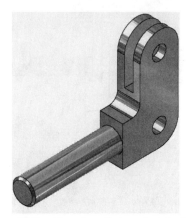

Figure 7-61 *Model after creating the join feature*   **Figure 7-62** *After chamfering the join feature*

Creating the Threads

1. Choose the **Thread** button from the **Features** toolbar to invoke the **Thread Feature** dialog box. You will be prompted to select the body as work surface. Select the cylindrical join feature. The preview of the threads will be displayed on the model.

2. Choose the **Specification** tab to display the options related to the specifications of the threads. Select **ANSI Metric M Profile** from the **Thread Type** drop-down list and **14** from the **Nominal Size** drop-down list.

3. Select **M14x2** from the **Pitch** drop-down list and **6g** from the **Class** drop-down list. Make sure the **Right hand** radio button is selected. Choose **OK** to exit the dialog box and create the threads. The model after creating the threads is shown in Figure 7-63.

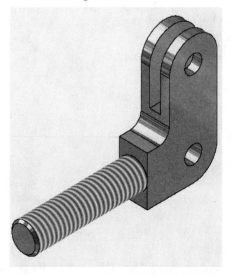

Figure 7-63 *Final model for Tutorial 2*

4. Save the model with the name \PersonalProject\c07**Tutorial2.ipt**.

Tutorial 3

In this tutorial you will create a model of the hexagonal nut shown in Figure 7-64a. The dimensions for the nut are shown in Figure 7-64b. The thread that should be created are **ANSI Metric M Profile** with nominal size of 10 and pitch of M10x1.5. The class of thread is 6H and it is a right-handed thread. After creating the model, save it with the name given below:

\PersonalProject\c07**Tutorial3.ipt**   (**Expected time: 30 min**)

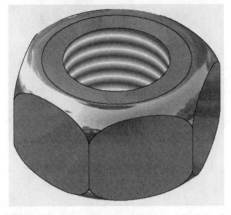

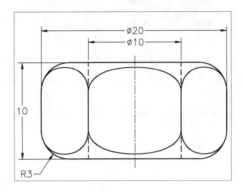

Figure 7-64a *Hexagonal nut with threads*   *Figure 7-64b* *Dimensions of the nut*

The steps that will be followed to create the model are listed below:

a. The hexagonal nut shown in Figure 7-64a will be created using the **Intersect** operation. The base feature for this model is a cylindrical feature with a hole inside.
b. Fillet the top and bottom faces of the cylindrical feature.
c. Define a new sketch plane on the top face of the base feature. On this plane draw a hexagon and extrude it using the **Intersect** operation.
d. Finally create the internal threads using the **Thread** tool.

Creating the Base Feature

1. Create the base feature for the nut as shown in Figure 7-65. The diameter of the outer cylinder is 20 mm and that of hole is 10 mm.

   You can draw the smaller circle inside the bigger circle for creating the hole. This will reduce one step of creating the hole feature.

Filleting the Faces of the Base Feature

1. Fillet the top and bottom faces of the base feature using the **Fillet** tool. The radius of fillet is 3 mm. The model after creating the fillet is shown in Figure 7-66.

Creating the Intersect Feature

The next feature is the intersect feature and will be created by defining a new sketch plane on either the top face of the model or on the bottom face of the model. After defining the sketch plane you will draw an inscribed hexagon. The diameter of the hexagon should be

Figure 7-65 *Base feature for the hexagonal nut*

Figure 7-66 *After filleting the faces*

equal to the diameter of the circle. You can use the **Precise Input** toolbar for drawing the hexagon.

1. Define a new sketch plane on the top face of the base feature. Draw an inscribed hexagon on the new sketch plane.

    The diameter of the circle in which the hexagon is inscribed should be equal to the diameter of the base feature. You can use the **Precise Input** toolbar to specify the value of diameter of the circle in which the hexagon is inscribed.

2. Exit the sketching environment and extrude the sketch using the **Intersect** operation and **All** extents. The model after creating the intersect feature is shown in Figure 7-67.

Creating the Threads

1. Choose the **Thread** button from the **Features** toolbar to invoke the **Thread Feature** dialog box.

2. Select the inner hole as the face for creating the threads.

3. Choose the **Specification** tab and select **ANSI Metric M Profile** from the **Thread Type** drop-down list.

4. Select **10** from the **Nominal Size** drop-down list and **M10x1.5** from the **Pitch** drop-down list.

5. Select **6H** from the **Class** drop-down list and choose **OK** to exit the **Thread Feature** dialog box and create the threads. The final model after creating the threads is shown in Figure 7-68.

6. Save the model with the name given below:

    \PersonalProject\c07**Tutorial3.ipt**

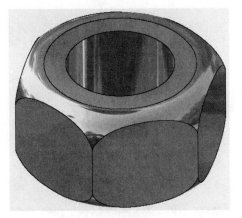

Figure 7-67 *After creating the intersect feature*

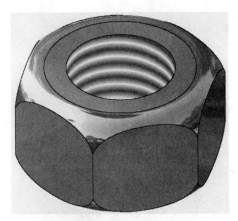

Figure 7-68 *Final model of nut*

Tutorial 4

In this tutorial you will create the model shown in Figure 7-69a. The dimensions for the model are shown in Figure 7-69b and Figure 7-69c. After creating the model, apply face draft on both the faces of 58 mm dimension. The angle for the face draft should be 1°. After creating the model, save it with the name given below:

\PersonalProject\c07**Tutorial4.ipt**   **(Expected time: 45 min)**

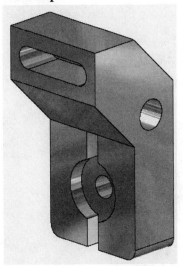

Figure 7-69a *Model for Tutorial 4*

The steps that will be followed to complete the model are listed below:

a.   Draw the sketch of the base feature with a hole on the YZ plane.
b.   Add two cut features and holes to the base feature.

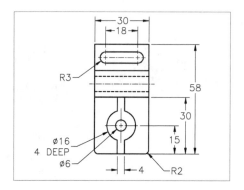

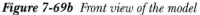

Figure 7-69b *Front view of the model*

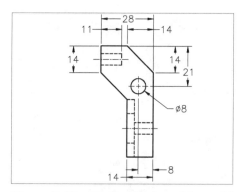

Figure 7-69c *Right side view of the model*

c. Create the face draft. To create the face draft, select the top face of the model as the pull direction. Make sure it is pointing downwards. Select the two faces to apply the face draft. You will notice that the width of the model at the upper end will remain the same and decrease from the lower end, thus applying the face draft.

d. Finally create the fillet. Remember that the fillet should be created after the face draft. The reason for this is that if you create the fillet first, the two faces will be taken as the faces tangent to the filleted edges. Therefore, the width of the model will remain constant at the bottom and will change from the top.

Creating the Base Feature

1. Open a new file and then create the base feature of the model on YZ plane as shown in Figure 7-70.

Adding the Remaining Features

1. Add the remaining cut features to the model as shown in Figure 7-71.

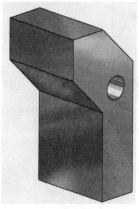

Figure 7-70 *Base feature of the model*

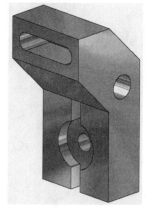

Figure 7-71 *Model after creating the remaining features*

Creating the Face Draft

1. Choose the **Face Draft** button from the **Features** toolbar to invoke the **Face Draft** dialog box. You will be prompted to select the pull direction.

2. Select the top face of the model as the pull direction and make sure that the arrow points downwards.

    If the direction points upwards, choose the **Flip Direction** button provided on the right of the **Pull Direction** button. The direction will reverse.

3. As soon as you specify the pull direction, the **Faces** button will be chosen and you will be prompted to select the face and the fixed edge.

4. Select both the faces one by one using a point close to the upper horizontal edge of the two faces, see Figure 7-72.

    When you take the cursor close to the face, it will be highlighted. Also, an edge on the face will be highlighted. This edge will be the fixed edge. In this model, the fixed edge should be the upper horizontal edge of both the faces. Therefore, to select the face, specify a point close to the upper horizontal edge of the faces.

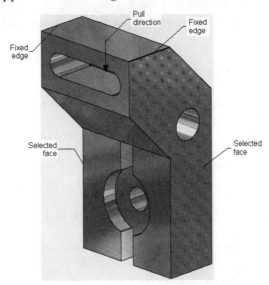

Figure 7-72 Selecting the options for face draft

5. Choose **OK** to exit the **Face Draft** dialog box and apply the face draft on the model.

6. Apply fillet to the model. The final model for Tutorial 4 is shown in Figure 7-73.

7. Save the model with the name given below:

    \PersonalProject\c07**Tutorial4.ipt**

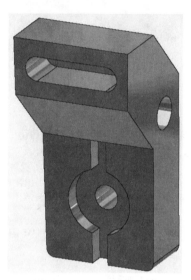

Figure 7-73 *Final model for Tutorial 4*

Self-Evaluation Test

Answer the following questions and then compare your answers with the answers provided at the end of this chapter.

1. To create the sweep feature, the path and the profile may or may not intersect. (T/F)

2. The lofted features are created by blending more than one dissimilar geometries. (T/F)

3. You can also apply different wall thicknesses to different faces in a shell feature. (T/F)

4. You cannot define a negative value for the length of the threads or the offset of the threads. (T/F)

5. The _____ method is used to create a spiral coil in a single plane.

6. _____ is defined as the process of scooping out material from the model and making it hollow from inside.

7. The _____ button in the **Shell** dialog box is used to select the faces of the model that should not be displayed in the resultant model.

8. _____ is applied to the faces of a model for its easy removal from casting.

9. The face draft feature will be displayed as the _____ feature in the browser.

10. If the faces selected to apply the face draft have some _____, they will also be selected for applying the face draft.

Review Questions

Answer the following questions.

1. The _____ operation of the **Coil** tool can also be used for creating internal or external threads in the model.

2. In Autodesk Inventor the _____ tool can be used to split the faces of the models or the complete model.

3. The _____ dialog box is used to directly create external or internal threads.

4. The path for the sweep feature can be open or closed but the profile has to be necessarily _____ .

5. The _____ edit box in the **Loft** dialog box is used to specify the distance to which the resultant feature will maintain the angle value at the start or the end sections.

6. Which of the following options allow you to create a coil in a single plane?

   (a) **Revolution and Height**   (b) **Pitch and Revolution**
   (c) **Spiral**   (d) **Pitch and Height**

7. Which one of the following options cannot be used to split a part?

   (a) Sketched lines   (b) Work Axis
   (c) Planar faces   (d) Work Plane

8. Which check box in the **Thread** dialog box is selected to create the threads through the length of the selected face.

   (a) **Length**   (b) **Full Length**
   (c) **Full**   (d) None

9. You can clear which one of the following check boxes in the **Thread Feature** dialog box to turn the display of the threads in the solid model.

   (a) **Display in Model**   (b) **Display**
   (c) **Off**   (d) None

10. Using which area in the **Loft** dialog box can you select the points on the sketches that will be used to map the shape of the loft feature?

    (a) **Point Mapping**   (b) **Mapping**
    (c) **Mapping Point**   (d) None

Exercises

Exercise 1

Create a solid model of the Offset shown in Figure 7-74a. The dimensions to be used are given in Figure 7-74b, Figure 7-74c, and Figure 7-74d. After creating the model save it with the name given below:

\PersonalProject\c07**Exercise1.ipt**   **(Expected time: 30 min)**

Note
The path for the sweep feature in Exercise 1 comprises of two lines of 5 mm length and an arc of radius 36 mm. If you apply the tangent constraint between the two lines and the arc, you will not be required to specify the center of the arc.

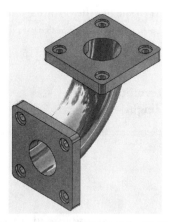

Figure 7-74a Solid model of Offset

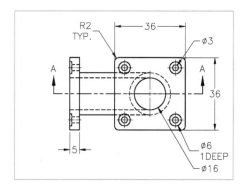

Figure 7-74b Top view of the model

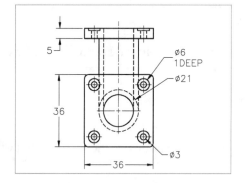

Figure 7-74c Left side view of the model

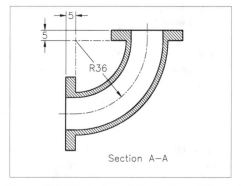

Figure 7-74d Sectioned front view of the model

Exercise 2

Create a solid model of the hexagonal headed cap screw shown in Figure 7-75a. The dimensions for the model are shown in Figure 7-75b. The threads to be created are **ANSI Metric M Profile** with nominal size of 10 and pitch value of M10x1.5. The class of the threads is 6g. Make sure that the threads are right handed. After creating the model save it with the name given below:

\PersonalProject\c07**Exercise2.ipt**   **(Expected time: 30 min)**

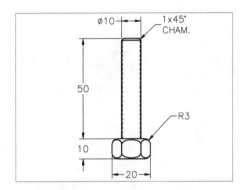

Figure 7-75a Solid model of the nut   *Figure 7-75b Dimensions for the nut*

Answers to Self-Evaluation Test
1. F, **2.** T, **3.** T, **4.** T, **5. Spiral**, **6.** Shelling, **7. Remove Faces**, **8.** Face draft, **9.** TaperEdge, **10.** tangent faces.

Chapter 8

Assembly Modeling-I

Learning Objectives

After completing this chapter you will be able to:

- *Understand the concept of bottom-up and top-down assemblies.*
- *Create components of top-down assemblies in assembly file.*
- *Insert components of bottom-up assemblies in assembly file.*
- *Understand various assembly constraints and use them to assemble the components.*
- *Move and Rotate individual components in assembly file.*

ASSEMBLY MODELING

An assembly is defined as a design consisting of more than one component bonded together at their respective working positions. In Autodesk Inventor, the components of assembly will be bonded using the parametric assembly constraints. Since the assembly constraints are parametric in nature, you can modify or delete them whenever you want. In Autodesk Inventor, the assemblies are created in the **Assembly** mode. To proceed to the assembly mode, invoke the **Open** dialog box and select the **Standard (mm).iam** file as shown in Figure 8-1.

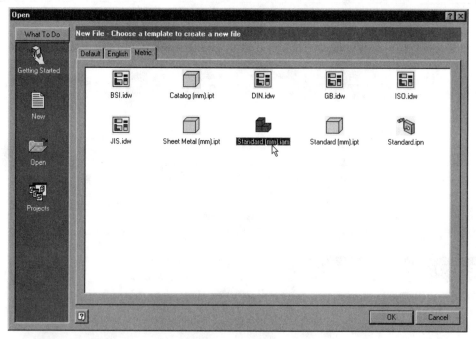

*Figure 8-1 Opening an assembly file from the **Metric** tab of the **Open** dialog box*

When you select the assembly file, the assembly environment will be activated. The screen display of Autodesk Inventor in the **Assembly** mode is shown in Figure 8-2. This figure also displays the **Assembly** panel bar, browser, and the **Assembly** toolbar for creating assemblies.

Note
*When you enter the **Assembly** mode, you will notice that very few tools in the **Assembly** panel bar and **Assembly** tool are available. All these tools will be available once you insert a component or create a component.*

TYPES OF ASSEMBLIES

In Autodesk Inventor, you can create two types of assemblies: top-down assemblies and bottom-up assemblies. Both these assemblies are discussed next.

Top-down Assemblies

A top-down assembly is an assembly whose all components are created in the same assembly

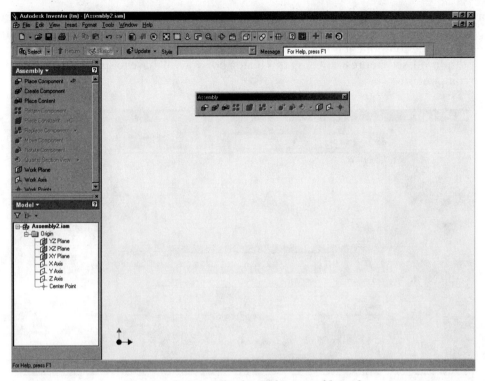

Figure 8-2 *Screen display in the* **Assembly** *mode*

file. In this type of assembly the components are created in the assembly file and then assembled using the assembly constraints. Generally, in case of large assemblies consisting of a number of components, the assembly files will become very large and will take a lot of space on the hard disk of your system. Moreover, the complete data related to the individual components as well as to the assembly will also be lost if there is any error in the assembly file. Considering all this, the process of creating the components in the **Assembly** mode of Autodesk Inventor is designed in such a way that the components you create in the **Assembly** mode are also saved as individual part or assembly files. This eliminates the risk of loosing the individual components in case there is an error in the assembly file. Also the size of the assembly file will be small because the components are also saved as individual part files. Therefore, the assembly file will have information related to only the assembly.

Bottom-up Assemblies

A bottom-up assembly is an assembly whose all components are created as separate part files and are referenced in the assembly file as external components. In this type of assembly, the components are created in the **Part** mode as *.ipt file. Once all components of the assembly are created, you will open an assembly file (.iam) and then insert all the component files using the tool provided in the **Assembly** mode. After inserting the components, they are assembled using the assembly constraints. Since the assembly file has information related only to assembling of components, these files are not very heavy and so require less hard disk space. However, remember that if any of the components referenced in the assembly is moved from its original location, it will not show up when you open the assembly next time. This is because Autodesk Inventor will look for the component only in the folder in which it was originally stored. Since the component is not found at its original location, the **Resolve Link** dialog box will be displayed, see Figure 8-3. Using this dialog box you will have to specify the new location of the component.

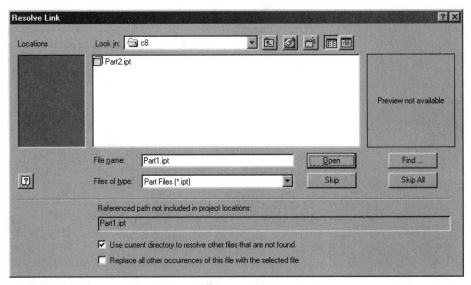

Figure 8-3 Resolve Link dialog box

CREATING TOP-DOWN ASSEMBLIES

As mentioned earlier, top-down assemblies are assemblies in which all the components are created in the same assembly file. However, to create the components you require an environment where you can draw the sketches of the sketched features and the environment where you can convert the sketches into features. In other words, to create the components in the assembly file, you require sketching environment as well as the part modeling environment (**Part** mode). Autodesk Inventor provides you the liberty to invoke both these environments in the **Assembly** mode also by using the **Create Component** tool. The use of this tool is discussed next.

Creating Components in the Assembly Mode

Toolbar:	Assembly > Create Component
Panel bar:	Assembly > Create Component

In Autodesk Inventor, you can create components in the **Assembly** mode also. One of the advantages of creating the components in the **Assembly** mode is that the component created in the **Assembly** mode can also be saved as a separate part file (*.ipt) or an assembly file (*.iam). Therefore, in case you again require any component created in the **Assembly** mode, you can use the individual part or assembly file. The components in the **Assembly** mode are created using the **Create Component** tool. When you invoke this tool, the

Create In-Place Component dialog box will be displayed, see Figure 8-4. The options under this dialog box are discussed next.

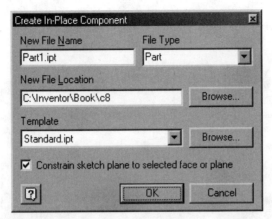

Figure 8-4 Create In-Place Component dialog box

New File Name

The **New File Name** text box is used to specify the name of the component that you create.

File Type

The **File Type** drop-down list is used to select the type of file format in which the new component will be saved. The options provided in this drop-down list are **Part** and **Assembly**. If you select **Part**, the new component will be saved as a part file in **.ipt** format. If you select **Assembly**, the new component will be saved as an assembly file in **.iam** format.

 Tip. *The Assembly option is used to create smaller subassemblies that consist of a few components. These smaller assemblies can be later assembled in a separate assembly file to form the main assembly.*

New File Location

The **New File Location** edit box is used to specify the location for saving the new file. You can either specify the location in this edit box or choose the **Browse** button to specify the location. When you choose this button, the **Browse for Folder** dialog box will be displayed, see Figure 8-5. Using this dialog box you can select the directory in which you can save the new file.

Template

The **Template** drop-down list is used to select the template for the new file. There are three default templates available in this drop-down list. They are **Sheet Metal.ipt**, **Standard.iam**, and **Standard.ipt**. You can also select the template by choosing the **Browse** button. When you choose this button, the **Open Template** dialog box will be displayed, see Figure 8-6. Using this dialog box you can select the required template for the new file.

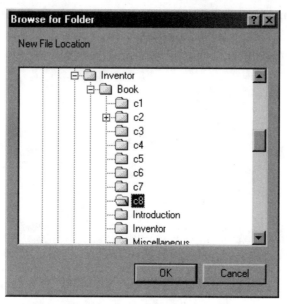

Figure 8-5 Browser for Folder dialog box

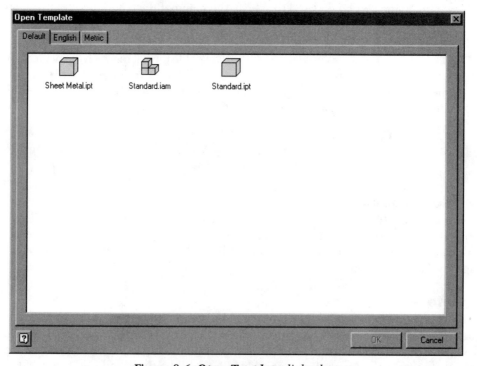

Figure 8-6 Open Template dialog box

Constrain sketch plane to selected face or plane

The **Constrain sketch plane to selected face or plane** check box is used to constrain the plane on which the base feature of the model will be created to the selected face of an existing model or work plane. If the component that you are creating is the first component, it will be grounded. A grounded component is the first component of the assembly using which the remaining components will be assembled. All the degrees of freedom of the grounded component will be eliminated so that it is not able to move from its original location. Even if you are placing external components, by default, the first component will be grounded.

Tip. *In an assembly it is very easy to distinguish between a grounded component and an ungrounded component. A grounded component will have a push pin icon on left of its name in the browser. You can make a grounded component ungrounded by using the shortcut menu displayed upon right-clicking on it in the browser. When you right-click on a grounded component in the browser, you will notice that there is a check mark in front of the **Grounded** option in the shortcut menu. To unground the component, choose this option again. The push pin icon will be replaced by the original part icon, suggesting that the component is ungrounded.*

After setting all the options in the **Create In-Place Component** dialog box, choose **OK**. When you choose **OK**, the sketching environment will be activated and you can draw the sketch for the base feature of the model. After creating the sketch, choose the **Return** button. The part modeling environment will be activated with all the part modeling tools, similar to the **Part** mode. Once you have created a part using the sketching environment and part modeling environment, you can switch back to the **Assembly** mode by again choosing **Return** from the **Command Bar**. The **Features** panel bar will be replaced by the **Assembly** panel bar and you will notice that all the tools in the **Assembly** panel bar will be available.

Similarly, you can create as many components as you want in the assembly. Once all the components are created, you can start assembling them using the assembly constraints.

CREATING BOTTOM-UP ASSEMBLIES

As mentioned earlier, bottom-up assemblies are those in which all the components are created as separate part files. All the individual part files are then inserted in an assembly file and are assembled using the assembly constraint. The first component inserted in the assembly will be grounded and the origin of the first component will coincide with that of the assembly file. Also, the three default planes of the part file will be placed in the same orientation as that of the default planes of the assembly file. The individual components are inserted in the assembly file using the **Place Component** tool discussed next.

Placing Components in the Assembly File

Toolbar:	Assembly > Place Component
Panel bar:	Assembly > Place Component

The **Place Component** tool is used to insert any inventor file in the current assembly file. When you invoke this tool, the **Open** dialog box will be displayed, see Figure 8-7. This dialog box is similar to the simple **Open** dialog box for opening the files. You can also preview the component before inserting using this dialog box. The type of file you want to insert can be selected from the **Files of type** drop-down list.

Figure 8-7 Open dialog box

Select the file to be placed from this dialog box and then choose the **Open** button. If it is the first component in the assembly file, one instance of the selected component will be placed automatically in the current file and you will be prompted to place another instance of the selected component. You can place as many copies of the selected component by specifying the point on the screen. Once you have placed the required number of instances of the component, right-click and choose **Done** from the shortcut menu. As mentioned earlier, the first component will be a grounded component. Therefore, the origin of the first component that will be placed automatically will coincide with the origin of the assembly file.

Similarly, you can place the other components using the **Place Component** tool. However, remember that if one or more components are already placed in the current assembly file, no instance of the selected component will be placed automatically. You will have to manually specify the location of the first instance of the component also.

ASSEMBLING THE COMPONENTS

Toolbar:	Assembly > Place Constraint
Panel bar:	Assembly > Place Constraint

 In Autodesk Inventor, the components are assembled using four types of assembly constraints, two types of motion constraints, and a transitional constraint. All these constraints can be applied using the various tabs of **Place Constraint** dialog box. This dialog box is displayed when you invoke the **Place Constraint** tool. All the seven types of constraints that can be applied using the **Place Constraint** dialog box are discussed next.

Mate Constraint

The **Mate** constraint is applied using the first button provided under the **Type** area of the **Assembly** tab of the **Place Constraint** dialog box, see Figure 8-8. The **Mate** constraint is used to make the selected planar face, axis, or point of a component coincident with that of another component. Depending upon the solution selected from the **Solution** area, the components will be assembled with the normal of the faces pointing in the same direction or in the opposite direction. The options that will be available in the **Assembly** tab of the **Place Constraint** dialog box when you choose the **Mate** button are discussed next.

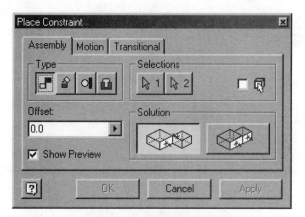

Figure 8-8 *The* **Mate** *constraint options in the* **Assembly**
tab of the **Place Constraint** *dialog box*

Selections Area

The options provided under this area are used to select the faces, axes, edges, or points of the
selected model for applying the **Mate** constraint. These options are discussed next.

1

The **1** button is chosen to select a face, axis, edge, or point on the first component for
applying the **Mate** constraint. Choose this button and then move the cursor close to the
component. If the cursor is close to a face, it will be highlighted and an arrow will be
displayed along with a cross. This arrow will point in the direction of the normal of the
selected face. The components are assembled in the direction of the normal of the faces.
Similarly, if you move the cursor close to an edge, axis, or a point, it will be highlighted.

2

The **2** button is chosen to select a face, axis, edge, or point on the second component for
applying the **Mate** constraint. Figure 8-9 shows the **Mate** constraint being applied on the
faces of two components. As evident from Figure 8-9, an arrow is displayed on the selected
face of both the components. These arrows point in the direction of the normal of the
selected face. The selected components will be assembled in the direction of these faces.

Pick part first

The **Pick part first** check box is provided on the right side of the **Selections** area. This
check box is used for the assembly that has a number of components. In such an assembly
it is hard to select the axis, edge, face, or point of one of the components due to the
complicacy. If this check box is selected, you will first have to select the component and
then select the option in that component for applying the constraint.

Tip. *You will notice that if after selecting the* **Pick part first** *check box you move
the cursor close to a component, the entire component will be highlighted instead of
faces, edges, axes, or points. Once you select the component, these options will be
highlighted.*

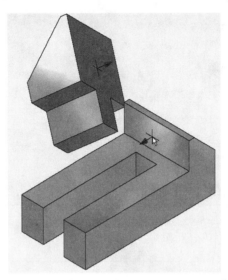

Figure 8-9 *Applying the **Mate** constraint on faces*

Note
*You can preview the assembling of the components on the screen after you have selected both the components to apply the constraint. However, remember that until you choose the **Apply** button in the **Place Constraint** dialog box, the constraint will not be applied and therefore, the components will not be actually assembled.*

Offset

The **Offset** edit box is used to specify the offset distance between the mating components. If the offset distance between the components is zero, they will touch each other. However, if there is an offset distance between the mating components, they will be placed at a distance from each other. Figure 8-10 shows the components assembled with an offset distance of 0 mm and Figure 8-11 shows the components assembled with an offset distance of 10 mm between the faces.

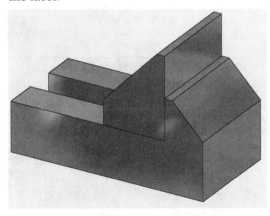

Figure 8-10 *Components assembled with an offset of 0 mm*

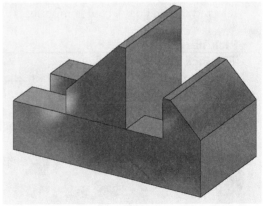

Figure 8-11 *Components assembled with an offset of 10 mm*

Tip. *Generally, the components are not assembled with a single constraint. Depending upon the components, you require two to three. It can be these many number of the same constraint or a combination of different constraints.*

Show Preview

The **Show Preview** check box is selected to display the preview of the assembling components. When you select two components to apply the constraint, a preview of the assembly will be displayed even if you have not chosen the **Apply** button. This is because the **Show Preview** check box is selected. If this check box is cleared, the preview of the assembly will not be displayed.

Solution Area

The buttons provided under the **Solution** area are used to specify whether the components being assembled should be placed in a mating position or in a flushing position. A mating position is a position where the normal of the faces are facing in the opposite direction, see Figure 8-12. A flushing position is a position where the normal of faces are facing in the same direction, see Figure 8-13.

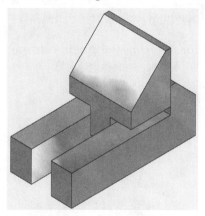

Figure 8-12 Mating position

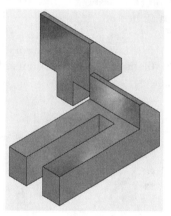

Figure 8-13 Flushing position

Angle Constraint

The **Angle** constraint is applied by using the second button in the **Type** area of the **Assembly** tab of the **Place Constraint** dialog box. This constraint is used to specify the angular position between the selected planar faces or edges of two components. The options that will be displayed in the **Assembly** tab of the **Place Constraint** dialog box are displayed in Figure 8-14. These options are discussed next.

Angle

This edit box is used to specify the angle between the selected planar faces or edges of two components. The components will be separated by an angle value specified in this edit box. You can specify a positive or negative value in this edit box.

Figure 8-14 *The **Angle** constraint options in the* ***Assembly*** *tab of the **Place Constraint** dialog box*

Solution Area

The options provided under this area are used to rotate the first and the second component by 180°. If you choose the **1** button, the first component will be rotated by 180°. Similarly, if you choose the **2** button, the second component will be rotated by 180°.

Figure 8-15 shows the components being selected for applying the **Angle** constraint and Figure 8-16 shows the components after applying the **Angle** constraint of 90° between the selected faces.

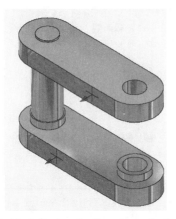

Figure 8-15 *Selecting the faces to apply the angle constraint*

Figure 8-16 *After applying the **Angle** constraint of 90°*

Note

*The remaining options under the **Angle** constraint are the same as those discussed under the **Mate** constraint.*

Tangent Constraint

The **Tangent** constraint is applied by choosing the third button in the **Type** area of the **Assembly** tab of the **Place Constraint** dialog box. This constraint forces the selected circular face of the component to become tangent to the circular face of the other component. The options that are displayed when you choose the **Tangent** button are displayed in Figure 8-17. These options are discussed next.

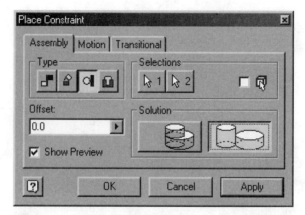

Figure 8-17 *The* ***Tangent*** *constraint options in the* ***Assembly*** *tab of the* ***Place Constraint*** *dialog box*

Solution Area

The options provided under the **Solution** area are used to specify whether the tangent constraint will be applied on the outer tangent faces or the inner tangent faces.

Figure 8-18 shows the components being selected for applying the **Tangent** constraint and Figure 8-19 shows the components after applying the **Tangent** constraint.

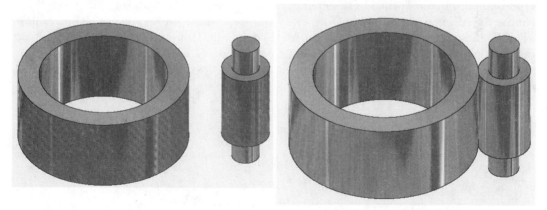

Figure 8-18 *Selecting the components to apply the* ***Tangent*** *constraint*

Figure 8-19 *Components after applying the* ***Tangent*** *constraint*

Note
The remaining options under the ***Tangent*** *constraint are the same as those discussed under the* ***Mate*** *constraint.*

Insert Constraint

The **Insert** constraint is applied by using the fourth button in the **Type** area of the **Assembly** tab of the **Place Constraint** dialog box. This constraint is used to force two different cylindrical or conical components or features of components to share the same orientation of the central axis. This constraint also makes the selected face of the first component coplanar with the selected face of the other component. The options that will be displayed in the **Assembly** tab of the **Place Constraint** dialog box are shown in Figure 8-20. These options are discussed next.

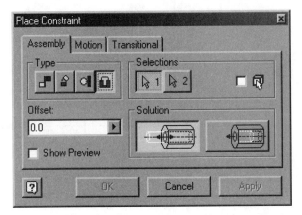

*Figure 8-20   The **Insert** constraint options in the Assembly tab of the **Place Constraint** dialog box*

Solution Area

The options provided under the **Solution** area are used to specify whether the normal of the mating faces will point in the same direction or in the opposite direction. If you choose the **Opposed** button, the normal of the mating faces will point in the opposite direction. If you choose the **Aligned** button, the mating faces will point in the same direction. This position will be similar to the flush situation of the **Mate** constraint. However, the central axes of both the components will share the same orientation. Figure 8-21 shows the components being selected to apply the **Insert** constraint and Figure 8-22 shows the components after applying the **Insert** constraint.

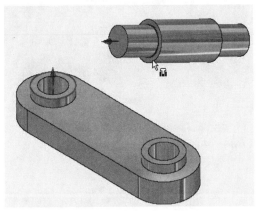

Figure 8-21 Selecting the components

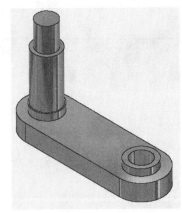

Figure 8-22 Components after assembling

Note

*The remaining options under the **Insert** constraint are the same as those discussed under the **Mate** constraint.*

Rotation Constraint

The **Rotation** constraint is applied by choosing the first button in the **Type** area of the **Motion** tab of the **Place Constraint** dialog box. This constraint is used to rotate one of the component in relation with the other component. The components rotate about the specified central axis. The options that are displayed when you choose the **Rotation** button from the **Type** area of the **Motion** tab of the **Place Constraint** dialog box are shown in Figure 8-23. These options are discussed next.

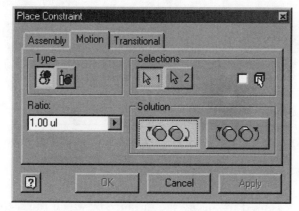

*Figure 8-23 The **Rotation** constraint options in the **Motion** tab of the **Place Constraint** dialog box*

Ratio

The **Ratio** edit box is used to specify the ratio by which the second component will rotate with respect to the first component. For example, if you enter a value of 2 in this edit box, the second component will rotate two times if the first component will rotate once. Similarly, if you enter a value of 10, the second component will rotate ten times if the first component is rotated once.

Solution

The options provided under the **Solution** area are used to specify the direction of rotation of the components. Choose the **Forward** button to rotate the components in the forward direction or choose the **Reverse** button to rotate the components in the reverse direction.

Note

*The constraints available in the **Motion** tab of the **Place Constraint** dialog box work only with the degree of freedom that is not removed. These constraints do not interfere with the other assembly constraints.*

*The remaining options under the **Rotation** constraint are the same as those discussed under the **Mate** constraint.*

Rotation-Translation Constraint

The **Rotation-Translation** constraint is applied by choosing the second button in the **Type** area of the **Motion** tab of the **Place Constraint** dialog box. This constraint is used to rotate the first component in relation with the translation of the second component. The options that are available in the **Motion** tab of the **Place Constraint** dialog box are shown in Figure 8-24. These options are discussed next.

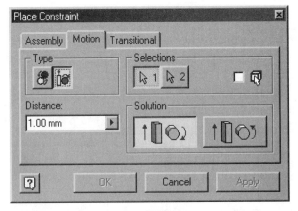

*Figure 8-24 The **Rotation-Translation** constraint options in the **Motion** tab of the **Place Constraint** dialog box*

Distance

The **Distance** edit box is used to specify the distance by which the second component will move in relation with one complete rotation of the first component. For example, if you enter a value of 2 mm in this edit box, the second component will move a distance of 2 mm for one complete rotation of the first component.

Note
*The remaining options under the **Rotation-Translation** constraint are same as those discussed under the **Rotation** constraint.*

Transitional Constraint

The **Transitional Constraint** is applied by choosing its button from the **Type** area of the **Transitional** tab of the **Place Constraint** dialog box, see Figure 8-25. A transitional constraint ensures that the selected face of the cylindrical component maintains contact with the other selected face when you slide the cylindrical component about the degree of freedom that is not eliminated. The options under this tab are similar to those discussed in the previous constraints.

MOVING INDIVIDUAL COMPONENTS

Toolbar:	Assembly > Move Component
Panel bar:	Assembly > Move Component

Figure 8-25 *The **Transitional** constraint options in the* ***Transitional** tab of the **Place Constraint** dialog box*

Autodesk Inventor allows you to move the individual unconstrained components in the assembly file without disturbing the position and location of the other components in the assembly file. This is done using the **Move Component** tool. When you invoke this tool, you will be prompted to drag the component to a new location. As you move the cursor close to any component, it will be highlighted. Select the component and then drag it to the desired location. The component will be relocated and the other components in the assembly file will not be disturbed.

ROTATING INDIVIDUAL COMPONENTS IN 3D SPACE

Toolbar:	Assembly > Rotate Component
Panel bar:	Assembly > Rotate Component

You can also rotate individual unconstrained components in the current assembly file without changing the orientation of the other components. This is done using the **Rotate Component** tool. When you invoke this tool, you will be prompted to drag the component to a new location. Select the component that you want to reorient. As soon as you select the component, the rim along with the handles will be displayed around the model. Also, the cursor will be changed to rotation mode cursor.

You can use the same tool to rotate other individual components also. After you have finished rotating a component, click on the other component using the rotation mode cursor. You will notice that the rim is now displayed around the component that you selected. Similarly, you can select any individual component to rotate in 3D space.

TUTORIALS

Tutorial 1

In this tutorial you will create all the components of the Butterfly Valve and then assemble them. The Body and the Shaft will be created in the assembly file and the remaining components will be created as individual parts in separate part files. The dimensions for the various components are given in Figure 8-26 through Figure 8-32. Assume the missing dimensions for the components and the parameters for the threads.   **(Expected time: 3 Hrs 30 min)**

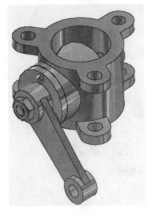

Figure 8-26 *Butterfly Valve assembly*

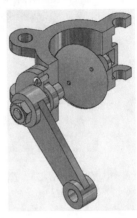

Figure 8-27 *Inside view of the Butterfly Valve*

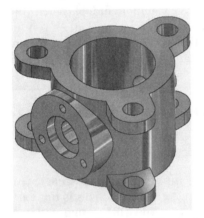

Figure 8-28a *Solid model of the Body*

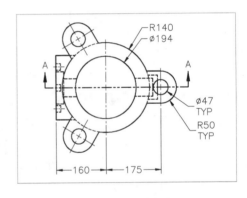

Figure 8-28b *Top view of the Body*

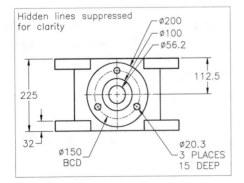

Figure 8-28c *Left side view of the Body*

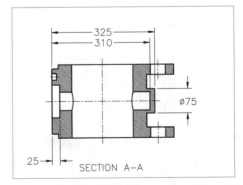

Figure 8-28d *Sectioned front view of the Body*

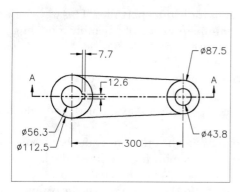

Figure 8-29a *Top view of the Arm*

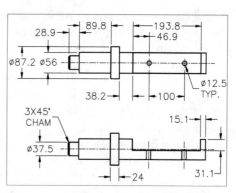

Figure 8-30 *Dimensions of the Shaft*

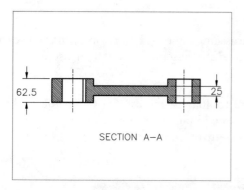

Figure 8-29b *Sectioned front view of the Arm*

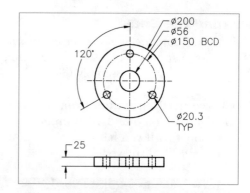

Figure 8-31 *Dimensions of the Retainer*

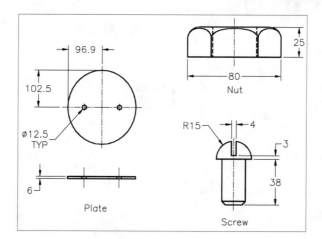

Figure 8-32 *Dimensions of the Plate, the Nut, and the Screw*

The steps that will be followed to create the assembly are listed below:

a.   As mentioned in the tutorial, you need to draw the Body and the Shaft in the assembly file. The remaining components will be created as individual part files. This way you will use the top-down approach as well as the bottom-up approach of assembly modeling.

b. To create this assembly, you will open a new metric assembly file and create Body and Shaft. Although these components will be created in the assembly file, they will also be stored as individual part files so that you can refer to these components whenever you require.

c. After creating the Body and Shaft, you will assemble these two components using the **Place Constraint** dialog box. Once these two components are assembled, you will close the assembly file.

d. Next, you will open new part files and one by one create the other individual components. Once all components are created, you will open the assembly file and insert the individual components in the assembly file. The components will be inserted using the **Place Component** tool. Then using the **Place Constraint** dialog box, assemble all the components to create the Butterfly Valve assembly.

Creating the Body

The Body and the Shaft will be created in the assembly file and therefore, you will use the top-down approach of assembly modeling. To create these two components, you will have to first open a new assembly file.

1. Choose the **New** button from the **Standard** toolbar to invoke the **Open** dialog box. Double-click on **Standard (mm).iam** in the **Metric** tab (Figure 8-33) to open a metric assembly file. If you have started the Autodesk Inventor session, this dialog box will be automatically displayed.

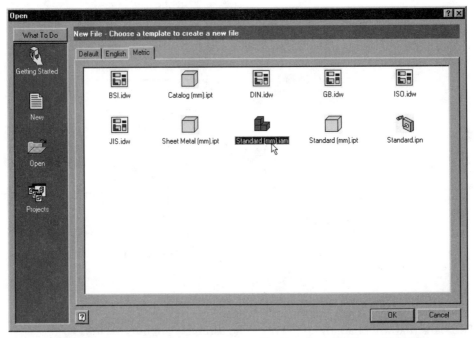

*Figure 8-33 Opening a new metric assembly file using the **Open** dialog box*

The assembly modeling environment will be activated with the **Assembly** panel bar at the left of the screen as shown in Figure 8-34.

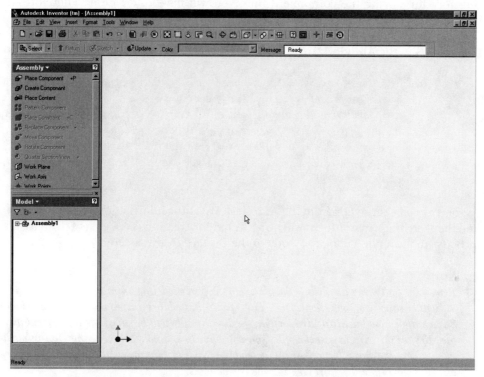

*Figure 8-34 Screen display in the **Assembly** mode*

You will notice that very few tools are available in the **Assembly** panel bar. This is because no component is present in the assembly file. Once a component is placed or created, all the other tools will be available for use.

2. Choose the **Create Component** button from the **Assembly** toolbar or choose **Create Component** from the **Assembly** panel bar to invoke the **Create In-Place Component** dialog box.

3. Enter the name of the new part file as **Body.ipt** in the **New File Name** edit box. Select **Part** from the **File Type** drop-down list.

4. Specify the location of the new part file in the **New File Location** edit box as **\PersonalProject\c08\Butterfly Valve**. Select **Standard.ipt** from the **Template** drop-down list.

5. Clear the **Constrain sketch plane to selected plane or face** check box. Choose the **OK** button.

The **Autodesk Inventor** information box will be displayed. This dialog box will inform you that the directory you have mentioned does not exist. It will also ask you whether you want to create this directory. Since, before starting the assembly you did not create any directory for storing the component files, you will have to create it. Therefore, if you choose **OK** in the **Autodesk Inventor** information box, it will create the directory for you.

6. Choose **OK** in the **Autodesk Inventor** information box.

Tip. *It is recommended that you create separate directories for storing the individual component files of assemblies. The reason for this is that lot of assemblies have the components that have similar names. For example, the name Body is common to a number of assemblies. Therefore, if you create the Body and store it in the directory of a particular assembly, there will be no confusion in placing the components. Also, when you open the assembly next time, there will be no confusion in referring to the component.*

As soon as you choose **OK** from the **Autodesk Inventor** information box, it will be closed and the sketching environment will be activated for creating the sketch of the base feature of Body. You can now create the Body of the Butterfly Valve assembly.

Note
Remember that if you are saving the file when the part modeling environment is active, the part file will be saved not the assembly file. This means that while creating the Body if you choose the ***Save*** *button from the* ***Standard*** *toolbar, the Body.ipt file will be saved not the current assembly file. To save the current assembly file, you will have to exit the part modeling environment and then choose the* ***Save*** *button in the assembly modeling environment. You can also save the assembly file before you start creating the components.*

7. Create the Body of the Butterfly Valve using the given dimensions. The screen display of the assembly file after creating the Body is shown in Figure 8-35.

   You will notice that the part modeling environment is still active in the assembly file. To proceed further, you will have to exit the part modeling environment. You can exit the part modeling environment by choosing the **Return** button from the **Command Bar**.

8. Choose the **Return** button from the **Command Bar** to exit the part modeling environment.

   When you choose the **Return** button, you will notice that the assembly modeling environment is activated and the **Features** panel bar of the part modeling environment is replaced by the **Assembly** panel bar of the assembly modeling environment.

9. Choose the **Save** button from the **Standard** toolbar and save the assembly with the name **Butterfly Valve.iam** in the **Butterfly Valve** directory.

   As mentioned earlier, until you exit the part modeling environment, only the part file will be saved when you choose the **Save** button. The assembly file will be saved only after you exit the part modeling environment.

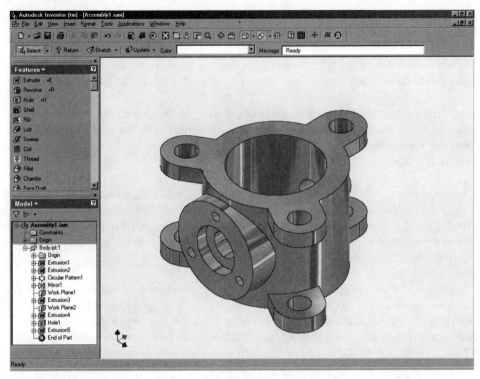

Figure 8-35 *Assembly file in the part modeling environment after creating the Body*

Creating the Shaft

The second component that has to be created in the assembly file is the Shaft. Therefore, you will again have to activate the sketching environment and the part modeling environment to create the Shaft. However, since the Body is already present in the assembly file, there are chances that it might start interfering with the part that you create next. Considering this, the part modeling environment in the assembly file is designed such that when you start creating the components in the assembly file, all the existing components become light in color and also become transparent so that they do not restrict you from viewing the new part that you create.

1. Choose the **Create Component** button from the **Assembly** toolbar or choose **Create Component** from the **Assembly** panel bar to invoke the **Create In-Place Component** dialog box.

2. Enter the name of the new part file as **Shaft.ipt** in the **New File Name** edit box. Select **Part** from the **File Type** drop-down list.

3. Specify the location of the new part file in the **New File Location** edit box as **\PersonalProject\c08\Butterfly Valve**. Select **Standard.ipt** from the **Template** drop-down list.

4. Clear the **Constrain sketch plane to selected plane or face** check box. Choose **OK**.

5. You will be prompted to select the plane on which you want to sketch the base feature. Select the XY plane from the browser.

    As soon as you select the XY plane, the sketching environment will be activated and the Body will become transparent. You can now proceed with creating the Shaft.

6. After creating the Shaft, save it before exiting the part modeling environment so that the Shaft.ipt file is saved. Exit the part modeling environment by choosing the **Return** button from the **Command Bar**. Save the assembly file by choosing the **Save** button from the **Standard** toolbar.

    When you exit the part modeling environment, you will notice that the Body is no more transparent. Also, both the components in the assembly file are interfering with each other. Therefore, before proceeding with assembling these components, you will have to move one of the components such that it does not interfere with the other. You can move the individual component using the **Move Component** tool.

7. Choose the **Move Component** button from the **Assembly** toolbar or choose **Move Component** from the **Assembly** panel bar. You will be prompted to drag the component to a new location. Select Body and drag it to a new location where it does not interfere with the Shaft. Choose the **Zoom All** button to increase the display area. The screen display of the assembly file with both the components is shown in Figure 8-36.

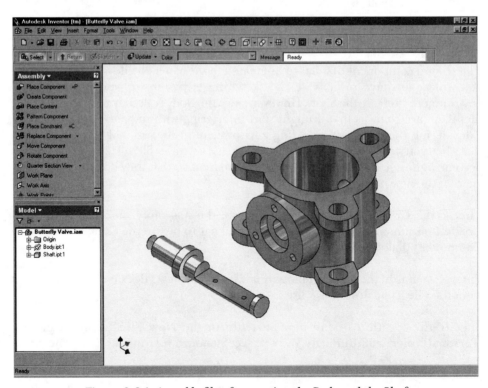

Figure 8-36 *Assembly file after creating the Body and the Shaft*

Note

*If the orientation of the Shaft and the Body is different from the one shown in Figure 8-36, you can reorient them using the **Rotate Component** tool.*

Assembling the Components

The Shaft is a circular part that has to be inserted in the counterbore hole of the Body. Therefore, you can use the **Insert** constraint to assemble these components. As mentioned earlier, the **Insert** constraint forces the selected components or features to share the same orientation of the central axis and at the same time makes the selected faces coplanar. Therefore, the Shaft will be assembled with the Body using the **Insert** constraint. Now, the flat part of the Shaft has to be at an angle to the top face of the Body. To assemble it at an angle with the top face, you will have to use the **Angle** constraint. Therefore, the second constraint that will be used is the **Angle** constraint.

1. Choose the **Place Constraint** button from the **Assembly** toolbar or choose **Place Constraint** from the **Assembly** panel bar to display the **Place Constraint** dialog box.

    By default, the **Mate** constraint is selected. For assembling the Shaft with the Body you require the **Insert** constraint. Therefore, you will have to choose the **Insert** button from the **Type** area of the **Assembly** tab of the **Place Constraint** dialog box.

2. Choose the **Insert** button from the **Type** area.

    You will notice that the **Insert** constraint symbol is attached to the cursor. This symbol will be displayed along with the cursor when you move the cursor on the graphics screen.

3. Select the face on the Shaft as shown in Figure 8-37.

    You will notice that the selected face is highlighted and an arrow along the direction of the central axis of the Shaft is displayed. This arrow will also point in the direction in which the Shaft will be assembled. Also, the **2** button in the **Selections** area of the **Place Constraint** dialog box is automatically chosen.

4. Select the inner face of the counterbore hole as shown in Figure 8-37.

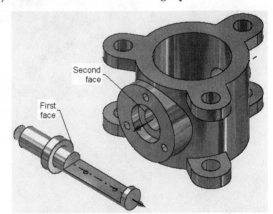

*Figure 8-37 Selecting the faces to apply the **Insert** constraint*

    As soon you select the second face for applying the constraint, the Shaft will assemble with the Body. This is because by default, the **Show Preview** check box in the **Place Constraint** dialog box is selected.

5. Choose the **Apply** button in the **Place Constraint** dialog box to assemble the Shaft with the Body.

6. Choose the **Angle** button to apply the **Angle** constraint.

    Since the model is in the Isometric view, the flat face of the Shaft is not visible. Therefore, you will have to reorient the assembly using the **Rotate** tool. This tool can be used when you are inside another tool and so when you invoke this tool, you will temporarily switch to assembly rotating mode. The assembling of components will resume when you exit the **Rotate** tool.

7. Choose the **Rotate** button from the **Standard** toolbar and rotate the assembly such that the flat face of the Shaft is visible. Right-click to display the shortcut menu and choose **Done** to exit this tool.

8. The symbol of the **Angle** constraint will be reattached to the cursor suggesting that the assembling of components is resumed. Select the flat face of the Shaft as the first face to apply the **Angle** constraint, see Figure 8-38.

9. Select the top face of the Body as the second face to apply the **Angle** constraint, see Figure 8-38.

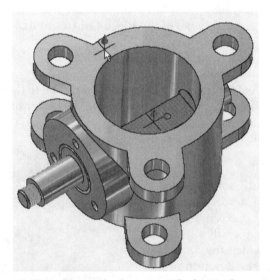

*Figure 8-38 Selecting the faces to apply the **Angle** constraint*

10. Enter the value of angle in the **Angle** edit box as **45**. The flat face rotate towards the right side. Choose **Apply** to apply the constraint. Exit the dialog box by choosing the **Cancel** button. Change the view back to the previous view by pressing the F5 key.

Creating other Components

1. Exit the current assembly file by choosing **Close** from the **File** menu.

2. Create the other components as individual part files and save them with their names in the **Butterfly Valve** directory.

3.   Exit the part file and then again open the **Butterfly Valve.iam** file.

Assembling the Retainer

The next component that has to be assembled is the Retainer. The Retainer is also a circular part and so can be assembled using the **Insert** constraint. However, since the central hole of the Retainer has to match with the Shaft and the other three holes with the holes on the left flat face of the Body, therefore, you will have to apply the **Insert** constraint twice. The first time it will be used for the central hole and the second time to align one of the smaller holes on the Retainer with one of the smaller holes on the left flat face of the Body. First of all, you will have to place the component in the current assembly file. The components can be placed using the **Place Component** tool.

1.   Choose the **Place Component** button from the **Assembly** toolbar or choose **Place Component** from the **Assembly** panel bar to invoke the **Open** dialog box.

By default, the current directory in the **Open** dialog box will be the **Butterfly Valve** directory. All the components that you created are displayed in this directory.

2.   Double-click on Retainer. You can also select the Retainer and then choose the **Open** button.

The **Place Component** dialog box will be closed. The Retainer will be attached to the cursor and you will be prompted to place the component.

3.   Place the Retainer at a location where it does not interfere with the other components.

After you have placed an instance of the Retainer, you will again be prompted to place the component. Since you have to place only one instance of the Retainer, you can exit the component placement option.

4.   Right-click in the graphics screen to display the shortcut menu and choose **Done** to exit the component placement option.

5.   Choose the **Place Constraint** button from the **Assembly** toolbar or choose **Place Constraint** from the **Assembly** panel bar. The **Place Constraint** dialog box will be displayed. If the **Place Constraint** dialog box is restricting the viewing of the components on the screen, you can move it by picking it from the blue strip on top.

6.   Choose the **Insert** button from the **Type** area. Select one of the smaller holes on the top face of the Retainer as the first face for applying the constraint, see Figure 8-39.

7.   Select one of the smaller holes on the flat face of the circular feature on the Body as the second face to apply the constraint, see Figure 8-39. Choose **Apply**.

As soon as you select the second face, the Retainer will move from its location and will be assembled with the Body such that both the selected holes are in line and the top face of the Retainer is coplanar with the flat face of the left circular feature on the Body. However,

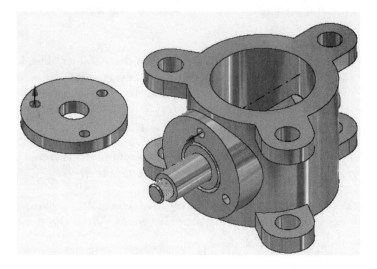

Figure 8-39 *Selecting the faces to apply the **Insert** constraint*

you will notice that the central hole of the Retainer is not in line with the central hole of the left circular feature of Body and Shaft. Therefore, you will have to apply the **Insert** constraint once again to align them.

8. Select the inner face of the Retainer that is coplanar with the Body as the first face to apply the constraint, see Figure 8-40. You may have to rotate the model to select this face.

9. Select the flat face of the left circular feature on the Body as the second face to apply the constraint, see Figure 8-40. Choose **Apply** and then choose **Cancel** to assemble the component and exit the dialog box.

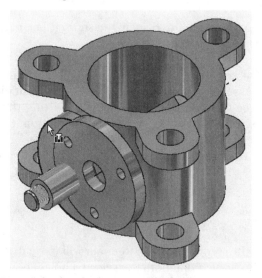

Figure 8-40 *Selecting the faces to apply the **Insert** constraint again*

Assembling the Arm

The next component that has to be assembled is the Arm. Since the Arm is assembled at a certain angle with respect to the Body, therefore, you will have to use two constraints to assemble it. The first constraint will be the **Insert** constraint that will insert the already assembled Retainer in the bigger hole of the Arm. The second constraint will be the **Angle** constraint that will be used to apply an angle between the XZ plane of the Arm and the top face of the Body. You will place the Arm using the **Place Component** tool.

1. Choose the **Place Component** button from the **Assembly** toolbar or choose **Place Component** from the **Assembly** panel bar to invoke the **Open** dialog box.

2. Double-click on the Arm.

3. Place the Arm at a location where it does not interfere with the other components.

4. Right-click in the graphics screen to display the shortcut menu and choose **Done** to exit the component placement option.

5. Choose the **Place Constraint** button from the **Assembly** toolbar or choose **Place Constraint** from the **Assembly** panel bar. The **Place Constraint** dialog box will be displayed.

6. Choose the **Insert** button and then select the hole on the top face of the bigger cylindrical feature in the Arm as the first face, see Figure 8-41.

7. Select the left face of the Retainer as the second face to apply the **Insert** constraint, see Figure 8-41. Choose the **Apply** button.

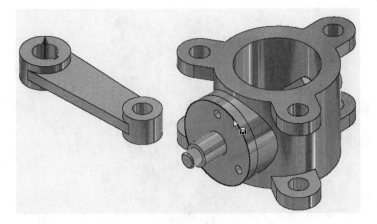

*Figure 8-41 Selecting the faces to apply the **Insert** constraint*

The Arm will be assembled with the Retainer and the Shaft will be inserted in the bigger hole of the Arm. The second constraint will be used to reorient the Arm such that it is assembled at an angle to the top face of the Body. This angle is the same as the angle between the top face of the Body and the flat face of the Shaft.

Note

*In this case it is presumed that the cylindrical features of the Arm are created on the XY plane. Also, the bigger and smaller cylindrical features are created from left to right respectively along the X axis direction when placed on the XY plane. Therefore, the XZ plane will pass through the center of the two cylindrical features. This XZ plane will be used to apply the **Angle** constraint.*

8. Choose the **Angle** button from the **Type** area. Select the top face of the Body as the first face to apply the constraint.

    The second face that has to be selected to apply the constraint is the XZ plane of the Arm. The XZ plane of the Arm will not be displayed in the browser. You will have to click on the + sign on the left of the Arm in the browser to display the **Origin** folder and then from this folder select the XZ plane.

9. Click on the + sign on the left of the Arm in the browser to display the **Origin** folder. Click again on the + sign on the left of the **Origin** folder to display all the planes of the Arm. Select the XZ plane.

    When you move the cursor on the XZ plane in the browser, it will be highlighted in the graphics screen.

10. Enter the value of the angle in the **Angle** edit box as **-135**. Choose **Apply** and then choose **Cancel** to apply the constraints and close the dialog box. Click on the - sign on the left of the Arm to close the folders. The assembly after assembling the Arm is shown in Figure 8-42.

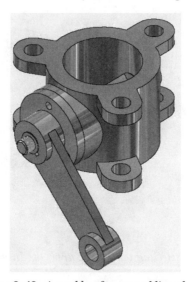

Figure 8-42 *Assembly after assembling the Arm*

Assembling the Plate

The next component that has to be assembled is the Plate. You will have to place the Plate in the assembly file and then assemble it on the flat feature of the Shaft. You will have to apply the **Insert** constraint twice to assemble the Plate properly with the Shaft. The first constraint will align one of the holes on the Plate with the one of the holes on the Shaft and the second constraint will align the second hole on the Plate with that on the Shaft.

However, since the Shaft is assembled inside the Body, therefore, the Body might cause a restriction in viewing the components being assembled. To avoid this situation, Autodesk Inventor allows you to turn off the display of the components that you do not require in assembling the other components. Therefore, before proceeding with the assembling of the Plate, you can turn off the display of the Body. This is done using the browser.

1. Right-click on the Body in the browser to display the shortcut menu. You will notice that in the shortcut menu, there is a check mark in front of the **Visibility** option, see Figure 8-43. This suggests that the display of this component is turned on. Choose the **Visibility** option again to turn off the display.

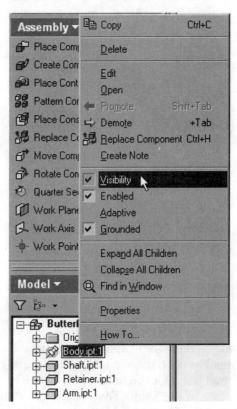

Figure 8-43 Turning off the display of the Body

The component whose visibility is turned off will be displayed in gray color in the browser. If you right-click on it again, you will notice that the check mark is removed.

2. Choose the **Place Component** button from the **Assembly** toolbar or choose **Place Component** from the **Assembly** panel bar to invoke the **Open** dialog box.

3. Double-click on the Plate.

4. Place the Plate at a location where it does not interfere with the other components.

5. Right-click in the graphics screen to display the shortcut menu and choose **Done** to exit the component placement option.

6. Choose the **Place Constraint** button from the **Assembly** toolbar or choose **Place Constraint** from the **Assembly** panel bar. The **Place Constraint** dialog box will be displayed.

7. Choose the **Insert** button and then select one of the holes on the top face of the Plate as the first face to apply the constraint, see Figure 8-44.

8. Select the right hole on the flat face of the Shaft as the second face to apply the constraint, see Figure 8-44. Choose the **Apply** button to apply the constraint.

Figure 8-44 *Selecting the faces to apply the constraint*

As soon as you select the second face to apply the constraint, the Plate will move from its location and will be assembled with the Shaft. Now, the second constraint has to be applied on the other hole of the Plate. But the hole has to be selected on the face that is made coplanar with the flat face of the Shaft. Therefore, you will have to reorient the model such that the back face of the Plate is visible and you can select the hole on that face to apply the constraint.

9. Reorient the assembly using the **Rotate** button so that the back face of the Plate is visible.

When you choose the **Rotate** button, you will be shifted to the rotate mode temporarily. Once you exit the rotate options, the assembling of components will resume.

10. Select the hole on the back face of the Plate as the first face to apply the constraint.

Since you rotated the model such that the back face of the Plate is visible, the flat face of the Shaft is not visible in the current view. Therefore, you will have to switch back to the previous view. Now, as you are inside the **Place Constraint** tool, you cannot use the F5 key to switch back to the previous view. You will have to invoke the **Rotate** tool again and then right-click to display the shortcut menu and choose **Previous View** from this menu.

11. Choose the **Rotate** button from the **Standard** toolbar and then right-click in the graphics screen to display the shortcut menu. Choose **Previous View** from this menu to switch back to the previous view. Again right-click and choose **Done** to exit the **Rotate** tool.

Tip. *You can also switch to the previous view by pressing the F5 key when you are inside the **Rotate** tool. Also, once you change the view using the F5 key, you can use it as well as SHIFT+F5 to change the view even when you are inside the **Place Constraint** tool and the **Rotate** tool is not active.*

12. Select the other hole on the flat face of the Shaft to apply the constraint. Choose the **Apply** button and then choose the **Cancel** button to exit the dialog box. The assembly after assembling the Plate is shown in Figure 8-45.

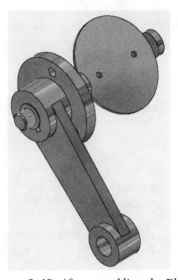

Figure 8-45 After assembling the Plate

Assembling the Screws

There are three instances of the Screw that have to be assembled such that they are inserted in the three holes on the Retainer. But before assembling the Screws, you have to turn off the display of the Arm so that it does not interfere in the display.

1. Right-click on the Arm in the browser and choose **Visibility** to turn off the display of the Arm in the assembly.

2. Choose the **Place Component** button from the **Assembly** toolbar or choose **Place Component** from the **Assembly** panel bar to invoke the **Open** dialog box.

3. Double-click on the Screw.

4. Place three instances of the Screw at a location where they do not interfere with the other components.

5. Choose the **Place Constraint** button from the **Assembly** toolbar or choose **Place Constraint** from the **Assembly** panel bar. The **Place Constraint** dialog box will be displayed.

6. Choose the **Insert** button and then select the flat face of the head of the Screw as the first face to apply the constraint.

7. Select one of the holes on the front face of the Retainer as the second face to apply the constraint. Choose **Apply** to apply the constraint.

8. Similarly, assemble the other two Screws with the two holes on the Retainer.

Assembling the Nut

The Nut has to be assembled with the Shaft. Since the threaded portion of the Shaft has to be inserted inside the hole of the Nut, you will use the **Insert** constraint to assemble this component.

1. Choose the **Place Component** button from the **Assembly** toolbar or choose **Place Component** from the **Assembly** panel bar to invoke the **Open** dialog box.

2. Double-click on the Nut.

3. Place the Nut at a location where it does not interfere with the other components. Rotate the Nut using the **Rotate Component** tool such that the flat face of the Nut is visible in the current view.

4. Choose the **Place Constraint** button from the **Assembly** toolbar or choose **Place Constraint** from the **Assembly** panel bar. The **Place Constraint** dialog box will be displayed.

5. Choose the **Insert** button and then select the hole on the flat face of the Nut as the first face to apply the constraint.

6. Select the end face of the threaded feature of the Shaft. Choose **Apply** and then choose **Cancel** to exit the dialog box.

Turning on the Display of the Body and the Arm

1. Right-click on the Body in the browser and choose **Visibility** from the shortcut menu to turn on the display of the Body in the assembly.

2. Similarly, right-click on the Arm in the browser and choose **Visibility**. The display of the Arm will be turned on in the assembly. Choose the **Zoom All** button from the **Standard** toolbar. The final Butterfly Valve assembly is shown in Figure 8-46.

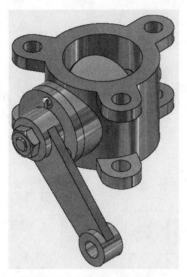

Figure 8-46 *Final Butterfly Valve assembly*

3. Choose the **Save** button from the **Standard** toolbar to save the assembly.

Tutorial 2

In this tutorial you will create the various components of the Plummer Block assembly and then assemble them in the assembly file. All the components should be created as separate part files. After creating the components, place them in the assembly file and then assemble them. The dimensions of the components are shown in Figure 8-47 through Figure 8-52. Assume the missing dimensions and the parameters for the threads.

(Expected time: 3 Hrs 30 min)

Note
The orientation of the Casting you draw should match the orientation of the Casting shown in the assembly in Figure 8-47. This is because when you place the first component in the assembly file, it is placed on the same plane on which it was originally created in the part file. Since the Casting will be the first component you place in the assembly file, the base of it should be created on the XY plane. Therefore, when you place it in the assembly file, it is placed on the XY plane. The orientation of the other components also depends upon the first component that you place in the assembly file.

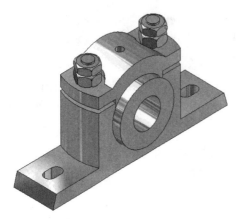

Figure 8-47 *Plummer Block assembly*

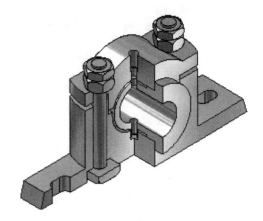

Figure 8-48 *Inside view of the Plummer Block assembly*

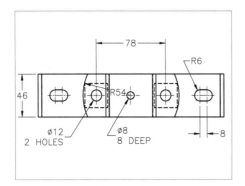

Figure 8-49a *Top view of the Casting*

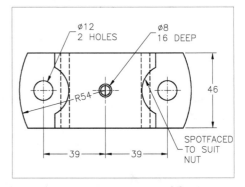

Figure 8-50a *Top view of the Cap*

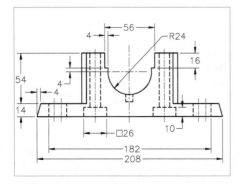

Figure 8-49b *Front view of the Casting*

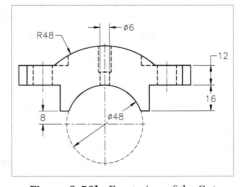

Figure 8-50b *Front view of the Cap*

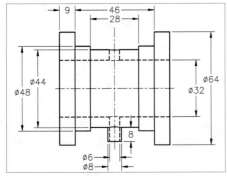

Figure 8-51 *Dimensions of the Brasses*

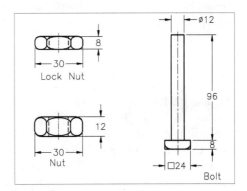

Figure 8-52 *Dimensions of the Lock Nut, the Nut, and the Bolt*

The steps that will be followed to create the assembly are listed below:

a. As mentioned in the tutorial description, you have to create all the components as separate part files and then insert them in the assembly file. Therefore, in this tutorial you will use the bottom-up approach of creating the assemblies. Create all components in individual part files and save them. The part files will be saved in the directory \PersonalProject \c08**Plummer Block**.

b. Open a new assembly file and using the **Place Component** tool, place the components in the assembly file. The first component that will be placed is the Casting. After placing the Casting, you will place the Cap. Then you will assemble them using the assembly constraint.

c. Next, you will turn off the display of the Cap and then place the Brasses. You will assemble the Brasses with the Casting and then turn off the display of the Brasses also.

d. Next, you will place two instance of the Bolt in the assembly file. Both the instances of the Bolt will be assembled with the Casting. Then you will turn on the display of the Cap and place two instances of the Nut and the Lock Nut. You will first assemble both the instances of the Nut with the Cap and then the Lock Nut with the Nut.

e. Finally you will turn on the display of the Brasses to complete the Plummer Block assembly.

Creating the Components

1. Create all the components of the Plummer Block assembly as separate part files. Specify the names of the files as shown in Figure 8-49 through Figure 8-52. The files should be saved in the directory /PersonalProject/c08/**Plummer Block**.

Assembling the Casting and the Cap

The Casting and the Cap will be assembled using two constraints. The first constraint is the **Insert** constraint that will align one of the holes on the top face of the Cap with its corresponding hole on one of the horizontal face of the Casting. You will also apply an offset of 4 mm between the mating faces in this constraint. The other constraint is the **Mate** constraint that will align the front face of the Cap with the front face of the Casting.

1. Open a new assembly file. Save it with the name **Plummer Block.iam** in the folder

/PersonalProject/c08/**Plummer Block**. This is the directory in which all the individual part files are saved.

1. Choose the **Place Component** button from the **Assembly** toolbar or choose **Place Component** from the **Assembly** panel bar to invoke the **Open** dialog box.

2. Double-click on the Casting.

   You will notice that one instance of the Casting is automatically placed in the assembly file. This instance is grounded and will have a push pin icon in front of it in the browser. You will again be prompted to place the component.

3. Right-click and choose **Done** from the shortcut menu. Similarly, place one instance of the Cap in the current assembly file. The location of the Cap should be such that it does not interfere with the Casting.

4. Choose **Rotate Component** from the **Assembly** panel bar and rotate the Cap such that its bottom face is visible in the current view.

5. Choose the **Place Constraint** button from the **Assembly** toolbar or choose **Place Constraint** from the **Assembly** panel bar. The **Place Constraint** dialog box will be displayed.

6. Choose the **Insert** button and then select the right hole on the bottom face of the Cap as the first face to apply the constraint.

7. Select the right hole on the top face of the Casting as the second face to apply the constraint. Enter the value of the offset as **4** in the offset edit box. Choose the **Apply** button.

   The Cap will be assembled with the Casting. However, the alignment of the front face of the Cap will not match the alignment of the front face of the Casting. Therefore, you will have to apply the **Mate** constraint.

8. Choose the **Mate** button from the **Type** area and then select the front face of the Cap as the first face to apply the constraint.

9. Select the front face of the Casting as the second face to apply the constraint. Select the **Flush** button from the **Solution** area. Choose **Apply** and then choose **Cancel** to exit the dialog box. The assembly after assembling the Cap and the Casting is shown in Figure 8-53.

Assembling the Brasses

The Brasses is a circular part and so can be assembled using the **Insert** constraint. Notice that in the Brasses there is a circular join feature created on the cylindrical face. The central axis of this feature has to be aligned with that of the hole on the circular face of the Casting. You can align these axes using the **Mate** constraint. However, to proceed with assembling the Brasses you will turn off the display of the Cap since it is not required in assembling the Brasses.

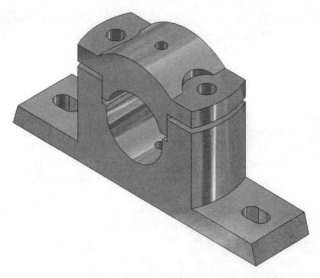

Figure 8-53 *After assembling the Cap with the Casting*

1. Right-click on the Cap in the browser and choose **Visibility** from the shortcut menu to turn off its display.

2. Place the Brasses using the **Place Component** tool. Invoke the **Place Constraint** dialog box using the **Place Constraint** tool. Choose the **Insert** button from the **Type** area and select the semicircular face of the Casting to apply the constraint, see Figure 8-54.

3. Select the face of the Brasses shown in Figure 8-54 to apply the constraint. Make sure the arrow points in the backward direction. Choose the **Apply** button.

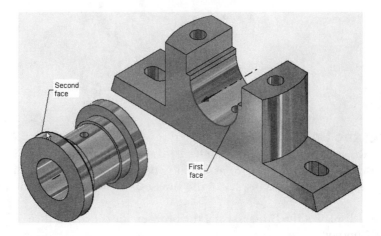

Figure 8-54 *Selecting the faces to apply the **Insert** constraint*

The next constraint will be used to align the central axis of the circular join feature created on the cylindrical face of the Brasses with that of the hole on the cylindrical face of the Casting. However, since the hole in the casting will not be visible even if you change the orientation of the assembly, you will have to change the display mode from shaded to wireframe. In the wireframe display, the inside holes and features will also be displayed.

4. Change the display mode to wireframe by choosing the down arrow on the right side of the **Shaded Display** button in the **Standard** toolbar and choosing **Wireframe Display**. Select the **Mate** button from the **Type** area and move the cursor close to the hole on the tangent face of the Brasses. When you move the cursor close to the hole, the central axis of the hole will be displayed. Select the central axis of the hole as the first selection set.

5. Select the central axis of the hole in the cylindrical face of the Casting as the second selection set. Choose the **Apply** button and then choose the **Cancel** button to apply the constraint and exit the dialog box.

6. Turn on the visibility of the Cap using the browser and change the display type to **Shaded Display**. The assembly is shown in Figure 8-55.

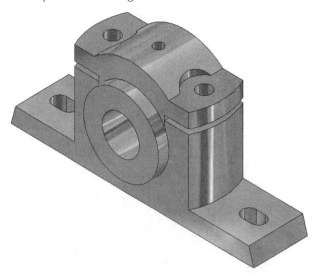

Figure 8-55 *After assembling the Brasses*

Assembling the Bolts

There are two instances of the Bolts that have to be assembled in the current assembly. But since the Brasses is not required for assembling the Bolts or the Nuts, you can turn off its display. After turning off the display of the Brasses, you will assemble the Bolts.

1. Turn off the display of the Brasses using the browser. Place two instances of the Bolt using the **Place Component** tool.

2. Invoke the **Place Constraint** dialog box and then choose the **Insert** button from the **Type** area. Select the circular face on the top face of the base square feature of the Bolt as the

first face to apply the constraint, see Figure 8-56.

3. Change the display type to wireframe and then select the circular face on the top face of the square cut on the bottom face of the Casting, see Figure 8-56. Choose **Apply**.

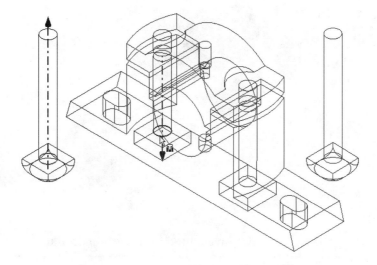

Figure 8-56 Selecting the faces to apply the constraint

4. Similarly, assemble the other Bolt and then change the display type to **Shaded Display**.

Assembling the Nuts and the Lock Nuts

Since the Nuts will be assembled with the Cap and the Lock Nuts with the Nuts, therefore, you do not require the Bolts. You can turn off the display of both the Bolts.

1. Turn off the display of both the Bolts using the browser. Place two instances each of the Nut and the Lock Nut using the **Place Component** tool.

2. Invoke the **Place Constraint** dialog box and then choose the **Insert** button from the **Type** area. Select the hole on the top face of one of the Nut as the first face to apply the constraint.

3. Select the left hole on the top face of the Cap as the second face to apply the constraint. The Nut will be assembled with the Cap. Choose the **Apply** button to apply the constraint.

4. Select the hole on the top face of one of the Lock Nut as the first face to apply the constraint.

5. Select the hole on the top face of the Nut that is assembled with the Cap as the second face to apply the constraint. The Lock Nut will be assembled with the Nut. Choose the **Apply** button to apply the constraint. Exit the dialog box by choosing the **Cancel** button.

6. Similarly, assemble the other Nut and the Lock Nut. Turn on the display of all the invisible components using the browser. The final Plummer Block assembly is shown in Figure 8-57.

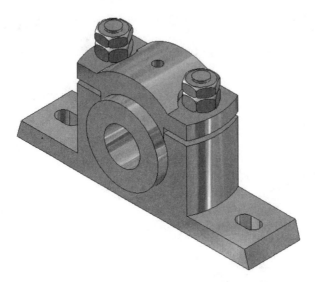

Figure 8-57 Final Plummer Block assembly

7.   Save the assembly by choosing the **Save** button from the **Standard** toolbar.

Self-Evaluation Test

Answer the following questions and then compare your answers with the answers given at the end of this chapter.

1.   In Autodesk Inventor you can use the bottom-up approach as well as the top-down approach for creating the assemblies. (T/F)

2.   If the assembly is created using the top-down approach, the components files are also saved as individual part files. (T/F)

3.   You can rotate individual components in the assembly file. (T/F)

4.   You cannot invoke the sketching environment in the assembly file. (T/F)

5.   The _____ tool is used to place the components in the assembly file.

6.   The _____ icon is displayed in front of the grounded component in the browser.

7.   When you invoke the **Place Constraint** tool, the _____ dialog box is displayed.

8.   The _____ constraint is used to make the selected planar face, axis, or point of a component coincident with that of another component.

9. By default, the first component placed in the assembly file is _____.

10. The individual components in the assembly file can be moved using the _____ tool.

Review Questions

Answer the following questions.

1. You can change the display type of the components even when you are using a tool to perform a function. (T/F)

2. The components that are not grounded by default can also be grounded when you want. (T/F)

3. The display of the components that are not required for assembling the other component can be turned off using the browser. (T/F)

4. If the component files are moved from their original location, the next time you open the assembly file, they will not show up in the assembly. (T/F)

5. The top-down assemblies are those in which all the components are created as individual part files and are placed in the assembly file. (T/F)

6. How many types of assembly constraints are available in Autodesk Inventor?

    (a) 4   (b) 5
    (c) 7   (d) 8

7. How many types of motion constraints are available in Autodesk Inventor?

    (a) 2   (b) 3
    (c) 4   (d) 5

8. Which tool is used to rotate the individual components in the assembly file.

    (a) **Rotate Component**   (b) **Move Component**
    (c) **Rotate**   (d) You cannot rotate the individual components

9. Which constraint is used to rotate one of the component in relation with the other component?

    (a) **Rotation**   (b) **Rotation-Translation**
    (c) **Mate**   (d) **Tangent**

Exercise

Exercise 1

Create the components of the Drill Press Vice assembly and then assemble them as shown in Figure 8-58. The dimensions for the components are shown in Figure 8-60 through 8-63b. Create a directory with the name \PersonalProject\c08**Drill Press Vice** and save all the component files and the assembly file in this directory. Assume the missing dimensions.

You will use the bottom-up approach for creating this assembly.   **(Expected time: 3 Hrs 15 min)**

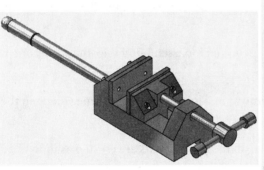

Figure 8-58 Drill Press Vice assembly

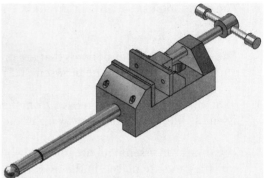

Figure 8-59 Drill Press Vice assembly

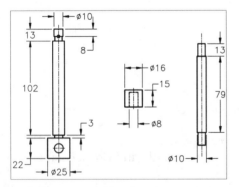

Figure 8-60 Dimensions of the Clamp Screw, the Handle Stop and the Clamp Screw Handle

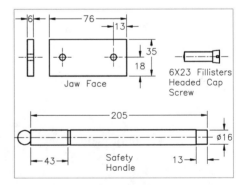

Figure 8-61 Dimensions of the Jaw Face, the Cap Screw and the Safety Handle

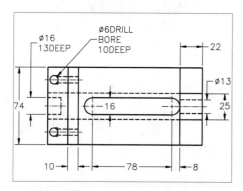

Figure 8-62a *Top view of the Base*

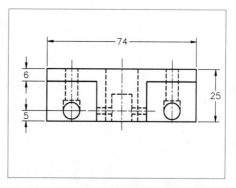

Figure 8-63a *Top view of the Movable Jaw*

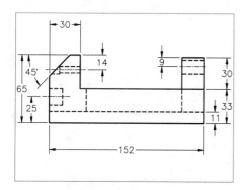

Figure 8-62b *Front view of the Base*

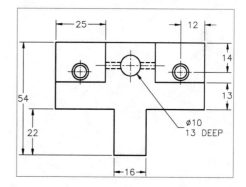

Figure 8-63b *Front view of the Movable Jaw*

Answers to Self-Evaluation Test

1. T, **2.** T, **3.** T, **4.** F, **5. Place Constraint**, **6.** push pin, **7. Open**, **8. Mate**, **9.** grounded, **10. Move Component**

Chapter 9

Assembly Modeling-II

Learning Objectives

After completing this chapter you will be able to:

- *Edit assembly constraints.*
- *Edit the components of an assembly.*
- *Check the degrees of freedom of a component.*
- *Create the pattern of the components in the assembly file.*
- *Replace a component in the assembly file with another component.*
- *Delete components in the assembly file.*
- *Edit the pattern of components.*
- *Delete assembly constraints.*
- *Create the section view of the assemblies in the assembly file.*
- *Analyze the assemblies for interference.*
- *Create the design views of the assemblies.*
- *Drive assembly constraints.*
- *Reorder the components in the assembly file.*

EDITING ASSEMBLY CONSTRAINTS

Generally, after creating the assembly or during the process of assembling the components, you have to edit the assembly constraints that are used to assemble the components. The editing operations that can be performed on the assembly constraints include modifying the type of assembly constraint, modifying the offset or angle values, modifying the type of solution, or changing the component to which the constraint was applied. In Autodesk Inventor, the assembly constraints are edited using the browser. By default, the constraints that are applied on the components will not be displayed in the browser. To display the assembly constraint applied on a component, click on the + sign on the left of the component in the browser. The **Origin** folder will be displayed along with the list of constraints that are applied to that component. To edit the constraint, right-click on it in the browser and choose **Edit** from the shortcut menu, see Figure 9-1.

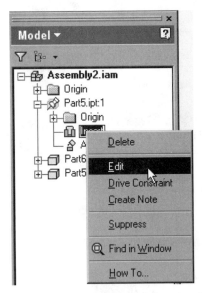

Figure 9-1 Editing assembly constraints using the browser

Tip. *If you move the cursor on the assembly constraint in the browser, the components on which that constraint is applied are highlighted in the assembly. The highlighted components will be displayed in red color on the graphics screen.*

Note

When you select the assembly constraint in the browser, an edit box is displayed below the browser. This edit box will display the value of the offset or the angle for the selected constraint. If you want to modify only the angle or the offset value, you can modify it using this edit box.

When you choose **Edit** from the shortcut menu that is displayed upon right-clicking on the assembly constraint in the browser, the **Edit Constraint** dialog box will be displayed, see Figure 9-2. This dialog box is similar to the **Place Constraint** dialog box and can be used to

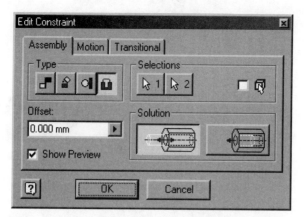

Figure 9-2 Edit Constraint dialog box for editing the assembly constraints

edit the assembly constraints. This dialog box can be used to change the constraint type, edit the offset or the angle value, modify the solution, or change the components to which the constraints are applied.

EDITING THE COMPONENTS

Sometimes after assembling the components of the assembly, you have to edit the components. In Autodesk Inventor, you can edit the components by two methods. These two methods of editing the components of an assembly are discussed next.

Editing the Components in the Assembly File

The first method of editing the components is to invoke the part modeling environment and the sketching environment in the assembly file and edit the component. This method of editing the components is similar to the top-down approach of assembly modeling. To edit the component in the assembly file, right-click on the component in the browser. The shortcut menu will be displayed. In this menu choose the **Edit** option, see Figure 9-3.

When you choose the **Edit** option, the part modeling environment will be activated in the assembly file. You will notice that the other components in the assembly file have become transparent. Also, they are displayed with a gray background in the browser and the component that you selected for editing is displayed with a white background. The component that is displayed in the white background is called the active component. You can edit the active component in the assembly file. Remember that only one component can be active at a time in the assembly file. Once you have edited the component, choose **Return** from the **Command Bar**. You will shift back to the **Assembly** mode. You will notice that now no component is displayed with a gray background.

After making the changes in the component in the assembly file, when you save the assembly file, the **Save** dialog box will be displayed. This dialog box will prompt you to specify whether you want to save the changes to the part file also or not. To view the components that have been modified, choose the button with two arrows on the bottom right corner of the dialog

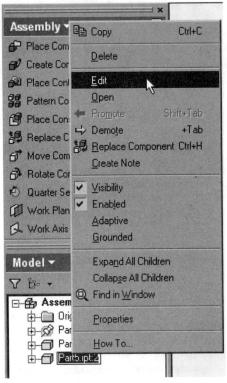

Figure 9-3 Editing the components

box. The **Save** dialog box will expand and will provide the list of all the components that have been modified, see Figure 9-4. If you want to save the changes in the part files, choose **OK**. If you do not want to save the changes in the part files, choose **No To All**.

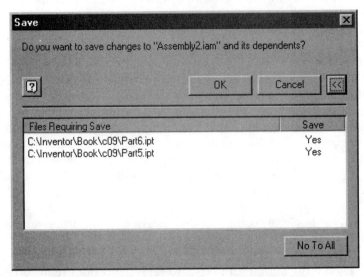

*Figure 9-4 **Save** dialog box for saving the part files*

Editing the Components by Opening their Part Files

The second method of editing the components is by opening their part files and making the necessary changes in the part files. Once you have made the required changes in the part files, save them and then exit the part files by choosing **Close** from the **File** menu. You will notice that the changes that you made in the part files are already reflected in the assembly file. This is because Autodesk Inventor is bidirectionally associative. This means that if you make changes in the components in any of the modes of Autodesk Inventor, the changes will be automatically reflected in the other modes.

To open the part file for editing, right-click on the component in the browser. The shortcut menu will be displayed. Choose **Open** in this shortcut menu as shown in Figure 9-5.

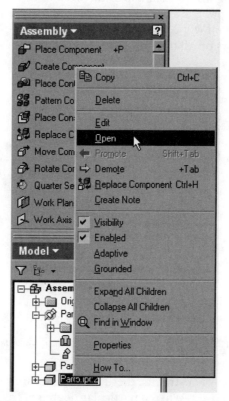

Figure 9-5 Opening the part file for editing

When you choose the **Open** option, the part file of the selected component will be opened. Make the necessary changes in the part file and then save the changes by choosing the **Save** button from the **Standard** toolbar. Now, exit the part file by choosing **Close** from the **File** toolbar. Since the assembly file was already opened, it will be displayed now. The changes that you made in the part file will be automatically reflected in that component in the assembly file.

CHECKING THE DEGREES OF FREEDOM OF A COMPONENT

As mentioned earlier, you restrict the degrees of freedom of a component by applying assembly constraints to it. You can view the degrees of freedom that are not restricted in a component by choosing **Degrees of Freedom** from the **View** menu. By default, this option is not selected and therefore, the degrees of freedom of the components are not visible on the screen. However, when you choose this option, a check mark will be displayed on the right side of this option in the **View** menu and the symbol of degrees of freedom will be displayed on the screen. In Autodesk Inventor, every component has six degrees of freedom. They are linear movement along X, Y, and Z axes and rotational movement along X, Y, and Z axes. These degrees of freedom are displayed using an icon similar to the 3D Indicator available on the lower left corner of the drawing window. For a component whose all degrees of freedom are open, the symbol of degrees of freedom will consist of three linear axes pointing in X, Y, and Z axes direction and circular arrows on all the three axes, see Figure 9-6.

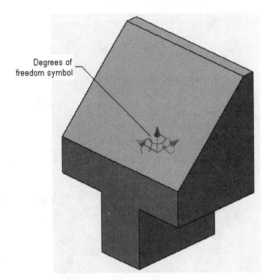

Degrees of freedom symbol

Figure 9-6 Component with all degrees of freedom open

When you apply the assembly constraints, these movements are restricted and therefore, the degrees of freedom are removed. When a particular degree of freedom is removed, it will no more be displayed in the symbol of degrees of freedom. For example, if you apply the assembly constraint such that the linear movement of the component is restricted along the Z axis, the linear axis along the Z axis will not be displayed in the symbol of degrees of freedom. However, the circular axis along the Z axis will still be displayed since you have not restricted that movement. Therefore, for a component whose all degrees of freedom are restricted, there will be no symbol of degrees of freedom.

Tip. *By default, the first component you place or create in the assembly file is grounded. A grounded component has all its degrees of freedom restricted and therefore, the symbol of degrees of freedom will not be displayed on it. However, if you unground the grounded component after assembling other components with it, you will notice that the symbol of degrees of freedom is displayed on it. This symbol will indicate that all the degrees of freedom of the component are open. You will also notice that a small green color cube is displayed on all the other components that were assembled with the grounded component. This cube suggests that all these components are assembled with an underconstrained component. The component became underconstrained when you ungrounded it. To view the underconstrained component, move the cursor on the green color cube on any one of the assembled components. The green color cube will turn red in color and the underconstrained component also changes to red color. It will also be displayed in red color in the browser. The component will be changed back to its original color when you move the cursor away from the cube.*

CREATING THE PATTERN OF THE COMPONENTS IN ASSEMBLY

Toolbar:	Assembly > Pattern Component
Panel bar:	Assembly > Pattern Component

While creating the assemblies, you have to sometime assemble more than one instance of a component about a specified arrangement. For example, in case of Butterfly Valve assembly, you have to assemble three instances of Screw with the Retainer and the Body (refer to Tutorial 1 of Chapter 8). All these three instances were recalled in the current assembly file and then assembled using the assembly constraint. Also, if you have to increase the number of holes in the Retainer and the Body from three to four, you will have to recall another instance of the Screw and insert it using the assembly constraint. However, this is a very tedious and time-consuming process. Therefore, to reduce the time for assembling the components, Autodesk Inventor has provided a tool for creating the pattern of the components. You can create circular or rectangular pattern of the components. This will reduce the assembling time as well the time taken in recalling number of instances of the components. Another advantage of creating the pattern of the components is that if you increase the number of instances in the pattern feature on the original part, the number of instances of the components in the pattern will also increase automatically. For example, if you increase the number of holes from three to four in the Retainer of the Butterfly Valve assembly, one more instance of the Screw will be automatically recalled in the assembly file and will be automatically inserted in the fourth hole of the Retainer.

The pattern of the components in the assembly file is created using the **Pattern Component** tool. When you invoke this tool, the **Pattern Component** dialog box will be displayed. The options under the various tabs of this dialog box are discuss next.

Component

The **Component** button is chosen to select the component in the assembly file that you want to pattern. When you invoke the **Pattern Component** dialog box, this button will be chosen automatically and you will be prompted to select the component to be patterned.

Associative Tab

The **Associative** tab (Figure 9-7) will be active by default when you invoke this tool.

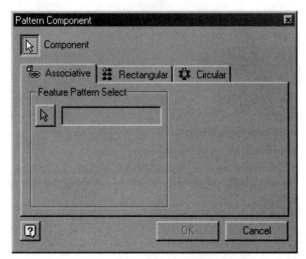

Figure 9-7 Associative tab of the Pattern Component dialog box

The options under this tab are used to select the pattern of feature on the base part to which the pattern of components will be associated. The pattern of feature can be selected by choosing the **Associated Feature Pattern** button provided under the **Feature Pattern Select** area of this tab. When you choose this button, you will be prompted to select the feature pattern to which the pattern of components will be associated. You can select the pattern of feature on the base part. Depending upon whether the pattern selected is rectangular or circular, it will be displayed in the display box provided on the right side of **Associated Feature Pattern** button. Also, the selected component will be assembled with all the instances of the feature pattern. Remember that the number of instances of components assembled using this tool will be modified upon modification in the number of instances in the pattern of feature only if the pattern of the component is created using the **Associative** tab.

Rectangular Tab

The options under this tab are used to create rectangular pattern of the selected components in the assembly file, see Figure 9-8. The options under this tab are similar to those discussed under the **Rectangular Pattern** dialog box in Chapter 5.

Note
Similar to the Rectangular Pattern dialog box, the options under the Rectangular tab of the Pattern Component dialog box will be available only after you specify the directions for column placement and row placement.

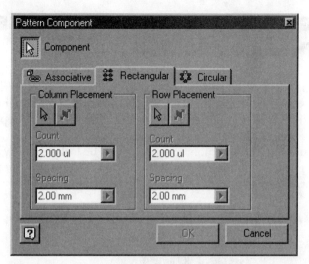

Figure 9-8 Rectangular tab of the Pattern Component dialog box

Circular Tab

The options under the **Circular** tab of the **Pattern Component** dialog box are used to create circular pattern of the selected component, see Figure 9-9. The options under this tab are similar to those discussed under the **Circular Pattern** dialog box in Chapter 5.

Figure 9-9 Circular tab of the Pattern Component dialog box

Note

The Angle edit box in the Circular tab is used to specify the incremental angle between the individual instances of the pattern.

REPLACING A COMPONENT IN THE ASSEMBLY FILE WITH ANOTHER COMPONENT

Autodesk Inventor allows you to replace any component in the assembly file with another component that you specify. You can either replace the single instance of the component or all the instances of the selected component with another specified component. If the shape of the new component is similar to that of the original component that you replaced, the assembly constraints will be retained. However, if the shape of the new component is not similar to that of the original component, the assembly constraints will be lost and you will have to apply the constraints again. The new component will be placed at the same location as that of the original component. The methods of replacing the components are discussed next.

Replacing Single Instance of the Selected Component

Toolbar: Assembly > Replace Component
Panel bar: Assembly > Replace Component

The single instance of the selected component can be replaced by the **Replace Component** tool. When you invoke this tool, you will be prompted to select the component to be replaced. When you select the component to be replaced, the **Open** dialog box will be displayed as shown in Figure 9-10.

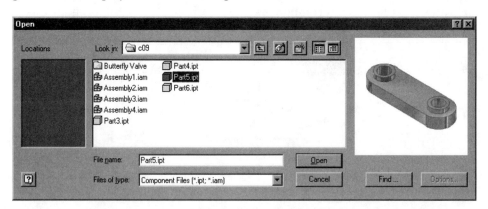

Figure 9-10 Open dialog box for selecting the new component

You can use this dialog box to specify the name and location of the new component. You can either double-click on the component or select the component and choose the **Open** button. The selected component will be placed at the location of the previous component. Remember that the assembly constraints will be retained only if the shape of the new component is similar to that of the original component.

If there are chances that the assembly constraints that you have applied on the component to be replaced are going to be lost, the **Possible Constraint Loss** dialog box will be displayed as shown in Figure 9-11. This dialog box will inform you that the constraints and notes associated with the component may be lost. Choose the **OK** button to continue with the process of replacement of the component. To abort the process, choose the **Cancel** button.

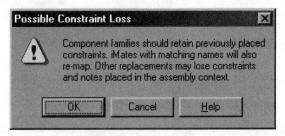

Figure 9-11 Possible Constraint Loss dialog box

Replacing All the Instances of the Selected Component

Toolbar: Assembly > Replace Component > Replace All
Panel bar: Assembly > Replace Component > Replace All

You can replace all the instances of the selected component by choosing the down arrow on the right side of the **Replace Component** button and then choosing the **Replace All** button. When you choose this button, you will be prompted to select the component to be replaced. Select the component to be replaced from the screen. As soon as you select the component to be replaced, the **Open** dialog box will be displayed. You can use this dialog box to select the new component. All the instances of the selected component will be replaced with the component selected in the **Open** dialog box.

 Tip. *The components assembled using the **Pattern Component** tool cannot be replaced using the **Replace Component** or the **Replace All** tool.*

DELETING THE COMPONENTS

You can delete the unwanted instances or the unwanted components from the assembly file using the browser. In the browser, right-click on the component that you do not require in the assembly file. The shortcut menu will be displayed. From the shortcut menu, choose **Delete**. The selected component will be deleted and will not be displayed on the screen.

To delete the components that are assembled using the **Pattern Component** tool, right-click on **Component Pattern** in the browser. The shortcut menu will be displayed. In this menu choose **Delete**. All the instances of the component assembled using the **Pattern Component** tool will be deleted. However, the original component will not be deleted and will be retained on the screen. You can deleted the original instance also by right-clicking on it in the browser and choosing **Delete** from the shortcut menu.

EDITING THE PATTERN OF COMPONENTS

Autodesk Inventor allows you to edit the pattern of the components created using the **Pattern Component** tool. This is done using the browser. To edit the pattern of the component, right-click on **Component Pattern** in the browser and choose **Edit** from the shortcut menu. The **Edit Component Pattern** dialog box will be displayed. Note that this dialog box will have only the tab that was used for creating the pattern of the component. For example, if the pattern of the component was created using the **Associative** tab of the **Pattern Component** dialog box, the **Edit Component Pattern** dialog box will have only the **Associative** tab. Similarly, if the pattern of component was created using the **Circular** tab of the **Pattern Component** dialog box, the **Edit Component Pattern** dialog box will have only the **Circular** tab. Figure 9-12 shows the **Edit Component Pattern** dialog box for editing the pattern created using the **Associative** tab of the **Pattern Component** dialog box.

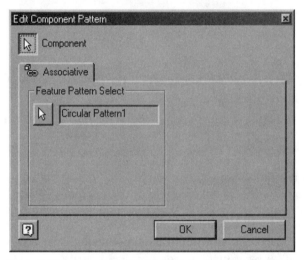

Figure 9-12 Edit Component Pattern dialog box for the pattern created using the Associative tab of the Pattern Component dialog box

Note
The options under the Edit Component Pattern dialog box are similar to those discussed under the Pattern Component dialog box.

Tip. *You can also make the selected component among the pattern of component independent. The independent component will be displayed as a separate component in the browser and will not be deleted when you delete the pattern of the component. To make the selected instance independent, click on the + sign on the left of Component Pattern in the browser. All the instances of the pattern will be displayed as elements in the browser. The first element is the original component and you cannot make this element independent since it is already not dependent on the pattern. Right-click on any of the other elements and choose Independent. You will notice that the selected element will have a red color cross on it in the browser and another instance of the selected element will be displayed in the browser as a separate component.*

You can again make the independent element dependent using the same process. However, in this case the instance of the component that was placed in the assembly as a separate component and displayed in the browser will not be removed.

DELETING ASSEMBLY CONSTRAINTS

You can delete unwanted assembly constraints using the browser. To delete the assembly constraint, click on the + sign on the left of the component in the browser. The **Origin** folder along with all the constraints that are applied on the component will be displayed. Now, right-click on the constraint to be deleted and choose **Delete** from the shortcut menu. The selected component will be deleted.

CREATING THE ASSEMBLY SECTION VIEW IN THE ASSEMBLY FILE

Sometimes while assembling the components in the assembly, some of the components are hidden behind the other components of the assembly. To visualize such components, Autodesk Inventor allows you to create the section views of the assembly. However, remember that these section views are for reference only and components are not actually chopped when you create the section views. You can create three types of section views. They are **quarter section view**, **half section view**, and **three quarter section view**.

You can create the quarter section view by choosing **Quarter Section View** from the **Assembly** toolbar or panel bar. When you choose this tool, you will be prompted to select the work planes or planar faces that will be used to section the assembly. Select two planar faces, two work planes, or a planar face and a work plane to section the assembly. The assembly will be sectioned as soon as you select two planes. You can flip the quarter to be displayed by right-clicking and choosing **Flip Section** from the shortcut menu. You can continue to choose this option until the required quarter is displayed. Once the required quarter is displayed, right-click and choose **Done** from the shortcut menu. Using the same shortcut menu you can create three quarter section view also. You can also create the three quarter section view by choosing the down arrow on the right side of the **Quarter Section View** tool and choosing **Three Quarter Section View**. You will be prompted to select the work plane or the planar face for creating the section view. When you select the work plane or the planar face, you will again be prompted to select the work plane or the planar face. As soon as you select the second work plane or planar face, the three quarter section view will be created.

Similarly, to create the half section view, choose the down arrow on the right of the **Quarter Section View** and choose **Half Section View**. You will be prompted to select the planar face or the work plane for creating the section view. Since for creating a half section you require only one plane, therefore, as soon as you select the planar face or the work plane, the assembly will be sectioned about that plane. You can flip the section by right-clicking and choosing **Flip Section** from the shortcut menu. Once the required section is displayed, right-click and choose **Done** from the shortcut menu.

You can exit the section views by choosing the down arrow on the right side of the **Quarter Section View** and choosing the **End Section View**. The complete assembly will be displayed when you choose this option. Figure 9-13 shows the quarter section view of an assembly and Figure 9-14 shows the three quarter section view of the same assembly.

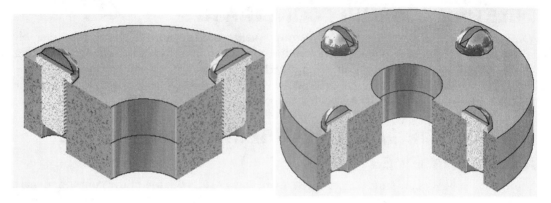

Figure 9-13   *Quarter section view of an assembly*   *Figure 9-14*   *Three quarter section view of the same assembly*

ANALYZING THE ASSEMBLIES FOR INTERFERENCE

Menu: Tools > Analyze Interference

Whenever you assemble the components of an assembly, no component should interfere with the other components of the assembly. If there is an interference between the components, this suggests that the dimensions of the components are not correct. You will have to eliminate this interference of components in the assembly to increase the efficiency of the assembly and also eliminate the material loss. In Autodesk Inventor, you can analyze the assemblies for interference using the **Analyze Interference** tool. This tool can be invoked from the **Tools** menu. When you invoke this tool, the **Interference Analysis** dialog box will be displayed as shown in Figure 9-15. The options provided under this dialog box are discussed next.

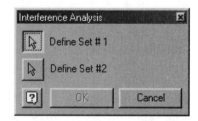

Figure 9-15 Interference Analysis dialog box

Define Set # 1

When you invoke the **Interference Analysis** dialog box, this button is chosen automatically and you will be prompted to select the component to add to the selection set. This button is chosen to select the first set of components. The selected components will be highlighted and will be displayed with a blue outline.

Define Set # 2

The **Define Set # 2** button is chosen to select the second set of components for analyzing interference. When you choose this button, the objects selected using the **Define Set # 1** button will be displayed with a green outline. The components that you select now will be displayed with a blue outline.

OK

After selecting the components in the first and the second set, choose this button to analyze the assembly. If there is no interference between the components, the **Autodesk Inventor** dialog box will be displayed. This dialog box will inform you that there is no interference between the components. However, if there is an interference between the components, the **Interference Detected** dialog box will be displayed and the portion of the components that are interfering will be displayed in red color in the assembly. The **Interference Detected** dialog box will inform you about the number of interferences found and the total volume of interference. This dialog box has a button with two arrows on the lower right corner. If you choose this button, this dialog box will expand and will provide you additional information about the interfering components, see Figure 9-16. You can copy this information on the Clipboard so that you can later copy it in a file or take a printout of this information.

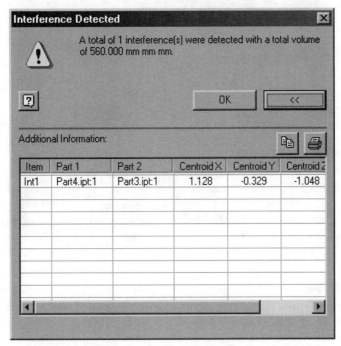

*Figure 9-16 Expanded **Interference Detected** dialog box*

CREATING DESIGN VIEWS

Menu: View > Design Views

In Autodesk Inventor, the design views are user defined views that can be used to view the assemblies. You can specify any orientation of the assembly by using a combination of drawing display tools and then save the assembly view with that orientation. Once the view is saved, you can recall that view whenever you require. In addition to the assembly file, you can also use design views for generating the views in the presentation file as well as in the drawing file.

When you invoke this tool, the **Design Views** dialog box will be displayed, see Figure 9-17. By default, the *****.default** design view will be created. This is the default view that is created automatically. You can create additional design views using this dialog box. The options available under this dialog box are discussed next.

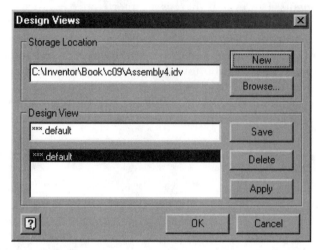

Figure 9-17 Design Views dialog box

Storage Location Area

The edit box provided in this area displays the location of the file in which the design views will be saved. By default, a file with the same name as that of the current assembly file and with the extension idv will be created. This file will store the design views of the current assembly. You can specify a new file for storing the design view by specifying a new name in the edit box and then choosing the **New** button provided in this area. You can also change the location of the file by changing its path in the edit box.

Design View Area

The options under this area are used to create a new design view, delete a design view, or make a design view current. To create a new design view, enter the name of the view in the edit box provided in this area and then choose the **Save** button. You will notice that the new design view is displayed in the list box provided below the edit box. You can delete the design view by selecting it from the list box and then choosing the **Delete** button. Note that you can also delete the default design view.

An existing design view can be made the current view by selecting it from the list box and then choosing the **Apply** button. You will notice that the assembly on the graphic view is reoriented such that it is displayed using the selected design view.

SIMULATING THE MOTION OF COMPONENTS OF AN ASSEMBLY BY DRIVING ASSEMBLY CONSTRAINTS

Autodesk Inventor allows you to simulate the motion of the components of an assembly by driving the assembly constraints. Remember that in the **Assembly** mode, you can simulate the motion of the component using only one constraint at a time. However, you can create some relation parameters and equations for simulating the motion of the components using more than one constraint at a time. To drive a constraint, right-click on it in the browser and choose **Drive Constraint**, see Figure 9-18.

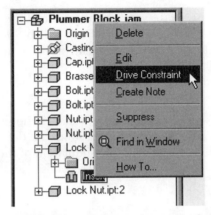

Figure 9-18 *Driving the constraints using the browser*

When you choose **Drive Constraint** from the shortcut menu, the **Drive Constraint** dialog box will be displayed, see Figure 9-19.

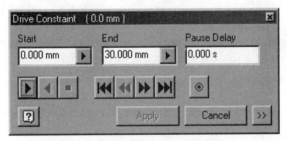

Figure 9-19 **Drive Constraint** *dialog box*

The options provided under this dialog box are discussed next.

Start

The **Start** edit box is used to specify the value of the position of the starting point of simulation. The value in this edit box depends upon the type of constraint you have selected to drive. For example, if the constraint you have selected to drive is the **Insert** constraint, the value in this edit box will be entered in terms of mm. If the constraint you have selected to simulate is the **Angle** constraint, the value in this edit box will be entered in terms of degrees. The default value of angle or offset in this edit box will be the value that you have specified for the constraint. For example, if you have applied an angle value of 90° between two components, the default value in the **Start** edit box will be 90.

Note

*The value of the **Start** edit box will also be displayed on the right side of the name of the **Drive Constraint** dialog box. Therefore, if the value of start point of the constraint simulation is -90°, the name of the dialog box will be **Drive Constraint (-90 deg)**.*

End

The **End** edit box is used to specify the value of the position for ending the simulation. Similar to the **Start** edit box, the values in this edit box will be dependent upon the type of constraint selected for simulation. The default value in this edit box will be the default value in the **Start** edit box plus 10.

Pause Delay

The **Pause Delay** edit box is used to specify some delay in the simulation of the components. The value in this edit box is entered in terms of seconds. Be default, the value in this edit box is zero. Therefore, there will be no delay in the simulation of the components. If you enter a value of 2 in this edit box, there will be a delay of 2 seconds between the steps of the simulation.

Forward

The **Forward** button is used to start the simulation of the component in the forward direction.

Reverse

The **Reverse** button is used to start the simulation of the component in the reverse direction.

Pause

The **Pause** button is used to temporarily stop the simulation of the component. The simulation can be resumed by choosing the **Forward** or the **Reverse** button again.

Minimum

The **Minimum** button is chosen to reset the simulation such that the component is positioned at the start point of the simulation.

Reverse Step

The **Reverse Step** button is chosen to position the component one step behind the current step in the simulation. This button will not be available if the component is positioned at the start point of the simulation.

Forward Step

The **Forward Step** button is chosen to position the component one step ahead of the current step in the simulation. This button will not be available if the component is positioned at the endpoint of the simulation.

Maximum

The **Maximum** button is chosen to reset the simulation such that the component is positioned at the endpoint of the simulation.

Record

The **Record** button is chosen to record the simulation of the component in the form of an avi file. When you choose this button, the **Open** dialog box will be displayed. Using this dialog box you can specify the name of the avi file in which you want to record the simulation. After specifying the name and location of the avi file, choose the **Open** button. The **Video Compression** dialog box will be displayed. This dialog box is used to specify the compressor and the compression quality of the avi files. After specifying the compression options, choose the **Forward** or the **Reverse** button to record the simulation. You can also choose both the buttons one by one to record the complete cycle of simulation. After recording the simulation, choose this button again to exit the recording.

Note

While recording the simulation, whatever is displayed inside the graphics window will be recorded. Remember that if you activate another application while the simulation is being recorded, the work done in that application will also be recorded in the avi file.

More

The **More** button is the button with two arrows and is available on the lower right corner of the **Drive Constraint** dialog box. When you choose this button, the dialog box expands and displays more options for simulating the components, see Figure 9-20. These options are discussed next.

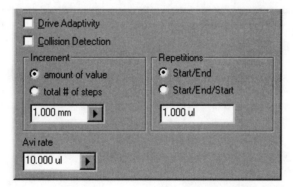

Figure 9-20 *More options in the* **Drive Constraint** *dialog box*

Drive Adaptivity

If the **Drive Adaptivity** check box is selected, the component will adapt during the process of its simulation. If you select this check box, the **Collision Detection** check box will not be available.

Collision Detection

If the **Collision Detection** check box is selected, the simulation will stop at the point where the collision is detected. The collision will be displayed in red color and the **Autodesk Inventor** dialog box will be displayed. This dialog box will inform you that a collision has been detected. If you select this check box, the **Drive Adaptivity** check box will not be available.

Increment Area

The options provided under the **Increment** area are used to specify the method for defining the increment during the simulation of the component. These options are discussed next.

amount of value

The **amount of value** radio button is used to specify the increment of simulation in terms of value of the steps. The value of the steps can be entered in the edit box available in the **Increment** area.

total # of steps

The **total # of steps** radio button is used to specify the increment of simulation in terms of the total number of steps in the simulation. The number of steps can be entered in the edit box available in the **Increment** area.

Repetitions Area

The options provided under the **Repetitions** area are used to specify the method for defining the number of repetitions of the cycles in the simulation. These options are discussed next.

Start/End

The **Start/End** radio button is selected to simulate the component such that the simulation is between the start position and the end position. If the number of repetitions is more than one, the component will be repositioned at the start position after the first cycle is over and before the second cycle starts. Since the component is repositioned at the start position after the first cycle is completed, the second cycle will again start from the start position.

Start/End/Start

The **Start/End/Start** radio button is selected to simulate the component such that the simulation is between the start position and the end position and then again from the end position to the start position. If the number of repetitions is more than one, the second cycle will be between the end position and the start position. The third cycle will be between the start position and the end position. Similarly, the fourth cycle will be between the end position and the start position.

In addition to these radio buttons, there is an edit box available in the **Repetitions** area. This edit box is used to specify the number of cycles in the simulation.

Avi rate

The **Avi rate** edit box is used to specify the number of steps that will be removed before a step of simulation is recorded in the avi file.

REORDERING THE COMPONENTS IN THE ASSEMBLY

Autodesk Inventor allows you to change the order in which the components were assembled in the assembly file. This is done using the browser. You can reorder the components such that the selected component is moved up or down in the browser. To reorder the component, select it in the browser and then drag it up or down in the browser, see Figure 9-21. The selected component will be displayed in the new order in the browser.

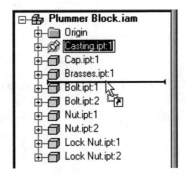

Figure 9-21 *Reordering the components*

Note

*Sometimes when you reorder the components, the **Autodesk Inventor - Restructure Assembly** dialog box will be displayed. This dialog box will inform you that the constraints were placed on the geometry that is no longer available. If you accept, the constraints applied to the selected component will become invalid. In such cases you should avoid reordering of components.*

TUTORIALS

Tutorial 1

In this tutorial you will open the Butterfly Valve assembly created in Tutorial 1 of Chapter 8 and then analyze the assembly for interference. After analyzing the assembly, you will delete the last two instances of the Screw and assemble the remaining instances by creating a pattern of the first instance. **(Expected time: 30 min)**

Before you start working on the tutorial, it is important to understand the procedure of completing the tutorial. The procedure for completing the tutorial is listed below.

a. Copy the Butterfly Valve directory from the c08 directory to the c09 directory.
b. Open the **Butterfly Valve.iam** file and analyze it for interference using the **Analyze Interference** tool.
c. Delete two instances of the Screw assembled with Retainer and then create two instances using the **Pattern Component** tool.

Saving the Butterfly Valve Assembly

In this tutorial you will open the Butterfly Valve assembly created in Chapter 8. However, it is recommended that before you open the Butterfly Valve assembly created in Chapter 8, you should copy the entire folder of Butterfly Valve in the c09 folder. This way when you make the modifications in the Butterfly Valve Assembly, the assembly of Chapter 8 is not affected. Therefore, you will first copy the Butterfly Valve folder in c09 folder and then open the **Butterfly Valve.iam** file from this folder.

1. Open a new session of Autodesk Inventor. Choose **Open** in the **Open** dialog box and then open the directory \PersonalProject\c08.

    You will notice that there is a directory with the name **Butterfly Valve** in c08 directory. This is the directory in which you have stored all the part files and the assembly file of Butterfly Valve.

2. Right-click on the Butterfly Valve directory and choose **Copy** from the shortcut menu.

3. Now, open the directory \PersonalProject\c09.

    If this directory does not exist, you can create it using the **Create New Folder** button in the **Open** dialog box.

4. Right-click in the folder and paste the Butterfly Valve directory in c09 directory. Open the Butterfly Valve directory and from this directory, open the **Butterfly Valve.iam** file.

    The Butterfly Valve assembly will be opened on the screen.

Analyzing the Assembly for Interference

When the assembly file is displayed on the screen, you will invoke the **Analyze Interference** tool and analyze the assembly for interference. There should be no interference in the assembly. The **Analyze Interference** tool can be invoked from the **Tools** menu.

1. Choose **Analyze Interference** from the **Tools** menu to display the **Interference Analysis** dialog box.

    The **Define Set # 1** button will be chosen and you will be prompted to select the components to add to the selection set.

2. Select Body from the graphics screen and then choose the **Define Set # 2** button from the dialog box. You will again be prompted to select the components to add to the selection set. Select the remaining components using the browser.

3. Choose the **OK** button. The **Analyzing Interference** dialog box will be displayed and you will notice that the system is analyzing the assembly for interference. After the analysis is complete, the **Autodesk Inventor** dialog box will be displayed that will inform you that no interference was detected. Choose **OK** in this dialog box to exit it.

Creating the Pattern of the Screw

While creating the Butterfly Valve assembly in Chapter 8, you assembled three instances of the Screw with the Retainer. You will retain the first instance of the Screw and delete the other two instances from the assembly. The other two instances will be assembled using the **Pattern Component** tool.

1. Select **Screw.ipt:2** from the browser and then press the SHIFT key and select **Screw.ipt:3** from the browser. You will notice that both the selected components are displayed in blue

color in the browser and with blue outline in the graphics screen.

2. Press the DELETE key to delete the two instances of the Screw.

    Since the holes on the Retainer are not visible in the current view, you will have to turn off the visibility of the Arm.

3. Turn off the visibility of the Arm using the browser.

4. Choose the **Pattern Component** button from the **Assembly** toolbar or choose **Pattern Component** from the **Assembly** panel bar to invoke the **Pattern Component** dialog box.

    The **Component** button will be chosen and you will be prompted to select the component to pattern.

5. Select the Screw as the component to pattern. Choose the **Associated Feature Pattern** button from the **Feature Pattern Select** area of the **Associative** tab. You will be prompted to select the feature pattern to associate to.

6. Select the hole on the lower right side of the Retainer. You will notice that the two instances of the Screw are assembled with the two holes on the Retainer. Also, the display box on the right of the **Associate Feature Pattern** button will display **Circular Pattern1**. This is the name of the pattern of holes on the Retainer.

    Note
    *If you have created the holes on the Retainer as circles while creating its basic sketch, you cannot use them to create the pattern. The reason is that you can associate the pattern to only the pattern of the feature and not of the sketch. In this case you can create a non-associative pattern using the **Circular** tab of the **Pattern Component** dialog box. However, as mentioned earlier, the pattern created using a tab other than the **Associative** tab will not be modified if the number of instances of the feature in the feature pattern is increased.*

7. Choose **OK** to create the pattern of the component and exit the **Pattern Component** dialog box.

    You will notice that the Screw is no more displayed in the browser. Instead, **Circular Pattern1** will be displayed. If you click on the + sign on the left of this, there will be three instances of the Screw with the name **Element:1**, **Element:2**, **Element:3**.

8. Turn on the display of the Arm using the browser. Choose the **Save** button from the **Standard** toolbar to save the changes in the assembly. The display of the browser after making all the modifications in the assembly is shown in Figure 9-22.

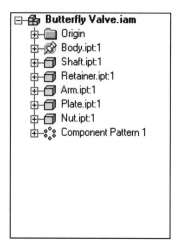

Figure 9-22 Display of the browser for Tutorial 1

Tutorial 2

In this tutorial you will open the Drill Press Vice assembly created in Exercise 1 of Chapter 8 and then check the interference between the Base and the remaining components of the assembly. After checking the interference you will drive the **Insert** constraint applied between the Clamp Screw and the Movable Jaw.   **(Expected time: 30 min)**

The following steps outline the procedure of completing this tutorial.

a. Copy the Drill Press Vice assembly from c08 directory to c09 directory.
b. Open the **Drill Press Vice.iam** file and analyze it for interference.
c. Drive the **Insert** constraint applied between the Clamp Screw and the Movable Jaw.

Saving the Drill Press Vice Assembly

Since you do not want to modify the assembly created in Chapter 8, you will have to copy the entire folder of Drill Press Vice assembly to c09 directory. After copying the files, you will open the assembly file and check the components for interference. There should be no interference between the components.

1. Invoke the **Open** dialog box by choosing the **Open** button. Open the directory \PersonalProject\c08.

    You will notice that there is a directory with the name Drill Press Vice in c08 directory.

2. Right-click on the Drill Press Vice directory and choose **Copy** from the shortcut menu.

3. Open the directory \PersonalProject\c09. Right-click and choose **Paste** to paste the Drill Press Vice directory in c09 directory.

4. Open the **Drill Press Vice.iam** file from this Drill Press Vice directory.

Checking the Assembly for Interference

1. Choose **Analyze Interference** from the **Tools** menu to invoke the **Interference Analysis** dialog box.

    The **Define Set # 1** button will be chosen by default and you will be prompted to select the components to add to the selection set.

2. Select the Base from the graphics screen. Choose the **Define Set # 2** button from the dialog box and then select the remaining components from the browser. Choose **OK**.

    The **Analyzing Interference** dialog box will be displayed informing that the interference is being analyzed.

3. After the analysis is complete, the **Autodesk Inventor** dialog box will be displayed and it will inform you that no interference was found in the assembly.

Driving the Constraint to Simulate the Motion of Assembly

The Clamp Screw Handle and the two instances of the Handle Stop were assembled with the Clamp Screw using the assembly constraints. Therefore, when you simulate the Clamp Screw by driving its constraint, you will notice that the Clamp Screw Handle and both the instances of the Handle Stop will also move along with the Clamp Screw.

1. Click on the + sign located on the left side of the Clamp Screw in the browser. It will expand and the **Origin** folder along with the different constraints applied to it are displayed.

2. Move the cursor over the **Insert** constraint. The Clamp Screw and the Movable Jaw will be highlighted in the graphics screen. This is to make sure that the constraint you select is the correct constraint. Right-click on the **Insert** constraint and choose **Drive Constraint** from the shortcut menu. The **Drive Constraint** dialog box will be displayed.

3. Enter 30 in the **End** edit box as the end value of the simulation.

4. Choose the **More** button to expand the dialog box. Select the **Start/End/Start** radio button from the **Repetitions** area and then enter 2 in the edit box provided under the same area.

    The value of 2 is entered in the edit box to have two cycles of simulation. The first cycle will be from the start position to the end position and the second cycle will be from the end position to the start position.

5. Choose the **Forward** button. You will notice the simulation of the Clamp Screw along its central axis. Also the other components assembled to it are moved along with it. Since there are two repetitions, the components will first move to a distance of 30 mm away from the Movable Jaw and then move back to the start position.

6. Exit the **Drive Constraint** dialog box by choosing the **Cancel** button.

7. Choose the **Save** button from the **Standard** toolbar to save the changes to the assembly.

Tutorial 3

In this tutorial you will create different components of the Double Bearing assembly and then assemble them as shown in Figure 9-23. Figure 9-24 shows the exploded view of the assembly. Use the **Pattern Component** tool while assembling the Bolts. The dimensions of various components are given in Figure 9-25 to Figure 9-27. After assembling the components, drive the **Insert** constraint of the first Bolt such that the remaining three instances are also simulated.

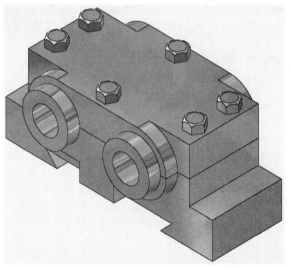

Figure 9-23 *Double Bearing assembly*

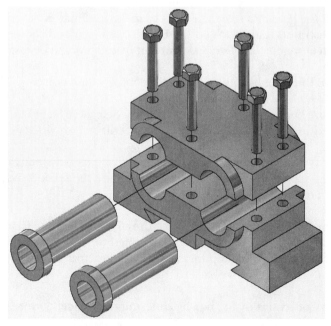

Figure 9-24 *Exploded view of Double Bearing assembly*

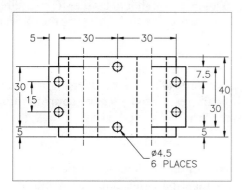

Figure 9-25a *Top view of the Cap*

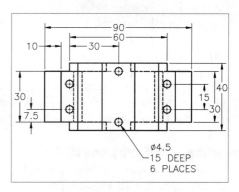

Figure 9-26a *Top view of the Base*

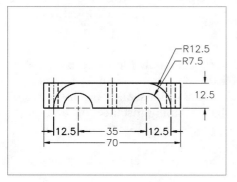

Figure 9-25b *Front view of the Cap*

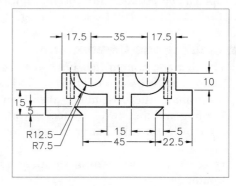

Figure 9-26b *Front view of the Base*

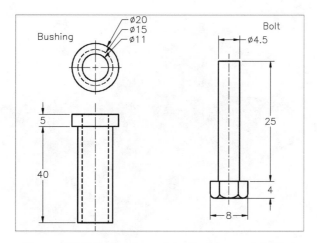

Figure 9-27 *Dimensions of the Bushing and the Bolt*

As mentioned earlier, before you start working on tutorial, you should list the steps required to complete the tutorial. The following steps outline procedure of completing the tutorial.

a. Create a directory with the name **Double Bearing** inside the c09 directory. Create all the components of Double Bearing assembly and store them in this directory.
b. Open a new assembly file and assemble the components of Double Bearing assembly. Only two instances of Bolt should be assembled and the rest should be created by patterning.
c. Drive the **Insert** constraint applied between one of the Bolt and the Cap.

Creating the Components

1. Create a directory with the name **Double Bearing** in the \PersonalProject\c09 directory and then create all the components in the individual part files and save them in this directory.

2. Open a new assembly file and save it with the name **Double Bearing.iam** in the directory \PersonalProject\c09\Double Bearing.

Assembling the Components

The first component that has to be recalled in the assembly file is the Base. After this component, you will recall the Cap and assemble these two components using the assembly constraints. After assembling these components, you will assemble two instances of the Bushing and then two instances of the Bolt. The remaining instances of the Bolt will be assembled using the **Pattern Component** tool.

1. Place one instance each of the Base and the Cap in the assembly file using the **Place Component** tool.

2. Assemble these components using the **Place Constraint** tool. The assembly after assembling the Base and the Cap is shown in Figure 9-28.

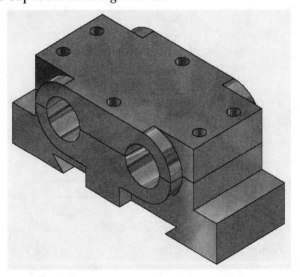

Figure 9-28 Assembly of the Base and the Cap

3. Place two instances of the Bushing and then assemble them using the **Place Constraint** tool.

4. Similarly, place two instances of the Bolt and assemble them as shown in Figure 9-29.

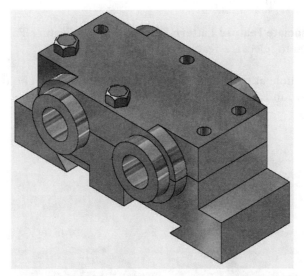

Figure 9-29 After assembling two instances each of the Bolt and the Bushing

It is presumed that one of the four holes at the corners of the Cap was created and the other three were patterned. Similarly, one of the holes in the middle of the Cap was created and the other was patterned. Since all the six holes were not created using the single pattern, you will have to use the **Pattern Component** tool twice. The first time it will assemble the Bolt on the remaining three holes at the corners and the second time it will assemble the Bolt in the remaining hole in the middle of the Cap.

5. Choose **Pattern Component** button from the **Assembly** toolbar or choose **Pattern Component** from the **Assembly** panel bar to invoke the **Pattern Component** dialog box. You will be prompted to select the component to pattern.

6. Select the Bolt at the lower left corner of the Cap.

7. Choose the **Associate Feature Pattern** button from the **Feature Pattern Select** area. You will be prompted to select the feature pattern to associate to.

8. Select one of the three holes at the corners of the Cap. Three instances of the Bolt will be assembled at the three holes.

    Since the **Pattern Component** tool is still active, you will again be prompted to select the component to pattern. However, to complete the assembling of the Bolts using the **Pattern Component** tool, you will have to choose **OK** and exit this dialog box. If you select the Bolt again, the pattern that will be created is not the one that you want.

10. Choose **OK** to exit this dialog box and assemble the remaining three instances of the Bolt.

11. Again invoke the **Pattern Component** tool and select the Bolt assembled with the hole at the middle of the Cap.

12. Choose the **Associate Feature Pattern** button from the **Feature Pattern Select** area. You will be prompted to select the feature pattern to associate to.

13. Select the other hole at the middle of the Cap. Choose **OK**. The final Double Bearing assembly is shown in Figure 9-30.

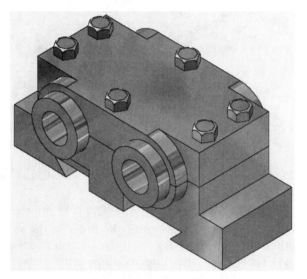

Figure 9-30 *Double Bearing assembly*

14. Choose the **Save** button from the **Standard** toolbar to save the assembly.

Driving the Constraint of the Bolt

When you drive the constraint of the first Bolt at the lower left corner of the Cap, you will notice that the remaining three instances at the corners of the Cap also simulate along with the first Bolt. This is because the remaining three instances were assembled using the **Pattern Component** tool. This tool will force the three instances to behave similar to the original Bolt.

1. Click on the + sign located on the left of **Component Pattern 1**. You will notice that four instances of Bolts will be displayed with the name **Element:1**, **Element:2**, **Element:3**, and **Element:4**.

2. Click on the + sign on the left of **Element:1**. The **Bolt.ipt:1** will be displayed. Click on the left of **Bolt.ipt:1** to display the **Origin** folder and the **Insert** constraint.

3. Right-click on the **Insert** constraint and choose **Drive Constraint** from the shortcut menu.

The **Drive Constraint** dialog box will be displayed.

4. Enter 30 as the value in the **End** edit box. Choose the **More** button to expand the dialog box.

5. Select **Start/End/Start** radio button from the **Repetitions** area and then enter 2 in the edit box available in this area.

6. Choose the **Forward** button.

All four bolts at the corners will be simulated and moved to a distance of 30 mm in the upward direction. All bolts are then moved back to their original position without any pause between the cycles. Figure 9-31 displays the assembly with the four bolts at the top-most position, just before the downward cycle begins.

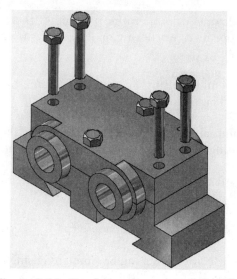

Figure 9-31 Simulating the motion of the Bolts

7. Exit the **Drive Constraint** dialog box by choosing the **Cancel** button. Choose the **Save** button to save the assembly.

Self-Evaluation Test

Answer the following questions and then compare your answers with the answers provided at the end of this chapter.

1. The components assembled using the **Pattern Component** tool can be replaced by other components. (T/F)

2. You can edit the components in the assembly file. (T/F)

3. The degrees of freedom symbol for a grounded component will not be displayed. (T/F)

4. The pattern of the component created using the **Circular** tab of the **Pattern Component** dialog box will be automatically modified if the pattern of the feature is modified. (T/F)

5. Autodesk Inventor allows you to open the part file of the component for editing the component. This is done by right-clicking on it in the browser and choosing _____ from the shortcut menu.

6. If a component is assembled using an underconstrained component, a green color _____ is displayed on the component.

7. The assembly constraints applied on a component can be edited by right-clicking on it in the browser and choosing _____ from the shortcut menu.

8. The three types of assembly section views that can be created in the assembly file are _____, _____, and _____.

9. To analyze the assembly for interference, choose _____ from the _____ menu.

10. The motion of assembly components can be simulated using the _____ dialog box.

Review Questions

Answer the following questions.

1. You can replace all the instances of a component in the assembly file. (T/F)

2. Any instance of a component assembled using the **Pattern Component** tool can be made independent. (T/F)

3. You can flip the section of the section view in the assembly. (T/F)

4. The information of interference between the components can be printed. (T/F)

5. The simulation of the components of assembly can be saved to an avi file. (T/F)

6. You can use which one of the following tools to replace only one instance of a component in the assembly?

    (a) **Replace**   (b) **Replace All**
    (c) **Replace Component**   (d) None

7. You can store the information related to the simulation of the components in the avi file by using which one of the following buttons in the **Drive Constraint** dialog box?

    (a) **Record**   (b) **Forward**
    (c) **Reverse**   (d) None

8. By default, the design view files are saved in which of the following format?

    (a) avi   (b) idv
    (c) ipt   (d) iam

9. Which one of the following buttons should be chosen to exit the section views in the assembly file?

    (a) **Full Section View**   (b) **No Section View**
    (c) **Half Section View**   (d) **End Section View**

10. If the pattern of a component is created using the **Circular** tab of the **Pattern Component** dialog box, which one of the following tab will be available in the **Edit Component Pattern** dialog box?

    (a) **Associative**   (b) **Rectangular**
    (c) **Circular**   (d) None

Exercise

Exercise 1

Open the Plummer Block assembly created in Tutorial 2 of Chapter 8 (Figure 9-32) and then create a design view with the name **Plummer Block**. After creating the design view, analyze the assembly for interference and then simulate the motion of the two Bolts. The bolts should move in the downward direction.   **(Expected time: 30 min)**

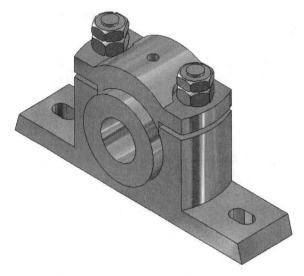

Figure 9-32 Plummer Block assembly created in Chapter 8

Answers to Self-Evaluation Test
1. F, 2. T, 3. T, 4. F, 5. **Open**, 6. cube, 7. **Edit**, 8. quarter section view, half section view, three quarter section view, 9. **Analyze Interference**, **Tools**, 10. **Drive Constraint**

Chapter 10

Drawing Mode-I

Learning Objectives

After completing this chapter you will be able to:

• *Understand the use of drawing views.*
• *Understand different types of drawing views in Autodesk Inventor.*
• *Create different types of drawing views.*
• *Edit drawing views.*
• *Delete drawing views.*
• *Move drawing views.*
• *Copy drawing views.*
• *Rotate drawing views.*
• *Assign different hatch patterns to different components in assembly section views.*
• *Suppress components in assembly section views.*

THE DRAWING MODE

Once you have created a solid model or an assembly, you will have to generate their drawing views. Drawing views are two-dimensional representations of a solid model or an assembly. Autodesk Inventor provides you with a specialized environment for generating drawing views. This specialized environment is called **Drawing** mode and has only those tools that are required to create or modify the drawing views and their options. As mentioned earlier, all the modes of Autodesk Inventor are bidirectionally associative. This property ensures that whenever you make any modification in a part or an assembly, the changes are reflected in the drawing views. Also, if you change the dimensions of a component or an assembly in the **Drawing** mode, the changes are also reflected in the part or assembly file. You can invoke the **Drawing** mode for generating the drawing views by selecting any **.idw** format file from the **Metric** tab of the **Open** dialog box, see Figure 10-1. Autodesk Inventor has provided different .idw files with predefined drafting standards such as ISO standard, BIN standard, DIN standard, and so on. You can use the required standard file and proceed to the **Drawing** mode for generating the drawing views. The selected sheet will follow its standard in generating and dimensioning the drawing views. However, you can change the standards that will be followed by modifying the standards in the sheet.

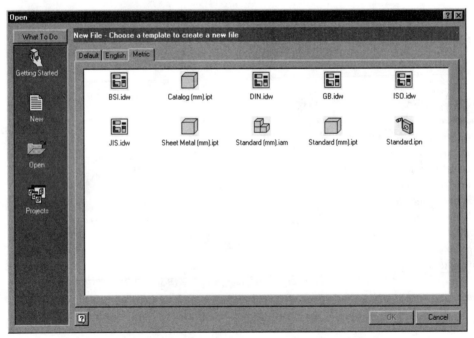

*Figure 10-1 Various .idw format files for proceeding to the **Drawing** mode*

The default screen appearance of the **Drawing** mode is shown in Figure 10-2. You will notice that a sheet is available in this mode. This sheet also has a title block on the lower right corner. This drawing sheet is similar to the drawing sheet on which drawing views are drawn using manual methods. This sheet is your working environment and you can generate as many views as you want of the selected component or assembly on this sheet. You can also change the sheet style, title block style, or add more sheets for generating the drawing views.

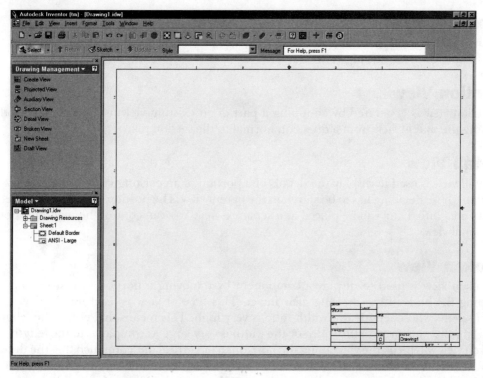

*Figure 10-2 Screen display in **Drawing** mode*

TYPE OF VIEWS

Autodesk Inventor allows you to create six type of views. They are discussed next.

Base View

The base view is the first view generated in the drawing sheet. This view is generated using the original model, assembly, or presentation. The base view is an independent view and is not affected by changes in any other view in the drawing sheet. Most of the other views in the sheet will be generated taking this view as the parent view.

Note
*The base view is created using the **Create View** tool. This tool is discussed in the next section.*

Projected View

The projected view is generated using any of the existing views as the parent view. This view is generated by projecting the lines either normal to the parent view or at an angle of 30° to the parent view. If the lines are projected normal to the parent view, the resultant view will be an orthographic view such as top view, front view, side view, and so on. If the lines are projected at 30°, the resultant view will be an isometric view. An isometric view is a two-dimensional representation of a three-dimensional model. You can view all three axes of a 3D model in the isometric view.

Auxiliary View

An auxiliary view is a drawing view that is generated by projecting the lines normal to a specified edge of an existing view.

Section View

A section view is generated by chopping a part of an existing view using a plane and then viewing the parent view from a direction normal to the section plane.

Detail View

A detail view is used to display the details of a portion of an existing view. You can select the portion whose detailing has to be shown in the parent view. The portion that you have selected will be magnified and will be placed as a separate view. You can control the magnification of the detail view.

Broken View

A broken view is used to display a component by removing a portion of it from between, keeping the ends of the drawing view intact. This type of view is used for displaying the components whose length and width ratio is very high. This means that either the length is very large as compared to the width or the width is very large as compared to the length. The broken view will break the view along the horizontal or vertical direction such that the drawing view fits the area you require. Note that in these views, the dimension of the edge that is broken will still be displayed as the actual value. However, that dimension will have a broken symbol that will suggest that this dimension value is for the edge that is broken in the view.

GENERATING THE DRAWING VIEWS

The method of generating all the six type of views is discussed next.

Generating Base View

Toolbar:	Drawing Management > Create View
Panel bar:	Drawing Management > Create View

As mentioned earlier, the first view that will be generated in the drawing sheet is the base view. This view is generated using the **Create View** tool. You can also invoke this tool by right-clicking on the sheet in the drawing window or in the browser and choosing **Create View**. When you invoke this tool, the **Create View** dialog box will be displayed as shown in Figure 10-3. The options provided under this dialog box are discussed next.

Component Area

The options provided under the **Component** area are used to select the component or the assembly whose drawing view you want to generate. These options are discussed next.

File

The **File** drop-down list displays the files that are selected for creating the drawing views. By default, this drop-down list displays the **<select document>** option. This is because

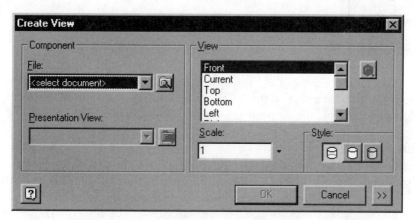

Figure 10-3 Create View dialog box

until now, no file is selected. To select a file whose drawing views you want to generate, choose the **Explore directories** button on the right of the **File** drop-down list. When you choose this button, the **Open** dialog box will be displayed, see Figure 10-4.

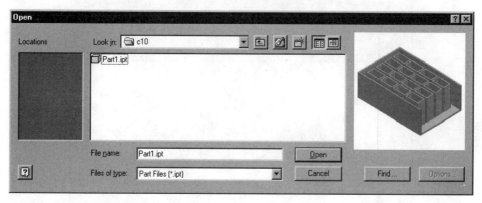

Figure 10-4 Open dialog box for selecting the file whose drawing views will be generated

This dialog box can be used to select the file whose drawing views you want to generate. By default, this dialog box allows you to select the part file that is saved in the .ipt format. However, you can also select the assembly file or the presentation file by selecting the option for those files from the **Files of type** drop-down list.

Note
If the file that you selected for generating the drawing views is not in the current directory, the ***Autodesk Inventor*** *information box will be displayed. This box will inform you that the location of the selected file is not in the current project folder. It will also inform you that to make sure that the file is found the next time you open the files in which that file is referenced, add the location of the file in the project or move the file in the current project folder.*

After you have selected the file, you will notice that its name and location is now displayed in the **File** drop-down list. Similarly, if you select any other file, its information will also be displayed in the **File** drop-down list.

Presentation View

If the selected file has some design views associated to it, they will be displayed in the **Presentation View** drop-down list. If the design view files of the selected file are not saved in the current directory, choose the **Explore directories** button available on right of this drop-down list to select the directory in which the design view files are saved.

View Area

The options under this area are used to specify the type of view, the scale factor of the view, and the display type of the view. The view to be created can be selected from the list box provided in this area. You can select any predefined view such as top, front, right, left, isometric top-right, isometric top-left, and so on. The resultant view will be based on the option selected from this list box. You can also create a drawing view with user-defined orientation by choosing the **Change view orientation** button provided on the right side of the list box. When you choose this button, the **Custom View** window will be displayed as shown in Figure 10-5.

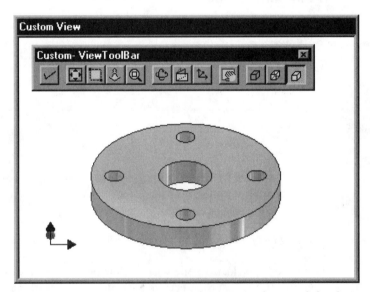

Figure 10-5 Custom View window for creating the user-defined view

The default view of the model will be displayed in this window. This window also provides you with the **Custom-View ToolBar**. This toolbar has different drawing display tools that can be used to modify the view orientation and display in the **Custom View** window. Once you have achieved the required view orientation, choose the **Exit Custom View** button that is the first button in the **Custom-View ToolBar**. The **Custom View** window will be closed and the **Create View** dialog box will be redisplayed. Also, the preview of the view created using the **Custom View** window will be displayed on the drawing sheet in the background.

Scale

The **Scale** edit box is used to specify the scale for the drawing view. You can specify the scale in this edit box or select the predefined standard scales. The predefined standard scales can be selected by choosing the down arrow on the right of the **Scale** edit box. When you choose this down arrow, the list of standard predefined scales will be displayed. Select the scale that you require from this list.

Style Area

The buttons provided under the **Style** area are used to specify the display type for the drawing views. You can view the drawing view with hidden lines, without hidden lines, or with the shaded display by choosing their respective buttons from this area. Figure 10-6 shows the drawing view with hidden lines and Figure 10-7 shows the drawing view without hidden lines.

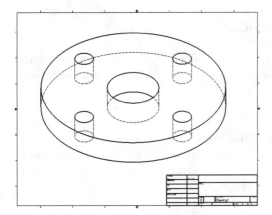

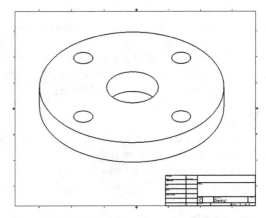

Figure 10-6 Drawing view with hidden lines   *Figure 10-7 Drawing view without hidden lines*

More

This is the button with two arrows provided on the lower right corner of the **Create View** dialog box. When you choose this button, the **Create View** dialog box expands and displays additional options for generating the drawing views, see Figure 10-8.

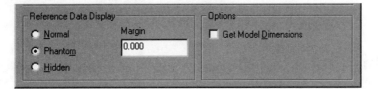

*Figure 10-8 More options displayed upon choosing the **More** button*

Reference Data Display

The options under the **Reference Data Display** area are used to select the display type for the reference data. These options are discussed next.

   Normal. The **Normal** radio button is selected to display the reference data using normal options without giving special consideration to it.

Phantom. The **Phantom** radio button is used to give special consideration to the reference data. If the drawing view is generated with the wireframe display type, the reference data will be displayed on top of the product data. However, the reference data and the product data do not hide each other. Also, the tangent edges of the reference data will not be displayed and the remaining edges of the reference data will be displayed using the phantom linetype. If the drawing view is generated with the shaded display type, the product data is displayed on top of the reference data using the shaded display type. The reference data will be displayed using the wireframe display type and the tangent edges of the reference data will be suppressed. The remaining edges of the reference data will be displayed using the phantom linetype.

Hidden. If the **Hidden** radio button is selected, the reference data will be suppressed and will not be displayed in the drawing view.

Margin. The **Margin** edit box is used to specify the value by which the view boundaries will be extended on all sides. The view boundaries are extended to display additional reference data in the drawing view.

Options
The **Options** area displays the **Get Model Dimensions** check box for displaying the dimensions that were used to create the model in the **Part** mode. The dimensions will be automatically placed when you place the drawing view. However, only those dimensions will be displayed that are normal to the selected view.

Note
*The Get Model Dimensions check box in the **Options** area will not be available if you are generating the drawing view of an assembly file or a presentation file.*

Tip. *By default, the model dimensions are displayed in the drawing view using the default dimensioning standards and dimension style. If the default dimension standard use dimensions in inches, the dimensions in the drawing views will be displayed in inches even if the dimensions were specified in millimeters in the model. However, you can modify the dimension standards as well as dimension style. This will be discussed in later chapters.*

Generating Projected Views

Toolbar:	Drawing Management > Projected View
Panel bar:	Drawing Management > Projected View

As mentioned earlier, the projected views are generated by projecting the lines from an existing view. To generate a projected view, invoke this tool and then select the parent view using which you want to generate the projected view. After selecting the parent view, you will be prompted to specify a location for the projected view. Specify a location for the projected view using the left mouse button. If you move the cursor in the horizontal or the vertical direction, an orthographic view will be generated. Similarly, if you move the cursor at an angle from the parent view, an isometric view will be generated. You can preview the resultant view on the drawing sheet. Once you have specified the location for the projected view, a rectangle will be displayed at that location and you will again be prompted to specify the location for the projected view. To generate the view, right-click on the drawing sheet and choose **Create** from the shortcut menu, see Figure 10-9.

Figure 10-9 *Choosing the **Create** option*

Note
The display type of the projected views will be the same as that of the parent view. However, you can modify the display type of the projected view.

Tip. *While generating the projected view, if you move the cursor in the horizontal or the vertical direction from the parent view, a center line will be displayed from the center of the parent view to the center of the projected view. This center line will suggest that the view is being projected normal to the parent view. Therefore, the resultant view will be an orthographic view.*

Figure 10-10 shows the drawing sheet with a base view and two projected views. The base view is the top view placed on the top of the drawing sheet and the projected views are the front view and the isometric view.

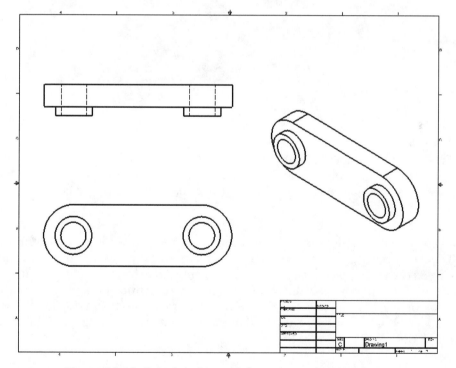

Figure 10-10 *Drawing sheet with base view and projected views*

Generating Auxiliary Views

Toolbar:	Drawing Management > Auxiliary View
Panel bar:	Drawing Management > Auxiliary View

As mentioned earlier, auxiliary views are generated by projecting the lines normal to a specified edge in the parent view. To generate an auxiliary view, invoke the **Auxiliary View** tool and then select the parent view. When you select the parent view, the **Auxiliary View** dialog box will be displayed as shown in Figure 10-11. The options under this dialog box are discussed next.

Figure 10-11 Auxiliary View dialog box

Label Area

The edit box provided under the **Label** area is used to enter the label for the auxiliary view. By default, this label will not be displayed on the drawing view. However, if you select the **Show Label** check box, the label of the view will be displayed on the drawing sheet.

Scale Area

The edit box provided under the **Scale** area is used to specify the scale factor for the auxiliary view. By default, the scale of the auxiliary view will be the same as that of the parent view. However, you can create an auxiliary view with a different scale by specifying the scale factor in this edit box. You can also select the predefined scale factors by choosing the down arrow on the right of this edit box and selecting the scale factor from the list that is displayed. The **Show Scale** check box can be selected to display the scale factor on the drawing view. This check box is cleared by default.

Style Area

The buttons provided in the **Style** area are used to specify the display type for the drawing view. By default, it will be the same as that of the parent view. However, you can specify the required display type by choosing its button from this area.

After you select the parent view, you will notice that an inclined line will be attached to the cursor. This inclined line is attached to the cursor for reminding you to select the edge in the parent view that will be used for generating the auxiliary view. When you select the edge, the preview of the view that will be generated is displayed on the sheet. You will notice that the view that is being generated is parallel to the selected edge. Also, a center line will be displayed that will be normal to the edge as well as the auxiliary view, see Figure 10-12. This center line and the **Auxiliary View** dialog box will be automatically removed once you place the view.

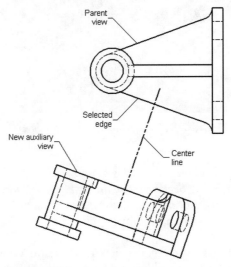

Figure 10-12 *Generating the auxiliary view*

Generating Section Views

Toolbar:	Drawing Management > Section View
Panel bar:	Drawing Management > Section View

As mentioned earlier, section views are generated by chopping a portion of an existing view using a cutting plane and then viewing the parent view from the direction normal to the cutting plane. To create a section view, invoke this tool and then select the parent view. After you select the parent view, a red rectangle will be created about the parent view and the cursor, that was originally an arrow, will be replaced by a + cursor. Using this cursor you will define the cutting plane. In Autodesk Inventor, the cutting plane will be defined by sketching one or more than one lines. You can use the temporary tracking option for drawing the lines that will define the section plane. After you have drawn the lines, right-click on the drawing sheet and choose **Continue** from the shortcut menu. The **Section View** dialog box will be displayed as shown in Figure 10-13 and you will be prompted to enter the location for the drawing view. You will notice that the line that you had drawn is converted into a section plane now and the preview of the section view is displayed on the drawing sheet. This preview will move as you move the cursor on the drawing sheet. However, it will always remain parallel to the section plane.

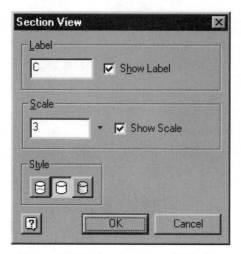

Figure 10-13 Section View dialog box

 Note

*The options under the **Section View** dialog box are similar to those under the **Auxiliary View** dialog box. However, in the **Section View** dialog box, the **Show Label** and the **Show Scale** check boxes will be selected by default. You can clear these check boxes if you do not want to display the label and the scale on the drawing view.*

When you specify the location of the section view, the **Section View** dialog box will be closed and the section view will be generated. The part of original view that is sectioned will be displayed with hatching lines in the section view. Figure 10-14 shows the section view generated from the parent view.

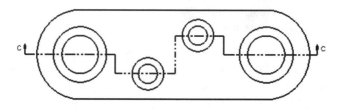

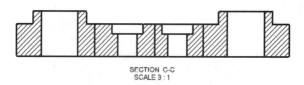

Figure 10-14 Base view and section view

Generating Detail Views

Toolbar:	Drawing Management > Detail View
Panel bar:	Drawing Management > Detail View

Detail views are used to display the details of a portion of an existing view by magnifying that portion and displaying it as a separate view. To create a detail view, invoke this tool and then select the parent view. When you select the parent view, the **Detail View** dialog box will be displayed as shown in Figure 10-15. The options under this dialog box are similar to those discussed under the **Auxiliary View** dialog box.

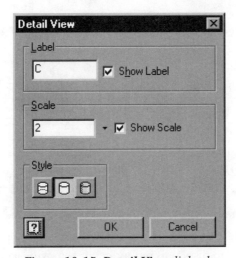

Figure 10-15 Detail View dialog box

You will notice that when you select the parent view, you will be prompted to specify the start point of the fence and a circle is attached to the cursor. The fence is actually the boundary that will enclose the portion of the parent view that will be magnified. Select a point on the parent view. This point should lie on the area that you want to magnify. The start point of the fence will be taken as the center and a circle will be displayed and you will be prompted to specify the endpoint of the fence. This circle will act as the boundary for the portion that will be magnified. Specify the endpoint of the fence by selecting another point. As soon as you specify the second point, the portion that you have magnified will be displayed as a view and will be attached to the cursor. You will be prompted to specify the location for the view. Specify the placement point for the drawing view. The detail view will be placed at the point that you specify. Figure 10-16 shows the drawing sheet with base view, two projected views, and a detail view.

Note
In Figure 10-16, the isometric view is generated using the front view as the base view.

Generating Broken Views

Toolbar:	Drawing Management > Broken View
Panel bar:	Drawing Management > Broken View

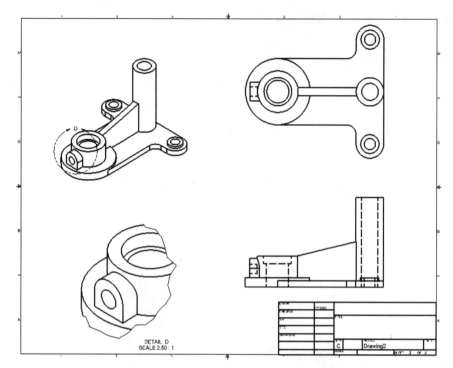

DETAIL D
SCALE 2.50 : 1

Figure 10-16 *Drawing sheet with base view, projected views, and detail view*

A broken view is used to display a component by removing a portion of it from between, keeping the ends of the drawing view intact. These views are generally used to display the models that have a high length to width ratio. Note that this tool will not create a separate view. This tool will break an existing view such that specified portion of the view is removed and the remaining portion of the view is displayed along with the ends of the views. The views will be broken with the help of two planes defined by lines. You do not have to draw the lines for defining the cutting planes. You just have to specify the location of the first and the second cutting plane. The portion of view that lies inside the two cutting planes will be removed and the remaining view will be displayed. To break the view, invoke this tool and then select the view you want to break. The **Broken View** dialog box will be displayed as shown in Figure 10-17 when you select the view to be broken. The options under this dialog box are discussed next.

Style Area

The buttons under the **Style** area are used to specify the style for displaying the break symbol. The style options provided under this area are discussed next.

Rectangular Style

The **Rectangular Style** button is used to break the views of a noncylindrical component.

Structural Style

The **Structural Style** button is used to break the views of a cylindrical component.

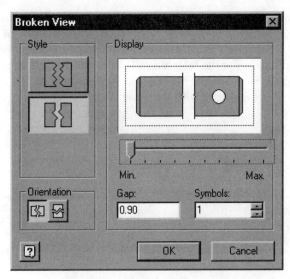

Figure 10-17 Broken View dialog box

Orientation Area

The buttons under the **Orientation** area are used specify the break in the horizontal or the vertical direction. Depending upon whether the view is vertical or horizontal, the option from this area will be selected.

Display Area

The options under the **Display** area are used to control the display of break lines in the broken view. The preview window in this area will display the break lines that will be displayed on the broken view. As you modify the options in the **Display** area, the preview in the preview window will also change. The scale of break lines can be modified using the slider bar in this area. The preview of change in scale will be displayed in the preview window and on the drawing sheet when you move the cursor on the drawing sheet.

Gap

The **Gap** edit box is used to specify the value of break gap in the broken view.

Symbol

The **Symbol** spinner is used to specify the number of break spinners in the break line when the **Structural Style** button is selected from the **Style** area. The maximum number of symbols that are allowed are three. This spinner will not be available if you choose the **Rectangular Style** button from the **Style** area.

You will notice that when you select the view to be broken, two lines with break symbol will be attached to the cursor and you will be prompted to specify the start point for the material to be removed. This point will be the point where the first cutting plane will be placed. After you specify the first point, you will notice that two break lines are placed at that point. These break lines will be based on the style that you have selected from the **Style** area. You will now be prompted to specify the endpoint for the material to be removed. This point will define the position of the second cutting plane. After you specify the location of the second cutting plane, you will notice that the view will shrink as the material between the two cutting planes is removed. Also, the break lines of the selected style will be displayed on the view. Figure 10-18 shows a broken view created using the rectangular style and Figure 10-19 shows a broken view created using the structural style with three symbols.

Figure 10-18 *Broken view created using the rectangular style*

Figure 10-19 *Broken view created using the structural style*

*Tip. If you break a projected orthographic view or a section view using the **Broken View** tool, the parent view will also be converted into a broken view. The scale and style of the broken parent view will be similar to that of the projected or section view. Similarly, if you break a view that is used as a parent view for generating other views, the dependent views will also be converted into broken views. Note that the isometric view generated by projecting the lines from an existing view is not dependent upon the parent view and so will not be converted into a broken view.*

SKETCHING THE DRAWING VIEWS

Toolbar:	Drawing Management > Draft View
Panel bar:	Drawing Management > Draft View

In addition to generating all the above-mentioned views, Autodesk Inventor also allows you to sketch a drawing view using the sketching tools. After sketching, these views will behave similar to the generated views. The drawing views can be sketched using the **Draft View** tool. When you invoke this tool, the **Draft View** dialog box will be displayed as shown in Figure 10-20. The options provided under this dialog box are discussed next.

Label Area

The edit box available in the **Label** area is used to specify the label of the view. The label of the view will be displayed in the browser.

Scale Area

The edit box available in the **Scale** area is used to specify the scale of the view. You can enter

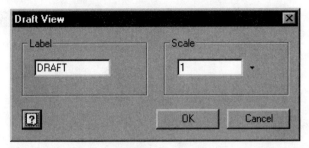

Figure 10-20 Draft View dialog box

the scale in the edit box or select the predefined scales by using the list that is displayed when you choose the down arrow on the right of the edit box.

After specifying the label and the scale for the view, choose the **OK** button. The sketching environment will be activated. All the sketching tools will be available in this environment that can be used to sketch the drawing view.

EDITING THE DRAWING VIEWS

In Autodesk Inventor, you can edit a drawing view by using the shortcut menu displayed upon right-clicking on the drawing view in the browser or on the sheet. If you move the cursor over a drawing view in the sheet, you will notice that a red box is drawn around the view using dotted lines. This box is the bounding box of the view. To edit a view, right-click when the box is displayed on the view and then choose **Edit View** from the shortcut menu. The **Edit View** dialog box will be displayed as shown in Figure 10-21. You can also display this dialog box by double-clicking on the drawing view when a red dotted box is displayed or by double-clicking on the required view in the browser.

Note
The options under this dialog box will be available based on the type of view selected for editing.

The options available under the **Edit View** dialog box are discussed next.

Label Area

The edit box available in the **Label** area is used to enter the name of the view. You can modify the current name by entering the new name in this edit box. The **Show Label** check box is available for displaying the name of the view on the drawing sheet. If you select this check box, the name of the view will be displayed on the drawing sheet.

Style Area

The buttons available in the **Style** area are used to specify the display style of the view. Some of the views acquire the display style from the parent view. Therefore, the buttons in this area will not be available. However, these buttons will be available if you clear the **Style from Base** check box. For the base view, the **Style from Base** check box will not be available. The **Tangent Edges** check box is selected to display the tangent edges at the end of the curves or the arcs in the drawing view. If this check box is cleared, the tangent edges drawn at the end of a curve or

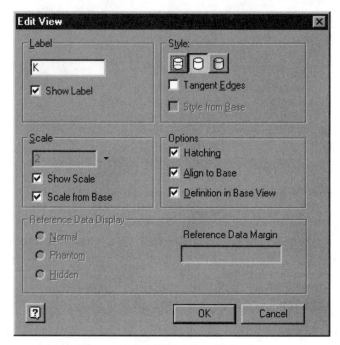

Figure 10-21 Edit View dialog box

an arc in the drawing view will be removed. If the **Style from Base** check box is available and is selected, this check box will not be available.

Scale Area

The options under this area are related to the scale of the drawing view. The edit box in this area is used to modify the current view scale. This edit box will be available only when the **Scale from Base** check box is not available or when it is cleared. The **Show Scale** check box is selected to show the scale of a view on the drawing sheet. The **Scale from Base** check box will not be available for the views that are not dependent on any view.

Options Area

The check boxes available in the **Options** area are discussed next.

Hatching

The **Hatching** check box is available for the section views. This check box is selected for displaying the hatching lines in the section view. If this check box is cleared, the hatching lines will not be displayed in the section view.

Align to Base

The **Align to Base** check box is available for the views that are dependent upon an existing view. This check box is selected for aligning the view to the parent view. The alignment of this view will change automatically if the alignment of the parent view is changed. If you clear this check box, the dependent views will not be modified if you reorient or relocate the parent view.

Definition in Base View

The **Definition in Base View** check box is available for the views that have some of their information in the parent view that was used to generate this view. For example, section views that have section plane in the parent view or the detail views that have their boundary in the parent view. If this check box is cleared, the information related to the selected view will not be displayed in the parent view.

Reference Data Display Area

The **Reference Data Display** area provides the options related to the reference data in the parent view. These options are similar to those discussed in the **Create View** dialog box.

DELETING THE DRAWING VIEWS

The unwanted drawing views can be deleted from the sheet by using the browser or from the sheet. To delete the drawing view using the browser, right-click on the drawing view in the browser and choose **Delete** from the shortcut menu, see Figure 10-22.

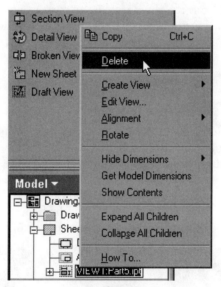

Figure 10-22 Deleting the drawing view using the browser

If the selected drawing views have some dependent drawing views, the **Delete View** dialog box will be displayed. This dialog box will confirm whether you want to delete the selected view and its dependent views. Choose **OK** if you want to delete the views. To view the views that are dependent upon the selected view, choose the **More** button with two arrows on the bottom right corner of this dialog box. The dialog box will expand and will provide the list of the dependent views, see Figure 10-23. By default, this dialog box will show **Yes** for all the views in the **Delete** column of the expanded area. This suggests that all the dependent views will be deleted if you delete the parent view. However, if you do not want to delete a dependent view, click on **Yes** once using the left mouse button. You will notice that **Yes** is replaced by **No**. This suggests that the selected dependent view will not be deleted if you delete the parent view.

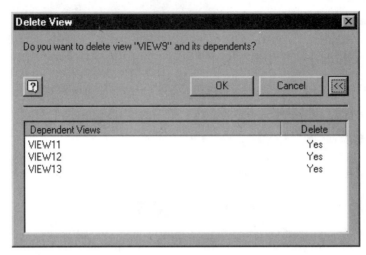

Figure 10-23 *Expanded* **Delete View** *dialog box*

To delete the drawing view from the sheet, move the cursor over the drawing view. A dotted rectangle, that is actually the bounding box of the drawing view, will be displayed. When this dotted rectangle is displayed, right-click and choose **Delete** from the shortcut menu. You can also pick a point on the drawing view when the dotted rectangle is displayed and then press the DELETE key from the keyboard.

MOVING THE DRAWING VIEWS

You can relocate the existing drawing view by moving it from its current location to a new location. However, remember that if the selected view has some dependent views, they will also move along with the parent view. To move the view, move the cursor over the view. When the dotted rectangle is displayed, press and hold the left mouse button down and drag the view to a new location in the sheet. Note that the section views, auxiliary views, and the projected orthographic views can be moved only along the axis in which they were projected. The isometric views and detail views can be moved to any location in the drawing sheet.

Tip. *You can suppress the option to move the dependent views along with the parent view if you do not want to move them with the parent view. This is done by clearing the* **Align to Base** *option from the* **Options** *area of the* **Edit View** *dialog box. This dialog box is displayed upon right-clicking on the dependent views.*

COPYING THE DRAWING VIEWS

Autodesk Inventor allows you to copy an existing view at a new location in the current sheet or in a new sheet. You can also copy the existing view in a new drawing file. To copy the view, move the cursor over the view and right-click when the dotted rectangle is displayed. Choose **Copy** from the shortcut menu that is displayed upon right-clicking. You can also right-click on the drawing view in the browser and choose **Copy** from the shortcut menu. You can paste this drawing view at a new location, in a new sheet, or in a new drawing file. Note that if the selected drawing view has some dependent views, they will not be copied along with the parent view.

Note

The process of adding more sheets will be discussed in the next chapter.

ROTATING THE DRAWING VIEW

Autodesk Inventor allows you to rotate the selected drawing view about its center point. If you rotate a drawing view that has some dependent views, they will also be affected. However, if you rotate the dependent view, the parent view is not affected. You can rotate an existing drawing view by right-clicking on it in the browser or on the sheet and choosing **Rotate** from the shortcut menu. When you choose this option, the **Rotate View** dialog box will be displayed as shown in Figure 10-24. The options available under this dialog box are discussed next.

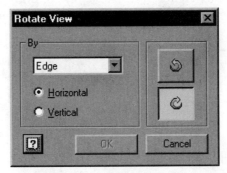

Figure 10-24 Rotate View dialog box

By Area

The drop-down list available under the **By** area is used to select the method of rotating the selected drawing view. There are two methods for rotating the drawing views. These methods are discussed next.

Edge

The **Edge** method is used to force the orientation of the selected view such that the selected edge becomes horizontal or vertical. The orientation will depend upon whether you select the **Horizontal** or **Vertical** radio button. These buttons will be displayed in the **By** area when you select **Edge** from the drop-down list. To rotate the view using this method, select the **Horizontal** or **Vertical** radio button and then select the edge in the selected view.

Angle

The **Angle** method is used to rotate the selected view by specifying the rotation angle of the view. The angle can be specified in the edit box that is displayed in the **By** area when you select the **Angle** option from the drop-down list.

Counter clockwise

The **Counter clockwise** button is the first button in the area that is on the right of the **By** area. This button is chosen to rotate the selected view in the counterclockwise direction.

Clockwise

The **Clockwise** button is available below the **Counter clockwise** button. This button is chosen to rotate the selected view in the clockwise direction.

ASSIGNING DIFFERENT HATCH PATTERNS TO THE COMPONENTS IN THE ASSEMBLY SECTION VIEWS

Whenever you generate section views of an assembly that has multiple components, by default, all of them are assigned similar hatch patterns. The angle of hatching lines between the adjacent components is different, but if the assembly has a number of components, this creates confusion. For example, Figure 10-25 shows the drawing views of Plummer Block assembly. In this figure, the components in the section view are assigned similar hatch patterns.

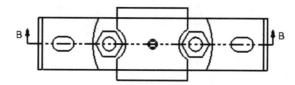

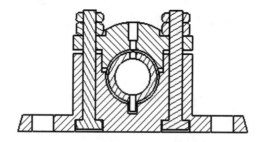

Figure 10-25 Similar hatch patterns of components in the section view

This confusion can be avoided by assigning different hatch patterns to the components of the assembly. To modify the hatch pattern, move the cursor over the hatching lines in the component in section view. The hatch pattern will turn red in color. Once the hatch pattern turns red in color, right-click to display the shortcut menu. In this shortcut menu, choose the **Modify Hatch** option. When you choose this option, the **Modify Hatch Pattern** dialog box will be displayed, see Figure 10-26. The options available under this dialog box are discussed next.

Pattern

The **Pattern** drop-down list is used to select the hatch pattern for the selected hatching. You can select the required hatch pattern from the list of patterns available in this drop-down list. The preview of the selected pattern can be displayed on the sheet. The hatch pattern that you select from this drop-down list will be assigned to the selected component. However, note that this hatch pattern will not be assigned to the other instances of the selected component. The other instances of the selected component will still be hatched using the default hatch pattern.

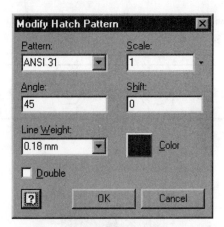

Figure 10-26 Modify Hatch Pattern dialog box

Angle

The **Angle** edit box is used to specify the angle of the hatching lines. You can specify the required angle by entering its value in this edit box.

Line Weight

The **Line Weight** drop-down list is used to specify the line weight of the hatching lines. You can specify the required line weight by selecting it from the predefined line weights available in this drop-down list.

Scale

The **Scale** edit box is used to specify the scale factor of the hatching lines. You can specify the required scale factor by entering its value in this edit box. You can also select the predefined scale factors by selecting them from the list displayed upon choosing the down arrow on the right of this dialog box.

Shift

The **Shift** edit box is used to offset the hatch pattern from its location through the specified distance. The hatch pattern is shifted to avoid the confusion with the hatch pattern of the adjacent component. Generally, the shift value should lie between 1 and 5. You can view the effect of shifting the hatch pattern on the sheet when you enter a value in this edit box.

Color

The **Color** button is used to modify the color of the selected hatch pattern. When you choose this button, the **Color** dialog box is displayed for selecting the required color.

Double

The **Double** check box is used to double the hatching lines by drawing another set of lines normal to the original lines in the hatch pattern.

Figure 10-27 shows the drawing views of Plummer Block assembly with different hatch patterns assigned to the components.

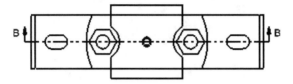

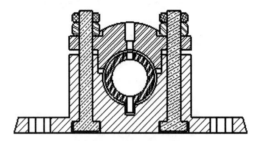

Figure 10-27 Different hatch patterns of components in the section view

SUPPRESSING THE COMPONENTS IN THE ASSEMBLY SECTION VIEWS

When you generate the section views of an assembly, all the components that are intersected by the cutting plane are sectioned as shown in Figure 10-28.

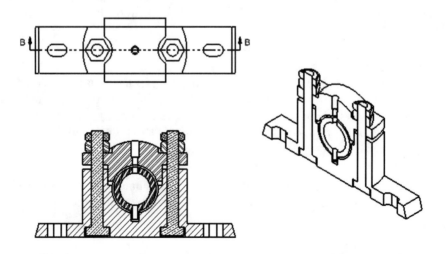

Figure 10-28 All components sectioned by the cutting plane

However, according to the drawing standards, the components such as nuts, bolts, lock nuts, and so on should not be sectioned while generating the section view. Therefore, you will have to suppress these components while generating the assembly section view. You can also suppress these components after generating the section view. The suppressed components will not be sectioned by the cutting plane.

To prevent the components from sectioning, right-click on the parent view in which the section plane is displayed and choose **Show Contents** from the shortcut menu. Click on the + sign located on the left of the view in the browser. You will notice that the name of the assembly is also displayed along with the dependent views. Click on the + sign located on the left of the assembly name to display all the components of the assembly in the browser. Now, hold the CTRL key down and using the left mouse button, select all the components that you want to exclude from sectioning. Once all the components are selected, they will be displayed with blue background in the browser. Right-click on any of the selected component to display the shortcut menu. You will notice that there will be a check mark in front of the **Section** option in the shortcut menu. Choose this option again to clear this option. All selected components will be excluded from sectioning and will not be displayed in section, see Figure 10-29.

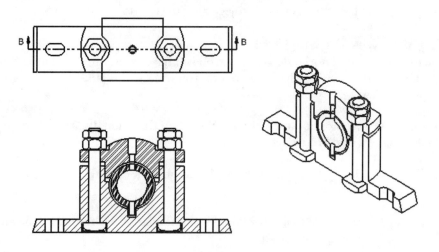

Figure 10-29 *Drawing views with components suppressed from sectioning*

TUTORIALS

Tutorial 1

In this tutorial you will generate the top view, full sectioned front view, and isometric view of the sectioned front view of the model created in Tutorial 2 of Chapter 6. Use the JIS standard template file for generating the views. After generating the drawing views, save the sheet with the name \PersonalProject\c10**Tutorial1.idw**. **(Expected time: 30 min)**

The following steps outline the procedure for generating the drawing views:

a. Copy the model whose drawing views you want to generate in the current directory.
b. Open a JIS template file and generate the base view using the **Create View** tool.
c. Generate the section view by sketching the section plane.
d. Using the **Projected View** tool, project the lines at an angle from the section view to generate the isometric view.

Copying the Model in the Current Directory

Before you start generating the drawing views of the model, it is important to copy the model whose drawing views are to be generated in the current directory. The reason is that when you open the drawing file next time, the component will be searched in the current c10 directory. Since the component is not available in the current directory, the **Resolve Link** dialog box will be displayed, which will prompt you to specify the location and path of the component file. Therefore, all the components or assemblies should be copied in the current directory or the drawing file should be saved in the directory in which the component and assembly file is located.

1. Create a directory with the name c10 in the PersonalProject directory and copy the **Tutorial2.ipt** file from the \PersonalProject\c06 directory to this directory.

Opening the New Drawing File

As mentioned in the tutorial description, you will have to use the JIS standard template for generating the drawing views. Therefore, you will use the **JIS.idw** file for generating the drawing views.

1. Start Autodesk Inventor and then choose **New** from the **What To Do** area to display the **Default**, **English**, and **Metric** tabs.

2. Choose the **Metric** tab to display the metric templates. Select the **JIS.idw** file and then choose the **OK** button, see Figure 10-30.

The standard template file that will follow the JIS standards for drafting will be opened on the screen as shown in Figure 10-31.

Note
The color of sheet is changed to white for the purpose of clarity. The sheet that will be displayed on your screen will be of yellow shade.

Generating the Base View

As mentioned earlier, the base view is the first view in the drawing sheet. Once you have generated the base view, you can use it as the parent view for generating the other views. The base view is generated using the **Create View** tool.

1. Choose the **Create View** button from the **Drawing Management** toolbar or choose **Create View** from the **Drawing Management** panel bar. The **Create View** dialog box will be displayed.

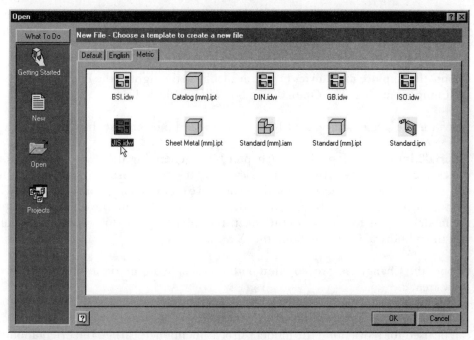

Figure 10-30 *Opening the JIS standard drawing template from the **Open** dialog box*

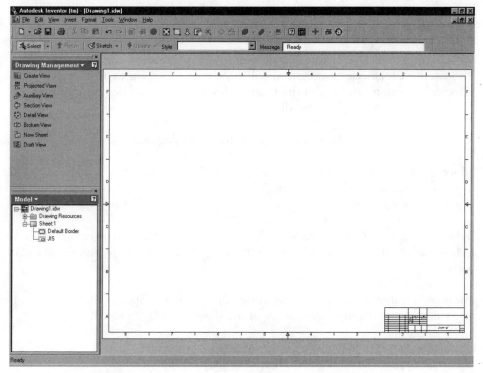

Figure 10-31 *Screen display of the JIS standard drawing file*

The preview of the drawing view will not be displayed on the sheet because you have not selected any part file whose drawing view you want to generate. Therefore, you will have to first select the part file whose drawing view will be generated.

2. Choose the **Explore directories** button available on the right of the **File** drop-down list in the **Component** area. The **Open** dialog box will be selected.

3. Select the file \PersonalProject\c10**Tutorial2.ipt** and then choose the **Open** button.

    Tutorial2.ipt file was copied from Chapter 6 for generating the drawing views. You will notice that the preview of the drawing view using the default orientation is now visible on the sheet. The drawing view will move as you move the cursor and will be generated at the point that you specify on the screen. In the default orientation, the cylindrical feature of the model is along the -Y axis of the sheet. You will have to first reorient the model such that the cylindrical feature is along the -X axis.

4. Choose the **Change view orientation** button available on the right of the list box in the **View** area.

    As soon as you choose this button, the **Custom View** window will be displayed. This window can be used for reorienting the model. Also, as mentioned earlier, the orientation that is achieved in this window will be selected as the orientation of the drawing view.

5. Choose the **Rotate at Angle** button from the **Custom- View ToolBar** to display the **Incremental View Rotate** dialog box.

6. Enter **90** as the value of rotation of view in the **Increment** edit box and then choose the **Clockwise** button. You will notice that as soon as you choose the   **Clockwise** button, the view in the **Custom View** window will be rotated through an angle of 90° in the clockwise direction.

7. Choose **OK** to exit the **Incremental View Rotate** dialog box.

8. Since the orientation of view is what you require, you can now exit the **Custom View** window. Choose the **Exit Custom View** button provided on the extreme left of the **Custom- View Toolbar**.

    When you exit the **Custom View** window, the drawing sheet will be redisplayed. Also, the cylindrical feature of the model is shown along the -X axis in the preview of the drawing view.

9. Modify the value of the scale in the **Scale** edit box to **1.5**. Specify the placement point of the view close to the top right corner of the sheet, see Figure 10-32.

   Note
*If the **Create View** dialog box is restricting you from specifying the point on the sheet, you can move it on the left side by holding it from the blue area on top of it.*

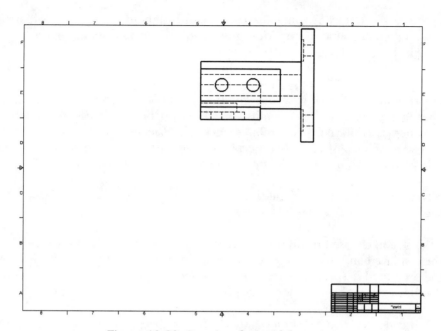

Figure 10-32 Drawing sheet with base view

Generating the Section View

The section view can be generated using the **Section View** tool. However, if you generate the view using this tool, you will first need to select the drawing view that has to be sectioned and then define the section plane. However, if you use the shortcut menu displayed by right-clicking on the base view in the browser or in the drawing sheet, you do not need to select the drawing view since it is already selected. Therefore, you will generate the section view using the shortcut menu.

1. Move the cursor over the base view on the sheet to display the dotted rectangle. When the dotted rectangle is displayed, right-click and choose **Create View > Section** from the shortcut menu.

    The dotted rectangle will be converted into a continuous line rectangle of red color. This suggests that you have to sketch the sectioning plane now.

2. Move the cursor close to the midpoint of the extreme left vertical edge of the base view. The cursor will snap to the midpoint and will turn green in color.

3. After the cursor snaps to the midpoint of the edge, move the mouse to a small distance in the horizontal direction towards the left of the view. You will notice that an imaginary horizontal line is being drawn from the midpoint of the left vertical edge. This is due to the temporary tracking option.

4. Specify a point after moving the cursor to a small distance towards left of the view in the horizontal direction. The specified point is selected as the first point of the section plane.

5. Move the cursor in the horizontal direction towards right of the view. You will notice that a horizontal line is being drawn. Move the cursor to a small distance on the right of the extreme right vertical edge of the base view. Make sure that the cursor do not snap to the midpoint of the right vertical edge and the line that is being drawn is horizontal.

    When you move the cursor towards right, the symbol of perpendicular constraint will be attached to the cursor. You can reconfirm that the line defining the section view is horizontal if this symbol is displayed. This symbol suggests that the line is normal to the extreme left vertical edge of the base view. This perpendicular constraint will be applied because you snapped to the midpoint of the left vertical edge of the base view.

6. Specify a point on the right of the right vertical edge of the base view. This point will be selected as the second point of the section plane.

7. Right-click and choose **Continue** from the shortcut menu. The **Section View** dialog box will be displayed and the preview of the section view will be displayed on the sheet. You will be prompted to specify the location of the section view. Note that hatching lines will not be displayed in the preview of the section view.

8. Specify the location of the section view below the base view, see Figure 10-33. The **Section View** dialog box will be automatically closed when you specify the location of the section view.

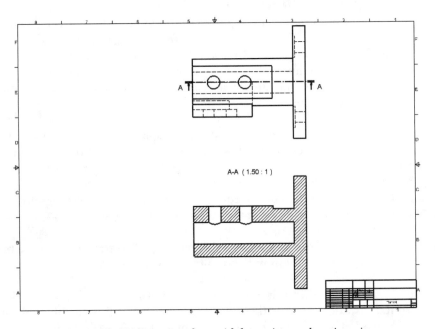

Figure 10-33 Drawing sheet with base view and section view

Generating the Isometric View of the Section View

The isometric view of the section view can also be generated using the shortcut menu.

1. Move the cursor over the section view and when the dotted rectangle is displayed, right-click to display the shortcut menu.

2. Choose **Create View > Projected** from the shortcut menu.

3. Move the cursor towards left of the section view and then move it upwards until the preview of isometric view is displayed. Specify the location of the view once the preview of isometric view is displayed. Right-click and choose **Create** to create the drawing view. The sheet after generating all the views is shown in Figure 10-34.

4. Save the drawing file with the name \PersonalProject\c10**Tutorial1.idw**.

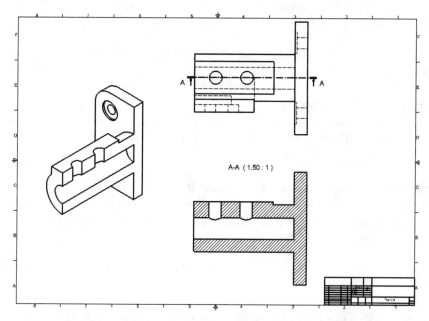

Figure 10-34 Drawing sheet after generating all the views

Tutorial 2

In this tutorial you will generate the top view, full sectioned front view, and isometric view of the section view of Plummer Block assembly created in Tutorial 2 of Chapter 8. The nuts and bolts should not be sectioned in the section view. Also, all the sectioned components should have different hatch patterns. Use the JIS standard drawing file for generating the drawing views. **(Expected time: 45 min)**

As mentioned earlier, it is better to outline the procedure of completing the tutorial. The following steps outline the procedure for generating the drawing views.

a. Copy the Plummer Block directory from the c08 directory to the c10 directory.

b.   Generate the top view of the assembly.
c.   Show the contents of the base view and then suppress bolts, nuts, and lock nuts so that they are not sectioned.
d.   Taking the top view as the parent view, generate full section front view.
e.   Modify the hatch of Casting and Cap.
f.   Generate the projected isometric view of the sectioned front view.

Copying the Plummer Block Directory

As mentioned earlier, you will have to copy the file that will be used to generate the drawing views in the current directory. Since in this tutorial the drawing views of an assembly will be generated, you will have to copy the directory in which the files of the assembly are stored. Also, note that the drawing file will be saved in the directory of the assembly and not in the c10 directory.

1.   Copy the Plummer Block directory from \PersonalProject\c08 directory to \PersonalProject \c10 directory.

Starting a new Drawing File

1.   Choose the **New** button from the **Standard** toolbar to invoke the **Open** dialog box. Choose the **Metric** tab and then double-click on the **JIS.idw** file to open a JIS standard drawing file.

Generating the Top View of the Assembly

1.   Choose the **Create View** button from the **Drawing Management** toolbar or choose **Create View** from the **Drawing Management** panel bar. The **Create View** dialog box will be displayed.

2.   Choose the **Explore directories** button from the **Component** area to display the **Open** dialog box.

3.   Select **Assembly Files (*.iam)** from the **Files of type** drop-down list. Open the directory \PersonalProject\c10\Plummer Block and then select **Plummer Block.iam** file. Choose the **Open** button to select the assembly for generating the drawing views.

You will return to the drawing sheet and the preview of the top view of the assembly will be displayed on the sheet. You will also be prompted to specify the location of the view.

4.   Modify the scale to **1.25** in the **Scale** edit box. Now, specify the location of the drawing view close to the upper right corner of the sheet, see Figure 10-35.

Suppressing the Components from Sectioning

As mentioned in the tutorial description, the nuts, bolts, and lock nuts should not be sectioned by the cutting plane. Therefore, you will have to suppress these components such that they are not sectioned in the section view.

1.   Move the cursor over the top view and right-click when a dotted rectangle is displayed.

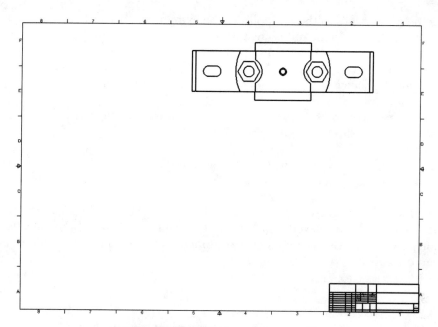

Figure 10-35 *Top view of the assembly*

Choose **Show Contents** from the shortcut menu.

You will notice that + sign is displayed on the left of **VIEW1:Plummer Block** in the browser.

2. Click on the + sign located on the left of the view in the browser to display **Plummer Block.iam**. The assembly name will also have a + sign located on left of it in the browser.

3. Click on the + sign located on the left of **Plummer Block.iam** to display all the components of the assembly. Press and hold the CTRL key down and select both the instances of Nut, Bolt, and Lock Nut using the left mouse button. The selected components will be displayed in blue background.

4. Right-click on any selected component to display the shortcut menu. In the shortcut menu, the **Section** option will be selected and will have a check mark in front of it.

5. Choose the **Section** option. If you right-click on any selected component again, you will notice that the check mark in front of the **Section** option is not displayed. This suggests that the selected components will not be sectioned.

6. Pick a point on the sheet to clear the selection of components.

Generating the Section View

1. Move the cursor over the top view and right-click when a dotted rectangle is displayed. Choose **Create View > Section** from the shortcut menu.

2. Move the cursor close to the midpoint of the extreme left vertical edge of the top view. The cursor will snap to the midpoint and will turn green in color.

3. When the cursor snaps to the midpoint, move it in the horizontal direction towards the left to a small distance and specify a point there as the start point of the section plane.

4. Move the cursor towards the right in the horizontal direction. The perpendicular constraint symbol will be displayed with the cursor.

5. Specify a point on the right of the extreme right vertical edge of the top view as the second point of the section plane. Note that the line should be horizontal and not inclined.

6. Right-click and choose **Continue** to display the **Section View** dialog box. The preview of section view will be displayed and you will be prompted to specify the location of the section view. Specify the location of the sectioned front view below the top view as shown in Figure 10-36.

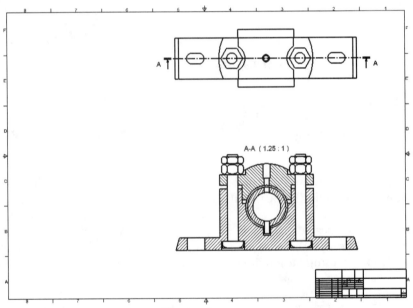

Figure 10-36 Sheet with top view and sectioned front view

Modifying the Hatch Patterns

The section view displays three components in section. These are Casting, Cap, and Brasses. One of these three components can retain the current hatching style and the style in remaining two will have to be modified. In this tutorial, Brasses will retain the current style and you will modify the hatching in Casting and Cap.

1. Move the cursor over the hatching in Casting. The hatching lines will turn red in color. After hatching turns red in color, right-click to display the shortcut menu. Choose **Modify Hatch** from the shortcut menu to display the **Modify Hatch Pattern** dialog box.

2. Select **ISO02W100** from the **Pattern** drop-down list and then select the **Double** check box. Choose **OK** to exit this dialog box.

3. Move the cursor over the hatching in Cap and right-click when the hatching turns red in color. Choose **Modify Hatch** from the shortcut menu to display the **Modify Hatch Pattern** dialog box.

4. Select the **Double** check box and then choose **OK** to exit this dialog box. All three components that are sectioned will have different hatch patterns now.

Generating the Isometric View of the Section View

The third view that has to be generated is the isometric view of the section view. This view will also be generated using the shortcut menu.

1. Move the cursor on the section view to display the dotted rectangle. Note that the cursor should not be over any hatch pattern. When the rectangle is displayed, right-click to display the shortcut menu. Choose **Create View > Projected** from the shortcut menu.

2. Move the cursor towards the left of the section view in the horizontal direction and then move the cursor upwards until the preview of the isometric view is displayed. When the isometric view is displayed, specify the point to define the location of this view.

3. Right-click and choose **Create** from the shortcut menu. The isometric view of the section view will be generated. The drawing sheet with all the drawing views is shown in Figure 10-37.

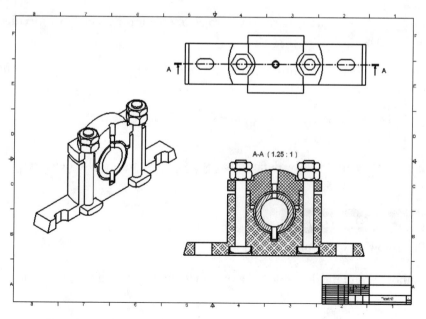

Figure 10-37 Drawing sheet after generating all the three views

4. Save the drawing sheet with the name given below:

\PersonalProject\c10\Plummer Block**Tutorial2.idw**

The file is saved in the Plummer Block directory because the Plummer Block assembly file that is used to generate the drawing views is stored in this directory.

Self-Evaluation Test

Answer the following questions and then compare your answers with the answers given at the end of this chapter.

1. You cannot generate the drawing views of an assembly file. (T/F)

2. The **Drawing** mode of Autodesk Inventor is not bidirectional in nature. (T/F)

3. You can add more sheets for generating the drawing views.

4. The display type of the view once set can be modified. (T/F)

5. While generating the base view, you can display the model dimensions by selecting the _____ check box in the **Create View** dialog box.

6. By default, the display type of the projected views will be the same as that of the _____.

7. The _____ views are generated by projecting the lines normal to a specified edge in the parent view.

8. In Autodesk Inventor, the cutting plane will be defined by _____ one or more than one lines.

9. The part of original view that is sectioned will be displayed with _____ in the section view.

10. When you delete any view, by default its _____ views are also deleted.

Review Questions

Answer the following questions.

1. You cannot prevent the dependent views from getting deleted if the parent view is deleted. (T/F)

2. The hatch pattern of a component in the section view can be modified. (T/F)

3. You can prevent some components from getting sectioned by the cutting plane in the section view. (T/F)

4. You can suppress the option to move the dependent views along with the parent view if you do not want to move them with the parent view. (T/F)

5. You can copy the selected drawing view in a new drawing file. (T/F)

6. Which one of the following tools is used to sketch a drawing view?

   (a) **Draft View**   (b) **Create View**
   (c) **New View**   (d) You cannot sketch a drawing view

7. Which one of the following windows is displayed using the **Create View** dialog box for modifying the orientation of the base view?

   (a) **Rotate View**   (b) **Orient View**
   (c) **Custom View**   (d) None

8. Which one of the following tools is used to generate a drawing view by removing a portion of it from between, keeping the ends of the component intact.

   (a) **Draft View**   (b) **Create View**
   (c) **Broken View**   (d) You cannot remove a portion of a drawing view

9. Which one of the following tools is used to display the details of a portion of an existing view by magnifying that portion and displaying it as a separate view.

   (a) **Detail View**   (b) **Create View**
   (c) **New View**   (d) None

10. Autodesk Inventor allows you to generate the isometric views using which one of the following tools?

   (a) **Draft View**   (b) **Create View**
   (c) **Projected View**   (d) None

Exercise

Exercise 1

Generate the top view, the right half sectioned front view, and the isometric view of the section view of the Double Bearing assembly with a scale of 2.5:1. This assembly was created in Tutorial 3 of Chapter 9. The Nut that is intersected by the cutting plane should not be sectioned as shown in Figure 10-37. Also, all the components should have different hatch patterns. Use the JIS standards for generating the views.   **(Expected time: 45 min)**

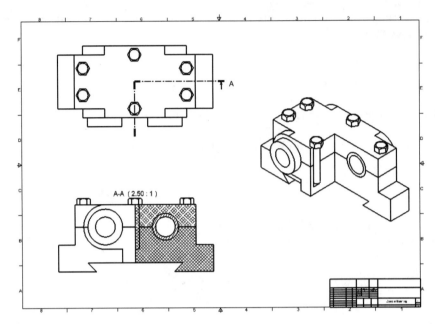

Figure 10-37 Drawing views to be generated for Exercise 1

Answers to Self-Evaluation Test
1. F, **2.** F, **3.** T, **4.** T, **5. Get Model Dimensions**, **6.** parent view, **7.** auxiliary, **8.** sketching, **9.** hatching lines, **10.** dependent.

Chapter 11

Drawing Mode-II

Learning Objectives

After completing this chapter you will be able to:
- *Modify drawing standards.*
- *Insert additional sheets in the current drawing.*
- *Make a drawing sheet active.*
- *Add parametric and reference dimensions to the drawing views.*
- *Modify the current sheet style.*
- *Create dimension styles.*
- *Modify dimension appearance using the shortcut menu.*
- *Create and edit the parts list for the assembly drawing views.*
- *Set the standards of the parts list.*
- *Add balloons to the assembly drawing views.*

MODIFYING DRAWING STANDARDS

As mentioned in Chapter 10, by default, the selected sheet will follow its standards in generating and dimensioning the drawing views. However, you can modify the standards of the current sheet. For example, you can open a JIS standard drawing file and assign the ANSI standards to it such that when you generate the drawing views and dimension them, the ANSI drafting standards are followed. You can modify the standards of the current sheet by choosing **Format > Standards** from the menu bar. When you choose this option, the **Drafting Standards** dialog box is displayed. It displays the current sheet standard in the **Select Standard** area. When you choose the **More** button provided on the bottom right corner of this dialog box, the dialog box will expand and provide the options related to the selected standard, see Figure 11-1.

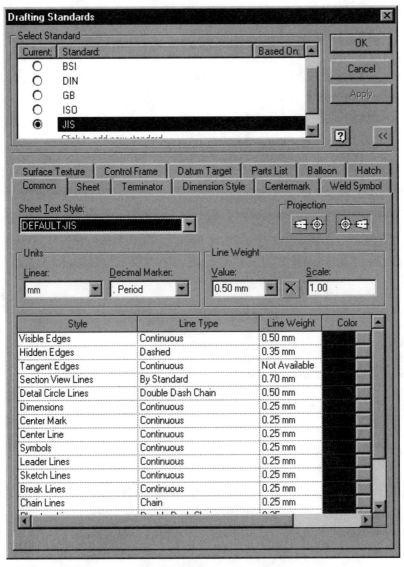

Figure 11-1 Drafting Standards dialog box

Using different tabs of this dialog box, you can modify the drafting standards. For example, if you want to change the projection type from third angle to first angle, choose the **Common** tab and then in the **Projection** area, choose the **First angle of projection** button.

If you want to change the drafting standard of the current drawing, select the required drafting standard from the **Select Standard** area and then choose the **Apply** button. You will notice that if the **Drafting Standards** dialog box is expanded, the options under the tabs will change if you select a different standard from the **Select Standard** area.

INSERTING ADDITIONAL SHEETS

Panel Bar:	Drawing Management > New Sheet
Toolbar:	Drawing Management > New Sheet

When you open a new drawing file, only one sheet is available. However, you can insert more drawing sheets for generating the drawing views using the **New Sheet** tool. You can also insert a new drawing sheet by right-clicking on the name of the drawing file on the top of the browser and choosing **New Sheet** from the shortcut menu. When you invoke this tool, a new sheet is automatically added. Note that the new sheet added will be the active sheet. An active sheet is one on which you can generate the drawing views. The active sheet will be displayed with white background in the browser. The other drawing sheets will be displayed with gray background in the browser.

MAKING A SHEET ACTIVE

You can make any sheet active by right-clicking on it in the browser and choosing **Activate** from the shortcut menu, see Figure 11-2. Note that if any sheet is already activated, this option will not be available when you right-click on a sheet in the browser.

Figure 11-2 Activating a drawing sheet using the browser

DISPLAYING DIMENSIONS IN THE DRAWING VIEWS

As mentioned in Chapter 10, you can display the model dimensions on the drawing views when you generate them. Model dimensions are also called parametric dimensions and are the dimensions that were used to create the model in the part file. These are the dimensions that were applied on the sketches of the features while defining them. You can also display the model dimensions after placing the drawing views. In addition to the model dimensions, Autodesk Inventor also allows you to add reference dimensions to the drawing views. The reference dimensions are those dimensions that were not applied to the model in the **Part** mode. These dimensions are used only for reference and are not used during manufacturing of a part. The method of adding model and reference dimensions are discussed next.

Displaying Parametric Dimensions in the Drawing Views

The parametric dimensions or the model dimensions can be displayed while generating the base view if you select the **Get Model Dimensions** check box from the **Options** area of the **Create View** dialog box. To display the model dimensions on an existing view, right-click on it in the browser or on the sheet and choose **Get Model Dimensions** from the shortcut menu. When you choose this option, the parametric dimensions that were used while creating the model will be displayed. However, note that the dimensions of only those features that are clearly visible will be displayed in the view. The remaining dimensions can be displayed in the projected views. If you modify the value of model dimensions, the dimensions of the actual part will also be modified.

 Tip. *You can move the model dimensions by dragging them. To move a model dimension, move the cursor over it on a drawing sheet. The dimension will turn red in color. Now, press and hold the left mouse button down and drag the dimension to a new location.*

Adding Reference Dimensions

Panel Bar:	Drawing Annotation > General Dimension
Toolbar:	Drawing Annotation > General Dimension

 Autodesk Inventor allows you to add reference dimensions to the drawing view using the **General Dimension** tool. This tool is similar to the **General Dimension** tool in the **Part** mode. The method of adding the dimensions is also similar for both the tools.

MODIFYING THE MODEL DIMENSIONS

Autodesk Inventor allows you to modify the model dimensions displayed on the drawing view. However, as mentioned earlier, all modes of Autodesk Inventor are bidirectionally associative. This nature of Autodesk Inventor will ensure that if you modify any dimension value in the **Drawing** mode, the changes will be reflected in the model in **Part** mode. Therefore, you will have to be very careful while modifying the model dimensions. To modify the model dimension, right-click on it and choose **Edit Model Dimension**, see Figure 11-3. When you choose this option, the **Edit Dimension** toolbar will be displayed with the current dimension value. You can modify the dimension value in this toolbar. After specifying the new dimension

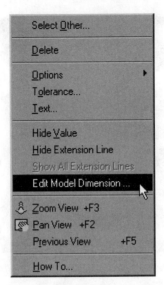

Figure 11-3 Editing model dimensions

value, choose the check mark button on the right of this toolbar. You will notice that the dimension is modified and it is reflected in the feature in drawing views. The selected feature will be modified based on the new dimension value.

EDITING DRAWING SHEETS

Autodesk Inventor allows you to edit the active drawing sheet. You can modify the size of the sheet, relocate the title block, modify the orientation of the drawing sheet, and so on. To edit the drawing sheet, right-click on the sheet in the browser or in the graphics screen and choose **Edit Sheet**. When you choose this option, the **Edit Sheet** dialog box is displayed as shown in Figure 11-4. The options provided under this dialog box are discussed next.

Format Area

The options provided under the **Format** area are used to define the name and size of the drawing sheet. These options are discussed next.

Name

The **Name** edit box is used to enter the name of the drawing sheet. The name you enter in this edit box will be displayed in the browser.

Size

The **Size** drop-down list is used to define the size of the drawing sheet. You can select predefined drawing sheet sizes from this drop-down list. If you want to specify a user-defined size, select **Custom Size (inches)** or **Custom Size (mm)** from this drop-down list. Using these options you can specify a user-defined size in inches or in millimeter. The height and width of the user-defined size will be defined in the **Height** and **Width** edit box. These edit boxes will be available below the **Size** drop-down list when you select the option to specify the user-defined size.

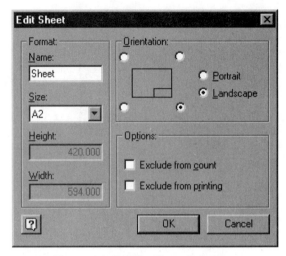

Figure 11-4 Edit Sheet dialog box

Orientation Area

The options provided under the **Orientation** area are used to specify the orientation of the sheet and the location of the title block. This area displays a sheet and has four radio buttons close to the four corners of the sheet. These radio buttons define the location of the title block in the sheet. By default, the radio button provided close to the lower right corner of the sheet is selected. This will force the title block to be placed on the lower right corner of the sheet. You can place the title block on any of the four corners by selecting their respective radio buttons. You can also define whether the orientation of the drawing sheet should be portrait or landscape by selecting the **Portrait** or **Landscape** radio button.

Options Area

The options provided under the **Options** area are discussed next.

Exclude from count

By default, when you open a drawing file, one sheet is available. This sheet is assigned number 1. If you add more sheets, they will be numbered 2, 3, and so on. The **Exclude from count** check box is selected it you do not want the current sheet to be included in this count. If you select this check box, the current sheet will not be assigned any number and the sheet number of the other sheets will be adjusted automatically.

Exclude from printing

The **Exclude from printing** check box is selected to exclude the current sheet from printing. If this check box is selected, the current sheet will not be considered while printing the drawing sheets.

CREATING DIMENSION STYLES

Dimension styles are used to control the appearance and positioning of the parameters related to the dimensions. Autodesk Inventor provides a number of dimension styles that you can use for displaying the dimensions. However, if the predefined dimension style do not meet your requirements, you can define a new dimension style and set the options related to the dimensions as per your requirement. To create a new dimension style, choose **Format > Dimension Styles** from the menu bar. The **Dimension Styles** dialog box will be displayed as shown in Figure 11-5.

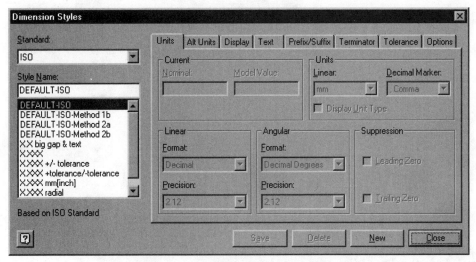

Figure 11-5 Dimension Styles dialog box

The default dimension styles are displayed in the **Style Name** list box. On the right of the dialog box are various tabs for setting the options related to the dimension style. You will notice that the options under these tabs are not available. The reason is that you cannot modify the default dimension styles. These options will be available only for new dimension styles. To create a new dimension style, choose the **New** button and then enter the name of the dimension style in the **Style Name** edit box. Now make the necessary changes in the parameters related to the dimensions in various tabs of the **Dimension Styles** dialog box. After making all the necessary changes, choose the **Save** button. All the new drawing views will be dimensioned using this dimension style.

Note
*If any existing drawing view is dimensioned, the dimensions in that drawing view will not be modified based on the new dimension style. To modify the dimension style of existing dimensions, select them and change the dimension style from the **Style** drop-down list in the **Command Bar**.*

MODIFYING THE DIMENSION APPEARANCE USING THE SHORTCUT MENU

You can also modify the dimension appearance using the shortcut menu that is displayed when you right-click on it. Depending upon the type of dimension selected, the options in this shortcut menu are displayed. Figure 11-6 shows a shortcut menu for a linear dimension. You can use this menu to control the display of extension lines, dimension text, leaders, arrowheads,

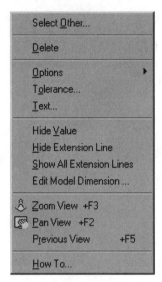

Figure 11-6 *Shortcut menu to modify the dimension appearance*

and so on. You can also hide the dimension value using this shortcut menu. If you choose the option to hide the dimension value, it will not be displayed in the drawing view. However, you can show the dimension value again using the shortcut menu that is displayed when you right-click on the dimension.

ADDING PARTS LIST (BILL OF MATERIAL) TO THE ASSEMBLY DRAWING VIEWS

Panel Bar:	Drawing Annotation > Parts List
Toolbar:	Drawing Annotation > Parts List

The parts list, also called Bill of Material or BOM is extremely useful in providing the information related to the components of assembly in the drawing views. It is a table that provides the information related to the number of components in an assembly, their names, their quantity, and other related information. In Autodesk Inventor, the parts list is added using the **Part List** tool. The parts list will be placed by taking the reference of one of the views in the drawing sheet. Therefore, when you invoke this tool, you will have to first select a view that will be used to generate the parts list. To select a view, move the cursor over the view and press the left mouse button when a red color dotted rectangle is displayed. When you select the view, the **Part List - Item Numbering** dialog box will be displayed, see Figure 11-7. This dialog box will be used to set the parameters related to the parts list and the components in the parts list. These options are discussed next.

Level Area

This area provides the options for selecting the components that will be listed in the parts list. These options are discussed next.

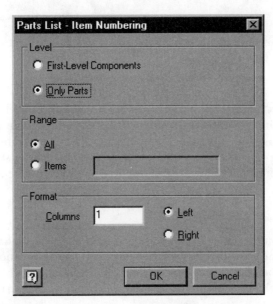

Figure 11-7 Part List - Item Numbering dialog box

First-Level Components

If all the components of an assembly are assembled in one assembly file, they are termed as the first-level components. However, if you assemble some of the components in a separate assembly file and reference the subassembly in the current assembly file, the components of the subassembly are termed as second-level components. If the **First-Level Components** radio button is selected, only first-level components will be listed in the parts list. This means that if the current assembly consists of a subassembly also, the components of the subassembly will not be listed in the parts list.

Only Parts

The **Only Parts** radio button is selected to list all the components in the parts list. Even the components of the subassembly will be listed. However, note that the subassemblies will not be listed in the parts list.

Range Area

The options under the **Range** area are used to specify the range of components that will be listed in the parts list. These options are discussed next.

All

The **All** radio button is selected to list all the components in the parts list.

Items

The **Items** radio button is selected to list only the specified components in the parts list. The range of components can be specified in the edit box available on the right of this radio button. Note that this radio button will not be available if you select the **First-Level Components** radio button from the **Level** area.

Format Area

The options under the **Format** area are used to specify the format of the parts list. These options are discussed next.

Columns

The **Columns** edit box is used to specify the number of columns in which the parts list will be split. Note that this edit box is not used to specify the number of columns in the parts list. This edit box is generally used for the assemblies that have a large number of components. The parts list of such components get very lengthy. Therefore, you can split it into two or three columns so that the length of the parts list can be reduced. However, in such parts lists, the length increases as the columns are increased by two or three times.

Left/Right

The **Left** and **Right** radio buttons are used to specify the side that will be attached to the cursor while placing the parts list. Note that if you select the **Left** radio button, the cursor will be attached to the upper right corner of the parts list. Similarly, if you select the **Right** radio button, the cursor will be attached to the upper left corner of the parts list.

After setting the options in the **Part List - Item Numbering** dialog box, choose the **OK** button. The dialog box will be closed and you will return to the drawing sheet. You will notice that the parts list is attached to the cursor. Place the parts list at the desired point. Figure 11-8 shows the drawing views of Double Bearing assembly with the parts list.

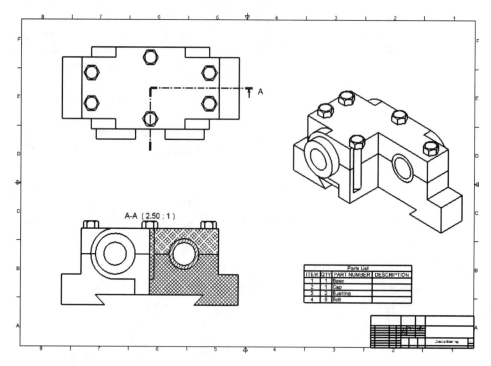

Figure 11-8 Drawing views of an assembly with the parts list

EDITING PARTS LIST

The default parts list that is placed has only the selected columns. If you want to add more columns to the parts list or delete some of the columns, you will have to edit it. You can edit the parts list by double-clicking on it or by right-clicking on it and choosing **Edit Parts List** from the shortcut menu. The **Edit Parts List** dialog box will be displayed as shown in Figure 11-9. The default columns and their values are displayed in this dialog box. You will notice that some of the values are displayed in red color and some in black color. To modify the value of any field, click on it and enter the new value. However, note that the fields displayed in red color cannot be modified. The other options under this dialog box are discussed next.

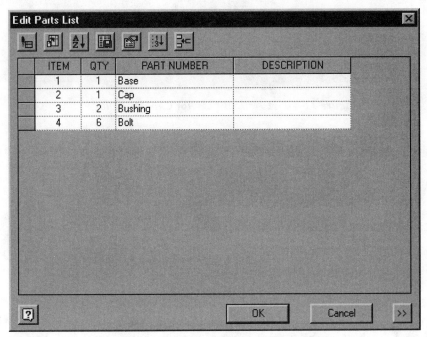

Figure 11-9 Edit Parts List dialog box

Compare

The **Compare** button is the first button and is provided on the top left corner of this dialog box. When you choose this button, the system compares the current parts list to the original parts list. If there are any changes in the parts list, they will be highlighted.

Column Chooser

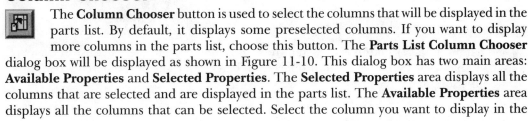
The **Column Chooser** button is used to select the columns that will be displayed in the parts list. By default, it displays some preselected columns. If you want to display more columns in the parts list, choose this button. The **Parts List Column Chooser** dialog box will be displayed as shown in Figure 11-10. This dialog box has two main areas: **Available Properties** and **Selected Properties**. The **Selected Properties** area displays all the columns that are selected and are displayed in the parts list. The **Available Properties** area displays all the columns that can be selected. Select the column you want to display in the

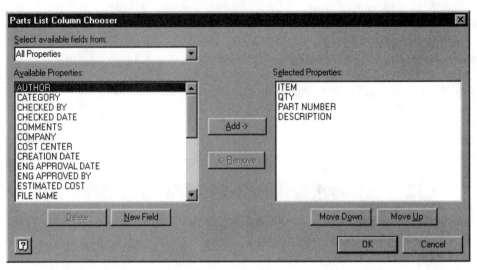

Figure 11-10 Parts List Column Chooser dialog box

parts list from the **Available Properties** area and then choose the **Add** button. The selected
column will be displayed in the **Selected Properties** area. Similarly, if you want to remove any
column from the **Selected Properties** area, select the column and choose the **Remove** button.

Sort

The **Sort** button is chosen to sort the items in the parts list. When you choose this
button, the **Sort Parts List** dialog box is displayed. Using this dialog box you can sort
the items in the parts list.

Export

The **Export** button is chosen to export the parts list to an external file. When you
choose this button, the **Export Parts List** dialog box is displayed. You can use this
dialog box to specify the file type of the new file and its location.

Heading

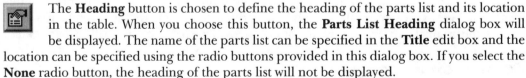The **Heading** button is chosen to define the heading of the parts list and its location
in the table. When you choose this button, the **Parts List Heading** dialog box will
be displayed. The name of the parts list can be specified in the **Title** edit box and the
location can be specified using the radio buttons provided in this dialog box. If you select the
None radio button, the heading of the parts list will not be displayed.

Renumber

The **Renumber** button is chosen to renumber the items in the parts list. If the parts
list has some items that are improperly numbered, they will be numbered according to
their original numbering.

Add Custom Parts

 The **Add Custom Parts** button is chosen to add another row to the parts list. You can manually enter the information in this row.

 Tip. *To delete a custom part row, move the cursor over the gray color button on the extreme left of the custom row. The cursor will be replaced by a small arrow that is pointing in the direction of the row. Now, press the left mouse button. The custom row will be selected and highlighted in black color. Right-click on any column of the selected row and choose* **Remove**. *The custom row will be removed.*

More

The **More** button is the button with two arrows and is provided on the lower right corner of the dialog box. When you choose this button, the dialog box will expand and more options related to the columns will be displayed, see Figure 11-11.

Figure 11-11 More options

You can use these options to set the properties of the selected column.

SETTING THE STANDARDS FOR THE PARTS LIST

You can set the standards for the parts list using the **Drafting Standards** dialog box. This dialog box is displayed when you choose **Format > Standards** from the menu bar. Choose the **More** button on the bottom right corner of this dialog box if it is not expanded. When you choose this button, the dialog box expands and displays various tabs for setting the standards. Choose the **Parts List** tab. The options related to the parts list will be displayed as shown in Figure 11-12. Using the options under this tab you can set the parameters related to the parts list. After you have made the necessary modifications in the parts list standards, choose the **Apply** button. You will notice that the changes are reflected in the parts list on the sheet. After you are satisfied with the changes, exit the **Drafting Standards** dialog box.

ADDING BALLOONS TO THE ASSEMBLY DRAWING VIEWS

Whenever you add the parts list to assembly drawing views, all the components in the assembly are listed in the parts list in a tabular form. Also, each component is assigned a unique number.

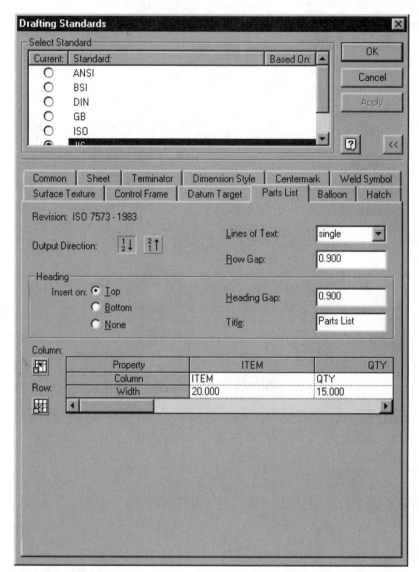

Figure 11-12 Parts List tab of the Drafting Standards dialog box

This means that if the assembly has ten components, all of them will be listed in the parts list with a different serial number assigned to them. However, in the drawing views, there is no reference about these components. Therefore, if you are not familiar with the names of the components, it is difficult to recognize them in the drawing view. To avoid this confusion, Autodesk Inventor allows you to add a callout called balloons to the components in the drawing view. These callouts are based on the serial number of the components in the parts list. If the component is assigned serial number 1 in the parts list, the callout will also show number 1. The balloons make it convenient to relate the components in the parts list to the components in the drawing view. You can add balloons to the selected components or to all the components in the drawing view. The method of adding balloons is discussed next.

Adding Balloons to the Selected Components

Panel Bar: Drawing Annotation > Balloon
Toolbar: Drawing Annotation > Balloon

You can add balloons to the selected components in the drawing view using the **Balloon** tool. After invoking this tool, move the cursor over the component to which you want to add the balloon. You will notice that one of the edges of the component is highlighted and it will turn red in color. Also, a symbol of coincident constraint will be attached to the cursor. This symbol suggests that the coincident constraint will be applied to one end of the balloon and the highlighted edge of the selected component. Select the edge of the component and move the cursor away from the component. One end of the balloon will be attached to the component and the other end will be attached to the cursor. Specify the point for the placement of the balloon and right-click to display the shortcut menu. From the shortcut menu, choose **Continue** to place the balloon. You will notice that a callout is added to the selected component and the name of the callout is the same as that in the parts list. Remember that you can add as many number of balloons as you want by selecting the components.

Adding Balloons to All the Components in the Drawing View

Panel Bar: Drawing Annotation > Balloon > Balloon All
Toolbar: Drawing Annotation > Balloon > Balloon All

You can also add balloons to all the components in the selected drawing view in a single attempt. This is done by choosing the down arrow on the right of the **Balloon** tool and choosing the **Balloon All** tool. After invoking this tool, select the drawing view in which balloons will be added. As soon as you select the drawing view, balloons will be added to all the components in that view. Note that if there is more than one instance of any component in the drawing view, balloons will be added to all of them. Since it is not necessary to add balloons to all the instances of a component, you will have to manually select the unwanted balloons and delete them. Also, when you add balloons using the **Balloon All** tool, the location of the balloons is not what is desired every time. Therefore, you will have to select and drag them to the desired location. Note that the start point of the balloon will be connected to the component using the coincident constraint. Therefore, it is recommended that you drag the balloons by selecting them from the other end.

Figure 11-13 shows a drawing sheet with parts list and balloons added to the components in the drawing view.

Tip. *You can modify the styles of balloons using the **Drafting Standards** dialog box. Invoke this dialog box and then choose the **Balloon** tab. Selected the desired style of balloons from this tab.*

*You cannot modify the size of arrowheads of balloons using the **Balloon** tab of the **Drafting Standards** dialog box. To modify the size of arrowheads, choose the **Terminator** tab of the **Drafting Standards** dialog box and set the value in the **Size** edit box. You can also modify other parameters of arrowheads using this tab.*

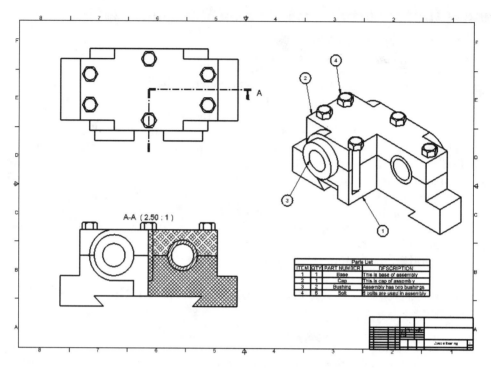

Figure 11-13 Drawing sheet with parts list and balloons

ADDING TEXT TO THE DRAWING SHEET

Autodesk Inventor allows you to add user-defined text to the drawing sheet. Depending upon your requirement, you can add multiline text with or without a leader. The methods of adding both types of text are discussed next.

Adding Multiline Text without Leader

Panel Bar:	Drawing Annotation > Text
Toolbar:	Drawing Annotation > Text

You can add multiline text without leader using the **Text** tool. When you invoke this tool, you will be prompted to specify the location of text or define a rectangle by dragging the mouse to define the bounding box of the text. After you specify the location of text or the bounding box of the text, the **Format Text** dialog box is displayed as shown in Figure 11-14. You can enter the text in the text box of this dialog box. You can also modify the format, style, and alignment of the text using this dialog box.

After writing the text in the text box, choose the **OK** button. The text will be placed at the specified location. Note that after placing the text, you will again be prompted to define the location of text or define a box using two points. This means that you can define text at as many locations as you want in a single attempt. You can exit this tool by pressing the ESC key.

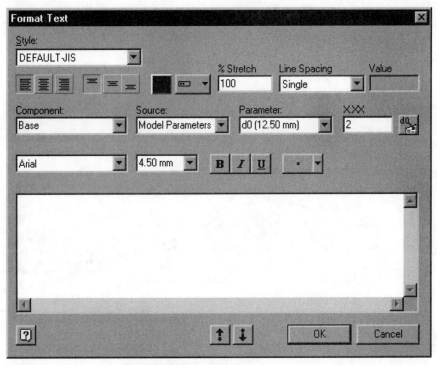

Figure 11-14 Format Text dialog box

Adding Multiline Text with Leader

Panel Bar:	Drawing Annotation > Leader Text
Toolbar:	Drawing Annotation > Leader Text

The text with leader is generally added to the entities to which you want to point and add some information. You can add the text with leader using the **Leader Text** tool. After invoking this tool, select the entity to which you want to add the leader text. As you move the cursor close to an entity, it will be highlighted and will turn red in color. Also, the symbol of coincident constraint will be attached to the cursor. This symbol suggests that the coincident constraint will be added to the selected entity and the arrowhead of leader. After selecting the entity, move the cursor away and define the second vertex of leader. You can define as many vertices in the leader line. Once you have defined the leader line, right-click to display the shortcut menu and choose **Continue**. The **Format Text** dialog box will be displayed. This dialog box is similar to the one that is displayed when you invoke the **Text** tool. You can define the text in this dialog box and then choose **OK**. The leader text will be added to the drawing sheet. Figure 11-15 shows a drawing sheet after adding text with and without leader.

Tip. *You can edit the text by double-clicking on it. When you double-click on a text, the **Format Text** dialog box is displayed with the current text.*

*To add center mark to a circle, choose the **Center Mark** tool from the **Drawing Annotation** toolbar or panel bar and select the circle.*

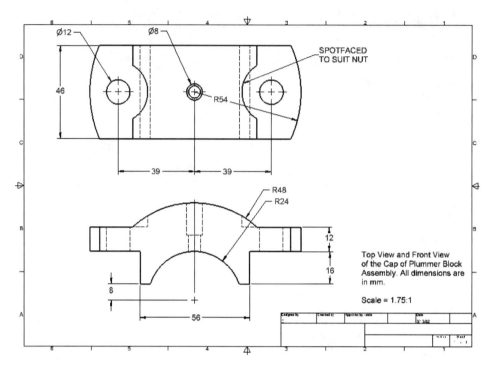

Figure 11-15 Drawing sheet after adding text with and without leader

TUTORIALS

Tutorial 1

In this tutorial you will generate the top view, front view, right side view, and isometric view of the model created in Exercise 1 of Chapter 4. You will use the ISO standard drawing sheet of A3 size but change the standard of the drawing sheet to ANSI. The line weight of visible lines in the drawing views should be 0.039 inches. The drawing views should be dimensioned as shown in Figure 11-16. Create a new dimension style with the name **Custom** for dimensioning the drawing view. The dimension style should have the following specifications:

Dimension Units: mm
Linear Precision: 0
Text Size: 5 mm
Terminator Size: 5 mm
Terminator Aspect Ratio: 1.5   **(Expected time: 1 Hr)**

Before you start generating the drawing views, it is recommended that you outline the steps for completing the tutorial. The steps that will be followed to complete this tutorial are listed below:

a.   Copy the model of Exercise 1 of Chapter 4 in the current directory and then open a new ISO standard drawing file.

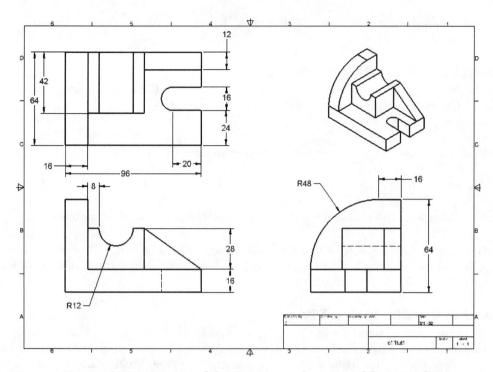

Figure 11-16 *Dimensioned drawing views to be generated for Tutorial 1*

b.   Modify the drafting standard to ANSI and modify the lineweight of visible edges.
c.   Create a new dimension style with the name **Custom** and modify the parameters as mentioned in the tutorial description.
d.   Generate the drawing views and display the model dimensions in the drawing views. Drag the dimensions so that they are displayed as desired.

Copying the Model in the Current Directory

As mentioned in the previous chapter, you should copy the model whose drawing views you are generating in the current directory.

1.   Create a directory with the name **c11** inside the directory \PersonalProject.

2.   Copy the file Exercise 1 from the directory \PersonalProject\c04 to the current directory.

Starting a New Drawing File

As mentioned in the tutorial description, you need to open a new ISO standard drawing file for generating the drawing views.

1.   Choose the **New** button to invoke the **Open** dialog box. Choose the **Metric** tab and open a new **ISO.idw** file.

The default ISO standard drawing sheet is displayed on the screen. Note that the default

ISO standard file is of A3 size and therefore, you do not need to modify the size of the drawing sheet.

Modifying the Drafting Standards

1. Choose **Format > Standards** from the menu bar to invoke the **Drafting Standards** dialog box. Choose the **More** button on the right of this dialog box to expand the dialog box if it is not already expanded.

2. Select the **ANSI** radio button from the **Select Standard** area.

   The options under the **Common** tab will be modified based on the ANSI standards.

3. Select **mm** from the **Linear** drop-down list in the **Units** area of the **Common** tab.

4. Click on the **Line Weight** field of the **Visible Edges** row. The field will be converted into a drop-down list. Select **0.039** from this drop-down list. Choose the **Apply** button and then choose **OK** to exit this dialog box.

Creating the Dimension Style

By default, the dimensions in the ANSI standard are displayed in inches. However, as mentioned in the tutorial description, you have to display the dimensions in millimeter. Therefore, you need to create a new dimension style using the **Dimension Styles** dialog box.

1. Choose **Format > Dimension Styles** from the menu bar to display the **Dimension Styles** dialog box.

2. Select **MM-ANSI** from the list box provided below the **Style Name** edit box. Choose the **New** button.

   The name in the **Style Name** edit box will change to **Copy of MM-ANSI**. This is the default name of the new dimension style. You need to change the name of the dimension style to **Custom**.

3. Enter the name of new dimension style as **Custom** in the **Style Name** edit box.

4. Select **0** from the **Precision** drop-down list in the **Linear** area of the **Units** tab.

   The precision for linear dimension will be forced to 0. This means that no digit will be displayed after decimal in the dimensions.

5. Choose the **Text** tab to display the text options. Choose the **Vertical Dimensions** flyout in the **Orientation** area and choose the first button in this flyout. This will force the text of the vertical dimension to be placed horizontally.

6. Choose the **Aligned Dimensions** flyout and then choose the first button. Similarly, choose the **Angular Dimensions** flyout and then choose the first button. The text of aligned and angular dimensions will also be placed horizontally.

7. Select **5.00 mm** from the **Size** drop-down list.

8. Choose the **Terminator** tab to display the options related to the arrowheads. Enter **5** as the size in the **Size** edit box. Also, enter **1.5** as the ratio in the **Aspect** edit box. Choose **Save** to save the changes in the dimension style and then choose **Close** to exit the dialog box.

    The new dimension style is created and all the new dimensions will be created using this dimension style.

Generating the Drawing Views

In this tutorial you need to generate four drawing views. The base view is the top view and the remaining views are projected views. The front view is generated by using the top view as the parent view, and the right side view and the isometric view are generated by using the front view as the parent view. Note that while generating the drawing views, the dimensions will not be displayed. They will be displayed after generating the drawing views.

1. Invoke the **Create View** tool and generate the top view of the model. Select the **Front** option from the list box provided under the **View** area to generate the top view. The scale of the view is 1.25. Place the view close to the top left corner of the drawing sheet.

2. Taking the top view as the parent view, generate the front view. Place the view below the top view. Similarly, taking the front view as the parent view, generate the right side view and the isometric view. Modify the scale of isometric view to 0.75, see Figure 11-17.

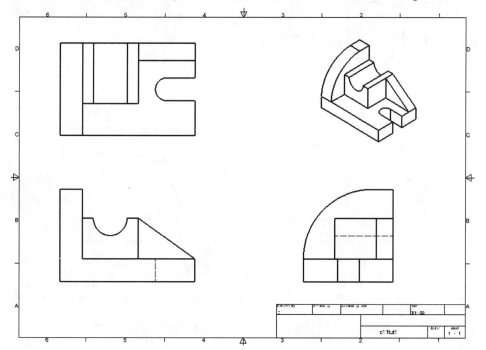

Figure 11-17 Drawing sheet after generating the drawing views

Displaying the Model Dimensions

As mentioned earlier, the model dimensions are the dimensions that were used while creating the model. Since you created a dimension style and that style is current, therefore, the dimensions will be placed based on this dimension style.

1. Move the cursor over the top view and right-click when the dotted rectangle is displayed. The shortcut menu will be displayed.

2. From the shortcut menu, choose **Get Model Dimensions**. The model dimensions that are applicable to the features in the top view are displayed.

3. Similarly, right-click on the front view and the side view and display the model dimensions on these views. All the dimensions shown in Figure 11-16 are displayed. If some of the dimensions are missing, add them by using the **General Dimension** tool from the **Drawing Annotation** toolbar or the **Drawing Annotation** panel bar.

    You will notice that the dimensions that are displayed on these drawing views are staggered and are not aligned. You will have to align these dimensions by dragging them.

4. One by one select the dimensions and drag them to place them neatly in the drawing views. The sheet after aligning the dimensions is shown in Figure 11-18.

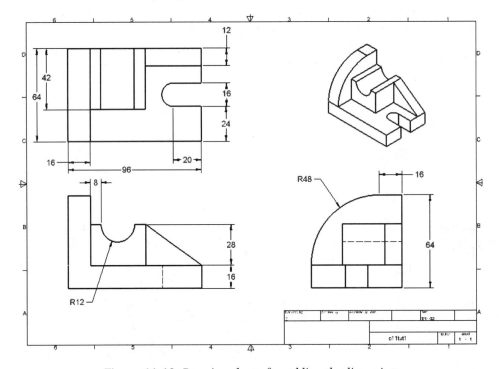

Figure 11-18 *Drawing sheet after adding the dimensions*

5. Save the file with the name \PersonalProject\c11**Tutorial1.idw**

Tutorial 2

In this tutorial you will open the drawing views of the Double Bearing assembly generated in Exercise 1 of Chapter 10. After opening the drawing views you will add the parts list and balloons to the components. The balloons should be added in the isometric view of the sectioned front view. The parts list should appear as shown in Figure 11-19.   (**Expected time: 45 min**)

Parts List			
ITEM	QTY	NAME	DESCRIPTION
1	1	Base	Bronze
2	1	Cap	Steel
3	2	Bushing	Steel
4	6	Bolt	.50—13UNC X 4.00

Figure 11-19 Parts list for Tutorial 2

The steps that will be followed to complete the model are listed below:

a.   Copy the **Double Bearing** directory from the \PersonalProject\c10 directory to the current directory.
b.   Open the file **Exercise1.idw** from this directory. Modify the lineweight of visible edges from the **Drafting Standards** dialog box.
c.   Place the default parts list by using the **Parts List** tool. Use the isometric view of the sectioned front view for placing the parts list.
d.   Modify the parts list such that it resembles the one shown in Figure 11-19.
e.   Use the **Balloon** tool to place the balloons using the components in the isometric view.

Copying the Double Bearing Directory in the Current Directory

1.   Copy the **Double Bearing** directory from the \PersonalProject\c10 directory to the current directory.

2.   Open the file \PersonalProject\c11\Double Bearing**Exercise1.idw**.

The drawing file is opened with top view, sectioned front view, and isometric view that were generated in Exercise 1 of Chapter 10.

Modifying the Drafting Standards

1.   Choose **Format > Standards** from the menu bar to invoke the **Drafting Standards** dialog box. Choose the **More** button available at the lower right corner if the dialog box is not expanded.

2.   Click on the field below the **Line Weight** column in the **Visible Edge** row to display the drop-down list. Select **1.00 mm** from this drop-down list as the value of the lineweight of the visible edges. Choose **Apply** and then choose **OK** to exit the dialog box.

Placing the Parts List

As mentioned earlier, the parts list is placed using the **Parts List** tool. However, when you place the parts list, the data will be listed in it using the default parameters. For example, the fields under the **DESCRIPTION** column will not display any data. You will have to modify the parts list after placing so that it appears similar to the one that is given in Figure 11-19.

1. Choose the **Parts List** button from the **Drawing Annotation** toolbar to invoke the **Parts List** tool. You can also invoke this tool by choosing **Parts List** from the **Drawing Annotation** panel bar.

   As mentioned earlier, the parts list is placed taking the reference of a drawing view. It is recommended that the drawing view you use as a reference for placing the parts list should have all the components so that all of them are listed in the parts list.

2. Select the isometric view as the reference view for placing the parts list.

   As soon as you select the drawing view, the **Parts List - Item Numbering** dialog box will be displayed.

3. Select the **All** radio button from the **Range** area. Accept the other default options in this dialog box and choose the **OK** button to exit this dialog box.

   You will be prompted to click on the location of the parts list. Notice that a rectangle is displayed on the screen and is attached to the cursor. This rectangle is the parts list that will be placed at the point that you specify.

4. Specify the location of the parts list close to the bottom right corner of the sheet above the title block. The sheet with the default parts list is shown in Figure 11-20.

   Note that in the default parts list the fields below the **DESCRIPTION** column do not display any data. This is because by default, there is no data specified for this field. You will have to manually define the data in these fields.

Modifying the Parts List

Whenever you place a parts list in the drawing views, it is displayed in the drawing sheet and in the browser. You can modify the parts list by double-clicking on it in the browser or in the drawing sheet. You need to modify the heading **PART NUMBER** to **NAME**, enter the data in the fields below the **DESCRIPTION** column, and center align the data in this column.

1. Double-click on the parts list in the drawing sheet. The **Edit Parts List** dialog box is displayed.

2. Using the left mouse click on the field below the **DESCRIPTION** column to enter the description related to the first component, that is, Base.

3.   Enter the description in this field as shown in Figure 11-19. Similarly, enter the description in the remaining fields.

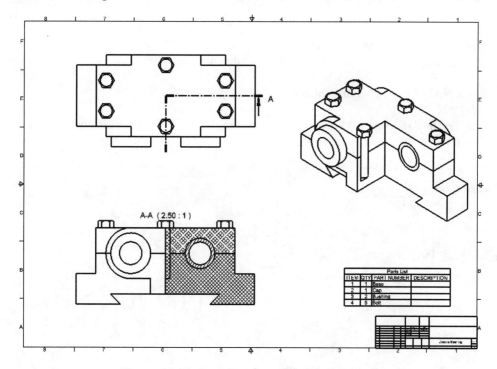

Figure 11-20 Drawing sheet with default parts list

By default, the data in the **DESCRIPTION** column is left aligned. You need to modify the alignment such that the text is center aligned.

4.   Move the cursor over the heading **DESCRIPTION**. You will notice that the cursor is replaced by an arrow that points in downward direction.

5.   Left-click when the arrow is displayed. The **DESCRIPTION** column and all the fields under this heading are selected.

6.   Choose the **More** button provided on the lower right corner of the dialog box. The dialog box will expand and provide more options.

7.   Enter **60** as the value in the **Width** edit box of the **Column Properties** area.

     This will increase the width of the fields below the **DESCRIPTION** heading.

8.   Choose the **Center** button in front of **Data Alignment** to center align the data in the fields below the **DESCRIPTION** heading.

     You will notice that the data in the selected field are center aligned now.

By default, the heading of the column that displays the name of the components is **PART NUMBER**. You need to modify this heading to **NAME**.

9. Move the cursor over the heading **PART NUMBER** and left-click when the cursor is replaced by an arrow. All the fields under this column will be selected and the heading will be displayed in the **Name** edit box of the **Column Properties** area.

10. Enter **NAME** in the **Name** edit box.

11. Choose the **OK** button to exit the dialog box. The sheet after editing the parts list is shown in Figure 11-21.

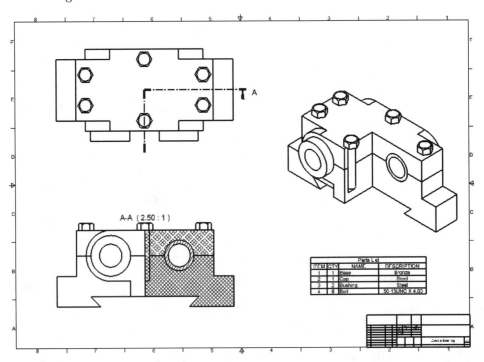

Figure 11-21 Drawing sheet after modifying the parts list

Adding Balloons to the Components

As mentioned earlier, the balloons are callouts attached to the components in the drawing view so that they can be referred to in the parts list. These are based on the item numbers in the parts list. You can add balloons using the **Balloon** tool or the **Balloon All** tool. However, as mentioned earlier, if you add balloons using the **Balloon All** tool, all instances of the components will be ballooned and you will have to delete the unwanted balloons. Also, the location of balloons need to be modified if you add them using this tool. Therefore, it is recommended that the balloons should be added using the **Balloon** tool.

1. Invoke the **Drafting Standards** dialog box and choose **Terminator** tab. Enter **6** as the value in the **Size** edit box and **1.5** as the value in **Aspect** edit box. Exit the dialog box.

2. Choose the **Balloon** button from the **Drawing Annotation** toolbar or choose **Balloon** from the **Drawing Annotation** panel bar.

3. Move the cursor over the Bolt on the upper left corner of the assembly in the isometric view. One of the edges of the component is highlighted and turned red in color. The symbol of coincident constraint is also displayed.

4. Select the component when the symbol of coincident constraint is displayed. You will notice that the start point of the balloon is attached to the selected edge and the other end of the balloon is attached to the cursor.

5. Specify the location of the other end of the balloon above the view.

6. Now, right-click and choose **Continue** from the shortcut menu.

   The balloon is created and display number 4 inside the circle. Number 4 corresponds to Bolt in the parts list.

7. Since you are already inside the **Balloon** tool, you do not need to invoke this tool again. Move the cursor over the circular edge of the Bushing that is not sectioned in the isometric view. Select when the circular edge is highlighted. One end of the balloon is attached to the edge.

8. Specify the location of the other end on the left of the view and then right-click to display the shortcut menu. Choose **Continue** from the shortcut menu to place the balloon.

9. Similarly, place the balloon on Base and Cap and place them on the right side.

10. After placing all the balloons, right-click to display the shortcut menu. Choose **Done** from this shortcut menu to exit this tool.

11. The drawing sheet after adding the parts list and the balloons is shown in Figure 11-22.

   Tip. *After adding the balloons to the components if you double-click on the parts list, you will notice that the symbol of balloon is displayed in front of all the components that are ballooned. This suggests that the balloons corresponding to the components are added to the drawing sheet.*

   *To change the arrowhead of balloon, right-click on it and choose **Edit Arrowhead**. The **Change Arrowhead** toolbar will be displayed with a drop-down list. You can select the arrowhead style from this drop-down list.*

12. Save the file with the name **Tutotial2.idw** in \PersonalProject\c11\Double Bearing directory.

Note
If the drawing file consists of more than one sheet, irrespective of which sheet was active at the time of closing the file, the first sheet will be active when you open the drawing file next time.

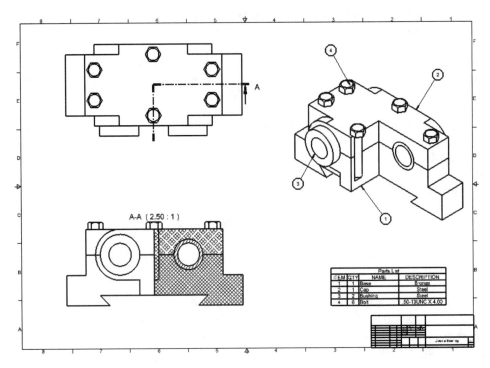

Figure 11-22 Drawing sheet after adding balloons

Tutorial 3

In this tutorial you will generate the drawing views of the Drill Press Vice assembly created in Exercise 1 of Chapter 8. The drawing views that need to be created are shown in Figure 11-23. After creating the drawing views, add parts list and balloons to the components. The parts list should resemble the one shown in Figure 11-24. You will use the GB standard file and then set the standards to ANSI. The units for linear distances should be in millimeters. Use the A3 size sheet for generating the drawing views.   **(Expected time: 1 Hr 15 min)**

The steps that will be followed to complete this tutorial are listed below:

a. Copy the Drill Press Vice assembly from c08 directory to c11 directory. Open a new GB standard drawing file using the **Metric** tab of the **Open** dialog box.
b. Modify the sheet to A3 size sheet.
c. Modify the drafting standards and generate the required drawing views.
d. Add the parts list and modify it such that it resembles the one shown in Figure 11-24.
e. Finally add the balloons to the components.

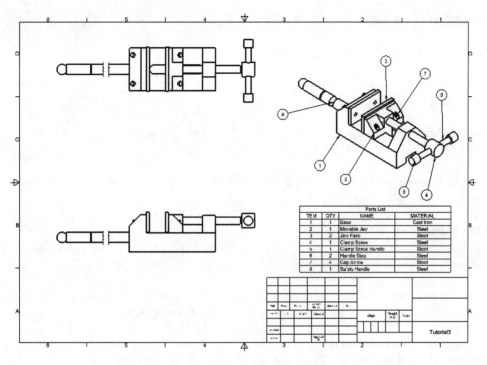

Figure 11-23 *Drawing sheet for Tutorial 3*

Parts List			
ITEM	QTY	NAME	MATERIAL
1	1	Base	Cast Iron
2	1	Movable Jaw	Steel
3	2	Jaw Face	Steel
4	1	Clamp Screw	Steel
5	1	Clamp Screw Handle	Steel
6	2	Handle Stop	Steel
7	4	Cap Screw	Steel
8	1	Safety Handle	Steel

Figure 11-24 *Parts list to be added*

Copying the Drill Press Vice Assembly

1. Copy the Drill Press Vice assembly from the \PersonalProject\c08 directory to the current directory.

Opening a New GB Standard File

1. Open a new metric file with GB standards.

    The default GB standard drawing sheet will be displayed. The size of default sheet is A2. You need to change this size to A3.

2. Right-click on **Sheet:1** in the browser and choose **Edit Sheet** from the shortcut menu. The **Edit Sheet** dialog box is displayed.

3. Select **A3** from the **Size** drop-down list in the **Format** area. Choose **OK** to exit the dialog box.

Generating the Drawing Views

Before generating the drawing views, you need to modify the standards of the current sheet based on the tutorial description.

1. Choose **Format > Standards** from the menu bar to display the **Drafting Standards** dialog box. Select the **ANSI** radio button from the **Select Standard** area.

2. Choose the **More** button if the dialog box is not already expanded. Select **mm** from the **Linear** drop-down list in the **Units** area. Select **0.039 in mm** from the **Line Weight** drop-down list of the **Visible Edges** row.

3. Choose the **Terminator** tab and enter **4** in the **Size** edit box. Choose **Apply** and then choose **OK** to exit this dialog box.

    This is done to increase the size of arrowheads in the balloons.

4. Generate the top view of the Drill Press Vice assembly with a scale of 0.5. Break the view such that the length of Safety Handle is reduced.

5. Generate the front view and the Isometric view as shown in Figure 11-25.

Placing the Parts List

1. Choose the **Parts List** button from the **Drawing Annotation** toolbar to invoke the **Parts List** tool. You can also invoke this tool by choosing **Parts List** from the **Drawing Annotation** panel bar.

2. Select the isometric view as the reference view for placing the parts list.

    As soon as you select the isometric view, the **Parts List - Item Numbering** dialog box will be displayed.

3. Accept the default options in this dialog box and choose **OK**.

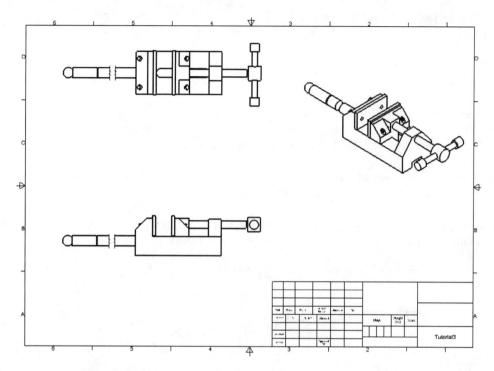

Figure 11-25 Drawing sheet after generating the drawing views

A rectangle that is actually the parts list will be attached to the cursor and you will be prompted to specify the location of the parts list.

4. Place the parts list on top of the title block.

Modifying the Parts List

1. Double-click on the parts list to display the **Edit Parts List** dialog box.

2. Select the **DESCRIPTION** column and choose the **More** button to expand the dialog box. Enter the heading of this column as **MATERIAL** in the **Name** edit box of the **Column Properties** area. Choose the **Center** button to center align the data in this column.

3. Select the **PART NUMBER** column and modify its heading to **NAME** in the **Name** edit box of the **Column Properties** area.

4. Enter the data in the **MATERIAL** field based on the parts list shown in Figure 11-24.

Adding Balloons to the Components

The final step in this tutorial is to add the balloons to the components in the isometric view. In this assembly it is better to add the balloons using the **Balloon All** tool. When you add the balloons using this tool, the balloons will be added to all the components. You will have to delete the balloons added to three instances of the Cap Screw, one instance of the

Handle Stop, and one instance of the Jaw Face. You also need to drag the balloons such that they are placed at a proper location in the drawing sheet.

1. Choose the down arrow on the right of the **Balloon** tool and choose the **Balloon All** tool from the **Drawing Annotation** toolbar or panel bar.

2. Select the isometric view for placing the balloons.

   The balloons will be added to all the components in the isometric view.

3. Delete the balloons added to three instances of the Cap Screw, one instance of the Jaw face, and one instance of the Handle Stop.

4. Drag the balloons to a proper location in the drawing sheet. The final drawing sheet after adding the parts list and the balloons is shown in Figure 11-26.

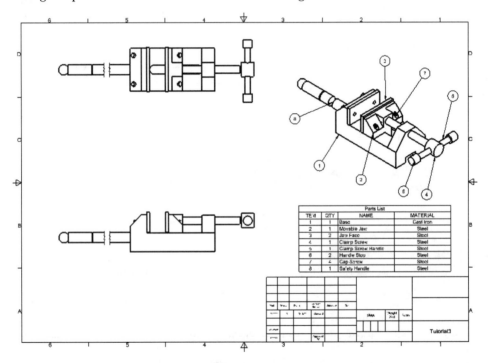

Figure 11-26   *Final drawing sheet for Tutorial 3*

5. Save this file with the name given below:

   \PersonalProject\c11\Drill Press Vice**Tutorial3.idw**

Self-Evaluation Test

Answer the following questions and then compare your answers with the answers given at the end of this chapter.

1. The drafting standards of a drawing sheet can be modified using the **Drawing Standards** dialog box. (T/F)

2. You can add parametric dimensions and reference dimensions to the drawing views. (T/F)

3. When you create a new dimension style, all existing dimensions will be modified based on the new style. (T/F)

4. The default parts list cannot be modified. (T/F)

5. You can add Bill of Material to the assembly drawing views using the _____ tool.

6. You can add multiline text without leader using the _____ tool.

7. When you open a new drawing file, only _____ sheet is available by default.

8. The _____ make it convenient to relate the components in the parts list to the components in the drawing views.

9. If you assemble some of the components in a separate assembly file and reference the subassembly in the current assembly file, the components of the subassembly are termed as _____ components.

10. You can modify the size of the drawing sheet by using the _____ dialog box.

Review Questions

Answer the following questions.

1. You cannot control the lineweight of lines in the drawing views. (T/F)

2. Whenever you open an old drawing file that has more than one sheet, the sheet that was active last time will be displayed as the active sheet. (T/F)

3. You cannot modify the size of arrowheads of balloons using the **Balloon** tab of the **Drafting Standards** dialog box. (T/F)

4. Autodesk Inventor allows you to add user-defined text to the drawing sheet. (T/F)

5. You can edit the text by double-clicking on it. (T/F)

6. Which one of the following tools can be used to add text with leader?

    (a) **Text**   (b) **Leader**
    (c) **Leader Text**   (d) None

7. Which one of the following tools can be used to add center marks to the circles in the drawing views?

    (a) **Center Mark**   (b) **Center Line**
    (c) **Center**   (d) None

8. Which one of the following tabs of **Drafting Settings** dialog box can be used to modify the size of arrowheads of balloons?

    (a) **Balloon**   (b) **Terminator**
    (c) **Common**   (d) **Sheet**

9. Which one of the following dialog boxes can be used to create a new dimension style?

    (a) **Dimension Style**   (b) **Dimension Text**
    (c) **Drafting Standards** (d) None

10. Which one of the following dialog boxes is displayed when you double-click on the parts list to edit it?

    (a) **Parts List**   (b) **Edit Parts List**
    (c) **Edit**   (d) You cannot edit parts list

Exercise

Exercise 1

Open the drawing views of Plummer Block assembly created in Tutorial 2 of Chapter 10 and then add the parts list and the balloons to the components. The drawing sheet after adding the parts list and the balloons is shown in Figure 11-27. The parts list to be added is shown in Figure 11-28. As evident in Figure 11-27, the balloons should be added in the isometric view.

(Expected time: 45 min)

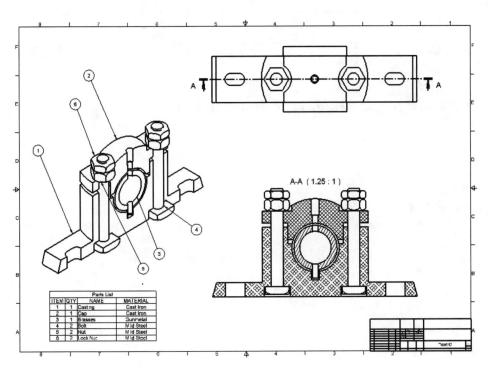

Figure 11-27 Drawing sheet for Exercise 1

Parts List			
ITEM	QTY	NAME	MATERIAL
1	1	Casting	Cast Iron
2	1	Cap	Cast Iron
3	1	Brasses	Gunmetal
4	2	Bolt	Mild Steel
5	2	Nut	Mild Steel
6	2	Lock Nut	Mild Steel

Figure 11-28 *Parts list for Exercise 1*

Answers to Self-Evaluation Test

1. F, **2.** T, **3.** F, **4.** F, **5. Parts List**, **6. Text**, **7.** one, **8.** balloons, **9.** second-level, **10. Edit Sheet**

Chapter 12

Presentation Mode

Learning Objectives

After completing this chapter you will be able to:
- *Create or restore the assembly view for creating the presentation.*
- *Tweak the components and add trails to them.*
- *Rotate the views using the Precise View Rotation tool.*
- *Animate the tweaked view.*

THE PRESENTATION MODE

As mentioned earlier, Autodesk Inventor allows you to animate the assemblies created in the **Assembly** mode. You can view some of the assemblies in motion by animating them. The animation of assemblies can be created in the **Presentation** mode. You can also use the **Presentation** mode for creating the exploded views of an assembly. An exploded view is a view in which the assembled components are moved to a defined distance from their original location. To invoke the **Presentation** mode, double-click on the **Standard.ipn** file in the **Metric** tab of the **Open** dialog box, see Figure 12-1.

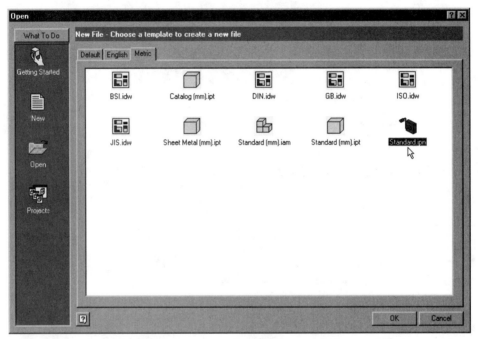

Figure 12-1 *Opening a new presentation file from the **Metric** tab of the **Open** dialog box*

The default screen appearance of the **Presentation** mode is shown in Figure 12-2.

Note
*You will notice that when you open a new presentation file, only the **Create View** tool is available in the **Presentation** panel bar. This is because you need to first create the presentation view of the assembly. Once the presentation view is created, other tools will become available in this mode.*

*As mentioned earlier, all the modes of Autodesk Inventor are bidirectionally associative. Therefore, if you make any modification in the assembly or components of the assembly, the changes will be automatically reflected in the **Presentation** mode.*

*You cannot modify the assembly or its components in the **Presentation** mode.*

*Figure 12-2 Screen display in the **Presentation** mode*

CREATING THE PRESENTATION VIEW

Toolbar:	Presentation > Create View
Panel Bar:	Presentation > Create View

 After proceeding to the **Presentation** mode, the first step is to create the presentation view. The presentation view can be used to animate the assembly or to create an exploded state of the assembly. The presentation views can be created by using the **Create View** tool. You can also invoke this tool by right-clicking in the drawing window and choosing **Create View** from the shortcut menu. When you invoke this tool, the **Select Assembly** dialog box will be displayed as shown in Figure 12-3. The options that are available in this dialog box are discussed next.

Assembly Area

The options under the **Assembly** area are used to select the assembly for creating the presentation view. These options are discussed next.

File

The **File** drop-down list displays the assembly file selected for creating the presentation view. By default, this drop-down list displays the **<select assembly document>** option. This is because no assembly file is selected. To select an assembly file, choose the **Explore Directories**

Figure 12-3 Select Assembly dialog box

button on the right of this drop-down list. When you choose this button, the **Open** dialog box will be displayed, see Figure 12-4. You can use this dialog box for selecting the assembly file that will be used for creating the presentation.

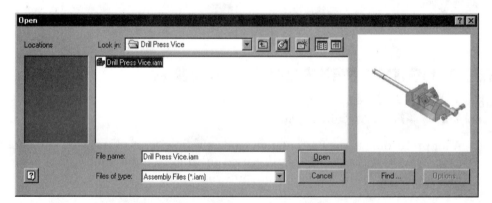

Figure 12-4 Open dialog box for selecting the assembly file

The selected assembly file and its location is displayed in the **File** drop-down list. Similarly, you can select other assemblies for generating the presentation views. The name of the selected assemblies and their location is displayed in the **File** drop-down list.

   Tip. *In the Open dialog box, the **Files of type** drop-down list displays only the **Assembly Files (*.iam)** option. This is because you can create the presentation views of only assembly files.*

Design View

The **Design View** drop-down list displays the design views associated with the selected assembly. If there is no assembly selected, this drop-down list is not available. Once this drop-down list is available, you can select the **Explore Directories** button to invoke the **Open** dialog box for selecting the design view files.

Explosion Method Area

As mentioned earlier, an exploded view is a view in which the components of assembly are moved to a specified distance from their original location in the assembly. The options under the **Explosion Method** area are used to select the method for exploding the selected assembly. These options are discussed next.

Manual

If the **Manual** radio button is selected, the assembly in the presentation view will not be exploded. This option is selected when you want to explode the assembly manually using other tools. Note that since the assembly will not be exploded, no other option in the **Explosion Method** area will be available if the **Manual** radio button is selected.

Automatic

The **Automatic** radio button is selected to automatically explode the assembly when the presentation view is created. The components of the assembly will move in the direction of the constraint that is used to assemble them. The distance to which the components will move is specified in the **Distance** edit box. This edit box will be available when you select the **Automatic** radio button.

Create Trails

Trails are defined as the parametric lines that display the path and direction of the assembled components. These lines can be used as a reference for determining the path and the direction in which the components are assembled. The **Create Trails** check box is selected to create the trails when the assembly is exploded. This check box will be available only when the **Automatic** radio button is selected.

Figure 12-5 shows the Drill Press Vice assembly exploded using the **Automatic** option. The distance of explosion is 25 mm. This figure also shows the trails that define the path and direction of assembled components.

Tip. *If the explosion distance is large, the result of exploding the assemblies using the **Automatic** method may not be what is desired. This is because if the explosion distance is large, the components of the assembly will move to a large distance and start interfering with the other components. Therefore, it is recommended that if the components need to be moved to a large distance, you should explode the assemblies using the manual method.*

*To increase the value of automatic explosion after creating the presentation view, click on the + sign located on left of **Explosion1** in the browser to display the name of the assembly. Right-click on the name and choose **Auto Explode** from the shortcut menu to display the **Auto Explode** dialog box. Enter the value of distance in the **Distance** edit box. The new value of distance will be added to the previous distance value. Remember that you cannot enter a negative value in this edit box.*

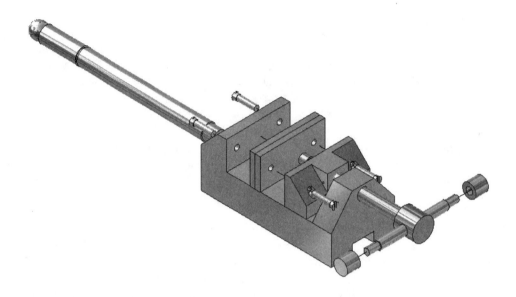

Figure 12-5 *Exploded assembly with trails*

TWEAKING THE COMPONENTS

Toolbar:	Presentation > Tweak Components
Panel Bar:	Presentation > Tweak Components

As mentioned earlier, if the distance by which the components should move in the exploded view is large, the components in the automatically created exploded view start interfering with the other components. For example, see Figure 12-6. This figures shows an automatic exploded view in which the components are moved to a distance of 42 mm. Notice the interference between the Movable Jaw and the Base, between the two Jaw Faces, and between the Clamp Screw and the Base. To avoid such situations, it is recommended that if the components need to be exploded to a large distance, you should create the exploded view manually by tweaking the components. Tweaking is defined as the process of adjusting the position of the assembled components with respect to the other components of the assembly by transforming them in the specified direction. The components can be tweaked by using the **Tweak Components** tool. The tweaked components can also be animated, thus creating the animation of the assemblies.

When you invoke this tool, the **Tweak Component** dialog box will be displayed as shown in Figure 12-7. The options provided under this dialog box are discussed next.

Create Tweak Area

The options under the **Create Tweak** area are used to select the component to be tweaked, the

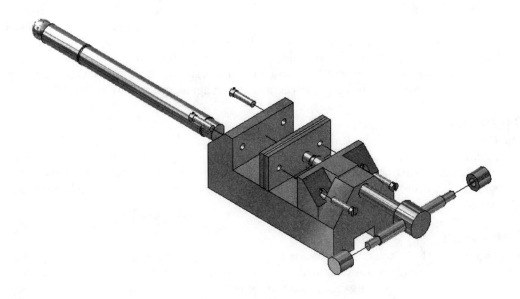

Figure 12-6 Exploded assembly displaying interfering components

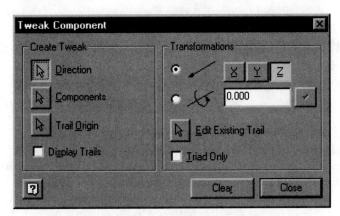

Figure 12-7 Tweak Component dialog box

direction of tweaking, and options related to the trails. These options are discussed next.

Direction

The **Direction** button is the first button in the **Create Tweak** area and is used to select the direction of moving or rotating the components. This button is chosen by default when you invoke the **Tweak Component** dialog box. When this button is chosen, you will notice that the direction symbol is attached to the cursor. This symbol will be visible when you move the cursor on the graphics screen. You can define the direction of rotation or moving by using any linear edge, face, or feature of the components in the assembly. If you select a cylindrical component, you can use its central axis as the direction of tweaking. When you move the cursor close to any component for selecting the direction, you will notice that a triad is displayed. This triad displays the X, Y, and Z directions. After you select the direction of tweaking, the triad will be fixed at the selected component. Also, the **Direction** button is no more chosen. Instead, the **Components** button will be chosen in the **Create Tweak** area. You can change the direction of tweaking by choosing the **Direction** button again and redefining the direction.

Components

The **Components** button is chosen to select the components that will be tweaked. This button will be automatically chosen when you define the direction of tweaking. When you choose this button, you will notice that a symbol of a 3D model and an arrow is attached to the cursor. This symbol suggests that you need to select the components to be tweaked. You will also be prompted to select the components to be tweaked.

Trail Origin

As mentioned earlier, trails are parametric lines defining the direction and path of assembled components. By default, when you tweak the components, the trails are created at the center of the components. You can use the **Trail Origin** button to redefine the origin of trail using two points.

Display Trails

The **Display Trails** check box is selected to display the trails in the exploded view. If this check box is cleared, the trails will not be displayed in the exploded view of the assembly.

Transformations Area

The options under the **Transformations** area are used to specify the type of transformation, direction of transformation, and the distance of transformation. These options are discussed next.

Linear

 The **Linear** option is used to tweak the selected components in the linear direction. Whenever you select the direction of tweaking by using the **Direction** button in the **Create Tweak** area, a triad is displayed with three axes. If the **Linear** option is selected, the selected components will be tweaked in the linear direction along one of these three axes. The distance of tweaking will be entered in the edit box provided in this area. Note that after entering the value in the edit box, choose the **Apply** button provided on the right of the edit box. Until you choose the **Apply** button, the components will not be tweaked. By default, the components will be tweaked in the Z direction. This axis is displayed in blue in the triad. The remaining two axes will be displayed in green. This is because the **Z** button is chosen in the **Transformations** area. If you want to tweak the components in the X or Y direction, choose the respective button from the **Transformations** area. The selected axis will be displayed in blue and the remaining two axes will be displayed in green.

Rotational

 The **Rotational** option is used to rotate the selected components around a specified axis of the triad. The triad is displayed when you select the direction by using the **Direction** button from the **Create Tweak** area. You can select the required axis by choosing its button from the **Transformations** area. The angle of rotation will be entered in the edit box provided on the right of the **Rotational** radio button. After entering the angle of rotation in the edit box, choose the **Apply** button to tweak the components.

Edit Existing Trail

The **Edit Existing Trail** button is chosen to edit an existing trail. When you choose this button, the remaining options in the **Tweak Component** dialog box will not be available. Choose this button and then select the trail from the graphics screen. The **Direction** button in the **Create Tweak** area and the edit box in the **Transformations** area will be available. You can modify the direction and distance/angle of the existing trail.

Triad Only

The **Triad Only** check box is selected to rotate the triad around the axis selected in the triad. The angle of rotation will be specified in the edit box provided on the right of the **Rotational** option. This check box is generally selected when you want to rotate the triad through a certain angle and then use the directions of rotated triad to add tweaks to the components. Remember that you cannot move the triad without moving the components. However, you can rotate it without rotating the components. After rotating the triad, you can add linear or rotation tweak to the components.

Figure 12-8 shows the exploded view of the Drill Press Vice assembly.

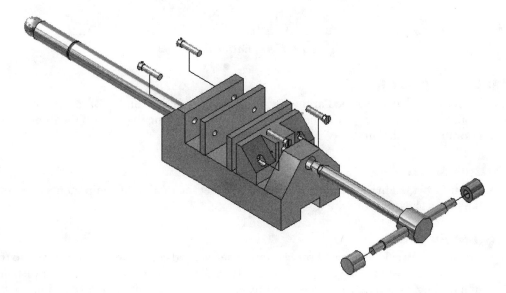

Figure 12-8 *Exploded view of the Drill Press Vice assembly*

Clear

The **Clear** button is chosen to clear the current settings in the **Tweak Component** dialog box. When you choose this button, all the current settings are reset to the default values and you can proceed with tweaking other components.

> **Tip**. *To modify the individual tweak values of the components, click on the + sign located on left of the name of the assembly in the browser. All components in the assembly will be displayed. Click on the + sign located on left of any component to display the tweak value. Select the tweak and an edit box will appear below the browser. Modify the value of the tweak in this edit box.*

ANIMATING THE ASSEMBLIES

Toolbar:	Presentation > Animate
Panel Bar:	Presentation > Animate

 The tweaked or exploded assemblies can be animated by using the **Animate** tool. When you invoke this tool, the **Animation** dialog box will be displayed as shown in Figure 12-9. The options provided under this dialog box are discussed next.

Figure 12-9 Animation dialog box

Parameter Area

The spinner provided under the **Parameter** area is used to set the number of repetitions in the animation. You can directly set the number of repetitions by setting the value of the **Repetitions** spinner or enter a value in this edit box.

Motion Area

The options provided in the **Motion** area are used to set the motion of components or record the animation. These options are discussed next.

Forward By Tweak

The **Forward By Tweak** button is chosen to force the tweaked components to be moved to the end value of tweak distance. If you have tweaked the selected components to a linear distance of 25 mm in the Z direction, then choosing this button will move all the tweaked components forward by the complete tweak distance, that is 25 mm in this case.

Forward By Interval

Whenever you create an animation, the total tweak distance or tweak angle is automatically divided into small intervals that are used as animation sequence. The **Forward By Interval** button is chosen to force the tweaked components to move forward by one interval in the animation.

Tip. *To set the interval value, choose the **Browser Filter** button on top of the browser. From the flyout that is displayed, choose the **Sequence View** option. You will notice that **Task1** option appears below **Explosion1** in the tree view of the browser. Right-click on **Task1** in the browser and choose **Edit** from the shortcut menu to display the **Edit Task & Sequences** dialog box. Set the value of interval in the **Interval** edit box provided in the **Sequences** area. Remember that more the value of interval, smother is the animation.*

Reverse By Interval

The **Reverse By Interval** button is chosen to force the tweaked components to move backward by one interval in the animation.

Reverse By Tweak

The **Reverse By Tweak** button is chosen to force the tweaked components to be moved to the start value of tweak distance. This button will work only if one cycle of animation is completed or the components are moved to the end position by using the **Forward By Tweak** button.

Play Forward

The **Play Forward** button is chosen to play the animation of assembly in the forward direction. The number of cycles in the animation will be based on the value of **Repetitions** spinner in the **Parameter** area. If the number of repetitions is more than one, the components will be repositioned at the start point of the forward cycle after the first repetition is completed and the second repetition will again begin from the start point of animation.

Auto Reverse

If the **Auto Reverse** button is chosen, the animation of assembly will be first played in the forward direction and then automatically played in the reverse direction. The number of forward and reverse cycles will depend upon the value of the **Repetitions** spinner. Note that in this case the forward and reverse movement of components is considered as one cycle.

Tip. *If the components are already moved to the end value of the tweak distance, that is, at the start position of the animation in the reverse direction, choosing the **Auto Reverse** button will animate the components in only the reverse direction if the number of repetitions is one.*

Play Reverse

The **Play Reverse** button is chosen to play the animation of assembly in the backward direction. The number of cycles in the animation will be based on the value of **Repetitions** spinner in the **Parameter** area. If the number of repetitions is more than one, the components will be repositioned at the start point of the reverse cycle after the first repetition is completed and the second repetition will again begin from the end point of animation.

Pause

The **Pause** button is chosen to temporarily stop the animation of assembly.

Record

The **Record** button is chosen to store the animation of an assembly in the form of an avi file. When you choose this button, the **Save As** dialog box will be displayed to specify the name and location of the avi file, see Figure 12-10.

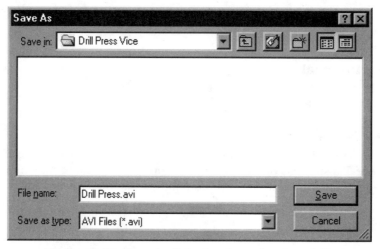

Figure 12-10 Save As dialog box for saving the avi file

After you specify the name of the avi file for saving the animation, the **Video Compression** dialog box will be displayed, see Figure 12-11. Set the values in this dialog box and then choose **OK**.

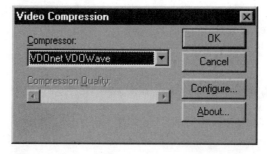

Figure 12-11 Video Compression dialog box

Once the video compression parameters are set, you are ready for creating the avi file. Now, choose the **Play Forward**, **Play Reverse**, or the **Auto Reverse** button to create the avi file of the animation. After the animation is recorded, choose this button again to exit recording.

Note

The avi files can be viewed using Windows Media Player.

Minimize dialog during recording

The **Minimize dialog during recording** check box is selected to minimize the **Animation** dialog box during the period the animation is being recorded. This is done because if the dialog box is not minimized, it will also appear in the avi file. This is because when the animation is being recorded, whatever appears on the graphics screen will also be recorded in the avi file.

Apply

The **Apply** button is chosen to apply the changes made to the parameters in this dialog box.

Reset

The **Reset** button is chosen to reset the parameters in the **Animation** dialog box to the default values.

More

This is the button with two arrows provided on the lower right corner of the **Animation** dialog box. When you choose this button, the **Animation** dialog box expands to display the **Animation Sequence** area, see Figure 12-12. All the tweaked components along with their tweak values are displayed in the list box available in this area. Note that all the components that were selected together while tweaking are displayed as a single sequence. The buttons provided in this area are discussed next.

Sequence	Component	Tweak Value
1	Handle Stop.ipt:1	Tweak (720.0 deg)
1	Handle Stop.ipt:2	Tweak (720.0 deg)
1	Clamp Screw Handle.ipt:1	Tweak (720.0 deg)
1	Clamp Screw.ipt:1	Tweak (720.0 deg)
2	Jaw Face.ipt:1	Tweak (25.000 mm)
2	Cap Screw.ipt:1	Tweak (25.000 mm)
2	Cap Screw.ipt:2	Tweak (25.000 mm)
2	Movable Jaw.ipt:1	Tweak (25.000 mm)
2	Handle Stop.ipt:1	Tweak (25.000 mm)
2	Handle Stop.ipt:2	Tweak (25.000 mm)
2	Clamp Screw Handle.ipt:1	Tweak (25.000 mm)
2	Clamp Screw.ipt:1	Tweak (25.000 mm)

Move Up   Move Down   Group   Ungroup

*Figure 12-12 The **Animation Sequence** area displayed upon choosing the **More** button*

Move Up

The **Move Up** button is chosen to move the selected sequence up in the order in the list box. Remember that the sequence that is displayed on top in the list box will be played first in the animation.

Move Down

The **Move Down** button is chosen to move the selected sequence down in the order in the list box.

Group

The **Group** button is chosen to group various sequences in the animation. All the grouped sequences will show the same sequence number after grouping.

> **Tip**. *The **Group** button is chosen when you want to club different tweak sequences together. Grouping a rotational and a linear tweak will provide the effect of linear and rotational movement together.*

Ungroup

The **Ungroup** button is chosen to ungroup the grouped sequences in the animation.

Note
*After grouping or ungrouping the sequences, choose the **Apply** button. If you do not choose the **Apply** button, the buttons to start animation in the **Motion** area will not be available.*

ROTATING THE PRESENTATION VIEW PRECISELY

Toolbar:	Presentation > Precise View Rotation
Panel Bar:	Presentation > Precise View Rotation

 Autodesk Inventor allows you to precisely rotate the presentation view in the **Presentation** mode. This is done by using the **Precise View Rotation** tool. When you invoke this tool, the **Incremental View Rotate** dialog box is displayed, see Figure 12-13. The options provided in this dialog box are discussed next.

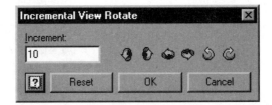

Figure 12-13 Incremental View Rotate dialog box

Increment

The **Increment** edit box is used to specify the value through which the presentation view will be rotated.

Rotate Down

The **Rotate Down** button is chosen to rotate the presentation view in the downward direction. The angle through which the view will be rotated is specified in the **Increment** edit box. Enter the increment value and then choose this button to rotate the view.

Rotate Up

The **Rotate Up** button is chosen to rotate the presentation view in the upward direction. The angle through which the view will be rotated is specified in the **Increment** edit box. Enter the increment value and then choose this button to rotate the view.

Rotate Left

The **Rotate Left** button is chosen to rotate the presentation view toward left. The angle through which the view will be rotated is specified in the **Increment** edit box. Enter the increment value and then choose this button to rotate the view.

Rotate Right

The **Rotate Right** button is chosen to rotate the presentation view toward right. The angle through which the view will be rotated is specified in the **Increment** edit box. Enter the increment value and then choose this button to rotate the view.

Roll Counter Clockwise

The **Roll Counter Clockwise** button is chosen to rotate the presentation view in the counterclockwise direction. The angle through which the view will be rotated is specified in the **Increment** edit box. Enter the increment value and then choose this button to rotate the view.

Roll Clockwise

The **Roll Clockwise** button is chosen to rotate the presentation view in the clockwise direction. The angle through which the view will be rotated is specified in the **Increment** edit box. Enter the increment value and then choose this button to rotate the view.

Reset

The **Reset** button is chosen to reset the current view to the isometric view. Irrespective of the current orientation of the view, if you choose this button, the isometric view will be restored.

TUTORIALS

Tutorial 1

In this tutorial you will explode the Plummer Block Assembly and then create an animation of disassembling (exploding) and assembling (unexploding) of the assembly. The exploded state of the Plummer Block assembly is shown in Figure 12-14.   **(Expected time: 45 min)**

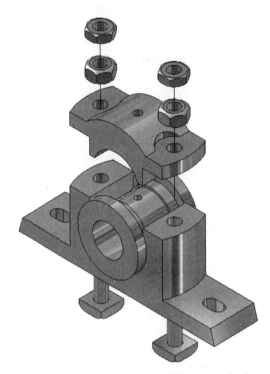

Figure 12-14 Exploded view of the Plummer Block Assembly

It is recommended that before you start with the tutorial, you should outline the procedure for completing the tutorial. The following points outline the steps that will be followed in completing this tutorial:

a. Copy the Plummer Block directory from the c11 directory to the c12 directory.
b. Open a new metric presentation file and create a new presentation view by using the **Create View** tool. In this view the assembly will not be exploded automatically.
c. Manually explode the assembly in four sequences. The first sequence will tweak the two Bolts. The second sequence will tweak the Cap, the Lock Nuts, and the Nuts. The third sequence will tweak the Lock Nuts. The final sequence will tweak the Nuts.
d. Invoke the **Animate** tool and then combine all the four sequences.
e. Finally, animate the sequences by using the **Auto Reverse** button in the **Animation** dialog box.

Copying the Folder

The presentation view is generated by using the Plummer Block assembly. Therefore, you need to copy the Plummer Block folder from the c11 folder to the c12 folder.

1. Create a folder with the name c12 inside the \PersonalProject directory.

2. Copy the Plummer Block folder from the c11 folder to the c12 folder.

Opening a New Presentation File

1. Choose **New** in the **Open** dialog box and then choose the **Metric** tab.

2. Double-click on **Standard.ipn** file, see Figure 12-15. A new presentation file is opened.

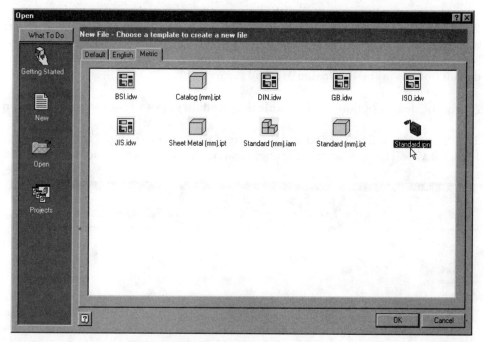

*Figure 12-15 Opening a new presentation file from the **Metric** tab of the **Open** dialog box*

Creating the Presentation View

When you open a new presentation file, only the **Create View** tool is available in the **Presentation** panel bar. This is because you first need to create the presentation view.

1. Choose the **Create View** button from the **Presentation** toolbar or choose **Create View** from the **Presentation** panel bar to invoke the **Select Assembly** dialog box.

2. Choose the **Explore Directories** button provided on the right of the **File** drop-down list in the **Assembly** area to invoke the **Open** dialog box.

3. Open the directory \PersonalProject\c12**Plummer Block**.

   You will notice that only the **Plummer Block.iam** file is available in this folder. This is because you can select only the assembly file for creating the presentation view.

4. Double-click on the **Plummer Block.iam** file to select this assembly for creating the presentation view.

The **Open** dialog box will be closed and the **File** drop-down list in the **Assembly** area of the **Select Assembly** dialog box will display the name and path of the selected assembly. Also, the **Design View** drop-down list displays the current design view.

5. Select *****.default** from the **Design View** drop-down list if it is not already selected.

    By default, the **Manual** radio button is selected in the **Explosion Method** area. This radio button is chosen when you do not want to automatically add tweaks to the components. Since in this tutorial you need to manually explode the assembly, you will accept the default options in the **Explosion Method** area.

6. Accept the default options in the **Explosion Method** area and choose the **OK** button.

    The design view will be created and the current view will be changed automatically to the Isometric view. The presentation file after creating the design view is shown in Figure 12-16.

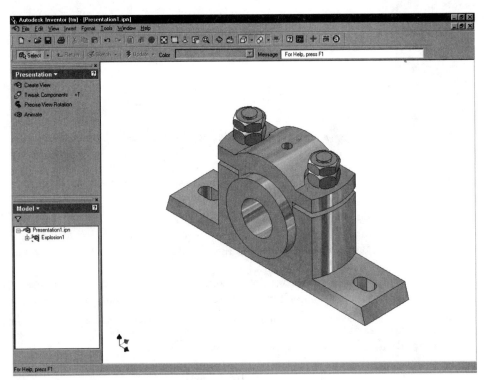

Figure 12-16 Presentation file after creating the presentation view

Tweaking the Components

As mentioned earlier, you can explode the assembly or add tweaks to the components of the assembly by using the **Tweak Components** tool.

1. Choose the **Tweak Components** button from the **Presentation** toolbar or choose **Tweak Components** from the **Presentation** panel bar to invoke the **Tweak Component** dialog box.

    When you invoke the **Tweak Component** dialog box, the **Direction** button in the **Create Tweak** area is chosen by default and you are prompted to select the direction for the tweak.

2. Select the vertical edge on the front face of the Base as the direction for the tweak, see Figure 12-17.

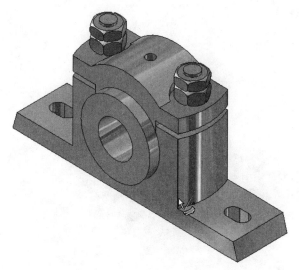

Figure 12-17 Selecting the direction for the tweak

As soon as you select the direction of the tweak, the selected edge will turn blue and a triad is displayed on the front face of the Base. The X, Y, and Z axes of the triad are along the X, Y, and Z axes of the current coordinate symbol displayed on the lower left corner of the graphics screen. Also, the Z axis of the triad is displayed in blue color. This suggests that the current tweak direction is along the Z axis.

Notice that after you define the direction of tweak, the **Components** button in the **Create Tweak** area is automatically chosen and you are prompted to select the components to be tweaked.

3. One by one select both the Bolts to tweak at the point where they extend out of the Lock Nuts.

    The top faces of the Bolts are displayed in blue outline. This suggests that the components are selected and can be tweaked.

4. Make sure that the **Display Trail** check box in the **Create Tweak** area is selected.

You need to add **Linear** tweak to the components and by default, the **Linear** radio button is selected in the **Transformations** area. Therefore, you just need to enter the value of linear tweak. Note that the Z axis of the triad points in the upward direction. But you need to tweak the components in the downward direction. Therefore, you need to enter a negative value of tweak.

5. Enter **-50** as the value in the edit box provided on the right of the **Rotational** radio button. Then choose the **Apply** button provided on the right of the edit box.

    The two Bolts will move in the downward direction, see Figure 12-18. This is the first sequence of tweak.

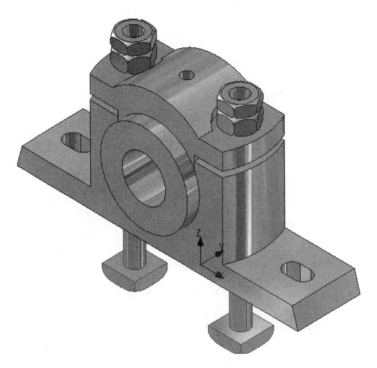

Figure 12-18 *Assembly after tweaking the two Bolts*

Since you are still inside the **Tweak Components** tool, you will again be prompted to select the components to be tweaked. Also, notice that the two Bolts are still displayed with a blue outline. This suggests that these components are still selected and if you enter a tweak value in the edit box, these components will be tweaked by that distance. Therefore, you first need to remove these components from the selected set.

6. Press and hold the SHIFT key down and then one by one click on both the Bolts. You will notice that the Bolts are no more displayed with a blue outline.

7. Select the Cap, the two Nuts, and the two Lock Nuts. All the selected components are displayed with a blue outline.

8. Enter **50** as the value in the edit box available on the right of the **Rotational** radio button in the **Transformations** area. Then choose the **Apply** button provided on the right of the edit box.

    The selected components will move in the upward direction by a distance of 50 mm. This is the second tweak sequence.

9. Next, press and hold the SHIFT key down and then one by one click on the Cap and both the Nuts to remove them from the current selection set. You will notice that only the two Lock Nuts are displayed with a blue outline now.

10. Choose the **Apply** button available on the right of the edit box in the **Transformations** area to move the two Lock Nuts further up by a distance of 50 mm.

    This is the third tweak sequence. You will notice that the blue trails are also created as you tweak the components. This is because the **Display Trails** check box in the **Create Tweak** area is selected.

11. Choose the **Zoom All** button from the **Standard** toolbar to increase the drawing display area such that the complete exploded assembly is displayed on the graphics screen.

12. Press and hold the SHIFT key down and then one by one click on the two Lock Nuts to remove them from the selection set. Release the SHIFT Key and then select the two Nuts.

    You will notice that the two Nuts are displayed with a blue outline.

13. Enter **25** as the value in the edit box provided on the right of the **Rotational** radio button in the **Transformations** area. Then choose the **Apply** button provided on the right of the edit box.

    The two Nuts will move in the upward direction by a distance of 25 mm and are now placed between the Cap and the two Lock Nuts. This is the fourth and the final tweak sequence.

14. Choose the **Close** button to exit the **Tweak Component** dialog box.

    You will notice that the triad that was displayed on the front face of the Base is removed from the screen and the edge selected to define the tweak direction is no more displayed in blue color. The assembly after creating the four tweak sequences is shown in Figure 12-19.

Animating the Assembly

The next step after tweaking the assembly is to animate it. The animation will carry out the simulation of exploding and unexploding of assembly. Note that when you tweak the components, the assembly is exploded and the components move to the tweaked position. Therefore, the first cycle in the animation will be to unexplode the assembly by moving the components back to their original assembled position and the second cycle will be to explode the assembly by moving the components to the tweaked position.

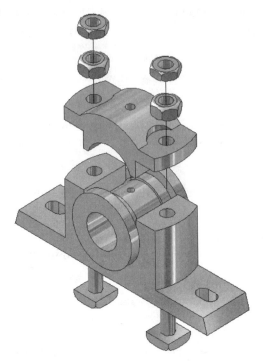

Figure 12-19 *Exploded assembly*

1. Choose the **Animate** button from the **Presentation** toolbar or choose **Animate** from the **Presentation** panel bar to invoke the **Animation** dialog box.

2. Choose the **More** button provided on the lower right corner of the dialog box to expand it.

    You will notice that there are four sequences in the **Animation Sequence** area. If you animate the assembly now, you will notice that the assembly will animate in four steps. These four steps are actually the four sequences displayed in the **Animation Sequence** area. Remember that the next step will start only after the previous step is completed. In order to animate the assembly such that all the sequences animate together, you need to select all of them and group them together.

3. Press and hold the SHIFT key down and select all the sequences displayed in the **Animation Sequence** area.

    You will notice that all the sequences are displayed with a blue background. Also, only the **Group** button is available in the **Animation Sequence** area.

4. Choose the **Group** button from the **Animation Sequence** area to group all the sequences together.

    All the tweaks are now grouped together under sequence 1.

5. Choose the **Apply** button to apply the changes to the assembly.

6. Hold the **Animation** dialog box from the blue portion and drag it to the left of the graphics screen such that it does not overlap with the assembly.

7. Choose the **Auto Reverse** button from the **Motion** area.

    You will notice that all the tweaked components in the animation move together to their original assembled position and then move back to the tweaked position.

8. Choose the **Cancel** button in the **Animation** dialog box to exit it. Save the assembly with the name given below:

    \PersonalProject\c12\Plummer Block**Tutorial1.ipn**

Tutorial 2

In this tutorial you will animate the Drill Press Vice assembly. The animation should consist of rotational tweak and the linear tweak. Save the animation in an avi file with the name **Drill Press Vice.avi**.   (Expected time: 1 Hr)

The following steps outline the procedure for completing the tutorial:

a. Copy the Drill Press Vice directory from the c11 directory to the c12 directory.
b. Open a new metric presentation file and create the presentation view of the Drill Press Vice assembly by using the **Create View** tool.
c. Tweak the components by using the **Tweak Components** tool.
d. Invoke the **Animation** dialog box and group the sequences.
e. Create the avi file and store the animation in the avi file.

Copying the Drill Press Vice Assembly
1. Copy the Drill Press Vice assembly from the c11 directory to the c12 directory.

Opening a New Presentation File
1. Choose the **New** button from the **Standard** toolbar to invoke the **Open** dialog box.

2. Choose the **Metric** tab and double-click on the **Standard.ipn** file to open a new metric presentation file.

Creating the Presentation View
1. Choose the **Create View** button from the **Presentation** toolbar or choose **Create View** from the **Presentation** panel bar to invoke the **Select Assembly** dialog box.

2. Choose the **Explore Directories** button provided on the right of the **File** drop-down list in the **Assembly** area to invoke the **Open** dialog box.

3. Open the directory \PersonalProject\c12**Drill Press Vice**. The **Drill Press Vice.iam** file will be displayed in this folder.

4. Double-click on the **Drill Press Vice.iam** file.

   The assembly will be selected and will be displayed along with its path in the **File** drop-down list in the **Assembly** area.

5. Select *****.default** from the **Design View** drop-down list if it is not already selected.

6. Accept the remaining default options and choose the **OK** button.

   The design view will be created and the current view will be changed to the Isometric view, see Figure 12-20.

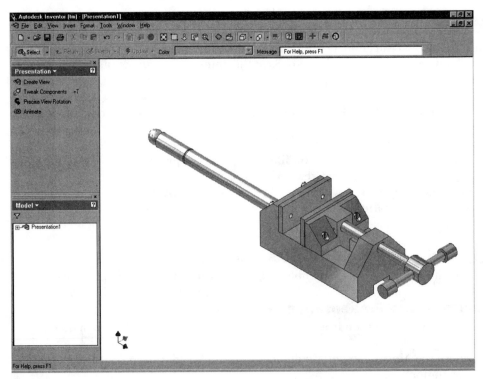

Figure 12-20 Presentation file after creating the presentation view of the Drill Press Vice assembly

Tweaking the Components

In this assembly you need to apply the rotational tweak to the Clamp Screw, the Clamp Screw Handle, and to the two Handle Stops. After that you need to apply the linear tweak to the above-mentioned components and also to the Movable Jaw, the Jaw Face assembled with the Movable Jaw, and to the two Cap Screws that are used to assemble the Jaw Face and the Movable Jaw.

1. Choose the **Tweak Components** button from the **Presentation** toolbar or choose **Tweak Components** from the **Presentation** panel bar to invoke the **Tweak Component** dialog box.

   As mentioned earlier, when you invoke the **Tweak Component** dialog box, the **Direction** button in the **Create Tweak** area is chosen by default and you are prompted to select the direction for the tweak.

2. Move the cursor close to the cylindrical face of the head of the Clamp Screw, see Figure 12-21.

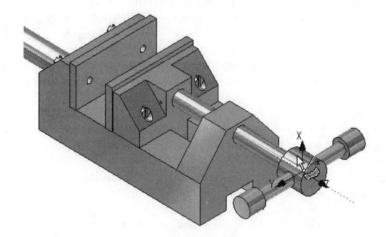

Figure 12-21 Defining the tweak direction on the head of the Clamp Screw

You will notice that the head of the Clamp Screw is displayed with a red outline and a triad is displayed on the component. Also, as shown in Figure 12-21, the Z axis of the triad coincides with the central axis of the Clamp Screw. This is displayed with a red dotted line.

3. Select the Clamp Screw when the triad is displayed and the Z axis of the triad coincides with the central axis of the Clamp Screw.

   Remember that if the Z axis of the triad is not coinciding with the central axis of the Clamp Screw, the resultant animation will not be what is actually required. In case you have selected a wrong direction of tweaking, choose the **Direction** button in the **Create Tweak** area again. You will be prompted to select the direction for the tweak.

   Now you will be prompted to select the components to be tweaked.

4. Select the Clamp Screw, the Clamp Screw Handle, and the two Handle Stops. The selected components are displayed with a blue outline.

5. Clear the **Display Trail** check box in the **Create Tweak** area.

This will ensure that the trails are not created when you tweak the components.

6.   Choose the **Rotational** radio button from the **Transformations** area.

Elliptical arrows indicating a positive direction of rotation will be displayed on all the three axes of the triad. The Z axis of the triad and the elliptical arrow on it will be displayed in blue color.

7.   Enter **720** as the value in the edit box provided on the right of the **Rotational** radio button. Choose the **Apply** button provided on the right of the edit box.

The rotational tweak will be applied to the selected components. This is the first sequence of the tweak. Note that the effect of the rotational tweak will not be evident on the screen at this time.

Next, you need to apply the linear tweak to the components. Some of the components are already selected and you need to select the remaining components to apply the linear tweak.

8.   Select the Movable Jaw, the Jaw Face assembled with the Movable Jaw, and the two Cap Screws that are used to fasten the Jaw Face with the Movable Jaw.

All the selected components are displayed with a blue outline. However, the rotational tweak is still active and you need to change it to the linear tweak.

9.   Select the **Linear** radio button from the **Transformations** area.

The elliptical arrows are no more displayed on the triad, but the Z axis of the triad is still displayed in blue color. This suggests that the selected components will move along the Z axis of the triad.

10. Enter **25** as the value in the edit box provided in the **Transformations** area and then choose the **Apply** button provided on the right of the edit box.

The selected components are moved to a distance of 25 mm along the Z axis of the triad. This is the second sequence of the tweak.

11. Choose the **Close** button to exit the **Tweak Component** dialog box. Now, choose the **Zoom All** button to increase the drawing display area and fit the assembly in the current view. The assembly after tweaking is shown in Figure 12-22.

Animating the Assembly

1.   Choose the **Animate** button from the **Presentation** toolbar or choose **Animate** from the **Presentation** panel bar to invoke the **Animation** dialog box.

2.   Choose the **More** button provided on the lower right corner of the dialog box to expand it.

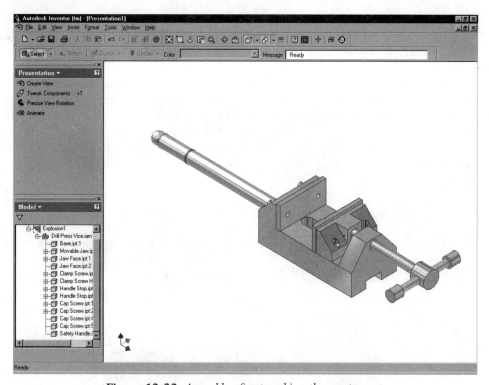

Figure 12-22 *Assembly after tweaking the components*

You will notice that two sets of sequences are displayed in the **Animation Sequence** area. You need to group these sequences to rotate and move the components at the same time.

3. Press and hold the SHIFT key down and then select all the sequences from the **Animation Sequence** area. All the sequences are displayed with a blue background.

4. Choose the **Group** button to group all the sequences in a single sequence.

5. Choose the **Apply** button so that the changes are applied to all the tweaked components.

    It is recommended that before you store the animation in the avi file, you should play it once to make sure the animation is correct.

6. Move the dialog box to the left of the screen such that it does not overlap with the assembly. Now, choose the **Auto Reverse** button to play the animation in the forward and the reverse direction.

    You will notice that all the tweaked components are moving in the forward direction and at the same time the Clamp Screw, the Clamp Screw Handle, and the two Handle Stops are rotating in the clockwise direction around the central axis of the Clamp Screw. This is because you applied rotational tweak to the Clamp Screw, the Clamp Screw Handle, and the two Handle Stops. After the forward cycle is completed, all the components will move in the reverse direction and the components to which the rotational tweak is applied will rotate in the counterclockwise direction. This gives the effect of working of the Drill Press Vice assembly.

Now, you can store the animation of the assembly in an avi file. However, before you proceed with storing the animation in the avi file, it is recommended that you increase the interval of the sequence. This is because higher the interval value, smoother is the avi file.

7. Choose the **Cancel** button from the **Animation** dialog box to close it. Now, choose the **Browser Filters** button provided on the top left corner of the browser to display the cascading menu.

8. Choose the **Sequence View** option from the cascading menu.

    You will notice that **Task1** and the **Drill Press Vice.iam** options are displayed below the **Explosion1** heading in the browser. If these options are not displayed, click on the + sign located on left of **Explosion1**. These options will be displayed.

9. Right-click on **Task1** and then choose **Edit** from the shortcut menu to display the **Edit Task & Sequence** dialog box, see Figure 12-23.

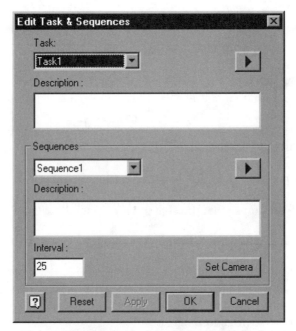

Figure 12-23 Edit Task & Sequence dialog box

> **Tip**. *Notice that there is only one sequence with the name **Sequence1** in the drop-down list provided under the **Sequences** area. This is because you grouped the two sequences together in a single sequence. If you invoke this dialog box before grouping the sequences, all the sequences you created will be displayed in the drop-down list.*

10. Enter **75** as the value in the **Interval** edit box and then choose the **Apply** button. Choose **OK** to close this dialog box.

11. Invoke the **Animation** dialog box again and then choose the **Record** button. When you choose this button, the **Save As** dialog box will be displayed for defining the name and location of the avi file.

    The **Drill Press Vice** directory is open by default. If not, open this directory.

12. Enter the name of the avi file as **Drill Press Vice** in the **File name** edit box and then choose the **Save** button.

    The avi file will be saved with the name **Drill Press Vice.avi** in the folder \PersonalProject \c12\Drill Press Vice.

13. As soon as you choose the **Save** button in the **Save As** dialog box, the **Video Compression** dialog box is displayed. Accept the default options from this dialog box and choose **OK** to close this dialog box.

14. Make sure the **Minimize dialog during recording** check box in the **Motion** area is selected. Now, choose the **Auto Reverse** button.

    The assembly will start animating and the dialog box will be minimized. After the animation is completed and the avi file is created, the dialog box will be restored on the screen.

15. Choose the **Record** button to exit the recording and then close the **Animation** dialog box.

    The avi file is created and you now can view it by using the Windows Media Player.

16. Save the presentation file with the name give below:

    \PersonalProject\c12\Drill Press Vice**Tutorial2.ipn**

Self-Evaluation Test

Answer the following questions and then compare your answers with the answers given at the end of this chapter.

1. Autodesk Inventor allows you to explode the assemblies in a special environment called the **Presentation** mode. (T/F)

2. Different type of presentation templates are provided in the **Metric** tab of the **Open** dialog box for creating different types of presentations. (T/F)

3. If the explosion distance in the automatic explosion is large, the components start interfering with each other. (T/F)

4. When you open a new presentation file, only the **Create View** tool is available. (T/F)

5. The **Open** dialog box that is displayed while creating the design view can be used to select only the _____ files.

6. The animation of the assemblies can be stored in a file of extension _____.

7. There are two types of tweaks. They are _____ and _____.

8. You can animate the assemblies in the forward direction as well as in the reverse direction by choosing the _____ button available in the **Motion** area of the **Animation** dialog box.

9. After you specify the name of the avi file in the **Save As** dialog box, the _____ dialog box is displayed.

10. The _____ button in the **Animation** dialog box is chosen when you want to club different tweak sequences together in a single sequence.

Review Questions

Answer the following questions.

1. You can modify the individual tweak values of the components. (T/F)

2. You can modify the interval value of an animation. (T/F)

3. You cannot ungroup the sequences grouped together. (T/F)

4. After grouping an animation, you need to choose the **Apply** button. (T/F)

5. The avi files can be viewed in the Windows Media Player. (T/F)

6. You cannot move the triad without moving the components but you can rotate it without rotating the components. (T/F)

7. Autodesk Inventor allows you to precisely rotate the presentation view in the **Presentation** mode with the help of which one of the following tools?

    (a) **Rotate View**   (b) **Precise View**
    (c) **Precise View Rotation**   (d) None

8. Which type of tweak will be used to rotate the selected components about a specified rotational axis?

    (a) Linear   (b) Circular
    (c) Rotational   (d) None

9. The assemblies can be exploded with the help of which one of the following dialog boxes?

    (a) **Tweak Component**   (b) **Explode Component**
    (c) **Tweak Assemblies**   (d) None

10. Which one of the following check boxes in the **Animation** dialog box is used to display the trails in the exploded view.

    (a) **Trail**   (b) **Trail On**
    (c) **Display Trail**   (d) None

Exercise

Exercise 1

Create the animation of exploding and unexploding the Butterfly Valve assembly. The exploded view of the Butterfly Valve is shown in Figure 12-24. Save the animation in an avi file with the name given below:

\PersonalProject\c12\Butterfly Valve**Butterfly Valve.avi**   **(Expected time: 1 Hr)**

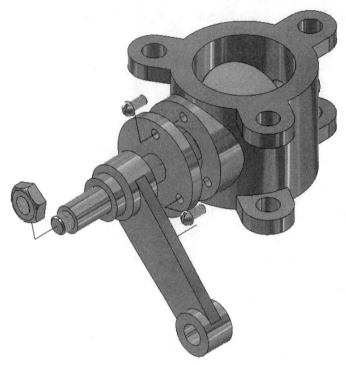

Figure 12-24 *Exploded view of the Butterfly Valve assembly*

Answers to Self-Evaluation Test
1. T, **2.** F, **3.** T, **4.** T, **5.** assembly, **6.** avi, **7.** linear, rotational, **8. Auto Reverse**, **9. Video Compression**, **10. Group**

Chapter 13

Modifying Inventor Options and Using Special Tools

Learning Objectives

After completing this chapter you will be able to:
- *Modify application options.*
- *Modify drawing settings.*
- *Modify lighting options.*
- *Create adaptive parts.*
- *Define parameters for creating parts.*
- *Create 3D Sketches.*

MODIFYING APPLICATION OPTIONS

To modify the application options, choose **Tools > Application Options** from the menu bar. When you choose this option, the **Options** dialog box will be displayed. This dialog box has eleven tabs that are used to set various options of Autodesk Inventor. The options under these tabs are discussed next.

General Tab

The options under the **General** tab of the **Options** dialog box (Figure 13-1) are used to set general parameters of Autodesk Inventor. These options are discussed next.

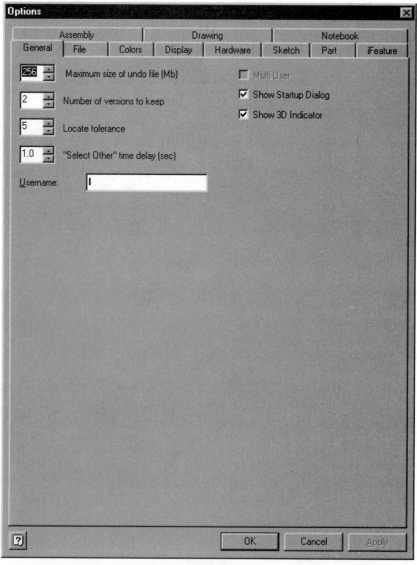

Figure 13-1 General tab of the Options dialog box

Maximum size of undo file (Mb)

This spinner is used to specify the maximum size of the file that will store the information about the actions undone by using the **Undo** tool.

Number of versions to keep

Every time you save a model, a new version file is created. This spinner is used to specify the number of old versions to keep for the model.

Locate tolerance

This spinner is used to specify the maximum distance by clicking where the object will be selected. This distance is specified in terms of pixels.

"Select Other" time delay (sec)

Whenever you move the cursor over an entity on the graphics screen, the cycling tool is displayed to select the other entities. This spinner is used to specify the time in seconds after which the cycling tool will be displayed to select other entities.

Username

This edit box is used to set the user name for the Inventor functions.

Multi User

When you are working in an environment where multiple users are involved, you need to introduce some safety measures or warning systems for your files. If this check box is selected, a warning will be issued when multiple users edit the files.

Show Startup Dialog

This check box is selected to display the **Open** dialog box when you start a new session of Autodesk Inventor. If this check box is cleared, the **Open** dialog box will not be displayed when you start a new session of Autodesk Inventor.

Show 3D Indicator

This check box is selected to display the 3D Indicator at the lower left corner of the drawing window.

File Tab

The options under the **File** tab (Figure 13-2) are used to specify the location of undo files, template files, project folders, and so on. To modify the location of these files, choose the **Browse** button available on the right of these options and specify the new location.

When you choose the **Browse** buttons, the **Browse for Folder** or the **Open** dialog box will be displayed. Using these dialog boxes you can specify the new location.

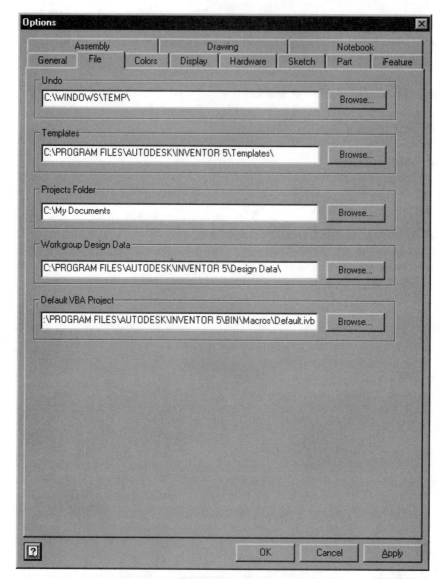

*Figure 13-2 **File** tab of the **Options** dialog box*

Colors Tab

The options under the **Colors** tab (Figure 13-3) are used to specify the color scheme for Autodesk Inventor. There are some standard color schemes available in Autodesk Inventor from which you can select the desired scheme.

 Note

*In the text of this book, the **Presentation** color scheme was used and the **Background Gradient** check box was cleared. If you used a different color scheme, the display of the model or the highlighted entities will be different than what is displayed or mentioned in this book.*

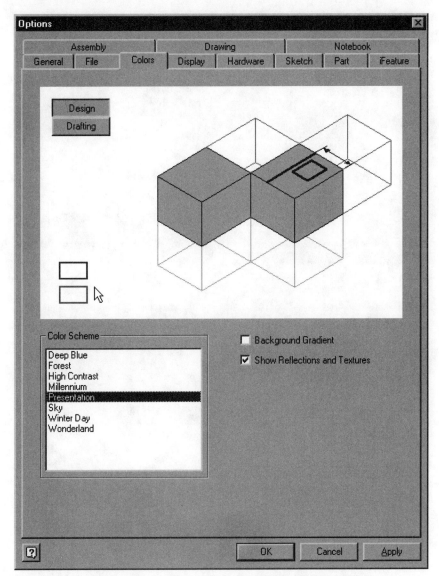

Figure 13-3 Colors tab of the Options dialog box

Display Tab

The options under the **Display** tab (Figure 13-4) are used to set the parameters related to the display type and quality of the model. You can set these parameters for the wireframe mode or for the shaded model.

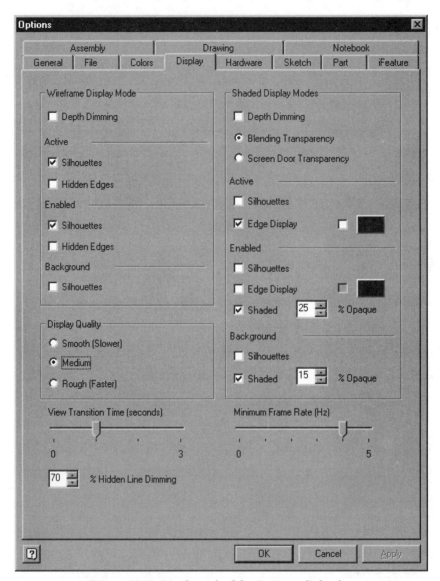

Figure 13-4 Display tab of the Options dialog box

Hardware Tab

The options under the **Hardware** tab (Figure 13-5) are used to set the parameters related to the hardware or the graphics settings. You can select the desired setting by selecting its radio button from this tab.

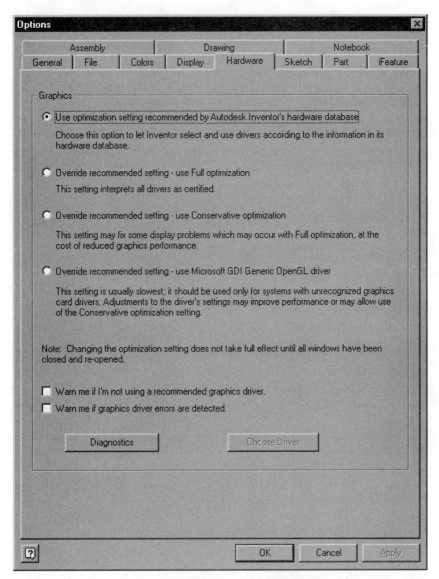

*Figure 13-5 **Hardware** tab of the **Options** dialog box*

Sketch Tab

The options under the **Sketch** tab (Figure 13-6) are used to set the parameters related to the sketching environment of Autodesk Inventor. You can set the parameters related to the constraints, axes, and other related parameters. Some of these options were discussed in previous chapters.

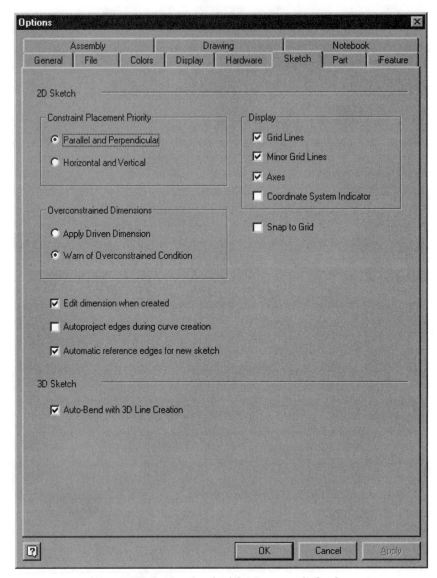

Figure 13-6 Sketch tab of the Options dialog box

Part Tab

The options under the **Part** tab (Figure 13-7) are used to set the parameters related to the **Part** mode of Autodesk Inventor.

Note
By default, when you open a new file, the sketches are created on the XY plane. However, by using the options in this tab you can define the plane on which the sketches will be created every time you open a new file.

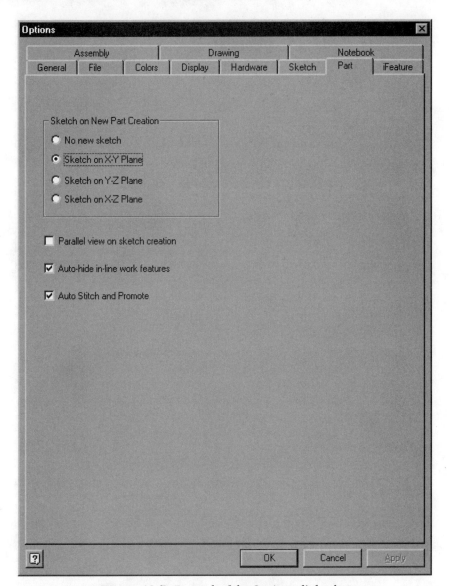

Figure 13-7 **Part** *tab of the* **Options** *dialog box*

iFeature Tab

The options under the **iFeature** tab (Figure 13-8) are used to set the parameters related to the ifeatures. You can set the program for viewing the ifeatures using this tab. You can also set the root of the ifeatures by using the options in this tab.

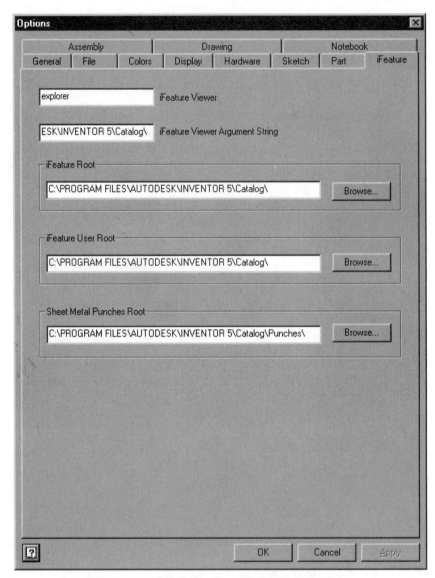

Figure 13-8 iFeature tab of the Options dialog box

Assembly Tab

The options under the **Assembly** tab (Figure 13-9) are used to set the options related to the **Assembly** mode of Autodesk Inventor.

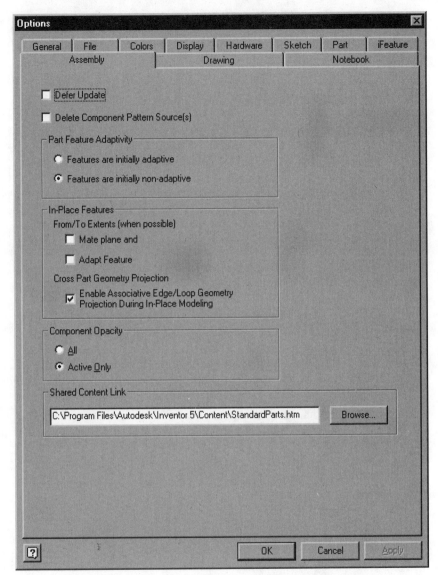

Figure 13-9 Assembly tab of the Options dialog box

Drawing Tab

The options under the **Drawing** tab (Figure 13-10) are used to set the options related to the **Drawing** mode of Autodesk Inventor.

Note

By default, when you open a new drawing file, the title block is located at the lower right corner of the screen. You can specify the location of the title block on any other corner by using the options provided in the Drawing tab of the Options dialog box.

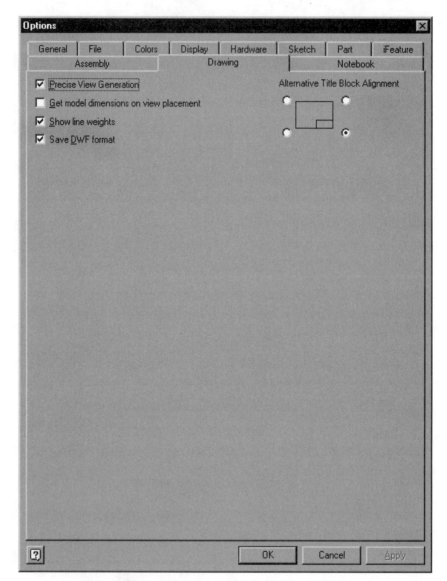

Figure 13-10 **Drawing** *tab of the* **Options** *dialog box*

Notebook Tab

The options under the **Notebook** tab (Figure 13-11) are used to set the options related to the notebook feature of Autodesk Inventor.

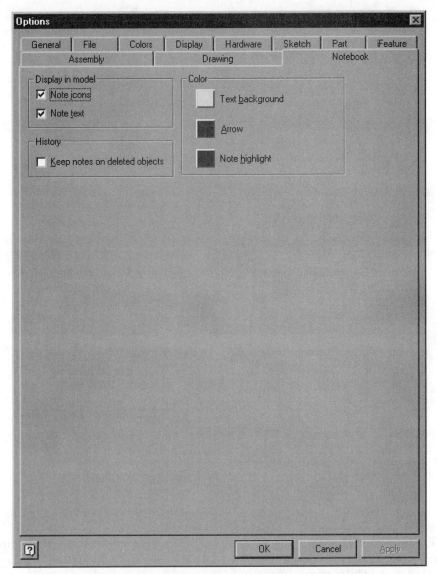

Figure 13-11 Notebook tab of the Options dialog box

MODIFYING DOCUMENT OPTIONS

To modify the document options, choose **Tools > Document Options** from the menu bar. When you choose this option, the **Document Options** dialog box is displayed. The options under the various tabs of the **Document Options** dialog box are discussed next.

Units Tab

The options under the **Units** tab (Figure 13-12) are used to set the options related to the units of the current document. These options are discussed next.

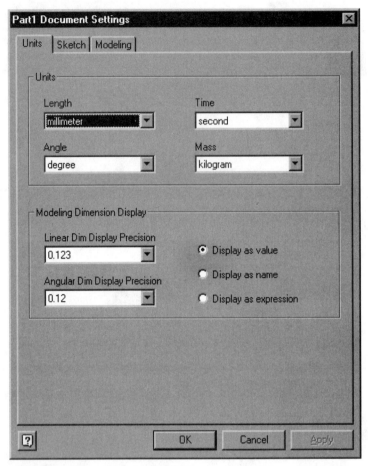

*Figure 13-12 **Units** tab of the **Document Options** dialog box*

Units Area
The options under the **Units** area are used to select the units for the length, angle, time, and mass in the current file. You can specify these options by selecting them from the drop-down lists provided in the **Units** area.

Modeling Dimension Display Area
Linear Dim Display Precision
The **Linear Dim Display Precision** drop-down list is used to specify the number of decimal places for the linear dimensions. You can select the required number of decimal places from this drop-down list.

Angular Dim Display Precision
The **Angular Dim Display Precision** drop-down list is used to specify the number of decimal places for the angular dimensions. You can select the required number of decimal places from this drop-down list.

Display as value

Whenever you add a dimension to an entity in Autodesk Inventor, the dimension is assigned a name. For example, the first dimension in the sketching environment of a part file will have a name of d0, the second dimension will have a name of d1, and so on. By default, the names of dimensions are not displayed in the sketching environment, only the values are displayed. This is because the **Display as value** radio button is selected in the **Modeling Dimension Display** area.

Display as name

If the **Display as name** radio button is selected, the names of dimensions will be displayed instead of the values.

Display as expression

If the **Display as expression** radio button is selected, the dimensions will be displayed in terms of the expression equating the name of the dimension with the value that you assigned to that dimension. For example, if you modify the value of the first dimension to 25 mm, the resultant dimension will be displayed as d0 = 25 mm in the drawing.

Note
The options under the Sketch tab were discussed in previous chapters.

MODIFYING LIGHTING OPTIONS

Autodesk Inventor has provided lighting options that allow you to view the solid model. You can modify these options or create a new lighting style for viewing the model. To modify the light options, choose **Format > Lighting** from the menu bar. When you choose this option, the **Lighting** dialog box is displayed as shown in Figure 13-13. You can use the same dialog box for modifying the current lighting style or creating a new lighting style. The options provided under this dialog box are discussed next.

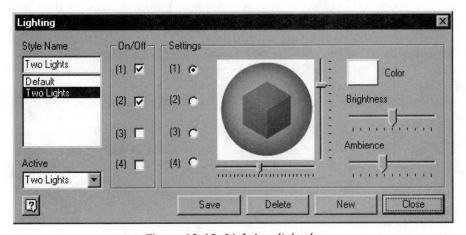

Figure 13-13 Lighting dialog box

Note

*To properly view the effect of different lighting styles, it is recommended that you create or open a solid model and then invoke the **Lighting** dialog box.*

Style Name Area

The list box provided in the **Style Name** area displays the lighting styles that are available. To create a new lighting style, choose the **New** button and specify the name of the new lighting style in the edit box. Then make the necessary changes and choose the **Save** button. Note that until you choose the **Save** button, the name of the new lighting style will not be displayed in the list box provided in this area.

Active

The **Active** drop-down list displays the current lighting style that is active. All the lighting styles will be available in this drop-down list and you can select the desired style from this list. The selected style will be made current.

Note

The current lighting style that is active cannot be deleted.

On/Off Area

The check boxes under the **On/Off** area are used to select the settings for lighting. The effect of the selected check boxes will be displayed. If you select more than one check box, their combined effect will be used for lighting the material.

Settings Area

The radio buttons provided in the **Settings** area are used to define the lighting settings. Depending upon the lighting setting defined, the check boxes in the **On/Off** area will be selected. The slider bars in this area are used to specify the location of the light source with respect to the model. Select the radio button of the setting from the **Settings** area, then select its corresponding check box from the **ON/Off** area, and then modify the location of the light source by using the sliders. You can dynamically view the effect in the model displayed on the graphics screen. You can also specify the color, brightness, and ambience of the selected light source by using the options provided in this area.

Note

*Remember that after making the changes in the lighting style, choose the **Save** button to save the changes to the lighting style. If you choose the **Close** button without saving the editing changes in the lighting style, the **Autodesk Inventor** dialog box will be displayed and you will be prompted to specify whether or not you want to save the changes in the lighting style.*

ADAPTIVE PARTS

Adaptive parts are the parts that automatically change their dimensions based on the dimensions and functions of the other parts to which they are assembled. Remember that to create an adaptive part or an adaptive feature, they should not be fully constrained. The part or the feature should be underdimensioned. The missing dimension will then be modified based on the dimensions of the other components. You can any time remove the adaptivity of the components and add the missing dimensions so that they do not change their dimensions. To convert a feature or sketch into an adaptive feature or sketch, right-click on it in the browser and choose **Adaptive** from the shortcut menu. Similarly, to convert a part into an adaptive part in the **Assembly** mode, right-click on it in the browser and choose **Adaptive** from the shortcut menu. Two arrows pointing in the counterclockwise direction will be displayed on the left of the adaptive part, feature, or sketch in the browser. Remember that the components that are originally created in other solid modeling tools and are imported in the Inventor file cannot be converted into an adaptive part.

DEFINING PARAMETERS

Menu:	Tools > Parameters
Toolbar:	Standard > Parameters

As mentioned earlier, every dimension in Autodesk Inventor is assigned a unique name. This unique name is also termed as parameter. When you specify the value for the dimension, the dimension parameter is equated in an expression with the value that you specified. Autodesk Inventor allows you to use parameters or expressions instead of entering the value while dimensioning a sketch or in the edit boxes of a dialog box while defining a feature. You can also create a new parameter by defining it in terms of the other parameter in an expression. The new parameters can be created before creating a sketch or after creating the sketch. The new parameters are created by using the **Parameters** tool. When you invoke this tool, the **Parameters** dialog box will be displayed, see Figure 13-14.

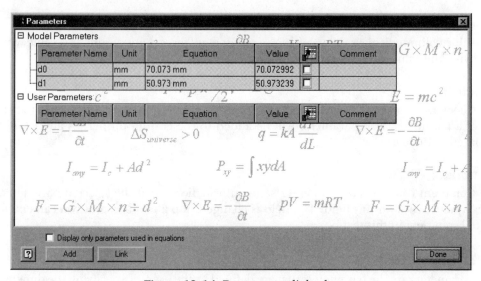

Figure 13-14 Parameters dialog box

This dialog box has two types of parameters. These are discussed next.

Model Parameters

Model parameters are the parameters that are automatically created when you apply the dimensions to the entities, or create a feature. The model parameters are displayed in a tabular form as shown in Figure 13-14. The options under this table are discussed next.

Parameter Name

The **Parameter Name** column displays the names of parameters. To modify the name of a parameter, click on its field in the **Parameter Name** column. The field will change to an edit box and you can enter the new name in this edit box. Note that you cannot duplicate the name of parameters. This means you cannot have two parameters with the same name.

Unit

The **Unit** column displays the unit of measuring the parameters. Note that you cannot modify the unit of a parameter.

Equation

Equations are mathematical expressions in which the parameters are equated with the algebraic or the trigonometric functions. Autodesk Inventor allows you to define the parameters using other existing parameter and equations. For example, to define a parameter d2, you can use the equation such as $d2=(d0/2+d1)*1.25$, where d0 and d1 are existing parameters. However, in the d2 field of the **Equation** column, you will not enter "d2=". All you need to enter is $(d0/2+d1)*1.25$ as the equation. Since it is entered in the d2 field of the **Equation** column, Autodesk Inventor will automatically equate it with the d2 parameter.

Value

The **Value** column displays the value of the parameter. You cannot modify this value without modifying the value in the **Equation** column.

Check Box

The **Check Box** column displays the check boxes for each parameter. If you select the check box of a parameter, that parameter will be added to the custom properties and cannot be displayed in the parts list.

Comment

The **Comment** column is used to enter some information about the selected parameter. To enter a value, click on this field. The field is changed into a text box and you can enter the desired comment in this text box.

User Parameters

User parameters are the parameters that are defined by the user for specifying the dimensions of entities and features. To create a user-defined parameter, choose the **Add** button. A new row will be displayed in the **User Parameter** table. You can specify the new settings of the user-defined parameters in the table. Note that you can modify the units of the user-defined parameter. To modify the units, click on the field below the **Unit** column. The **Unit Type** dialog box will be displayed as shown in Figure 13-15 and you can select the desired units

Figure 13-15 Unit Type dialog box

from this dialog box.

Note

*The options under the **User Parameters** table are similar to those under the **Model Parameters** table.*

Display only parameters used in equations

If the **Display only parameters used in equations** check box is selected, only those parameters will be displayed that are used in equations for defining other parameters.

Link

In addition to the model parameters and the user-defined parameters, Autodesk Inventor also allows you to create link parameters. The link parameters are those that are created in a separate Microsoft Excel spreadsheet. Note that the model parameters and the user-defined parameters can be used only in the current file, whereas the link parameters can be used in as many number of files as you require. This is because the link parameters are external parameters that can be imported to any file. To import a link parameter, choose the **Link** button. When you choose this button, the **Open** dialog box is displayed as shown in Figure 13-16. You can specify the name and the location of the Microsoft Excel spreadsheet by using the **Open** dialog box.

When you select the spreadsheet, the location and the name of the spreadsheet will be displayed in the dialog box and a new table will be displayed. This table will show the parameters imported from the selected spreadsheet.

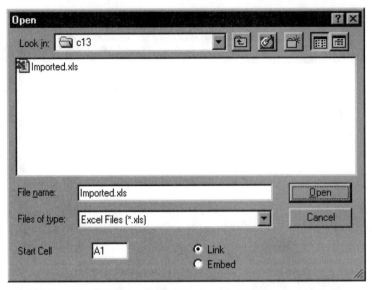

Figure 13-16 Open dialog box for selecting the spread sheet

CREATING 3D SKETCHES

Command bar: Sketch > 3D Sketch

🖉 3D Sketch   In previous chapters you have learned about creating 2D sweeps by defining the path in 2D space. In this chapter you will learn about creating a 3D sketch that can be used for creating sweep features in 3D space as shown in Figure 13-17.

Figure 13-17 Pipe created by sweeping a profile about a 3D path

To create a 3D sketch, choose the down arrow located on the right of **Sketch** in the **Command Bar** and then choose **3D Sketch**. When you choose this option, the 3D sketching environment will be activated. Note that since the sketch has to be created in 3D, you will not be prompted to select the sketching plane. As soon as you enter the 3D sketching environment, the **3D Sketch** panel bar will be displayed above the browser. Notice that there are only six tools for creating a 3D sketch. Out of these six tools, three are for creating the work features. The functions of the remaining three tools are discussed next.

Line

The **Line** tool is used to create a line in the 3D space. Note that unlike the line in a 2D sketch, you cannot create a line by specifying the points on the graphics screen. The 3D line can only be created by using work points or the vertices of an existing model. By default, the 3D lines are automatically bent at the corners and the bend radius is displayed. This is because the **Auto-Bend** option is on by default. To turn off this option, invoke the **Line** tool in the 3D sketching environment and then right-click on the graphics screen to display the shortcut menu. You will notice that the **Auto-Bend** option is chosen in this shortcut menu. To turn off this option, choose **Auto-Bend** again from the shortcut menu. Now, when you draw a 3D line, it will not be bent at the corners. Figure 13-18 shows a 3D line created by using a combination of work points and vertices of an existing model.

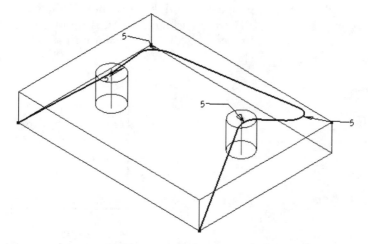

Figure 13-18 3D line created using work points and vertices of a model

Tip. *Unlike sweeping the profile about the 2D paths, the profile that will be swept about a 3D path need not be normal to the start point of the path. You can draw the profile at an angle to the 3D path. However, remember that the resultant sweep feature will still be normal to the start point of the 3D path*

Bend

The **Bend** tool is used to manually create the bends at the corners of the 3D line. When you invoke this tool, the **3D Sketch Bend** toolbar is displayed as shown in

Figure 13-19. You can specify the radius of the bend in this toolbar and then select the two lines that comprise the corner where the bend will be created. Note that at the corners at which the bend cannot be created, a cross will be displayed when you move the cursor over the line to select it. This cross suggests that you cannot select this line for creating a bend.

Figure 13-19   3D Sketch Bend toolbar

Include Geometry

The **Include Geometry** tool is used to include an existing 2D geometry in the 3D sketch. You can also select an edge of an existing model to be included in the 3D sketch.

Note
You cannot save a file in the 3D sketching environment. You need to exit the 3D sketching environment if you want to save the part file.

TUTORIALS

Tutorial 1

In this tutorial you will create new parameters and then use them in sketching and extruding the model shown in Figure 13-20. The dimensioned sketch is shown in Figure 13-21. The sketch should be extruded to a distance of EXT. The dimensions in the sketch should be displayed as equations as shown in Figure 13-21. **(Expected time: 30 min)**

Figure 13-20 Model for Tutorial 1

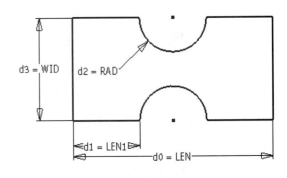

Figure 13-21 Sketch for the model

The numeric values of the parameters are given below:

LEN = 60
LEN1 = LEN/3
WID = LEN/2
RAD = LEN/6
EXT = LEN1

Before you start working on the tutorial, it is recommended that you outline the procedure for completing the tutorial. The steps that will be required to complete the tutorial are listed below.

a.   Start Autodesk Inventor and open a new metric part file.

b.   Create the sketch and add the required constraints.

c.   Invoke the **Parameters** tool and create the required parameters by using the **Parameters** dialog box.

d.   Invoke the **Document Settings** dialog box and select the option to display the dimensions as equations.

e.   Invoke the **General Dimension** tool and dimension the sketch by entering parameters instead of values in the **Edit Dimension** toolbar.

f.   Exit the sketching environment and extrude the sketch. Enter the parameter instead of value in the extrusion distance edit box.

Opening a New Part File

1.   Start Autodesk Inventor and then choose **New** from the **Open** dialog box.

2.   Choose the **Metric** tab and open a new metric part file. Exit the sketching environment and define a new sketch plane on the XZ plane.

Drawing the Sketch

1.   Draw the sketch for the model by using the sketching tools. Add the required constraints. The sketch is shown in Figure 13-22.

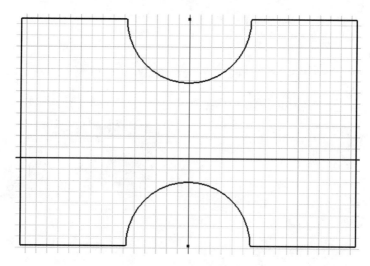

Figure 13-22   *Sketch after adding the required constraints*

Creating the Parameters

As mentioned earlier, the parameters are created by using the **Parameters** dialog box. You can invoke this dialog box by choosing the **Parameters** button from the **Standard** toolbar.

1. Choose the **Parameters** button from the **Standard** toolbar to invoke the
    Parameters dialog box.

2. Choose the **Add** button to enter a new row in the **User Parameters** table. Enter the name
    of the parameter as **LEN** in the **Parameter Name** field. Now, press ENTER.

    You will notice that a new row with the name LEN is created. The unit of the parameter is
    mm and the equation and value is 1. You now need to modify the value of the parameter.

3. Click on the **Equation** field of the LEN row. It will change into an edit box. Enter **60** as the
    value of this parameter in this edit box and then press ENTER.

    You will notice that the value of the **Value** field is automatically changed to **60.000000**.

4. Again, choose the **Add** button to add another row in the **User Parameters** table.

5. Enter **LEN1** as the name of the parameter in the **Parameter Name** field.

6. Click on the **Equation** field and enter **LEN/3** in this field and then press ENTER.

    You will notice that the value in the **Value** field is automatically changed to **20.000000**.
    This is because the value of the LEN parameter is 60 and LEN1 = LEN/3 = 60/3 = 20.
    Also, notice that **ul** is automatically added on right of the equation. You do not have to
    enter this while defining the equation as it is added by Autodesk Inventor.

7. Similarly, create the remaining parameters. The **Parameters** dialog box after creating all
    the parameters is shown in Figure 13-23. Choose **Done** to exit the **Parameters** dialog box.

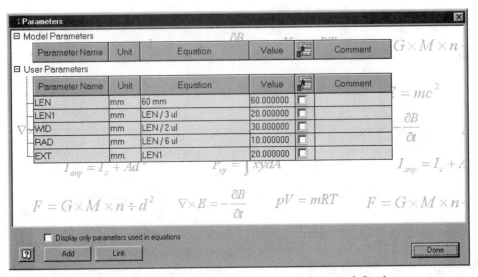

Figure 13-23 Parameters dialog box after creating the user-defined parameters

Note

Since you have not dimensioned the sketch until now, no row will be displayed in the **Model Parameter** *table. Once you add dimensions to the sketch, the parameters will be added in the* **Model Parameter** *table.*

Displaying the Dimensions as Equations

It is mentioned in the tutorial description that you need to display the dimensions as equations. Therefore, you need to select this option from the **Document Settings** dialog box.

1. Choose **Tools > Document Settings** from the menu bar to invoke the **Document Settings** dialog box.

2. Select the **Display as expression** radio button from the **Modeling Dimension Display** area of the **Units** tab. Choose **Apply** and then choose **OK** to exit the dialog box.

Dimensioning the Sketch

Now, you can dimension the sketch by using the parameters. Note that the parameters are case sensitive. This means that if you have specified the name of the parameter in capital letters, you need to enter the name in the **Edit Dimension** toolbar in capital letters. If you do not enter the name of the parameter as you specified it in the **Parameters** dialog box, the **Autodesk Inventor** dialog box will be displayed and you will be informed that this expression cannot be evaluated.

1. Invoke the **General Dimension** tool and then one by one select the vertical lines at the two ends of the sketch. Place the dimension below the sketch to display the **Edit Dimension** toolbar.

2. Enter **LEN** as the value in the **Edit Dimension** toolbar and then press ENTER.

   You will notice that the dimension is automatically modified and is displayed as an equation on the graphics screen. This is because you selected the option of displaying the dimensions as equations.

3. Select the lower left horizontal line and then place the dimension above the previous dimension. Enter **LEN1** as the value in the **Edit Dimension** toolbar and press ENTER.

4. Select the left vertical line and the place the dimension on the left of the sketch. Enter **WID** as the value in the **Edit Dimension** toolbar and then press ENTER.

5. Select the upper arc and then place the dimension on the left of the arc. Enter **RAD** as the value in the **Edit Dimension** toolbar and then press ENTER.

   This completes the dimensioning of the sketch. The sketch after adding the dimensions is shown in Figure 13-24. In this figure, the grid lines and the axes are not displayed for the clarity of the sketch.

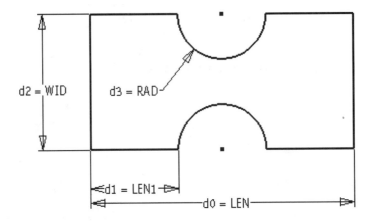

Figure 13-24 Sketch displaying the dimensions as equations

Extruding the Sketch

1. Exit the sketching environment and then change the current view to the Isometric view.

2. Invoke the **Extrude** dialog box and then enter **EXT** as the value in the edit box provided in the **Extents** area. Accept the remaining default options and then choose the **OK** button.

   The sketch will be extruded through a distance defined by the EXT parameter.

3. Save the model with the name \PersonalProject\c13**Tutorial1.ipt**.

Tutorial 2

In this tutorial you will create the assembly of the Outer Plate and the Inner Plate shown in Figure 13-25. The dimensions of the Outer Plate are shown in Figure 13-26. Create the Inner Plate as an adaptive part that should automatically adjust its size to fit inside the Outer Plate. Apply the **Mate** constraints with an offset of 10 mm to all the outer faces of the Inner Plate and the inner faces of the groove in the Outer Plate. After assembling the components, edit the inner cavity of the Outer Plate such that the Inner Plate again adjusts its dimensions automatically.   **(Expected time: 1 Hr)**

Note
Since the Inner Plate has to be an adaptive part, its dimensions are not required.

The following steps outline the procedure for completing this tutorial:

a. Open a new metric assembly file and then create the Outer Plate.
b. Invoke the **Create Component** tool and then select the top face of the Outer Plate as the sketching plane for the Inner Plate.
c. Make the sketch of the Inner Plate adaptive and then set the parameters in the **Assembly**

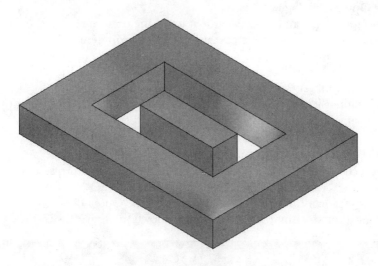

Figure 13-25 *Assembly for Tutorial 2*

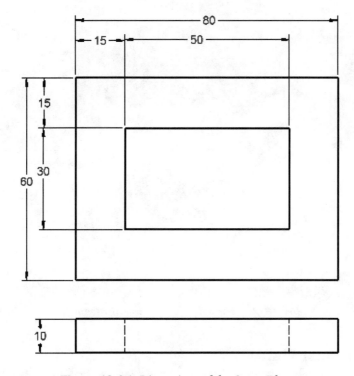

Figure 13-26 *Dimensions of the Outer Plate*

tab of the **Options** dialog box.

d.   Sketch the Inner Plate and then extrude it up to the bottom face of the Outer Plate.

e.   Save the model and then exit the part modeling environment.

f.   Add the **Mate** constraint to all the inner faces of the groove in the Outer Plate and outer faces of the Inner Plate. The size of the Inner Plate will automatically change in order to adjust inside the Outer Plate.

g.   Modify the dimensions of the inner cavity of the Outer Plate. The size of the Inner Plate will again change automatically in order to retain the design intent.

Creating the Outer Plate

You can directly create the Outer Plate and the Inner Plate in the assembly file.

1.   Open a new metric assembly file and then create the Outer Plate on the XY plane. The assembly file after creating the Outer Plate is shown in Figure 13-27.

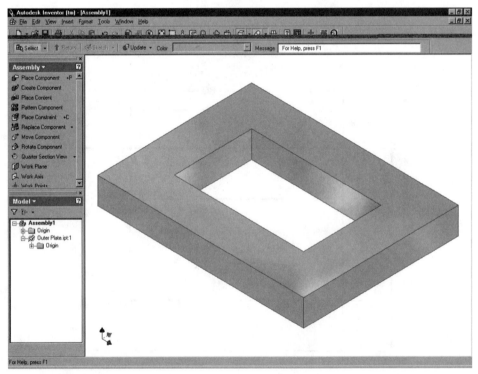

Figure 13-27 *Assembly after creating the Outer Plate*

Creating the Inner Plate

The Inner Plate will be sketched by taking the top face of the Outer Plate as the sketching plane. Remember that the sketch plane should be constrained to the selected face.

1.   Invoke the **Create Component** tool and then select the top face of the Outer Plate as the sketching plane. Make sure that the **Constrain sketch plane to selected face or plane**

check box is selected in the **Create In-Place Component** dialog box. The name of the component should be Inner Plate.

2. Right-click on **Sketch1** in the browser and choose **Adaptive** from the shortcut menu. This will make the Inner Plate adaptive and this component will now adjust its size automatically based on the surrounding environment.

3. Choose **Tools > Application Options** from the menu bar to display the **Options** dialog box. Choose the **Assembly** tab to display the options under this tab.

4. Select all the check boxes under the **In-Place Features** area.

    This is done so that the model created should be adaptive. Also, since you will extrude the model to the bottom face of the Inner Plate, selecting these options will automatically modify the new part when the parent part is modified.

5. Choose **Apply** and then choose **OK**. Draw the sketch for the Inner Plate and then extrude it to the bottom face of the Outer Plate. Save the part file and then exit the part modeling environment.

    You will not add dimensions to the Inner Plate since it is an adaptive part. The assembly after creating the Inner Plate is shown in Figure 13-28.

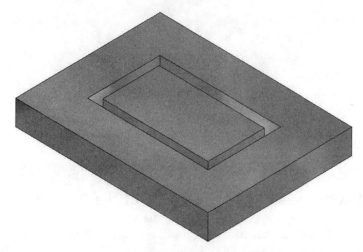

Figure 13-28 Assembly after creating the Inner Plate

6. Now, apply the **Mate** constraint with an offset of 10 mm on the inner left vertical face of the Outer Plate and the outer left vertical face of the Inner Plate. The Inner Plate will shift toward right.

7. Change the display type to wireframe and then apply the **Mate** constraint with an offset of 10 mm on the inner lower horizontal face of the Outer Plate and the outer lower horizontal face of the Inner Plate. The Inner Plate will shift upwards.

8. Now, apply the **Mate** constraint with an offset of 10 mm on the inner right vertical face of the Outer Plate and the outer right vertical face of the Inner Plate.

    Notice that the size of the Inner Plate is reduced in order to fit inside the cavity of the Outer Plate. This is because of the adaptive property of the Inner Plate.

9. Similarly, apply the **Mate** constraint with an offset of 10 mm on the inner upper horizontal face of the Outer Plate and the outer upper horizontal face of the Inner Plate.

    Notice that the size of the Inner Plate is further reduced in order to fit inside the cavity of the Outer Plate.

10. Close the **Place Constraint** dialog box and then change the display type back to shaded. The assembly after applying the constraint is shown in Figure 13-29. Notice the change in the size of the Inner Plate.

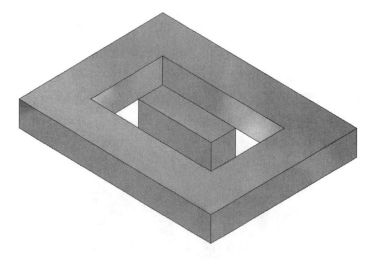

Figure 13-29 *Assembly after applying the constraint*

Modifying the Dimensions of the Cavity of the Outer Plate

You can edit the dimensions of the cavity of the Outer Plate in the assembly file itself. Since the Inner Plate is an adaptive part, it will automatically change its dimensions when the dimensions of the cavity are modified.

1. Double-click on the **Outer Plate.ipt:1** in the browser to activate this component.

2. Modify the dimensions of the cavity as shown in Figure 13-30.

3. Now, choose **Return** from the **Command Bar** to exit the sketching environment.

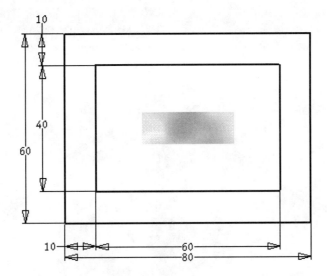

Figure 13-30 Modifying the dimensions of the cavity

4. Again, choose **Return** from the **Command Bar** to exit the part modeling environment. Change the current view to the Isometric view.

    You will notice that the dimensions of the Inner Plate are again modified in order to retain the design intent of assembly. The assembly after modifying the dimensions of the cavity is shown in Figure 13-31. Notice the change in the dimensions of the Inner Plate.

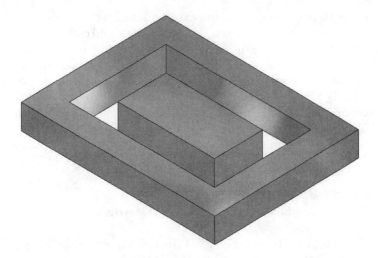

Figure 13-31 Modified assembly

5. Save the assembly with the name \PersonalProject\c13**Tutorial2.iam**. You will be prompted to save the individual part files. Save the changes in the part files also.

Tutorial 3

In this tutorial you will create the pipe in 3D space as shown in Figure 13-32. Assume the
dimensions of the pipe.   **(Expected time: 30 min)**

Figure 13-32 Pipe for Tutorial 3

The following steps outline the procedure for completing this tutorial:

a. Create the first 2D sketch consisting of three lines on the XY plane and then exit the
   sketching environment.
b. Define a new work plane normal to the existing sketch and then create the second 2D
   sketch on this new work plane. The second 2D sketch should consist of two lines. The start
   point of the first line should be the endpoint of the last line in the first sketch.
c. Exit the sketching environment and then invoke the 3D sketching environment.
d. Using the **Include Geometry** tool, select all the lines to be included in the 3D sketch.
e. Add bends on all corners and then exit the 3D sketching environment.
f. Select the work plane defined earlier as the sketching plane and then sketch the profile of
   the pipe. Take the reference of the start point of the first line for drawing the sketch.
g. Exit the sketching environment and sweep the sketch about the 3D path to create the 3D
   pipe.

Drawing the First 2D Sketch

1. Invoke the **Open** dialog box and then choose the **Metric** tab.

2. Open a new metric part file and then draw the first sketch on the XY plane as shown in
   Figure 13-33.

Drawing the Second 2D Sketch

The second 2D sketch will be created on a work plane that is defined normal to the third
line of the first 2D sketch. Therefore, first you need to define a new work plane normal to
the third line of the sketch.

1. Define a new work plane normal to the third line of the sketch and then select it as the sketching plane for drawing the next 2D sketch.

2. Draw the next sketch starting from the origin of the sketch plane. The origin of the sketch plane is the endpoint of the third line of the first sketch.

Note

*While dimensioning, if the lines move from their original location, you can move them back by using the **Move** tool such that the start point of the first line lies at the origin of the sketch plane. The from point of move can be the start point of the first line and the to point of move can be the origin that can be specified in the **Precise Input** toolbar.*

3. Exit the sketching environment. The first and the second 2D sketches are shown in Figure 13-34.

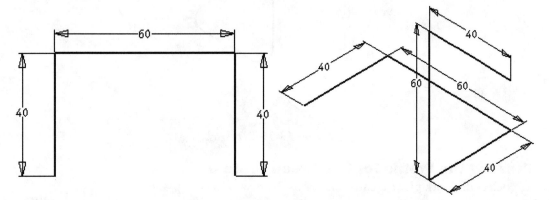

Figure 13-33 First 2D sketch   *Figure 13-34* After drawing the second 2D sketch

Creating the 3D Sketch

1. Choose the down arrow on the right of **Sketch** in the **Command Bar** and choose **3D Sketch** to invoke the 3D sketching environment.

2. Choose the **Include Geometry** button from the **3D Sketch** toolbar or choose **Include Geometry** from the **3D Sketch** panel bar.

3. One by one select all the lines in first 2D sketch and the second 2D sketch.

4. Choose the **Bend** button to display the **3D Sketch Bend** toolbar. Enter **10** as the value in this toolbar and then select all the lines that form corners of the 3D sketch.

   You will notice that a fillet kind of bend is created on all the corners and the dimension is displayed on all the bends.

5. Exit the 3D sketching environment.

6. Now, one by one delete the two 2D sketches by using the browser. Note that the dependent entities should not be deleted.

    The 3D sketch turns magenta in color. The 3D sketch after deleting the 2D sketches is shown in Figure 13-35.

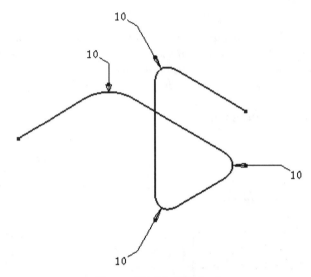

Figure 13-35 3D sketch

Creating the Profile for the Sweep Feature

1. Select the work plane created earlier as the new sketching plane.

2. Draw the sketch of the profile of the sweep feature. The sketch of the profile consist of two concentric circles and the center of the circles should be at the start point of the first line of the 3D path. Specify 6 mm as the diameter of the outer circle and 4 mm as the diameter of the inner circle.

3. Exit the sketching environment.

Sweeping the Profile about the 3D Path

1. Invoke the **Sweep** dialog box and select the two circles as the profile of the sweep feature. The two circles turn blue in color.

2. Choose the **Path** button in the **Shape** area of the **Sweep** dialog box and then select the 3D path as the path of the sweep feature. The complete 3D path turns blue.

3. Choose **OK** to close the **Sweep** dialog box.

4. The **Autodesk Inventor (tm) - Create Sweep Feature** dialog box will be displayed. Choose **Accept** in this dialog box to close it and create the pipe in 3D space. The final pipe for Tutorial 3 is shown in Figure 13-36.

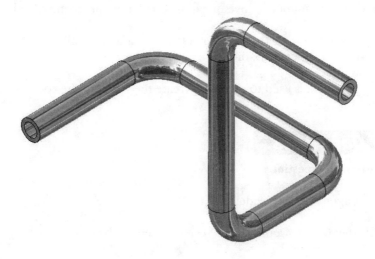

Figure 13-36 *Pipe for Tutorial 3*

5.　Save this model with the name \PersonalProject\c13**Tutorial3.ipt**.

Self-Evaluation Test

Answer the following questions and then compare your answers with the answers given at the end of this chapter.

1.　You can set the option of increasing the size of the undo file by using the **General** tab of the **Options** dialog box. (T/F)

2.　The options under the **Display** tab (Figure 13-3) are used to specify the color scheme for Autodesk Inventor. (T/F)

3.　By using the **Part** tab of the **Options** dialog box you can set the plane on which the sketch will be drawn when you open a new part file. (T/F)

4.　Autodesk Inventor does not allow you to display the dimensions as equations. (T/F)

5.　To modify the light options, choose _____ from the menu bar.

6.　After making the changes in the lighting style, choose the _____ button to save the changes to the lighting style.

7.　_____ parts are the parts that automatically change their dimensions based on the dimensions and functions of the other parts to which they are assembled.

8. Every dimension in Autodesk Inventor is assigned a unique name called _____.

9. _____ parameters are the parameters that are automatically created when you apply the dimensions to the entities, or create a feature.

10. The _____ tool is used to manually create the bends at the corners of the 3D line.

Review Questions

Answer the following questions.

1. The current light style can be deleted. (T/F)

2. The profile that will be swept about a 3D path need not be normal to the start point of the path. (T/F)

3. Unlike the 2D sketching environment, you can save the file in the 3D sketching environment. (T/F)

4. The options under the **Hardware** tab (Figure 13-5) are used to set the parameters related to the hardware or the graphics settings.

5. User parameters are the parameters that are defined by the user for specifying the dimensions of entities and features. (T/F)

6. Which one of the following tabs of the **Options** dialog box is used to specify the location of the title block in the drawing sheet?

    (a) **Drawing**   (b) **Sketch**
    (c) **Display**   (d) **Part**

7. Which one of the following is not a type of parameter?

    (a) Drawing   (b) Model
    (c) User   (d) Link

8. Using which one of the following tabs can you display the dimensions as equations?

    (a) **Units**   (b) **Sketch**
    (c) **Modeling**   (d) None

9. Using which one of the following tabs of the **Options** dialog box can you set the options related to the constraints, axes, and grid lines?

    (a) **Drawing**   (b) **Sketch**
    (c) **Part**   (d) None

10. Which one of the following tools is used to merge a 2D sketch entity into a 3D sketch?

(a) **Line**   (b) **Bend**
(c) **Include Geometry**   (d) None

Exercise

Exercise 1

Create the following sketch with the help of parameters. After dimensioning the sketch, display
the dimensions as equations as shown in Figure 13-37.   **(Expected time: 30 min)**

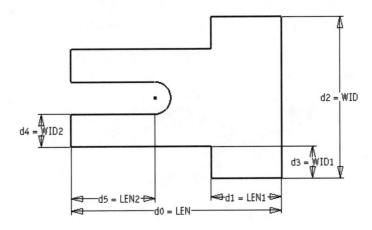

Figure 13-37 *Sketch with dimensions as equations*

The numeric values of the parameters is given below:
LEN = 60
LEN1 = LEN/3
LEN2 = LEN/2.5
WID = LEN*0.75
WID1 = WID/5
WID2 = WID1

After displaying the dimensions as equations, display the dimensions as names.

Note
*After selecting the option of displaying the dimensions as equations or names, sometimes the
dimension display do not change on the graphics screen. In this case double-click on any dimension
and then press ENTER to close the **Edit Dimension** toolbar. The dimension display will
automatically change.*

Answers to Self-Evaluation Test
1. T, **2.** F, **3.** T, **4.** F, **5. Format > Lighting**, **6. Save**, **7.** Adaptive, **8.** parameter, **9.** Model, **10. Bend**

Chapter *14*

Sheet Metal Mode

Learning Objectives

After completing this chapter you will be able to:
- *Set the parameters for creating the sheet metal parts.*
- *Use the Face tool.*
- *Fold a part of the sheet metal part by using the Fold tool.*
- *Create a flange by using the Flange tool.*
- *Add corner seam to the sheet metal parts by using the Corner Seam tool.*
- *Use the Punch Tool tool.*
- *Add a hem to the sheet metal part by using the Hem tool.*
- *Create a cut feature in the sheet metal part by using the Cut tool.*
- *Fillet the corners of the sheet metal part by using the Corner Fillet tool.*
- *Chamfer the corners of the sheet metal part by using the Corner Chamfer tool.*
- *Create the flat pattern of the sheet metal component by using the Flat Pattern tool.*

SHEET METAL MODE

A sheet metal component is a component created by bending, cutting, or deforming an existing sheet of metal of uniform thickness, see Figure 14-1.

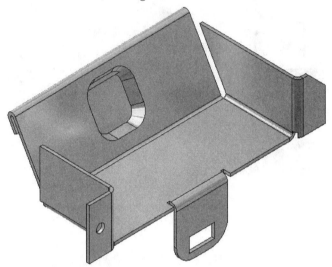

Figure 14-1 *Sheet metal component*

Now, since it is not possible to manufacture such a model, therefore, after creating the sheet metal component, you need to flatten it in order to manufacture it. Figure 14-2 shows the flattened view of the sheet metal component shown in Figure 14-1.

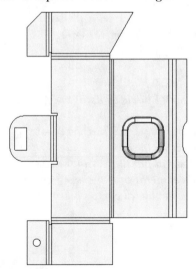

Figure 14-2 *Flattened view of the sheet metal component*

Autodesk Inventor allows you to create the sheet metal components in a special environment, called the **Sheet Metal** mode, provided specially for the sheet metal components. This environment provides all the tools that will be required for creating the sheet metal component. To invoke the **Sheet Metal** mode, double-click on **Sheet Metal (mm).ipt** from the **Metric** tab of the **Open** dialog box, see Figure 14-3.

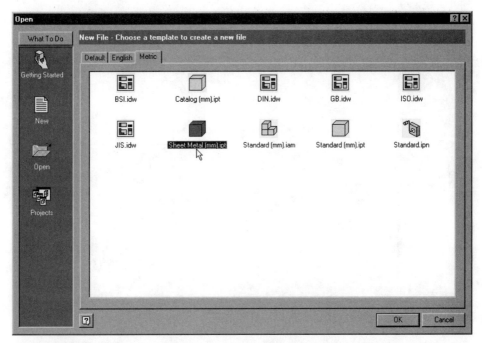

*Figure 14-3 Opening a new sheet metal file from the **Metric** tab of the **Open** dialog box*

When you select this file, you will proceed to the **Sheet Metal** mode. Notice that when you open a new sheet metal file, by default the sketching environment is activated as shown in Figure 14-4. This is because similar to the part modeling environment, you first need to create the sketch of the base feature of the sheet metal component. After creating the base feature of the sheet metal component, the remaining tools will be available in the **Sheet Metal** mode.

Note
*To make sure that you are in the sketching environment of the **Sheet Metal** mode, choose **Applications** from the menu bar. You will notice that the **Modeling** and the **Sheet Metal** options are displayed. These options are not activated but a check mark is displayed on the left of the **Sheet Metal** option. This confirms that you are inside the sketching environment of a sheet metal file.*

*The **Modeling** and the **Sheet Metal** options in the **Applications** will be available when you exit the sketching environment. You can switch from the **Sheet Metal** mode to the **Part** mode by choosing **Applications > Modeling** from the menu bar. Similarly, if you are in the **Part** mode, you can switch to the **Sheet Metal** mode by choosing **Applications > Sheet Metal** from the menu bar.*

*Sheet metal files are also saved in the ***.ipt* format.*

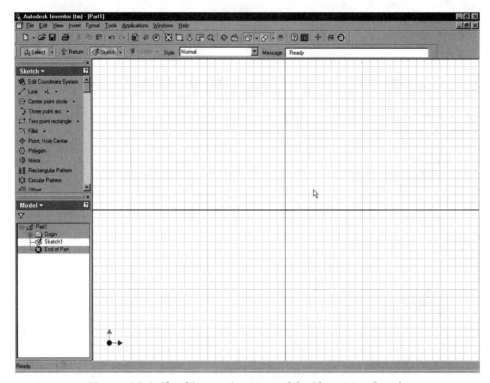

*Figure 14-4 Sketching environment of the **Sheet Metal** mode*

After creating the sketch for the base of the sheet metal component, exit the sketching environment. You will notice that the **Sketch** panel bar is replaced by the **Sheet Metal** panel bar. Note that very few tools are available in this panel bar. More tools will be available when you create the base of the sheet metal part.

Before proceeding with converting the sketch into the sheet metal base, it is recommended that you set the options related to the sheet metal part. You can set these options by using the **Styles** tool discussed next.

SETTING SHEET METAL PART OPTIONS

Toolbar:	Sheet Metal > Styles
Panel bar:	Sheet Metal > Styles

The **Styles** tool is used to set the options related to the sheet metal component. When you invoke this tool, the **Sheet Metal Styles** dialog box will be displayed. The **Default** style is created by default. To create a new sheet metal style, choose the **New** button and enter the name of the style in the edit box provided in the **Style List** area. The **Sheet Metal Styles** dialog box provides three tabs for setting the parameters of the sheet metal components. The options under these three tabs are discussed next.

Sheet Tab

The options under the **Sheet** tab (Figure 14-5) are discussed next.

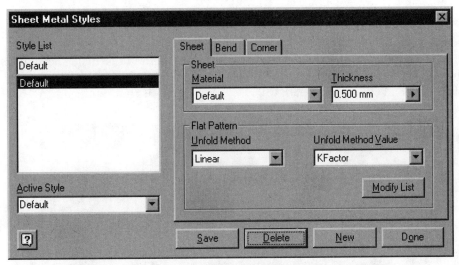

Figure 14-5 Sheet tab of the Sheet Metal Styles dialog box

Sheet Area

The options under the **Sheet** area are used to specify the material and thickness of the sheet. These options are discussed next.

Material

The **Material** drop-down list is used to specify the material of the sheet. You can select the desired material from the predefined materials available in this drop-down list.

Thickness

The **Thickness** edit box is used to specify the thickness of the sheet. You can enter the thickness of the sheet in this edit box or select from the predefined thicknesses available by choosing the arrow available on the right of this edit box.

Flat Pattern Area

The options under the **Flat Pattern** area are used to specify the parameters related to the unfolding of the sheet metal component for manufacturing. These options are discussed next.

Unfold Method

The **Unfold Method** drop-down list is used to specify the method that will be used while unfolding the sheet metal component. This drop-down list provides two methods for unfolding the sheet metal component, The first method is the **Linear** method and it uses a simple unfolding technique for flattening the component. The second method is the **Bend Table** method. When you select this method, the **Open** dialog box is displayed by using which you can select the file in which the bend table is stored. The bend tables are stored in the .txt files.

Unfold Method Value

The **Unfold Method Value** drop-down list is used to specify the value of the unfold method. The options in this drop-down list will depend upon the method selected from the **Unfold Method** drop-down list.

Modify List

When you choose the **Modify List** button, the **Unfold Method List** dialog box is displayed. This dialog box has the list of the unfold methods, their type, and their values. If you have selected a bend table file, its path will also be displayed as shown in Figure 14-6.

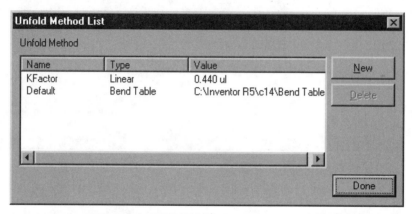

Figure 14-6 Unfold Method List dialog box

Bend Tab

The options under the **Bend** tab (Figure 14-7) are used to set the parameters related to the bending of the sheet. These options are discussed next.

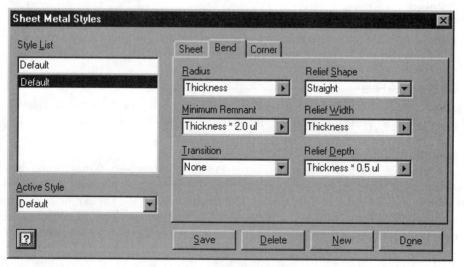

Figure 14-7 Bend tab of the Sheet Metal Styles dialog box

Radius

The **Radius** edit box is used to set the radius of the bend or the fold. The default value of the radius of the bend is equal to the thickness of the sheet. You can enter a numeric value in this edit box to select it as the bend radius. Figure 14-8 shows a sheet folded with a radius of 1 mm and Figure 14-9 shows a sheet folded with a radius of 5 mm.

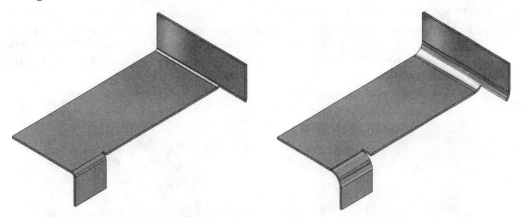

Figure 14-8 *Sheet with 1 mm bend radius*   *Figure 14-9* *Sheet with 5 mm bend radius*

 Tip. *If you modify the bend radius after bending or folding a sheet metal component, the model will automatically update and acquire the new bend radius value when you choose the **Save** button and exit the **Sheet Metal Styles** dialog box.*

Relief Shape

Whenever you bend or fold a sheet metal component such that the bend does not extend throughout the length of the edge, a groove is added at the end of the bend so that the walls of the sheet metal part do not intersect when folded or unfolded. This groove is known as relief. The **Relief Shape** drop-down list is used to select the shape of the relief. Be default, a straight relief is added as shown in Figure 14-10. You can also add a round relief by selecting **Round** from this drop-down list. Figure 14-11 shows a round relief.

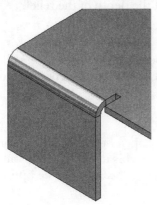
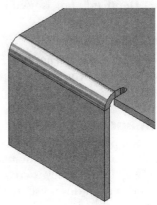

Figure 14-10 *Straight relief added while folding*   *Figure 14-11* *Round relief added while folding*

Minimum Remnant

The **Minimum Remnant** edit box is used to set the value of the material between the relief created by bending or folding and the edge of the sheet metal component.

Relied Width

The **Relief Width** edit box is used to enter the value of the width of the relief. The default value of the relief width is equal to the thickness of the sheet. You can enter the desired value of the relief width in this edit box. Figure 14-12 shows a sheet metal component with a relief width of 1 mm and Figure 14-13 shows a sheet metal component with a relief width of 4 mm.

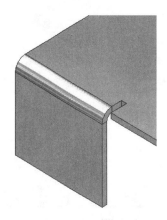 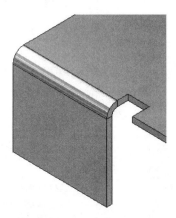

Figure 14-12 *Relief width 1 mm*   *Figure 14-13* *Relief width 4 mm*

Transition

The **Transition** drop-down list is used to specify the transition type in the unfolded view when no relief is specified. The default value of this drop-down list is **None**. You can select the **Intersection**, **Straight Line**, or the **Arc** transition type from this drop-down list.

Relied Depth

The **Relief Depth** edit box is used to enter the value of the depth of the relief.

Corner Tab

The options under the **Corner** tab (Figure 14-14) are used to set the parameters related to the relief at the corners where the three faces of the sheet metal component are folded. These options are discussed next.

Relief Shape

The **Relief Shape** drop-down list is used to specify the shape of the relief at the corner where the three faces are folded. Remember that the options in this drop-down list will work only when one of the three faces is created by using the **Corner Seam** too. The options that are available in this drop-down list are discussed next.

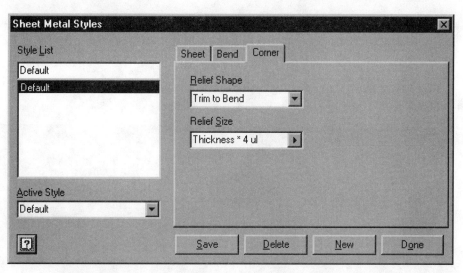

Figure 14-14 Corner tab of the Sheet Metal Styles dialog box

Note

*It is recommended that to view a better effect of different corner relief shapes, flatten the sheet metal component by using the **Flat Pattern** tool.*

Trim to Bend

The **Trim to Bend** is the default option in this drop-down list and is used when you do not want any relief at the corner where the three faces are folded. Figure 14-15 shows an unfolded sheet metal part with no relief at the corner.

Round

The **Round** option is used to create a round corner relief as shown in Figure 14-16.

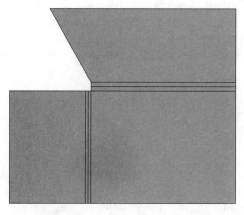

Figure 14-15 Flattened sheet metal part with no corner relief

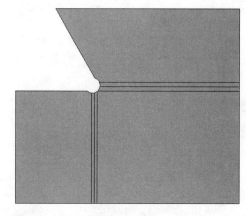

Figure 14-16 Flattened sheet metal part with round corner relief

Square

The **Square** option is used to create a square corner relief as shown in Figure 14-17.

Tear

The **Tear** option is used to create a corner relief that appears torn at the corners as shown in Figure 14-18.

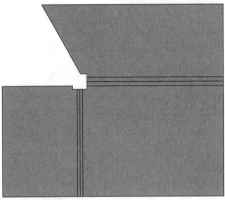

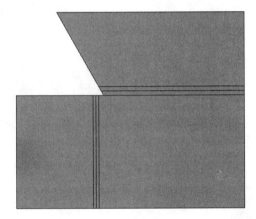

Figure 14-17 *Flattened sheet metal part with square corner relief*

Figure 14-18 *Flattened sheet metal part with torn corner relief*

Relief Size

The **Relief Size** edit box is used to specify the size of the corner relief. You can enter the value as an equation in terms of the thickness of the sheet or as a numeric value.

After making the necessary modifications, choose the **Save** button to save the changes and then choose the **Done** button to close the dialog box. As soon as you close the dialog box, the changes you made in the sheet metal style will be highlighted in the sheet metal component.

Once you have made the necessary initial settings, you are ready to create the sheet metal component. The tools that are required to create the sheet metal component are discussed next.

CREATING THE SHEET METAL COMPONENT

Toolbar:	Sheet Metal > Face
Panel bar:	Sheet Metal > Face

The **Face** tool is used to create the base of the sheet metal component or for adding additional faces on the sheet metal component. As mentioned earlier, when you open a new sheet metal file, the sketching environment is activated. After creating the sketch for the base of the sheet metal component, exit the sketching environment and invoke this tool. When you invoke this tool, the **Face** dialog box will be displayed. This dialog box has three tabs. But since you are creating the base, the options in these tabs will not be required. Note that since there is only one sketch on the graphics screen, it will be automatically selected.

The sheet thickness will be taken as the thickness defined in the **Sheet** tab of the **Sheet Metal Styles** dialog box. Figure 14-19 shows the sketch before converting it into a sheet metal component and Figure 14-20 shows the sheet metal component created using the given sketch.

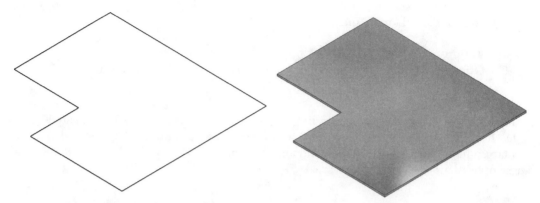

Figure 14-19 *Sketch before converting into sheet metal part*

Figure 14-20 *Sheet metal part created using the given sketch*

After creating the base of the sheet metal component, if you create a sketch and invoke the **Face** tool, the other options in the **Face** dialog box will be used. The options under the various tabs of the **Face** dialog box are discussed next.

Face Shape Tab

The options under the **Face Shape** tab (Figure 14-21) are used to specify the shape and bend options of the face. These options are discussed next.

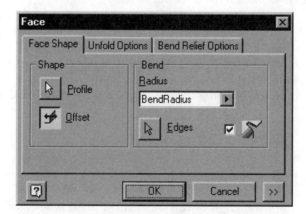

Figure 14-21 *Face Shape tab of the Face dialog box*

Shape Area

The options under the **Shape** area are used to specify the shape of the face. These options are discussed next.

Select Profile

The **Select Profile** button is chosen to select the sketch of the face. If there is only one unconsumed sketch on the screen, it will be automatically selected. However, if there are more than one unconsumed sketches or the sketch consists of multiple closed loops, you will have to select them manually by using this button.

Offset Flip

The **Offset Flip** button is chosen to flip the direction of the face creation.

Bend Area

Whenever you create a face on an existing sheet metal component, a bend is created at the edge where the new face joins the existing component. Also, a bend relief will be added to the new face. The options related to the bend and the bend relief are available in the **Bend** area. These options are discussed next.

Radius

The **Radius** edit box is used to specify the radius of the bend. By default, the bend radius defined in the **Bend** tab of the **Sheet Metal Styles** dialog box is selected as the bend radius. You can also specify a new bend radius by entering a numeric value in this edit box.

Select Edge

The **Select Edge** button is chosen to select the edge that will be joined with the existing sheet metal component. If one of the edges of the sketch is coincident with an edge of the existing sheet metal part, the common edge will be automatically selected. However, if the edge of the sketch is not coincident with an edge of the sheet metal component, you will have to select the edge manually. You can also use this button to select additional faces that you want to be added in the bend.

Bend Relief

The **Bend Relief** check box is selected to create a bend relief. If this check box is cleared, the bend relief will not be created. By default, the bend relief options are taken based on the parameters defined in the **Sheet Metal Styles** dialog box. However, you can define new relief parameters by using the options in the **Bend Relief Options** tab of this dialog box.

Figure 14-22 shows the sketch that will be used for creating the face of the sheet metal component and Figure 14-23 shows the sheet metal component created after adding the face. Notice the bend and the bend relief created with the face. Figure 14-24 shows a sketch that has no edge that is coincident with the edge of the sheet metal part. Notice that in this figure the edge of the sheet metal base is selected for creating the bend. Figure 14-25 shows the sheet metal component created by using the given sketch.

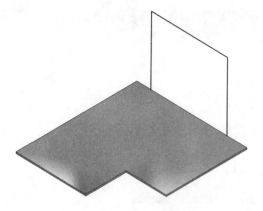

Figure 14-22 *Sketch before converting into a new face of the sheet metal part*

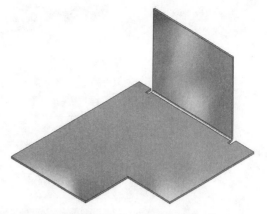

Figure 14-23 *Sheet metal part after creating the new face*

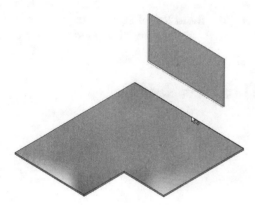

Figure 14-24 *Selecting the sketch and edge for creating the face of sheet metal part*

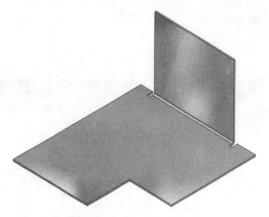

Figure 14-25 *Sheet metal part after creating the new face*

Unfold Options Tab

The options under the **Unfold Options** tab are used to specify the parameters related to unfolding of the face of the sheet metal component. By default, the options specified in the **Sheet** tab of the **Sheet Metal Styles** dialog box are used. This is the reason no option in this tab is available. However, if you want to override the options specified in the **Sheet Metal Styles** dialog box, clear the **Use Default Settings** check box. You will notice that the options in the **Unfold Options** tab are available as shown in Figure 14-26. These options are similar to the options discussed in the **Sheet Metal Styles** dialog box.

Bend Relief Options Tab

The options under the **Bend Relief Options** tab are used to specify the parameters related to bend relief. By default, the options specified in the **Bend** tab of the **Sheet Metal Styles**

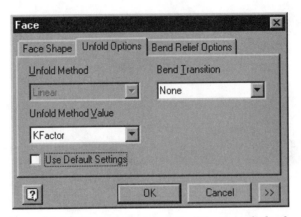

Figure 14-26 Unfold Options tab of the Face dialog box

dialog box are used. This is the reason no option in this tab is available. However, if you want to override the options specified in the **Sheet Metal Styles** dialog box, clear the **Use Default Settings** check box. You will notice that the options in the **Bend Relief Options** tab are available as shown in Figure 14-27. These options are similar to the options discussed in the **Sheet Metal Styles** dialog box.

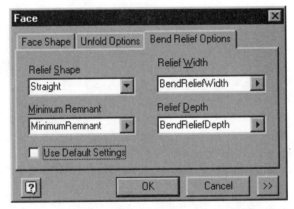

Figure 14-27 Unfold Options tab of the Face dialog box

FOLDING A PART OF THE SHEET METAL COMPONENT

Toolbar:	Sheet Metal > Fold
Panel bar:	Sheet Metal > Fold

Autodesk Inventor allows you to fold a part of the sheet metal component by using the **Fold** tool. Remember that the sheet metal part will be folded with the help of a sketched line. This line will act as the folding line. When you invoke the **Fold** tool, the **Fold** dialog box will be displayed. The various options provided in the **Fold** dialog box are discussed next.

Fold Shape Tab

The options under the **Fold Shape** tab (Figure 14-28) are used to specify the shape of fold. These options are discussed next.

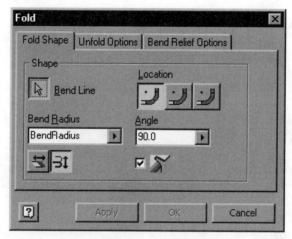

Figure 14-28 Fold Shape tab of the Fold dialog box

Shape Area

Select Sketched Bend Line

The **Select Sketched Bend Line** button is chosen to select the bend line that will be used to fold the component. When you invoke the **Fold** dialog box, this button is chosen by default. Note that only the line that has both its endpoints at the edges of the sheet metal component can be selected to bend the component. As soon as you select the bend line, two green arrows are displayed on the bend line. The first arrow will point in the direction of the portion of the sheet metal part that will be folded and the second arrow points in the direction of bending.

Bend Radius

The **Bend Radius** edit box is used to specify the radius of the bend. By default, the value specified in the **Bend** tab of the **Sheet Metal Styles** dialog box is taken as the bend radius. You can also enter any desired value in this edit box.

Flip Side

The **Flip Side** button is chosen to flip the side of the sheet metal part that will be folded.

Flip Direction

The **Flip Direction** button is chosen to flip the direction in which the sheet metal component will be folded.

Location

The **Location** buttons are chosen to specify the location of bend with respect to the sketch line selected as the bend line. There are three buttons that can be used to specify the location of the bend with respect to the bend line. These three buttons are discussed next.

Centerline of Bend. The **Centerline of Bend** is the first button below the **Location** heading. By default, this button is chosen for creating the bend. If you choose this button, the bend line will be considered as the centerline of the bend and the bend will be created equally in both the directions of the bend line.

Start of Bend. The **Start of Bend** button is provided on the right of the **Centerline of Bend** button. If this button is chosen, the bend will be created such that the bend line is located at the start of the bend.

End of Bend. The **End of Bend** button is provided on the right of the **Start of Bend** button. If this button is chosen, the bend will be created such that the bend line is located at the end of the bend.

Angle
The **Angle** edit box is used to specify the angle of fold for the sheet metal component. The default value in this edit box is **90.0**. You can specify any desired value in this edit box.

Bend Relief
The **Bend Relief** check box is used to create the bend relief. If this check box is cleared, the bend relief will not be created when you fold the sheet metal part.

Figure 14-29 shows a line that will be used to fold the sheet metal part and Figure 14-30 shows the sheet metal part folded through an angle of 60° by using the given line.

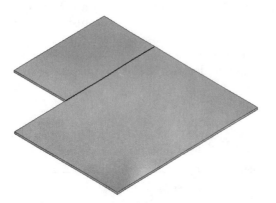

Figure 14-29 Line that will be used to fold the sheet metal part

Figure 14-30 Sheet metal part after folding it through an angle of 60° by using the line

Note
*The options under the **Unfold Options** and the **Bend Relief Options** tabs are the same as those discussed in the previous sections of this chapter.*

ADDING FLANGE TO THE SHEET METAL COMPONENT

Toolbar:	Sheet Metal > Flange
Panel bar:	Sheet Metal > Flange

 Autodesk Inventor allows you to directly add a folded face to the existing sheet metal component. This is done by using the **Flange** tool. When you invoke this tool, the **Flange** dialog box will be displayed. The options under the various tabs of the **Flange** dialog box are discussed next.

Flange Shape Tab

The options provided under the **Flange Shape** tab (Figure 14-31) are used to set the parameters related to the shape and bend of the flange. These options are discussed next.

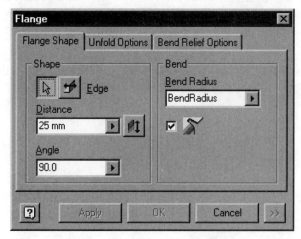

Figure 14-31 Flange Shape tab of the Flange dialog box

Shape Area

The options under the **Shape** area are used to set the parameters related to the shape of the flange. These options are discussed next.

Select Edge

The **Select Edge** button is the first button in the **Shape** area and is used to select the edge on which the flange will be created. When you invoke the **Flange** dialog box, the **Select Edge** button is chosen by default and you are prompted to select the edge. Note that if you select the edge on the upper face of the sheet metal component, by default the flange will be created in the upward direction. Similarly, if you select the edge on the lower face of the sheet metal component, by default the flange will be created in the downward direction.

Flip Offset

The **Flip Offset** button is provided on the right of the **Select Edge** button and is used to specify whether the inner edge or the outer edge of the flange will be aligned with the edge of the sheet metal component.

Distance

The **Distance** edit box is used to specify the height of the flange. The height of the flange will be calculated from the edge that was selected to create the flange.

Flip Direction

The **Flip Direction** button is chosen to flip the direction of flange creation. As mentioned earlier, if you select the edge on the upper face of the sheet metal component, by default the flange will be created in the upward direction. But if you choose this button, the flange will be created in the downward direction. However, note that the selected edge will still be the starting edge of the flange.

Angle

The **Angle** edit box is used to specify the angle through which the flange will be bent with respect to the sheet metal component. The default value in this edit box is **90.0** and therefore, the flange will be bent through an angle of 90°. The angle value of the flange can vary from 0° to 180°.

Tip. *If a flange is created through an angle of 180°, it will not be visible as it will be merged with the face of the sheet metal component. If a flange is created through an angle of 170°, it will create a face similar to a hem.*

Note
The hems will be discussed later in this chapter.

Bend Area

The options in the **Bend** area are used to set the parameters related to the bending of the flange. These options are discussed next.

Bend Radius

The **Bend Radius** edit box is used to enter the radius of the bend. By default, the value set in the **Sheet Metal Styles** dialog box is taken as the bend value. However, you can set any bend radius by entering its value in this edit box.

Bend Relief

The **Bend Relief** check box is selected to create the bend relief. If this check box is cleared, the relief will not be created.

Figure 14-32 shows the edge being selected for creating the flange and Figure 14-33 shows the sheet metal component after creating the flange.

More Button

The **More** button is the button with two arrows and is available on the lower right corner of the **Flange** dialog box. When you choose this button, the **Flange** dialog box expands and provides more options. These options are discussed next.

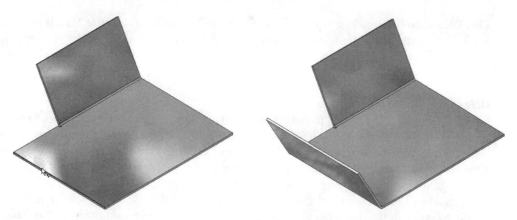

Figure 14-32 *Selecting the edge for creating the flange*

Figure 14-33 *Sheet metal component after creating the flange at an angle of 60°*

Extents Area

The options in the **Extents** area (Figure 14-34) are used to set the parameters related to the extents of the flange. These options are provided in the **Type** drop-down list and are discussed next.

Figure 14-34 **Extents** *area displayed by choosing the* **More** *button*

Edge

The **Edge** option is the option that is selected by default in this drop-down list. This option ensures that the flange is created through the edge selected form the sheet metal component.

Width

The **Width** option is used to create a flange through a specified width of the selected edge and at a specified offset distance. When you select this option, the **Select Start Point** button, the **Offset** edit box, the **Flip Direction** button, and the **Width** edit box are displayed in the **Extents** area and you are prompted to select the start point of the flange. You can select a vertex, work point, or a work plane for defining the start point of the flange. The offset distance is specified in the **Offset** edit box and it is the distance by which the flange will be offset from the start point. You can reverse the direction of offset by choosing the

Flip Direction button. The width of the flange will be specified in the **Width** edit box. Figure 14-35 shows the flange created at an offset of 5 mm from the selected start point and with a width of 15 mm. Notice the bend relief that is automatically created on both the sides.

Offset

The **Offset** option is selected to define the width of the flange in terms of offset from two points on the selected edge. When you invoke this option, the **Select Start Point** button, **Select End Point** button, **Offset1** edit box, and **Offset2** edit box are displayed in the **Extents** area and you are prompted to select the flange start point. Select the start point of the flange on the selected edge. Then you will be prompted to select the endpoint of the flange. Select the endpoint of the flange on the selected edge. After selecting the two points, you can define the offset from the first point and the second point in the **Offset1** and the **Offset2** edit boxes respectively. Based on the two offset values and the known length of the edge, the width of the flange is automatically calculated. Figure 14-36 shows a flange created with the offset 1 value as 10 mm and the offset 2 value as 5 mm.

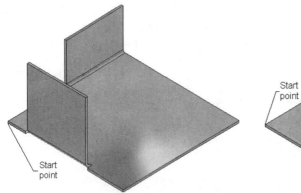

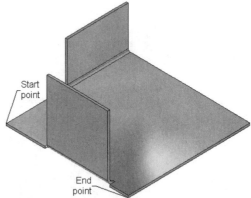

Figure 14-35   Flange created with an offset of 5 mm and width of 15 mm

Figure 14-36   Flange created with the offset 1 value as 10 mm and offset 2 value as 5 mm

Note
*The options in the **Unfold Options** and the **Bend Relief Options** tabs of the **Flange** dialog box are similar to those discussed in the previous sections of this chapter.*

CREATING CUT IN THE SHEET METAL COMPONENT

Toolbar:	Sheet Metal > Cut
Panel bar:	Sheet Metal > Cut

You can create any type of cut in the sheet metal component by drawing its sketch and then cutting it by using the **Cut** tool. Note that if you invoke this tool without creating a sketch, you will be informed that there is no unconsumed sketch. When you invoke this tool, the **Cut** dialog box will be displayed as shown in Figure 14-37. The options under this dialog box are discussed next.

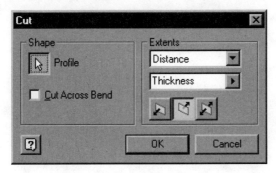

Figure 14-37 Cut dialog box

Shape Area

The options under the **Shape** area are used to specify the shape of the cut. These options are discussed next.

Profile

The **Profile** button is chosen to select the profile of the cut. When you invoke the **Cut** dialog box, this button is chosen by default. If there is only one unconsumed sketch on the screen, it will be automatically selected for creating the cut. However, if there are more than one unconsumed sketches, you will be prompted to select the profile.

Cut Across Bend

The **Cut Across Bend** check box is selected to cut the material throughout the thickness of the sheet. If you select this check box, the options in the **Extents** area will not be available. This is because when you are cutting the material throughout the thickness of the sheet, you do not require to specify the extents of the cut.

Extents Area

The options in the **Extents** area are used to specify the extents of the cut. You can select the options for defining the extents of the cut from the drop-down list provided in this area. The options in this drop-down list are similar to those discussed for the solid model components.

Figure 14-38 shows two unconsumed sketches before creating the cut in the sheet metal component. Figure 14-39 shows the sheet metal component after creating the cut by using the two sketches.

CREATING SEAMS AT THE CORNERS OF THE SHEET METAL COMPONENT

Toolbar:	Sheet Metal > Corner Seam
Panel bar:	Sheet Metal > Corner Seam

 Autodesk Inventor allows you to create the corner seams in a sheet metal component with the help of the **Corner Seam** tool. When you invoke this tool, the **Corner Seam**

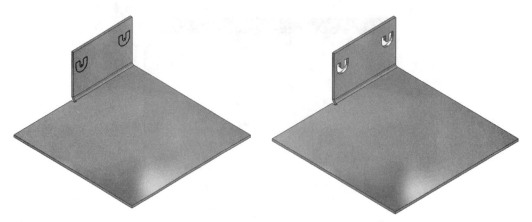

Figure 14-38 *Unconsumed sketches before creating the cut*   **Figure 14-39** *Sheet metal component after creating the cut*

dialog box will be displayed. The options that are provided in this dialog box are discussed next.

Corner Seam Shape Tab

The options under the **Corner Seam Shape** tab (Figure 14-40) are used to set the parameters related to the shape of the seam. These options are discussed next.

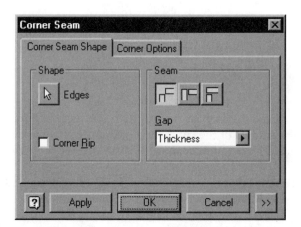

Figure 14-40 Corner Seam Shape *tab of the* **Corner Seam** *dialog box*

Shape Area

Select Edge

The **Select Edge** button is chosen to select the edges for creating the corner seam. When you invoke this dialog box, the **Select Edge** button is chosen by default and no option in the **Seam** area is available. The options in the seam area will be available only after you have selected the edges for creating the corner seam.

Corner Rip

The **Corner Rip** check box is selected when you want to rip a corner of a sheet metal component that has three faces meeting at a corner. This is generally used when you want to convert a shelled solid model into a sheet metal component and rip its corner in order to open it. To rip a corner of such a component, select the vertical edge at the corner. The corner will be automatically ripped and the solid model will be converted into a sheet metal component. Figure 14-41 shows a shelled solid model component before ripping the corners and Figure 14-42 shows the solid model component after its corners are ripped and it is converted into a sheet metal component.

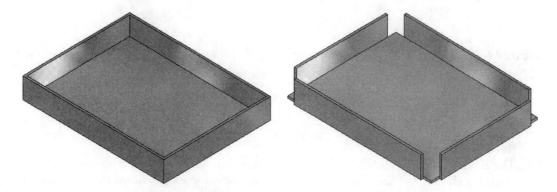

Figure 14-41 *Model before ripping the corners*   *Figure 14-42* *Model after ripping the corners*

> **Tip**. *To convert a solid model into a sheet metal component, you first need to shell it. Remember that the wall thickness in the shell should be equal to or less than the thickness of the sheet specified in the **Sheet Metal Styles** dialog box. If the wall thickness in the shell is more than the thickness of the sheet, you will not be able to rip the corners of the shelled model. After shelling the component, rip its corners by using the **Corner Seam** tool. By ripping the corners of a solid model component, you will convert it into a sheet metal component. Once the solid model is converted into a sheet metal component, you can apply sheet metal operations on it.*

Seam Area

No Overlap

The **No Overlap** button is the first button in the **Seam** area. This button is chosen by default and it ensures that there is no overlapping of the faces whose edges are selected for creating the corner seam. Figure 14-43 shows the two faces that are selected to create the corner seam and Figure 14-44 shows the sheet metal component after creating the corner seam. Notice that there is no overlapping of the faces. Also notice that the bend relief in both the faces is automatically adjusted with reference to the corner seam.

Overlap

The **Overlap** button is provided on the right of the **No Overlap** button. If this button is

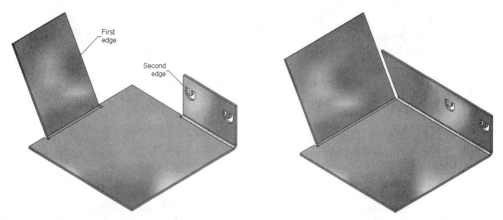

Figure 14-43 *Selecting the edges to create seam*   **Figure 14-44** *Model after creating the corner seam*

chosen, the face that is defined by the first selected edge will overlap the face defined by the second selected edge, see Figure 14-45. In this figure the sequence of selecting the edges is the same as that in Figure 14-43.

Reverse Overlap

The **Reverse Overlap** button is provided on the right of the **Overlap** button and if this button is chosen, the face defined by the second selected edge will overlap the face defined by the first selected edge as shown in Figure 14-46. In this figure also the sequence of selecting the edges is the same as that in Figure 14-43.

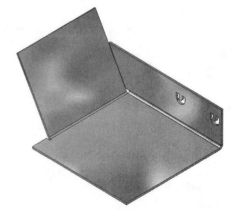

Figure 14-45 *Overlapping of faces*   **Figure 14-46** *Reverse overlapping of faces*

Gap

The **Gap** edit box is used to define the gap between the two faces in the corner seam. By default, the value in this edit box is **Thickness**. This means that the thickness of the sheet will be taken as the gap between the faces. You can enter any desired value in this edit box.

Mitter Area

The **Mitter** area replaces the **Seam** area when the two edges selected for defining the corner seam are coplanar. Similar to the **Seam** area, this area also provides three buttons in addition to the **Gap** edit box. The function of the three buttons is discussed next.

45 Degrees

The **45 Degrees** button is the first button in the **Mitter** area. This button is chosen to create a mitter corner between the selected faces. Figure 14-47 shows the two edges selected to create a mitter corner and Figure 14-48 shows a 45° mitter corner.

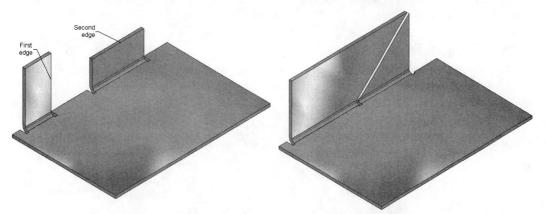

Figure 14-47 Selecting the edges to create a mitter   *Figure 14-48 45° mitter corner*

90 Degrees

The **90 Degrees** button is available on the right of the **45 Degrees** button and this button is chosen to create a 90° mitter corner as shown in Figure 14-49.

Reverse 90 Degrees

The **Reverse 90 Degrees** button is available on the right of the **90 Degrees** button and this button is chosen to create a reverse 90° mitter corner as shown in Figure 14-50.

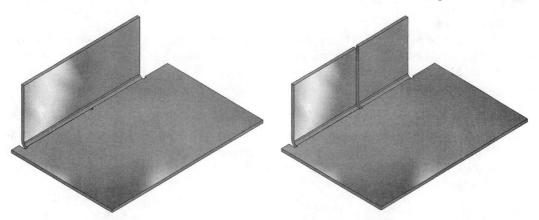

Figure 14-49 90° mitter corner   *Figure 14-50 Reverse 90° mitter corner*

BENDING THE SHEET METAL FACES

Toolbar: Sheet Metal > Bend
Panel bar: Sheet Metal > Bend

 Autodesk Inventor allows you to create a new face by adding a new bent face between the two existing faces. This is done by using the **Bend** tool. When you invoke this tool, the **Bend** dialog box will be displayed. The options that are provided in the **Bend** dialog box are discussed next.

Bend Shape Tab

The options in the **Bend Shape** tab (Figure 14-51) are used to set the parameters related to the shape of the bent face. These options are discussed next.

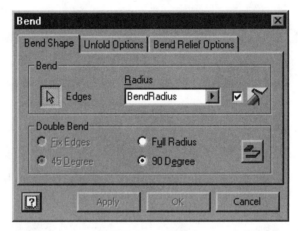

Figure 14-51 Bend Shape tab of the Bend dialog box

Bend Area

Select Edge

The **Select Edge** button is chosen to select the edges on the two faces between which the bent face will be added. When you invoke the **Bend** dialog box, this button is chosen by default and you are prompted to select the edge. Remember that until you select the edges for creating the bent face, the options in the **Double Bend** area will not be available.

Radius

The **Radius** edit box is used to specify the radius of the bend. The default value of this edit box is the bend radius specified in the **Sheet Metal Styles** dialog box. However, you can override the value specified in the **Sheet Metal Styles** dialog box and specify any desired value in this edit box.

Bend Relief

The **Bend Relief** check box is selected to create the bend relief while bending the faces. If this check box is cleared, the bend relief will not be created while bending.

Double Bend Area

The options in the **Double Bend** area are used to create a bend between two noncoplanar parallel faces. These options are discussed next.

Fix Edges

The **Fix Edges** radio button is selected to create a bend of equal dimensions between the selected edges.

45 Degree

The **45 Degree** radio button is selected to create a 45° bend between the selected edges. Note that when you select the edges for defining the bend, the edge selected first is taken as the fixed edge. While creating the bent face, if the sizes of the two selected edges are different, the size of the fixed edge and the face defined by this edge remains constant by default. However, the size of the other edge and the face defined by this edge is either trimmed or extended in order to adjust the new face.

Full Radius

The **Full Radius** radio button is selected to create a half circle bent face between the two selected edges. Figure 14-52 shows the two edges selected for creating the bend and Figure 14-53 shows a full radius bend created between the selected faces. Notice that in Figure 14-53, the face defined by the second edge is modified to adjust the new bent face.

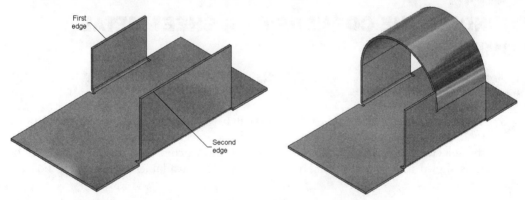

Figure 14-52 Selecting the edges   *Figure 14-53 Full radius bent face*

90 Degree

The **90 Degree** radio button is selected to create a 90° bend between the selected edges as shown in Figure 14-54. In this figure, the sequence of selecting the edges is the same as that in Figure 14-52.

Flip Fixed Edge

The **Flip Fixed Edge** check box is selected to change the fixed edge. As mentioned earlier, the edge selected first is taken as the fixed edge and the face defined by the other edge is modified in order to adjust the new bent face. However, if you choose this button, the edge selected second will be taken as the fixed edge and the face defined by the first edge will be modified in order to adjust the new bent face. Figure 14-55 shows a bent face that is added by selecting two edges in an order similar to that shown in Figure 14-52. Notice that the size of the face defined by the first edge is modified to adjust the new bent face.

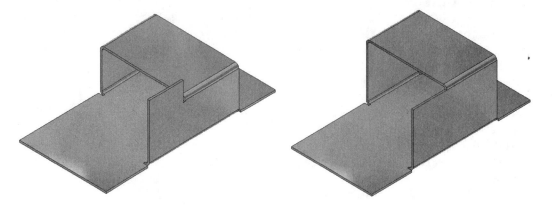

Figure 14-54 90° bent   *Figure 14-55 90° bent after flipping the fixed edge*

Note
*The options under the **Unfold Options** and the **Bend Relief Options** tabs are the same as those discussed in the previous sections of this chapter.*

ROUNDING THE CORNERS OF A SHEET METAL COMPONENT

Toolbar:	Sheet Metal > Corner Round
Panel bar:	Sheet Metal > Corner Round

The corners of a sheet metal components can be rounded by using the **Corner Round** tool. You can use this tool for rounding a single selected corner or all the corners of the selected face. When you invoke this tool, the **Corner Round** dialog box will be displayed as shown in Figure 14-56. The options that are available in this dialog box are discussed next.

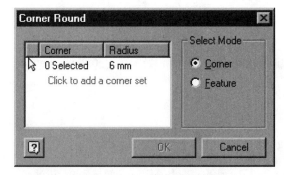

*Figure 14-56 **Corner Round** dialog box*

Corner

The **Corner** column displays the corners that are selected to be rounded. When you invoke the **Corner Round** dialog box, you are prompted to select a corner to be rounded. By default, this column displays **0 Selected**. This is because no corner is selected for rounding. To round a corner, select the edge that defines the corner of the sheet metal plate. The selected corner will be rounded. When you select a corner, this column displays **1 Selected**. Similarly, if you select more corners, the **Corner** column displays the number of corners that you have selected. You can preview the corner round on the graphics screen.

Radius

The **Radius** column displays the radius of the corner round. To modify the radius, click on this column and enter the new value of the radius.

Select Mode

The options in the **Select Mode** area are used to select the mode for selecting the object to be filleted. The options that are available in this area are discussed next.

Corner

The **Corner** radio button is selected by default in the **Select Mode** area and it allows you to individually select the corners that should be rounded.

Feature

The **Feature** radio button is selected to select a feature whose all corners will be rounded. When you select this radio button, you will be prompted to select the feature to be rounded. As soon as you select a feature, you will notice that all its corners are selected to be rounded. Note that if a feature has some faces that are folded, even the corners at the folded face are selected to be rounded. Figure 14-57 shows a feature being selected for rounding the corners. Notice that the dotted lines display the original feature before the face is folded. Figure 14-58 shows the sheet metal component after all the corners of the selected feature are rounded. Since the two flanges were not a part of the actual base feature, their corners are not rounded.

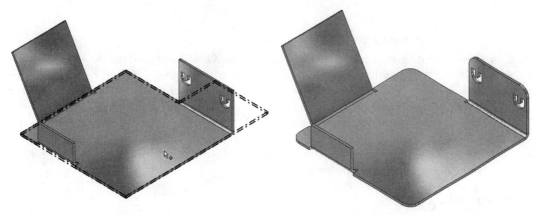

Figure 14-57 *Selecting the feature to be rounded*   ***Figure 14-58*** *After rounding the corners*

CHAMFERING THE CORNERS OF A SHEET METAL COMPONENT

Toolbar:	Sheet Metal > Corner Chamfer
Panel bar:	Sheet Metal > Corner Chamfer

 You can chamfer the corners of a sheet metal component by using the **Corner Chamfer** tool. When you invoke this tool, the **Corner Chamfer** dialog box will be displayed as shown in Figure 14-59. The options provided in this dialog box are discussed next.

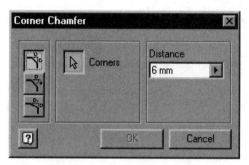

Figure 14-59 Corner Chamfer dialog box

One Distance

The **One Distance** button is the first button in the area that is on the extreme left of the **Corner Chamfer** dialog box. This button is chosen when you want to create a chamfer with equal distance in both the directions of the chamfer corner. When you invoke the **Chamfer Corner** dialog box, the **One Distance** button is chosen by default and you are prompted to select a corner to chamfer. The chamfer created by using this method is at a 45° angle. The chamfer distance can be specified in the **Distance** edit box that is available in the area that is on the extreme right of this dialog box. Since you have to specify only one distance value, only one edit box will be available in this area.

Distance and Angle

The **Distance and Angle** button is provided below the **One Distance** button. This button is chosen to define the chamfer by using one distance and one angle. When you choose this button, the **Edge** button is displayed in the area that is in the middle of the **Corner Chamfer** dialog box and you are prompted to select a face to chamfer. This is the face along which the distance value will be calculated. After you select the face, you will be prompted to select the corner to chamfer. You can define the distance value in the **Distance** edit box and the angle value in the **Angle** edit box. These edit boxes are displayed in the area that is located on the extreme right of the **Corner Chamfer** dialog box.

Two Distances

The **Two Distances** button is provided below the **Distance and Angle** button and is used to create a chamfer by defining two distances of the chamfer. The two distances can be entered in the **Distance1** and **Distance2** edit boxes. These edit boxes are displayed in the area that is located on the extreme right of the **Corner Chamfer** dialog box. Figure 14-60 shows a sheet metal component before chamfering the corners and Figure 14-61 shows the component after chamfering the corners.

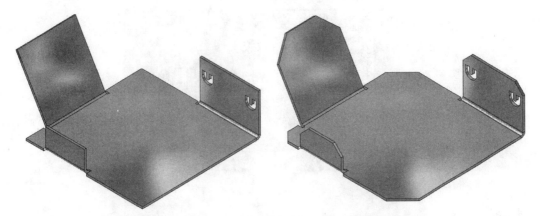

Figure 14-60 Model before chamfering   *Figure 14-61 Model after chamfering*

PUNCHING A 3D SHAPE INTO A SHEET METAL COMPONENT

Toolbar:	Sheet Metal > Punch Tool
Panel bar:	Sheet Metal > Punch Tool

You can punch a 3D shape into a sheet metal component with the help of the **Punch Tool** tool. Remember that the 3D shape can be punched only on a sketched point, endpoints of a line or an arc, or center points of arcs and circles. When you invoke this tool, the **Punch Tool** dialog box is displayed. This dialog box has different pages that guide you through the process of punching the selected 3D shape into the sheet metal component.

Shape Page

The **Shape** page is the first page that is displayed when you invoke this dialog box, see Figure 14-62. This page allows you to select the shape that you want to punch on the sheet metal component. The options that are available on this page are discussed next.

File Name

The **File Name** display box displays the name and the path of the library file that is selected to punch the shape. To select a new punch shape library file, choose the **Browse** button. When you choose this button, the **Browse for Folder** dialog box is displayed. You can use this dialog box to select the library file that stores the punch shapes. The library file and its path will be displayed in the display box that is provided on the right of the **Browse** button.

List Box

The **List Box** displays the list of the punch shapes that are available in the selected library file.

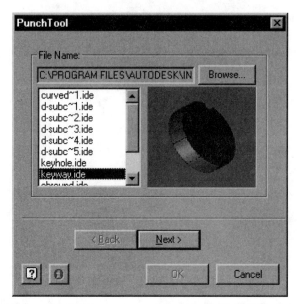

Figure 14-62 Shape page of the Punch Tool dialog box

You can select the required punch shape from the list box. The preview of the selected shape will be displayed in the preview window provided on the right of this list box.

Next

The **Next** button is chosen to proceed to the next page of the **Punch Tool** dialog box. Remember that if you choose the **Next** button in this page, you cannot return to this page. Therefore, you need to be very careful in selecting the shape that you want to punch. If you have selected a wrong punch shape and chosen the **Next** button, you will have to exit the **Punch Tool** dialog box and then invoke it again to select a different shape.

Geometry Page

The options in the **Geometry** page (Figure 14-63) are used to specify the location and orientation of the punch shape. If there is a sketched point on the sheet metal component, it will be automatically selected as the center of the punch shape. However, if you want to use the endpoints of lines or arcs, or the center point of circle or ellipse, you will have to select them manually. As soon as you select the location of the punch shape, its preview will be displayed on the screen. You can change the orientation of the punch shape by entering its value in the **Angle** edit box. After setting these parameters, choose the **Next** button.

 Note
*If you choose the **Next** button in the **Geometry** page to proceed to the next page, you can come back to the **Geometry** page by choosing the **Back** button in the next page.*

Size Page

The Size page of the **Punch Tool** dialog box is used to set the size of the punch shape by modifying its dimensions. The name and the value of the dimension will be displayed in the

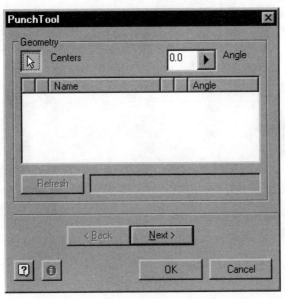

Figure 14-63 Geometry page of the Punch Tool dialog box

Name and the **Value** columns respectively as shown in Figure 14-64. To modify a dimension value, click on its field. The field will turn into an edit box or a drop-down list. If it turns into an edit box, you can enter the desired value in it. If the field turns into a drop-down list, you can select the desired value from the drop-down list. After setting the dimensions, choose the **OK** button to exit the dialog box and punch the shape on the sheet metal component.

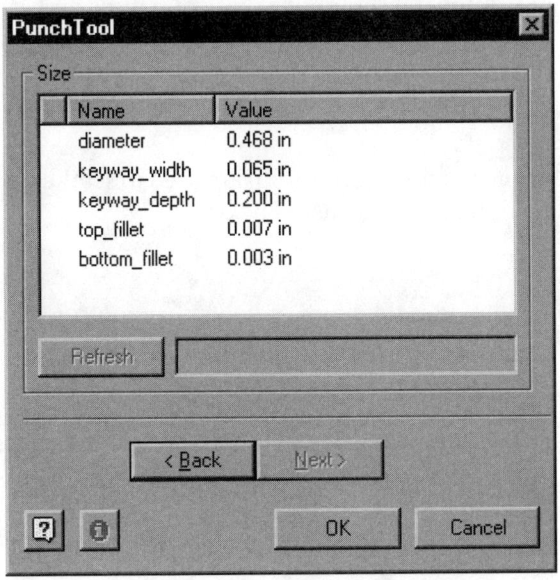

Figure 14-64 Size page of the Punch Tool dialog box

Figure 14-65 shows a sheet metal component after punching the keyway in the flange face.

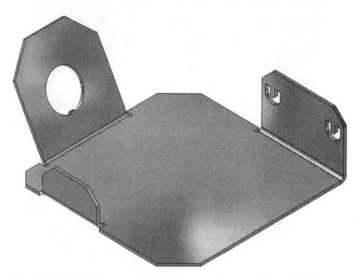

Figure 14-65 Sheet metal component after punching the keyway

CREATING HEMS

Toolbar:	Sheet Metal > Hem
Panel bar:	Sheet Metal > Hem

The hems are defined as the rounded faces that are created on sharp edges of a sheet metal component in order to reduce the area of sharpness in a sheet metal component. This makes that sheet metal component easy to handle and assemble. You can create the hems by using the **Hem** dialog box. The options that are available in the **Hem** dialog box are discussed next.

Hem Shape Tab

The options in the **Hem Shape** tab (Figure 14-66) are used to set the parameters related to the shape of the hem. These options are discussed next.

Type

The **Type** drop-down list provides the types of hems that you can create. These options are discussed next.

Single

The **Single** is the default hem type and it creates a single hem as shown in Figure 14-67.

Teardrop

The **Teardrop** type creates a teardrop hem as shown in Figure 14-68.

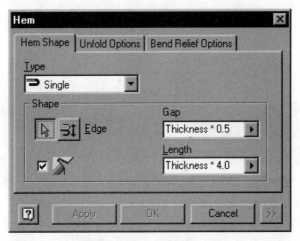

Figure 14-66 Hem Shape tab of the Hem dialog box

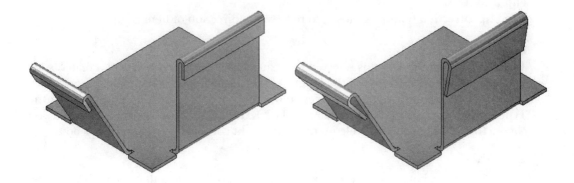

Figure 14-67 Single hem on flanges   *Figure 14-68 Teardrop hem on flanges*

Rolled
The **Rolled** type creates a rolled hem that does not have a face extending beyond the curve as shown in Figure 14-69.

Double
The **Double** type creates a double hem by rotating the hem twice as shown in Figure 14-70. This type of hem do not have any shared edge and so are very easy to handle.

Shape Area
Select Edge
When you invoke the **Hem** dialog box, this button is chosen by default and you are prompted to select the edge. The hem will be created on the selected edge. Note that you can select only one edge at a time for creating the hem. After selecting the edge, set the parameters and choose the **Apply** button to create the hem. Once the hem is created on one edge, this button will be chosen automatically and you are prompted to select the

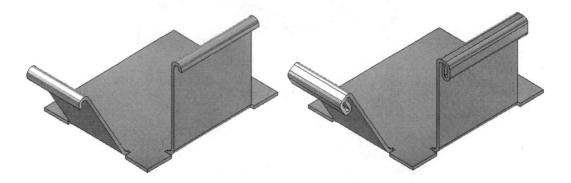

Figure 14-69 Rolled hem on flanges   *Figure 14-70* Double hem on flanges

edge to create the hem.

Flip Direction
The **Flip Direction** button is chosen to reverse the direction of hem creation.

Bend Relief
The **Bend Relief** check box is selected to create the relief when the hem is created such that it does not extend through the length of the selected edge. The effect of this check box will be visible only when you select an option other than the **Edge** option from the **Type** drop-down list in the **Extents** area. The **Extents** area will be displayed when you choose the **More** button available on the lower right corner of the **Hem** dialog box.

Gap
The **Gap** edit box is used to set the value of the hem gap. The default value in this edit box is **Thickness*0.5**. You can enter any desired value as the gap of the hem value in this edit box.

Length
The **Length** edit box is used to set the length of the hem. The default value in this edit box is **Thickness*4.0**. You can enter any desired value as the length of the hem in this edit box.

 Note
*The options in the **More** area are the same as those discussed in the **Flange** dialog box.*

*The options in the **Unfold Options** tab and the **Bend Relief Options** tab are the same as those discussed in the **Sheet Metal Styles** dialog box.*

CREATING CONTOUR FLANGE

Toolbar:	Sheet Metal > Contour Flange
Panel bar:	Sheet Metal > Contour Flange

Contour flanges are the flanges that are created by using an open sketched shape. To create a contour flange, you need to first sketch an open shape. After sketching the shape, invoke the **Contour Flange** tool. Note that until you draw an open sketch, you cannot invoke this tool. When you invoke this tool, the **Contour Flange** dialog box will be displayed. The options that are available in this dialog box are discussed next.

Contour Flange Shape Tab

The options under the **Contour Flange Shape** tab (Figure 14-71) are used to set the parameters related to the shape of the contour flange. These options are discussed next.

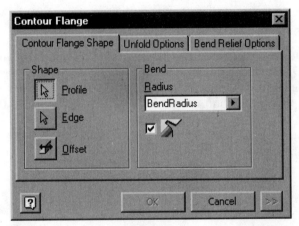

Figure 14-71 Contour Flange Shape tab of the Contour Flange dialog box

Shape Area

Select Profile

The **Select Profile** button is chosen to select the profile that will be used to create the contour flange. When you invoke the **Contour Flange** dialog box, this button is chosen by default and you are prompted to select an open profile.

Select Edge

The **Select Edge** button is chosen to select the edge on which the flange will be created. As soon as you select the profile, this button is chosen automatically and you are prompted to select the edge.

Flip Offset

The **Flip Offset** button is chosen to reverse the direction of offset of the contour flange.

Bend Area

Radius

The **Radius** edit box is used to set the value of the radius of the bend in the contour flange. The default value in this edit box is the value set in the **Sheet Metal Styles** dialog box. You can set any desired value in this edit box.

Bend Relief

The **Bend Relief** check box is selected to create a bend relief if the contour flange is not created through the length of the edge.

More

The **More** button is the button with two arrows and is available on the lower right corner of the **Contour Flange** dialog box. When you choose this button, the **Contour Flange** dialog box expands and displays the **Extents** area. This area has the **Type** drop-down list for specifying the extents of the flange. All the options in this drop-down list, except for the **Distance** option, are the same as those discussed in the previous sections of this chapter. The **Distance** option is discussed below.

Distance

The **Distance** option is used to specify the distance of the contour flange. When you select this option, the **Distance** edit box appears in the **Extents** area. You can define the distance of the contour flange in this edit box. You can reverse the direction of flange creation by choosing the **Flip Direction** button that is available on right of the **Distance** edit box.

Figure 14-72 shows the profile and the edge selected for creating the contour flange and Figure 14-73 shows the contour flange created with some width and at an offset.

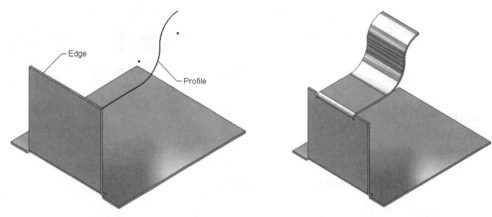

Figure 14-72 Selecting the edge and the profile   *Figure 14-73 Contour flange*

Note
*The options in the **Unfold Options** and the **Bend Relief Options** tabs are the same as those discussed in the previous sections of this chapter.*

UNFOLDING THE SHEET METAL COMPONENTS

Toolbar:	Sheet Metal > Flat Pattern
Panel bar:	Sheet Metal > Flat Pattern

You can unfold the sheet metal components by using the **Flat Pattern** tool. When you invoke this tool, the sheet metal component is unfolded and is displayed in a separate graphics window. Note that you cannot make any modifications in the unfolded sheet metal component. However, if you make the changes in the sheet metal component, they are reflected in the flat pattern. When you create the flat pattern, it is added in the browser on top of the sheet metal component. Figure 14-74 shows a sheet metal component and Figure 14-75 shows the flat pattern of the same component.

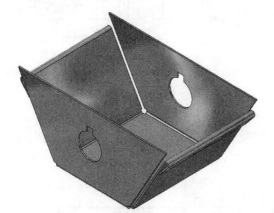

Figure 14-74 Sheet metal part

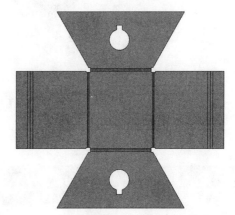

Figure 14-75 Flat pattern of the sheet metal part

Tip. *If you want to open a flat pattern window that was earlier closed by you, right-click on it in the browser and choose* **Open Window**. *The flat pattern window will be opened on the graphics screen.*

Note

The remaining tools in the **Sheet Metal** *mode and their working is similar to the tools and their working in the* **Part** *mode.*

TUTORIALS

Tutorial 1

In this tutorial you will create the sheet metal component of the Holder Clip shown in Figure 14-76a. The flat pattern of the component is shown in Figure 14-76b. The dimensions of the component are shown in Figure 14-76c and Figure 14-76d. The thickness of the sheet is 1 mm. After creating the sheet metal component, create the flat pattern of the component. Save the component with the name given below:

\PersonalProject\c14**Tutorial1.ipt**   **(Expected time: 1 Hr)**

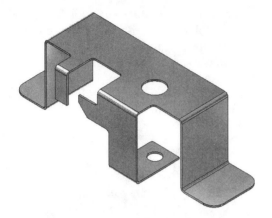

Figure 14-76a *Sheet metal model of Holder Clip*

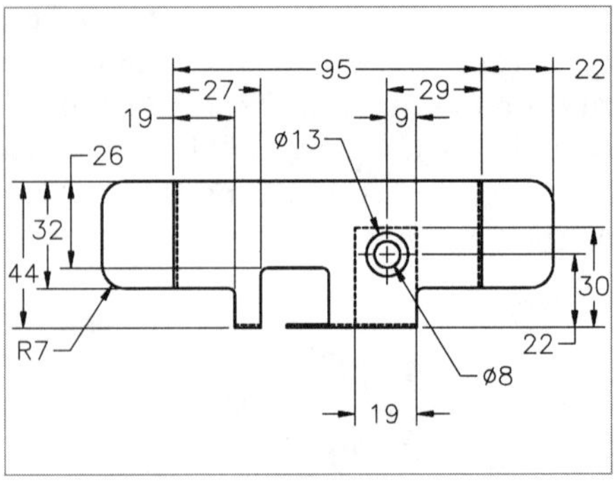

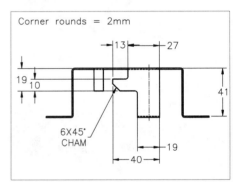

Figure 14-76c *Top view of the Holder Clip*

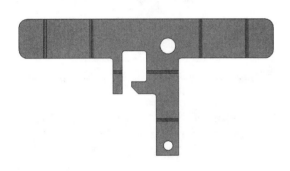

Figure 14-76b *Flat pattern of the component*

Figure 14-76d *Front view of the Holder Clip*

It is recommended that before you start creating the model, you should outline the steps that will be followed to complete the tutorial. The steps that will be followed to complete the tutorial are listed below:

a. Open a new metric sheet metal file and then draw the sketch of the top face of the sheet metal component.
b. Set the parameters in the **Sheet Metal Styles** dialog box and convert the sketch into the sheet metal face.
c. Add the contour flange on the right and the left faces of the top feature.
d. Add the contour flange on the front face of the feature.
e. Create a cut feature on the front face of the new flange and then add another face and chamfer to it.
f. Create the last flange and then create the two holes. Finally, create the flat pattern.

Opening a New Metric Sheet Metal File
1. Start Autodesk Inventor and then choose **New** in the **Open** dialog box.

2. Choose the **Metric** tab and then double-click on the **Sheet Metal (mm).ipt** file to open a new metric sheet metal file.

    The sketching environment will be activated where you can draw the sketch for the top face of the sheet metal component.

3. Draw the sketch for the top face of the Holder Clip as shown in Figure 14-77.

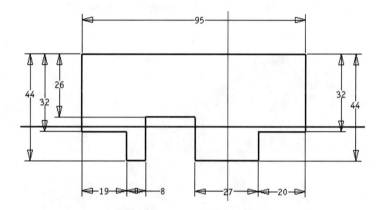

Figure 14-77 Sketch for the top face of the Holder Clip

Note
In Figure 14-77, the grid lines are hidden for clarity of the sketch.

4. Exit the sketching environment by choosing **Return** from the **Command Bar**.

Converting the Sketch into a Sheet Metal Face

Before you convert the sketch into a sheet metal face, it is recommended that you set the parameters in the **Sheet Metal Styles** dialog box. These parameters will control the thickness of the sheet, the radius of bend, the parameters of relief, and so on.

1. Choose the **Styles** button from the **Sheet Metal** toolbar or choose **Styles** from the **Sheet Metal** penal bar to invoke the **Sheet Metal Styles** dialog box.

    When you invoke the **Sheet Metal Styles** dialog box, the **Sheet** tab is active by default. You can set the parameters related to the sheet thickness in this tab. Since all the other parameters are based on the thickness of the sheet, they will automatically change when you change the sheet thickness.

2. Enter **1** as the value in the **Thickness** edit box in the **Sheet** area.

    This will increase the sheet thickness to 1 mm.

3. Choose **Save** and then choose **Done** to save the changes and exit the dialog box.

4. Choose the **Face** button from the **Sheet Metal** toolbar or choose **Face** from the **Sheet Metal** panel bar to invoke the **Face** dialog box.

    Since there is only one unconsumed sketch, it will be automatically selected and highlighted to create the sheet metal component face.

5. Choose **OK** to create the face and exit the **Face** dialog box. Change the current view to the Isometric view. The top of the Holder Clip is shown in Figure 14-78.

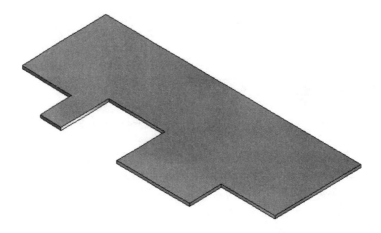

Figure 14-78 Top face of the Holder Clip

Creating the Contour Flange

As mentioned earlier, the contour flange is created with the help of a sketched contour. Therefore, you first need to sketch the contour that will be used to create the flange.

1. Define a new sketch plane on the face shown in Figure 14-79.

2. Draw the sketch for the contour flange as shown in Figure 14-80.

3. Exit the sketching environment and then choose the **Contour Flange** button from the **Sheet Metal** toolbar or choose **Contour Flange** from the **Sheet Metal** panel bar to invoke the **Contour Flange** dialog box.

    The **Profile** button in the **Shape** area of the **Contour Flange Shape** tab will be chosen by default and you will be prompted to select the profile for creating the contour flange.

4. Select one of the two sketched lines as the contour for creating the flange. Since the other line is a part of the same sketch, it will also be automatically selected and the sketch will turn blue in color.

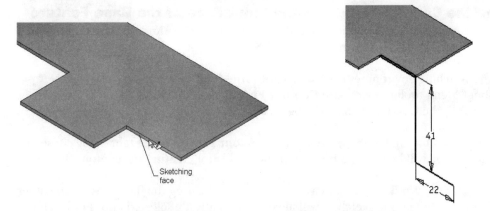

Figure 14-79 *Selecting the sketching plane*   **Figure 14-80** *Sketch for the contour flange*

As soon as you select the profile, the **Select Edge** button in the **Shape** area will be chosen and you will be prompted to select the edge on which the flange will be created.

5. Select the extreme right vertical edge on the top face to create the flange.

6. Accept the remaining default options and choose **OK** to create the flange. You will notice that a bend is automatically created between the base sheet and the flange. The dimensions and parameters of this bend will be taken as the parameters defined in the **Sheet Metal Styles** dialog box.

7. Similarly, create the flange on the other side of the top face. You will have to flip the direction by using the **Flip Offset** button in the **Shape** area of the **Contour Flange Shape** tab so that the front face of the flange is coplanar with the left face of the base sheet. The sheet metal model of the Holder Clip after creating the two contour flanges is shown in Figure 14-81.

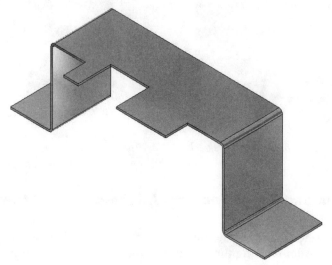

Figure 14-81 *Sheet metal component after creating the two contour flanges*

Creating the Contour Flange on the Front Face of the Base Feature

1. Define a new sketch plane on the planar face of the base feature and then create the sketch for the contour flange as shown in Figure 14-82.

2. Exit the sketching environment and then choose the **Contour Flange** button from the **Sheet Metal** toolbar or choose **Contour Flange** from the **Sheet Metal** panel bar to invoke the **Contour Flange** dialog box.

   The **Profile** button in the **Shape** area of the **Contour Flange Shape** tab will be chosen by default and you will be prompted to select the profile for creating the contour flange.

3. Select one of the two sketched lines as the contour for creating the flange. Since the other line is a part of the same sketch, it will also be automatically selected and the sketch will turn blue in color.

   As soon as you select the profile, the **Select Edge** button in the **Shape** area will be chosen and you will be prompted to select the edge on which the flange will be created.

4. Select the horizontal edge on the top face to create the flange.

5. Choose the **Flip Offset** button to reverse the direction in which the flange face will be created.

6. Accept the remaining default options and choose **OK** to create the flange. The sheet metal component after creating the third contour flange is shown in Figure 14-83.

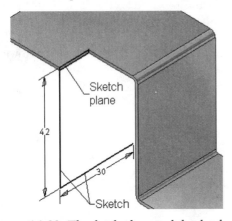
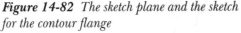

Figure 14-82 *The sketch plane and the sketch for the contour flange*

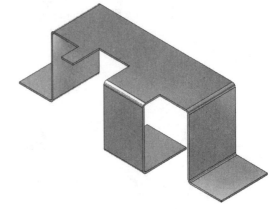

Figure 14-83 *Sheet metal component after creating the contour flange*

Creating a Cut and a New Face on the Front Face of the Previous Flange

1. Define a new sketch plane on the front face of the previous flange and create a sketch for the cut feature. After creating the sketch, exit the sketching environment.

2. Invoke the **Cut** tool and create the cut feature by using the **All** extents. The sheet metal component after creating the cut is shown in Figure 14-84.

3. Similarly, again define a sketch plane on the front face of the previous flange and create a new rectangular face by using the **Face** tool.

4. Next, add the corner chamfer by using the **Corner Chamfer** tool as shown in Figure 14-85.

Figure 14-84 *Sheet metal component after creating the cut feature*

Figure 14-85 *Sheet metal component after creating the new face and corner chamfer*

Creating the Last Flange

1. Choose the **Flange** button from the **Sheet Metal** toolbar or choose **Flange** from the **Sheet Metal** panel bar to invoke the **Flange** dialog box. You will be prompted to select the edge for creating the flange.

2. Select the edge on the top face of the base feature as shown in Figure 14-86.

3. Enter **19** as the value in the **Distance** edit box and then choose the **Flip Direction** button.

4. Accept the remaining default options and choose the **OK** button to create the flange and exit the dialog box.

   The sheet metal component after creating the flange is shown in Figure 14-87.

Creating the Rounds and Holes

1. Create all the rounds by using the **Corner Round** tool.

2. Define new sketch planes on the required faces and then create the two holes.

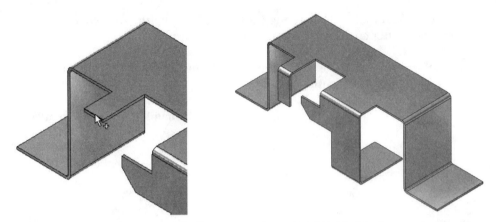

Figure 14-86 *Selecting the edge to create the flange*   ***Figure 14-87*** *Model after creating the flange*

This completes the sheet metal component for the Holder Clip. The final sheet metal component for the Holder Clip is shown in Figure 14-88.

3. Save the sheet metal component with the name \PersonalProject\c14**Tutorial1.ipt**.

Creating the Flat Pattern

The flattened view of a sheet metal component plays a very important role in process planning while designing the punch tools and dies for creating the sheet metal component. Therefore, the flattened view is a very important part of any sheet metal component. As mentioned earlier, you can unfold the sheet metal component and display its flattened view in a separate graphics window. This is done by using the **Flat Pattern** tool.

1. Choose the **Flat Pattern** button from the **Sheet Metal** toolbar or choose **Flat Pattern** from the **Sheet Metal** panel bar.

The sheet metal component will be unfolded and will be displayed in a separate window as shown in Figure 14-89.

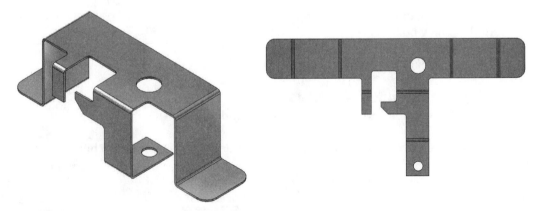

Figure 14-88 *Final model of Holder Clip*   ***Figure 14-89*** *Flat Pattern of the sheet metal part*

Note

If the orientation of the flat pattern is not similar to the one shown in Figure 14-89, close the flat pattern window and then right-click on **Flat Pattern** *in the browser. Choose the* **Select Base Face** *option from the shortcut menu and then select the top face as the base face. Now, again right-click on* **Flat Pattern** *in the browser and choose* **Open Window** *to open the flat pattern window. You will notice that the orientation of the flat pattern is similar to the one shown in Figure 14-89.*

Tutorial 2

In this tutorial you will create the sheet metal component shown in Figure 14-90a. The dimensions of the component are shown in Figure 14-90b, Figure 14-90c, and Figure 14-90d. The flat pattern of the component is shown in Figure 14-91. The thickness of the sheet is 1 mm. The dimensions of the hems are not given. Select the default parameters as the dimensions for creating the hems on the two faces. **(Expected time: 45 min)**

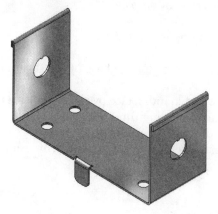

Figure 14-90a Sheet metal component

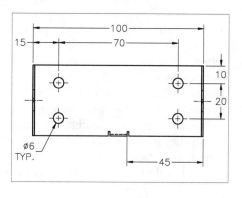

Figure 14-90b Top view of the model

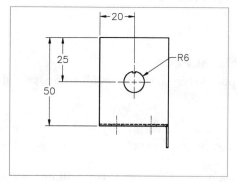

Figure 14-90c Left side view of the model

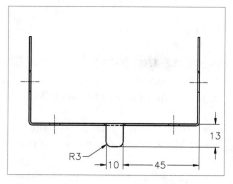

Figure 14-90d Front view of the model

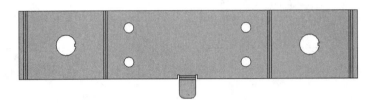

Figure 14-91 *Flat pattern of the sheet metal component*

The following steps outline the procedure for creating the model:

a.   Open a new metric sheet metal file and create the sketch for the base of the sheet metal component on the XY plane.
b.   Exit the sketching environment and convert the sketch into a face by using the **Face** tool.
c.   Create one hole and then pattern it to create the remaining three instances.
d.   Create the flange on the left and right faces of the sheet metal base.
e.   Create hems on the two flanges and then create the circle with a keyway by using the **Punch Tool** dialog box.
f.   Create the flange on the front face of the base.

Creating the Sketch for the Base Feature

1.   Choose **New** from the **Standard** toolbar to invoke the **Open** dialog box.

2.   Choose the **Metric** tab and open a new metric sheet metal file.

3.   Create the sketch for the base as shown in Figure 14-92.

Converting the Sketch into a Sheet Metal Face

As mentioned earlier, you should first set the parameters in the **Sheet Metal Styles** dialog box and then convert the sketch into a face.

1.   Choose the **Styles** button from the **Sheet Metal** toolbar or choose **Styles** from the **Sheet Metal** panel bar to invoke the **Sheet Metal Styles** dialog box.

2.   Enter **1** as the value in the **Thickness** edit box in the **Sheet** area. This will increase the sheet thickness to 1 mm. Choose **Save** and then choose **Done** to close the dialog box.

3.   Choose the **Face** button from the **Sheet Metal** toolbar or choose **Face** from the **Sheet Metal** panel bar to invoke the **Face** dialog box.

Since there is only one unconsumed sketch, it will be automatically selected and highlighted to create the sheet metal component face.

5. Choose **OK** to create the face and exit the **Face** dialog box.

6. Define a new sketch plane on the top face of the base and create a hole center for creating a hole.

7. Exit the sketching environment and create the hole at the hole center.

8. Create a rectangular pattern of the hole. Change the current view to the Isometric view. The base of the sheet metal component after creating the hole pattern is shown in Figure 14-93.

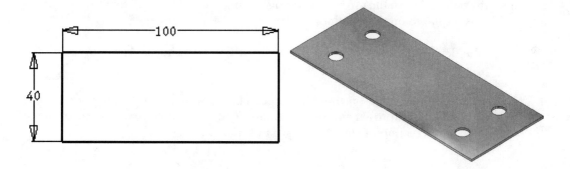

Figure 14-92 *Sketch for the base feature*   *Figure 14-93* *Base after creating the hole pattern*

Creating the Two Flanges

1. Choose the **Flange** button from the **Sheet Metal** toolbar or choose **Flange** from the **Sheet Metal** panel bar to invoke the **Flange** dialog box. You will be prompted to select the edge for creating the flange.

2. Select the right vertical edge on the bottom face of the base. You will notice that the preview of the flange is shown in the downward direction.

3. Choose the **Flip Direction** button and enter **50** as the value in the **Distance** edit box.

4. Choose the **Apply** button.

You will notice that the flange is created on the right edge and the **Flange** dialog box is still available. This is because you did not exit the dialog box after creating the flange. You cannot use the same parameters to create the flange on the other side.

5. Press and hold the F4 key down and rotate the model such that the bottom vertical edge on the other side of the base is visible.

6. Release the F4 key and select the vertical edge on the bottom face of the base.

   You will notice that the flange is created in the upward direction. This is because the parameters are already set in the **Flange** dialog box.

7. Choose the **OK** button from the **Flange** dialog box to create the flange and exit the dialog box. Change the current view to the Isometric view. The sheet metal component after creating the flanges is shown in Figure 14-94.

Creating the Hems

1. Choose the **Hem** button from the **Sheet Metal** toolbar or choose **Hem** from the **Sheet Metal** panel bar to invoke the **Hem** dialog box. You will be prompted to select an edge to create the hem.

2. Select the outer edge on the top face of the right flange. You will notice that the preview of the hem is displayed on the graphics screen.

3. Accept the default parameters in the **Hem** dialog box and choose **Apply** to create the hem.

4. Now, select the outer edge on the left flange. The preview of the flange is displayed. Choose the **OK** button to create the flange and exit the dialog box. The sheet metal component after creating the hems is shown in Figure 14-95.

Figure 14-94   *Model after creating the flanges*   *Figure 14-95*   *Model after creating the hems*

Creating the Cut Feature

Next, the cut feature with the keyway needs to be created. This feature will be created by punching the predefined shape on one of the flanges and will then be mirrored on the other side. However, as mentioned earlier, the shapes are punched by using a sketched point. Therefore, you first need to sketch a point in the middle of one of the flanges. But before creating the cut feature, it is recommended that you suppress the hems. This is because after creating the hems, the actual dimensions of the face are reduced and you cannot get the proper dimensions of the face.

1. Using the browser, suppress the two hems. Now, define a new sketch plane on the outer face of the right flange.

2. Create a sketch point at the middle of the face. The vertical dimension of the point from the top edge should be 25 mm.

3. Exit the sketching environment and then choose the **Punch Tool** button from the **Sheet Metal** toolbar or choose **Punch Tool** from the **Sheet Metal** panel bar to invoke the **Shape** page of the **Punch Tool** dialog box.

4. Select **keyway.ide** from the list box. The preview of the keyway is displayed in the preview window. Choose the **Next** button to proceed to the **Geometry** page.

   Since there is only one sketched point, it will be selected as the center of the keyway and a preview of the keyway will be displayed on the graphics screen. You will notice that in the preview, the keyway is toward the right of the circle. You need to rotate it in order to get the proper orientation of the keyway.

5. Enter **90** as the value in the **Angle** edit box on the **Geometry** page. Choose the **Next** button to proceed to the next page. Accept the default dimension values and choose **OK** to create the keyway.

   Note
   *The punched 3D shapes are displayed as **iFeature** in the browser.*

6. Create a work plane in the middle of the sheet metal component and then mirror the punched feature on the other flange by using the **Mirror Feature** tool. The sheet metal component after creating the punched feature on both the flanges is shown in Figure 14-96.

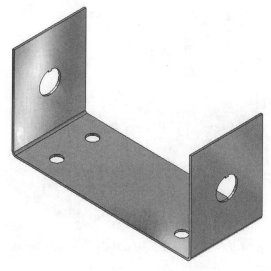

Figure 14-96 Sheet metal component after creating the punched features

Creating the Next Flange

1. Choose the **Flange** button from the **Sheet Metal** toolbar or choose **Flange** from the **Sheet Metal** panel bar to invoke the **Flange** dialog box. You will be prompted to select the edge for creating the flange.

2. Select the upper edge on the front face of the base of the sheet metal component. The preview of the flange will be displayed on the graphics screen.

3. Enter **13** as the value in the **Distance** edit box. Choose the **More** button located on the lower right corner of the dialog box to expand the dialog box.

4. Select **Width** from the **Type** drop-down list in the **Extents** area. The **Offset** and **Width** edit boxes will appear in the **Extents** area and you will be prompted to select the flange start point.

5. Select the right endpoint of the selected edge as the start point of the flange. Enter **43** as the flange offset value in the **Offset** edit box and then choose the **Flip Direction** button.

6. Enter **10** as the value of the width of the flange in the **Width** edit box. Choose **OK** to create the flange and exit the dialog box.

7. Create rounds on the two corners of the previous flange by using the **Corner Round** tool. The radius of the corner round is 3 mm.

   This completes the sheet metal component. Unsuppress all the suppressed features. The final sheet metal component is shown in Figure 14-97.

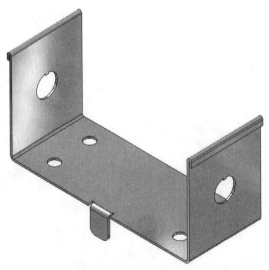

Figure 14-97 Completed sheet metal component for Tutorial 2

Creating the Flat Pattern

1. Choose the **Flat Pattern** button from the **Sheet Metal** toolbar or choose **Flat Pattern** from the **Sheet Metal** panel bar. The flat pattern of the sheet metal component will be displayed in a separate window as shown in Figure 14-98.

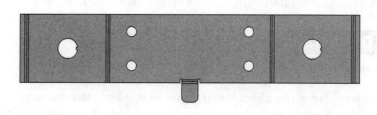

Figure 14-98 *Flat pattern of the component*

2. Save the model with the name given below:

   \PersonalProject\c14**Tutorial2.ipt**

Self-Evaluation Test

Answer the following questions and then compare your answers with the answers given at the end of this chapter.

1. The sheet metal files are saved as the *.ipt files. (T/F)

2. When you invoke a new sheet metal file, you are by default in the sketching environment. (T/F)

3. The contour flange will be created only with the help of a sketched contour. (T/F)

4. A sketched point will automatically be selected as the center of the punched 3D shape. (T/F)

5. You can unfold a sheet metal component by using the _____ tool.

6. By default, the value of the bend radius is equal to the _____ of the sheet.

7. In Autodesk Inventor you can fold a sheet metal face only by using a _____ line that acts as the _____ line.

8. Autodesk Inventor allows you to create the corner seams in a sheet metal component with the help of the _____ tool.

9. If a flange is created through an angle of _____, it will not be visible as it will be merged with the face of the sheet metal component.

10. To convert a solid model into a sheet metal component, you first need to _____ it.

Review Questions

Answer the following questions.

1. If you modify a value in the **Sheet Metal Styles** dialog box after creating the sheet metal component, the changes will be reflected in the sheet metal component when you exit the dialog box after saving the changes. (T/F)

2. The flat pattern is displayed in a separate window. (T/F)

3. You can set the material for the sheet metal component from the **Sheet Metal Styles** dialog box. (T/F)

4. The value of the bend and unfold parameters that are set in the **Sheet Metal Styles** dialog box cannot be overridden from the dialog boxes of any tool. (T/F)

5. You can set the value of an edit box as an equation in terms of the thickness of the sheet. (T/F)

6. A punched 3D shape cannot be mirrored. (T/F)

7. The flange that follows a sketched shape in a sheet metal component can be created using which one of the following tools?

    (a) **Flange**   (b) **Contour Flange**
    (c) **Face**   (d) **Hem**

8. Which one of the following is not a type of hem?

    (a) **Single**   (b) **Double**
    (c) **Tripple**   (d) **Teardrop**

9. The base of the sheet metal component can be created by using which one of the following tools?

    (a) **Flange**   (b) **Contour Flange**
    (c) **Face**   (d) **Hem**

10. You can fillet all the corners of the base feature by using which one of the following tools?

(a) **Round**   (b) **Corner Round**
(c) **Face**   (d) **Hem**

Exercise

Exercise 1

Create the sheet metal component shown in Figure 14-99a. The flat pattern of the component is shown in Figure 14-99b. The dimensions of the model are shown in Figure 14-99c and Figure 14-99d. Assume the missing dimensions. **(Expected time: 30 min)**

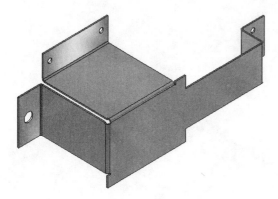

Figure 14-99a Sheet metal part for Exercise 1

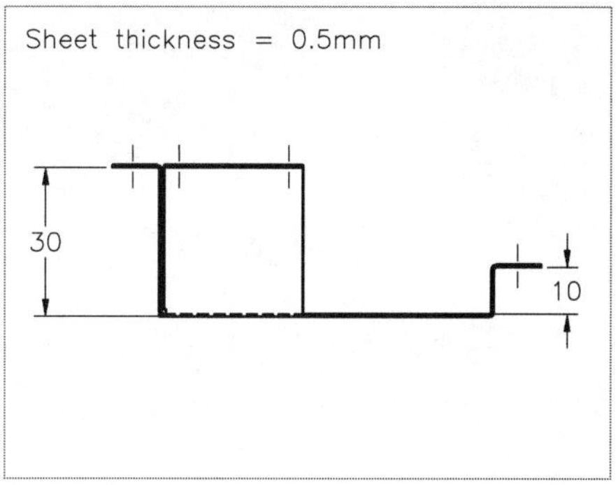

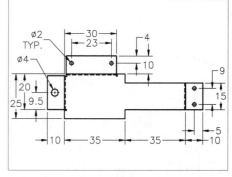

Figure 14-99c Top view of the component

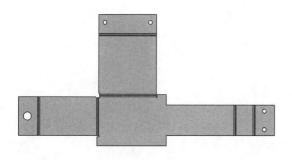

Figure 14-99b Flat pattern of the component

Figure 14-99d Front view of the component

Hint
*The flanges on the top face and the left face can be created to some width and then by using the **Corner Seam** tool, you can force them to close together. This way the corner relief will also be created.*

Answers to Self-Evaluation Test
1. T, **2.** T, **3.** T, **4.** T, **5. Flat Pattern**, **6.** thickness, **7.** sketched, folding, **8. Corner Seam**, **9.** 180°, **10.** shell

Chapter 15

Projects

After completing this chapter you will be able to:
- *Use Autodesk Inventor tools to create the component of the project assemblies.*
- *Use the assembly tools to assemble the project assemblies.*
- *Use the presentation tools to create the presentation of the project assemblies.*
- *Use the drawing tools to generate the drawing views of the project assemblies and add balloons and parts list to the drawing views.*

Tutorial 1

In this tutorial you will create all the components of the Wheel Support assembly and then assemble them together as shown in Figure 15-1. You will use the bottom-up approach of assembly modeling in creating this assembly. After creating the assembly, create an animation of exploding and unexploding of the components. The exploded view of the assembly is shown in Figure 15-2. Finally, generate the following drawing views of the assembly:

1. Top view
2. Front view
3. Left side view
4. Isometric view

Use the drawing ISO standard drawing sheet for generating the drawing views. The drawing sheet should also display the parts list and the balloons. The parts list that needs to be added is shown in Figure 15-3. The dimensions of the components are shown in Figure 15-4, Figure 15-5, Figure 15-6, and Figure 15-7.   **(Expected time: 4 Hrs)**

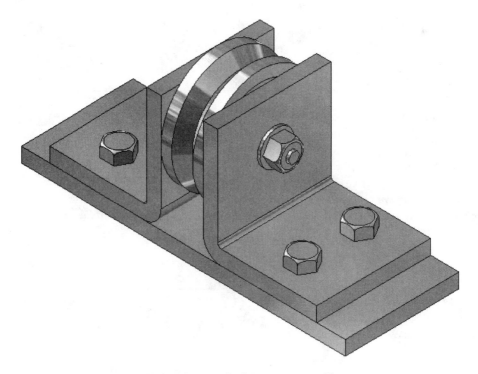

Figure 15-1 *Wheel Support assembly*

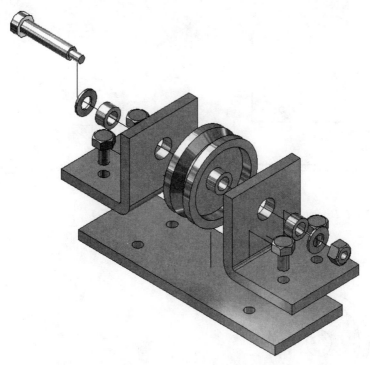

Figure 15-2 *Exploded view of the Wheel Support assembly*

PARTS LIST			
ITEM	QTY	NAME	MATERIAL
1	1	Base	Steel
2	2	Support	Steel
3	2	Bushing	Bronze
4	1	Wheel	Cast Iron
5	4	Bolt	Steel
6	2	Washer	Bronze
7	1	Shoulder Screw	Steel
8	1	Nut	Steel

Figure 15-3 *Parts list for the assembly*

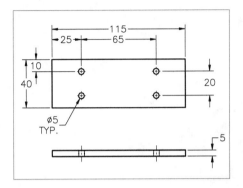

Figure 15-4 *Dimensions of the Base*

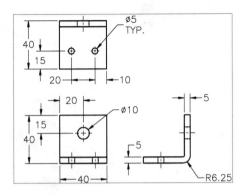

Figure 15-5 *Dimensions of the Support*

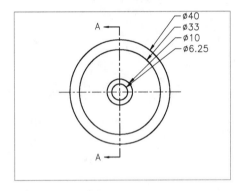

Figure 15-6a *Front view of the Wheel*

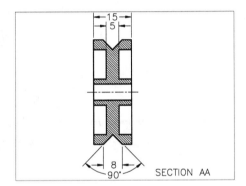

Figure 15-6b *Sectioned side view of the Wheel*

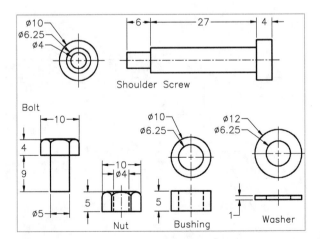

Figure 15-7 *Dimensions of the Shoulder Screw, Bolt, Nut, Bushing, and Washer*

The following steps outline the procedure for completing this tutorial.

a. Create the individual components in separate part files.
b. Open a new assembly file and place one instance of the Base and two instances of the Support.
c. Assemble the Base and the two instances of the Support by using the assembly constraints.
d. Place two instances of the Bushing and assemble them with the two Supports.
e. Place the Wheel and assemble it by using the assembly constraints.
f. Place one instance of the Bolt and assemble it. Assemble the remaining three instance of the Bolt with the help of the associated pattern.
g. Place two instances of the Washer, one instance of the Shoulder Screw, and one instance of the Nut and assemble them.
h. Analyze the assembly for interference. Then save the assembly file and close it. Open a new presentation file and generate the presentation view.
i. Add tweaks to the components and then animate them.
j. Save and close the presentation file and open a new ISO standard drawing sheet.
k. Set the parameters in the **Drafting Standards** dialog box and then generate the drawing views.
l. Place the parts list and balloons in the drawing sheet.

Creating the Base

The individual component files are created in the part files and are saved in the .ipt format. You will use the metric standard part file to create the individual components.

1. Start Autodesk Inventor and then choose **New** from the **What To Do** area.

2. Choose the **Metric** tab to display the metric standard files.

3. Double-click on **Standard (mm).ipt** to open a metric standard part file.

   When you open a new part file, by default you are in the sketching environment where you can draw the sketch for the base feature. In the Base part, the sketch for the base feature will be a rectangle. Note that you will not create the holes while drawing the sketch for the base feature. This is because one of the hole will be created as the second feature and the remaining three instances will be created with the help of the **Rectangular Pattern** tool. This rectangular pattern will then be used to create the associative pattern of the Bolts in the assembly file.

4. Choose **Two point rectangle** from the **Sketch** panel bar and draw the rectangle.

5. Choose **General Dimension** from the **Sketch** panel bar and select the top horizontal line of the rectangle.

6. Place the dimension on top of the sketch to display the **Edit Dimension** toolbar.

7. Enter **115** as the value in the **Edit Dimension** toolbar and choose the check mark button located on the right of the **Edit Dimension** toolbar to assign the dimension value to the

selected entity. You can also press the ENTER key to assign the value. You will notice that the two horizontal lines of the rectangle are driven to a length of 115 mm.

8. Press the F3 key and dynamically zoom to get the complete display of the sketch on the graphics screen. After you get the proper display of the rectangle and the dimension, release the F3 key.

   Since you are still inside the **General Dimension** tool, you will be prompted to select the geometry to dimension.

9. Select the left vertical line and place the dimension on the left of the sketch. Enter **40** as the value in the **Edit Dimension** toolbar and then press ENTER.

   You will notice that the two vertical lines of the rectangle are driven to 40 mm length. This completes the dimensioning of the sketch for the base feature.

10. Choose **Return** from the **Command Bar** to exit the sketching environment. The fully dimensioned sketch of the base feature is shown in Figure 15-8.

11. Choose **Extrude** from the **Features** panel bar.

    The **Extrude** dialog box will be displayed. Since there is only one unconsumed sketch on the graphics screen, it will be selected and highlighted.

12. Enter **5** as the value in the edit box provided in the **Extents** area. Choose **OK** to create the base feature and exit the **Extrude** dialog box.

13. Right-click on the graphics screen to display the shortcut menu. Choose **Isometric View** from the shortcut menu to change the current view to the Isometric view, see Figure 15-9.

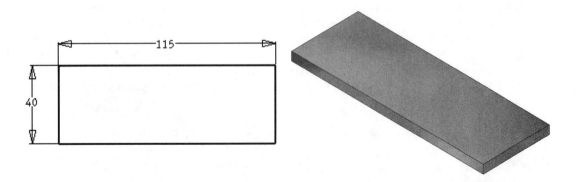

Figure 15-8 *Dimensioned sketch of the base feature*   *Figure 15-9* *Base feature*

Now, you need to create the holes. You will create one of the holes and the remaining holes will be created by using the **Rectangular Pattern** tool. The holes in Autodesk Inventor are created by using a point/hole center, endpoints of lines or arcs, and center points of arcs, circles, or ellipses. Therefore, you need to first define a sketch plane and then place a point for creating the hole.

14. Choose **Sketch** from the **Command Bar** and select the top face of the base feature as the sketching plane.

    You will notice that the sketching environment is activated and a sketch defining the contour of the top face, which is actually the rectangle, is created.

15. Press the F5 key. This key is used to switch to the previous view. Now, choose **Point, Hole Center** from the **Sketch** panel bar. You will be prompted to select the hole center point.

16. Specify a point close to the lower left corner of the top face as the location of the hole center.

17. Choose **General Dimension** from the **Sketch** panel bar and select the hole center. The hole center will turn blue in color. Now, select the left vertical edge of the top face and place the dimension below the base feature. The **Edit Dimension** toolbar will be displayed.

18. Enter **25** as the value in the **Edit Dimension** toolbar and then press ENTER. You will notice that the hole center will move from its original location such that it is now at a distance of 25 mm from the left vertical edge.

19. Since you are still inside the **General Dimension** tool, you will again be prompted to select the geometry to dimension. Select the hole center and then select the bottom horizontal line. Now, place the dimension on the left of the base feature to display the **Edit Dimension** toolbar.

20. Enter **10** as the value in the **Edit Dimension** toolbar and then press ENTER. This completes the dimensioning of the hole center. Right-click on the graphics screen and choose **Isometric View** from the shortcut menu to change the current view to the Isometric view.

21. Choose **Return** from the **Command Bar** to exit the sketching environment and then choose **Hole** from the **Features** panel bar.

    Since there is only one hole center, it will be automatically selected to place the hole and the preview of the hole as it will be created using the current values of the **Hole** dialog box will be displayed on the graphics screen.

22. Select **Through All** from the drop-down list provided in the **Termination** area. Modify the dimension of the diameter of the hole in the preview window to **5** and then choose the **OK** button to create the hole, see Figure 15-10.

    Next, you need to create a rectangular pattern of the hole to create the remaining instances of the hole. A rectangular pattern is the one in which the selected entities are arranged along the edges of an imaginary rectangle. The pattern will be created by using the **Rectangular Pattern** tool.

23. Choose **Rectangular Pattern** from the **Features** panel bar to invoke the **Rectangular Pattern** dialog box.

You will notice that the **Features** button is chosen by default and you are prompted to select the features to pattern.

24. Select the hole as the feature to pattern. The hole will be displayed with blue outline.

25. Choose the **Direction** button in the **Direction1** area to select the first direction of arranging the holes. You will be prompted to select the direction to pattern.

26. Select the lower horizontal edge of the top face of the base feature as the first direction.

You will notice that a green arrow and a circle is displayed. The direction of the arrow is toward the left of the existing hole. But, this direction needs to be toward the right of the existing hole. Therefore, you need to reverse the direction of pattern.

27. Choose the **Flip** button provided in the **Direction1** area. You will notice that the direction of the arrow and the circle is reversed on the graphics screen and is now toward the right of the existing hole.

28. Enter **65** as the value in the **Spacing** edit box in **Direction1** area.

29. Now, choose the **Direction** button in the **Direction2** area and select the right vertical edge of the top face of the base feature to define the second direction of pattern.

You will notice that another green arrow is displayed on the right vertical edge of the top face and the direction of this edge is downwards from the existing hole. Therefore, you need to reverse the second direction of pattern.

30. Choose the **Flip** button in the **Direction2** area to reverse the second direction of pattern.

31. Enter **20** as the value in the **Spacing** edit box in **Direction2** area.

32. Choose the **OK** button to create the hole pattern and exit the dialog box. You will notice that three new instances of the hole are created.

This completes the Base component. The final base component is shown in Figure 15-11.

32. Save the component with the name given below:

\PersonalProject\c15\Wheel Support**Base.ipt**

If the Wheel Support directory is not created, you can create it by using the **Create New Folder** button in the **Save As** dialog box.

33. Close the current file by choosing **File > Close** from the menu bar.

Figure 15-10 *Component after creating the hole*   *Figure 15-11* *Final Base component*

Creating the Support

The next component that needs to be created is the Support. The assembly requires two instances of the Support. You will create one file and place it twice in the assembly file so that there are two instances of the Support in the assembly file.

1. Choose **New** from the **Standard** toolbar to display the **Open** dialog box.

2. Choose the **Metric** tab and then double-click on the **Standard (mm).ipt** file to open a new metric standard part file.

    As mentioned earlier, by default the sketching environment is activated when you open a new part file. However, the sketch for the base feature of the Support will not be created on the default XY plane that is selected when you open a new part file. You need to exit the sketching environment and then define a new sketch plane on the XZ plane.

3. Choose **Return** from the **Command Bar** to exit the sketching environment and then right-click on the graphics screen to display the shortcut menu. Choose **Isometric View** from the shortcut menu to change the current view to the Isometric view. Now, click on the + sign located on the left of the **Origin** directory in the browser. You will notice that the three default planes, the three default axes, and the center point is displayed.

4. Choose **Sketch** from the **Command Bar** and then select the XZ plane from the browser. The sketching environment will be activated but it will not be parallel to the screen of the monitor. In order to draw the sketch, you need to reorient the sketching plane such that the sketching plane is parallel to the screen of the monitor.

5. Choose the **Rotate** button from the **Standard** toolbar and then press the SPACEBAR to activate the common views option.

    You will notice that a cube is displayed with an arrow on all the faces and all the corners. Two of the faces of the cube are parallel to the XZ plane. You need to select the arrow that is in the middle of the front face that is parallel to the XZ plane in order to reorient the sketching plane and make it parallel to the screen of the monitor.

6. Select the arrow that is in the middle of the front face of the cube that is parallel to the XZ plane. The sketching plane will be reoriented.

7. Draw the sketch for the base feature and then add the required constraints and dimensions to it as shown in Figure 15-12. The grid lines and the axes are not displayed in this figure for clarity.

8. Exit the sketching environment and then choose **Extrude** from the **Features** panel bar. Since there is only one unconsumed sketch on the graphics screen, it will be selected and highlighted.

9. Enter **40** as the value in the edit box provided in the **Extents** area and then choose **OK** to create the feature. The extruded feature is shown in Figure 15-13.

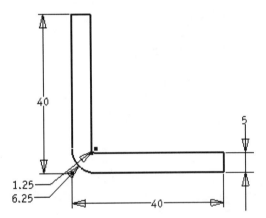

Figure 15-12 Sketch for the base of the Support

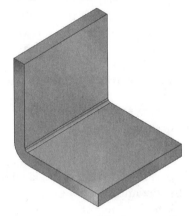

Figure 15-13 Model after extruding

10. Now, you need to create holes on the horizontal and the vertical face. First, the two holes on the horizontal face will be created. Choose **Sketch** from the **Command Bar** and define a new sketching plane on the top horizontal face of the base feature. The sketching environment will be activated.

11. Place two hole centers on the sketching plane and add the required constraints and dimensions to it as shown in Figure 15-14. In this sketch, the **Vertical** constraint is added to the two hole centers that will force them to be in the same vertical line. Therefore, when you add the 15 dimension to one of the hole centers, the other one is also driven to the same value.

12. Exit the sketching environment and choose **Hole** from the **Features** panel bar. The two hole centers will be automatically selected as the center points of the holes.

13. Select **Through All** from the drop-down list provided in the **Termination** area and then

enter **5** as the value of the diameter of the holes in the preview window. You will notice that the diameter of the preview of the holes on the graphics screen is also modified

14. Choose **OK** to create the holes, see Figure 15-15.

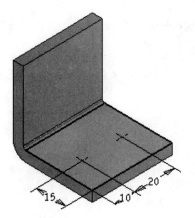

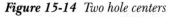

Figure 15-14 *Two hole centers*

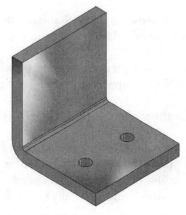

Figure 15-15 *Holes created on the hole center*

15. Similarly, create the hole on the vertical face of the base feature. The final model of the Support is shown in Figure 15-16.

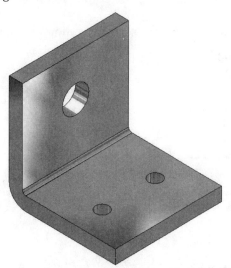

Figure 15-16 *Final model of the Support*

16. Save this model with the name given below:

\PersonalProject\c15\Wheel Support**Support.ipt**

17. Close this window by choosing **File > Close** from the menu bar.

Creating the Wheel

The next component that needs to be created is the Wheel. This is a revolved component and the sketch for this component will be created on the default XY plane. After creating the sketch, it will be revolved through an angle of 360°.

1. Choose **New** from the **Standard** toolbar and then choose the **Metric** tab to display the metric standard files.

2. Double-click on the **Standard (mm).ipt** file to open a new metric standard part file. The sketching environment will be activated.

3. Draw the sketch for the revolved feature and then draw a center line to add the dimensions.

4. Add the dimensions to the sketch as shown in Figure 15-17. The linear diameter dimensions are added by selecting the center line first and then selecting the line to which the linear diameter dimensions needs to be added. You will notice that the linear diameter dimension is automatically created.

5. Change the current view to the Isometric view and then exit the sketching environment. Choose **Revolve** from the **Features** panel bar to display the **Revolve** dialog box. You will notice that the sketch is selected to be revolved and the axis of revolution is the center line that you created to apply the linear diameter dimensions.

6. Choose **OK** to create the revolved component as shown in Figure 15-18.

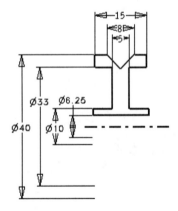

Figure 15-17 *Dimensioned sketch of the Wheel*

Figure 15-18 *Component after revolving*

7. Save the model with the name given below:

   \PersonalProject\c15\Wheel Support**Wheel.ipt**

8. Close the file by choosing **File > Close** from the menu bar.

Creating the Remaining Components

Similarly, create the remaining components in the separate part files. Save all the files in the \PersonalProject\c15**Wheel Support** folder.

Assembling the Components

In Autodesk Inventor, the components are assembled in the assembly file and these files are saved in the .iam format. Therefore, to assemble the components, you first need to open a new assembly file.

1. Choose **New** from the **Standard** toolbar to invoke the **Open** dialog box. Choose the **Metric** tab and then double-click on the **Standard (mm).iam** file to open a new metric standard assembly file.

    You will notice that very few tools are available in the **Assembly** panel bar. This is because no component is available in the assembly file. Once you place some components or create some components in the assembly file, other tools in the **Assembly** panel bar will be available.

2. Choose **Place Components** from the **Assembly** panel bar to invoke the **Open** dialog box. You will notice that the **Wheel Support** directory is opened by default in the **Look in** drop-down list and all the components of the Wheel Support assembly are displayed in the dialog box.

3. Double-click on the **Base.ipt** file to place this component in the assembly file.

    As soon as you double-click on the file, the **Open** dialog box will be closed and you will return to the graphics screen. Notice that one instance of the Base is placed in the current file and you are prompted to place another instance of the component. Also, the current view will be changed to the Isometric view.

4. Right-click on the graphics screen and choose **Done** from the shortcut menu. Again choose **Place Component** from the **Assembly** panel bar to invoke the **Open** dialog box. Double-click on the **Support.ipt** file and place one instance of the Support at a location where it does not interfere with the Base.

5. Choose the down arrow on the right of the **Shaded Display** button in the **Standard** toolbar and choose **Wireframe** display to turn the display of the components to wireframe.

6. Choose the **Zoom All** button from the **Standard** toolbar to increase the drawing display area.

7. Choose **Place Constraint** from the **Assembly** panel bar to invoke the **Place Constraint** dialog box.

    By default, the **Mate** constraint button is chosen in the **Type** area of the **Assembly** tab. The Support will be assembled with the Base by using the **Insert** constraint. Therefore, you need to choose the button of the **Insert** constraint from the **Type** area.

8. Choose the **Insert** button from the type area to invoke the **Insert** constraint. Select the lower face of the upper hole on the horizontal face of the Support as the first face to apply the constraint as shown in Figure 15-19.

9. Select the top face of the hole close to the top right corner of the Base as the second face to apply the constraint, see Figure 15-19.

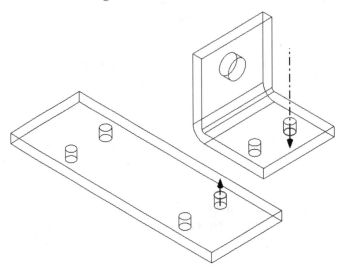

*Figure 15-19 Selecting the faces to apply the **Insert** constraint*

As soon as you select the second face to apply the constraint, the Support will move from its current location and assemble with the Base. This is because the **Show Preview** check box is selected by default. If this check box is cleared, the component will not move until you choose **Apply**.

10. Choose **Apply** to apply the constraint. The Support will be assembled with the Base. However, you need to apply one more constraint in order to remove all the degrees of freedom.

11. Select the **Pick part first** check box from the **Selections** area. This check box allows you to select the component first and then select the face to apply the constraint.

12. Move the cursor over the Support and select it when the component turns red. Now, move the cursor close to the lower face of the lower hole on the Support and when it is highlighted, select it as the first face to apply the constraint.

13. Move the cursor over the Base and select it when it turns red. Now, move the cursor close to the upper face of the hole on the lower right corner of the Base and select it as the second face to apply the constraint.

14. Choose **Apply** to apply the constraint and then choose **Cancel** to close the dialog box. Change the display type back to shaded. The assembly is shown in Figure 15-20.

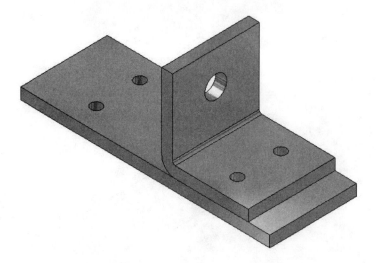

Figure 15-20 *Assembly of the Base and the Support*

15. Now, right-click on **Support.ipt:1** in the browser and choose the **Visibility** option to turn off the display of this component. Change the display type to wireframe.

16. Choose **Place Component** from the **Assembly** panel bar and place one more instance of the **Support** at a location where it does not interfere with the Base.

17. Choose **Place Constraint** from the **Assembly** panel bar to invoke the **Place Constraint** dialog box. Choose the **Insert** button from the **Type** area and make sure the **Select part first** check box in the **Selections** area is cleared.

18. Select the lower face of the upper hole on the Support as the first face to apply the constraint, see Figure 15-21.

19. Select the upper face of the hole close to the lower left corner of the Base as the second face to apply the constraint, see Figure 15-21.

20. Choose the **Apply** button to apply the constraint. Now, select the lower face of the lower hole on the Support as the first face to apply the constraint, see Figure 15-22.

21. Select the upper face of the hole close to the upper left corner of the Base as the second face to apply the constraint, see Figure 15-22.

22. Choose the **Apply** button to apply the constraint and then choose the **Cancel** button to close the dialog box.

23. Using the browser, turn on the visibility of **Support.ipt:1**.

Next, you need to assemble the Bushing with the Supports. Two instances of the Bushing

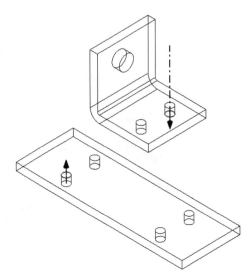

Figure 15-21 *Selecting the faces to apply the **Insert** constraint*

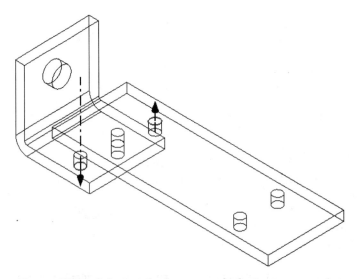

Figure 15-22 *Selecting the faces to apply the **Insert** constraint*

are required to be assembled with the two Supports and therefore, you need to place two
instances of the Bushing.

24. Choose **Place Component** from the **Assembly** panel bar and place two instances of the
Bushing at locations where they do not interfere with the assembled components.

25. Choose **Place Constraint** from the **Assembly** panel bar to invoke the **Place Constraint**
dialog box. Choose the **Insert** button from the **Type** area and then select the top face of
one of the Bushing as the first face to apply the constraint, see Figure 15-23.

26. Select the back face of the hole on the vertical face of the Base as the second face to apply the constraint, see Figure 15-23.

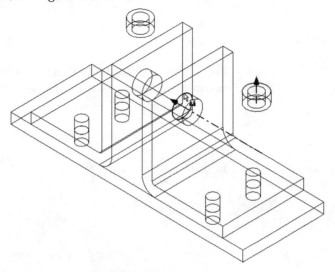

*Figure 15-23 Selecting the faces to apply the **Insert** constraint*

27. Now, choose the **Aligned** button from the **Solution** area to align the two components. This will insert the Bushing inside the hole on the vertical face of the Base. Similarly, assemble the other Bushing inside the hole on the vertical face of the other Support. Change the display type to shaded. The assembly after assembling the two Bushings is shown in Figure 15-24.

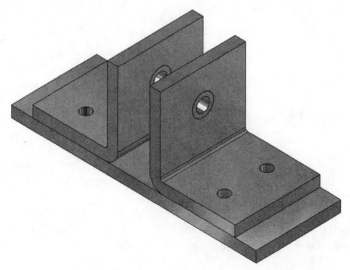

Figure 15-24 Assembly after assembling the two Bushings

Next, you will assemble the Wheel. You can assemble the Wheel with one of the Bushings and so you do not require the Supports to assemble the Wheel. Therefore, you can turn off the display of the two Supports.

28. Turn off the visibility of the two Supports by using the browser. Now, choose **Place Component** from the **Assembly** panel bar and place one instance of the Wheel at a location where it does not interfere with the assembly.

29. Change the display type to wireframe and then choose **Place Constraint** from the **Assembly** panel bar to invoke the **Place Constraint** dialog box. Choose the **Insert** button from the **Type** area.

30. Select the right face of the Wheel as the first face to apply the constraint, see Figure 15-25.

31. Select the left face of the right Bushing as the second face to apply the constraint, see Figure 15-25.

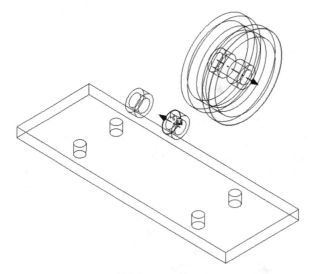

*Figure 15-25 Selecting the faces to apply the **Insert** constraint*

32. Choose the **Apply** button to apply the constraint and then choose **Cancel** to close the dialog box.

    Now you will assemble one of the Bolts and the remaining three instances of the Bolts will be assembled by using the associative pattern. To create the associative patter, you will use the rectangular pattern of holes on the Base.

33. Turn off the display of the Wheel and both the Bushings and then turn on the display of **Support.ipt:2** by using the browser. This is the Support that is assembled on the left side of the Base.

34. Choose **Place Component** from the **Assembly** panel bar and place one instance of the Bolt at a location where it does not interfere with the assembly.

35. Choose **Place Constraint** from the **Assembly** panel bar to invoke the **Place Constraint** dialog box and then choose the **Insert** button from the **Type** area.

36. Select the start face of the cylindrical feature of the Bolt as the first face to apply the constraint, see Figure 15-26.

37. Select the top face of the lower hole on the Support as the second face to apply the constraint, see Figure 15-26.

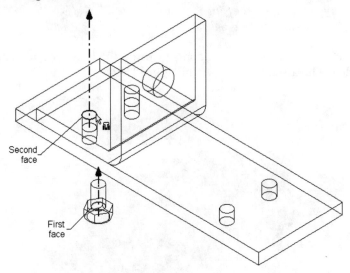

*Figure 15-26 Selecting the faces to apply the **Insert** constraint*

38. Choose the **Apply** button to apply the constraint and then choose **Cancel** to close the dialog box.

39. The remaining three instances of the Bolt will be assembled by using the **Pattern Component** tool. Choose **Pattern Component** from the **Assembly** panel bar to invoke the **Pattern Component** dialog box. You will be prompted to select the component to pattern.

40. Select the Bolt that was assembled with the Support. Now, choose the **Associated Feature Pattern** button available in the **Feature Pattern Select** area of the **Associative** tab. You will be prompted to select the feature pattern to associate to.

    To create the pattern of the component, you can use any of the instance of the hole created by using the rectangular pattern. Remember that you cannot select the original instance of the hole as this hole was created and not patterned.

41. Move the cursor close to the lower right hole on the Base.

    As soon as you move the cursor over the lower right hole, the three instances of the hole created by using the rectangular pattern will be highlighted and displayed with a red outline.

42. Select the lower right hole on the Base when it is highlighted and displayed with a red outline. As soon as you select the hole, three instance of the Bolts will be placed on the three holes on the Base. Choose **OK** to close the **Pattern Component** dialog box.

Tip. *In step 33, if you turned on the display of the first support (**Support.ipt:1**) and assembled the Bolt with it, then when you create the pattern of the components, the Bolts will be assembled toward the right side of the Base instead of the left side. This is because the pattern of the hole in the Base was originally created from left to right. Therefore, the pattern of the component will also be created from left to right. In this case the Bolts will be placed outside the Base on the right side.*

43. Turn on the display of all the components by using the browser and change the display type to shaded. The assembly is shown in Figure 15-27.

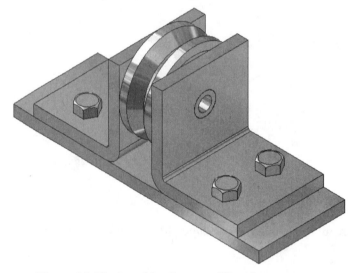

Figure 15-27 Assembly after assembling the components

Note
*The four Bolts will be stored inside **Component Pattern 1** in the browser. If you click on the + sign located on the left of **Component Pattern 1** in the browser, the four Bolts will be displayed as **Element:1**, **Element:2**, **Element:3**, and **Element:4**.*

Tip. *If you want to turn off the visibility of a component that is assembled by using the **Pattern Component** tool, click on the + sign located on the left of **Component Pattern** in the browser to display the elements in the pattern. Then click on the + sign located on the left of the element whose visibility you want to turn off. The name of the component will be displayed. Now, right-click on the name of the component and choose **Visibility** from the shortcut menu.*

44. Similarly, assemble the two Washers, the Shoulder Screw, and the Nut, in the same sequence. The final Wheel Support assembly is shown in Figure 15-28.

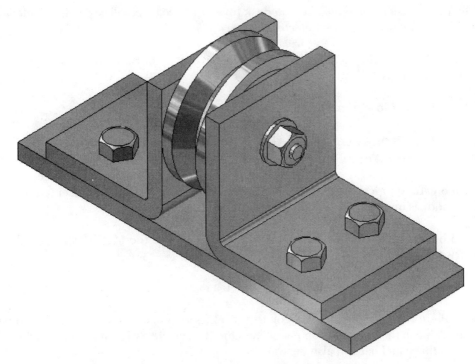

Figure 15-28 *Final Wheel Support assembly*

45. Save the assembly with the name given below:

\PersonalProject\c15\Wheel Support**Wheel Support.iam**

Checking the Assembly for Interference

To make sure there is no interference of the components in the assembly, you need to check the assembly for interference.

1. Choose **Tools > Analyze Interference** from the menu bar to display the **Interference Analysis** dialog box.

   The **Define Set # 1** button is chosen by default and you will be prompted to select the component to add to select set.

2. Select the Base from the graphics window as the component in set 1. The Base will be displayed with a blue outline.

3. Now, choose the **Define Set # 2** button. You will notice that the Base is now displayed with a green outline and you are prompted to select the component to add to select set.

4. Select all the remaining components of the assembly from the graphics window or from the browser and then choose **OK**.

5. After the analysis is complete, the **Autodesk Inventor** dialog box will be displayed informing you that no interference was detected.

6. Choose **OK** in this dialog box and then choose **Save** from the **Standard** toolbar to save the Wheel Support assembly.

7. Choose **File > Close** from the menu bar to close the assembly file.

Creating the Presentation of the Wheel Support Assembly

Next, you need to create the presentation of the Wheel Support assembly. The presentation will include assembling and disassembling of the components of the Wheel Support assembly. In Autodesk Inventor, the presentations are created in the **Presentation** mode. This mode is invoked by opening a presentation file.

1. Choose **New** from the **Standard** toolbar and then choose the **Metric** tab to display the metric templates.

2. Double-click on the **Standard.ipn** file to open a metric standard presentation file.

    Since there is no presentation view on the graphics screen, only the **Create View** tool will be available in the **Presentation** panel bar. Once you create a presentation view, the other tools in this panel bar will also be available.

3. Choose **Create View** from the **Presentation** panel bar to invoke the **Select Assembly** dialog box.

4. Choose the **Explore Directories** button available on the right of the **File** edit box in the **Assembly** area to display the **Open** dialog box.

    Since the Wheel Support directory is current, it will be displayed in the **Look in** drop-down list and the **Wheel Support.iam** file will be displayed in this dialog box.

5. Double-click on the **Wheel Support.iam** file. The name and the path of the file will be displayed in the **File** edit box. Also, the current design view associated with it will be displayed in the **Design View** drop-down list.

6. Accept the remaining default options and choose **OK** to create the presentation view, see Figure 15-29. When you create a presentation view, **Explosion1** is displayed in the browser below the **Presentation1** heading.

8. Click on the + sign located on the left of **Explosion1** to display **Wheel Support.iam**. Click on the + sign located on the left of **Wheel Support.iam** to display all the components of the assembly in the browser.

    Notice that the components are displayed in the same sequence in which they were placed in the assembly file. If you move the cursor over any component in the browser, it will be highlighted on the graphics screen.

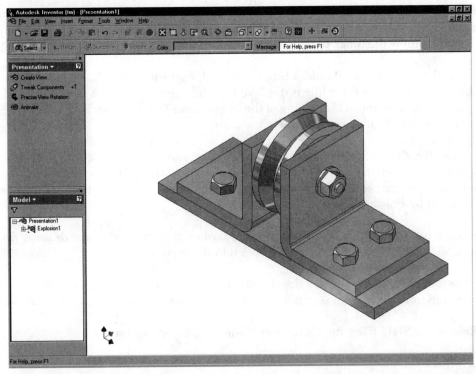

Figure 15-29 *Presentation file with the presentation view of the Wheel Support assembly*

7. Choose **Tweak Component** from the **Presentation** panel bar to invoke the **Tweak Component** dialog box.

   The **Direction** button in the **Create Tweak** area is chosen by default and you are prompted to select the direction for tweak.

8. Move the cursor close to the longer edge of the Base. This edge is along the direction displayed by the red arrow in the coordinate system icon available on the lower left corner of the graphics screen.

9. As soon as you move the cursor close to the edge, it will turn red in color. Select the edge when it turns red in color.

   The selected edge will turn blue in color and a triad is displayed with three axes. The Z axis of the triad is displayed in blue color. This suggests that the current direction of tweak is along the Z axis of the triad. Also, notice that the **Components** button in the **Create Tweak** area will be chosen and you are prompted to select the components to tweak.

10. From the browser, select Shoulder Screw as the component to tweak. It will now be displayed with a blue outline. Make sure the **Display Trails** check box in the **Create Tweak** area is selected.

11. Choose the **X** button from the **Transformations** area and then enter **-75** as the value in the edit box provided on the right of the **Rotational** radio button. Now, choose the **Apply** button to apply the tweak to the component.

    You will notice that the Shoulder Screw is moved to a distance of 75 mm in the backward direction and a blue color line is displayed on the component. This line is the trail that displays the direction of assembling of the component. The Shoulder Screw is still selected and is displayed with a blue outline.

12. Choose the **Z** button from the **Transformations** area and then enter **20** as the value in the edit box provided in this area. Choose the **Apply** button provided on the right of the edit box to apply the tweak to the component. The Shoulder Screw will move in the upward direction by a distance of 20 mm.

13. Choose the **Zoom All** button from the **Standard** toolbar to increase the drawing display area so that the Shoulder Screw is displayed in the current view.

14. Press and hold the SHIFT key down and select Shoulder Screw. This component will be removed from the current selection set and will no more be displayed with a blue outline.

15. Release the SHIFT key and then select Washer.ipt:1 from the browser.

Note
It is assumed that Washer.ipt:1 is the Washer that is assembled with the left Support. In case you have assembled Washer.ipt:1 with the right Support, you need to select Washer.ipt:2 from the browser. The selected instance of the Washer will be displayed with a blue outline. Since the Washer assembled with the left Support will not be visible in the current display, you can change the display to wireframe. This way you can confirm that the selected component is correct.

16. Choose the **X** button from the **Transformations** area and then enter **-40** as the value in the edit box provided in this area. Now, choose the **Apply** button available on the right of the edit box to apply the tweak value to the component.

    The Washer will move by a distance of 40 mm toward the left side of the assembly.

17. Press and hold the SHIFT key down and from the graphics screen select the Washer that is moved. The Washer is removed from the selection set and is no more displayed with a blue outline.

18. Release the SHIFT key and then select Bushing.ipt:1 from the browser. It is assumed that this is the Bushing that is assembled with the left Support. In case this is not the Bushing that is assembled with the Support in your assembly, select the other Bushing and remove this from the selected set.

19. The **X** button is already selected in the **Transformations** area. Enter **-30** as the value in the edit box provided in this area and then choose the **Apply** button available on the right of the edit box. The Bushing will move toward left by a distance of 30 mm.

20. Remove the Bushing from the selection set and then select the Nut from the graphics screen. The selected component will be displayed with a blue outline.

21. Enter **40** as the value in the edit box provided in the **Transformations** area and then choose the **Apply** button. The Nut will move to a distance of 40 mm toward the right of the assembly.

22. Remove the Nut from the selection set and then from the graphics screen select the Washer that is assembled with the right Support.

23. Enter **30** as the value in the edit box and then choose the **Apply** button. The Washer will move to a distance of 30 mm toward the right of the assembly.

24. Remove the Washer from the current selection set and select the Bushing that is assembled inside the right Support. Enter **20** as the value in the edit box and then choose the **Apply** button. The Bushing will move to a distance of 20 mm toward the right of the assembly.

25. Remove the Bushing from the current selection set and then select all the four Bolts from the browser. The four Bolts will be displayed with a blue outline.

26. Choose the **Z** button from the **Transformations** area. Enter **15** as the value in the edit box and then choose the **Apply** button. The four Bolts will move to a distance of 15 mm in upward direction.

27. Remove the four Bolts from the current selection set and then select the Base from the graphics screen. Enter **-15** as the value in the edit box and then choose the **Apply** button. The assembly after tweaking these components is shown in Figure 15-30.

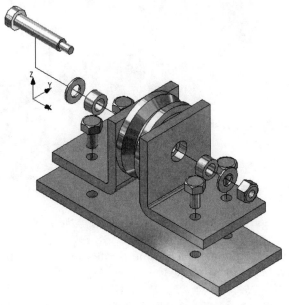

Figure 15-30 Tweaked assembly

28. Remove the Base from the current selection set and then select the right Support, the two Bolts on the right, the Nut, the Bushing on the right, and the Washer on the right from the graphics screen. All the selected components will be displayed with a blue outline.

29. Choose the **X** button from the **Transformations** area. Enter **25** as the value in the edit box and then choose the **Apply** button. All the selected components will move toward right by a distance of 25 mm.

30. Remove all the components from the current selection set and then select the Support, two Bolts, Washer, Bushing, and the Shoulder Screw that are on the left of the Wheel. The selected components will be displayed with a blue outline.

31. Enter **-25** as the value in the edit box and then choose the **Apply** button. The selected components will move toward the left by a distance of 25 mm.

32. Choose **Close** in the **Tweak Components** dialog box to close the dialog box. Choose the **Zoom All** button from the **Standard** toolbar. The assembly after tweaking all the components is shown in Figure 15-31.

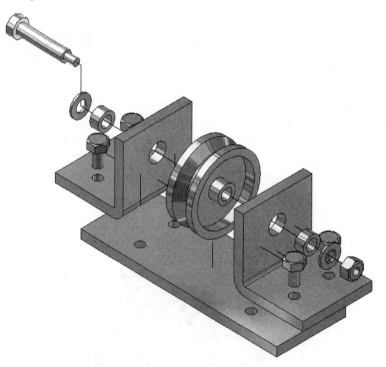

Figure 15-31 Assembly after tweaking the assembly

Next, you need to animate the assembly and create the avi file. The tweaked assembly is animated by using the **Animate** tool.

33. Choose **Animate** from the **Assembly** panel bar to invoke the **Animation** dialog box.

34. Choose the **Record** button from the **Motion** area. The **Save As** dialog box will be displayed in which you can enter the name of the avi file.

35. Enter **Wheel Support** in the **File name** edit box of the **Save As** dialog box and then choose the **Save** button. As soon as you choose the **Save** button, the **Video Compression** dialog box will be displayed.

36. Accept the default options in the **Video Compression** dialog box and choose **OK** to close this dialog box.

37. You will return to the Autodesk Inventor window. Make sure the **Minimize dialog during recording** check box in the **Motion** area is selected. Now, choose the **Auto Reverse** button to start creating the avi file of the animation.

    You will notice that as soon as you choose the **Auto Reverse** button, the **Animation** dialog box will be minimized and the animation of the assembly will start. After the animation is completed, the **Animation** dialog box will be restored on the screen.

38. Choose the **Cancel** button to close the **Animation** dialog box.

 Note
You can view the avi files by using the Windows Media Player.

39. Save the presentation file with the name given below:

    \PersonalProject\c15\Wheel Support**Wheel Support.ipn**

40. Choose **File > Close** to close the presentation file.

Generating the Drawing Views

In Autodesk Inventor, the drawing views are generated in the **Drawing** mode. Autodesk Inventor allows you to select the sheet of the predefined drafting standards for generating the drawing views.

1. Choose the **New** button from the **Standard** toolbar to invoke the **Open** dialog box. Choose the **Metric** tab to display the metric standard files.

2. Double-click on the **ISO.idw** file to open an ISO standard drawing file.

    Before you start generating the drawing views, you need to make some changes in the default standard of this file.

3. Choose **Format > Standards** from the menu bar to invoke the **Drafting Standards** dialog box. Choose the **More** button provided on the lower right corner of the dialog box if the dialog box is not already expanded.

4. In the **Common** tab, click on the **Line Weight** field of the **Visible Edges** row. The field will

be converted into a drop-down list. Select **1.00 mm** from the drop-down list.

5. Choose the **Third angle of projection** button from the **Projection** area to change the projection type to third angle.

6. Choose the **Sheet** tab to display the options related to the sheet. Choose the **Sheet** button in the **Colors** area. The **Color** dialog box will be displayed.

7. Select white color from this dialog box and then choose **OK**. You will notice that the color of the **Sheet** button is changed to white. Choose **Apply** and then choose **OK**. The color of the drawing sheet will change to white.

8. Choose **Create View** from the **Drawing Management** panel bar to invoke the **Create View** dialog box.

9. Choose the **Explore Directories** button available on the right of the **File** drop-down list in the **Component** dialog box. The **Open** dialog box will be displayed. The **Wheel Support** directory will be opened and displayed in the **Look in** drop-down list.

10. Select **Assembly Files (*.iam)** from the **Files of type** drop-down list. The **Wheel Support.iam** file will be displayed.

11. Double-click on the **Wheel Support.iam** file. The name and the path of the selected file will be displayed in the **File** drop-down list. The preview of the assembly will be attached to the cursor and it will move as you move the cursor on the sheet.

12. Select **Front** from the list box available in the **View** area and enter **1.25** as the value in the **Scale** edit box.

13. Specify the view placement point close to the top right corner of the drawing sheet. This will place the top view of the assembly. The drawing sheet after generating the top view is shown in Figure 15-32.

14. Double-click on the top view to display the **Edit View** dialog box.

15. Select the **Tangent Edges** check box in the **Style** area to display the tangent edges on all the drawing views. Choose **OK** to exit the dialog box.

16. Move the cursor over the previous view. You will notice that a red rectangle of dotted lines is displayed. When the red dotted rectangle appears, right-click on the drawing view to display the shortcut menu.

17. Choose **Create View > Projected** from the shortcut menu.

18. Now, move the cursor downwards. You will notice that the preview of the front view is attached to the cursor.

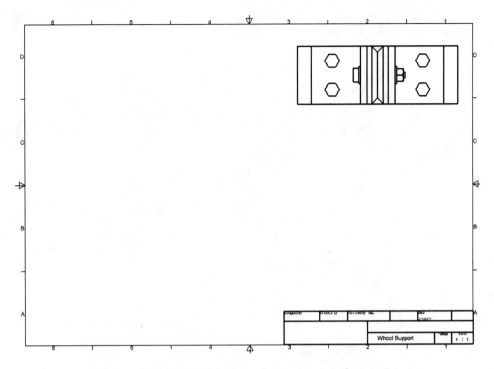

Figure 15-32 Drawing sheet after generating the top view

19. Specify the location of the drawing view below the top view as shown in Figure 15-33. The drawing view that is generated is the front view of the assembly. After placing the view, move the cursor toward the left side. You will notice that a preview of another view is attached to the cursor. But the next view needs to be generated by using the front view as the parent view, therefore, you will exit the current sequence of view generation.

20. Right-click to display the shortcut menu and then choose **Create** to create the view.

21. Move the cursor over the front view and when the red dotted rectangle appears, right-click to display the shortcut menu.

22. Choose **Create View > Projected** from the shortcut menu. Move the cursor toward the left of the sheet. You will notice that the preview of the left side view is attached to the cursor. Specify the location of the left side view on the left of the front view as shown in Figure 15-33.

23. Now, move the cursor toward the top left corner of the sheet. You will notice that the preview of the isometric view is attached to the cursor. Specify the location of the isometric view close to the top right corner of the sheet, see Figure 15-33.

24. Right-click and choose **Create** from the shortcut menu to create both the projected views. The drawing sheet after generating all the drawing views is shown in Figure 15-33.

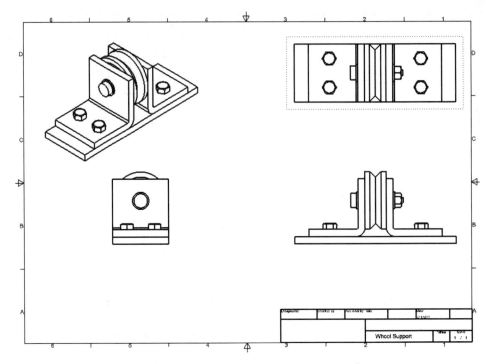

Figure 15-33 *Drawing sheet after generating all the views*

Next, you need to place the parts list and the balloons in the drawing sheet. The parts list will be placed on the lower left corner of the sheet and the balloons will be placed in the isometric view.

25. Right-click anywhere on the **Drawing Management** panel bar to display the shortcut menu. Choose **Drawing Annotation** from the shortcut menu. You will notice that the **Drawing Management** panel bar is replaced by the **Drawing Annotation** panel bar.

26. Choose **Parts List** from the **Drawing Annotation** panel bar and then select the isometric view as the reference view to place the parts list.

    As soon as you select the isometric view, the **Parts List - Item Numbering** dialog box will be displayed.

27. Select the default options from this dialog box and choose **OK**. You will notice that the upper right corner of the parts list is attached to the cursor.

28. Place the parts list close to the lower left corner of the drawing sheet.

    Notice that the sequence of the components in the parts list is the same in which the components were assembled in the assembly file. However, the parts list is not what is required and so you need to modify the parts list.

29. Double-click on the parts list to display the **Edit Parts List** dialog box.

30. Move the cursor over the heading **PART NUMBER**. The cursor is replaced by an arrow that points in the downward direction.

31. Press the left mouse button when the arrow is displayed. You will notice that all the fields in the **PART NUMBER** column are selected and displayed with a black background.

32. Now, choose the **More** button available on the lower right corner of the dialog box. Enter the name of the column as **NAME** in the **Name** edit box in the **Column Properties** area.

33. Choose the **Center** button available on the right of **Data Alignment**. This will centrally align the text in all the fields in the **NAME** column.

34. Next, move the cursor over the heading **DESCRIPTION** and left click when the cursor is replaced by the arrow to select this column. Enter the name of this column as **MATERIAL** in the **Name** edit box of the **Column Properties** area and choose the **Center** button available on the right of **Data Alignment**.

35. Now, one by one enter the material corresponding to the component in the fields provided below the **MATERIAL** column.

36. After entering the material in the fields, choose **OK** to close the **Edit Parts List** dialog box. The edited parts list is shown in Figure 15-34.

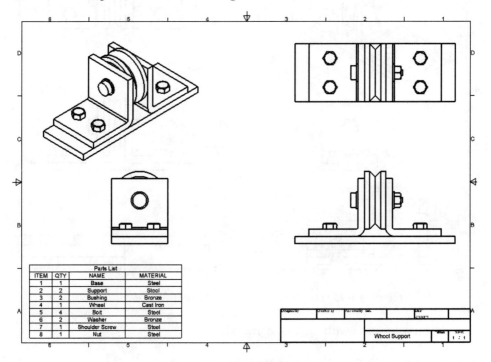

Figure 15-34 Drawing sheet with the drawing views and the part list

Finally, you will place the balloons in the isometric view. You will place all the balloons and then remove the balloons that are not required.

37. Choose the down arrow available on the right of **Balloon** in the **Drawing Annotation** panel bar and choose **Balloon All**.

38. Move the cursor over the isometric view and select this view when the red color dotted rectangle is displayed.

    You will notice that the balloons will be attached to all the components but will not be attached to the two Washers and the Nut. This is because these components are not visible in the current view. You can add the balloon to the Nut in the front view.

39. Retain the balloons that are required and delete the remaining balloons. Drag the balloons to the proper location.

40. Choose the down arrow available on the right of **Balloon All** in the **Drawing Annotation** panel bar and choose **Balloon**. Now, place the balloon on the Nut in the front view. The final drawing sheet after attaching the balloons is shown in Figure 15-35.

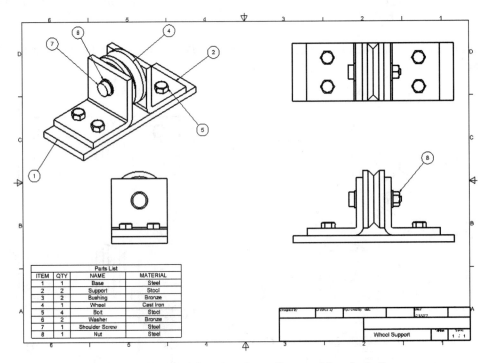

Figure 15-35 *Final drawing sheet after attaching the balloons*

41. Save the drawing sheet with the name given below:

\PersonalProject\c15\Wheel Support**Wheel Support.idw**

Project 1

Create all the components of the Bracket Support assembly and then assemble them as shown in Figure 15-36. The exploded view of the assembly is shown in Figure 15-37. After assembling the components, create a presentation for assembling and disassembling the components and record the animation in an avi file. Next, generate the following drawing views of the assembly:

1. Top view
2. Front view
3. Side view
4. Isometric view
5. Detailed view of the V-face of the Pulley

Use the JIS standard drawing sheet for generating the drawing views. After generating these views, add another sheet and then generate the Isometric view of the exploded view in that sheet. Add parts list and balloons to the exploded view in the second sheet. The parts list that needs to be added is shown in Figure 15-38. The dimensions of the components are given in Figure 15-39, Figure 15-40, Figure 15-41, and Figure 15-42.   **(Expected time: 3 Hrs 30 min)**

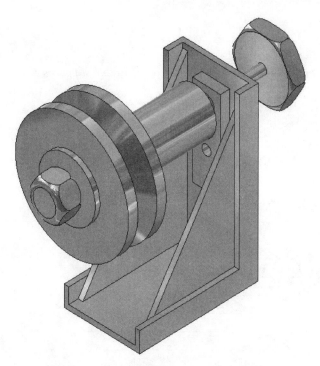

Figure 15-36 *Pulley Support assembly*

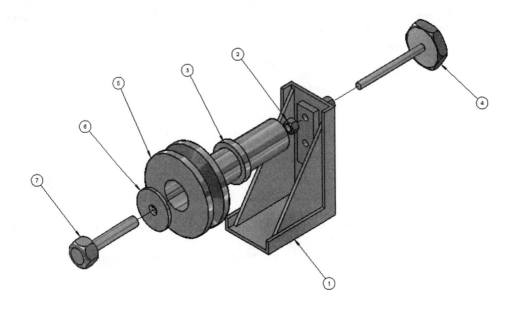

Figure 15-37 Exploded view of the Pulley Support assembly

PARTS LIST			
ITEM	QTY	NAME	MATERIAL
1	1	Bracket	Steel
2	2	Nut	Steel
3	1	Bushing	Steel
4	1	Turn Screw	Steel
5	1	Pulley	Steel
6	1	Washer	Steel
7	1	Cap Screw	Steel

Figure 15-38 Parts list for the Pulley Support assembly

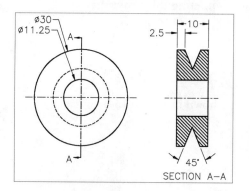

Figure 15-39 *Dimensions of the Pulley*

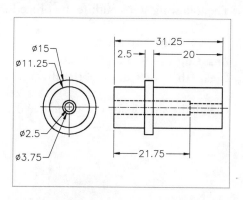

Figure 15-40 *Dimensions of the Bushing*

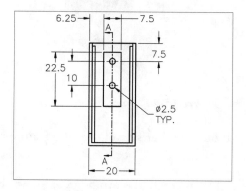

Figure 15-41a *Left side view of the Bracket*

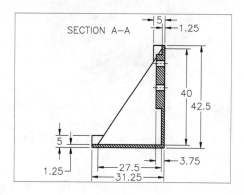

Figure 15-41b *Sectioned front view of the Bracket*

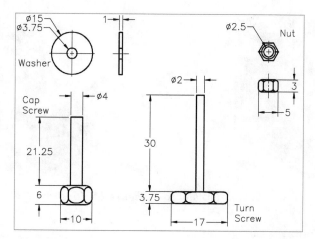

Figure 15-42 *Dimensions of the Washer, Cap Screw, Turn Screw, and Nut*

The following steps outline the procedure for completing this project:

Creating the Components
Creating the Bracket
1. Create the base feature of the Bracket as shown in Figure 15-43.

2. Create the shell feature and remove the faces as shown in Figure 15-44.

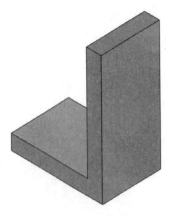

Figure 15-43 *Base feature of the Bracket*   **Figure 15-44** *Bracket after shelling*

3. Create one of the two braces and then mirror it on the other side of the base feature as shown in Figure 15-45.

4. Add the support feature to the base feature and then create the two holes as shown in Figure 15-46. This completes the Bracket part.

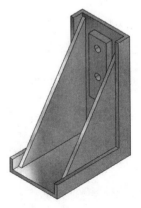

Figure 15-45 *Bracket after adding the two braces*   **Figure 15-46** *Bracket after adding the support*

Creating the Pulley
1. Draw the sketch for the Pulley as shown in Figure 15-47.

2. Revolve the sketch to create the Pulley as shown in Figure 15-48

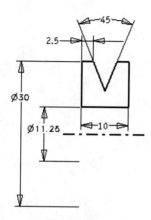

Figure 15-47 *Sketch of the Pulley*

Figure 15-48 *Model of the Pulley*

Creating the Bushing

1. Create the sketch for the Bushing as shown in Figure 15-49.

2. Revolve the sketch to create the Bushing and add the two holes as shown in Figure 15-50.

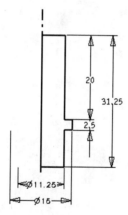

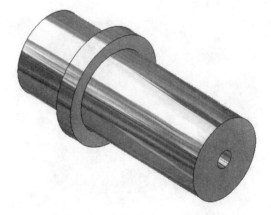

Figure 15-47 *Sketch of the Bushing*

Figure 15-48 *Model of the Bushing*

Creating the Turn Screw

1. Create the base of the head of the Turn Screw as shown in Figure 15-49.

2. Add fillets on both the planar faces of the base feature as shown in Figure 15-50.

Figure 15-49 *Base of the Turn Screw*   *Figure 15-50* *Base after adding fillets*

3. Define a new sketch plane on the top face of the base feature and then draw the circumscribed hexagon. The diameter of the circle in which the hexagon is inscribed should be equal to the diameter of the base feature. Extrude the sketch by using the **Intersect** option as shown in Figure 15-51.

4. Add the final feature on the top face as shown in Figure 15-52.

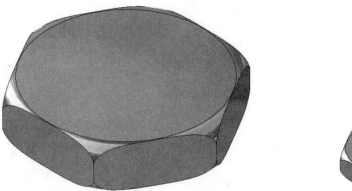

Figure 15-51 *After adding the intersect feature*   *Figure 15-52* *Final model of the Turn Screw*

Creating the Nut
1. Create the base of the Nut as shown in Figure 15-53.

2. Create the next intersect feature on the base feature and then add the hole as shown in Figure 15-54.

Creating the Remaining Components
Similarly, create the remaining components of the Pulley Support assembly.

Figure 15-53 Base feature of the Nut

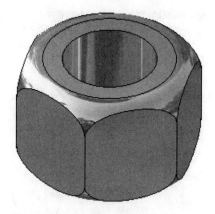

Figure 15-54 Final model of the Nut

Assembling the Components
Assembling the Bracket and the Nuts

1. Place one instance of the Bracket and two instances of the Nut in the assembly file.

2. Assemble one of the Nut with the hole on the right face of the Bracket as shown in Figure 15-55.

3. Assemble the second Nut with the hole on the support feature of the Bracket as shown in Figure 15-56.

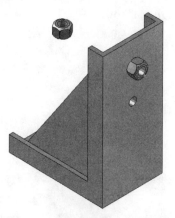

Figure 15-55 Assembly after assembling one of the two Nuts with the Bracket

Figure 15-56 Assembly after assembling both the Nuts with the Bracket

Assembling the Bushing

1. Assemble the Bushing with the Nut assembled with the support feature of the Bracket as shown in Figure 15-57.

Assembling the Turn Screw

1. Assemble the Turn Screw with the Nut assembled on the right face of the Bracket as shown in Figure 15-58. The offset distance is 5 mm.

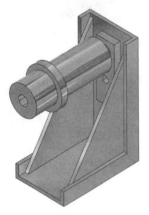

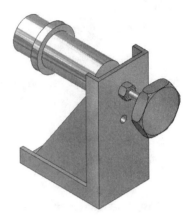

Figure 15-57 *Assembly after assembling the Bushing with the Nut*

Figure 15-58 *Assembly after assembling the Turn Screw with the Nut*

Assembling the Pulley

1. Turn off the visibility of the Turn Screw and the Nut on the right and then assemble the Pulley with the Bushing as shown in Figure 15-59.

Assembling the Washer

1. Assemble the Washer with the Pulley as shown in Figure 15-60.

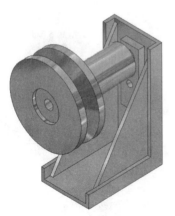

Figure 15-59 *Assembly after assembling the Pulley*

Figure 15-60 *Assembly after assembling the Washer with the Pulley*

Assembling the Cap Screw

1. Assemble the Cap Screw with the Washer. Turn on the display of the invisible components. The final assembly is shown in Figure 15-61. The offset distance is 5 mm.

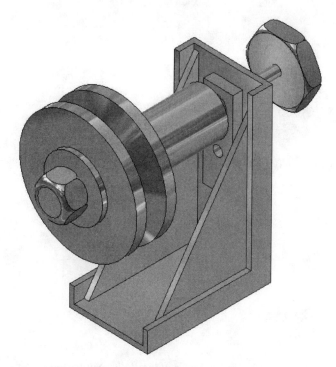

Figure 15-61 *Final Wheel Support assembly*

2. Save the assembly file with the name given below:

    \PersonalProject\c15\Pulley Assembly**Pulley Assembly.iam**

Creating the Presentation

1. Open a new presentation file and add the tweaks to the components.

2. Create the animation of the assembly and store the animation in an avi file with the following name:

    \PersonalProject\c15\Pulley Support**Pulley Support.avi**

3. The exploded assembly is shown in Figure 15-62. Save the presentation file with the name given below:

    \PersonalProject\c15\Pulley Support**Pulley Support.ipn**

Generating the Drawing Views

1. Open a new JIS standard drawing file and then generate the top view, front view, side view, isometric view, and the detailed view as shown in Figure 15-63. The scale of the top view is 3. The remaining views are based on the top view.

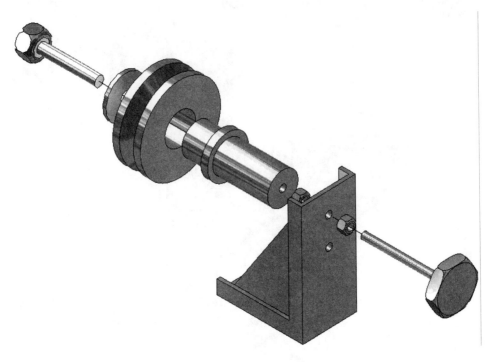

Figure 15-62 *Tweaked view of the Pulley Support assembly*

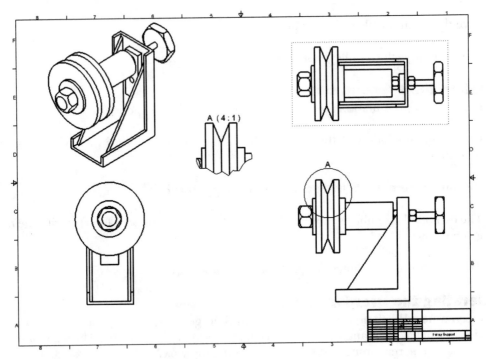

Figure 15-63 *Drawing views in the first sheet*

2. Insert a new sheet and generate the isometric view of the presentation file.

3. Add the parts list and the balloons to the components as shown in Figure 15-64.

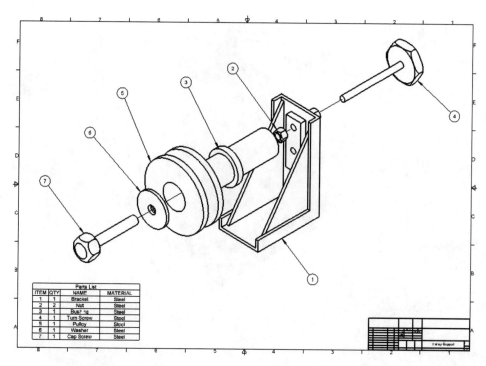

Parts List			
ITEM	QTY	NAME	MATERIAL
1	1	Bracket	Steel
2	2	Nut	Steel
3	1	Bushing	Steel
4	1	Turn Screw	Steel
5	1	Pulley	Steel
6	1	Washer	Steel
7	1	Cap Screw	Steel

Figure 15-64 Exploded view of the Pulley Support assembly with the parts list and the balloons

4. Save the drawing sheet with the name given below:

\PersonalProject\c15\Pulley Support**Pulley Support.idw**

Project 2

Create all the components of the Pipe Vice assembly and then assemble them as shown in Figure 15-65. The exploded view of the assembly is shown in Figure 15-66. The dimensions of the components of the assembly are shown in Figure 15-67, Figure 15-68, and Figure 15-69. After creating the assembly, create a presentation for moving and rotating the components of the assembly. Also, generate the following drawing views in the JIS standard drawing sheet:

1. Top view
2. Front view
3. Side view
4. Isometric view
5. Detailed view of the teeth of the Jaw   **(Expected time: 3 Hrs)**

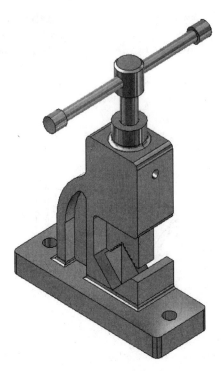

Figure 15-65 *Pipe Vice assembly*

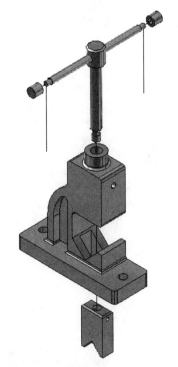

Figure 15-66 *Exploded view of the Pipe Vice assembly*

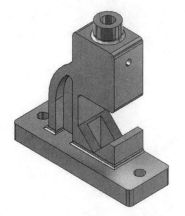

Figure 15-67a *Solid model of the Base*

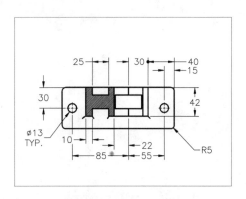

Figure 15-67b *Sectioned top view of the Base*

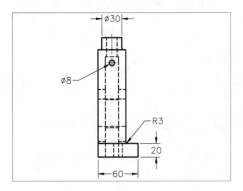

Figure 15-67c *Side view of the Base*

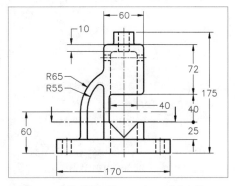

Figure 15-67d *Front view of the Base*

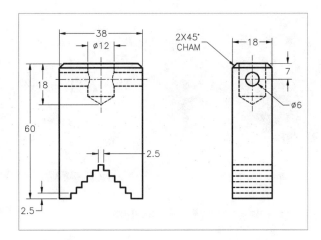

Figure 15-68 *Dimensions of the Movable Jaw*

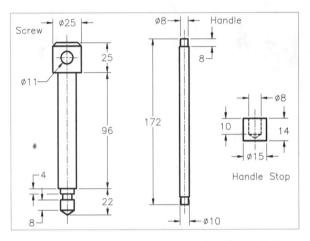

Figure 15-69 *Dimensions of the Screw, Handle, and the Handle Stop*

The following steps outline the procedure for completing this project.

Creating the Components
Creating the Base

1. Create the base feature of the Base and then add the fillets as shown in Figure 15-70.

2. Define a new sketching plane on the back face of the base feature and draw the sketch for the next feature as shown in Figure 15-71.

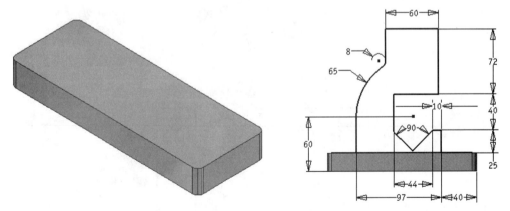

Figure 15-70 *Base feature after filleting*   ***Figure 15-71*** *Sketch of the second feature*

3. Extrude the sketch to a distance of 42 mm as shown in Figure 15-72.

4. Create the next cut feature and the fillets as shown in Figure 15-73.

Figure 15-72 *After creating the second feature*   **Figure 15-73** *After creating the cut feature*

5. Create the remaining features in the model. The final model for the Base is shown in Figure 15-74.

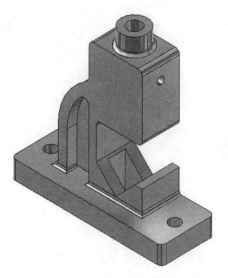

Figure 15-74 *Completed model of the Base*

Creating the Jaw

The next component that needs to be created is the Jaw.

1. Draw the sketch for the base of the Jaw as shown in Figure 15-75.

2. Extrude the sketch to a distance of 18 to create the Jaw and then add the chamfer and holes to it as shown in Figure 15-76.

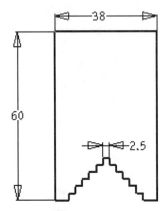

Figure 15-75 *Sketch of the base of the Jaw*

Figure 15-76 *Final model of the Jaw*

Creating the Screw

1. Create the revolved base feature of the Screw as shown in Figure 15-77.

2. Add the chamfer and the hole as shown in Figure 15-78.

Figure 15-77 *Base feature of the Screw*

Figure 15-78 *Final model of the Screw*

Creating the Remaining Components
Similarly, create the Handle and the Handle Stop.

Assembling the Components

1. Open a new file and then assemble the Base with the Jaw as shown in Figure 15-79.

2. Make the Base invisible and place one instance of the Screw. Assemble the Screw with the Jaw as shown in Figure 15-80.

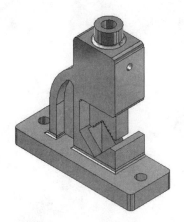

Figure 15-79 *Assembly of the Base and the Jaw*   *Figure 15-80* *After assembling the Screw*

3. Place one instance of the Handle and assemble it with the Screw as shown in Figure 15-81.

4. Place two instances of the Handle Stop and assemble them with the Handle as shown in Figure 15-82.

Figure 15-81 *After assembling the Handle*   *Figure 15-82* *After assembling the two Handle stops*

5. Turn on the visibility of the Base. The final Pipe Vice assembly is shown in Figure 15-83.

6. Save the assembly with the name given below:

    \PersonalProject\c15\Pipe Vice**Pipe Vice.iam**

Creating the Presentation

1. Create the presentation of the Pipe Vice assembly showing the animation of moving and rotating the components. The components that will rotate are the Screw, the Handle, and the two Handle Stops. The components that will move are all the above-mentioned components and the Jaw. Save the file with the name \PersonalProject\c15\Pipe Vice**Pipe Vice.ipn**.

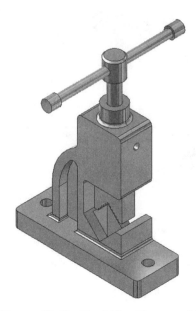

Figure 15-83 *Final Pipe Vice assembly*

Generating the Drawing Views

1.   Open a new JIS standard file and generate the drawing views as shown in Figure 15-84.

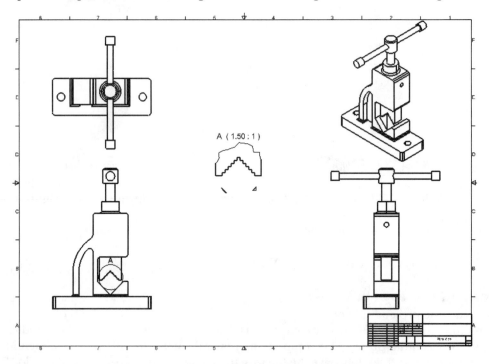

Figure 15-84 *Drawing views of the Pipe Vice assembly*

2. Add the parts list and the balloons to the drawing views as shown in Figure 15-85.

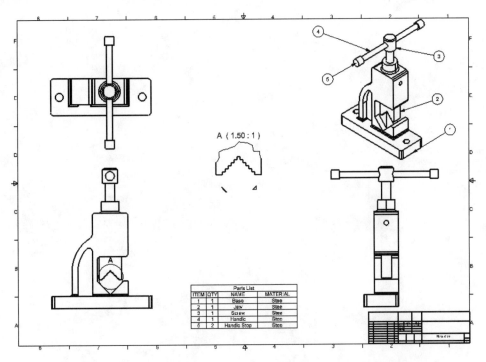

Figure 15-85 *Drawing views after adding the parts list and the balloons*

3. Save the sheet with the name given below:

\PersonalProject\c15\Pipe Vice**Pipe Vice.idw**

Appendix A

System Requirements and Installing Autodesk Inventor

SYSTEM REQUIREMENTS

The following are the minimum system requirements for running Autodesk Inventor release 5:

1. For training and assemblies smaller than 100 parts (minimum): Intel® Pentium® based PC with 266MHz processor or better with 128MB RAM.
2. For small assembly modeling (up to 1000 parts): Pentium II or Pentium II Xeon or equivalent processor, 450MHz or faster, with 256MB RAM.
3. For large assembly modeling: Pentium II or Pentium II Xeon or equivalent processor, 600MHz or faster, with 512MB RAM.
4. Microsoft® Windows® XP Professional, Windows 2000 Professional (SP1 or better recommended), Windows NT® 4 (SP6 recommended), or Windows Me (for training or home use only).
5. 360MB free disk space (460MB if Content Library is installed).
6. Microsoft Internet Explorer version 5.5.
7. Microsoft Excel 97 or newer.
8. Microsoft NetMeeting 3.01 (for online collaboration).

INSTALLING AUTODESK INVENTOR

The following steps describe the installation process of Autodesk Inventor release 5:

1. Insert the Autodesk Inventor release 5 CD in the CD-ROM drive of your computer.

2. If AutoPlay is enabled, the **Autodesk Setup Wizard** dialog box will be displayed as shown in Figure A-1.

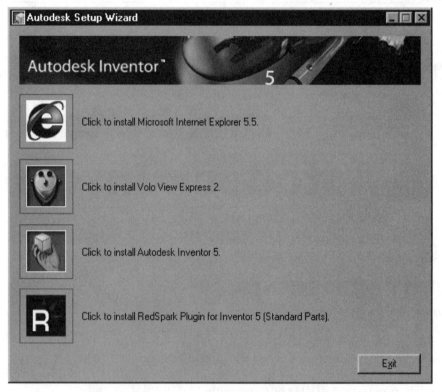

Figure A-1 Autodesk Setup Wizard dialog box

It is assumed that Internet Explorer 5.5 and Volo View Express 2 is already installed on your system. If these applications are not installed, you can install them by choosing their respective buttons in the **Autodesk Setup Wizard** dialog box.

3. Choose the **Click to install Autodesk Inventor 5.** button from this dialog box.

4. The **Autodesk Inventor 5 Setup** dialog box will be displayed as shown in Figure A-2. Choose the **Next** button.

5. After reading the Autodesk software license agreement, select the **I accept the license agreement** radio button and then choose **Next**.

Figure A-2 Autodesk Inventor 5 Setup dialog box

6.   From the **License Type** page, select whether the type of license to install is for single user or network system, see Figure A-3 and then choose **Next**.

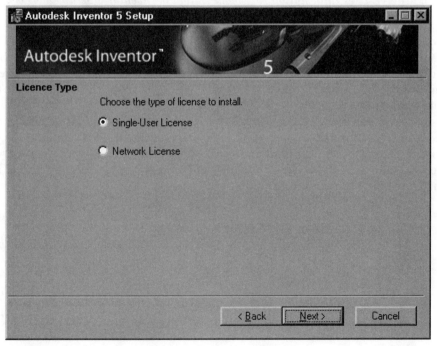

Figure A-3 License Type page of the Autodesk Inventor 5 Setup dialog box

7. In the **User Information** page (Figure A-4), enter the user information, serial number, and the CD Key number in the respective fields and then choose **Next**.

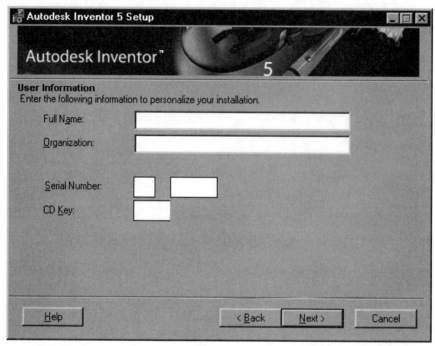

*Figure A-4 **User Information** page of the **Autodesk Inventor 5 Setup** dialog box*

8. By default, the destination folder for installing Autodesk Inventor is C:\Program Files\Autodesk. If you want to select any other folder for installing Autodesk Inventor, choose the **Browse** button in the **Destination Folder** page (Figure A-5) and specify the name and the location of the destination folder. After specifying the name and the location of the destination folder, choose **Next**.

9. Specify the type of installation by selecting its radio button in the **Installation Type** page shown in Figure A-6. It is recommended that to get the complete productive use of Autodesk Inventor, you select the complete installation. After selecting the type of installation, choose the **Next** button.

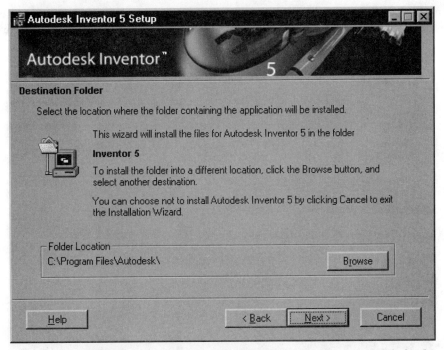

Figure A-5 Destination Folder page of the Autodesk Inventor 5 Setup dialog box

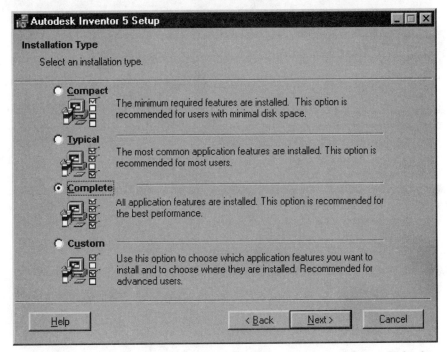

Figure A-6 Installation Type page of the Autodesk Inventor 5 Setup dialog box

10. The **Measurement units** page is displayed and is used to select the unit for measuring length while using Autodesk Inventor, see Figure A-7. This books uses the millimeter as the unit for measuring length. Select the measurement unit and then choose the **Next** button.

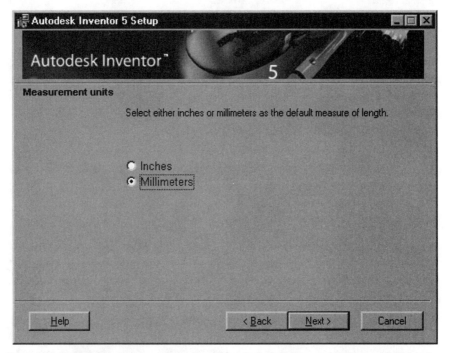

Figure A-7 Measurement units page of the Autodesk Inventor 5 Setup dialog box

11. From the **Drawing standards** page (Figure A-8), select the default drawing standard by selecting the radio button of the standard. This is the standard that will be followed by the default file in the **Default** tab of the **Open** dialog box. After selecting the standard, choose the **Next** button.

12. The **Part modification** page is displayed as shown in Figure A-9. This page is used to specify whether or not you want to enable the part modification from within the drawing. It is recommended that you enable the part modification from within the drawing. After selecting the option, choose the **Next** button.

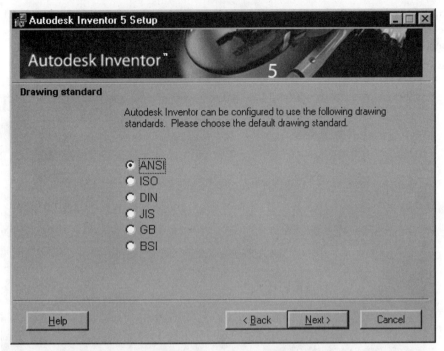

Figure A-8 Drawing standards page of the Autodesk Inventor 5 Setup dialog box

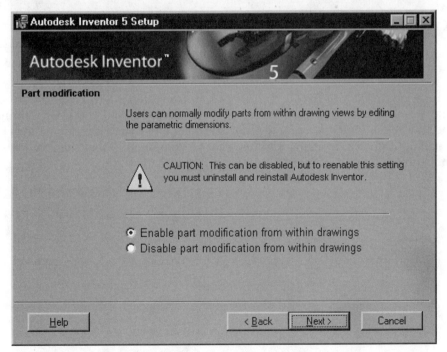

Figure A-9 Part modification page of the Autodesk Inventor 5 Setup dialog box

13. The **Ready to Install the Application** page is displayed as shown in Figure A-10. Choose the **Next** button to start installing Autodesk Inventor. The program files are installed on your system and when the installation is complete, you will be informed that Autodesk Inventor has been successfully installed on your system. Choose the **Finish** button.

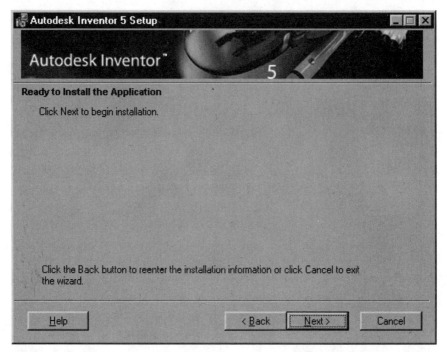

Figure A-8 Ready to Install the Application page of the *Autodesk Inventor 5 Setup* dialog box

14. The **Installer Information** dialog box will be displayed and you will be prompted to specify whether or not you want to restart the computer now. It is recommended that after installing Autodesk Inventor, you restart your computer so that the program files are configured for your system. Choose **Yes** from this dialog box to restart the computer.

Appendix B

Interface

OPENING OTHER FORMAT FILES

Autodesk Inventor allows you to import or open a file created and saved in other file formats. The method of importing or opening some of these files is discussed next.

Opening an AutoCAD (DWG) file

 If the file is originally created in AutoCAD, you can place it in the sketch mode. However, note that if the file is opened in the sketch mode, it will be placed as a sketch even if the AutoCAD file has solid models. To open an AutoCAD file in the sketch mode, choose **Insert AutoCAD File** from the **Sketch** panel bar or choose **Insert AutoCAD File** from the **Sketch** toolbar. The **Open** dialog box that can be used to specify the name and the location of the AutoCAD file will be displayed.

Note
*You may need to increase the drawing display area in the inventor file by using the **Zoom All** button after placing the AutoCAD file.*

Opening a Mechanical Desktop File

Autodesk Inventor allows you to directly open a Mechanical Desktop file with a parametric solid model in Autodesk Inventor. However, note that before you open a Mechanical Desktop file in Autodesk Inventor, both these applications should be opened on your system. If you try to open a Mechanical Desktop file in Autodesk Inventor without opening Mechanical Desktop application, an error message will be displayed and you will be informed that you need to first open Mechanical Desktop before importing the file in Autodesk Inventor.

When you import the Mechanical Desktop file in Autodesk Inventor, the file will be opened in an assembly file (.iam file) of Autodesk Inventor. The entire data related to the parametric features of the Mechanical Desktop solid model will be retained in Autodesk Inventor also. To view these features, activate the imported part file by using the browser. The features and their sequence in the model will be displayed in the browser. If you double-click on any of the feature, its dimensions will be displayed on the graphics screen. This suggests that each and every dimension related to the solid model in Mechanical Desktop will be imported in Autodesk Inventor. Therefore, there is a complete flexibility of opening a Mechanical Desktop file in Autodesk Inventor without loosing any information about the components.

Autodesk Inventor also allows you to set various options related to the DWG file that you are opening. You can set the units in which the solid model will be measured, the layout you want to import from the DWG file, and other related options. To set these options, select the Mechanical Desktop file by using the **Open** dialog box of Autodesk Inventor and then choose the **Options** button provided on the left of the **Open** button in the dialog box. The **DWG File Import Options** dialog box will be displayed as shown in Figure B-1.

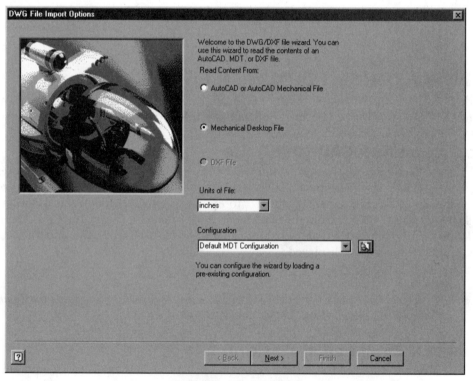

Figure B-1 DWG File Import Options dialog box

Select the options in this dialog box and then choose the **Next** button. The **MDT Model/ Layout Import options** dialog box will be displayed as shown in Figure B-2.

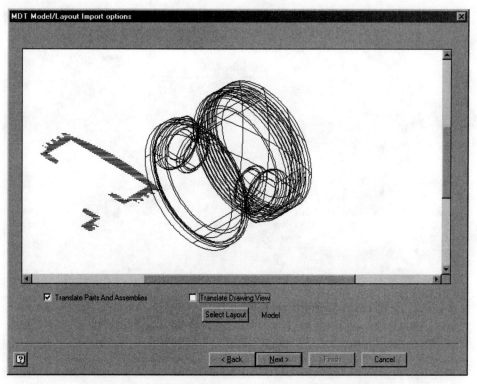

Figure B-2 MDT Model/Layout Import options dialog box

Using this dialog box you can select whether you want to import the data from the model space or from the layout. In case you need to import the data from the layout, you will be given the options of selecting the layout from which the data will be imported. After selecting the option from this dialog box, choose the **Next** button. The **MDT Import Destination Options** dialog box will be displayed as shown in Figure B-3.

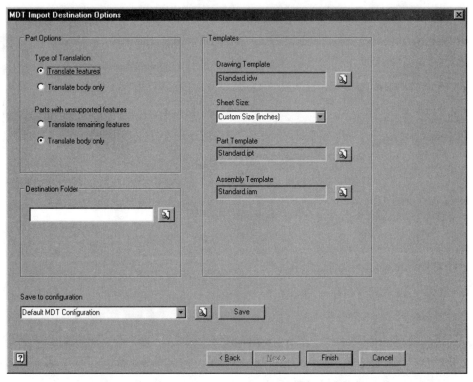

Figure B-3 MDT Import Destination Options dialog box

You can set the options related to the resultant Autodesk Inventor file from this dialog box. After setting the options, choose **Finish** in this dialog box. You will return to the **Open** dialog box. You can now open the Mechanical Desktop file in Autodesk Inventor by choosing the **Open** button. When you choose the **Open** button, the **Multiple Part Definitions** dialog box will be displayed (Figure B-4) and you will be prompted to select the parts that you want to import in Autodesk Inventor. Select the parts that you want to import and then choose **OK**. The component will be placed exactly as it was placed in Mechanical Desktop.

Figure B-4 Multiple Part Definitions dialog box

Note
Similarly, you can also open an AutoCAD or an AutoCAD LT file as 2D entities in Autodesk Inventor.

IMPORTING OTHER FORMAT FILES

You can also import the files stored in other formats like STEP, IGES, SAT, and so on. To import these files, invoke the **Open** dialog box in Autodesk Inventor and choose their format from the **Files of type** drop-down list in the **Open** dialog box. Figure B-5 shows the STEP format file being selected from the **Open** dialog box.

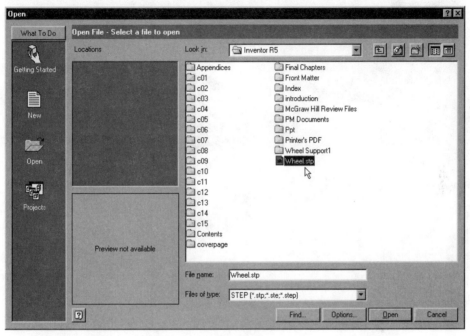

Figure B-5 *Selecting the STEP format file from the **Open** dialog box*

Unlike importing MDT files where even a single part file is opened in Autodesk Inventor assembly file, the step files are opened in a part file of Autodesk Inventor. Remember that the information related to the features of the solid model are not imported with the solid. This can be confirmed in the browser where only one feature is displayed, which is the **Base** feature. This is because when a solid is stored in the STEP format, the information related to the features and other parameters of the solid is lost.

EDITING THE IMPORTED FILES

As mentioned earlier, if you import the files in a format other than the DWG format, the information related to the features in the model is not imported. The imported model is composed of only one feature, that is, the base feature. Therefore, it is not possible to edit the features of the imported model. However, Autodesk Inventor allows you to perform some editing operations on these imported models in the **Solids** mode. To invoke the **Solids** mode, double-click on **Base** in the browser. You will notice that the **Features** panel bar is replaced by the **Solids** panel bar with the tools to edit the imported solid. You can also invoke the **Solids** toolbar to edit the imported solid. The editing operations that you can perform by using the tools in the **Solids** panel bar or the **Solids** toolbar include moving the faces of the model, extending or contracting the model, and so on. Figure B-6 shows an imported solid that was originally created in Pro/E and imported in the STEP format.

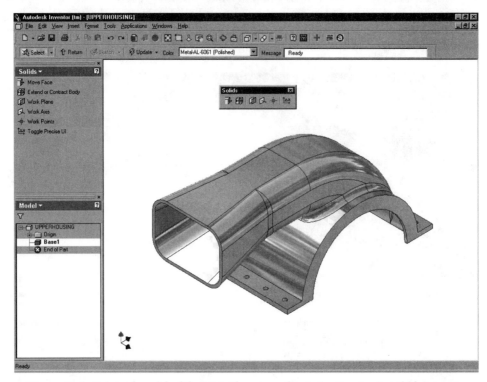

Figure B-6 *Original model of the Upperhousing after importing in Autodesk Inventor*

Figure B-7 shows the same model after extending the right face of the model by using the **Extend or Contract Body** tool. Notice that the right face has moved toward the right to some distance, thus expanding the model.

After making the necessary changes in the model, choose the **Return** button to switch back to the **Part** mode. As soon as you choose **Return**, the **Solids** panel bar will be replaced by the **Features** panel bar. Remember that you cannot save a model in the **Solids** mode. You need to exit this mode by choosing **Return** from the **Command Bar** and save the file in the **Part** mode. As mentioned earlier, the models saved in the **Part** mode are saved in the .ipt format.

Note
*When you save the model by choosing the **Save** button from the **Standard** toolbar, the model will be saved with the name of the imported file. This means that if you have opened a STEP file with the name upperhousing.stp, the model will be saved as upperhousing.ipt. However, if you want to save the model with some other name and in some other location, choose **File > Save Copy As** from the menu bar and specify the name and the location of the file in the **Save Copy As** dialog box.*

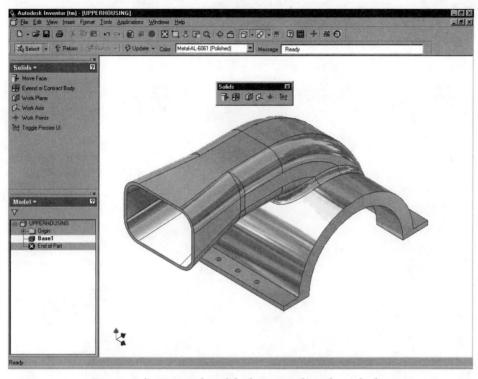

Figure B-7 *Imported model after expanding the right face*

Tip. *You can also import the files stored in the IGES and the SAT format in an existing part file by choosing **Insert > Import** from the menu bar. When you choose this option from the menu bar, the **Import** dialog box will be displayed. You can select the format for importing the files from the **Files of type** drop-down list.*

*Remember that the files of other formats that are opened by using the **Open** dialog box are opened as a solid model file. However, the files inserted in the current file by using the **Import** dialog box are imported as surface models and not the solid models.*

EXPORTING THE FILES

Autodesk Inventor allows you to export the Inventor files into various other formats such as STEP, SAT, IGES, STL, and so on. To export a file, choose **File > Save Copy As** from the menu bar. The **Save Copy As** dialog box will be displayed. Select the required file format for exporting the file from the **Save as type** drop-down list. You will notice a number of predefined formats in which you can export the file.

Index

List of other Publications by Sham Tickoo and CADCIM Technologies

The following is the list of the other publications by Sham Tickoo and CADCIM Technologies.

Pro/ENGINEER Book

* Pro/ENGINEER for Designers, Release 2001
  CADCIM Technologies

Mechanical Desktop Book

* Mechanical Desktop Instructor, Release 5
  McGraw Hill Publishing Company

AutoCAD Books (US Edition)

* AutoCAD 2002: A Problem-Solving Approach
  Autodesk Press
* AutoCAD LT 2002: A Problem-Solving Approach
  Autodesk Press
* Customizing AutoCAD 2002
  Autodesk Press
* AutoCAD 2000: A Problem Solving Approach
  Autodesk Press
* Customizing AutoCAD 2000
  Autodesk Press
* AutoCAD LT 2000: A Problem-Solving Approach
  Autodesk Press
* Customizing AutoCAD R14
  Autodesk Press
* AutoCAD LT 97: Problem Solving Approach
  Autodesk Press
* AutoCAD Release 13 Update Guide DOS/Windows
  Autodesk Press
* AutoCAD LT 2.0 for Windows: A Problem Solving Approach
  Autodesk Press
* AutoCAD: A Problem Solving Approach DOS R 13 - 3 Hole Punch
  Autodesk Press
* Customizing AutoCAD: Release 13 for DOS and Windows
  Autodesk Press
* AutoCAD: A Problem Solving Approach Release 13/DOS
  Autodesk Press
* Customizing AutoCAD Release 12
  Autodesk Press

AutoCAD Books (Italian Edition)

* AutoCAD 2000 Fondamenti
* AutoCAD 2000 Techniche Advantaze

AutoCAD Book (Chinese Edition)
*   AutoCAD 2000

AutoCAD Books (Indian Edition)
*   AutoCAD 2002 with Applications
    Tata McGraw Hill Publishers
*   Understanding AutoCAD 2002
    Tata McGraw Hill Publishers
*   Advanced Techniques in AutoCAD 2002
    Tata McGraw Hill Publishers
*   AutoCAD 2000 with Applications
    Galgotia Publishers
*   Understanding AutoCAD 2000
    Galgotia Publishers
*   Advanced Techniques in AutoCAD 2000
    Galgotia Publishers
*   AutoCAD 14 Bible
    Galgotia Publishers
*   Understanding AutoCAD 14
    Galgotia Publishers
*   Advanced Techniques in AutoCAD 14
    Galgotia Publishers

3D Studio MAX and VIZ Books
*   Learning 3DS Max: A Tutorial Approach, Release 4
    Goodheart-Willcox Publishers (USA)
*   Learning 3D Studio VIZ: A Tutorial Approach
    Goodheart-Willcox Publishers (USA)
*   Learning 3D Studio R4: A Tutorial Approach
    Goodheart-Willcox Publishers (USA)
*   Learning 3D Studio MAX/VIZ 3.0: A Tutorial Approach
    BPB Publishers (India)